STUDY GUIDE
to accompany
McConnell and Brue
MACROECONOMICS

STUDY GUIDE
to accompany
McConnell and Brue
MACROECONOMICS

Fourteenth Edition

WILLIAM B. WALSTAD
PROFESSOR OF ECONOMICS
UNIVERSITY OF NEBRASKA–LINCOLN

ROBERT C. BINGHAM
LATE PROFESSOR OF ECONOMICS
KENT STATE UNIVERSITY

Irwin
McGraw-Hill

Boston   Burr Ridge, IL   Dubuque, IA   Madison, WI   New York   San Francisco   St. Louis
Bangkok   Bogotá   Caracas   Lisbon   London   Madrid
Mexico City   Milan   New Delhi   Seoul   Singapore   Sydney   Taipei   Toronto

Irwin/McGraw-Hill

A Division of The McGraw·Hill Companies

Study Guide to Accompany Macroeconomics Principles, Problems, and Policies

4 5 6 7 8 9 0   QPD QPD   9 4 3 2 1 0 9

ISBN 0-07-289839-9

Editorial director: Michael Junior
Publisher: Gary Burke
Sponsoring editor: Lucille Sutton
Developmental editor: Marilea Fried
Marketing manager: Nelson Black
Project manager: Eva Marie Strock
Production supervisor: Louis Swaim
Cover designer: Francis Owens
Editorial assistant: Lee Hertel
Compositor: York Graphic Services, Inc.
Typeface: Helvetica
Printer: Quebecor Printing

Back cover illustration by Jacques Cournoyer

http://www.mhhe.com

About the Authors

William B. Walstad is a professor of economics at the University of Nebraska–Lincoln, where he directs the National Center for Research in Economic Education. He received his Ph.D. degree from the University of Minnesota. Professor Walstad has been honored with a Distinguished Teaching Award at Nebraska. He also received the Henry H. Villard Research Award for his published research in economic education. He coedited *Teaching Undergraduate Economics: A Handbook for Instructors* (McGraw-Hill) and serves as an associate editor of the *Journal of Economic Education*.

Robert C. Bingham was an undergraduate student at DePauw University and obtained M.A. and Ph.D. degrees from Northwestern University. He taught at the University of Nebraska–Lincoln, where he was a colleague of Professor McConnell before moving to Kent State University, from which he retired in 1985. He was the author of several other study guides and supplements for the principles of economics courses.

To
Tammie, Laura, and Kristin, and Eileen

Contents

How to Use the Study Guide to Learn Economics

This *Study Guide* is designed to help you read and understand Campbell R. McConnell and Stanley L. Brue's textbook, *Macroeconomics,* fourteenth edition. If used properly, a study guide can be a great aid to you for what is probably your first course in economics.

No one pretends that the study of economics is easy, but it can be made easier. Of course, a study guide will not do your work for you, and its use is no substitute for reading the text. You must be willing to read the text, spend time on the subject, and work at learning if you wish to understand economics.

Many students do read their text and work hard on their economics course and still fail to learn the subject. This occurs because principles of economics is a new subject for these students, and they have had no previous experience in learning economics. They want to learn but do not know just how to go about it. Here is where the *Study Guide* can help. Let's first see what the *Study Guide* contains and then how to use it.

■ WHAT THE STUDY GUIDE IS

The *Study Guide* contains 23 chapters—one for each chapter in *Macroeconomics*—and a **glossary.** Each *Study Guide* chapter has 11 sections. The first 5 sections identify and explain the basic content and concepts in each chapter.

1. An **introduction** explains what is in the chapter of the text and how it is related to material in earlier and later chapters. It points out topics to which you should give special attention and reemphasizes difficult or important principles and facts.

2. A **checklist** tells you the things you should be able to do when you have finished the chapter.

3. A **chapter outline** shows how the chapter is organized and summarizes briefly the essential points made in the chapter.

4. Selected **hints and tips** for each chapter help you master the material and make connections with any previous discussion of a topic.

5. A list of the **important terms** in the chapter points out what you must be able to define in order to understand the material in the chapter. A definition of each term is in the glossary at the end of the *Study Guide.*

The next 6 sections of the *Study Guide* allow you to **self-test** your understanding of the chapter material.

6. Fill-in questions (short-answer and list questions) help you learn and remember the important generalizations and facts in the chapter.

7. True-false questions test your understanding of the material in the chapter.

8. Multiple-choice questions also give you a chance to check your knowledge of the chapter content and prepare for this type of course examination.

9. Problems help you learn and understand economic concepts by requiring different skills—drawing a graph, completing a table, or finding relationships—to solve the problems.

10. Short answer and **essay questions** can be used as a self-test, to identify important questions in the chapter, and to prepare for examinations.

11. Answers to fill-in questions, problems and projects, true-false questions, and multiple-choice questions are found at the end of each chapter. References to the specific pages in the textbook for each true-false, multiple-choice, and short answer or essay question are also provided.

■ HOW TO STUDY AND LEARN WITH THE HELP OF THE *STUDY GUIDE*

1. *Read and outline.* For best results, quickly read the introduction, outline, list of terms, and checklist in the *Study Guide* before you read the chapter in *Macroeconomics.* Then read the chapter in the text slowly, keeping one eye on the *Study Guide* outline and the list of terms. Highlight the chapter as you read it by identifying the *major and minor* points and by placing *Study Guide* outline numbers or letters (such as I or A or 1 or a) in the margins. When you have completed the chapter, you will have the chapter highlighted, and the *Study Guide* will serve as a handy set of notes on the chapter.

2. *Review and reread.* After you have read the chapter in the text once, return to the introduction, outline, and list of terms in the *Study Guide.* Reread the introduction and outline. Does everything there make sense? If not, go back to the text and reread the topics that you do not remember well or that still confuse you. Look at the outline. Try to recall each of the minor topics or points that were contained in the text under each of the major points in the outline. When you come to the list of terms, go over them one by one. *Define or explain each to yourself and then look for the definition of the term either in the text chapter or in the glossa*ry. Compare your own definition or explanation with that in the *text or glossary.* The quick way to find the definition of a term in the text is to look in the text index for the page(s) in which that term or concept is mentioned. Make any necessary correction or change in your own definition or explanation.

3. *Test and check answers.* When you have done all this, you will have a general idea of what is in the text chapter. *Now look at the fill-in questions, true-false questions, multiple-choice questions, and problems.* Tackle each of these four sections one at a time, using the following procedure. (**1**) Answer as many questions as you can without looking in the text or in the answers section. (**2**) Check the text for whatever help you need. It is a good idea to do more than merely look for answers in the text. Reread any section for which you were not able to answer questions. (**3**) Consult the answers section at the end of the chapter for the correct answers and reread any section of the text for which you missed questions. (See the text page references given with the answer to each true-false or multiple-choice question.)

The questions in these four sections are not all equally difficult. Do not expect to get them all right the first time. Some are designed to pinpoint things of importance that you will probably miss the first time you read the text and to get you to read about them again. None of the questions are unimportant. Even those that have no definite answers will bring you to grips with many important economic questions and increase your understanding of economic principles and problems.

The *short answer and essay questions* cover the major points in the chapter. For some of the easier questions, all you may do is mentally outline your answer. For the more difficult questions, you may want to write out a brief outline of the answer or a full answer. Do not avoid the difficult questions just because they are more work. Answering these questions is often the most valuable work you can do toward acquiring an understanding of economic relationships and principles.

Although no answers are given in the *Study Guide* to the short answer and essay questions, the answer section does list text page references for each question. You are *strongly* encouraged to read those text pages for an explanation of the question or for better insight into the question content.

4. *Double check.* Before you turn to the next chapter in the text and *Study Guide,* return to the checklist. If you cannot honestly check off each item in the list, you have not learned what the authors of the text and of this *Study Guide* hoped you would learn.

■ **ANSWERS TO KEY QUESTIONS IN *MACROECONOMICS***

In addition to the self-test in the *Study Guide,* there are end-of-chapter questions in *Macroeconomics* that you can answer to double check your understanding. Some of these questions are similar to the questions in the *Study Guide,* but none are identical. It is highly recommended that you try to answer the **key questions** at the end of each chapter in *Macroeconomics.* You can then check your work against the Answers sections in the *Study Guide.*

■ **SOME FINAL WORDS**

Perhaps the method of using the *Study Guide* outlined above seems like a lot of work. It is! Study and learning necessarily entail work on your part. This is a fact you must accept if you are to learn economics.

After you have used the *Study Guide* to study three or four chapters, you will find that some sections are more valuable to you than others. Let your own experience determine how you will use it. But do not discontinue use of the *Study Guide* after three or four chapters merely because you are not sure whether it is helping you. ***Stick with it.***

■ **ACKNOWLEDGMENTS**

The late Professor Robert Bingham prepared the first 10 editions of the *Study Guide.* He worked with great care and wanted the *Study Guide* to be a valuable aid for students. Many past users of the *Study Guide* will attest to his success. Although Professor Bingham did not participate directly in this revision, his work remains a major contribution to this edition.

I also want to acknowledge the help I received from many others. Campbell McConnell and Stanley Brue offered many insightful comments on the *Study Guide* over the years and encouraged my work. I received valuable suggestions and corrections for this edition from Loretta Fairchild, Joyce Gleason, Richard Harmstone, Ralph Lewis, Peter Kerr, Dave Rosenbaum, Mary Stevenson, and Joshua Stull. Ken Rebeck helped me proof and check the self-test questions and identify text page numbers for answers. Students in my principles of economics classes at the University of Nebraska–Lincoln continue to give me feedback that has helped improve the *Study Guide* with each edition. Sharon Nemeth was of invaluable assistance in helping proof portions of the manuscript. Finally, the team at McGraw-Hill, especially Lucille Sutton, provided good editorial and production support. Despite the many contributions from others, all responsibility for any errors or omissions are mine. I encourage *Study Guide* users to send me comments or suggestions at any time.

William B. Walstad

STUDY GUIDE
to accompany
McConnell and Brue
MACROECONOMICS

CHAPTER 1

The Nature and Method of Economics

Chapter 1 introduces you to economics—the study of how people decide how to use scarce productive resources to satisfy material wants. The purpose of this chapter is to explain the nature of the subject and to describe the methods that economists use to study economic questions.

The first section of the chapter describes the three key features of the *economic perspective.* This perspective first recognizes that all choices involve costs and that these costs must be involved in an economic decision. The economic perspective also incorporates the view that to achieve a goal, people make decisions which reflect their rational self-interest. The third feature considers that people compare marginal benefits against marginal costs when making decisions and will choose the situation where the marginal benefit is greater than the marginal cost. You will develop a better understanding of these features and the meaning of the economic perspective as you read about the economic issues in this book.

As you begin your study of economics, you might be wondering if the work you will do to learn the chapter material is worthwhile. It most certainly is. Knowledge of economics is important because it is essential for well-informed citizenship and has many practical applications to professional and personal decisions.

Economists use two different approaches to examine economic topics. Theoretical economics, or *economic analysis,* is the systematic gathering of relevant facts and the derivation of principles with these facts using inductive or deductive methods. *Policy economics* entails the formulation of policies or recommended solutions to economic problems.

The heart of the chapter is the discussion of *economic principles* in the economic methodology section. These principles are generalizations, imprecise and subject to exceptions because economists cannot conduct laboratory experiments to test the generalizations. Economics is a science, but not an exact science. Economic principles are also simplifications—approximations of a complex world—for analyzing problems in *microeconomics* and *macroeconomics* and for finding solutions to these problems.

The choice of an economic policy depends on economic principles *and* on the value judgments and weights given to economic goals. Here we move from *economic theory* and *positive economics,* which investigates what is, to *normative economics,* which incorporates subjective or value-laden views of what ought to be. Many of the apparent disagreements among economists are over normative policy issues and involve deciding which economic

goals for our economy are most important in making the case for a policy solution.

Clear thinking about economic questions requires that beginning students avoid many pitfalls. Errors of commission and omission can occur from bias, loaded terminology, imprecise definitions, fallacies of composition, and causation fallacies. Awareness of these pitfalls will help you think more objectively about the economic issues you will read about throughout this book.

■ CHECKLIST

When you have studied this chapter you should be able to

☐ Write a formal definition of economics.
☐ Describe the three key features of an economic perspective.
☐ Give examples of the application of an economic perspective.
☐ Give two good reasons for studying economics.
☐ Describe theoretical economics or economic analysis.
☐ Distinguish between induction and deduction in economic reasoning.
☐ Explain what an economic principle is and how economic principles are obtained.
☐ Discuss how economic principles are generalizations and abstractions.
☐ Explain what the "other things equal" (*ceteris paribus*) assumption is and why this assumption is employed in economics.
☐ Define policy economics.
☐ List three steps in economic policymaking.
☐ Identify eight economic goals widely accepted in the United States and many other nations.
☐ Discuss the conflicting or complementary nature of economic goals.
☐ Distinguish between macroeconomics and microeconomics.
☐ Give examples of positive and normative economics.
☐ Identify the five pitfalls to objective thinking when given examples.

■ CHAPTER OUTLINE

1. Economics is concerned with the efficient use of limited productive resources to achieve the maximum satisfaction of human material wants.

2. The *economic perspective* has three interrelated features.

    a. It recognizes scarcity requires choice and that all choices entail a cost.

    b. It views people as rational decision makers who make choices based on their self-interest.

    c. It uses marginal analysis to assess how the marginal costs of a decision compare with the marginal benefits.

3. Citizens in a democracy must understand elementary economics to comprehend the present-day problems of their society and to make intelligent decisions when they vote. Economics is an academic rather than a vocational subject, but a knowledge of it is valuable to business executives, consumers, and workers.

4. Economic methodology includes both theoretical economics and policy economics.

    a. *Theoretical economics* is the gathering and analysis of relevant facts to derive economic principles. Economists use both inductive and deductive reasoning to develop economic principles. Induction creates principles from factual observations, or goes from the particular to the general. Deduction formulates a hypothesis and then tests it for validity, or goes from the general to the particular. Economic principles and theories are meaningful statements about economic behavior in the economy.

    (1) They are also called laws and models.

    (2) Each principle and theory is a generalization that shows a tendency or average effect.

    (3) The "other things equal" (ceteris paribus) assumption is used to limit the influence of other factors when making a generalization.

    (4) Economic principles and theories are abstractions from reality.

    (5) Many economic principles or models can be illustrated graphically.

    b. *Policy economics* is the use of economic principles to develop a course of action to solve economic problems.

    (1) The three steps in creating economic policy are stating the goal, considering the options, and evaluating the results.

    (2) Eight major economic goals are considered important in the United States and many other nations: economic growth, full employment, economic efficiency, price-level stability, economic freedom, economic security, an equitable distribution of income, and a balance of trade. Economic goals can be complementary, or they can conflict and require tradeoffs. The interpretation of economic goals and the setting of priorities can be difficult and cause problems in economic policymaking.

5. Economic analysis is conducted at two levels, and might be positive or normative.

    a. *Macroeconomics* looks at the entire economy or its major aggregates or sectors, such as households, businesses, or government.

    b. *Microeconomics* studies the economic behavior of individuals, particular markets, firms, or industries.

    c. *Positive economics* focuses on facts and is concerned with what is, or the scientific analysis of economic behavior.

    d. *Normative economics* suggests what ought to be and answers policy questions based on value judgments. Most disagreements among economists involve normative economics.

6. Objective thinking in the study and use of economic principles requires strict application of the rules of logic, in which personal emotions are irrelevant, if not detrimental. The pitfalls beginning students encounter when studying and applying economic principles include the following:

    a. Bias of preconceived beliefs not warranted by facts

    b. Loaded terminology or the use of terms in a way which appeals to emotion and leads to a nonobjective analysis of the issues

    c. The definition of terms by economists in ways which may not be the same as the ways in which these terms are more commonly used

    d. The fallacy of composition or the assumption that what is true of the part is necessarily true of the whole

    e. Two causation fallacies confuse cause and effect.

    (1) The after this, therefore because of this fallacy **(post hoc, ergo propter hoc)** is the mistaken belief that when one event precedes another, the first event is the cause of the second.

    (2) The other fallacy is to confuse correlation with causation. Two factors may be related, but that does not mean that one factor caused the other.

■ HINTS AND TIPS

1. The economic perspective presented in the first section of the chapter has three features related to decision making: scarcity and the necessity of choice, rational self-interest in decision making, and marginal analysis of the costs and benefits of decisions. Although these features may seem strange to you at first, they are central to the economic thinking used to examine decisions and problems throughout the book.

2. The chapter introduces important pairs of terms: inductive and deductive reasoning; microeconomics and macroeconomics; and positive economics and normative economics. Make sure you understand what each pair means.

3. Objective thinking about economic problems is difficult and requires that you be able to recognize the major pitfalls—loaded terminology, inaccurate definitions, fallacy of composition, *post hoc* fallacy, and confusing correlation with causation. One way to remember these pitfalls is to associate each one with a practical example.

■ IMPORTANT TERMS

Note: See Glossary in the back of the book for definitions of terms.

economics

economic perspective

economic analysis

marginal analysis

economic theory

economic principles

induction

deduction

generalizations

ceteris paribus

policy economics

tradeoffs

macroeconomics

aggregate

microeconomics

positive economics

normative economics

fallacy of composition

post hoc, ergo propter hoc

SELF-TEST

■ **FILL-IN QUESTIONS**

1. Economics is the study of the efficient use of (unlimited, limited) _____ resources to achieve (minimum, maximum) _____ satisfaction of human wants.

2. The economic perspective recognizes that (resources, scarcity) _____ requires choice and that choice has an opportunity (benefit, cost) _____. "There is no such thing as a free lunch" in economics because scarce resources have (unlimited, alternative) _____ uses.

3. The economic perspective also assumes that people make choices based on their self-interest and that they are (irrational, rational) _____. It also is based on comparisons of the (partial, marginal) _____ costs and benefits of an economic decision.

4. An understanding of economics is essential if we are to be well-informed (citizens, technicians) _____, and such an understanding has many personal and professional applications even though it is a(n) (vocational, academic) _____ and not a(n) _____ subject.

5. The systematic arranging of facts, the interpretation of them, and the drawing of generalizations based on them is called (policy, theoretical) _____ economics.

6. When economists develop economic principles from studying facts, they are using the (deductive, inductive) _____ method, whereas the _____ method uses facts to test the validity of hypotheses or economic theories.

7. Economic principles are also called (facts, laws) _____, or (theories, policies) _____, or (models, tradeoffs) _____.

8. Economic principles are often imprecise quantitative statements or (fallacies, generalizations) _____ about people's economic behavior, and they necessarily involve (abstractions, distractions) _____ from reality to simplify complex situations.

9. When economists assume that other factors are held constant and do not change when studying an economic relationship, they are using the (*post hoc*, other things equal) _____ assumption.

10. The formulation of recommended solutions or remedies for economic problems is referred to as (theoretical, policy) _____ economics.

11. The three steps in the formulation of economic policy are (1) stating the economic (theory, goal) _____, (2) determining the policy (results, options) _____, and (3) implementing and evaluating policy (assumptions, effectiveness) _____.

12. Eight widely accepted economic goals in the United States and many nations are

a. _____

b. _____

c. _____

d. _____

e. _____

f. _____

g. _____

h. _____

13. Increases in economic growth that promote full employment would be an example of a set of (conflicting, complementary) _____ economic goals. Efforts to achieve an equitable distribution of income that at the same time reduce economic efficiency would be an example of a set of (conflicting, complementary) _____ economic goals, indicating that there are (tradeoffs, causal effects) _____ among economic goals.

14. The study of the total output of the economy or the general level of prices is the subject of (microeconomics, macroeconomics) _____, whereas the study of output in a particular industry or of a particular product is the subject of _____.

15. The collection of specific units which are being added and treated as if they were one unit is an (assumption, aggregate) _____.

16. Two different types of statements can be made about economic topics. A (positive, normative) _____ statement explains what is by offering a scientific proposition about economic behavior that is based on economic theory and facts, but a _____ statement includes a value judgment about an economic policy or the economy that suggests what ought to be. Many of the reported disagreements among economists usually involve (positive, normative) _____ statements.

17. Holding a preconceived notion, such as thinking that corporate profits are always excessive, is an example of a(n) (aggregate, bias) _____ pitfall in economic thinking.

18. Pitfalls to economic thinking can also occur because terminology is (theoretical, loaded) _____ and definitions are based on (common, economic) _____ usage.

19. The statement that "what is good for the individual is also good for the group" may not be correct because of the fallacy of (complexity, composition) _____.

20. The person who believes that "washing a car will cause it to rain tomorrow" is expressing a(n) (other things equal, *post hoc*) _____ fallacy.

■ **TRUE-FALSE QUESTIONS**

Circle the T if the statement is true, the F if it is false.

1. Economics deals with the activities by which humans can earn a living and improve their standard of living.　**T　F**

2. From an economic perspective, "there is no such thing as a free lunch."　**T　F**

3. Rational self-interest is the same thing as being selfish.　**T　F**

4. The economic perspective views individuals or institutions as making rational choices based on the marginal analysis of the costs and benefits of decisions.　**T　F**

5. Economics is academic and of little value because it does not teach the student how to earn a living.　**T　F**

6. Systematically arranging facts, interpreting them, and using them to derive economic principles is called economic analysis.　**T　F**

7. The deductive method is the scientific method and the method used to derive economic principles from economic facts.　**T　F**

8. Deduction and induction are complementary rather than opposing techniques of investigation.　**T　F**

9. Economic principles enable us to predict the economic consequences of many human actions.　**T　F**

10. In economics, the terms "law," "principle," "theory," and "model" essentially mean the same thing.　**T　F**

11. The "other things equal" or *ceteris paribus* assumption is made to simplify the reasoning process.　**T　F**

12. Economic principles, or theories, are abstractions.　**T　F**

13. The first step in the formulation of an economic policy, the statement of goals, may be occasion for disagreement because different people may have different and conflicting goals to be achieved.　**T　F**

14. Once a single goal or end has been determined as the sole objective of economic policy, there is seldom any question of which policy to adopt to achieve that goal.　**T　F**

15. One of the widely (although not universally) accepted economic goals of people in the United States is an equal distribution of income.　**T　F**

16. A tradeoff is a situation in which some of one economic goal is sacrificed to obtain some of another economic goal.　**T　F**

17. Macroeconomic analysis is concerned with the economic activity of specific firms or industries.　**T　F**

18. Microeconomic analysis is concerned with the performance of the economy as a whole or its major aggregates.　**T　F**

19. The statement that "the legal minimum wage should be raised to give working people a decent income" is an example of a normative statement.　**T　F**

20. When value judgments are made about the economy or economic policy, this is called positive economics.　**T　F**

21. The belief that lending money is always superior to borrowing money is an example of a bias in objective thinking about economic issues.　**T　F**

22. The fallacy of composition would be calling profits "excessive" or an unemployed worker "lazy."　**T　F**

23. If you speak of "capital" to most people, they understand that you are referring to money. The economist, therefore, is obligated to use the term "capital" to mean money.　**T　F**

24. The *post hoc, ergo propter hoc* fallacy is the belief that "what is true for the individual or part of a group is necessarily true for the group or whole."　**T　F**

25. A person who concludes that more education increases income may be confusing correlation with causation.　**T　F**

■ **MULTIPLE-CHOICE QUESTIONS**

Circle the letter that corresponds to the best answer.

1. What statement would best complete a short definition of economics? "Economics is the study of
  (a) how businesses produce goods and services"
  (b) the efficient use of scarce productive resources"
  (c) the equitable distribution of society's income and wealth"
  (d) the printing and circulation of money throughout the economy"

2. The idea in economics that "there is no such thing as a free lunch" means that

(a) the marginal benefit of such a lunch is greater than its marginal cost
(b) businesses cannot increase their market share by offering free lunches
(c) scarce resources have alternative uses or opportunity costs
(d) consumers are irrational when they ask for a free lunch

3. A major feature of the economic perspective is
   (a) equating rational self-interest with selfishness
   (b) comparing marginal benefits with marginal costs
   (c) the validity of normative economics for decision making
   (d) the recognition of the abundance of economic resources

4. From an economic perspective, when a business decides to employ more workers, the business decision maker has most likely concluded that the marginal
   (a) costs of employing more workers have decreased
   (b) benefits of employing more workers has increased
   (c) benefits of employing more workers are greater than the marginal costs
   (d) costs of employing more workers is not an opportunity cost for the business because more workers are needed to increase production

5. Economic analysis that derives economic principles about how individuals behave or institutions act is called
   (a) policy economics
   (b) macroeconomics
   (c) normative economics
   (d) theoretical economics

6. When economic principles or theories are derived from factual evidence, this method of economic reasoning is called
   (a) *post hoc*
   (b) deduction
   (c) induction
   (d) hypothesis testing

7. The development of an economic hypothesis through intuition, insight, or logic is associated with
   (a) induction
   (b) deduction
   (c) policy economics
   (d) normative economics

8. When economists state that "consumer spending rises when personal income increases," this is an example of
   (a) a generalization
   (b) loaded terminology
   (c) a normative statement
   (d) a fallacy of composition

9. Another term for the assumption that "other things are equal" is
   (a) *ceteris paribus*
   (b) the correlation fallacy
   (c) the fallacy of composition
   (d) *post hoc, ergo propter hoc*

10. An economic principle states that the lower the price of a product, the greater the quantity consumers will wish to purchase. This principle is based on the critical assumption that
   (a) the whole is not greater than the sum of the parts
   (b) economic goals are complementary and not conflicting
   (c) economic analysis is normative
   (d) there are no other important changes affecting the demand for the product

11. The three basic steps in economic policymaking are
   (a) gather facts, make abstractions, show findings
   (b) state the goal, determine the options, evaluate results
   (c) create the theory, analyze assumptions, derive conclusions
   (d) form hypotheses, simplify the model, assume other things are equal

12. The production of more goods and services and the development of higher standard of living would be associated with what economic goal?
   (a) economic security
   (b) economic freedom
   (c) economic growth
   (d) full employment

13. Which economic goal is associated with the idea that we want to get the maximum benefit at the minimum cost from the limited productive resources available?
   (a) economic security
   (b) economic freedom
   (c) economic growth
   (d) economic efficiency

14. Which economic goal would be most abstract and difficult to measure?
   (a) full employment
   (b) economic efficiency
   (c) economic freedom
   (d) price-level stability

15. To say that two economic goals are conflicting means
   (a) it is impossible to quantify both goals
   (b) there is a tradeoff in the achievement of the two goals
   (c) the two goals are not fully accepted as important economic goals
   (d) the attainment of one goal also results in the attainment of the other goal

16. If economic growth tends to produce a more equitable distribution of income among people in a nation, this relationship between the two economic goals appears to be
   (a) deductive
   (b) conflicting
   (c) complementary
   (d) mutually exclusive

17. When we look at the whole economy or its major aggregates, our analysis would be at the level of
   (a) microeconomics
   (b) macroeconomics
   (c) positive economics
   (d) normative economics

18. Which would be studied in microeconomics?
- **(a)** the output of the entire economy
- **(b)** the total number of workers employed in the United States
- **(c)** the general level of prices in the U.S. economy
- **(d)** the output and price of wheat in the United States

19. Which is a normative economic statement?
- **(a)** the consumer price index rose 5.6% last month
- **(b)** the unemployment rate of 6.8% is too high
- **(c)** the average rate of interest on loans is 8.6%
- **(d)** the economy grew at an annual rate of 2.6%

20. Sandra states that "there is a high correlation between consumption and income." Arthur replies that the correlation occurs because "people consume too much of their income and don't save enough."
- **(a)** Both Sandra's and Arthur's statements are positive.
- **(b)** Both Sandra's and Arthur's statements are normative.
- **(c)** Sandra's statement is positive and Arthur's statement is normative.
- **(d)** Sandra's statement is normative and Arthur's statement is positive.

21. What pitfall to objective thinking is reflected in a person's view that corporate profits are always excessive?
- **(a)** bias
- **(b)** definition
- **(c)** the fallacy of composition
- **(d)** confusing correlation and causation

22. During World War II, the United States used price control to prevent inflation; some people said this was "a fascist and arbitrary restriction of economic freedom," while others said it was "a necessary and democratic means of preventing ruinous inflation." Both labels are examples of
- **(a)** economic bias
- **(b)** the fallacy of composition
- **(c)** the misuse of commonsense definitions
- **(d)** loaded terminology

23. If a farmer grows a larger crop one year, he or she will likely receive more income. Therefore, to reason that if all farmers grew larger crops one year they will likely receive more income is an example of
- **(a)** the after this, therefore because of this fallacy
- **(b)** the fallacy of composition
- **(c)** economic bias
- **(d)** using loaded terminology

24. The government increases its expenditures for road construction equipment, and later the average price of this equipment falls. The belief that the lowered price was the result of the increase in government expenditures is an example of:
- **(a)** the after this, therefore because of this fallacy
- **(b)** the fallacy of composition
- **(c)** imprecise definition
- **(d)** using loaded terminology

25. You observe that more education is associated with more income and conclude that more income leads to more education. This would be an example of

- **(a)** the fallacy of composition
- **(b)** confusing correlation and causation
- **(c)** using the other things equal assumption
- **(d)** the after this, therefore because of this fallacy

■ PROBLEMS

1. Use the appropriate number to match the terms with the phrase.

1. economics
2. theoretical economics
3. policy economics
4. macroeconomics
5. microeconomics
6. positive economics
7. normative economics
8. empirical economics

a. The formulation of courses of action to bring about desired economic outcomes or to prevent undesired occurrences. _____

b. The attempt to establish scientific statements about economic behavior; a concern with "what is" rather than what ought to be." _____

c. Part of economics that involves value judgments about what the economy should be like or the way the economic world should be. _____

d. Social science concerned with the efficient use of scarce resources to achieve maximum satisfaction of human material wants. _____

e. Part of economics concerned with the whole economy or its major sectors. _____

f. The testing of economic hypotheses and theories. _____

g. Deriving economic principles from relevant economic facts. _____

h. Part of economics concerned with the economic behavior of individual units such as households, firms, and industries (particular markets). _____

2. *News report:* "The worldwide demand for wheat from the United States increased and caused the price of wheat in the United States to rise." This is a *specific* instance of a more *general* economic principle. Of which economic *generalization* is this a particular example? _____

_____

_____

3. Following are four statements. Each is an example of one of the pitfalls frequently encountered in the study of economics. Indicate in the space following each statement the type of pitfall involved.

a. "Investment in stocks and bonds is the only way to build real capital assets." _____

b. "An unemployed worker can find a job if the worker looks diligently and conscientiously for employment; therefore, all unemployed workers can find employment if they are diligent and conscientious in looking for a job."

_____

c. **McConnell:** "Regulation of public utilities in the United States is an immoral and unconscionable interference with the divine right of private property and, as you know, there is no private property in the socialist nations." **Brue:** "It is far from that. You know perfectly well that it is an attempt to limit the unmitigated avarice of mammoth corporations in order, as the Constitution commands, to promote the general welfare of a democratic America." _____

_____

d. "The stock market crash of 1929 was followed by and resulted in 10 years of depression." _____

_____

4. Following is a list of economic statements. Indicate in the space to the right of each statement whether it is positive (P) or normative (N). Then, in the last four lines below, write two of your own examples of positive economic statements and two examples of normative economic statements.

a. New York City should control the rental price of apartments. _____

b. Consumer prices rose at an annual rate of 5% last year. _____

c. Most people who are unemployed are just too lazy to work. _____

d. Generally, if you lower the price of a product, people will buy more of that product. _____

e. The profits of drug companies are too large and ought to be used to conduct research on new medicines. _____

f. Government should do more to help the poor. _____

g. _____ P

h. _____ P

i. _____ N

j. _____ N

■ SHORT ANSWER AND ESSAY QUESTIONS

1. Define economics in both a less and a more sophisticated way. In your latter definition, explain the meaning of "resources" and "wants."

2. What are the three interrelated features of the economic perspective?

3. What is the economic meaning of the statement "there is no such thing as a free lunch"?

4. What is the difference between rational self-interest and selfishness?

5. How do economists use marginal analysis?

6. What are the principal reasons for studying economics?

7. Define the terms "induction" and "deduction" and give an example of each.

8. Define and explain the relationships between economic theory and policy economics.

9. What is the relationship between fact and theory?

10. What is a "laboratory experiment under controlled conditions"? Does the science of economics have any kind of laboratory? Why do economists use the "other things equal" assumption?

11. Why are economic principles and models necessarily generalized and abstract?

12. What does it mean to say that economic principles can be used for prediction?

13. What procedure should be followed in formulating sound economic policies?

14. Of the eight economic goals listed in the text, which one would you *rank* first, second, third, etc.? Would you add any other goals to this list? If economic goals 2 and 4 were conflicting, which goal would you prefer? Why? If goals 1 and 5 were conflicting, which would you prefer? Why?

15. How can the concept "tradeoffs" be applied to the discussion of economic goals? Give an example.

16. Explain the difference between macroeconomics and microeconomics.

17. Why do economists disagree?

18. What are some current examples of positive economic statements and normative economic statements?

19. Explain each of the following terms:
   (a) fallacy of composition
   (b) loaded terminology
   (c) the *post hoc, ergo propter hoc* fallacy

20. Use an example to describe how correlation differs from causation.

ANSWERS

Chapter 1 The Nature and Method of Economics

FILL-IN QUESTIONS

1. limited, maximum
2. scarcity, cost, alternative
3. rational, marginal
4. citizen, academic, vocational
5. theoretical
6. inductive, deductive
7. laws, theories, models
8. generalizations, abstractions
9. other things equal (or *ceteris paribus*)
10. policy
11. goal, options, effectiveness
12. *a.* economic growth; *b.* full employment; *c.* economic efficiency; *d.* price stability; *e.* economic freedom; *f.* equitable distribution of income; *g.* economic security; *h.* balance of trade (*any order for a–h*)
13. complementary, conflicting, tradeoffs
14. macroeconomics, microeconomics

15. aggregate
16. positive, normative, normative
17. bias
18. loaded, common
19. composition
20. *post hoc*

TRUE-FALSE QUESTIONS

1. T, p. 3	**8.** T, p. 7	**15.** T, p. 9	**22.** F, p. 11
2. T, p. 4	**9.** T, p. 7	**16.** T, p. 9	**23.** F, p. 11
3. F, p. 4	**10.** T, p. 7	**17.** F, pp. 9-10	**24.** F, p. 11
4. T, pp. 4-5	**11.** T, p. 8	**18.** F, pp. 9-10	**25.** T, pp. 11-13
5. F, pp. 5-6	**12.** T, p. 8	**19.** T, p. 10	
6. T, pp. 6-7	**13.** T, pp. 8-9	**20.** F, p. 10	
7. F, p. 7	**14.** F, p. 8	**21.** T, pp. 10-11	

MULTIPLE-CHOICE QUESTIONS

1. b, p. 3	**8.** a, pp. 7–8	**15.** b, p. 9	**22.** d, p. 11
2. c, p. 4	**9.** a, p. 8	**16.** c, p. 9	**23.** b, p. 11
3. b, pp. 4-5	**10.** d, p. 8	**17.** b, pp. 9-10	**24.** a, p. 11
4. c, pp. 4-5	**11.** b, pp. 8-9	**18.** d, p. 10	**25.** b, pp. 11-13
5. d, pp. 6-7	**12.** c, p. 9	**19.** b, p. 10	
6. c, p. 7	**13.** d, p. 9	**20.** c, p. 10	
7. b, p. 7	**14.** c, p. 9	**21.** a, pp. 10-11	

PROBLEMS

1. *a.* 3; *b.* 6; *c.* 7; *d.* 1; *e.* 4; *f.* 8; *g.* 2; *h.* 5
2. An increase in the demand for an economic good will cause the price of that good to rise.
3. *a.* definitions; *b.* the fallacy of composition; *c.* loaded terminology; *d.* the after this, therefore because of this fallacy.
4. *a.* N; *b.* P; *c.* N; *d.* P; *e.* N; *f.* N

SHORT ANSWER AND ESSAY QUESTIONS

1. p. 3	**6.** pp. 5-6	**11.** pp. 7-8	**16.** pp. 9-10
2. pp. 4-5	**7.** p. 7	**12.** pp. 7-8	**17.** p. 10
3. p. 4	**8.** pp. 6-9	**13.** pp. 8-9	**18.** p. 10
4. p. 4	**9.** pp. 6-8	**14.** p. 9	**19.** p. 11
5. pp. 4-5	**10.** p. 8	**15.** p. 9	**20.** pp. 11-13

Graphs and Their Meaning

This appendix introduces graphing in economics. Graphs help illustrate and simplify the economic theories and models presented throughout this book. The old saying that "a picture is worth 1000 words" applies to economics; graphs are the way that economists "picture" relationships between economic variables.

You must master the basics of graphing if these "pictures" are to be of any help to you. The appendix explains how to achieve that mastery. It shows you how to construct a graph from a table of data of two variables, such as income and consumption. Economists usually, but not always, place the *independent variable* (income) on the horizontal axis and the *dependent variable* (consumption) on the vertical axis of the graph. Once the data points are plotted and a line drawn to connect the plotted points, you can determine whether there is a *direct* or an *inverse relationship* between the variables. Identifying a direct and an inverse relationship between variables is an essential skill used repeatedly in this book.

Information from data in graphs and tables can be written in an equation. This work involves determining the *slope* and *intercept* from a straight line in a graph or data in a table. Using values for the slope and intercept, you can write a *linear equation* that will enable you to calculate what the dependent variable would be for a given level of the independent variable.

Some graphs used in the book are *nonlinear*. With *nonlinear curves,* the slope of the line is no longer constant throughout but varies as one moves along the curve. This slope can be estimated at a point by determining the slope of a straight line that is drawn tangent to the curve at that point. Similar calculations can be made for other points to see how the slope changes along the curve.

■ APPENDIX CHECKLIST

After you have studied this appendix you should be able to

☐ Explain why economists use graphs.
☐ Construct a graph of two variables using the numerical data from a table.
☐ Make a table with two variables from data on a graph.
☐ Distinguish between a direct and an inverse relationship when given data on two variables.
☐ Identify dependent and independent variables in economic examples and graphs.

☐ Describe how economists use the other things equal (*ceteris paribus*) assumption in graphing two variables.
☐ Calculate the slope of a straight line between two points when given the tabular data, and indicate whether the slope is positive or negative.
☐ Describe how slopes are affected by the choice of the units of measurement for either variable.
☐ Explain how slopes are related to marginal analysis.
☐ Graph infinite or zero slopes and explain their meaning.
☐ Determine the vertical intercept for a straight line in a graph with two variables.
☐ Write a linear equation using the slope of a line and the vertical intercept; when given values for the dependent variable, determine values for the independent variable.
☐ Estimate the slope of a nonlinear curve at a point using a line that is tangent to the curve at that point.

■ APPENDIX OUTLINE

1. Graphs illustrate the relationship between variables and give economists and students another way, in addition to verbal explanation, of understanding economic phenomena. Graphs are aids in describing economic theories and models.

2. The construction of a simple graph involves plotting the numerical data of two variables from a table.

    a. Each graph has a horizontal and a vertical axis that can be labeled for each variable and then scaled for the range of the data point that will be measured on the axis.

    b. Data points are plotted on the graph by drawing perpendiculars from the scaled points on the two axes to the place on the graph where the perpendiculars intersect.

    c. A line or curve can then be drawn to connect the points plotted on the graph.

3. A graph provides information about relationships between variables.

    a. An upward-sloping line to the right on a graph indicates that there is a positive or *direct relationship* between two variables: an increase in one is associated with an increase in the other; a decrease in one is associated with a decrease in the other.

    b. A downward-sloping line to the right means that there is a negative or *inverse relationship* between the two variables: An increase in one is associated with a decrease in the other; a decrease in one is associated with an increase in the other.

4. Economists are often concerned with determining cause and effect in economic events.

a. A dependent variable changes (increases or decreases) because of a change in another variable.

b. An independent variable produces or "causes" the change in the dependent variable.

c. In a graph, mathematicians place an independent variable on the horizontal axis and a dependent variable on the vertical axis; economists are more arbitrary about which variable is placed on an axis.

5. Economic graphs are simplifications of economic relationships. When graphs are plotted, usually an implicit assumption is made that all other factors are being held constant. This "other things equal" or *ceteris paribus* assumption is used to simplify the analysis so the study can focus on the two variables of interest.

6. The *slope* of a straight line in a two-variable graph is the ratio of the vertical change to the horizontal change between two points.

a. A *positive* slope indicates that the relationship between the two variables is *direct.*

b. A *negative* slope indicates that there is an *inverse* relationship between the two variables.

c. Slopes are affected by the *measurement units* for either variable.

d. Slopes measure *marginal* changes.

e. Slopes can be *infinite* (line parallel to vertical axis) or *zero* (line parallel to horizontal axis).

7. The vertical *intercept* of a straight line in a two-variable graph is the point where the line intersects the vertical axis of the graph.

8. The slope and intercept of a straight line can be expressed in the form of a *linear equation,* which is written as $y = a + bx$. Once the values for the intercept (*a*) and the slope (*b*) are calculated, then given any value of the independent variable (*x*), the value of the dependent variable (*y*) can be determined.

9. The slope of a straight line is constant, but the slope of a nonlinear curve changes throughout. To estimate the slope of a nonlinear curve at a point, the slope of a line tangent to the curve at that point is calculated.

■ **HINTS AND TIPS**

1. This appendix will help you understand the graphs and problems presented throughout the book. Do not skip reading the appendix or working on the self-test questions and problems in this *Study Guide.* The time you invest now will pay off in improved understanding in later chapters. Graphing is a basic skill for economic analysis.

2. Positive and negative relationships in graphs often confuse students. To overcome this confusion, draw a two-variable graph with a positive slope and another two-variable graph with a negative slope. In each graph, show

what happens to the value of one variable when there is a change in the value of the other variable.

3. A straight line in a two-variable graph can be expressed in an equation. Make sure you know how to interpret each part of the linear equation.

■ **IMPORTANT TERMS**

vertical and horizontal axes

direct (positive) and inverse (negative) relationships

dependent and independent variables

slope of a straight line

vertical intercept

linear equation

nonlinear curve

tangent

SELF-TEST

■ **FILL-IN QUESTIONS**

1. The relationship between two economic variables can be visualized with the aid of a two-dimensional _____, which has a _____ axis and a _____ axis.

2. Customarily, the (dependent, independent) _____ variable is placed on the horizontal axis and the _____ is placed on the vertical axis. The _____ variable is said to change because of a change in the _____ variables.

3. The vertical and horizontal (scales, ranges) _____ of the graph are calibrated to reflect the _____ of values in the table of data points on which the graph is based.

4. The graph of a straight line that slopes downward to the right indicates that there is a(n) (direct, inverse) _____ relationship between the two variables. A graph of a straight line that slopes upward to the right tells us that the relationship is (direct, inverse) _____. When the value of one variable increases and the value of the other variable increases, then the relationship is _____; when the value of one increases, while the other decreases, the relationship is _____.

5. In interpreting an economic graph, the "cause" or the "source" is the (dependent, independent) _____ variable and the "effect" or "outcome" is the _____ variable.

6. Other variables, beyond the two in a two-dimensional graph, that might affect the economic relationship are assumed to be (changing, held constant) _____. This assumption is also referred to as the "other things

equal" assumption or as (*post hoc, ceteris paribus*)
_____.

7. The slope of a straight line between two points is defined as the ratio of the (vertical, horizontal) _____ change to the _____ change.

8. When two variables move in the same direction, the slope will be (negative, positive) _____; when the variables move in opposite directions, the slope will be _____.

9. The slope of a line will be affected by the (units of measurement, vertical intercept) _____.

10. The concept of a slope is important to economists because it reflects the (marginal, total) _____ change in one variable on another variable.

11. A graph of a line with an infinite slope is (horizontal, vertical) _____, while a graph of a line with a zero slope is _____.

12. The point at which the slope of the line meets the vertical axis is called the vertical (tangent, intercept) _____.

13. We can express the graph of a straight line with a linear equation that can be written as $y = a + bx$.

    a. *a* is the (slope, intercept) _____ and *b* is the _____

    b. *y* is the (dependent, independent) _____ variable and *x* is the _____ variable.

    c. If *a* were 2, *b* were 4, and *x* were 5, then *y* would be _____. If the value of *x* changed to 7, then *y* would be _____. If the value of *x* changed to 3, then *y* would be _____.

14. The slope of a (straight line, nonlinear curve) _____ is constant throughout; the slope of a _____ varies from point to point.

15. An estimate of the slope of a nonlinear curve at a certain point can be made by calculating the slope of a straight line that is (tangent, perpendicular) _____ to the point on the curve.

■ **TRUE-FALSE QUESTIONS**

Circle the T if the statement is true, the F if it is false.

  1. Economists design graphs to confuse people. **T F**

  2. If the straight line on a two-variable graph slopes downward to the right, then there is a positive relationship between the two variables. **T F**

  3. A variable that changes as a consequence of a change in another variable is considered a dependent variable. **T F**

  4. Economists always put the independent variable on the horizontal axis and the dependent variable on the vertical axis of a two-variable graph. **T F**

  5. *Ceteris paribus* means that other variables are changing at the same time. **T F**

  6. In the ratio for the calculation of the slope of a straight line, the vertical change is in the numerator and the horizontal change is in the denominator. **T F**

  7. If the slope of the linear relationship between consumption and income was .90, then it tells us that for every $1 increase in income there will be a $.90 increase in consumption. **T F**

  8. The slope of a straight line in a two-variable graph will *not* be affected by the choice of the units for either variable. **T F**

  9. The slopes of lines measure marginal changes. **T F**

10. The absence of a relationship between a change in the price of variable *A* and the quantity of variable *B* would be described by a line parallel to the horizontal axis. **T F**

11. A line with an infinite slope in a two-variable graph is parallel to the horizontal axis. **T F**

12. In a two-variable graph, income is graphed on the vertical axis and the quantity of snow is graphed on the horizontal axis. If income was independent of the quantity of snow, then this independence would be represented by a line parallel to the horizontal axis. **T F**

13. If a linear equation is $y = 10 + 5x$, the vertical intercept is 5. **T F**

14. When a line is tangent to a nonlinear curve, then it intersects the curve at a particular point. **T F**

15. If the slope of a straight line on a two-variable (x, y) graph were .5 and the vertical intercept were 5, then a value of 10 for *x* would mean that *y* is also 10. **T F**

16. A slope of -4 for a straight line in a two-variable graph indicates that there is an inverse relationship between the two variables. **T F**

17. If *x* is an independent variable and *y* is a dependent variable, then a change in *y* results in a change in *x.* **T F**

18. An upward slope for a straight line that is tangent to a nonlinear curve indicates that the slope of the nonlinear curve at that point is positive. **T F**

19. If one pair of *x, y* points was (13, 10) and the other pair was (8, 20), then the slope of the straight line between the two sets of points in the two-variable graph, with *x* on the horizontal axis and *y* on the vertical axis, would be 2. **T F**

20. When the value of **x** is 2, a value of 10 for **y** would be calculated from a linear equation of **y** = −2 + 6**x**.

T   F

■ **MULTIPLE-CHOICE QUESTIONS**

Circle the letter that corresponds to the best answer.

1. If an increase in one variable is associated with a decrease in another variable, then we can conclude that the variables are
 (a) nonlinear
 (b) directly related
 (c) inversely related
 (d) positively related

2. The ratio of the absolute vertical change to the absolute horizontal change between two points of a straight line is the
 (a) slope
 (b) vertical intercept
 (c) horizontal intercept
 (d) point of tangency

3. There are two sets of **x, y** points on a straight line in a two-variable graph, with **y** on the vertical axis and **x** on the horizontal axis. If one set of points was (0, 5) and the other set (5, 20), the linear equation for the line would be
 (a) **y** = 5**x**
 (b) **y** = 5 + 3**x**
 (c) **y** = 5 + 15**x**
 (d) **y** = 5 + .33**x**

4. In a two-variable graph of data on the price and quantity of a product, economists place
 (a) price on the horizontal axis because it is the independent variable and quantity on the vertical axis because it is the dependent variable
 (b) price on the vertical axis because it is the dependent variable and quantity on the horizontal because it is the independent variable
 (c) price on the vertical axis even though it is the independent variable and quantity on the horizontal axis even though it is the dependent variable
 (d) price on the horizontal axis even though it is the dependent variable and quantity on the vertical axis even though it is the independent variable

5. In a two-dimensional graph of the relationship between two economic variables, an assumption is usually made that
 (a) both variables are linear
 (b) both variables are nonlinear
 (c) other variables are held constant
 (d) other variables are permitted to change

6. When the slope of a straight line to a point tangent to a nonlinear curve is zero, then the straight line is
 (a) vertical
 (b) horizontal
 (c) upward sloping
 (d) downward sloping

Questions 7, 8, 9, and 10 are based on the following four data sets. In each set, the independent variable is in the left column and the dependent variable is in the right column.

(1)		(2)		(3)		(4)	
A	**B**	**C**	**D**	**E**	**F**	**G**	**H**
0	1	0	12	4	5	0	4
3	2	5	8	6	10	1	3
6	3	10	4	8	15	2	2
9	4	15	0	10	20	3	1

7. There is an inverse relationship between the independent and dependent variable in data sets
 (a) 1 and 4
 (b) 2 and 3
 (c) 1 and 3
 (d) 2 and 4

8. The vertical intercept is 4 in data set
 (a) 1
 (b) 2
 (c) 3
 (d) 4

9. The linear equation for data set 1 is
 (a) **B** = 3**A**
 (b) **B** = 1 + 3**A**
 (c) **B** = 1 + .33**A**
 (d) **A** = 1 + .33**B**

10. The linear equation for data set 2 is
 (a) **C** = 12 − 1.25**D**
 (b) **D** = 12 + 1.25**C**
 (c) **D** = 12 − .80**C**
 (d) **C** = 12 − .80**D**

Answer Questions 11, 12, 13, and 14 on the basis of the following diagram.

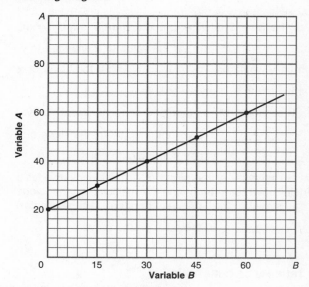

11. The variables **A** and **B** are:
 (a) positively related
 (b) negatively related
 (c) indirectly related
 (d) nonlinear

12. The slope of the line is
    (a) .33
    (b) .67
    (c) 1.50
    (d) 3.00

13. The vertical intercept is
    (a) 80
    (b) 60
    (c) 40
    (d) 20

14. The linear equation for the slope of the line is
    (a) $A = 20 + .33B$
    (b) $B = 20 + .33A$
    (c) $A = 20 + .67B$
    (d) $B = 20 + .67A$

Answer Questions 15, 16, and 17 on the basis of the following diagram.

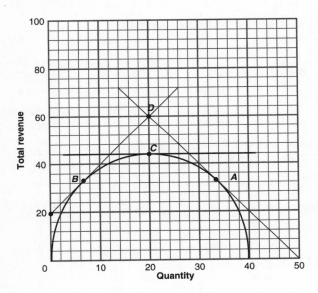

15. The slope of the line tangent to the curve at point **A** is
    (a) 2
    (b) −2
    (c) −1.5
    (d) −0.5

16. The slope of the line tangent to the curve at point **B** is
    (a) −2
    (b) 2
    (c) 3
    (d) 0.5

17. The slope of the line tangent to the curve at point **C** is
    (a) −1
    (b) 1
    (c) 0
    (d) undefined

18. Assume that the relationship between concert ticket prices and attendance is expressed in the equation $P =$ $25 - 1.25Q$, where **P** equals ticket price and **Q** equals concert attendance in thousands of people. On the basis of this equation, it can be said that
    (a) more people will attend the concert when the price is high compared to when the price is low
    (b) if 12,000 people attended the concert, then the ticket price was $10
    (c) if 18,000 people attend the concert, then entry into the concert was free
    (d) an increase in ticket price by $5 reduces concert attendance by 1000 people

19. If you know that the equation relating consumption (**C**) to income (**Y**) is $C = \$7,500 + .2Y$, then
    (a) consumption is inversely related to income
    (b) consumption is the independent variable and income is the dependent variable
    (c) if income is $15,000, then consumption is $10,500
    (d) if consumption is $30,000, then income is $10,000

20. If the dependent variable changes by 22 units when the independent variable changes by 12 units, then the slope of the line is
    (a) 0.56
    (b) 1.83
    (c) 2.00
    (d) 3.27

■ **PROBLEMS**

1. Following are three tables for making graphs. On the graphs, plot the economic relationships contained in each table. Be sure to label each axis of the graph and indicate the unit measurement and scale used on each axis.
    a. Use the table at the top of the next page to graph national income on the horizontal axis and consumption expenditures on the vertical axis below; connect the seven points and label the curve "Consumption." The relationship between income and consumption is

a(n) (direct, inverse) _____ one and the

consumption curve a(n) (up-, down-) _____ sloping curve.

National income, billions of dollars	Consumption expenditures, billions of dollars
$ 600	$ 600
700	640
800	780
900	870
1000	960
1100	1050
1200	1140

b. Use the next table to graph investment expenditures on the horizontal axis and the rate of interest on the vertical axis; connect the seven points and label the curve "Investment." The relationship between the rate of interest and investment expenditures is a(n) (direct, inverse) _____ one and the investment curve is a(n) (up-, down-) _____ sloping curve.

Rate of interest, %	Investment expenditures, billions of dollars
8	$220
7	280
6	330
5	370
4	400
3	420
2	430

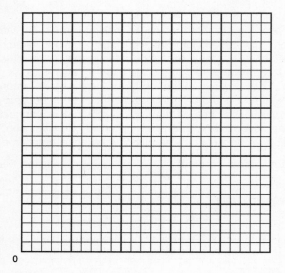

0

c. Use the next table to graph average salary on the horizontal axis and wine consumption on the vertical axis; connect the seven points.

Average salary, U.S. college professors	Annual per capita wine consumption in liters
$52,000	11.5
53,000	11.6
54,000	11.7
55,000	11.8
56,000	11.9
57,000	22.0
58,000	22.1

0

(1) The average salary of a college professor and wine consumption (are, are not) _____ *correlated.* The higher average salary (is, is not) _____ the *cause* of the greater consumption of wine.

(2) The relationship between the two variables may be purely _____; or, as is more likely, both the higher salaries and the greater consumption of wine may be the result of the higher _____ in the U.S. economy.

2. This question is based on the following graph.

a. Construct a table for points **A–I** from the data shown in the graph.

b. According to economists, price is the (independent, dependent) _____ variable and quantity is the _____ variable.

c. Write a linear equation that summarizes the data.

3. The following three sets of data each show the relationship between an independent variable and a dependent variable. For each set, the independent variable is in the left column and the dependent variable is in the right column.

(1)		(2)		(3)	
A	**B**	**C**	**D**	**E**	**F**
00	10	0	100	0	20
10	30	10	75	50	40
20	50	20	50	100	60
30	70	30	25	150	80
40	90	40	0	200	100

a. Write an equation that summarizes the data for sets (1), (2), and (3).

b. State whether each data set shows a positive or an inverse relationship between the two variables.

c. Plot data sets 1 and 2 on the following graph. Use the same horizontal scale for both sets of independent variables and the same vertical scale for both sets of dependent variables.

0

4. This problem is based on the following graph.

a. The slope of the straight line through point *a* is?
b. The slope of the straight line through point *b* is?
c. The slope of the straight line through point *c* is?

■ **SHORT ANSWER AND ESSAY QUESTIONS**

1. Why do economists use graphs in their work?

2. Give two examples of a graph that illustrates the relationship between two economic variables.

3. What does the slope tell you about a straight line? How would you interpret a slope of 4? A slope of −2? A slope of .5? A slope of −.25?

4. If the vertical intercept increases in value but the slope of a straight line stays the same, what happens to the graph of the line? If the vertical intercept decreases in value, what will happen to the line?

5. How do you interpret a vertical line on a two-variable graph? How do you interpret a horizontal line?

6. When you know that the price and quantity of a product are inversely related, what does this tell you about the slope of a line? What do you know about the slope when the two variables are positively related?

7. Which variable is the dependent and which is the independent in the following economic statement: "A decrease in business taxes had a positive effect on investment spending."

8. How do you tell the difference between a dependent and independent variable when examining economic relationships?

9. Why is an assumption made that all other variables are held constant when we construct a two-variable graph of the price and quantity of a product?

10. How do mathematicians and economists differ at times in how they construct two-dimensional graphs? Give an example.

11. How is the slope of a straight line in a two-variable graph affected by the choice of the units for either variable? Explain and give an example.

12. What is the relationship between the slopes of lines and marginal analysis?

13. Describe a case in which a straight line in a two-variable graph would have an infinite slope and a case in which the slope of a line would be zero.

14. If you know that the equation relating consumption (**C**) to income (**Y**) is $C = 10{,}000 + 5Y$, then what would consumption be when income is $5000? Construct an income-consumption table for five different levels of income.

15. How do the slopes of a straight line and a nonlinear curve differ? How do you estimate the slope of a nonlinear curve?

ANSWERS

Appendix to Chapter 1 Graphs and Their Meaning

FILL-IN QUESTIONS

1. graph, horizontal, vertical (either order for last two)
2. independent, dependent, dependent, independent
3. scales, ranges
4. inverse, direct, direct, inverse
5. independent, dependent
6. held constant, *ceteris paribus*
7. vertical, horizontal
8. positive, negative
9. units of measurement
10. marginal
11. vertical, horizontal
12. intercept
13. *a.* intercept, slope; *b.* dependent, independent; *c.* 22, 30, 14
14. straight line, nonlinear curve
15. tangent

TRUE-FALSE QUESTIONS

1. F, p. 15	**6.** T, p. 17	**11.** F, p. 18	**16.** T, pp. 17
2. F, pp. 15-16	**7.** T, pp. 17-18	**12.** T, p. 18	**17.** F, pp. 16-17
3. T, p. 16	**8.** F, p. 17	**13.** F, p. 18	**18.** T, p. 19
4. F, p. 17	**9.** T, p. 18	**14.** F, p. 19	**19.** F, pp. 16-17
5. F, p. 17	**10.** T, p. 18	**15.** T, pp. 18-19	**20.** T, pp. 18-19

MULTIPLE-CHOICE QUESTIONS

1. c, pp. 15-16	**6.** b, pp. 18-19	**11.** a, pp. 15-16	**16.** b, p. 17
2. a, p. 17	**7.** d, pp. 15-16	**12.** b, p. 17	**17.** c, pp. 17-19
3. b, pp. 17-19	**8.** d, p. 18	**13.** d, p. 18	**18.** b, pp. 18-19
4. c, p. 17	**9.** c, p. 18	**14.** c, pp. 18-19	**19.** c, pp. 18-19
5. c, p. 17	**10.** c, p. 18	**15.** b, p. 17	**20.** b, p. 17

PROBLEMS

1. *a.* direct, up-; *b.* inverse, down-; *c.* (1) are, is not; (2) coincidental, incomes (standard of living, or similar answer)
2. *a.*; *b.* independent, dependent; *c.* $P = 4.00 - .25Q$

Point	Price	Quantity
A	$4.00	0
B	3.50	2
C	3.00	4
D	2.50	6
E	2.00	8
F	1.50	10
G	1.00	12
H	.50	14
I	.00	16

3. *a.* (1) $B = 10 + 2A$; (2) $D = 100 - 2.5C$; (3) $F = 20 + .4E$; *b.* (1) positive; (2) inverse; (3) positive
4. *a.* 5; *b.* 0; *c.* -10

■ SHORT ANSWER AND ESSAY QUESTIONS

1. p. 15	**5.** p. 18	**9.** p. 17	**13.** p. 18
2. p. 16	**6.** pp. 15-16	**10.** pp. 18-19	**14.** pp. 18-19
3. p. 17	**7.** pp. 16-17	**11.** p. 17	**15.** p. 19
4. p. 18	**8.** pp. 16-17	**12.** p. 18	

CHAPTER 2

The Economizing Problem

Chapter 2 explains the central problem of economics: Resources—the ultimate means of satisfying material wants—are scarce *relative* to the insatiable wants of society. Economics as a science is the study of the various aspects of the behavior of society in its effort to allocate the scarce resources—land, labor, capital, and entrepreneurial ability—in order to satisfy as best it can its unlimited desire for consumption.

Economics is called the science of efficiency. To understand what efficiency means, however, you must first define its two characteristics: *full employment* and *full production.* Full employment means that all productive resources available to the economy are being used. Full production requires that two types of efficiency—allocative and productive—are being achieved. *Allocative efficiency* means that resources are being devoted to the production of the goods and services society most highly values. *Productive efficiency* entails producing this optimal product mix in the least costly way.

The *production possibilities curve* is used in this chapter's tables and graphs to discuss the major concerns of economics. The production possibilities model is a valuable device for illustrating the meaning of many concepts defined in the chapter—scarcity, choice, the law of increasing opportunity cost, allocative and productive efficiency, unemployment, and economic growth. It can also be applied to many real economic situations involving budgeting, wartime production, discrimination, productivity, economic growth comparisons, environmental protection, international trade, famine, and central planning. This basic economic model is the first and one of the most important ones presented in the text that you will be using to understand the economic world.

Every economy is faced with the problem of scarce resources and has to find ways to respond to the economic problem. No economy answers the problem in the same way that another economy does. Between the extremes of pure (or laissez-faire) capitalism and the command economy (socialism) are various economic systems; all these systems are different devices—different methods of organization—for finding an answer to the economic problem of relative scarcity. Chapters 3 through 6 explain in greater detail how the U.S. economy is organized and operates to address the economizing problem.

The *circular flow model* (or diagram) is a device which illustrates for a capitalistic economy the relation between households and businesses, the flow of money and economic goods and services between households and

businesses, their dual role as buyers and sellers, and the two basic types of markets essential to the capitalist process.

■ **CHECKLIST**

When you have studied this chapter you should be able to

☐ Explain the economizing problem in terms of wants and resources.
☐ Identify four types of economic resources.
☐ Describe the resource payments made in return for each economic resource.
☐ Write a definition of economics that incorporates the relationship between resources and wants.
☐ Explain why full employment and full production are necessary for the efficient use of resources.
☐ Distinguish between allocative efficiency and productive efficiency.
☐ State the four assumptions made when a production possibilities table or curve is constructed.
☐ Construct a production possibilities curve when you are given the appropriate data.
☐ Define opportunity cost and utilize a production possibilities curve to explain the concept.
☐ State the law of increasing opportunity costs.
☐ Show how the law of increasing opportunity cost is reflected in the shape of the production possibilities curve.
☐ Explain the economic rationale for the law of increasing opportunity cost.
☐ Use marginal analysis to define allocative efficiency.
☐ Explain how allocative efficiency determines the optimal point on a production possibilities curve.
☐ Use a production possibilities curve to illustrate unemployment and productive inefficiency.
☐ Use the production possibilities curve to illustrate economic growth.
☐ Explain how international trade affects a nation's production possibilities curve.
☐ Give examples of the application of the production possibilities model.
☐ Define pure capitalism, command economy, and traditional economy.
☐ Use two characteristics to compare and contrast pure capitalism with a command economy.
☐ Explain why many economies can be described as mixed economic systems.

☐ Draw the circular flow diagram; correctly label the real and money flows and the two major types of markets.

☐ Draw the circular flow model, correctly labeling the two markets and the real and money flows between the two sectors in this simplified economy.

■ CHAPTER OUTLINE

1. The study of economics rests on the bases of two facts:

a. Society's material wants are unlimited.

b. The economic resources which are the ultimate means of satisfying these wants are scarce in relation to the wants.

(1) Economic resources are classified as land, capital, labor, and entrepreneurial ability.

(2) The payments received by those who provide the economy with these four resources are rental income, interest income, wages, and profits, respectively.

(3) Because these resources are scarce (or limited), the output that the economy is able to produce is also limited.

2. Economics, then, is the study of how society's scarce resources are used (administered) to obtain the greatest satisfaction of its material wants. To be efficient in the use of its resources, an economy must achieve both full employment and full production.

a. *Full employment* means that the economy is using all available resources.

b. *Full production* means that all resources used for production should contribute to the maximum satisfaction of society's material wants. Full production implies that there is

(1) *productive efficiency,* in which the goods and services society desires are being produced in the least costly way.

(2) *allocative efficiency,* in which resources are devoted to the production of goods and services society most highly values.

c. The production possibilities table indicates the alternative combinations of goods and services an economy is capable of producing when it has achieved full employment and full production.

(1) The four assumptions usually made when a production possibilities table is constructed is that economic efficiency, fixed resources, fixed technology, and two products are being considered.

(2) The table illustrates the fundamental choice every society must make: what quantity of each product it wants produced.

d. The data in the production possibilities table can be plotted on a graph to obtain a production possibilities curve.

e. The opportunity cost of producing an additional unit of one product is the total amount of other products that are sacrificed. The law of increasing opportunity costs reflects that the opportunity cost of producing additional units of a product increases as more of that product is produced.

(1) The law of increasing opportunity costs results in a production possibilities curve that is concave (from the origin).

(2) The opportunity cost of producing additional units of a product increases as more of the product is produced because resources are not completely adaptable to alternative uses.

f. Allocative efficiency means that resources are devoted to the optimal product mix for society. This optimal mix is determined by assessing marginal costs and benefits.

(1) The marginal-cost curve for a product rises because of the law of increasing opportunity costs; the marginal-benefit curve falls because the consumption of a product yields less and less satisfaction.

(2) There will be *underallocation* of resources to production of a product when the marginal benefit is greater than the marginal cost, and *overallocation* when the marginal cost is greater than the marginal benefit.

(3) Allocative efficiency is achieved when the marginal cost of a product equals the marginal benefit of a product.

3. Different outcomes will occur when assumptions underlying the production possibilities model are relaxed.

a. *Unemployment.* The economy may be operating at a point inside the production possibilities curve if the assumption of full production and productive efficiency no longer holds. In this case, there will be an unemployment of resources and production will not occur in the least costly way.

b. *Economic Growth.* The production possibilities curve can move outward if the assumption of fixed resources or the assumption of no technological change is dropped.

(1) Economic growth can occur when there is an expansion in the quantity and quality of resources, or when there is technological advancement.

(2) The combination of goods and services an economy chooses to produce today helps determine its production possibilities in the future.

c. International trade and specialization allow a nation to obtain more goods and services than what is indicated by its production possibilities curve, and thus the effect is similar to an increase in economic growth.

4. There are many applications of the production possibilities model. Seven are discussed in the chapter: society's production of military or consumer goods, discrimination, land-use controversies, women in the labor force, economic growth in Japan and the United States, famine in Africa, and emerging technologies.

5. Different economic systems differ as to how they respond to the economizing problem.

a. At one extreme is pure capitalism, which relies on the private ownership of its economic resources and the market system.

b. At the other extreme, the command economy uses the public ownership of its resources and central planning.

c. Economies in the real world lie between these two extremes and are hybrid systems.

d. Some less-developed nations have traditional (or customary) economies which are shaped by the society's customs and traditions.

6. The circular flow model is a device used to clarify the relationships between households and business firms in a purely capitalistic economy.

    a. In resource markets, households supply and firms demand resources, and in product markets, the firms supply and households demand products. Households use the incomes they obtain from supplying resources to purchase the goods and services produced by the firms, and in the economy there is a real flow of resources and products and a money flow of incomes and expenditures.

    b. The circular flow model has several limitations.

■ HINTS AND TIPS

1. Chapter 2 presents many economic definitions and classifications. Spend time learning these definitions *now* because they are used in later chapters, and you must know them if you are to understand what follows.

2. The production possibilities graph is a simple and extremely useful economic model. Practice your understanding of it by using it to explain the following economic concepts: scarcity, choice, opportunity cost, the law of increasing opportunity costs, full employment, full production, productive efficiency, allocative efficiency, unemployment, and economic growth.

3. Opportunity cost is always measured in terms of a foregone alternative. From a production possibilities table, you can easily calculate how many units of one product you forgo when you get another unit of a product. The ratio of what you forgo to what you get measures the opportunity cost of a choice in a production possibilities table.

■ IMPORTANT TERMS

economizing problem

utility

economic resources

land, capital, labor, and entrepreneurial ability

investment

factors of production

economics

full employment

full production

allocative efficiency

productive efficiency

consumer goods

capital goods

production possibilities table

production possibilities curve

opportunity cost

law of increasing opportunity costs

economic growth

unemployment

economic systems

pure capitalism

market systems

command economies

traditional economies

resource market

product market

circular flow model

SELF-TEST

■ FILL-IN QUESTIONS

1. The economizing problem arises because society's material wants are (limited, unlimited) _____ and economic resources are _____.

2. Consumers want to obtain goods and services that provide (resources, utility) _____. Some products that meet this objective are (capital goods, necessities) _____, while others are (investment goods, luxuries) _____.

3. The four types of resources are

    a. _____

    b. _____

    c. _____

    d. _____

4. Both consumer goods and capital goods satisfy human wants. The consumer goods satisfy these wants (directly, indirectly) _____, and the capital goods satisfy them _____.

5. The income individuals receive from supplying land or natural resources is (interest, rental) _____ income, whereas the income received from supplying capital goods is _____ income. The income received by individuals who supply labor is (wage, profit) _____ income; the income received from entrepreneurial ability is _____ income.

6. Economics is the social science concerned with the problem of using (unlimited, scarce) _____ resources to attain the maximum fulfillment of society's _____ wants.

7. Economic efficiency requires full (employment, allocation) _____ so that all available resources can be used and that there be full (production, distribution) _____ so that the employed resources contribute to the maximum satisfaction of material wants.

8. Full production implies that two types of efficiency are achieved: Resources are devoted to the production of the mix of goods and services society most wants, or there is (allocative, productive) _____ efficiency and the goods and services will be produced in the least costly way, or there will be _____ efficiency.

9. When a production possibilities table or curve is constructed, four assumptions are made:

    a. _____

b. _____

c. _____

d. _____

10. In a two-product world, the quantity of other goods and services an economy must give up to produce more housing is the opportunity (benefit, cost) _____ of producing the additional housing.

11. The law of increasing opportunity costs explains why the production possibilities curve is (convex, concave) _____ from the origin. The economic rationale for the law is that economic resources (are, are not) _____ completely adaptable to alternative uses.

12. Allocative efficiency is determined by assessing the marginal costs and benefits of the output from the allocation of resources to production.

    a. The marginal cost curve for a product rises because of increasing (satisfaction, opportunity costs) _____, and the marginal benefit curve falls because of less _____ from the additional consumption of a product.

    b. When the marginal benefit is greater than the marginal cost, there will be (over, under) _____-allocation of resources to the production of a product, but when the marginal cost is greater than the marginal benefit, there will be an _____-allocation.

    c. Optimal allocation of resources occurs when the marginal costs of the product output are (greater than, less than, equal to) _____ the marginal benefits.

13. Following is a production possibilities curve for capital goods and consumer goods.

    a. If the economy moves from point **A** to point **B**, it will produce (more, fewer) _____ capital goods and (more, fewer) _____ consumer goods.

    b. If the economy is producing at point **X**, some resources in the economy are either (not available,

unemployed) _____ or (underemployed, overemployed) _____.

    c. If the economy moves from point **X** to point **B** (more, fewer) _____ capital goods and (more, fewer) _____ consumer goods will be produced.

    d. If the economy is to produce at point **Y,** there must be (unemployment, economic growth) _____. This can occur because of a resource supply (decrease, increase) _____ or a technological (decline, improvement) _____.

14. The more an economy consumes its current production, the (more, less) _____ it will be capable of producing in future years if other things are equal.

15. The United States' experience with World War II or the Vietnam War can be used to illustrate the production possibilities curve by placing (labor resources, military goods) _____ on one axis and (capital resources, civilian goods) _____ on the other axis and then drawing a curve (bowed out from, bowed into) _____ the origin.

16. Technological advance can shift a nation's production possibilities curve (inward, outward) _____ because the effects are similar to an increase in (economic growth, unemployment) _____.

17. The institutional arrangements and coordinating mechanisms used to respond to the economic problem is called (a traditional economy, an economic system) _____.

18. In pure capitalism, property resources are (publicly, privately) _____ owned. The means used to direct and coordinate economic acitivity is the (command, market) _____ system.

19. In a command economy, property resources are (publicly, privately) _____ owned. The coordinating device in this economic system is (planning, markets) _____.

20. In the circular flow model,

    a. Households are demanders and businesses are suppliers in (product, resource) _____ markets, and businesses are demanders and households are suppliers in _____ markets.

    b. The flow of economic resources and finished goods and services is the (money, real) _____ flow, and the flow of income and expenditures is the _____ flow.

■ TRUE-FALSE QUESTIONS

Circle the T if the statement is true, the F if it is false.

1. The conflict between the scarce material wants of society and its unlimited economic resources gives rise to the economizing problem. **T F**

2. The wants with which economics is concerned include only those wants which can be satisfied by goods and services. **T F**

3. Money is a resource and is classified as "capital." **T F**

4. From the economist's perspective, investment refers to the production and purchase of capital goods. **T F**

5. The payment to entrepreneurial ability is interest income. **T F**

6. Resources are scarce because society's material wants are unlimited and productive resources are limited. **T F**

7. Economic efficiency requires that there be both full employment of resources and full production. **T F**

8. Allocative efficiency means that goods and services are being produced by society in the least costly way. **T F**

9. Only allocative efficiency is necessary for there to be full production. **T F**

10. The opportunity cost of producing antipollution devices is the other goods and services the economy is unable to produce because it has decided to produce these devices. **T F**

11. The opportunity cost of producing a good tends to increase as more of it is produced because resources less suitable to its production must be employed. **T F**

12. Drawing a production possibilities curve concave to the origin is the geometric way of stating the law of increasing opportunity costs. **T F**

13. Economic rationale for the law of increasing opportunity cost is that economic resources are fully adaptable to alternative uses. **T F**

14. Allocative efficiency is determined by assessing the marginal costs and benefits of the output from the allocation of resources to production. **T F**

15. The marginal-cost curve for a product rises because of increasing satisfaction from the consumption of the product. **T F**

16. Given full employment and full production, it is not possible for an economy capable of producing just two goods to increase its production of both. **T F**

17. Economic growth means an increase in the production of goods and services, and it is shown by a movement of the production possibilities to the right. **T F**

18. The more capital goods an economy produces today, the greater will be the total output of all goods it can produce in the future, other things being equal. **T F**

19. International trade and specialization can shift the production possibilities of a nation outward, similar to what would occur if there were increased economic growth. **T F**

20. If a country has unemployed resources at the outset of a war, it can increase its production of military goods without having to decrease its production of civilian goods. **T F**

21. Pure capitalism is also called laissez-faire capitalism. **T F**

22. A command economy is characterized by the private ownership of resources and the use of markets and prices to coordinate and direct economic activity. **T F**

23. Most real-world economies contain features exhibiting both pure capitalism and a command economy. **T F**

24. In the circular flow model, the household functions on the demand side of the resource and product markets. **T F**

25. One limitation of the simple model of the circular flow is that flows of output and income are constant. **T F**

■ MULTIPLE-CHOICE QUESTIONS

Circle the letter that corresponds to the best answer.

1. Which is the correct match of an economic resource and payment for that resource?
   (a) land and wages
   (b) labor and interest income
   (c) capital and rental income
   (d) entrepreneurial ability and profit

2. An "innovator" is defined as an entrepreneur who
   (a) makes basic policy decisions in a business firm
   (b) combines factors of production to produce a good or service
   (c) invents a new product or process for producing a product
   (d) introduces new products on the market or employs a new method to produce a product

3. An economy is efficient when it has achieved
   (a) full employment
   (b) full production
   (c) either full employment or full production
   (d) both full employment and full production

4. Allocative and productive efficiency are conditions that best characterize
   (a) full employment
   (b) full production
   (c) traditional economies
   (d) command economies

5. When a production possibilities schedule is written (or a production possibilities curve is drawn) in this chapter, four assumptions are made. Which of the following is one of those assumptions?
   (a) more than two products are produced

(b) the state of technology changes
(c) the economy has both full employment and full production
(d) the quantities of all resources available to the economy are variable, not fixed

Answer Questions 6, 7, 8, and 9 based on the following graph.

6. At point **A** on the production possibilities curve in the above illustration,
    (a) wheat production is inefficient
    (b) tractor production is inefficient
    (c) the economy is employing all its resources
    (d) the economy is not employing all its resources

7. Unemployment and production inefficiency would best be represented in the graph by point:
    (a) **A**
    (b) **B**
    (c) **C**
    (d) **D**

8. The choice of point **B** over point **A** as the optimal product mix for society would be based on
    (a) productive efficiency
    (b) full employment of resources
    (c) the law of increasing opportunity costs
    (d) a comparison of marginal costs and benefits

9. Economic growth could be represented by
    (a) a movement from point **A** to point **B**
    (b) a movement from point **B** to point **A**
    (c) a shift in the production possibilities curve out to point **C**
    (d) a shift in the production possibilities curve out to point **D**

10. The production possibilities curve is
    (a) concave
    (b) convex
    (c) linear
    (d) positive

11. What is the economic rationale for the law of increasing opportunity cost?
    (a) full production and full employment of resources have not been achieved

(b) economic resources are not completely adaptable to alternative uses
(c) economic growth is being limited by the pace of technological advancement
(d) an economy's present choice of output is determined by fixed technology and fixed resources

12. If there is an increase in the resources available within the economy,
    (a) more goods and services will be produced in the economy
    (b) the economy will be capable of producing more goods and services
    (c) the standard of living in the economy will rise
    (d) the technological efficiency of the economy will improve

13. If the production possibilities curve below moves from position **A** to position **B,** then
    (a) the economy has increased the efficiency with which it produces wheat
    (b) the economy has increased the efficiency with which it produces tractors
    (c) the economy has put previously idle resources to work
    (d) the economy has gone from full employment to less than full employment

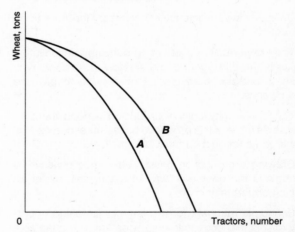

14. Which would be the best example of allocative efficiency? When society devoted resources to the production of
    (a) slide rules instead of hand-held calculators
    (b) horse-drawn carriages instead of automobiles
    (c) word processors instead of manual typewriters
    (d) long-playing records instead of compact discs or cassette tapes

15. Which situation would most likely shift the production possibilities curve for a nation in an outward direction?
    (a) deterioration in product quality
    (b) reductions in the supply of resources
    (c) increases in technological advances
    (d) rising levels of discrimination

16. The opportunity cost of a new public stadium is the
    (a) money cost of hiring guards and staff for the new stadium

(b) cost of constructing the new stadium in a future year

(c) change in the real estate tax rate to pay off the new stadium

(d) other goods and services that must be sacrificed to construct the new stadium

17. Which situation would most likely cause a nation's production possibilities curve to shift inward?

(a) investing more resources in new plants and equipment

(b) eliminating discrimination based on race and ethnic background

(c) increasing international trade or incurring a trade deficit

(d) going to war with another nation and suffering a major defeat

18. The combination of products in society's production possibilities table which is the most valued or optimal is determined

(a) at the midpoint of the production possibilities table

(b) at the endpoint of the production possibilities table

(c) where the marginal benefits equal marginal costs

(d) where the opportunity costs are maximized

19. The underallocation of resources by society to the production of a product means that the

(a) marginal benefit is greater than the marginal cost

(b) marginal benefit is less than the marginal cost

(c) opportunity cost of production is rising

(d) consumption of the product is falling

Answer Questions 20, 21, and 22 on the basis of the data given in the following production possibilities table.

	Production possibilities (alternatives)					
	A	B	C	D	E	F
Capital goods	100	95	85	70	50	0
Consumer goods	0	100	180	240	280	300

20. The choice of alternative **B** compared with alternative **D** would tend to promote

(a) a slower rate of economic growth

(b) a faster rate of economic growth

(c) increased consumption in the present

(d) central economic planning

21. If the economy is producing at production alternative **D**, the opportunity cost of 40 more units of consumer goods is about

(a) 5 units of capital goods

(b) 10 units of capital goods

(c) 15 units of capital goods

(d) 20 units of capital goods

22. In the table, the law of increasing opportunity costs is suggested by the fact that

(a) greater and greater quantities of consumer goods must be given up to get more capital goods

(b) smaller and smaller quantities of consumer goods must be given up to get more capital goods

(c) capital goods are relatively more scarce than consumer goods

(d) the production possibilities curve will eventually shift outward as the economy expands

23. The private ownership of property resources and use of the market system to direct and coordinate economic activity is characteristic of

(a) pure capitalism

(b) the command economy

(c) market socialism

(d) the traditional economy

24. The two kinds of markets found in the circular flow model are

(a) real and money markets

(b) real and traditional markets

(c) money and authoritarian markets

(d) product and resource markets

25. In the circular flow model, businesses

(a) demand both products and resources

(b) supply both products and resources

(c) demand products and supply resources

(d) supply products and demand resources

■ **PROBLEMS**

1. Following is a list of resources. Indicate in the space to the right of each whether the resource is land (LD), capital (C), labor (LR), entrepreneurial ability (EA), or some combinations of these resources.

a. Fishing grounds in the North Atlantic   _____

b. A cash register in a retail store   _____

c. Uranium deposits in Canada   _____

d. An irrigation ditch in Nebraska   _____

e. The work performed by Bill Gates   _____

f. The oxygen breathed by human beings   _____

g. An IBM plant in Rochester, Minnesota   _____

h. The food on the shelf of a grocery store   _____

i. The work done by a robot in an auto plant   _____

j. The tasks accomplished in perfecting a new computer for commercial sales   _____

k. A carpenter building a house   _____

2. Following is a production possibilities table for two commodities: wheat and automobiles. The table is constructed using the usual assumptions. Wheat is measured in units of 100,000 bushels and automobiles in units of 100,000.

Combination	Wheat	Automobiles
A	0	7
B	7	6
C	13	5
D	18	4
E	22	3
F	25	2
G	27	1
H	28	0

a. Follow the general rules for making graphs (see the appendix to Chapter 1); plot the data from the table on the graph below to obtain a production possibilities curve. Place wheat on the vertical axis and automobiles on the horizontal axis.

b. Fill in the following table showing the opportunity cost per unit of producing the 1st through the 7th automobile.

Automobiles	Cost of production
1st	_____
2d	_____
3d	_____
4th	_____
5th	_____
6th	_____
7th	_____

3. The graph in the next column is a production possibilities curve. Draw on this graph

    a. a production possibilities curve which indicates greater efficiency in the production of good **A**

    b. a production possibilities curve which indicates greater efficiency in the production of good **B**

    c. a production possibilities curve which indicates an increase in the resources available to the economy

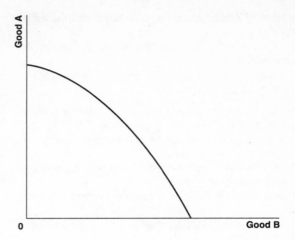

4. Following is a list of 12 economic goods. Indicate in the space to the right of each good whether it is a consumer good (CON), a capital good (CAP), or that it depends (DEP) on who is using it and for what purpose.

    a. An automobile _____

    b. A tractor _____

    c. A taxicab _____

    d. A house _____

    e. A factory building _____

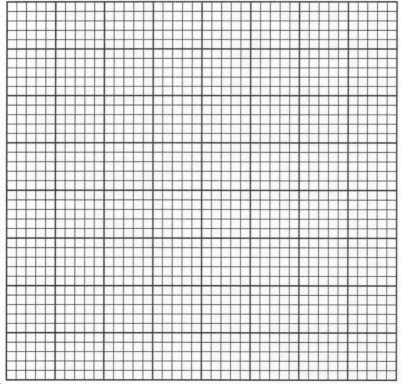

f. An office building _____

g. An ironing board _____

h. A refrigerator _____

i. A telephone _____

j. A quart of a soft drink _____

k. A cash register _____

l. A screwdriver _____

5. In the circular flow diagram below, the upper pair of flows (*a* and *b*) represent the resource market and the lower pair (*c* and *d*) the product market.

Supply labels or explanations for each of the four flows:

a. _____

b. _____

c. _____

d. _____

■ SHORT ANSWER AND ESSAY QUESTIONS

1. Explain what the term "economizing problem" means. Why are resources scarce?

2. In what sense are wants satiable or insatiable?

3. What are the four economic resources? How is each resource defined?

4. What is the income each economic resource earns?

5. When is a society economically efficient? What does "full production" mean, and how does it differ from "full employment"?

6. Explain why full production implies both allocative and productive efficiency.

7. What four assumptions are made in drawing a production possibilities curve or schedule?

8. What is opportunity cost? Give an example.

9. What is the law of increasing opportunity cost? Why do costs increase?

10. What determines the optimal product mix for society's production possibilities?

11. How can unemployment be illustrated with the production possibilities curve?

12. What will be the effect of increasing resource supplies on production possibilities?

13. Describe how technological advances will affect the production possibilities curve.

14. Explain the tradeoff between goods for the present and goods for the future and the effect on economic growth.

15. What qualification does international trade make for the interpretation of production possibilities?

16. Describe how going to war can be illustrated by the production possibilities curve.

17. Give examples of other real-world applications of the production possibilties curve.

18. Pure capitalism and the command economy differ in two important ways. Compare the two economic systems with each other and with authoritarian capitalism and market socialism.

19. In the circular flow model, what are the two markets? What roles do households play and what role do businesses play in each market?

20. In the circular flow model, what two income flows are pictured in money terms and in real terms? What two expenditure flows are pictured in money terms and in real terms?

ANSWERS

Chapter 2 The Economizing Problem

FILL-IN QUESTIONS

1. unlimited, limited
2. utility, necessities, luxuries
3 *a.* land or natural resources, *b.* capital, *c.* labor, *d.* entrepreneurial ability
4. directly, indirectly
5. rental, interest, wage, profit
6. scarce, unlimited
7. employment, production
8. allocative, productive
9. *a.* the economy is operating at full employment and full production; *b.* the available supplies of the factors of production are fixed; *c.* technology does not change during the course of the analysis; *d.* the economy produces only two products
10. cost
11. concave, are not
12. *a.* opportunity costs, satisfaction; *b.* under, over; *c.* equal to
13. *a.* fewer, more; *b.* unemployed, underemployed; *c.* more, more; *d.* economic growth, increase, improvement
14. less
15. military goods, civilian goods, bowed out from
16. outward, economic growth
17. economic system
18. privately, market
19. publicly, planning
20. *a.* product, resource; *b.* real, money

TRUE-FALSE QUESTIONS

1. F, pp. 22	**3.** F, pp. 23-24	**5.** F, p. 24	**7.** T, p. 24
2. T, pp. 22-23	**4.** T. p. 23	**6.** T, p. 24	**8.** F, p. 25

9. F, p. 25   **14.** T, pp. 28-29 **19.** T, pp. 32-33 **24.** F, pp. 36-37
10. T, pp. 27-28 **15.** F, pp. 27-28 **20.** T, p. 33   **25.** T, p. 36
11. T, pp. 27-28 **16.** T, pp. 26-27 **21.** T, p. 34
12. T, p. 28   **17.** T, pp. 30-31 **22.** F, p. 35
13. F, p. 28   **18.** T, pp. 31-32 **23.** T, p. 35

MULTIPLE-CHOICE QUESTIONS

1. d, p. 24   **8.** d, p. 28-29   **15.** c, pp. 30-31 **22.** a, pp. 27-28
2. d, p. 24   **9.** d, p. 31   **16.** d, p. 27   **23.** a, p. 34
3. d, p. 24   **10.** a, p. 28   **17.** d, p. 34   **24.** d, p. 36
4. b, p. 25   **11.** b, p. 28   **18.** c, pp. 28-29 **25.** d, p. 36
5. c, pp. 25-26 **12.** b, p. 30   **19.** a, pp. 28-29
6. c, p. 26   **13.** b, pp. 30-32 **20.** b, p. 31-32
7. c, pp. 29-30 **14.** c, pp. 28-29 **21.** d, p. 27-28

PROBLEMS

1. *a.* LD; *b.* C; *c.* LD; *d.* C; *e.* EA; *f.* LD; *g.* C; *h.* C; *i.* C; *j.* EA; *k.* LR

2. *b.* 1, 2, 3, 4, 5, 6, 7 units of wheat
3. *a.* curve will shift outward along good A axis but stay at the same point on good B axis; *b.* curve will shift outward along good B axis but stay at the same point on good A axis; *c.* entire curve will shift outward
4. *a.* DEP; *b.* CAP; *c.* CAP; *d.* DEP; *e.* CAP; *f.* CAP; *g.* DEP; *h.* DEP; *i.* DEP; *j.* DEP; *k.* CAP; *l.* DEP
5. *a.* money income payments (wages, rent, interest, and profit); *b.* services or resources (land, labor, capital, and entrepreneurial ability); *c.* goods and services; *d.* expenditures for goods and services

SHORT ANSWER AND ESSAY QUESTIONS

1. pp. 22-24   **6.** p. 25   **11.** p. 30   **16.** pp. 33-34
2. p. 23   **7.** pp. 25-26   **12.** p. 30   **17.** pp. 33-34
3. pp. 23-24   **8.** pp. 4; 27   **13.** pp. 30-31   **18.** pp. 34-35
4. p. 24   **9.** pp. 27-28   **14.** pp. 31-32   **19.** pp. 35-37
5. pp. 24-25   **10.** pp. 28-29   **15.** p. 32   **20.** pp. 36-37

Understanding Individual Markets: Demand and Supply

Chapter 3 introduces you to the most fundamental tools of economic analysis: demand and supply. To progress successfully into the later chapters, it is essential that you understand what is meant by demand and supply and how to use these powerful tools.

Demand and supply are simply "boxes" or categories into which all the forces and factors that affect the price and the quantity of a good bought and sold in a competitive market are placed. Demand and supply determine price and quantity exchange, and it is necessary to see *why* and *how* they do this.

Many students never do understand demand and supply because they never learn to *define* demand and supply *exactly.* They never learn (1) what an increase or decrease in demand or supply means, (2) the important distinctions between "demand" and "quantity demanded" and between "supply" and "quantity supplied," and (3) the equally important distinctions between an increase (or decrease) in demand and an increase (or decrease) in quantity demanded and between an increase (or decrease) in supply and an increase (or decrease) in quantity supplied.

Having learned these, however, it is no great trick to comprehend the so-called law of supply and demand. The equilibrium price—that is, the price which will tend to prevail in the market as long as demand and supply do not change—is simply the price at which **quantity demanded** and **quantity supplied** are equal. The quantity bought and sold in the market (the equilibrium quantity) is the quantity demanded and supplied at the equilibrium price. If you can determine the equilibrium price and quantity under one set of demand and supply conditions, you can determine them under any other set and so will be able to analyze for yourself the effects of changes in demand and supply upon equilibrium price and quantity.

This chapter includes a brief examination of the factors that determine demand and supply and the ways in which changes in these determinants will affect and cause changes in demand and supply. A graphic method is used in this analysis in order to facilitate an understanding of demand and supply, equilibrium price and quantity, changes in demand and supply, and the resulting changes in equilibrium price and quantity. In addition to understanding the *specific* definitions of demand and supply, it is necessary to understand the two counterparts of demand and supply: the **demand curve** and the **supply curve.** These are graphic (or geometric) representations of the same data contained in the schedules of demand and supply.

You will use supply and demand over and over. It will turn out to be as important to you in economics as jet propulsion is to the pilot of a Boeing 767: You can't get off the ground without it.

■ CHECKLIST

When you have studied this chapter you should be able to

☐ Define a market.
☐ Define demand and state the law of demand.
☐ Graph the demand curve when you are given a demand schedule.
☐ Explain the difference between individual and market demand.
☐ List the major determinants of demand and explain how each one shifts the demand curve.
☐ Distinguish between change in demand and change in the quantity demanded.
☐ Define supply and state the law of supply.
☐ Graph the supply curve when you are given a supply schedule.
☐ List the major determinants of supply and explain how each shifts the supply curve.
☐ Distinguish between change in supply and change in the quantity supplied.
☐ Define surplus and shortage.
☐ Describe how the equilibrium price and quantity are determined in a competitive market.
☐ Determine, when you are given the demand for and the supply of a good, the equilibrium price and the equilibrium quantity.
☐ Predict the effects of changes in demand and supply on equilibrium price and equilibrium quantity; and on the prices of substitute and complementary goods.
☐ Explain the meaning of the rationing function of prices.
☐ Explain why violations of the "other things equal" assumption may cause confusion about the validity of the laws of demand and supply.
☐ Give a real-world application of supply and demand.

■ CHAPTER OUTLINE

1. A market is any institution or mechanism that brings together buyers and sellers of a particular good or service. This chapter assumes that markets are highly competitive.

2. *Demand* is a schedule of prices and the quantities which buyers would purchase at each of these prices during a selected period of time.

    a. As price rises, other things being equal, buyers will purchase smaller quantities, and as price falls they will purchase larger quantities; this is the law of demand.

    b. The demand curve is a graphic representation of demand and the law of demand.

    c. Market (or total) demand for a good is a summation of the demands of all individuals in the market for that good.

    d. The demand for a good depends on the tastes, income, and expectations of buyers; the number of buyers in the market; and the prices of related goods.

    e. A change (either an increase or a decrease) in demand is caused by a change in any of the factors (in **d**) which determine demand and means that the demand schedule and demand curve have changed.

    f. A change in demand and a change in the quantity demanded are *not* the same thing.

3. *Supply* is a schedule of prices and the quantities which sellers will sell at each of these prices during some period of time.

    a. The supply schedule shows, other things equal, that as the price of the good rises larger quantities will be offered for sale, and that as the price of the good falls, smaller quantities will be offered for sale.

    b. The supply curve is a graphic representation of supply and the law of supply; the market supply of a good is the sum of the supplies of all sellers of the good.

    c. The supply of a good depends on the techniques used to produce it, the prices of the resources employed in its production, the extent to which it is taxed or subsidized, the prices of other goods which might be produced, the price expectations of sellers, and the number of sellers of the product.

    d. Supply will change when any of these determinants of supply changes; a change in supply is a change in the entire supply schedule or curve.

    e. A change in supply must be distinguished from a change in quantity supplied.

4. The market or *equilibrium price* of a product is that price at which quantity demanded and quantity supplied are equal; the quantity exchanged in the market (the equilibrium quantity) is equal to the quantity demanded and supplied at the equilibrium price.

    a. The rationing function of price is the elimination of shortages and surpluses of the commodity.

    b. A change in demand, supply, or both changes both the equilibrium price and the equilibrium quantity in specific ways.

    c. When demand and supply schedules (or curves) are drawn up, it is assumed that all the nonprice determinants of demand and supply remain unchanged. This assumption is often stated as "other things equal."

    d. There are many real-world examples of the application of supply and demand.

■ HINTS AND TIPS

1. This chapter is the most important one in the book. Make sure you spend extra time on it and master the material. If you do, your long-term payoff will be a much easier understanding of the applications in later chapters.

2. One mistake students often make is to confuse *change in demand* with *change in quantity demanded.* A change in demand causes the entire demand curve to *shift,* whereas a change in quantity demanded is simply a *movement* along an existing demand curve.

3. It is strongly recommended that you draw supply and demand graphs as you work on supply and demand problems so you can see a picture of what happens when demand shifts, supply shifts, or both demand and supply shift.

4. Make a chart and related graphs that show the eight possible outcomes from changes in demand and supply. Figure 3-6 in the text illustrates the *four single shift* outcomes:

    (1) $D\uparrow$: $P\uparrow$, $Q\uparrow$ (3) $S\uparrow$: $P\downarrow$, $Q\uparrow$

    (2) $D\downarrow$: $P\downarrow$, $Q\downarrow$ (4) $S\downarrow$: $P\uparrow$, $Q\downarrow$

Four shift combinations are described in Table 3-9 of the text. Make a figure to illustrate each combination.

    (1) $S\uparrow$, $D\downarrow$: $P\downarrow$, Q?   (3) $S\uparrow$, $D\uparrow$: P?, $Q\uparrow$

    (2) $S\downarrow$, $D\uparrow$: $P\uparrow$, Q?   (4) $S\downarrow$, $D\downarrow$: P?, $Q\downarrow$

5. Make sure you understand the other things equal assumption described at the end of the chapter. It will help you understand why the law of demand is not violated even if the price and quantity of a product increase over time.

■ IMPORTANT TERMS

market

demand

demand schedule (curve)

law of demand

diminishing marginal utility

quantity demanded

income effect

substitution effect

demand curve

individual demand

total or market demand

determinant of demand

increase (or decrease) in demand

normal good

inferior good

substitute goods

complementary goods

supply

supply schedule (curve)

quantity supplied

supply curve

determinant of supply

increase (or decrease) in supply

equilibrium price

equilibrium quantity

rationing function of prices

other things equal assumption

SELF-TEST

■ **FILL-IN QUESTIONS**

1. A market is the institution or mechanism that brings together buyers or (demanders, suppliers) _____ and sellers or _____ of a particular good or service.

2. In resource markets prices are determined by the demand decisions of (businesses, households) _____ and the supply decisions of _____.

3. In product markets prices are determined by demand decisions of (businesses, households) _____ and the supply decisions of _____.

4. The relationship between price and quantity in the demand schedule is a(n) (direct, inverse) _____ relationship; in the supply schedule the relationship is a(n) _____ one.

5. The added satisfaction or pleasure a consumer obtains from additional units of a product decreases as the consumer's consumption of the product increases. This phenomenon is called deminishing marginal (equilibrium, utility) _____.

6. A consumer tends to buy more of a product as its price falls because
    a. The purchasing power of the consumer is increased and the consumer tends to buy more of this product (and of other products), this is called the (income, substitution) _____ effect;
    b. The product becomes less expensive relative to similar products and the consumer tends to buy more of the original product and less of a similar product, which is called the _____ effect.

7. When demand or supply is graphed, price is placed on the (horizontal, vertical) _____ axis and quantity on the _____ axis.

8. The change from an individual to a market demand schedule involves (adding, multiplying) _____ the quantities demanded by each consumer at the various possible (incomes, prices) _____.

9. When the price of one product and the demand for another product are directly related, the two products are called (substitutes, complements) _____; however, when the price of one product and the demand for another product are inversely related, the two products are called _____.

10. When a consumer demand schedule or curve is drawn up, it is assumed that five factors that determine demand are fixed and constant. These five determinants of consumer demand are

    a. _____
    b. _____
    c. _____
    d. _____
    e. _____

11. A decrease in demand means that consumers will buy (larger, smaller) _____ quantities at every price, or will pay (more, less) _____ for the same quantities.

12. A change in income or in the price of another product will result in a change in the (demand for, quantity demanded of) _____ the given product, while a change in the price of the given product will result in a change in the _____ the given product.

13. An increase in supply means that producers will make and be willing to sell (larger, smaller) _____ quantities at every price, or will accept (more, less) _____ for the same quantities.

14. A change in resource prices or the prices of other goods that could be produced will result in a change in the (supply, quantity supplied) _____ of the given product, but a change in the price of the given product will result in a change in the _____.

15. The fundamental factors which determine the supply of any commodity in the product market are

    a. _____
    b. _____
    c. _____
    d. _____
    e. _____
    f. _____

16. If quantity demanded is greater than quantity supplied, price is (above, below) _____ the equilibrium price; and the (shortage, surplus) _____ will cause the price to (rise, fall) _____. If quantity demanded is less than the quantity supplied, price is (above, below) _____ the equilibrium price, and the (shortage, surplus) _____ will cause the price to (rise, fall) _____.

17. The equilibrium price of a product is the price at which quantity demanded is (greater than, equal to) _____ quantity supplied, and there (is, is not) _____ a surplus or a shortage at that price.

18. In the space next to **a–h,** indicate the effect [*increase* (+), *decrease* (−), or *indeterminate* (?)] on equilibrium price (**P**) and equilibrium quantity (**Q**) of each of these changes in demand and/or supply.

<table>
<tr><td></td><td>P</td><td>Q</td></tr>
<tr><td>**a.** Increase in demand, supply constant</td><td>____</td><td>____</td></tr>
<tr><td>**b.** Increase in supply, demand constant</td><td>____</td><td>____</td></tr>
<tr><td>**c.** Decrease in demand, supply constant</td><td>____</td><td>____</td></tr>
<tr><td>**d.** Decrease in supply, demand constant</td><td>____</td><td>____</td></tr>
<tr><td>**e.** Increase in demand, increase in supply</td><td>____</td><td>____</td></tr>
<tr><td>**f.** Increase in demand, decrease in supply</td><td>____</td><td>____</td></tr>
<tr><td>**g.** Decrease in demand, decrease in supply</td><td>____</td><td>____</td></tr>
<tr><td>**h.** Decrease in demand, increase in supply</td><td>____</td><td>____</td></tr>
</table>

19. If supply and demand establish a price for a good so that there is no shortage or surplus of a product, then price is successfully performing its (utility, rationing) _____ function. The price that is set is a market-(changing, clearing) _____ price.

20. To assume that all the determinants of demand and supply do not change is to employ the (marginal utility, other things equal) _____ assumption.

■ **TRUE-FALSE QUESTIONS**

Circle the T if the statement is true, the F if it is false.

1. A market is any arrangement that brings together the buyers and sellers of a particular good or service.
T F

2. Demand is the amount of a good or service which a buyer will purchase at a particular price. **T F**

3. The law of demand states that as price increases, other things being equal, the quantity of the product demanded increases. **T F**

4. The law of diminishing marginal utility is one explanation of why there is an inverse relationship between price and quantity demanded. **T F**

5. The substitution effect suggests that, at a lower price, you have the incentive to substitute the more expensive product for similar products which are relatively less expensive. **T F**

6. There is no difference between individual demand schedules and the market demand schedule for a product.
T F

7. In graphing supply and demand schedules, supply is put on the horizontal axis and demand on the vertical axis.
T F

8. If price falls, there will be an increase in demand.
T F

9. If consumer tastes or preferences for a product decreases, the demand for the product will tend to decrease.
T F

10. An increase in income will tend to increase the demand for a product. **T F**

11. When two products are substitute goods, the price of one and the demand for the other will tend to move in the same direction. **T F**

12. If two goods are complementary, an increase in the price of one will tend to increase the demand for the other.
T F

13. A change in the quantity demanded means that there has been a change in demand. **T F**

14. Supply is a schedule which shows the amounts of a product a producer can make in a limited time period.
T F

15. An increase in resource prices will tend to decrease supply. **T F**

16. A government subsidy for the production of a product will tend to decrease supply. **T F**

17. An increase in the prices of other goods that could be made by producers will tend to decrease the supply of the current good that the producer is making. **T F**

18. A change in supply means that there is a movement along an existing supply curve. **T F**

19. A surplus indicates that the quantity demanded is less than the quantity supplied at that price. **T F**

20. If the market price of a product is below its equilibrium price, the market price will tend to rise because demand will decrease and supply will increase.
T F

21. The equilibrium price of a good is the price at which the demand and the supply of the good are equal.
T F

22. The rationing function of prices is the elimination of shortages and surpluses. **T F**

23. If the supply of a product increases and demand decreases, the equilibrium price and quantity will increase.
T F

24. If the demand for a product increases and the supply of the product decreases, the equilibrium price will increase and equilibrium quantity will be indeterminant.
T F

25. Economists often make the assumption of other things equal to hold constant the effects of other factors when examining the relationship between prices and quantities demanded and supplied. **T F**

■ MULTIPLE-CHOICE QUESTIONS

Circle the letter that corresponds to the best answer.

1. The markets examined in this chapter
(a) sell nonstandard or differentiated products
(b) have buyers cooperating to determine prices
(c) are controlled by a single producer
(d) are highly competitive

2. A schedule which shows the various amounts of a product consumers are willing and able to purchase at each price in a series of possible prices during a specified period of time is called
(a) supply
(b) demand
(c) quantity supplied
(d) quantity demanded

3. The reason for the law of demand can best be explained in terms of
(a) supply
(b) complementary goods
(c) the rationing function of prices
(d) diminishing marginal utility

4. Assume that in a competitive market video tape players (VCRs) double in price. What will most likely happen in that market to the equilibrium price and quantity of video tapes?
(a) price will increase; quantity will decrease
(b) price will decrease; quantity will increase
(c) price will decrease; quantity will decrease
(d) price will increase; quantity will increase

5. Given the following individuals' demand schedules for product X, and assuming these are the only three consumers of X, which set of prices and output levels below will be on the market demand curve for this product?

Price X	Consumer 1 Q_{dx}	Consumer 2 Q_{dx}	Consumer 3 Q_{dx}
$5	1	2	0
4	2	4	0
3	3	6	1
2	4	8	2
1	5	10	3

(a) ($5, 2); ($1, 10)
(b) ($5, 3); ($1, 18)
(c) ($4, 6); ($2, 12)
(d) ($4, 0); ($1, 3)

6. Which factor will decrease the demand for a product?
(a) a favorable change in consumer tastes
(b) an increase in the price of a substitute good
(c) a decrease in the price of a complementary good
(d) a decrease in the number of buyers

7. The income of a consumer decreases and the consumer's demand for a particular good increases. It can be concluded that the good is
(a) normal
(b) inferior

(c) a substitute
(d) a complement

8. Which of the following could cause a decrease in consumer demand for product X?
(a) a decrease in consumer income
(b) an increase in the prices of goods which are good substitutes for product X
(c) an increase in the price which consumers expect will prevail for product X in the future
(d) a decrease in the supply of product X

9. If two goods are substitutes for each other, an increase in the price of one will necessarily
(a) decrease the demand for the other
(b) increase the demand for the other
(c) decrease the quantity demanded of the other
(d) increase the quantity demanded of the other

10. If two products, A and B, are complements, then
(a) an increase in the price of A will decrease the demand for B
(b) an increase in the price of A will increase the demand for B
(c) an increase in the price of A will have no significant effect on the price of B
(d) a decrease in the price of A will decrease the demand for B

11. If two products, X and Y, are independent goods, then
(a) an increase in the price of X will significantly increase the demand for Y
(b) an increase in the price of Y will significantly increase the demand for X
(c) an increase in the price of Y will have no significant effect on the demand for X
(d) a decrease in the price of X will significantly increase the demand for Y

12. The law of supply states that, other things being constant, as price increases
(a) supply increases
(b) supply decreases
(c) quantity supplied increases
(d) quantity supplied decreases

13. If the supply curve moves from S_1 to S_2 on the graph below, there has been
(a) an increase in supply
(b) a decrease in supply
(c) an increase in quantity supplied
(d) a decrease in quantity supplied

14. A decrease in the supply of a product would most likely be caused by
  (a) an increase in business taxes
  (b) an increase in consumer incomes
  (c) a decrease in resource costs for production
  (d) a decrease in the price of a complementary good

15. Which of the following could *not* cause an increase in the supply of cotton?
  (a) an increase in the price of cotton
  (b) improvements in the art of producing cotton
  (c) a decrease in the price of the machinery and tools employed in cotton production
  (d) a decrease in the price of corn

16. If the quantity supplied of a product is greater than the quantity demanded for a product, then
  (a) there is a shortage of the product
  (b) there is a surplus of the product
  (c) the product is a normal good
  (d) the product is an inferior good

17. When government sets the price of a good and that price is below the equilibrium price, the result will be
  (a) a surplus of the good
  (b) a shortage of the good
  (c) an increase in the demand for the good
  (d) a decrease in the supply of the good

Answer Questions 18, 19, and 20 on the basis of the data in the the following table. Consider the following supply and demand schedules for corn.

Price	Quantity demanded	Quantity supplied
$20	395	200
22	375	250
24	350	290
26	320	320
28	280	345
30	235	365

18. The equilibrium price in this market is
  (a) $22
  (b) $24
  (c) $26
  (d) $28

19. An increase in the cost of labor lowers the quantity supplied by 65 units at each price. The new equilibrium price would be
  (a) $22
  (b) $24
  (c) $26
  (d) $28

20. If the quantity demanded at each price increases by 130 units, then the new equilibrium quantity will be
  (a) 290
  (b) 320
  (c) 345
  (d) 365

21. A decrease in supply and a decrease in demand will
  (a) increase price and decrease the quantity exchanged
  (b) decrease price and increase the quantity exchanged
  (c) increase price and affect the quantity exchanged in an indeterminate way
  (d) affect price in an indeterminate way and decrease the quantity exchanged

22. An increase in demand and a decrease in supply will
  (a) increase price and increase the quantity exchanged
  (b) decrease price and decrease the quantity exchanged
  (c) increase price and the effect upon quantity exchanged will be indeterminate
  (d) decrease price and the effect upon quantity exchanged will be indeterminate

23. An increase in supply and an increase in demand will:
  (a) increase price and increase the quantity exchanged
  (b) decrease price and increase the quantity exchanged
  (c) affect price in an indeterminate way and decrease the quantity exchanged
  (d) affect price in an indeterminate way and increase the quantity exchanged

24. A cold spell in Florida devastates the orange crop. As a result, California oranges command a higher price. Which of the following statements best explains the situation?
  (a) the supply of Florida oranges decreases, causing the supply of California oranges to increase and their price to increase
  (b) the supply of Florida oranges decreases, causing their price to increase and the demand for California oranges to increase
  (c) the supply of Florida oranges decreases, causing the supply of California oranges to decrease and their price to increase
  (d) the demand for Florida oranges decreases, causing a greater demand for California oranges and an increase in their price

Answer Questions 25, 26, 27, 28, and 29 based on the following graph showing the market supply and demand for a product.

25. Assume that the market is initially in equilibrium where D_1 and S_1 intersect. If there is an increase in the number of buyers, then the new equilibrium would most likely be at point
(a) *W*
(b) *X*
(c) *Y*
(d) *Z*

26. Assume that the equilibrium price and quantity in the market are P_2 and Q_2. Which factor would cause the equilibrium price and quantity to shift to P_1 and Q_3?
(a) an increase in product price
(b) an increase in demand
(c) an increase in supply
(d) a decrease in quantity

27. If the market equilibrium was at point *Y* but the price of the product was set at P_1, then there would be a
(a) surplus of $Q_3 - Q_1$
(b) shortage of $Q_3 - Q_1$
(c) surplus of $Q_1 - Q_2$
(d) shortage of $Q_2 - Q_1$

28. What would cause a shift in the equilibrium price and quantity from point *Z* to point *X*?
(a) a decrease in prodution costs and more favorable consumer tastes for the product
(b) an increase in the number of suppliers and an increase in consumer incomes
(c) an increase in production costs and decrease in consumer incomes
(d) an improvement in production technology and decrease in the price of a substitute good

29. Assume that the market is initially in equilibrium where D_1 and S_1 intersect. If consumer incomes increased and the technology for making the product improved, then new equilibrium would most likely be at
(a) P_1 and Q_1
(b) P_2 and Q_2
(c) P_1 and Q_3
(d) P_3 and Q_1

30. The demand curve and its inverse relationship between price and quantity demanded is based on the assumption of
(a) other things equal
(b) changing expectations
(c) complementary goods
(d) increasing marginal utility

■ **PROBLEMS**

1. Using the demand schedule at the top of the next column, plot the demand curve on the graph below the schedule. Label the axes and indicate for each axis the units being used to measure price and quantity.

Price	Quantity demanded, 1000 bushels of soybeans
$7.20	10
7.00	15
6.80	20
6.60	25
6.40	30
6.20	35

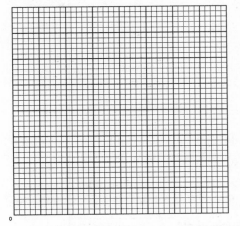

a. Plot the following supply schedule on the same graph.

Price	Quantity supplied, 1000 bushels of soybeans
$7.20	40
7.00	35
6.80	30
6.60	25
6.40	20
6.20	15

b. The equilibrium price of soybeans will be $_____.
c. How many thousand bushels of soybeans will be exchanged at this price? _____
d. Indicate clearly on the graph the equilibrium price and quantity by drawing lines from the intersection of the supply and demand curves to the price and quantity axes.
e. If the Federal government supported a price of $7.00 per bushel there would be a (shortage, surplus) _____ of _____ bushels of soybeans.

2. The demand schedules of three individuals (Robert, Charles, and Lynn) for loaves of bread are shown in the following table. Assuming there are only three buyers of bread, determine and graph the total or market demand schedule for bread.

Price	Quantity demanded, loaves of bread			Total
	Robert	Charles	Lynn	
$.40	1	4	0	_____
.36	3	5	1	_____
.32	6	6	5	_____
.28	10	7	10	_____
.24	15	8	16	_____

3. Following is a demand schedule for bushels of apples. In columns 3 and 4 insert *any* new figures for quantity which represent in column 3 an increase in demand and in column 4 a decrease in demand.

(1) Price	(2) Quantity demanded	(3) Demand increases	(4) Demand decreases
$6.00	400	____	____
5.90	500	____	____
5.80	600	____	____
5.70	700	____	____
5.60	800	____	____
5.50	900	____	____

4. Assume that O'Rourke has, when his income is $100 per week, the demand schedule for good A shown in columns 1 and 2 of the following table and the demand schedule for good B shown in columns 4 and 5. Assume that the prices of A and B are $.80 and $5, respectively.

Demand for A (per week)			Demand for B (per week)		
(1) Price	(2) Quantity demanded	(3) Quantity demanded	(4) Price	(5) Quantity demanded	(6) Quantity demanded
$.90	10	0	$5.00	4	7
.85	20	10	4.50	5	8
.80	30	20	4.00	6	9
.75	40	30	3.50	7	10
.70	50	40	3.00	8	11
.65	60	50	2.50	9	12
.60	70	60	2.00	10	13

a. How much A will O'Rourke buy? _____

How much B? _____

b. Suppose that as a consequence of a $10 increase in O'Rourke's weekly income, the quantities demanded of A become those shown in column 3 and the quantities demanded of B become those shown in column 6.

(1) How much A will he now buy? _____

How much B? _____

(2) Good A is (normal, inferior) _____.

(3) Good B is _____.

5. The market demand for good X is shown in columns 1 and 2 of the following table. Assume the price of X to be $2 and constant.

(1) Price	(2) Quantity demanded	(3) Quantity demanded	(4) Quantity demanded
$2.40	1,600	1,500	1,700
2.30	1,650	1,550	1,750
2.20	1,750	1,650	1,850
2.10	1,900	1,800	2,000
2.00	2,100	2,000	2,200
1.90	2,350	2,250	2,450
1.80	2,650	2,550	2,750

a. If as the price of good Y rises from $1.25 to $1.35 the quantities demanded of good X become those shown in column 3, it can be concluded that X and Y are (substitute, complementary) _____ goods.

b. If as the price of good Y rises from $1.25 to $1.35 the quantities of good X become those shown in column 4, it can be concluded that X and Y are _____ _____ goods.

6. In a local market for hamburger on a given date, each of 300 identical sellers of hamburger has the following supply schedule.

(1) Price	(2) Quantity supplied— one seller, lb	(3) Quantity supplied— all sellers, lb
$2.05	150	_____
2.00	110	_____
1.95	75	_____
1.90	45	_____
1.85	20	_____
1.80	0	_____

a. In column 3 construct the market supply schedule for hamburger.
b. Following is the market demand schedule for hamburger on the same date and in the same local market as that given above.

Price	Quantity demanded, lb
$2.05	28,000
2.00	31,000
1.95	36,000
1.90	42,000
1.85	49,000
1.80	57,000

If the Federal government sets a price on hamburger at $1.90 a pound, the result would be a (shortage, surplus) _____ of _____ pounds of hamburger in this market.

7. Each of the following events would tend to increase or decrease either the demand for or the supply of computer games and, as a result, will increase or decrease the price of these games. In the first blank indicate the effect on demand or supply (increase, decrease); in the second blank, indicate the effect on price (increase, decrease).
a. It becomes known that a local department store is going to have a sale on these games 3 months from now. _____;

_____
b. The workers who produce the games go on strike for over 2 months. _____; _____

c. The workers in the industry receive a $1 an hour wage increase. _____; _____

d. The average price of movie tickets increases.

_____; _____

e. The price of business software, a product also supplied by the computer software producers, rises.

_____; _____

f. It is announced by a private research institute that children who play computer games also improve their grades in school. _____; _____

g. Because of the use of mass production techniques, the amount of labor necessary to produce a game decreases._____; _____

h. The price of computers increases. _____;

_____

i. The average consumer believes that a shortage of games is developing in the economy. _____;

_____

j. The Federal government imposes a $5 per game tax on the manufacturers of computer games.

_____; _____

■ SHORT ANSWER AND ESSAY QUESTIONS

1. What is a market? Define it and give examples.

2. Define demand and the law of demand.

3. What are three possible explanations for the inverse relationship between price and quantity demanded?

4. Two decades ago, the price of coffee in the United States rose significantly as a result of bad weather in coffee-producing regions. Use the income effect and the substitution effect concepts to explain why the quantity of coffee demanded in the United States significantly decreased.

5. Use the diminishing marginal utility concept to explain why the quantity demanded of a product will tend to rise when the price of the product falls.

6. What is the difference between individual and market demand? What is the relationship between these two types of demand?

7. Explain the difference between an increase in demand and an increase in the quantity demanded.

8. What are the factors that cause a change in demand? Use supply and demand graphs to illustrate what happens to price and quantity when demand increases.

9. How are inferior, normal, and superior goods defined? What is the relationship between these goods and changes in income?

10. Why does the effect of a change in the price of related goods depend on whether a good is a substitute or complement? What are substitutes and complements?

11. A newspaper reports that "blue jeans have become even more popular and are now the standard clothing that people wear for both play and work." How will this change affect the demand and supply of blue jeans? What will happen to the price and quantity of blue jeans sold in the market? Explain and use a supply and demand graph to illustrate your answer.

12. Compare and contrast the supply schedule with the demand schedule.

13. Supply does not remain constant for long because the factors which determine supply change. What are these factors? How do changes in them affect supply?

14. Explain the difference between an increase in supply and an increase in the quantity supplied.

15. Describe and illustrate with a supply and demand graph the effect of an increase in supply on price and quantity. Do the same for a decrease in supply.

16. The U.S. Congress passes a law that raises the excise tax on gasoline by $1 per gallon. What effect will this change have on the demand and supply of gasoline? What will happen to gasoline price and quantity? Explain and use a supply and demand graph to illustrate your answer.

17. What is the relationship between the price of a product and a shortage of the product? What is the relationship between the price of a product and surplus of the product?

18. Given the demand for and the supply of a commodity, what price will be the equilibrium price of this commodity? Explain why this price will tend to prevail in the market and why higher (lower) prices, if they do exist temporarily, will tend to fall (rise).

19. Analyze the following quotation and explain the fallacies contained in it: "An increase in demand will cause price to rise; with a rise in price, supply will increase and the increase in supply will push price down. Therefore, an increase in demand results in little change in price because supply will increase also."

20. Suppose an industry sells 2000 units of a product at $10 per unit one year, 3000 units at $12 the next year, and 4000 units at $14 the third year. Is this evidence that the law of demand is violated? Explain.

ANSWERS

Chapter 3 Understanding Individual Markets: Demand and Supply

FILL-IN QUESTIONS

1. demanders, suppliers
2. businesses, households
3. households, businesses
4. inverse, direct
5. utility
6. *a.* income; *b.* substitution
7. vertical, horizontal

8. adding, prices
9. substitutes, complements
10. *a.* the tastes or preferences of consumers; *b.* the number of consumers in the market; *c.* the money income of consumers; *d.* the prices of related goods; *e.* consumer expectations with respect to future prices and income (any order for *a–e*)
11. smaller, less
12. demand for, quantity demanded of
13. larger, less
14. supply, quantity supplied
15. *a.* the technology of production; *b.* resource prices; *c.* taxes and subsidies; *d.* prices of other goods; *e.* price expectations; *f.* the number of sellers in the market (any order for *a–f*)
16. below, shortage, rise, above, surplus, fall
17. equal to, is not
18. *a.* +, +; *b.* −, +; *c.* −, −; *d.* +, −; *e.* ?, +; *f.* +, ?; *g.* ?, −; *h.* −, ?
19. rationing, clearing
20. other things equal

TRUE-FALSE QUESTIONS

1. T, p. 42	10. T, pp. 46-47	19. T, p. 52
2. F, pp. 43; 47-48	11. T, p. 47	20. F, pp. 52-53
3. F, P. 43	12. F, p. 47	21. F, pp. 52-53
4. T, p. 43	13. F, pp. 47-48	22. T, p. 53
5. F, p. 44	14. F, p. 48	23. F, pp. 53-54
6. F, pp. 44-45	15. T, pp. 49-50	24. T, pp. 54-55
7. F, p. 53	16. F, p. 50	25. T, p. 57
8. F, pp. 47-48	17. T, p. 50	
9. T, pp. 45-46	18. F, p. 51	

MULTIPLE-CHOICE QUESTIONS

1. d, p. 42	11. c, p. 47	21. d, p. 56
2. b, p. 43	12. c, p. 49	22. c, pp. 54-55
3. d, p. 43	13. a, p. 50	23. d, p. 55
4. c, pp. 47; 53	14. a, pp. 49-50; 53	24. b, pp. 47; 53
5. b, pp. 44-45	15. a, p. 51	25. c, pp. 46; 53
6. d, pp. 45-47	16. b, p. 52	26. c, p. 53
7. b, p. 47	17. b, p. 52	27. b, pp. 52; 54
8. a, pp. 45-47	18. c, pp. 52-53	28. c, pp. 45-47; 49-51; 56
9. b, p. 47	19. d, pp. 52-53	29. c, pp. 46-47; 50; 55
10. a, p. 47	20. d, pp. 52-53	30. a, pp. 43; 57

PROBLEMS

1. *b.* 6.60; *c.* 25,000; *e.* surplus, 20,000
2. Total: 5, 9, 17, 27, 39
3. Each quantity in column 3 is greater than in column 2, and each quantity in column 4 is less than in column 2.
4. *a.* 30, 4; *b.* (1) 20, 7; (2) inferior; (3) normal (superior)
5. *a.* complementary; *b.* substitute
6. *a.* 45,000; 33,000; 22,500; 13,500; 6,000; 0 *b.* shortage, 28,500
7. *a.* decrease demand, decrease price; *b.* decrease supply, increase price; *c.* decrease supply, increase price; *d.* increase demand, increase price; *e.* decrease supply, increase price; *f.* increase demand, increase price; *g.* increase supply, decrease price; *h.* decrease demand, decrease price; *i.* increase demand, increase price; *j.* decrease supply, increase price

SHORT ANSWER AND ESSAY QUESTIONS

1. p. 42	8. pp. 45; 53	15. p. 53
2. p. 43	9. p. 46-47	16. pp. 50; 53
3. pp. 43-44	10. p. 47	17. p. 52
4. p. 44	11. pp. 45-46; 53	18. pp. 52-53
5. p. 43	12. pp. 43; 48-49	19. p. 51
6. pp. 44-45	13. pp. 49-51	20. p. 53
7. pp. 47-48	14. p. 51	

CHAPTER 4

Pure Capitalism and the Market System

Chapter 4 describes the characteristics of pure capitalism, identifies three practices found in all modern economies, and offers a detailed explanation of the operation of the market system.

The first part of Chapter 4 describes the *ideological* and *institutional* characteristics of pure capitalism. In a pure capitalist system, most of the resources are owned by its citizens, who are free to use them as they wish in their own self-interest. Prices and markets express the self-interests of resource owners, consumers, and business firms. Competition regulates self-interest—to prevent the self-interest of any person or any group from working to the disadvantage of the economy and to make self-interest work for the benefit of the entire economy. The role of government is also limited under pure capitalism.

The three practices of all modern economies are the employment of large amounts of **capital,** the development of **specialization,** and the *use of money.* Economies use capital and engage in specialization because it is a more efficient use of their resources; it results in larger total output and the greater satisfaction of wants. When workers, business firms, and regions within an economy specialize, they become dependent on each other for the goods and services they do not produce for themselves. To obtain these goods and services they must engage in trade. Trade is made more convenient by using money as a medium of exchange.

The latter part of Chapter 4 describes the operation of the competitive market system. There are *Five Fundamental Economic Questions* that any economic system must answer in its attempt to use its scarce resources to satisfy its material wants. The five questions or problems are: (1) How much output is to be produced? (2) What is to be produced? (3) How is the output to be produced? (4) Who is to receive the output? (5) Can the economic system adapt to change? Only the last four questions will be discussed in this chapter; the first question will be discussed in the chapter on macroeconomics.

The explanation of how the market system finds answers to the last four of the Five Fundamental Economic Questions is only an approximation—a simplified version or a model—of the methods actually employed by the U.S. economy. Yet this simple model, like all good models, contains enough realism to be truthful and is general enough to be understandable. If the aims of this chapter are accomplished, you can begin to understand the market system and methods our economy uses to solve the economizing problem presented in Chapter 2.

■ **CHECKLIST**

When you have studied this chapter you should be able to

☐ Identify the six important institutional or ideological characteristics of capitalism.
☐ Describe the significance of property rights in capitalism.
☐ Distinguish between freedom of enterprise and freedom of choice.
☐ Explain why self-interest is a driving force of capitalism.
☐ Identify two features of competition.
☐ Explain the role of a market system in capitalism.
☐ Describe the size of government in capitalism.
☐ List three characteristics of all modern economies.
☐ Explain why the production of capital goods entails roundabout production.
☐ Discuss how specialization improves efficiency.
☐ Describe the advantages of money over barter for the exchange of goods and services.
☐ List the Five Fundamental Economic Questions about the operation of an economy.
☐ Explain how a competitive market system determines what will be produced.
☐ Distinguish between normal profit and economic profit.
☐ Predict what will happen to the price charged by and the output of an expanding and a declining industry, and explain why these events will occur.
☐ Explain how consumer sovereignty and dollar votes work in a market economy.
☐ Describe market restraints on economic freedom.
☐ Explain how production is organized in a competitive market system.
☐ Find the least costly combination of resources when given the technological data and the prices of the resources.
☐ Explain how a competitive market system determines the distribution of total output.
☐ Describe the guiding function of prices to accommodate change in the competitive market system.
☐ Explain how the competitive market system initiates change by fostering technological advances and capital accumulation.
☐ State how the "invisible hand" in the competitive market system tends to promote public or social interests.
☐ List three virtues of the competitive market system.

■ **CHAPTER OUTLINE**

1. The U.S. economy is not pure capitalism, but it is a

close approximation of pure capitalism. Pure capitalism has the following six features that distinguish it from other economic systems.

    a. Private individuals and organizations own and control their property resources by means of the institution of private property.

    b. These individuals and organizations possess both the freedom of enterprise and the freedom of choice.

    c. Each of them is motivated largely by self-interest.

    d. Competition prevents them, as buyers and sellers, from exploiting others.

    e. Markets and prices (the market system) are used to communicate and coordinate the decisions of buyers and sellers.

    f. The role of government is limited in a competitive and capitalist economy.

2. In common with other advanced economies of the world, the U.S. economy has three major characteristics.

    a. It employs complicated and advanced methods of production and large amounts of capital equipment to produce goods and services efficiently.

    b. It is a highly specialized economy, and this specialization increases the productive efficiency of the economy.

    c. It uses money extensively to facilitate trade and specialization.

3. Five Fundamental Economic Questions must be answered by the competitive market system.

    a. How much output is to be produced?

    b. What is to be produced?

    c. How is output to be produced?

    d. Who is to receive the output?

    e. Can the economic system adapt to change?

4. The system of prices and markets and households' and business firms' choices furnish the economy with answers to the last four Fundamental Economic Questions.

    a. The demands of consumers for products and the desires of business firms to maximize their profits determine what and how much of each product is produced and what price it will be set at.

    b. The desires of business firms to maximize profits by keeping their costs of production as low as possible guide them to use the most efficient techniques of production and determine their demands for and prices of the various resources; competition forces them to use the most efficient techniques and ensures that only the most efficient will be able to stay in business.

    c. With resource prices determined, the money income of each household is determined; and with product prices determined, the quantity of goods and services these money incomes will buy is determined.

    d. The market system is able to accommodate itself to changes in consumer tastes, technology, and resource supplies.

    (1) The desires of business firms for maximum profits and competition lead the economy to make the appropriate adjustments in the way it uses its resources.

    (2) Competition and the desire to increase profits promotes better techniques of production and capital accumulation.

5. Competition in the economy compels firms seeking to promote their own interests to promote (as though led by an "invisible hand") the best interest of society as a whole: an allocation of resources appropriate to consumer wants, production by the most efficient means, and the lowest possible prices.

    a. Three noteworthy merits of the market system are

    (1) The *efficient* use of resources

    (2) The *incentive* the system provides for productive activity

    (3) The personal *freedom* allowed participants as consumers, producers, workers, or investors.

■ HINTS AND TIPS

1. The first section of the chapter describes pure capitalism, which is an idealized framework based on *six* characteristics and institutions. After reading the section, check your understanding by listing the six points and writing a short explanation of each one.

2. There are *three* other characteristics of all modern economies that you should know. Can you list and explain them to yourself or to a fellow student? If not, make sure you reread that section of the chapter.

3. The section on the "Market System At Work" is both the most important and the most difficult part of the chapter. A market economy, or any economic system, must answer *Five Fundamental Economic Questions*. Detailed answers to four of the five questions are given in this section of the chapter. If you examine each one individually and in the order in which each is presented, you will more easily understand how the market system works. (Actually, the market system finds the answers simultaneously, but make your learning easier for now by considering them one by one.)

4. Be sure to understand the *importance* and *role* of each of the following in the operation of the market system: (1) the rationing and directing functions of prices, (2) the profit motive of business firms, (3) the entry into and exodus of firms from industries, (4) competition, and (5) consumer sovereignty.

■ IMPORTANT TERMS

private property	economic cost
freedom of choice	normal profit
freedom of enterprise	economic profit
self-interest	expanding industry
competition	declining industry
roundabout production	consumer sovereignty
specialization	dollar votes
division of labor	derived demand
medium of exchange	guiding function of prices
barter	invisible hand
coincidence of wants	
Five Fundamental Questions	

SELF-TEST

■ **FILL-IN QUESTIONS**

1. The ownership of property resources by private individuals and organizations is the institution of private (resources, property) _____. The freedom of private businesses to obain resources and use them to produce goods and services is the freedom of (choice, enterprise) _____, while the freedom to dispose of property or money as a person sees fit is the freedom of _____.

2. Self-interest means that each economic unit attempts to do what is best for itself, but this might lead to an abuse of power in a capitalist economy if it were not directed and constrained by (government, competition) _____. Self-interest and selfishness (are, are not) _____ the same thing in a market economy.

3. According to the economist, competition is present if two conditions prevail; these two conditions are

a. _____

_____

b. _____

_____

4. In a capitalist economy, individual buyers communicate their demands and individual sellers communicate their supplies in the system of (markets, prices) _____, and the outcomes from economic decisions are a set of product and resource _____ that are determined by demand and supply.

5. In the ideology of pure capitalism, government is assigned a(n) (limited, extensive) _____ role.

6. Modern economies make extensive use of capital goods and engage in roundabout production because it is more (efficient, inefficient) _____ than direct production; they practice specialization and the division of labor because the self-sufficient producer or worker tends to be an _____ one.

7. In modern economies money functions chiefly as a medium of (commerce, exchange) _____. Barter between two individuals will take place only if there is a coincidence of (resources, wants) _____.

8. List the Five Fundamental Economic Questions every economy must answer.

a. _____

b. _____

c. _____

d. _____

e. _____

9. A *normal profit* (is, is not) _____ an economic cost because it is a payment that (must, need not) _____ be paid to (workers, entrepreneurs) _____, but an *economic profit* (is, is not) _____ an economic cost because it (must, need not) _____ be paid to them to obtain and retain the services they provide to the firm.

10. Pure or economic profit is equal to the total (revenue, cost) _____ of a firm less its total _____.

11. Business firms tend to produce those products from which they can obtain at least a(n) (economic, normal) _____ profit and a maximum _____ profit.

12. If firms in an industry are obtaining economic profits, firms will (enter, leave) _____ the industry, the price of the industry's product will (rise, fall) _____, the industry will employ (more, fewer) _____ resources, produce a (larger, smaller) _____ output, and the industry's economic profits will (increase, decrease) _____ until they are equal to (zero, infinity) _____.

13. Consumers vote with their dollars for the production of a good or service when they (sell, buy) _____ it, and because of this, consumers are said to be (dependent, sovereign) _____ in a market economy. The buying decisions of consumers (restrain, expand) _____ the freedom of firms and resource suppliers.

14. Firms are interested in obtaining the largest economic profits possible, so they try to produce a product in the (most, least) _____ costly way. The most efficient production techniques depend on the available (income, technology) _____ and the (prices, quotas) _____ of needed resources.

15. The market system determines how the total output of the economy will be distributed among its households by determining the (incomes, expenditures) _____ of each household and by determining the (prices, quality) _____ for each good and service produced.

16. In industrial economies, change is almost continuous in consumer (preferences, resources) _____, in the supplies of _____, and in technology. To make the appropriate adjustments to these changes, a marekt economy allows price to perform its (monopoly, guiding) _____ function.

17. The competitive market system tends to foster technological change. The incentive for a firm to be the first to use a new and improved technique of production or to produce a new and better product is a greater economic (profit, loss) _____, and the incentive for other firms to follow its lead is the avoidance of _____.

18. Technological advance will require additional (capital, consumer) _____ goods, so the entrepreneur uses profit obtained from the sale of _____ goods to accquire (capital, consumer) _____ goods.

19. A purely competitive market system promotes (unity, disunity) _____ between private and public interests. Firms and resource suppliers seem to be guided by a(n) (visible, invisible) _____ hand to allocate the economy's resources efficiently.

20. The two *economic* arguments for a market system are that it promotes (public, efficient) _____ use of resources and that it uses (incentives, government) _____ for directing economic activity. The major *noneconomic* argument for the market system is that it allows for personal (wealth, freedom) _____.

■ **TRUE-FALSE QUESTIONS**

Circle the T if the statement is true, the F if it is false.

1. The U.S. economy can correctly be called "pure capitalism." **T F**

2. In the United States, there are legal limits to the right of private property. **T F**

3. The freedom of business firms to produce a particular consumer good is always limited by the desires of consumers for that good. **T F**

4. The pursuit of economic self-interest is the same thing as selfishness. **T F**

5. When a market is competitive, the individual sellers of the commodity are unable to reduce the supply of the commodity enough to drive its price upward. **T F**

6. The market system is also a communication system. **T F**

7. The employment of capital to produce goods and services requires that there be "roundabout production" and it is more efficient than "direct" production. **T F**

8. Increasing the amount of specialization in an economy generally leads to the more efficient use of its resources. **T F**

9. One way human specialization can be achieved is through a division of labor in productive activity. **T F**

10. Money is a device for facilitating the exchange of goods and services. **T F**

11. "Coincidence of wants" means that two persons want to acquire the same good or service. **T F**

12. Cigarettes may serve as money if sellers are generally willing to accept them as money. **T F**

13. One of the Five Fundamental Questions is who will control the output. **T F**

14. Business firms try to maximize their normal profits. **T F**

15. Industries in which economic profits are earned by the firms in the industry will attract the entry of new firms. **T F**

16. If firms have sufficient time to enter industries, the economic profits of an industry will tend to disappear. **T F**

17. Business firms are only free to produce whatever they want in any way they wish if they do not want to maximize profits or to minimize losses. **T F**

18. The derived demand of a resource depends on the demands for the products the resource produces. **T F**

19. Resources will tend to be used in those industries capable of earning normal or economic profits. **T F**

20. Economic efficiency requires that a given output of a good or service be produced in the least costly way. **T F**

21. If the market price of resource A decreases, firms will tend to employ smaller quantities of resource A. **T F**

22. Changes in the tastes of consumers are reflected in changes in consumer demand for products. **T F**

23. The incentive which the market system provides to induce technological improvement is the opportunity for economic profits. **T F**

24. The tendency for individuals pursuing their own self-interests to bring about results which are in the best interest of society as a whole is often called the "invisible hand." **T F**

25. A basic economic argument for the market system is that it promotes an efficient use of resources. **T F**

■ **MULTIPLE-CHOICE QUESTIONS**

Circle the letter that corresponds to the best answer.

1. Which is one of the main features of pure capitalism?
   (a) central economic planning
   (b) limits on freedom of choice

(c) the right to own private property

(d) an expanded role for government in the economy

2. In pure capitalism, freedom of enterprise means that

(a) businesses are free to produce products that consumers want

(b) consumers are free to buy goods and services that they want

(c) resources are distributed freely to businesses that want them

(d) government is free to direct the actions of businesses

3. The maximization of profit tends to be the driving force in the economic decision making of

(a) entrepreneurs

(b) workers

(c) consumers

(d) legislators

4. How do consumers typically express self-interest?

(a) by minimizing their economic losses

(b) by maximizing their economic profits

(c) by seeking the lowest price for a product

(d) by seeking jobs with the highest wages and benefits

5. Which of the following is a characteristic of competition as the economist sees it?

(a) the widespread diffusion of economic power

(b) a small number of buyers in product markets

(c) several sellers of all products

(d) the relatively difficult entry into and exit from industries by producers

6. To decide how to use its scarce resources to satisfy human wants pure capitalism relies on

(a) central planning

(b) roundabout production

(c) markets and prices

(d) barter

7. In pure capitalism, the role of government is best described as

(a) nonexistent

(b) limited

(c) significant

(d) extensive

8. What is roundabout production?

(a) the division of labor that results from specialization in the production of a good or service

(b) the production and use of capital goods to help make consumer goods

(c) the production of a good and service and the payment for it with money

(d) the production of a consumer good and its sale to consumers

9. In an economy that possesses full employment and full production, constant amounts of resources, and unchanging technology,

(a) increasing the production of capital goods requires an increase in the production of consumer goods

(b) decreasing the production of capital goods necessitates a decrease in the production of consumer goods

(c) increasing the production of capital goods is impossible

(d) increasing the production of capital goods requires a decrease in the production of consumer goods

10. When workers specialize in various tasks to produce a commodity, the situation is referred to as

(a) double coincidence of wants

(b) roundabout production

(c) freedom of choice

(d) division of labor

11. Which is a prerequisite of specialization?

(a) having a convenient means of exchanging goods

(b) letting government create a plan for the economy

(c) business firms making an economic profit

(d) business firms making a normal profit

12. The competitive market system is a method of

(a) communicating and synchronizing the decisions of consumers, producers, and resource suppliers

(b) centrally planning economic decisions

(c) promoting productive efficiency, but not allocative efficiency

(d) promoting allocative efficiency, but not productive efficiency

13. Which of the following best defines economic costs?

(a) total payments made to workers, landowners, suppliers of capital, and entrepreneurs

(b) only total payments made to workers, landowners, suppliers of capital, and entrepreneurs which must be paid to obtain the services of their resources

(c) total payments made to workers, landowners, suppliers of capital, and entrepreneurs less normal profits

(d) total payments made to workers, landowners, suppliers of capital, and entrepreneurs plus normal profits

14. If a business' total economic cost of producing 10,000 units of a product is $750,000 and this output is sold to consumers for $1,000,000, then the firm would earn

(a) a normal profit of $750,000

(b) an economic profit of $750,000

(c) an economic profit of $250,000

(d) a normal profit of $1,750,000

15. If less-than-normal profits are being earned by the firms in an industry, the consequences will be that

(a) lower-priced resources will be drawn into the industry

(b) firms will leave the industry, causing the price of the industry's product to fall

(c) firms will leave the industry, causing the price of the industry's product to rise

(d) the price of the industry's product will fall and thereby cause the demand for the product to increase

16. Which of the following would necessarily result, sooner or later, from a decrease in consumer demand for a product?

(a) a decrease in the profits of firms in the industry
(b) an increase in the output of the industry
(c) an increase in the supply of the product
(d) an increase in the prices of resources employed by the firms in the industry

17. The demand for resources is
(a) increased when the price of resources falls
(b) most influenced by the size of government in a capitalist economy
(c) derived from the demand for the products made with the resources
(d) decreased when the product that the resources produce becomes popular

Answer Questions 18, 19, and 20 on the basis of the following information.

Suppose 50 units of product X can be produced by employing just labor and capital in the four ways shown below. Assume the prices of labor and capital are $5 and $4, respectively.

	A	B	C	D
Labor	1	2	3	4
Capital	5	3	2	1

18. Which technique is economically most efficient in producing product X?
(a) A
(b) B
(c) C
(d) D

19. If the price of product X is $1, the firm will realize
(a) an economic profit of $28
(b) an economic profit of $27
(c) an economic profit of $26
(d) an economic profit of $25

20. Now assume that the price of labor falls to $3 and the price of capital rises to $5. Which technique is economically most efficient in producing product X?
(a) A
(b) B
(c) C
(d) D

21. Which is the primary factor determining the share of the total output of the economy received by a household?
(a) the tastes of the household
(b) the medium of exchange used by the household
(c) the prices at which the household sells its resources
(d) ethical considerations in the operation of a market economy.

22. If an increase in the demand for a product and the resulting rise in the price of the product cause the quantity of the product supplied, the size of the industry producing the product, and the amounts of resources devoted to the production of the product to expand, price is successfully performing its

(a) guiding function
(b) rationing function
(c) medium-of-exchange function
(d) standard-of-value function

23. In a capitalist economy characterized by competition, if one firm introduces a new and better method of production, other firms will be forced to adopt the improved technique
(a) to avoid less-than-normal profits
(b) to obtain economic profits
(c) to prevent the price of the product from falling
(d) to prevent the price of the product from rising

24. Which of the following would be an indication that competition does not exist in an industry?
(a) less-than-normal profits in the industry
(b) inability of the firms in the industry to expand
(c) inability of firms to enter the industry
(d) wages are lower than the average wage in the economy

25. The chief economic virtue of the competitive market system is that it
(a) allows extensive personal freedom
(b) efficiently allocates resources
(c) provides an equitable distribution of income
(d) eliminates the need for decision making

■ **PROBLEMS**

1. Use the appropriate number to match the term with the phrase.

1. invisible hand	**5. consumer sovereignty**
2. coincidence of wants	**6. derived demand**
3. division of labor	**7. specialization**
4. guiding function of prices	**8. roundabout production**

a. The construction and use of capital goods to aid in the production of consumer goods. _____
b. The ability of price changes to bring about changes in the quantities of products and resources demanded and supplied. _____
c. Using the resources of an individual, a firm, a region, or a nation to produce one (or a few) goods and services.

_____

d. The tendency of firms and resource suppliers seeking to further their own self-interest while also promoting the interests of society in a market economy. _____
e. The demand for a resource that depends on the demand for the product it can be used to produce. _____
f. Splitting the work required to produce a product into a number of different tasks that are performed by different workers. _____
g. A situation in which the product that one trader desires to obtain is the same as that which another trader desires to give. _____
h. Determination by consumers of the types and quanti-

ties of goods and services that will be produced in a market economy. _____

2. Assume that a firm can produce *either* product A, product B, or product C with the resources it currently employs. These resources cost the firm a total of $50 per week. Assume, for the purposes of the problem, that the firm's employment of resources cannot be changed. The market prices of and the quantities of A, B, and C these resources will produce per week are given below. Compute the firm's profit when it produces A, B, or C, and enter these profits in the table below.

Product	Market price	Output	Economic profit
A	$7.00	8	$_____
B	4.50	10	_____
C	.25	240	_____

a. Which product will the firm produce? _____

b. If the price of A rose to $8, the firm would _____
_____

(Hint: You will have to recompute the firm's profit from the production of A.)

c. If the firm were producing A and selling it at a price of $8, what would tend to happen to the number of firms producing A? _____
_____

3. Suppose that a firm can produce 100 units of product X by combining labor, land, capital, and entrepreneurial ability in three different ways. If it can hire labor at $2 per unit, land at $3 per unit, capital at $5 per unit, and entrepreneurship at $10 per unit, and if the amounts of the resources required by the three methods of producing 100 units of product X are indicated in the table, answer the following questions.

	Method		
Resource	1	2	3
Labor	8	13	10
Land	4	3	3
Capital	4	2	4
Entrepreneurship	1	1	1

a. Which method is the least expensive way of producing 100 units of X? _____

b. If X sells for 70 cents per unit, what is the economic profit of the firm? $_____

c. If the price of labor should rise from $2 to $3 per unit and if the price of X is 70 cents,
(1) the firm's use of

labor would change from _____ to _____

land would change from _____ to _____

capital would change from _____ to _____
entrepreneurship would not change

(2) The firm's economic profit would change from
$_____ to $_____

■ **SHORT ANSWER AND ESSAY QUESTIONS**

1. Explain the several elements—institutions and assumptions—embodied in pure capitalism.

2. What do each of the following seek if they pursue their own self-interest: consumers, resource owners, and business firms?

3. Explain what economists mean by competition. For a market to be competitive, why is it important that there be buyers and sellers and easy entry and exit?

4. What are the advantages of indirect or roundabout production?

5. How does an economy benefit from specialization and the division of labor?

6. Give an example of how specialization can benefit two separate and diversely endowed geographic regions.

7. What is money? What important function does it perform? Explain how money performs this function and how it overcomes the disadvantages associated with barter.

8. For an item to be useful as money, what is its necessary major characteristic? Can you think of other characteristics that might be favorable?

9. What are the Five Fundamental Economic Questions?

10. In what way do the desires of entrepreneurs to obtain economic profits and avoid losses make consumer sovereignty effective?

11. Why is the ability of firms to enter industries which are prosperous important to the effective functioning of competition?

12. Explain *in detail* how an increase in the consumer demand for a product will result in more of the product being produced and more resources being allocated to its production.

13. To what extent are firms "free" to produce what they wish by methods which they choose? Do resource owners have freedom to use their resources as they wish?

14. What are the two important functions of prices? Explain the difference between these two functions.

15. Households use the dollars obtained by selling resource services to "vote" for the production of consumer goods and services. Who "votes" for the production of capital goods, why do they "vote" for capital-goods production, and where do they obtain the dollars needed to cast these "votes"?

16. What is meant when it is said that competition is the mechanism which "controls" the market system? How does competition do this?

17. "An invisible hand operates to identify private and public interests." What are private interests and what is the public interest?

18. What is it that leads the economy to operate as if it were directed by an invisible hand?

19. If the basic economic decisions are not made in a capitalist economy by a central authority, how are they made?

20. Describe three virtues of the market system.

ANSWERS

Chapter 4 Pure Capitalism and the Market System

FILL-IN QUESTIONS

1. property, enterprise, choice
2. competition, are not
3. *a.* large numbers of independently acting buyers and sellers operating in the markets; *b.* freedom of buyers and sellers to enter or leave these markets
4. markets, price
5. limited
6. efficient, inefficient
7. exchange, wants
8. *a.* How much of a society's resources should be used?; *b.* What goods and services are to be produced?; *c.* How is that output to be produced?; *d.* How is the output to be distributed among economic units of the economy?; *e.* Can the economic system adapt to change?
9. is, must, entrepreneurs, is not, need not
10. revenue, cost
11. normal, economic
12. enter, fall, more, larger, decrease, zero
13. buy, sovereign, restrain
14. least, technology, prices
15. incomes, prices

16. preferences, resources, guiding
17. profit, losses
18. capital, consumer, capital
19. unity, invisible
20. efficient, incentives, freedom

TRUE-FALSE QUESTIONS

1. F, p. 61	**8.** T, p. 65	**15.** T, p. 68	**22.** T, pp. 71-72
2. T, p. 62	**9.** T, p. 65	**16.** T, p. 68	**23.** T, pp. 72-73
3. T, P. 62	**10.** T, pp. 65-66	**17.** T, p. 69	**24.** T, p. 73
4. F, p. 63	**11.** F, p. 66	**18.** T, p. 69	**25.** T, p. 73
5. T, p. 63	**12.** T, p. 66	**19.** T, pp. 69-70	
6. T, p. 64	**13.** F, p. 67	**20.** T, p. 70	
7. T, pp. 64-65	**14.** F, p. 68	**21.** F, p. 70	

MULTIPLE-CHOICE QUESTIONS

1. c, p. 61	**8.** b, ppw. 64-65	**15.** c, pp. 68-69	**22.** c, pp. 70-71
2. a, p. 62	**9.** d, p. 65	**16.** a, p. 69	**23.** a, p. 62
3. a, p. 63	**10.** d, p. 65	**17.** c, pp. 69-70	**24.** c, pp. 69-70
4. c, p. 63	**11.** a, pp. 65-66	**18.** b, p. 70	**25.** b, p. 70
5. a, p. 63	**12.** a, p. 67	**19.** a, pp. 68; 70	
6. c, p. 64	**13.** b, p. 68	**20.** d, p. 70	
7. b, p. 64	**14.** c, p. 68	**21.** c, pp. 70-71	

PROBLEMS

1. *a.* 8; *b.* 4; *c.* 7; *d.* 1; *e.* 6; *f.* 3; *g.* 2; *h.* 5
2. $6, −$5, $10; *a.* C; *b.* produce A and have an economic profit of $14; *c.* it would increase
3. *a.* method 2; *b.* 15; *c.* (1) 13, 8; 3, 4; 2, 4; (2) 15, 4

SHORT ANSWER AND ESSAY QUESTIONS

1. pp. 61-67	**6.** p. 65	**11.** pp. 68-69	**16.** p. 73
2. p. 63	**7.** pp. 65-66	**12.** p. 69	**17.** p. 73
3. p. 63	**8.** pp. 66-67	**13.** p. 69	**18.** p. 73
4. pp. 64-65	**9.** p. 67	**14.** pp. 68-69	**19.** p. 73
5. p. 65	**10.** p. 68	**15.** p. 73	**20.** pp. 73-74

The Mixed Economy: Private and Public Sectors

The U.S. economy is divided into a private sector and public sector. The first half of Chapter 5 discusses the private sector—the characteristics of the millions of households and business firms. The second half of Chapter 5 describes the public sector—the functions and financing of the Federal, state, and local governments. Learning about these two sectors will give you the basic facts and framework you need for understanding the U.S. economy.

Chapter 5 begins with an examination of the **households** of the economy, the distribution of income in the United States, and the uses to which the households put their incomes. Two different distributions of income are examined. Households in the United States earn five kinds of income and receive transfer payments. The way in which the total personal income received by all U.S. households is divided among the five types of earned income and transfer payments is called the **functional distribution of income.** The way in which the total personal income received by all households is distributed among the various income classes is called the **personal distribution of income.**

Business firms in the United States are also a focus of the chapter. It is apparent that what most characterizes U.S. business is the differences among firms in size and legal form, as well as in the products they produce. You should note the distinctions between a proprietorship, a partnership, and a corporation and the advantages and disadvantages of each form. Also, big business is an important characteristic of the U.S. economy because corporations account for the major source of production in the economy.

Chapter 5 also introduces you to the five basic functions performed by the Federal, state, and local governments in the mixed capitalist economy of the United States. The discussion points out the degree and the ways in which government causes the U.S. economy to differ from pure capitalism. The chapter does not attempt to list all the *specific* ways in which government affects the behavior of the economy; instead, it provides a *general* classification of the tasks government performs.

This chapter also discusses the two major functions of government: (1) the legal and social framework for the operation of the market system as provided by government; (2) government actions that can be taken to maintain competition in the economy. In addition, the chapter explains how government influences the market system in three other ways: by redistributing wealth and income, altering domestic output, and stabilizing the economy.

The chapter also returns to the **circular flow model** first presented in Chapter 2. The model has now been modified to include government along with businesses and households. The addition of government changes the real and monetary flows in the model. The 12 links among the household, business, and government sectors in the model are described in detail.

The facts of *government finance* in the United States are presented in the final sections of Chapter 5. The organization of the discussion is relatively simple. First, the trends for taxes collected and expenditures made by all levels of government—Federal, state, and local—are examined briefly. Second, a closer look is taken at the major items upon which the Federal government spends its income, the principal taxes it levies to obtain its income, and the relative importance of these taxes. Third, the chapter looks at the major expenditures and taxes of the state and local governments and will take a brief look at fiscal federalism and lotteries.

■ **CHECKLIST**

When you have studied this chapter you should be able to

☐ Define and distinguish between a functional and a personal distribution of income.

☐ State the relative size of the five sources of personal income in the functional distribution.

☐ List the three uses to which households put their personal incomes and state the relative size of each.

☐ Distinguish among durable goods, nondurable goods, and services in personal consumption expenditures.

☐ Explain the differences among a plant, a firm, a conglomerate, and an industry.

☐ State the difference between limited and unlimited liability.

☐ State the advantages and disadvantages of the three legal forms of business enterprise.

☐ Report the relative importance of each of the legal forms of business enterprise in the U.S. economy.

☐ Cite evidence to indicate that large corporations dominate the economy.

☐ Explain in one or two sentences why the U.S. economy is **mixed capitalism** rather than **pure capitalism.**

☐ Enumerate the five economic functions of government

in the United States and explain the difference between the purpose of the first two and the purpose of the last three functions.

☐ Define monopoly and explain why government wishes to prevent monopoly and to preserve competition in the economy.

☐ Explain why government feels it should redistribute income and list the three principal policies it employs for this purpose.

☐ Define spillover cost and spillover benefit.

☐ Explain why a competitive market fails to allocate resources efficiently when there are spillover costs and benefits.

☐ List two actions government can take to reduce spillover costs.

☐ List three actions goverment can take to encourage spillover benefits.

☐ Give definitions of a public good and a quasipublic good.

☐ Explain how the government reallocates resources from the production of private goods to the production of public or quasipublic goods.

☐ Describe the stabilization role of government and the two main economic problems it is designed to address.

☐ Draw the circular flow diagram that includes businesses, households, and government, labeling all the flows and illustrating the role of government.

☐ Explain the difference between government purchases and transfer payments and the affect of each on the composition of national output.

☐ Identify the four largest categories of Federal expenditures.

☐ List the three main sources of Federal tax revenues.

☐ Define and explain the differences between marginal and average tax rates.

☐ Identify the four largest sources of expenditures for state and local government.

☐ Describe how state and local governments raise tax revenue.

☐ Discuss the affect of fiscal federalism and lotteries on state and local government finance.

■ **CHAPTER OUTLINE**

1. *Households* play a dual role in the economy. They supply the economy with resources, and they purchase the greatest share of the goods and services produced by the economy. They obtain their personal incomes in exchange for the resources they furnish the economy and from the transfer payments they receive from government.

  a. The functional distribution of income indicates the way in which total personal income is divided among the five sources of earned income (wages and salaries, proprietors' income, corporate profits, interest, and rents) and transfer payments.

  b. The personal distribution of income indicates the way in which total personal income is divided among households in different income classes.

2. Households use their incomes to purchase consumer goods, to pay taxes, and to accumulate savings.

  a. Personal taxes constitute a deduction from a household's personal income; what remains after taxes can be either saved or spent.

  b. Saving is what a household does not spend of its after-tax income.

  c. Households spend for durable goods, nondurable goods, and services.

3. The *business population* of the U.S. economy consists of three major types of entities. A *plant* is a physical structure that produces a product. A <u>business firm</u> is an organization which owns and operates plants. (Multiplant firms may own horizontal, vertical, or conglomerate combinations of plants.) An *industry* is a group of firms producing the same or similar goods or services.

4. The three principal *legal forms* of business firms are the *proprietorship, partnership,* and *corporation.* Each has special characteristics and advantages and disadvantages.

  a. The proprietorship is easy to form, lets the owner be boss, and allows great freedom. Disadvantages are lack of access to large amounts of financial capital, difficulty of managerial specialization, and the owner's unlimited liability.

  b. The partnership is also easy to form and allows for more access to financial capital and permits more managerial specialization. Potential disadvantages are that partners may disagree, there are still limits to financial capital or managerial specialization, continuity of the firm over time is a problem, and partners face unlimited liability.

  c. The corporation can raise financial capital through the sale of stocks and bonds, has limited liability for owners, can become large in size, and has an independent life. Chief disadvantages are the double taxation of some corporate income, potential for abuse of this legal entity, and legal or regulatory expenses. There can also be a principal-agent problem with the separation of ownership and control of the firm.

  d. Large corporations are a major characteristic of the U.S. economy; they dominate most industries and produce most of the nation's output.

5. The U.S. economy is "mixed," with government and markets directing economic activity. *Government* performs five economic functions. The first two (**6** and **7** following) are designed to make the market systems operate more effectively; the other three (**8**, **9**, and **10**) are used to eliminate the shortcomings of a purely market-type economy.

6. The first of these functions is to provide the legal and social framework that makes the effective operation of the market system possible.

7. The second function is the maintenance of competition and the regulation of monopoly.

8. Government performs its third function when it redistributes income to reduce income inequality.

9. When government reallocates resources it performs its fourth function:

    a. It reallocates resources to take account of spillover costs and benefits.

    b. It also reallocates resources to provide society with public (social) goods and services.

    c. It levies taxes and uses the tax revenues to purchase or produce the public goods.

10. Its fifth function is stabilization of the price level and maintenance of full employment.

11. *A circular flow* diagram that includes the public sector as well as business firms and households in the private sector of the economy reveals that government purchases public goods from private businesses, collects taxes from and makes transfer payments to these firms, purchases labor services from households, collects taxes from and makes transfer payments to these households, and can alter the distribution of income, reallocate resources, and change the level of economic activity by affecting the real and monetary flows in the diagram.

12. Government spending consists of *purchases* of goods and services and *transfer* payments, but they have different effects on the economy. Purchases are exhaustive because they directly use the economy's resources, while transfers are nonexhaustive. Government spending is equal to about one-third of domestic output.

13. At the Federal level of government,

    a. most spending goes for pensions and income security, national defense, health care, or interest on the public debt.

    b. the major sources of revenue are personal income taxes, payroll taxes, and corporate income taxes.

14. At the other government levels,

    a. state governments depend largely on sales, excise, and personal income taxes, and they spend their revenues on public welfare, education, health care, and highways.

    b. local governments rely heavily on property taxes; they spend much of the revenue on education.

    c. state and local governments often receive transfers and grants from the Federal government in a process called fiscal *federalism*; they sometimes use *lotteries* to supplement tax revenues.

■ HINTS AND TIPS

1. This chapter is a long one, so do not try to learn everything at once. Break the chapter into its three natural parts and work on each one separately. The first part describes features of the private sector. The second part explains the functions of government. The third part looks at government finance.

2. There are many descriptive statistics about the private and public sectors. Avoid memorizing these statistics. Instead, look for the trends and generalizations which these statistics illustrate about the private or public sector. For example, the discussion of government finance

describes recent trends in government expenditures and taxes, and indicates the relative importance of taxes and expenditures at each level of government.

■ IMPORTANT TERMS

functional distribution of income	principal-agent problem
personal distribution of income	monopoly
	spillover (externality)
personal taxes	spillover cost
personal saving	spillover benefit
personal consumption expenditures	exclusion principle
	public goods
durable good	free-rider problem
nondurable good	quasipublic goods
services	government purchase
plant	government transfer payment
firm	personal income tax
horizontal combination	marginal tax rate
vertical combination	average tax rate
conglomerate combination	payroll tax
industry	corporate income tax
sole proprietorship	sales tax
partnership	excise tax
corporation	property tax
stocks	fiscal federalism
bonds	lotteries
limited liability	
double taxation	

SELF-TEST

■ FILL-IN QUESTIONS

1. The approximately 101 million (businesses, <u>households</u>) _____ in the United States play a dual role in the economy because they (sell, buy) _____sul_____ resources and _____buy_____ most of total output of the economy.

2. The largest single source of income in the United States is (profits, interest, <u>wages</u> and <u>salaries</u>) _____ and is equal to about (26, 51, ~~71~~) _____% of total income.

3. In the United States the poorest (1, 20) _20_ % of all families receive about 4% of total personal income, and the richest (1, 20) _20_ % of these families receive about 47% of total personal income.

4. The total income of households is disposed of in three ways: personal ___consumption___, personal ___saving___, and personal ___taxes___.

5. Households use about 14% of their total income to pay for personal (taxes, consumption expenditures) _____taxes_____ and about 80% for personal _____c.e._____.

6. If a product has an expected life of 3 years or more it is a (durable, nondurable) _____d_____ good, whereas if it has an expected life of less than 3 years it is a _____n/d_____ good.

7. Today there are about 22 million business (firms, industries) _____firms_____ in the United States. The legal form of the great majority of them is the (sole proprietorship, partnership, corporation) _____pro_____, but the legal form that produces 90 percent of the sales of the U.S. economy is the _____corp_____.

8. The liabilities of a sole proprietor and of partners are (limited, unlimited) _____, but the liabilities of stockholders in a corporation are _____lim_____.

9. The separation of ownership and control in a corporation may create a (free-rider, principal-agent) _____pr_____ problem. In this case, stockholders would be the (riders, principals, agents) _____pr_____ and managers would be the _____ag_____.

10. List the five economic functions of government.

a. _____L & S Framework_____

b. _____maintain comp_____

c. _____redis income_____

d. _____reallocate resources_____

e. _____stabilization_____

11. To control monopoly, the U.S. government has created commissions to (tax, regulate) _____ natural monopolies, and in cases at the local level, government has become an (agent, owner) _____. Government has also enacted (trust, antitrust) _____ laws to maintain competition.

12. The market system, because it is an impersonal mechanism, results in an (equal, unequal) _____ distribution of income. To redistribute income from the upper- to the lower-income groups, the government has provided (transfer, tax) _____ payments, engaged in (military, market) _____ intervention, and used the (income, sales) _____ tax to raise much of its revenues.

13. Government frequently reallocates resources when it finds instances of (market, public) _____ failure. The two major cases of such failure occur when the competitive market system either

a. _____produce wrong amount of goods_____

b. _____

_____

14. Competitive markets bring about an efficient allocation of resources only if there are no (private, spillover) _____ costs or benefits in the consumption and production of the good or service.

15. There is an externality whenever some of the costs of producing a product accrue to people other than the (seller, buyer) _____S_____ or some of the benefits from consuming a product accrue to people other than the _____b_____.

16. What two things can government do to

a. make the market reflect spillover costs?

(1) _____Legislation_____

(2) _____taxes_____

b. make the market reflect spillover benefits?

(1) _____Subsidize con & supp_____

(2) _____govt. finance_____

17. Public goods tend to be goods which are not subject to the (inclusion, exclusion) _____ex_____ principle and which are (divisible, indivisible) _____in_____. Quasipublic goods are goods which could be subjected to the (inclusion, exclusion) _____ex_____ principle but are provided by government because they have large spillover (costs, benefits) _____ben_____.

18. To reallocate resources from the production of private to the production of public and quasipublic goods, government reduces the demand for private goods by (taxing, subsidizing) _____tax_____ consumers and then uses the (profits, tax revenue) _____tax rev_____ to buy public or quasipublic goods.

19. To stabilize the economy with less than full employment, government will (increase, decrease) _____ total spending by (increasing, decreasing) _____ its expenditures for public goods and services and by (increasing, decreasing) _____ taxes. When there are inflationary pressures, the government will (decrease, increase) _____ total spending by (decreasing, increasing) _____ its expenditures for public goods and services and by _____ taxes.

20. An examination of the public sector of the U.S. economy reveals that
a. since 1960 government *purchases* of goods and services as a percentage of total output (increased, remained relatively constant) _____ and since the early 1950s have been about (10, 20, 30) _____% of the domestic output;
b. but government *transfer payments* as a percentage of domestic output during the past 35 years (increased, decreased, remained constant) _____;
c. and the tax revenues required to finance both government expenditures and transfer payments are today about (one-third, two-thirds) _____ of domestic output.

21. Government transfer payments are (exhaustive, nonexhaustive) _____, whereas government purchases of goods and services are _____ because they absorb resources.

22. The most important source of revenue for the Federal government is the (personal income, payroll) _____ tax; next in importance is the _____ tax. The three largest categories of Federal expenditures ranked by budget size are (health, national defense, pensions, and income security) _____, _____, and _____.

23. Federal income tax rates are progressive, which means that people with (lower, higher) _____ incomes pay a larger percentage of that income as taxes than do persons with _____ incomes. The tax paid on an additional unit of income is the (average, marginal) _____, while the total tax paid divided by the total taxable income is the _____ tax rate.

24. Many state governments rely primarily on (property, sales, and excise) _____ taxes and (personal, corporate) _____ income taxes for their revenue, which they spend mostly on (national defense, public welfare) _____ and (interest, education) _____.

25. At local levels of government the single most important source of revenue is the (income, property) _____ tax and the single most important expenditure is for (public safety, education) _____.

■ **TRUE-FALSE QUESTIONS**

Circle the T if the statement is true, the F if it is false.

1. The personal distribution of income describes the manner in which society's total personal income is divided among wages and salaries, corporate profits, proprietors' income, interest, and rents.   **T F**

2. In both relative and absolute terms, personal taxes have risen since World War II.   **T F**

3. Most of the personal saving in the U.S. economy is done by those households in the top 10% of its income receivers.   **T F**

4. *Dissaving* means that personal consumption expenditures exceed after-tax income.   **T F**

5. A durable good is defined as a good which has an expected life of 3 years or more.   **T F**

6. A plant is defined as a group of firms under a single management.   **T F**

7. An industry is a group of firms that produce the same or nearly the same products.   **T F**

8. Limited liability refers to the fact that all members of a partnership are liable for the debts incurred by one another.   **T F**

9. The corporate form of organization is the least used by firms in the United States.   **T F**

10. The corporation in the United States today always has a tax advantage over other legal forms of business organization.   **T F**

11. Whether a business firm should incorporate or not depends chiefly on the amount of money capital it must have to finance the enterprise.   **T F**

12. Corporations produce about 90% of the total sales (output) produced by privately owned business firms in the United States.   **T F**

13. The U.S. economy is a mixed economy because there are both households and businesses.   **T F**

14. The Pure Foods and Drug Act is an example of the reallocation function of government.   **T F**

15. When the Federal government provides for a monetary system, it is doing so primarily to maintain competition.   **T F**

16. Transfer payments are one means government uses to redistribute income.   **T F**

17. If demand and supply reflected all the benefits and costs of producing a product, there would be efficient resource use.   **T F**

18. When there are spillover costs, more resources are allocated to the production of the product and more is produced than is efficient.   **T F**

19. One way for government to correct for spillover costs from a product is to increase its demand.   **T F**

20. When there are spillover benefits from a product, there will be an overallocation of resources for its production. **T F**

21. One way for government to correct spillover benefits from a product is to subsidize consumers of the product. **T F**

22. Using the exclusion principle, government provides public goods so as to exclude private businesses from providing them. **T F**

23. Obtaining the benefits of private goods requires that they be purchased; obtaining benefits from public goods requires only that they be produced. **T F**

24. Governments have provided lighthouse services because these services have public benefits and because private producers of such services experience the free-rider problem. **T F**

25. When the Federal government takes actions to control unemployment or inflation it is performing the allocative function of government. **T F**

26. Government purchases of goods and services are called *nonexhaustive expenditures* and government transfer payments are called *exhaustive expenditures.* **T F**

27. When a government levies taxes and uses the tax revenue to make transfer payments, it shifts resources from the production of private goods to the production of public goods. **T F**

28. The chief source of revenue for the Federal government is the corporate income tax. **T F**

29. If the marginal tax rate is higher than the average tax rate, the average tax rate will fall as income rises. **T F**

30. Property taxes are the largest percentage of the total budget of local governments. **T F**

■ **MULTIPLE-CHOICE QUESTIONS**

Circle the letter that corresponds to the best answer.

1. The functional distribution for the United States shows that the largest part of the personal income is
  (a) wages and salaries
  (b) proprietors' income
  (c) corporate profits
  (d) interest and rents

2. The part of after-tax income which is not consumed is defined as
  (a) saving
  (b) capital investment
  (c) wages and salaries
  (d) nondurable goods expenditure

3. If personal consumption expenditures were 80% of income and personal taxes were 8% of income, then personal savings would be
  (a) 8% of income
  (b) 10% of income
  (c) 12% of income
  (d) 88% of income

4. Which is a true statement?
  (a) The durable goods and services parts of personal consumption expenditures vary more over time than do the expenditures for nondurables.
  (b) Expenditures for nondurables vary more than do the expenditures for durable goods and services.
  (c) Expenditures for nondurables vary more than the expenditures for services and less than the expenditures for durables.
  (d) Expenditures for nondurables vary more than the expenditures for durables and less than the expenditures for services.

5. A group of three plants which is owned and operated by a single firm and which consists of a farm growing wheat, a flour-milling plant, and a plant which bakes and sells bakery products is an example of
  (a) a horizontal combination
  (b) a vertical combination
  (c) a conglomerate combination
  (d) a corporation

6. Limited liability is associated with
  (a) only proprietorships
  (b) only partnerships
  (c) both proprietorships and partnerships
  (d) only corporations

7. Which form of business organization can most effectively raise money capital?
  (a) corporation
  (b) partnership
  (c) proprietorship
  (d) vertical combination

8. The separation of ownership and control in a corporation may create
  (a) a free-rider problem
  (b) a principal-agent problem
  (c) a horizontal combination
  (d) limited liability

9. One major means that government uses to deal with monopoly is to
  (a) increase the demand for its product
  (b) decrease the supply of its product
  (c) stabilize incomes
  (d) regulate the firm

10. Government uses all the following ways to redistribute income, *except*
  (a) transfer payments
  (b) market intervention
  (c) limited liability
  (d) taxation

11. To redistribute income from high-income to low-income households, government might
  (a) increase transfer payments to high-income and decrease transfer payments to low-income households

(b) increase the taxes paid by high-income and increase the transfer payments to low-income households

(c) increase the taxes paid by low-income and decrease the taxes paid by high-income households

(d) decrease the taxes paid by high-income and decrease the transfer payments to low-income households

12. Which is the best example of a good or service providing the economy with a spillover cost?
(a) a textbook
(b) an automobile
(c) a business suit
(d) an audit of a business firm's books

13. Which economic situation would result in overallocation of resources to the production of a good?
(a) spillover benefits
(b) spillover costs
(c) a free-rider program
(d) inflation

14. How does government correct for spillover benefits?
(a) by taxing consumers
(b) by taxing producers
(c) by subsidizing producers
(d) by separating ownership from control

15. Which is characteristic of public goods?
(a) they are indivisible
(b) they are sold in competitive markets
(c) they are subject to the exclusion principle
(d) they can be produced only if large spillover costs are incurred

16. There is a free-rider problem when people
(a) are willing to pay for what they want
(b) are not willing to pay for what they want
(c) benefit from a good without paying for its cost
(d) want to buy more than is available for purchase in the market

17. Quasipublic goods are goods and services
(a) to which the exclusion principle could not be applied
(b) which have large spillover benefits
(c) which would not be produced by private producers through the market system
(d) which are indivisible

18. In the circular flow model, government provides goods and services and receives net taxes from
(a) colleges and universities
(b) businesses and households
(c) resource and product markets
(d) foreign nations and corporations

19. Which accounts for the largest percentage of all Federal expenditures?
(a) income security
(b) national defense

(c) interest on the public debt
(d) veterans' services

20. Which is the largest source of the tax revenues of the Federal government?
(a) sales and excise taxes
(b) property taxes
(c) payroll taxes
(d) personal income taxes

21. A tax that would most likely alter consumer expenditures on a product would be
(a) an excise tax
(b) a general sales tax
(c) a personal income tax
(d) a corporate income tax

22. Which pair represents the chief source of income and the most important type of expenditure of state governments?
(a) personal income tax and expenditures for education
(b) personal income tax and expenditures for highways
(c) sales and excise taxes and expenditures for highways
(d) sales and excise taxes and expenditures for public welfare

23. Which pair represents the chief source of income and the most important type of expenditure of *local* governments?
(a) property tax and expenditures for highways
(b) property tax and expenditures for education
(c) sales and excise taxes and expenditures for public welfare
(d) sales and excise taxes and expenditures for police, fire, and general government

Questions 24 and 25 are based on the tax table given below.

Taxable income	Total tax
$ 0	$ 0
30,000	5,000
70,000	15,000
150,000	42,000

24. The marginal tax rate at the $70,000 level of taxable income is
(a) 16.6
(b) 21.4
(c) 25.0
(d) 28.0

25. The average tax rate at the $150,000 level of taxable income is
(a) 21.4
(b) 28.0
(c) 31.5
(d) 33.8

■ PROBLEMS

1. The following table shows the functional distribution of total income in the United States in 1997.

	Billions of dollars
Wages and salaries	$4,703
Proprietors' income	545
Corporate profits	804
Interest	450
Rents	148
Total earnings	6,650

Of the total earnings about _____% were wages and salaries, and about _____% were corporate profits.

2. Indicate in the space to the right of **a–i** whether these business characteristics are associated with the proprietorship (PRO), partnership (PART), corporation (CORP), two of these, or all three of these legal forms.

a. Much red tape and legal expense in beginning the

firm _____

b. Unlimited liability _____

c. No specialized management _____

d. Has a life independent of its owner(s) _____

e. Double taxation of income _____
f. Greatest ability to acquire funds for the expansion

of the firm _____

g. Permits some but not a great degree of specialized

management _____
h. Possibility of an unresolved disagreement among

owners over courses of action _____

i. The potential for the separation of ownership and

control of the business _____

3. Following is a list of various government activities. Indicate in the space to the right of each into which of the five classes of government functions the activity falls. If it falls under more than one of the functions, indicate this.

a. Maintaining an army _____
b. Providing for a system of unemployment compen-

sation _____

c. Establishment of the Federal Reserve Banks _____

_____

d. Insuring employees of business firms against in-

dustrial accidents _____
e. Establishment of an Antitrust Division in the De-

partment of Justice _____
f. Making it a crime to sell stocks and bonds under

false pretenses _____

g. Providing low-cost lunches to school children _____

_____

h. Taxation of whisky and other spirits _____

_____

i. Regulation of organized stock, bond, and com-

modity markets _____
j. Setting tax *rates* higher for larger incomes than for

smaller ones _____

4. The following circular flow diagram includes business firms, households, and the government (the public sector). Also shown are the product and resource markets.

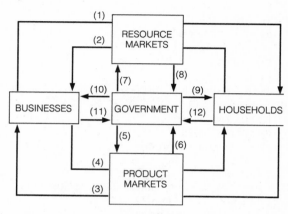

a. Supply a label or an explanation for each of the 12 flows in the model:

(1) _____

(2) _____

(3) _____

(4) _____

(5) _____

(6) _____

(7) _____

(8) _____

(9) _____

(10) _____

(11) _____

(12) _____

b. If government wished to
(1) expand output and employment in the economy, it

would increase expenditure flows _____

or _____, decrease net tax flows

_____ or _____, or do both;
(2) increase the production of public (social) goods and decrease the production of private goods in the

economy, it would increase flows _____

and _____ or _____;
(3) redistribute income from high-income to low-income households, it would (increase, decrease)

_____ the net taxes (taxes minus trans-

fers) paid by the former and _____ the net

taxes paid by the latter in flow _____.

5. In the following table are several levels of taxable income and hypothetical marginal tax rates for each $1000 increase in income.

Taxable income	Marginal tax rate, %	Tax	Average tax rate, %
$1500		$300	20
2500	22	520	20.8
3500	25	_____	_____
4500	29	_____	_____
5500	34	_____	_____
6500	40	_____	_____

a. At the four income levels compute the tax and the average tax rate

b. As the marginal tax rate

(1) increases the average tax rate (increases, decreases, remains constant) _____

_____.

(2) decreases the average tax rate _____.

c. This tax is _____ because the average tax rate increases as income _____.

■ SHORT ANSWER AND ESSAY QUESTIONS

1. Explain the difference between a functional and a personal distribution of income. Rank the five types of earned income in the order of their size.

2. Which would result in greater total saving and less consumption spending out of a national income of a given size: a more or less nearly equal distribution of income?

3. The purchase of what type of consumer goods is largely postponable? Why is this? How is it possible for a family's personal consumption expenditures to exceed its after-tax income?

4. What is the difference between a plant and a firm? Between a firm and an industry? Which of these three concepts is the most difficult to apply in practice? Why? Distinguish between a horizontal, a vertical, and a conglomerate combination.

5. What are the principal advantages and disadvantages of each type of the three legal forms of business organization? Which of the disadvantages of the proprietorship and partnership accounts for the employment of the corporate form among the big businesses of the U.S. economy?

6. Explain what "separation of ownership and control" of the modern corporation means. What problem does this separation create for stockholders and managers?

7. Is the U.S. economy and manufacturing in the United States dominated by big business? What evidence do you use to reach this conclusion?

8. Why is it proper to refer to the U.S. economy as "mixed"?

9. What are the five economic functions of government in the U.S. mixed capital economy? Explain what the performance of each function requires government to do.

10. Would you like to live in an economy in which government undertook only the first two functions listed in the text? What would be the advantages and disadvantages of living in such an economy?

11. Why does the market system provide some people with lower income than it provides others?

12. What is meant by a spillover in general and by spillover cost and spillover benefit in particular?

13. How does the existence of spillover costs and benefits affect the allocation of resources and the prices of products?

14. What methods does government use to
  (a) redistribute income
  (b) reallocate resources to take account of spillover costs
  (c) reallocate resources to take account of spillover benefits?

15. Distinguish between a private and a public good. Include in your answer an explanation of the "exclusion principle," the distinction between divisible and indivisible goods, and the free-rider problem.

16. What basic method does government in the United States use to reallocate resources away from the production of private goods and toward the production of public and quasipublic goods?

17. What is the stabilization function of government? What are the two economic problems that this function addresses?

18. In a circular flow diagram that includes not only business firms and households but also government (or the public sector), what are the four flows of money into or out of the government sector of the economy? Using this diagram, explain how government redistributes income, reallocates resources from the private to the public sector, and stabilizes the economy.

19. What is the present size of government spending and taxation in the U.S. economy?

20. Government expenditures fall into two broad classes: expenditures for goods and services and transfer payments. Explain the difference between these, and give examples of expenditures which fall into each of the two classes.

21. Explain precisely the difference between the marginal tax rate and the average tax rate.

22. Explain how the Federal personal income tax enables the Federal government to perform three (of the five) economic functions.

23. Explain in detail the differences that exist among Federal, state, and local governments in the taxes upon which they primarily rely for their revenues and the major purposes for which they use these revenues.

24. Why does the Federal government share its tax revenues with state and local governments? How has this fiscal federalism changed in recent years?

25. What points do critics and defenders make about the lotteries state or local governments use?

ANSWERS

Chapter 5 The Mixed Economy: Private and Public Sectors

FILL-IN QUESTIONS

1. households, sell, buy
2. wages and salaries, 71
3. 20, 20
4. consumption, saving, taxes (any order)
5. taxes, consumption expenditures
6. durable, nondurable
7. firms, sole proprietorship, corporation
8. unlimited, limited
9. principal-agent, principals, agents
10. *a.* provide legal foundation and social environment; *b.* maintain competition; *c.* redistribute income and wealth; *d.* reallocate resources; *e.* stabilize the economy (any order for *a–e*)
11. regulate, owner, antitrust
12. unequal, transfer, market, income
13. market; *a.* produces the "wrong" amounts of certain goods and services; *b.* fails to allocate any resources to the production of certain goods and services whose production is economically justified
14. spillover
15. seller, buyer
16. *a.* (1) enact legislation, (2) pass special taxes; *b.* (1) subsidize consumers, (2) subsidize suppliers, (3) government financing or production of the product
17. exclusion, indivisible, exclusion, benefits
18. taxing, tax revenue
19. increase, increasing, decreasing, decrease, decreasing, increasing
20. *a.* 20; *b.* increased; *c.* one-third
21. nonexhaustive, exhaustive
22. personal income, payroll, pensions and income security, national defense, health
23. higher, lower, marginal, average
24. sales and excise, personal, public welfare, education
25. property, education

TRUE-FALSE QUESTIONS

1. F, p. 78	9. F, p. 81	17. T, p. 86	25. F, p. 88-89
2. T, pp. 78-79	10. F, pp. 82-83	18. T, p. 86	26. F, p. 91
3. T, P. 79	11. T, p. 82	19. F, p. 86	27. F, p. 91
4. T, p. 79	12. T, p. 82	20. F, p. 86-87	28. F, p. 92
5. T, p. 79	13. F, p. 84	21. T, p. 87	29. F, p. 93
6. F, p. 80	14. F, p. 84	22. F, p. 87	30. T, p. 94-95
7. T, p. 80	15. F, pp. 84-85	23. T, p. 87	
8. F, p. 83	16. T, p. 85	24. T, p. 87-88	

MULTIPLE-CHOICE QUESTIONS

1. a, p. 77	8. b, p. 83	15. a, p. 87	22. d, p. 94
2. a, p. 78	9. d, p. 85	16. c, p. 88	23. b, p. 95
3. c, pp. 78-79	10. c, pp. 85-86	17. b, p. 88	24. c, p. 93
4. a, p. 79	11. b, pp. 85-86	18. b, p. 90	25. b, p. 93
5. b, p. 80	12. b, p. 86	19. a, p. 93	
6. d, p. 81-83	13. b, p. 86	20. d, p. 93	
7. a, p. 82-83	14. c, p. 87	21. a, p. 94	

PROBLEMS

1. 71, 12
2. *a.* CORP; *b.* PRO and PART; *c.* PRO; *d.* CORP; *e.* CORP; *f.* CORP; *g.* PART; *h.* PART; *i.* CORP
3. *a.* reallocates resources; *b.* redistributes income; *c.* provides a legal foundation and social environment *and* stabilizes the economy; *d.* reallocates resources; *e.* maintains competition; *f.* provides a legal foundation and social environment *and* maintains competition; *g.* redistributes income; *h.* reallocates resources; *i.* provides a legal foundation and social environment; *j.* redistributes income
4. *a.* (1) businesses pay costs for resources that become money income for households; (2) households provide resources to businesses; (3) household expenditures become receipts for businesses; (4) businesses provide goods and services to households; (5) government spends money in product market; (6) government receives goods and services from product market; (7) government spends money in resource market; (8) government receives resources from resource market; (9) government provides goods and services to households; (10) government provides goods and services to businesses; (11) businesses pay net taxes to government; (12) households pay net taxes to government; *b.* (1) 5, 7 (either order), 11, 12 (either order); (2) 9, 10, 11 (either order); (3) increase, decrease, 12
5. *a.* tax: $770, 1,060, 1,400, 1,800; average tax rate: 22%, 23.6%, 25.5%, 27.7%; *b.* (1) increases, (2) decreases; *c.* progressive, increases

SHORT ANSWER AND ESSAY QUESTIONS

1. pp. 77-78	8. p. 84	15. pp. 87-88	22. pp. 84, 92
2. p. 79	9. p. 84	16. p. 88	23. pp. 92-95
3. p. 79	10. pp. 84-85	17. pp. 88-89	24. pp. 95-96
4. p. 80	11. p. 85	18. pp. 89-91	25. p. 96
5. pp. 81-83	12. pp. 86-87	19. pp. 91-95	
6. p. 83	13. pp. 86-87	20. pp. 91-92	
7. p. 84	14. pp. 85-87	21. pp. 93-94	

The United States in the Global Economy

Chapter 6 introduces you to the global economy and its influence on the United States. International trade is important to the United States for many reasons, as you learn in the first section of the chapter. In *relative* terms, other nations have exports and imports which are a larger percentage of their GDPs—about 25 to 35%—because they often have a small domestic market and a limited resource base. By contrast, the United States exports and imports only about 12 to 14% of its GDP because it has a larger domestic market and a more abundant resource base. In *absolute* terms, however, the United States is the world's largest trading nation. Exports were $857 billion and imports were $972 billion in 1996, exceeding all other nations. Most of the trade is with other industrially advanced nations such as Canada, Japan, and Germany. This volume of trade has grown over the years with expansion of the global economy, the rise of multinational corporations, and with the emergence of new trading nations such as the "Asian tigers" [Hong Kong (now part of China), Singapore, South Korea, and Taiwan] and China.

The second section of the chapter briefly returns to the circular flow. Now the global economy ("rest of the world") can be added to the model by connecting it to the product market of that model to make it more complete. Four links are made to the model: *Export flows* are paid for by *foreign expenditure flows*; *import flows* are paid for by *U.S. expenditure flows.*

In the third section, you learn about the principle of **comparative advantage,** which is the basis for all trade between individuals, regions, and nations. A nation, for example, will specialize in the production of a product at which it has a lower domestic opportunity cost and trade to obtain those products for which its domestic opportunity cost is higher. Thus, specialization and trade increase productivity within a nation and increase a nation's output and standard of living.

Trading in a global economy requires a **foreign exchange market** in which national currencies are exchanged, as you discover in the fourth section of the chapter. This market is competitive, so the principles of supply and demand that you read about in Chapter 3 apply to it. Changes in supply and demand for currency will affect the price of a national currency. When the U.S. dollar price of another currency has increased, the value of the U.S. dollar has **depreciated** relative to the other currency. Conversely, when the U.S. dollar price of another currency has increased, the value of the U.S. dollar has **appreciated** in value relative to the other currency.

Government actions and policies can affect international trade in many ways. Governments can impose protective tariffs, import quotas, and nontariff barriers, or they can foster exports through subsidies. The reasons for the interventions are difficult to explain given the strong economic rationale for free trade based on the principle of comparative advantage. Nevertheless, as you learn in the fifth section of the chapter, public misunderstanding of the gains from trade, or political considerations designed to protect domestic industries, often lead to government policies that create trade barriers and distort the free flow of products between the nations, thus increasing costs for society.

The sixth section discusses *multilateral* agreements among nations and the creation of free-trade zones that have been designed to reduce trade barriers and increase world trade. In the United States, the process of gradual tariff reduction began with the Reciprocal Trade Agreement Act of 1934. Since 1947, worldwide multilateral negotiations to reduce trade barriers have been conducted through the General Agreements on Tariffs and Trade (GATT). The Uruguay round of GATT negotiations were completed in 1993, and this new agreement included many provisions to improve trade among nations. The other major development has been the formation of free-trade zones. The European Union (originally the Common Market) is a trading bloc of 15 European nations. In 1993, the North American Free Trade Agreement (NAFTA) created a free-trade zone covering the United States, Canada, and Mexico. These trade blocs have the potential to create more trade frictions or lead to freer worldwide trade.

The final section of the chapter explores the issue of whether U.S. businesses can *compete* in a global economy. Foreign competition has certainly changed production practices and employment in U.S. industry since the 1960s. Some industries face a comparative *dis*advantage in world markets. Many U.S. firms, however, have adapted to the changes in the global economy by increasing productivity to reduce costs, improve product quality, and expand export markets.

■ **CHECKLIST**

When you have studied this chapter you should be able to

☐ Explain the importance of international trade to the U.S. economy in terms of volume, dependence, trade patterns, and financial linkages.

☐ Describe several factors that have facilitated the rapid growth of international trade since World War II.

☐ Identify the key participating nations in international trade.

☐ Add the international trade dimension to the circular flow model.

☐ Explain the basic principle of comparative advantage based on an individual example.

☐ Compute the comparative costs of production from production possibilities data when you are given an example with cost data for 2 countries.

☐ Determine which of 2 economic countries have a comparative advantage in the example.

☐ Indicate the range in which the terms of trade will be found in the example.

☐ Show the gains from specialization and trade in the example.

☐ Define the main characteristics of the foreign exchange market.

☐ Demonstrate how supply and demand analysis applies to the foreign exchange market.

☐ Distinguish between the appreciation and depreciation of a currency.

☐ Identify four types of trade impediments and subsidies.

☐ Discuss two reasons why governments intervene in international trade.

☐ Estimate the cost to society from trade restrictions.

☐ List the major features of the Reciprocal Trade and Agreements Act of 1934 and the General Agreements on Tariffs and Trade (GATT) of 1947.

☐ Identify the major provisions of the Uruguay round of GATT negotiations.

☐ Describe the history, goals, and results from the European Union.

☐ Explain the features and significance of the North American Free Trade Agreement (NAFTA).

☐ Discuss the prospects for frictions among trading blocs or further trade integration among nations.

☐ Discuss the capability of U.S. business to compete in the global economy.

■ **CHAPTER OUTLINE**

1. *Trade* among nations is large and unique, and thus warrants special attention.

   a. Although the relative importance of international trade to the United States is less than it is for other nations, it is still of considerable importance.

   (1) Exports and imports are about 12–14% of GDP, and the United States is the largest trading nation in the world.

   (2) The U.S. economy depends on international trade for vital raw materials and a variety of finished products.

   (3) There are some patterns in U.S. trade: most are with industrially advanced nations, with Canada being the largest trade partner; overall imports exceed exports, but the deficits are greatest with Japan and OPEC countries.

   (4) International trade must be financed, and, in the case of the United States, large trade deficits have re-

quired the selling of business ownership (securities) to companies in other nations.

   b. Factors that have facilitated trade since World War II include improvements in transportation and communications technology, along with a general decline in tariffs and worldwide peace.

   c. The major participants in international trade are the United States, Japan, and the nations of western Europe. Newer participants include the Asian tigers (Hong Kong, Singapore, South Korea, and Taiwan) and China. The collapse of communism in the former Soviet Union and the nations of Eastern Europe significantly changed trade patterns in that region.

2. The **circular flow model** of Chapter 5 can be expanded to include the international trade dimension by adding the "rest of the world" box to the model. This box would be connected to the U.S. product market, through flows of imports and exports, and U.S. and foreign expenditures.

3. Specialization and trade among economic units (individuals, firms, states, regions, or nations) are based on the principle of *comparative advantage.* Specialization and trade increase productivity and the output of goods and services.

   a. The basic principle can be illustrated with an example using two individuals.

   (1) Suppose that an accountant wants to have her house painted. The accountant can either do it herself or hire a professional painter to do the job. The law of comparative advantage suggests that the accountant will specialize in that work where the opportunity cost is lower relative to the work where the opportunity cost is higher.

   (2) The same principle applies to the professional painter in deciding whether to prepare his own tax return or hire an accountant to prepare the tax return.

   (3) Given the hypothetical labor time and wage data in the textbook example, both the accountant and the painter reduce their opportunity costs when they specialize in their respective jobs and exchange money for other services they desire.

   b. The concept can also be illustrated with a hypothetical example of trade between two nations that produce two different products.

   (1) Suppose that the production possibilities for each nation are a straight line (there is a constant cost ratio).

   (2) Each nation will find it profitable to trade because there is a comparative (cost) advantage in the production of one of the two products; each nation can produce one of the products at a lower opportunity cost than the other.

   c. The terms of trade between nations—the ratio at which one product is traded for another—lies between the cost ratios for the two nations.

   d. Each nation gains from this trade because specialization allows for more total production from the same resources and permits a better allocation of resources; specialization and trade have the effect of easing the fixed constraints of the production possibilities curve for each nation.

4. National currencies are traded in a *foreign exchange market.* This market is competitive and establishes the exchange rate of a domestic currency for foreign currency. The price of a domestic currency, or its exchange rate, is the price paid in the domestic currency to buy 1 unit of another currency ($0.01 U.S. = 1 Japanese yen). Exchange rates are unusual prices because they link the prices of the currencies of nations.

   a. The exchange rate for a nation's currency is determined by the supply of and demand for that currency. When the supply or demand changes, then the exchange rate of the currency changes (for example, a change from $0.01 U.S. = 1 yen to $0.02 U.S. = 1 yen).

   b. The exchange value of a currency can depreciate or appreciate.

   (1) Increases in the exchange rate or price of a unit of foreign currency (the dollar price of a yen increases) means that there has been a *depreciation* in the value of one currency (the dollar) relative to the foreign currency.

   (2) Decreases in the exchange rate for a foreign currency (a decrease in the dollar price of yen) means that there has been an *appreciation* in the value of one currency (the dollar) relative to the foreign currency (the yen).

5. Governments develop *trade policies* that can reduce trade between nations.

   a. Government policies that restrict trade between nations include protective tariffs, import quotas, nontariff barriers, and export subsidies.

   b. The reason for trade restrictions is that governments may not understand the gains from trade, or there are political concerns, such as the protection of businesses or groups in a nation against international competition.

   c. But the costs of these restrictive trade policies outweigh the benefits, and as a consequence consumers pay higher prices and the nation makes less efficient use of its resources.

6. International trade policies have changed over the years with the development of *multilateral agreements* and *free-trade* zones.

   a. United States trade policy has been significantly affected by the Reciprocal Trade Agreements Act of 1934 and by the General Agreements on Tariffs and Trade (GATT) begun in 1947.

   (1) Until 1934, the United States steadily increased tariff rates to protect private-interest groups, but since the passage of the 1934 act, tariff rates have been substantially reduced. This act gave the president the authority to negotiate with foreign nations and included *most-favored-nation (MFN) status* clauses.

   (2) GATT provided equal treatment of all member nations and sought to reduce tariffs and eliminate import subsidies by multilateral negotiations.

   (3) The Uruguay round of GATT negotiations started in 1986 and was completed in 1993. The major provisions, which will be phased in through 2005, reduce tariffs on products, cut restrictive rules applying to services, phase out quotas on textiles and apparel, and decrease subsidies for agriculture. A World Trade Organization was established to settle disputes among nations.

   b. The European Union (EU) is an example of a regional free-trade zone or trade bloc among 15 nations. It abolished tariffs among member nations and developed common policies on various economic issues, such as the tariffs on goods to and from nonmember nations. The EU has produced freer trade and increased economies of scale for production in its member nations, but such a trading bloc creates trade frictions with nonmember nations like the United States.

   c. In 1993, the North American Free Trade Agreement (NAFTA) created a free-trade zone covering the United States, Mexico, and Canada. Critics of this agreement fear job losses and the potential for abuse by other nations using Mexico as a base for production. Defenders cite the mutual advantages from freer trade and the fact that increased worldwide investment in Mexico will stimulate growth in that nation and trade with the United States.

   d. Free-trade agreements may create hostile trading blocs or serve as leverage for reducing trade restrictions. The United States is working toward freer trade though the Asian-Pacific Economic Cooperation (APEC) forum and by expanding NAFTA coverage to Chile and Mercosur nations (Brazil, Argentina, Uruguay, and Paraguay).

7. Increased international trade has resulted in more competitive pressure on U.S. businesses, which raises the question of whether the United States can compete in global markets. Most firms have been able to meet the competitive change by lowering production costs, improving products, or using new technology. Some firms and industries have had difficulty remaining competitive and continue to lose market share and employment. Overall, increased trade has produced substantial benefits for U.S. consumers (lower prices and more products) and enabled the nation to make more efficient use of its scarce resources.

■ HINTS AND TIPS

1. Comparative advantage is directly related to the opportunity cost concept and production possibilities you learned about in Chapter 2.

   a. A nation has a comparative advantage in the production of a product when it can produce the product at a lower domestic opportunity cost than can a trading partner. A nation will specialize in the production of a product for which it is the low (opportunity) cost producer.

   b. When a production possibilities schedule for two nations and two products has a constant cost ratio, you can reduce the complicated production possibilities schedule to a 2 × 2 table. Put the two products in the two columns and the two nations in the two rows of the matrix. In each cell of the matrix put the *maximum* of each product that can be produced by a nation. Then for each nation, divide the maximum of one product into the maximum amount of the other product to get the domestic opportunity cost of one product in terms of the other.

c. This last point can be illustrated with an example from problem 2 in this study guide chapter. Lilliput can produce a *maximum* of 40 pounds of apples or 20 pounds of bananas. Brobdingnag can produce a *maximum* of 75 pounds of apples or 25 pounds of bananas. The 2 × 2 matrix would look like this:

	Apples	Bananas
Lilliput	40	20
Brobdingnag	75	25

For Lilliput, the domestic opportunity cost of producing 1 pound of apples is $\frac{1}{2}$ pound of bananas. In Brobdingnag, the domestic opportunity cost of producing 1 pound of apples is $\frac{1}{3}$ pound of bananas. Brobdingnag is the lower (opportunity) cost producer of apples and will specialize in the production of that product. Lilliput is the lower (opportunity) cost producer of bananas because producing 1 pound of bananas requires giving up 2 pounds of apples, whereas in Brobdingnag producing 1 pound of bananas requires giving up 3 pounds of apples.

2. Foreign exchange rates often confuse students because they can be expressed in two ways: the U.S. dollar price of a unit of foreign currency ($1.56 for 1 British pound), or the amount of foreign currency that can be purchased by one U.S. dollar ($1 can purchase .64 British pounds). If you know the exchange rate in one way, you can easily calculate it the other way. Using the information from the first way, dividing $1.56 into 1 British pound gives you the British pound price for 1 U.S. dollar (1/1.56 = .64 of a British pound). Using information from the second way, dividing .64 of a British pound into 1 U.S. dollar gives you the dollar price of a British pound (1/.64 = 1.56). Both ways may be used, although one way may be used more often than the other. Rates for British pounds or Canadian dollars are usually expressed the first way, in terms of U.S. dollars. Rates for the Swiss franc, Japanese yen, or German mark are expressed in the second way, per U.S. dollar.

■ IMPORTANT TERMS

multinational corporations	Reciprocal Trade Agreements Act
"Asian tigers"	free-trade zones
comparative advantage	most-favored-nation clauses
terms of trade	
foreign exchange market	General Agreements on Tariffs and Trade (GATT)
exchange rates	World Trade Organization
depreciation	European Union (EU)
appreciation	trade bloc
protective tariffs	North American Free Trade Agreement (NAFTA)
import quotas	
nontariff barriers	
export subsidies	
Smoot-Hawley Tariff Act	

SELF-TEST

■ FILL-IN QUESTIONS

1. The importance of international trade varies by nation. Nations in which exports account for a relatively high percentage of GDP tend to have a (limited, diversified) _____ resource base and domestic market, whereas nations in which exports account for a lower percentage of GDP tend to have a _____ resource base and domestic market. An example of a higher exporting nation would be the (United States, Netherlands) _____, and a lower exporting nation would be the _____.

2. In relative terms, the imports and exports of the United States amount to about (12–14, 25–27) _____% of the economy's GDP. In absolute terms, the United States is the world's (smallest, largest) _____ trading nation.

3. The bulk of the trade of the United States is with (less developed, industrially advanced) _____ nations. The largest trading partner for the United States is (Canada, Japan) _____. The United States has a large trade deficit with (Canada, Japan) _____.

4. Factors that have helped increase the growth of world trade since World War II include improvement in _____ and _____ technology, a general decline in _____, and _____ relations between the major trading partners in the world.

5. The top participants in international trade include the _____, _____ and the nations of western Europe. These participants serve as the headquarters for most (national, multinational) _____ corporations and dominate world trade. The new industrializing economies of Hong Kong, Singapore, South Korea, and Taiwan, known as the "_____," have expanded their share of the world trade to over 10%.

6. In the circular flow model that adds the "rest of the world," foreign expenditures pay for U.S. (imports, exports) _____ and U.S. expenditures pay for _____.

7. Specialization and trade (increase, decrease) _____ the productivity of a nation's resources and _____ total output more than would be the case without it.

8. When one nation has a lower opportunity cost of producing a product relative to another state or nation it

has a (nontariff barrier, comparative advantage) _____

_____. The amount of one product that must be given up to obtain 1 unit of another product is the (foreign exchange, terms of trade) _____.

9. When the dollar price of foreign currency increases, there has been a(n) (appreciation, depreciation) _____ in value of the dollar. When the dollar price of foreign currency decreases, there has been a(n) _____ in value of the dollar. For example, if the dollar price of a German mark (DM) decreases from $0.60 = 1 DM to $0.50 = 1 DM, then it means that there has been a(n) (appreciation, depreciation) _____ in the value of the dollar; but if the dollar price of a German mark increases from $0.40 = 1 DM to $0.55 = 1 DM, then it means that there has been a(n) _____ in the value of the dollar.

10. In the market for Japanese yen, an increase in the (demand for, supply of) _____ yen will decrease the dollar price of yen, while an increase in the _____ yen will increase the dollar price of yen. If the dollar price of the yen increases, then Japanese goods imported into the United States will be (more, less) _____ expensive.

11. The major government policies that restrict trade include
  a. excise taxes or duties on imported goods that are called _____,
  b. limits on the quantities or total value of specific items that may be imported, referred to as _____,
  c. licensing requirements, unreasonable standards, and red tape for a product, which are _____,
  d. government payments to domestic producers of export goods, known as _____.

12. Governments may intervene in trade between nations because they mistakenly think of (exports, imports) _____ as helpful and _____ as harmful for a national economy. In fact, there are important gains from trade in the form of the extra output obtained from abroad. Trade makes it possible to obtain (exports, imports) _____ at a lower cost than would be the case if they were produced using domestic resources, and the earnings from _____ help a nation pay for these lower cost (exports, imports) _____.

13. Another reason why governments interfere with free trade is based on (private, political) _____ considerations. Groups and industries seek protection from foreign competition through (GATT, tariffs) _____ and import (quotas, subsidies) _____, or other kinds of trade restrictions. The costs of trade protectionism are (clear to, hidden

from) _____ consumers in the protected product so there is little opposition to demands for protectionism.

14. Tariffs and quotas (benefit, cost) _____ domestic firms in the protected industries, but _____ domestic consumers in the form of (lower, higher) _____ prices than would be the case if there were free trade. They also (benefit, cost) _____ domestic firms that use the protected goods as inputs in their production processes.

15. Until 1934, the trend of tariff rates in the United States was (upward, downward) _____. The trend has been (upward, downward) _____ since the 1934 passage of the (Smoot-Hawley Tariff, Reciprocal Trade Agreements) _____ Act. This act empowered the President to lower (tariffs, quotas) _____ by up to 50% in return for a reduction in foreign restrictions on U.S. goods and incorporated (quotas, most-favored-nation) _____ clauses in U.S. trade agreements.

16. The three cardinal principles established in the General Agreements on Tariffs and Trade are
  a. _____
  b. _____
  c. _____

17. The major provisions of the Uruguay round of (NAFTA, GATT) _____ negotiations include (exchange rate, tariff) _____ reductions, coverage of legal, financial, and other (goods, services) _____ by GATT, cuts in agricultural (import quotas, subsidies) _____, and protection of (collective, intellectual) _____ property against piracy. It also created the successor to GATT, called the (Reciprocal, World) _____ Trade Organization.

18. An example of a free-trade zone or trade bloc is the (Mercosur, European) _____ Union that was originally started in 1958 as the Common Market.
  a. The specific aims of the Common Market were the abolition of (exchange rates, tariffs and quotas) _____, the establishment of (uniform, different) _____ tariffs on goods imported from outside the Common Market, the (restricted, free) _____ movement of capital and labor within the Common Market, and common policies on other matters.
  b. The Union created (small, large) _____ markets and stimulated production that has allowed in-

dustries to achieve (higher, lower) _____ costs. The economic effects of the Union on non-member nations such as the United States are mixed because economic growth in the Union will cause U.S. exports to the Union to (decrease, increase) _____ while the tariffs barrier will cause U.S. exports to _____.

19. The North American Free Trade Agreement (NAFTA) formed a trade (barrier, bloc) _____ among the United States, Canada, and Mexico. This agreement eliminated (terms of trade, tariffs) _____ among the nations. Critics in the United States say that it will (increase, decrease) _____ jobs, but defenders say that it will _____ total output.

20. The evidence shows that many U.S. firms (can, cannot) _____ compete and be successful in the global economy; however, some firms that have benefitted from past trade protection may find it difficult to adjust to foreign (control, competition) _____ and may go out of business.

■ TRUE-FALSE QUESTIONS

Circle the T if the statement is true, the F if it is false.

1. For the United States, the volume of international trade has been increasing relatively but not absolutely. **T F**

2. The U.S. economy's share of world trade has decreased since 1947. **T F**

3. The United States exports and imports goods and services with a dollar value greater than any other nation in the world. **T F**

4. The United States is completely dependent on trade for certain commodities which cannot be obtained in domestic markets. **T F**

5. Canada is the most important trading partner for the United States in terms of the volume of exports and imports. **T F**

6. If a person, firm, or region has a comparative advantage in the production of a particular commodity, it should specialize in the production of that commodity. **T F**

7. If one nation has a comparative advantage in the production of a commodity than another nation, then it has a higher opportunity cost of production relative to the other nation. **T F**

8. The economic effects of specialization and trade between nations are similar to increasing the quantity of resources or to achieving technological progress. **T F**

9. The interaction of the demand for, and supply of, Japanese yen will establish the dollar price of Japanese yen. **T F**

10. An increase in incomes in the United States would tend to cause the dollar price of the Japanese yen to fall. **T F**

11. When the dollar price of another nation's currency increases, there has been an appreciation in the value of the dollar. **T F**

12. When the dollar depreciates relative to the value of the currencies of the trading partners of the United States, then goods imported into the United States will tend to become more expensive. **T F**

13. Export subsidies are government payments to reduce the price of a product to buyers from other nations. **T F**

14. Nontariff barriers include excise taxes or duties placed on imported goods. **T F**

15. Through world trade, an economy can reach a point beyond its domestic production possibilities curve. **T F**

16. One reason that trade restrictions get public support is that the alleged benefits of the restrictions are often immediate and clear-cut, but the adverse affects are often obscure and dispersed over the economy. **T F**

17. Tariffs and quotas benefit domestic firms in the protected industries and also help domestic consumers by lowering the prices for those products. **T F**

18. The Smoot-Hawley Tariff Act of 1930 reduced tariffs in the United States to the lowest level ever in an attempt to pull the nation out of the Great Depression. **T F**

19. If the United States concludes a tariff agreement which lowers the tariff rates on goods imported from another nation and that trade agreement contains a most-favored-nation (MFN) clause, the lower tariff rates are then applied to those goods when they are imported from other MFNs. **T F**

20. The members of the European Union (EU) have experienced freer trade since it was formed. **T F**

21. The economic integration of nations creates larger markets for firms within the nations that integrate and makes it possible for these firms and their customers to benefit from the economies of large-scale (mass) production. **T F**

22. The formation of the European Union (EU) may make it more difficult for U.S. firms to compete for European customers with firms located within the Union. **T F**

23. The 1993 North American Free Trade Agreement (NAFTA) includes all Central American nations. **T F**

24. NAFTA is an example of the gains to be obtained from voluntary export restrictions. **T F**

25. The evidence is clear that major U.S. firms are unable to compete in world markets without significant protection from foreign competition. **T F**

■ MULTIPLE-CHOICE QUESTIONS

Circle the letter that corresponds to the best answer.

1. Which nation is the world's leading trading nation in terms of absolute volumes of imports and exports?

(a) Japan
(b) China
(c) Germany
(d) United States

2. Which nation is our most important trading partner in terms of the quantity of trade volume?
(a) Japan
(b) Canada
(c) Germany
(d) United Kingdom

3. Which of the following is true?
(a) Exports as a percentage of GDP is greatest in the United States.
(b) The United States is almost totally dependent on other nations for aircraft, machine tools, and coal.
(c) Most of the exports and imports trade of the United States is with industrially advanced nations.
(d) The United States has a trade surplus with Japan.

4. How is most of the trade deficit financed by a nation such as the United States?
(a) by buying securities or assets from other nations
(b) by selling securities or assets to other nations
(c) by borrowing from the Federal government
(d) by lending to the Federal government

5. Which factor has greatly facilitated international trade since World War II?
(a) expanded export subsidies
(b) greater import quotas
(c) increased nontariff barriers
(d) improved communications

6. "Asian tigers" refers to the
(a) nations of Japan and China
(b) nations of Hong Kong, Singapore, South Korea, and Taiwan
(c) aggressive export strategies of the Philippines and Thailand
(d) multinational corporations located in Asian countries

7. In the circular flow model of the economy, U.S.
(a) imports are paid for by foreign expenditures
(b) exports are paid for by U.S. expenditures
(c) imports are paid for by U.S. expenditures
(d) exports are paid for by U.S. multinational corporations

8. Why do nations specialize and engage in trade?
(a) to protect multinational corporations
(b) to increase output and income
(c) to improve communications
(d) to control other nations

Answer Questions 9, 10, 11, and 12 on the basis of the data given for two regions, Slobovia and Utopia, which have the following production possibilities tables.

SLOBOVIA PRODUCTION POSSIBILITIES TABLE

	Production alternatives					
Product	A	B	C	D	E	F
Cams	1,500	1,200	900	600	300	0
Widgets	0	100	200	300	400	500

UTOPIA PRODUCTION POSSIBILITIES TABLE

	Production alternatives				
Product	A	B	C	D	E
Cams	4,000	3,000	2,000	1,000	0
Widgets	0	200	400	600	800

9. In Slobovia, the comparative cost of
(a) 1 cam is 3 widgets
(b) 1 widget is $\frac{1}{3}$ cam
(c) 1 cam is $\frac{1}{3}$ widget
(d) 3 widgets is 1 cam

10. Which of the following statements is *not* true?
(a) Slobovia should specialize in the production of widgets.
(b) Slobovia has a comparative advantage in the production of widgets.
(c) Utopia should specialize in the production of widgets.
(d) Utopia has a comparative advantage in the production of cams.

11. The terms of trade will be
(a) greater than 7 cams for 1 widget
(b) between 7 cams for 1 widget and 5 cams for 1 widget
(c) between 5 cams for 1 widget and 3 cams for 1 widget
(d) less than 3 cams for 1 widget

12. Assume that if Slobovia did not specialize it would produce alternative C and that if Utopia did not specialize it would select alternative B. The gains from specialization are
(a) 100 cams and 100 widgets
(b) 200 cams and 200 widgets
(c) 400 cams and 500 widgets
(d) 500 cams and 400 widgets

13. If the dollar-yen exchange rate is $1 for 110 yen, then a Sony VCR priced at 27,500 yen would cost a U.S. consumer
(a) $200
(b) $250
(c) $275
(d) $300

14. If the equilibrium exchange rate changes so that the dollar price of Japanese yen increases
(a) the dollar has appreciated in value
(b) the dollar has depreciated in value
(c) U.S. citizens will be able to buy more Japanese goods
(d) Japanese will be able to buy fewer U.S. goods

15. A decrease in the United States demand for Japanese goods will
(a) increase the demand for Japanese yen and increase the dollar price of yen
(b) increase the demand for Japanese yen but decrease the dollar price of yen
(c) decrease the demand for Japanese yen and decrease the dollar price of yen
(d) decrease the demand for Japanese yen but increase the dollar price of yen

16. If the exchange rate for one United States dollar changes from 1.4 German marks to 1.7 German marks, then there has been
(a) an appreciation in the value of the mark
(b) a depreciation in the value of the dollar
(c) a depreciation in the value of the mark
(d) an increase in the price of the mark

17. Which of the following is designed to restrict trade?
(a) GATT
(b) NAFTA
(c) import quotas
(d) multinational corporations

18. Why do governments often intervene in international trade?
(a) to expand a nation's production possibilities
(b) to improve the position of multinational corporations
(c) to protect domestic industries from foreign competition
(d) to increase revenue from tariff duties and excise taxes

19. Tariffs and quotas in a nation benefit domestic
(a) consumers and foreign producers of the protected product
(b) consumers and producers of the protected product
(c) producers of the protected product, but harm domestic consumers of the product
(d) foreign producers of the protected product, but harm domestic producers of the product

20. Which one of the following specifically empowered the president of the United States to reduce its tariff rates up to 50% if other nations would reduce their tariffs on American goods?
(a) the Smoot-Hawley Tariff Act of 1930
(b) the Reciprocal Trade Agreements Act of 1934
(c) the General Agreement on Tariffs and Trade of 1947
(d) North American Free Trade Agreement of 1993

21. Which of the following is characteristic of the General Agreement on Tariffs and Trade? Nations signing the agreement were committed to
(a) the expansion of import quotas
(b) the reciprocal increase in tariffs by negotiation
(c) the nondiscriminatory treatment of all member nations
(d) the establishment of a world customs union

22. One important outcome from the Uruguay round of GATT was
(a) removal of voluntary export restraints in manufacturing
(b) reduction of trade barriers and subsidies in agriculture
(c) abolishment of patent, copyright, and trademark protection
(d) an increase in tariff barriers on services

23. One of the potential problems with the European Union is that
(a) an unregulated free flow of labor and capital may reduce productivity

(b) economies of large-scale production may increase consumer prices
(c) tariffs may reduce trade with nonmember nations
(d) governments may have difficulty covering the shortfall from the elimination of duties and taxes

24. An example of the formation of a trade bloc would be the
(a) Smoot-Hawley Tariff Act
(b) North American Free Trade Agreement
(c) Reciprocal Trade Agreements Act
(d) General Agreements on Tariffs and Trade

25. The Mercosur is
(a) the controlling body of the European Union
(b) one of the provisions of the North American Free Trade Agreement
(c) the name of the organization resulting from the latest GATT negotiations
(d) a free-trade zone covering Brazil, Argentina, Uruguay, and Paraguay

■ **PROBLEMS**

1. The following problem will help you understand the principle of comparative advantage and the benefits of specialization. A tailor named Hart has the production possibilities table for trousers and jackets as given. He chooses production alternative D.

HART'S PRODUCTION POSSIBILITIES TABLE

Product	Production alternatives					
	A	B	C	D	E	F
Trousers	75	60	45	30	15	0
Jackets	0	10	20	30	40	50

Another tailor, Schaffner, has the following production possibilities table and produces production alternative E.

SCHAFFNER'S PRODUCTION POSSIBILITIES TABLE

Product	Production alternatives						
	A	B	C	D	E	F	G
Trousers	60	50	40	30	20	10	0
Jackets	0	5	10	15	20	25	30

a. To Hart,

(1) the cost of one pair of trousers is _____ jackets

(2) the cost of one jacket is _____ pairs of trousers

b. To Schaffner,

(1) the cost of one pair of trousers is _____ jackets

(2) the cost of one jacket is _____ pairs of trousers

c. If Hart and Schaffner were to form a partnership to make suits,

(1) _____ should specialize in the making of trousers because he can make a pair of trousers at the cost of _____ of a jacket while it costs his partner _____ of a jacket to make a pair of trousers.

(2) _____ should specialize in the making of jackets because he can make a jacket at the cost of _____ pairs of trousers while it costs his partner _____ pairs of trousers to make a jacket.

d. Without specialization, Hart and Schaffner were able to make 50 pairs of trousers and 50 jackets. If each specializes completely in the item in the production of which he has a comparative advantage, their combined production will be _____ pairs of trousers and _____ jackets. Thus the gain from specialization is _____ _____.

e. When Hart and Schaffner come to divide the income of the partnership between them, the manufacture of a pair of trousers should be treated as the equivalent of from _____ to _____ jackets (or a jacket should be treated as the equivalent of from _____ to _____ pairs of trousers).

2. The countries of Lilliput and Brobdingnag have the production possibilities tables for apples and bananas shown below.

Note that the costs of producing apples and bananas are constant in both countries.

LILLIPUT PRODUCTION POSSIBILITIES TABLE

Product (lb)	Production alternatives					
	A	B	C	D	E	F
Apples	40	32	24	16	8	0
Bananas	0	4	8	12	16	20

BROBDINGNAG PRODUCTION POSSIBILITIES TABLE

Product (lb)	Production alternatives					
	A	B	C	D	E	F
Apples	75	60	45	30	15	0
Bananas	0	5	10	15	20	25

a. In Lilliput the cost of producing

(1) 8 apples is _____ bananas

(2) 1 apple is _____ bananas

b. In Brobdingnag the cost of producing

(1) 15 apples is _____ bananas

(2) 1 apple is _____ bananas

c. In Lilliput the cost of producing

(1) 4 bananas is _____ apples

(2) 1 banana is _____ apples

d. In Brobdingnag the cost of producing

(1) 5 bananas is _____ apples

(2) 1 banana is _____ apples

e. The cost of producing 1 apple is lower in the country of _____ and the cost of producing 1 banana is lower in the country of _____.

f. Lilliput has a comparative advantage in the production of _____ and Brobdingnag has a comparative advantage in the production of _____.

g. The information in this problem is not sufficient to determine the exact terms of trade, but the terms of trade will be *greater* than _____ apples for 1 banana and *less* than _____ apples for 1 banana. Put another way, the terms of trade will be between _____ bananas for 1 apple and _____ bananas for 1 apple.

h. If neither nation could specialize, each would produce production alternative C. The combined production of apples in the two countries would be _____ apples and the combined production of bananas would be _____ bananas.

(1) If each nation specializes in producing the fruit for which it has a comparative advantage, their combined production will be _____ apples and _____ bananas.

(2) Their gain from specialization will be _____ apples and _____ bananas.

3. Use the following table that shows 10 different currencies and how much of each currency can be purchased with a U.S. dollar.

Country	Currency	Currency per U.S. $		A or D
		Year 1	Year 2	
Brazil	Real	0.85	0.91	_____
Britain	Pound	0.65	0.59	_____
Canada	Dollar	1.41	1.51	_____
France	Franc	5.44	5.22	_____
Germany	Mark	1.58	1.69	_____
India	Rupee	31.39	34.55	_____
Japan	Yen	100.15	110.23	_____
Mexico	Peso	4.65	5.09	_____
Norway	Krone	6.88	6.49	_____
Thailand	Bhat	25.12	23.22	_____

a. In the far right column of the table, indicate whether the U.S. dollar has appreciated (A) or depreciated (D) from year 1 to year 2.

b. In year 1, a U.S. dollar would purchase _____ French francs, but in year 2, it would purchase _____ French francs. The U.S. dollar has (appreciated, depreciated) _____ against the French franc from year 1 to year 2.

c. In year 1, a U.S. dollar would purchase _____

Japanese yen, but in year 2, it would purchase _____
Japanese yen. The U.S. dollar has (appreciated, de-

preciated) _____ against the Japanese
yen from year 1 to year 2.

4. This problem asks you to calculate prices based on
exchange rates. Use the data in the table for Problem 3
to answer the following items.

    a. Using the exchange rates shown for year 1, what
would be the U.S. dollar cost for the following products?
    (1) Japanese television costing 30,000 yen.

                                                  $_____

    (2) French scarf costing 600 francs. $_____

    (3) Thai artwork costing 3,768 bhats. $_____

    (4) German auto costing 79,000 marks. $_____
    (5) Mexican silver bracelet costing 1,376 pesos.

                                                  $_____
    b. Using the exchange rates shown for year 2, what
would be the U.S. dollar cost of the following products?
    (1) Japanese television costing 30,000 yen.

                                                  $_____

    (2) French scarf costing 600 francs. $_____

    (3) Thai artwork costing 3,768 bhats. $_____

    (4) German auto costing 79,000 marks. $_____
    (5) Mexican silver bracelet costing 1,376 pesos.

                                                  $_____
    c. Indicate whether the U.S. dollar cost of each prod-
uct in **4b** has increased (+) or decreased (−) from year
1 to year 2. _____ _____ _____ _____
    d. What is the relationship between your answers in
4c to the ones you gave for the corresponding nations
in **3a**?
    (1) When the U.S. dollar *appreciates* in value against
a foreign currency, the U.S. dollar cost of a product from

that nation will (increase, decrease) _____.
    (2) When the U.S. dollar *depreciates* in value against
a foreign currency, the U.S. dollar cost of a product from

that nation will (increase, decrease) _____.

■ SHORT ANSWER AND ESSAY QUESTIONS

1. In relative and absolute terms, how large is the volume of the international trade of the United States? What
has happened to these figures over the past 30 or so
years?

2. What are the principal exports and imports of the U.S.
economy? What commodities used in the economy come
almost entirely from abroad, and what American industries sell large percentages of their outputs abroad?

3. Which nations are the principal trading partners of the
United States? How much of this trade is with the devel-

oped and how much of it is with the developing nations
of the world?

4. Give several factors that have facilitated trade since
World War II.

5. Who are the major participants in international trade?
Describe the relative influence of the key players.

6. Describe how the international trade component can
be added to the circular flow model of the economy.

7. Use an example of two individuals to describe the basic principle of comparative advantage.

8. What is meant by comparative cost and comparative
advantage?

9. Explain how comparative advantage determines the
terms of trade between nations.

10. What is the gain for a nation that results from specialization in the production of products for which there is
a comparative advantage?

11. Describe the characteristics of a foreign exchange
market and of exchange rates. Why is an exchange rate
an unusual price?

12. Illustrate with a supply and demand graph how equilibrium is determined in a dollar-yen market. Be sure to
label axes and curves.

13. Why might an appreciation of the value of the U.S.
dollar relative to the Japanese yen depress the U.S. economy and stimulate the Japanese economy? Why might a
government intervene in the foreign exchange market and
try to increase or decrease the value of its currency?

14. What are the major trade impediments and subsidies? How do they restrict international trade?

15. Why do governments intervene in international trade
and develop restrictive trade policies?

16. What is the cost to society from trade protectionism?
Who benefits and who is hurt by trade protectionism?

17. What was the Smoot-Hawley Tariff Act of 1930? What
international trade problems are illustrated by this act?

18. Explain the basic provisions of the Reciprocal Trade
Agreements Act of 1934.

19. What were the cardinal principles contained in the
General Agreements on Tariffs and Trade (GATT)?

20. What were the basic provisions and important results
of the Uruguay round of GATT negotiations?

21. What is the European Union? What were its original
goals under the Common Market?

22. Discuss the potential trade effects of the European
Union on the United States.

23. What is the North American Free Trade Agreement
(NAFTA)? What do its critics and defenders say about the
agreement?

24. What are the prospects for friction among trading blocs
or further integration of worldwide trade among nations?

25. Can U.S. firms compete in a global economy? Evaluate the competitive abilities of U.S. firms in a global economy.

ANSWERS

Chapter 6 The United States in the Global Economy

FILL-IN QUESTIONS

1. limited, diversified, Netherlands, United States
2. 12–14, largest
3. industrially advanced, Canada, Japan
4. transportation, communications (any order), tariffs, peaceful
5. United States, Japan (any order), multinational, Asian tigers
6. exports, imports
7. increase, increase
8. comparative advantage, terms of trade
9. depreciation, appreciation, appreciation, depreciation
10. supply of, demand for, more
11. *a.* protective tariffs; *b.* import quotas; *c.* nontariff barriers; *d.* export subsidies
12. exports, imports, imports, exports, imports
13. political, tariffs, quotas, hidden from
14. benefit, cost, higher cost
15. upward, downward, Reciprocal Trade Agreements, tariffs, most-favored-nation
16. *a.* equal, nondiscriminatory treatment of all member nations; *b.* reduction of tariffs by multilateral negotiations; *c.* elimination of import quotas
17. GATT, tariff, services, subsidies, intellectual, World
18. European; *a.* tariffs and quotas, uniform, free; *b.* large, large, lower, increase, decrease
19. bloc, tariffs, decrease, increase
20. can, competition

TRUE-FALSE QUESTIONS

1. F, p. 102
2. T, p. 102
3. T, p. 102
4. T, p. 102
5. T, p. 103
6. T, p. 109
7. F, p. 109
8. T, p. 110
9. T, p. 111
10. F, pp. 111-112
11. F, pp. 111-112
12. T, pp. 111-112
13. T, p. 113
14. F, p. 113
15. T, p. 113
16. T, pp. 113-114
17. F, pp. 113-114
18. F, p. 114
19. T, p. 114
20. T, p. 116
21. T, p. 116
22. T, p. 116
23. F, p. 116
24. F, pp. 116-117
25. F, pp. 117-118

MULTIPLE-CHOICE QUESTIONS

1. d, p. 102
2. b, p. 103
3. c, p. 103
4. b, p. 104
5. d, p. 104
6. b, p. 105
7. c, pp. 105-106
8. b, pp. 107-108
9. c, pp. 108-109
10. c, pp. 108-109
11. c, pp. 108-109
12. a, pp. 108-109
13. b, p. 111
14. b, p. 111
15. c, p. 111
16. c, pp. 111-112
17. c, p. 113
18. c, p. 113
19. c, p. 113
20. b, p. 114
21. c, pp. 115-116
22. b, pp. 115-116
23. c, p. 116
24. b, p. 116
25. d, p. 117

PROBLEMS

1. *a.* (1) 2/3, (2) 1 1/2; *b.* (1) 1/2, (2) 2; *c.* (1) Schaffner, 1/2, 2/3; (2) Hart, 1 1/2, 2; *d.* 60, 50, 10 pairs of trousers; *e.* 1/2, 2/3, 1 1/2, 2
2. *a.* (1) 4, (2) 1/2; *b.* (1) 5, (2) 1/3; *c.* (1) 8, (2) 2; *d.* (1) 15, (2) 3; *e.* Brobdingnag, Lilliput; *f.* bananas, apples; *g.* 2, 3, 1/3, 1/2; *h.* 69, 18, (1) 75, 20, (2) 6, 2
3. *a.* A, D, A, D, A, A, A, A, D, D; *b.* 5.44, 5.22, depreciated; *c.* 100.15, 110.23, appreciated
4. *a.* (1) 299.55 (2) 110.29 (3) 150 (4) 50,000 (5) 295.91; *b.* (1) 272.16 (2) 114.94 (3) 162.27 (4) 46,745.56 (5) 270.33; *c.* 1 − (2) + (3) + (4) − (5)−; *d.* (1) decrease (2) increase

SHORT ANSWER AND ESSAY QUESTIONS

1. p. 102
2. p. 103
3. p. 103
4. p. 104
5. pp. 104-105
6. pp. 105-107
7. p. 108
8. pp. 108-109
9. p. 109
10. pp. 109-110
11. pp. 110-111
12. p. 111
13. pp. 111-112
14. pp. 112-113
15. pp. 113-114
16. pp. 113-114
17. p. 114
18. pp. 114-115
19. p. 115
20. pp. 115-116
21. p. 116
22. p. 116
23. pp. 116-117
24. p. 117
25. pp. 117-118

Measuring Domestic Output, National Income, and the Price Level

The subject of Chapter 7 is national income accounting. The first measure that you will learn about in the chapter is the **gross domestic product (GDP).** The GDP is an important economic statistic because it provides the best estimate of the total market value of all final goods and services produced by our economy in 1 year. You will also discover why GDP is a monetary measure that counts only the value of final goods and services and excludes nonproductive transactions such as secondhand sales.

National income accounting involves estimating output, or income, for the nation's society as a whole, rather than for an individual business firm or family. Note that the terms "output" and "income" are interchangeable because the nation's domestic output and its income are identical. The value of the nation's output equals the total expenditures for this output, and these expenditures become the income of those who have produced this output. Consequently, there are two equally acceptable methods—expenditures or income—for determining GDP.

From an expenditure perspective, GDP is composed of four expenditure categories: personal consumption expenditures (**C**), gross private domestic investment (**I_g**), government purchases (**G**), and net exports (**X_n**). These expenditures become income for people when they are paid out in the form of employee compensation, rents, interest, proprietor's income, and corporate profits, with adjustments made for indirect business taxes, depreciation, and net foreign factor income earned in the United States. In national income accounting, the amount spent to purchase this year's total output is equal to money income derived from production of this year's output.

This chapter also explains the relationship of GDP to other national accounts. These accounts include **net domestic product** (NDP), **national income** (NI) as derived from NDP, **personal income** (PI), and **disposable income** (DI). The relationship between GDP, NDP, NI, PI, and DI is shown in Table 7-4 of the text. The circular flow using the expenditures and income approaches to GDP are illustrated in Figure 7-3 of the text.

By measuring the **price level,** economists are able to determine how much inflation (an increase in the price level) or deflation (a decrease in the price level) has occurred in the economy. This information is important because income-output measures are expressed in monetary units, so if accurate comparisons are to be made between years, these monetary measures must be adjusted to take account of changes in the price level. A simple example is presented to show how a GDP price in-dex, or deflator, is constructed, and then the index is used to adjust nominal GDP to determine real GDP for comparison purposes. The GDP price index and the consumer price index as measures of the rate of inflation will also be explained.

The last section of the chapter looks at the relationship between GDP and economic well-being. You will learn about economic factors that are excluded from GDP measurement—nonmarket or illegal transactions, changes in leisure and product quality, differences in the composition and distribution of output, and the environmental effects of GDP production—and how their exclusion can lead to an under- or overstatement of economic well-being. Although national income accounts are not perfect measures of all economic conditions, they are still reasonably accurate and useful indicators of the performance of the national economy.

Chapter 7 is the essential background for Parts 2 and 3 of the text, which explain the history of and the factors that determine the level of domestic output and income in the economy. Chapter 7 is important because it explains the several methods used to measure the performance of the economy in a given year and make the adjustments necessary to ensure accurate measurements of performance over time.

■ **CHECKLIST**

When you have studied this chapter you should be able to

☐ Identify three ways national income accounting can be used for economic decision making.
☐ Give a definition of the gross domestic product (GDP).
☐ Explain why GDP is a monetary measure.
☐ Describe how GDP measures value added and avoids multiple counting.
☐ Give examples of two types of nonproduction transactions that are excluded from GDP.
☐ Describe the relationship between the expenditures and income approaches to GDP accounting.
☐ List the two types of goods included in personal consumption expenditures (C).
☐ Identify three items included in gross private domestic investment (I_g).
☐ Explain why changes in inventories are an investment.
☐ Distinguish between gross and net investment.

☐ Discuss how differences in the amount of net investment affect economic growth in an economy.

☐ List the items included in government purchases (G).

☐ Describe the meaning and calculation of net exports (X_n).

☐ Compute GDP using the expenditures approach when given national income accounting data.

☐ Identify the five income items that make up U.S. national income.

☐ List three things that can happen to corporate profits.

☐ Explain the indirect business taxes adjustment to national income accounts.

☐ Define depreciation and discuss how it affects national income accounts.

☐ Describe the effect of net foreign factor income on national income accounts.

☐ Compute GDP using the income approach when given national income accounting data.

☐ Define net domestic product (NDP).

☐ Show how to derive U.S. national income (NI) from net domestic product (NDP).

☐ Define personal income (PI) in national income accounts.

☐ Explain how to obtain disposable income (DI) from personal income (PI).

☐ Use Figure 7-3 in the text to describe the circular flow model for GDP.

☐ Distinguish between nominal and real GDP.

☐ Construct a price index when given the necessary price and quantity data.

☐ Obtain a price index when given data on nominal and real GDP.

☐ Discuss some real-world factors that affect the GDP price index.

☐ Distinguish between the GDP and the consumer price index (CPI).

☐ List seven reasons why GDP may understate or overstate economic well-being.

■ CHAPTER OUTLINE

1. National income accounting consists of concepts which enable those who use them to measure the economy's output, to compare it with past outputs, to explain its size and the reasons for changes in its size, and to formulate policies designed to increase it.

2. The market value of all final goods and services produced in the economy during the year is measured by the gross domestic product (GDP).

 a. GDP is measured in dollar terms rather than in terms of physical units of output.

 b. To avoid multiple counting, GDP includes only *final* goods and services (goods and services that will not be processed further during the *current* year).

 c. Nonproduction transactions are not included in GDP; purely financial transactions and second-hand sales are therefore excluded.

 d. Measurement of GDP can be accomplished by either the expenditures or the income method, but the same result is obtained by the two methods.

3. Computation of the GDP by the **expenditures approach** requires the addition of the total amounts of the four types of spending for final goods and services.

 a. Personal consumption expenditures (C) are the expenditures of households for durable and nondurable goods and for services.

 b. Gross private domestic investment (I_g) is the sum of the spending by business firms for machinery, equipment, and tools; spending by firms and households for new buildings; and the changes in the inventories of business firms.

 (1) A change in inventories is included in investment because it is the part of output of the economy which was not sold during the year.

 (2) Investment does not include expenditures for stocks or bonds or for second-hand capital goods.

 (3) Gross investment exceeds net investment by the value of the capital goods worn out during the year.

 (4) An economy in which net investment is positive (zero, negative) is an expanding (a static, a declining) economy.

 c. Government purchases (G) are the expenditures made by all governments in the economy for products produced by business firms and for resource services from households.

 d. Net exports (X_n) in an economy equal the expenditures made by foreigners for goods and services produced in the economy less the expenditures made by the consumers, governments, and investors of the economy for goods and services produced in foreign nations.

 e. In equation form, $C + I_g + G + X_n =$ GDP

4. Computation of GDP by the **income approach** requires adding the income derived from the production and sales of final goods and services. The five income items are

 a. Compensation of employees (the sum of wages and salaries *and* wage and salary supplements).

 b. Rents.

 c. Interest (only the interest payments made by business firms are included, and the interest payments made by government are excluded).

 d. Proprietors' income (the profits or net income of unincorporated firms).

 e. Corporate profits which are subdivided into

 (1) Corporate income taxes

 (2) Dividends

 (3) Undistributed corporate profits

 f. Three additions are made to the income side to balance it with expenditures.

 (1) Indirect business taxes are added because they are initially income that later gets paid to government.

 (2) Depreciation, or the consumption of fixed capital, is added because it is initially income to businesses that later gets deducted in calculating profits.

 (3) Net foreign factor income is added because it reflects income from all domestic output regardless of the foreign or domestic ownership of domestic resources.

5. In addition to GDP, four other national income measures are important in evaluating the performance of the economy. Each has a distinct definition and can be computed by making additions to or deductions from another measure.

a. NDP is the annual output of final goods and services over and above the capital goods worn out during the year. It is equal to the GDP minus depreciation (consumption of fixed capital).

b. NI is the total income **earned** by U.S. owners of land and capital and by the U.S. suppliers of labor and entrepreneurial ability during the year. It equals NDP *minus* net foreign factor income earned in the United States and *minus* indirect business taxes.

c. PI is the total income **received**—whether it is earned or unearned—by the households of the economy before the payment of personal taxes. It is found by **adding** transfer payments to and **subtracting** social security contributions, corporate income taxes, and undistributed corporate profits from the NI.

d. DI is the total income available to households after the payment of personal taxes. It is equal to PI less personal taxes and also equal to personal consumption expenditures plus personal saving.

e. The relations among the five income-output measures are summarized in Table 7-4.

f. Figure 7-3 is a more realistic and complex circular flow diagram that shows the flows of expenditures and incomes among the households, business firms, and governments in the economy.

6. Because price levels change from year to year, it is necessary to adjust the nominal GDP (or money GDP) computed for any year to obtain the real GDP before year-to-year comparison between the outputs of final goods and services can be made.

a. There are two methods for deriving *real GDP* from *nominal GDP.* The first method involves computing a *price index.*

(1) This index is a ratio of the price of a market basket in a given year to the price of the same market basket in a base year, with the ratio multiplied by 100.

(2) To obtain real GDP, divide nominal GDP by the price index expressed in hundredths.

b. In the second method, nominal GDP is broken down into prices and quantities for each year. Real GDP is found by using base-year prices and multiplying them times each year's physical quantities. The GDP price index for a particular year is the ratio of nominal to real GDP for that year.

c. In the real world, complex methods are used to calculate the GDP price index. The price index is useful for calculating real GDP. The price index number for a reference period is arbitrarily set at 100.

(1) For years when the price index is below 100, dividing nominal GDP by the price index (in hundredths) inflates nominal GDP to obtain real GDP.

(2) For years when the price index is greater than 100, dividing nominal GDP by the price index (in hundredths) deflates nominal GDP to obtain real GDP.

d. The consumer price index (CPI) is a fixed-weight price index that measures the ratio of the current price of a fixed, base-period market basket to the base period price of the same market basket, multiplied by 100.

It is designed to measure the cost of a constant standard of living.

7. The GDP is not, for the following reasons, a measure of economic well-being.

a. It excludes the value of final goods and services not bought and sold in the markets of the economy.

b. It excludes the amount of leisure the citizens of the economy are able to have.

c. It does not record the improvements in the quality of products which occur over the years.

d. It does not measure changes in the composition and the distribution of the domestic output.

e. It is not a measure of per capita output because it does not take into account changes in the size of the economy's population.

f. It does not record the pollution costs to the environment of producing final goods and services.

g. It does not measure the market value of the final goods and services produced in the underground sector of the economy.

■ **HINTS AND TIPS**

1. This chapter is fairly difficult, and the only way to learn the material is to sit down and read through the chapter several times. A careful reading will enable you to avoid the necessity of memorizing. Begin by making sure you know precisely what GDP means and what is included in and excluded from measurement of this most important statistic.

2. Accounting is essentially an adding-up process. This chapter explains in detail and lists the items which must be added to obtain GDP by the *expenditures approach* or *income approach.* It is up to you to learn what to add on the expenditure side, and what to add on the income side. Figure 7-1 is an important accounting reference for this task.

3. Changes in the price level have a significant effect on the measurement of GDP, and thus it is critical that you practice converting nominal GDP to real GDP using a price index. Problems 4 and 5 in this *Study Guide* should help you understand nominal and real GDP and the conversion process.

4. GDP is a good measure of the market value of the output of final goods and services that are produced in an economy in 1 year; however, the measure is not perfect, so you should be aware of its limitations, which are noted at the end of the chapter.

■ **IMPORTANT TERMS**

national income accounting	multiple counting
price level	value added
gross domestic product (GDP)	expenditures approach
	income approach
final goods	personal consumption expenditures
intermediate goods	

gross private domestic investment

net private domestic investment

government purchases

net exports

national income (NI)

indirect business taxes

consumption of fixed capital (depreciation)

net domestic product (NDP)

personal income (PI)

disposable income (DI)

nominal GDP

real GDP

price index

consumer price index

SELF-TEST

■ FILL-IN QUESTIONS

1. National income accounting is valuable because it provides a means of keeping track of the level of (unemployment, production) _____ in the economy and the course it has followed over the long run and the information needed to make public (policies, payments) _____ that will improve the performance of the economy.

2. Gross domestic product (GDP) measures the total (market, nonmarket) _____ value of all (intermediate, final) _____ goods and services produced in a country (in 1 year, over 2 years) _____.

3. GDP for a country includes goods and services produced (within, outside) _____ its geographic boundaries and (does, does not) _____ treat resources supplied by U.S. citizens differently from resources supplied by citizens of other countries.

4. GDP is a (monetary, nonmonetary) _____ measure that permits comparison of the (relative, absolute) _____ worth of goods and services.

5. In measuring GDP only (intermediate, final) _____ goods and services are included; if _____ goods and services were included, the accountant would be (over, under) _____ stating GDP, or (single, multiple) _____ counting.

6. A firm buys materials for $2000 from other firms in the economy and produces from them a product which sells for $3015. The value added by the firm is ($1015, $2000, $3015) _____.

7. GDP accounting excludes (production, nonproduction) _____ transactions. These include (financial, nonfinancial) _____ transactions such as

public or private transfer payments or the sale of securities, and (first, second) _____ hand sales.

8. Personal consumption expenditures are the expenditures of households for goods such as automobiles, which are (durable, nondurable) _____, and goods such as food, which are _____, plus expenditures for (housing, services) _____.

9. Gross private domestic investment basically includes the final purchases of (capital, consumer) _____ goods by businesses, all (construction of new, sales of existing) _____ buildings and houses, and changes in (services, inventories) _____.

10. The difference between gross and net private domestic investment is equal to (depreciation, net exports) _____, or the (production, consumption) _____ of fixed capital.

11. If gross private domestic investment is less than depreciation, net private domestic investment is (positive, zero, negative) _____ and the production capacity of the economy is (static, declining, expanding) _____.

12. An economy's *net* exports equal its exports (minus, plus) _____ its imports. If exports are less than imports, net exports are (positive, negative) _____, but if exports are greater than imports, net exports are _____.

13. Using the expenditure approach, the GDP equation equals ($NDP + NI + PI, C + I_g + G + X_n$) _____.

14. The compensation of employees in the system of social accounting consists of actual wages and salaries (plus, minus) _____ wage and salary supplements. Salary supplements are the payments employers make to social security or (public, private) _____ insurance programs and to _____ pension, health, and welfare funds.

15. Corporate profits are disposed of in three ways: corporate income (taxes, interest) _____, (depreciation, dividends) _____, and undistributed corporate (taxes, profits) _____.

16. Three adjustments are added to national income to obtain (GDP, DI) _____. They are (direct, indirect) _____ business taxes, the consumption of (variable, fixed) _____ capital, and (gross, net) _____ foreign factor income earned in the United States.

17. Gross domestic product overstates the economy's production because it fails to make allowance for (multiple counting, depreciation) _____ or the need to replace (consumer, capital) _____ goods. When this adjustment is made, the calculations produce (net domestic product, national income) _____.

18. National income is equal to net domestic product (plus, minus) _____ indirect business taxes plus (gross, net) _____ foreign factor income earned in the United States.

19. Personal income equals national income (plus, minus) _____ transfer payments _____ the sum of social security contributions, corporate income taxes, and undistributed corporate profits.

20. Disposable income equals (national, personal) _____ income (plus, minus) _____ personal taxes.

21. A GDP which reflects the prices prevailing when the output is produced is called unadjusted, or (nominal, real) _____ GDP, but a GDP figure which is deflated or inflated for price level changes is called adjusted or _____ GDP.

22. To calculate a price index in a given year, the combined price of a market basket of goods and services in that year is (divided, multiplied) _____ by the combined price of the market basket in the base year. The result is then _____ by 100.

23. Real GDP is calculated by dividing (the price index, nominal GDP) _____ by _____. The price index expressed in hundredths is calculated by dividing (real, nominal) _____ GDP by _____ GDP.

24. The consumer price index (CPI) is a (variable, fixed) _____-weight price index that measures the change in the cost of a (constant, variable) _____ standard of living.

25. For several reasons, GDP is not a measure of social welfare in an economy.
   a. It does not include the (market, nonmarket) _____ transactions that result in the production of goods and services or the amount of (work, leisure) _____ of participants in the economy.

b. It fails to record improvements in the (quantity, quality) _____ of the products produced, or the changes in the (level, composition) _____, and distribution of the economy's total output.
   c. It does not take into account the undesirable effects of GDP production on the (government, environment) _____ or the goods and services produced in the (market, underground) _____ economy.
   d. Because it is a measure of the *total* output of the economy, it does not measure the (marginal, per capita) _____ output of the economy.

■ TRUE-FALSE QUESTIONS

Circle the T if the statement is true, the F if it is false.

1. National income accounting allows us to assess the performance of the economy and make policies to improve that performance. **T F**

2. Gross domestic product measures at their market values the total output of all goods and services produced in the economy during a year. **T F**

3. GDP is simply a count of the quantity of output and is not a monetary measure. **T F**

4. The total market value of the wine produced in the United States during a year is equal to the number of bottles of wine produced in that year multiplied by the (average) price at which a bottle sold during that year. **T F**

5. GDP includes the sale of intermediate goods and excludes the sale of final goods. **T F**

6. The total value added to a product and the value of the final product are equal. **T F**

7. Social security payments and other public transfer payments are counted as part of GDP. **T F**

8. The sale of stocks and bonds are excluded from GDP. **T F**

9. In computing gross domestic product, private transfer payments are excluded because they do not represent payments for currently produced goods and services. **T F**

10. The two approaches to the measurement of the gross domestic product yield identical results because one approach measures the total amount spent on the products produced by business firms during a year while the second approach measures the total income of business firms during the year. **T F**

11. Personal consumption expenditures only include expenditures for durable and nondurable goods. **T F**

12. The expenditure made by a household to have a new home built is a personal consumption expenditure. **T F**

13. In national income accounting, any increase in the inventories of business firms is included in gross private domestic investment. **T F**

14. If gross private domestic investment is greater than depreciation during a given year, the economy's production capacity has declined during that year. **T F**

15. Government purchases include spending by all units of government on the finished products of business, but excludes all direct purchases of resources such as labor. **T F**

16. The net exports of an economy equal its exports of goods and services less its imports of goods and services. **T F**

17. The income approach to GDP include compensation of employees, rents, interest income, proprietor's income, and corporate profits. **T F**

18. Indirect business taxes are the difference between gross private domestic investment and net private domestic investment. **T F**

19. Net foreign factor income is the difference between the earnings of foreign-owned resources in the United States and the earnings from U.S.-supplied resources abroad. **T F**

20. Comparison of a gross domestic product with the gross domestic product of an earlier year when the price level has risen between the two years necessitates "inflating" of the GDP figure in the later year. **T F**

21. To adjust nominal gross domestic product for a given year, it is necessary to divide nominal GDP by the price index—expressed in hundredths—for that year. **T F**

22. The consumer price index (CPI) is the price index used to adjust nominal GDP to measure real GDP. **T F**

23. The GDP is a good measure of the economic well-being of society. **T F**

24. The productive services of a homemaker are included in GDP. **T F**

25. The spillover costs from pollution and other activities associated with the production of the GDP are deducted from total output. **T F**

■ **MULTIPLE-CHOICE QUESTIONS**

Circle the letter that corresponds to the best answer.

1. Which is a primary use for national income accounting?
   (a) it provides a basis for assessing the performance of the economy.
   (b) it measures economic efficiency in specific industries.
   (c) it estimates expenditures on nonproduction transactions.
   (d) it analyzes the cost of pollution to the economy.

2. Gross domestic product (GDP) is defined as
   (a) personal consumption expenditures and gross private domestic investment
   (b) the sum of wage and salary compensation of employees, corporate profits, and interest income
   (c) the market value of final goods and services produced within a country in 1 year
   (d) the market value of all final and intermediate goods and services produced by the economy in 1 year

3. GDP provides an indication of society's evaluation of the relative worth of goods and services because it
   (a) provides an estimate of the value of secondhand sales
   (b) gives increased weight to security transactions
   (c) is an estimate of income received
   (d) is a monetary measure

4. To include the value of the parts used in producing the automobiles turned out during a year in gross domestic product for that year would be an example of
   (a) including a nonmarket transaction
   (b) including a nonproduction transaction
   (c) including a noninvestment transaction
   (d) multiple counting

5. Which of the following is a security transaction?
   (a) the sale of a used (secondhand) ironing board at a garage sale
   (b) the sale of shares of stock in the United States Steel Corporation
   (c) the payment of social security benefits to a retired worker
   (d) the birthday gift of a check for $5 sent by a grandmother to her grandchild

6. The sale in 1999 of an automobile produced in 1998 would not be included in the gross domestic product for 1999; doing so would involve
   (a) including a nonmarket transaction
   (b) including a nonproduction transaction
   (c) including a noninvestment transaction
   (d) multiple counting

7. The service a babysitter performs when she stays at home with her baby brother while her parents are out and for which she receives no payment is not included in the gross domestic product because
   (a) this is a nonmarket transaction
   (b) this is a nonproduction transaction
   (c) this is a noninvestment transaction
   (d) multiple counting would be involved

8. According to national income accounting, money income derived from the production of this year's output is equal to
   (a) corporate profits and indirect business taxes
   (b) the amount spent to purchase this year's total output
   (c) the sum of interest income and the compensation of employees
   (d) gross private domestic investment less the consumption of fixed capital

9. Which would be considered an investment according to economists?

  (a) the purchase of newly issued shares of stock in Microsoft

  (b) the construction of a new computer chip factory by Intel

  (c) the resale of stock originally issued by the General Motors Corporation

  (d) the sale of a retail department store building by Sears to JC Penney

10. A refrigerator was produced by its manufacturer in 1998, sold to a retailer in 1998, and sold by the retailer to a final consumer in 1999. The refrigerator was

  (a) counted as consumption in 1998

  (b) counted as investment in 1999

  (c) counted as investment in 1998

  (d) not included in the gross domestic product of 1998

11. If gross private domestic investment is greater than depreciation, the economy will most likely be

  (a) static

  (b) expanding

  (c) declining

  (d) experiencing inflation

12. GDP in an economy is $3452 billion. Consumer expenditures are $2343 billion, government purchases are $865 billion, and gross investment is $379 billion. Net exports are

  (a) +$93 billion

  (b) +$123 billion

  (c) −$45 billion

  (d) −$135 billion

13. The annual charge which estimates the amount of capital equipment used up in each year's production is called

  (a) indirect business taxes

  (b) inventory reduction

  (c) depreciation

  (d) investment

14. The income approach to GDP sums the total income earned by U.S. resource suppliers, adds net foreign factor income earned in the United States, and also adds two adjustments:

  (a) net investment and the consumption of fixed capital

  (b) the consumption of fixed capital and indirect business taxes

  (c) indirect business taxes and undistributed corporate profits

  (d) undistributed corporate profits and financial transactions

15. What can happen to the allocation of corporate profits?

  (a) It is paid to proprietors as income.

  (b) It is paid to to stockholders as dividends.

  (c) It is paid to the government as interest income.

  (d) It is retained by the corporation as rents.

Questions 16 through 22 use the national income accounting data given in the following table.

	Billions of dollars
Net private domestic investment	$ 32
Personal taxes	39
Transfer payments	19
Indirect business taxes	8
Corporate income taxes	11
Personal consumption expenditures	217
Consumption of fixed capital	7
U.S. exports	15
Dividends	15
Government purchases	51
Net foreign factor income earned in the U.S.	0
Undistributed corporate profits	10
Social security contributions	4
U.S. imports	17

16. Gross private domestic investment is equal to

  (a) $32 billion

  (b) $39 billion

  (c) $45 billion

  (d) $56 billion

17. Net exports are equal to

  (a) −$2 billion

  (b) $2 billion

  (c) −$32 billion

  (d) $32 billion

18. The gross domestic product is equal to

  (a) $298 billion

  (b) $302 billion

  (c) $317 billion

  (d) $305 billion

19. Corporate profits are equal to

  (a) $15 billion

  (b) $25 billion

  (c) $26 billion

  (d) $36 billion

20. The net domestic product is equal to

  (a) $298 billion

  (b) $302 billion

  (c) $317 billion

  (d) $321 billion

21. National income is equal to

  (a) $245 billion

  (b) $278 billion

  (c) $290 billion

  (d) $310 billion

22. Personal income is equal to

  (a) $266 billion

  (b) $284 billion

  (c) $290 billion

  (d) $315 billion

23. If both nominal gross domestic product and the level of prices are rising, it is evident that

  (a) real GDP is constant

  (b) real GDP is rising but not so rapidly as prices

(c) real GDP is declining

(d) no conclusion can be drawn concerning the real GDP of the economy on the basis of this information

24. Suppose nominal GDP rose from $500 billion to $600 billion while the GDP deflator increased from 125 to 150. The real GDP

(a) remained constant

(b) increased

(c) decreased

(d) cannot be calculated from these figures

25. In an economy, the total expenditures for a market basket of goods in year 1 (the base year) was $4000 billion. In year 2, the total expenditure for the same market basket of goods was $4500 billion. What was the GDP price index for the economy in year 2?

(a) .88

(b) 1.13

(c) 188

(d) 113

26. Nominal GDP is less than real GDP in an economy in year 1. In year 2, nominal GDP is equal to real GDP. In year 3, nominal GDP is slightly greater than real GDP. In year 4, nominal GDP is significantly greater than real GDP. Which year is most likely to be the base year that is being used to calculate the price index for this economy?

(a) 1

(b) 2

(c) 3

(d) 4

27. Nominal GDP was $3774 billion in year 1 and the GDP deflator was 108 and nominal GNP was $3989 in year 2 and the GDP deflator that year was 112. What was real GDP in years 1 and 2, respectively?

(a) $3494 billion and $3562 billion

(b) $3339 billion and $3695 billion

(c) $3595 billion and $3725 billion

(d) $3643 billion and $3854 billion

28. A price index one year was 145, and the next year it was 167. What is the approximate percentage change in the price level from one year to the next as measured by that index?

(a) 12%

(b) 13%

(c) 14%

(d) 15%

29. GDP accounting includes

(a) the goods and services produced in the underground economy

(b) expenditures for equipment to reduce the pollution of the environment

(c) the value of the leisure enjoyed by citizens

(d) the goods and services produced but not bought and sold in the markets of the economy

30. Which is a major reason why GDP is *not* an accurate index of society's economic well-being?

(a) It includes population changes.

(b) It excludes many improvements in product quality.

(c) It includes transactions from the underground economy.

(d) It excludes transactions from the buying and selling of stocks.

■ PROBLEMS

1. Following are national income accounting figures for the United States.

	Billions of dollars
Exports	$ 367
Dividends	60
Consumption of fixed capital	307
Compensation of employees	1722
Government purchases	577
Rents	33
Indirect business taxes	255
Gross private domestic investment	437
Corporate income taxes	88
Transfer payments	320
Interest	201
Proprietors' income	132
Personal consumption expenditures	1810
Imports	338
Social security contributions	148
Undistributed corporate profits	55
Personal taxes	372
Net foreign factor income earned in the U.S.	0

a. In the following table, use any of these figures to prepare an Income Statement for the economy similar to the one found in Table 7-3 of the text.

Receipts: Expenditures approach		Allocations: Income approach	
Item	**Amount**	**Item**	**Amount**
_____	$_____	_____	$_____
_____	$_____	_____	$_____
_____	$_____	_____	$_____
_____	$_____	_____	$_____
		_____	$_____
		_____	$_____
		_____	$_____
		National income	$_____
		_____	$_____
		_____	$_____
		_____	$_____
Gross domestic product	$_____	Gross domestic product	$_____

b. Use the other national accounts to find

(1) Net domestic product is $_____

(2) National income is $_____

(3) Personal income is $_____

(4) Disposable income is $_____

2. A farmer owns a plot of ground and sells the right to pump crude oil from his land to a crude oil producer. The crude oil producer agrees to pay the farmer $20 a barrel for every barrel pumped from the farmer's land.

a. During one year 10,000 barrels are pumped.

(1) The farmer receives a payment of $_____ from the crude oil producer.

(2) The value added by the farmer is $_____.

b. The crude oil producer sells the 10,000 barrels pumped to a petroleum refiner at a price of $25 a barrel.

(1) The crude oil producer receives a payment of $_____ from the refiner.

(2) The value added by the crude oil producer is $_____.

c. The refiner employs a pipeline company to transport the crude oil from the farmer's land to the refinery and pays the pipeline company a fee of $1 a barrel for the oil transported.

(1) The pipeline company receives a payment of $_____ from the refiner.

(2) The value added by the company is $_____.

d. From the 10,000 barrels of crude oil, the refiner produces 315,000 gallons of gasoline and various by-products which are sold to distributors and gasoline service stations at an average price of $1 per gallon.

(1) The total payment received by the refiner from its customers is $_____.

(2) The value added by the refiner is $_____.

e. The distributors and service stations sell the 315,000 gallons of gasoline and by-products to consumers at an average price of $1.30 a gallon.

(1) The total payment received by distributors and service stations is $_____.

(2) The value added by them is $_____.

f. The total value added by the farmer, crude oil producer, pipeline company, refiner, and distributors and service stations is $_____, and the market value of the gasoline and by-products (the final good) is $_____.

3. Following is a list of items which may or may not be included in the five income-output measures of the national income accounts (GDP, NDP, NI, PI, DI). Indicate in the space to the right of each which of the income-output measures includes this item; it is possible for the item to be included in none, one, two, three, four, or all of the measures. If the item is included in none of the measures, indicate why it is not included.

a. Interest on the national debt _____

_____

b. The sale of a used computer _____

c. The production of shoes which are not sold by the manufacturer _____

d. The income of a bootlegger in a dry state _____

e. The purchase of a share of common stock on the New York Stock Exchange _____

f. The interest paid on the bonds of the General Motors Corporation _____

g. The labor performed by a homemaker _____

h. The labor performed by a paid babysitter _____

i. The monthly check received by an idler from his rich aunt _____

j. The purchase of a new tractor by a farmer _____

k. The labor performed by an assembly line worker in repapering his own kitchen _____

l. The services of a lawyer _____

m. The purchase of shoes from the manufacturer by a shoe retailer _____

n. The monthly check received from the Social Security Administration by a college student whose parents have died _____

o. The rent a homeowner would receive if she did not live in her own home _____

4. Following is hypothetical data for a market basket of goods in year 1 and year 2 for an economy.

a. Compute the expenditures for year 1.

MARKET BASKET FOR YEAR 1 (BASE YEAR)

Products	Quantity	Price	Expenditures
Toys	3	$10	$_____
Pencils	5	2	$_____
Books	7	5	$_____
Total			$_____

b. Compute the expenditures for year 2.

MARKET BASKET FOR YEAR 2

Products	Quantity	Price	Expenditures
Toys	3	$11	$_____
Pencils	5	3	$_____
Books	7	6	$_____
Total			$_____

c. In the space below, show how you computed the GDP price index for year 2.

_____

5. The following table shows nominal GDP figures for 3 years and the price indices for each of the 3 years. (The GDP figures are in billions.)

Year	Nominal GDP	Price index	Real GDP
1929	$104	121	$_____
1933	56	91	$_____
1939	91	100	$_____

a. Use the price indices to compute the real GDP in each year. (You may round your answers to the nearest billion dollars.) Write answers in the table.

b. Which of the 3 years appears to be the base year?

_____

c. Between
(1) 1929 and 1933 the economy experienced (inflation, deflation) _____.

(2) 1933 and 1939 it experienced _____.
d. The nominal GDP figure
(1) for 1929 was (deflated, inflated, neither) _____

_____.

(2) for 1933 was _____.

(3) for 1939 was _____.
e. The price level

(1) fell by _____ % from 1929 to 1933.

(2) rose by _____ % from 1933 to 1939.

■ **SHORT ANSWER AND ESSAY QUESTIONS**

1. Of what use is national income accounting to economists and policymakers?

2. What is the definition of GDP? How are the values of output produced at a U.S.-owned factory in the United States and a foreign-owned factory in the United States treated in GDP accounting?

3. Why is GDP a monetary measure?

4. How does GDP accounting avoid multiple counting and exaggeration of the value of GDP?

5. Why does GDP accounting exclude nonproduction transactions?

6. What are the two principal types of nonproduction transactions? List examples of each type.

7. What are the two sides to GDP accounting? What is the meaning and relationship between the two sides?

8. What would be included in personal consumption expenditures by households?

9. How is gross private domestic investment defined?

10. Is residential construction counted as investment or consumption? Explain.

11. Why is a change in inventories an investment?

12. How do you define a static, an expanding, and a declining production capacity using the concepts of gross private domestic investment and depreciation?

13. What do government purchases include and what do they exclude?

14. How are imports and exports handled in GDP accounting?

15. What are five income components of GDP that add up to national income? Define and explain the characteristics of each component.

16. What are three adjustments made to the income approach to GDP accounting to get it to balance with expenditures? Define and explain the characteristics of each one.

17. Explain how to calculate net domestic product (NDP), national income (NI), personal income (PI), and disposable income (DI).

18. What is the difference between real and nominal GDP? Describe two methods economists use to determine real GDP. Illustrate each method with an example.

19. Explain the difference between the GDP price index and the consumer price index (CPI).

20. Why might GDP not be considered an accurate measure of the economic well-being of society? Identify seven reasons why GDP might understate or overstate economic well-being.

ANSWERS

Chapter 7 Measuring Domestic Output, National Income, and the Price Level

FILL-IN QUESTIONS

1. production, policies
2. market, final, in 1 year
3. within, does not
4. monetary, relative
5. final, intermediate, over, multiple
6. $1015
7. nonproduction, financial, second
8. durable, nondurable, services
9. capital, construction of new, inventories
10. depreciation, consumption
11. negative, declining
12. minus, negative, positive
13. $C + I_g + G + X_n$
14. plus, public, private
15. taxes, dividends, profits
16. GDP, indirect, fixed, net
17. depreciation, capital, net domestic product
18. minus, net
19. plus, minus
20. personal, minus
21. nominal, real
22. divided, multiplied
23. nominal GDP, the price index, nominal, real
24. fixed, constant
25. *a.* nonmarket, leisure; *b.* quality, composition; *c.* environment, underground; *d.* per capita

TRUE-FALSE QUESTIONS

1. T, p. 125	**4.** T, p. 125	**7.** F, p. 126	**10.** F, p. 127
2. F, p. 125	**5.** F, pp. 125-126	**8.** T, p. 127	**11.** F, p. 128
3. F, P. 125	**6.** T, p. 126	**9.** T, pp. 126-127	**12.** F, p. 128

13. T, pp. 128-129 **18.** F, p. 133 **23.** F, p. 140
14. F, pp. 129-131 **19.** T, p. 134 **24.** F, p. 140
15. F, p. 131 **20.** F, pp. 135-137 **25.** F, p. 142
16. T, p. 131 **21.** T, p. 138
17. T, pp. 132-133 **22.** F, pp. 137-138, 140

MULTIPLE-CHOICE QUESTIONS

1. a, pp. 124-125 **11.** b, p. 129 **21.** c, p. 135
2. c, p. 125 **12.** d, p. 132 **22.** b, p. 135
3. d, p. 125 **13.** c, p. 133 **23.** d, pp. 136-138
4. d, pp. 125-126 **14.** b, pp. 132-134 **24.** b, pp. 138-139
5. b, p. 127 **15.** b, p. 133 **25.** d, p. 139
6. b, p. 127 **16.** b, p. 129 **26.** b, pp. 138-139
7. a, p. 140 **17.** a, p. 131 **27.** a, p. 139
8. b, p. 127 **18.** d, p. 132 **28.** d, p. 141
9. b, p. 128 **19.** d, p. 133 **29.** b, pp. 140-144
10. c, pp. 128-129 **20.** a, p. 134 **30.** b, p. 143

PROBLEMS

1. *a.* See the following table; *b.* (1) 2546, (2) 2291, (3) 2320, (4) 1948

Receipts: Expenditures approach		Allocations: Income approach	
Personal consumption expenditures	$1810	Compensation of employees	$1722
Gross private domestic investment	437	Rents	33
		Interest	201
Government purchases	577	Proprietors' income	132
Net exports	29	Corporate income taxes	88
		Dividends	60
		Undistributed corporate profit	55
		National income	$2291
		Indirect business taxes	255
		Consumption of fixed capital	307
		Net foreign factor income earned in the U.S.	0
Gross domestic product	$2853	Gross domestic product	$2853

2. *a.* (1) 200,000, (2) 200,000; *b.* (1) 250,000, (2) 50,000; *c.* (1) 10,000, (2) 10,000; *d.* (1) 315,000, (2) 55,000; *e.* (1) 409,500, (2) 94,500; *f.* 409,500, 409,500
3. *a.* personal income and disposable income, a public transfer payment; *b.* none, a secondhand sale; *c.* all, represents investment (additions to inventories); *d.* all, illegal production and incomes are included when known; *e.* none, a purely financial transaction; *f.* all; *g.* none, a nonmarket transaction; *h.* all; *i.* none, a private transfer payment; *j.* all; *k.* none, a nonmarket transaction; *l.* all; *m.* all, represents additions to the inventory of the retailer; *n.* personal income and disposable income, a public transfer payment; *o.* all, estimate of rental value of owner-occupied homes is included in rents as if it were income and in personal consumption expenditures as if it were payment for a service
4. *a.* 30, 10, 35, 75; *b.* 33, 15, 42, 90; *c.* ($90/$75) 100 = 120
5. *a.* 86, 62, 91; *b.* 1939; *c.* (1) deflation, (2) inflation; *d.* (1) deflated, (2) inflated, (3) neither; *e.* (1) 24.8 (2) 9.9

SHORT ANSWER AND ESSAY QUESTIONS

1. pp. 124-125 **8.** p. 128 **15.** pp. 132-133
2. p. 125 **9.** p. 128 **16.** pp. 133-134
3. p. 125 **10.** p. 128 **17.** pp. 134-135
4. pp. 125-126 **11.** pp. 128-129 **18.** pp. 136-140
5. p. 126 **12.** pp. 129-131 **19.** p. 141
6. pp. 126-127 **13.** p. 131 **20.** pp. 141-144
7. p. 127 **14.** p. 131

Macroeconomic Instability: Unemployment and Inflation

In the last chapter you learned how to define and how to compute the gross and net domestic product and domestic, personal, and disposable income in any year. This chapter begins the explanation of what determines how large each of these five income-output measures will be. In the chapters that follow, you will learn what influences the income and output levels of the economy, what causes them to change, and how they might be controlled for the welfare of society.

Chapter 8 is concerned with the instability of the American economy. The first major section of the chapter discusses the **business cycle:** the ups and downs in the employment of labor and the real output of the economy that occur over the years. That there have been expansions and contractions in economic (or business) activity since the end of the American Civil War is evident from even a casual look at U.S. economic history. What is not immediately evident, however, is that these alternating and relatively short periods of prosperity and hard times have taken place over a longer period in which the trends in output, employment, and the standard of living have been upward. During this long history booms and busts have occurred quite irregularly; their duration and intensity have been so varied that it is better to think of economic instability than of business cycles.

Two principal problems result from the instability of the economy. The first problem is described in the second major section of the chapter. Here you will find an examination of the **unemployment** that accompanies a downturn in the level of economic activity in the economy. You will discover that there are three different kinds of unemployment, that **full employment** means about 5.5% of the labor force is unemployed, and that there are at least three problems encountered in measuring the percentage of the labor force actually unemployed at any time. You will also learn that unemployment has an **economic cost,** and that this cost is unequally distributed among different sectors of our society. You probably will not be too surprised to discover that widespread unemployment can be the cause of other social problems.

The second problem that results from economic instability is **inflation;** it is examined in the remainder of the chapter. Inflation is an increase in the general (or average) level of prices in an economy. It does not have a unique cause: It may result from increases in demand, from increases in costs, or from both. Regardless of its cause, it works a real hardship on certain sectors within

the economy. If it occurs at too rapid a rate, it may bring about a severe breakdown in the economy.

Understanding the meaning of unemployment and inflation is important. They are the twin problems of the macroeconomy.

■ **CHECKLIST**

When you have finished this chapter you should be able to

☐ Explain what the business cycle means.
☐ Describe the four phases of an idealized business cycle.
☐ Identify the immediate determinant or cause of the cyclical changes in the levels of real output and employment.
☐ Identify the two types of noncyclical fluctuations.
☐ Distinguish the differences among the impact of cyclical fluctuations on industries producing capital and consumer durable goods, the impact on those producing consumer nondurable goods, and the impact on high- and low-concentration industries.
☐ Distinguish among frictional, structural, and cyclical unemployment, and explain the causes of these three kinds of unemployment.
☐ Define full employment and the full-employment unemployment rate (the natural rate of unemployment).
☐ Describe the process used by the Bureau of Labor Statistics (BLS) to measure the rate of unemployment, and list the two criticisms of the BLS data.
☐ Identify the economic cost of unemployment.
☐ Define the GDP gap and state Okun's law.
☐ Discuss the unequal burdens of unemployment.
☐ Define inflation and the rate of inflation.
☐ Make international comparisons of inflation rate and unemployment rate data.
☐ Define demand-pull inflation and explain its effects in ranges 1, 2, and 3 of a price level and real domestic output graph.
☐ Define cost-push inflation and its relation to per unit production costs.
☐ Identify two variants of cost-push or supply-side inflation.
☐ Describe the complexities involved in distinguishing between demand-pull and cost-push inflation.
☐ Distinguish between real and nominal income and calculate real income when given data on nominal income and the price level.

☐ List groups that are hurt by and groups that benefit from unanticipated inflation.

☐ Describe how the redistributive effects of inflation are changed when it is anticipated.

☐ Present three scenarios that describe the possible effects of inflation on real output and employment.

■ CHAPTER OUTLINE

1. The history of the U.S. economy is a record of exceptional economic growth.

  a. But this growth has been accompanied by periods of inflation, recession, or both.

  b. The **business cycle** means alternating periods of prosperity and recession. These recurrent periods of ups and downs in employment, output, and prices are irregular in their duration and intensity, but the typical pattern is **peak, recession, trough,** and **recovery** to another peak.

  c. Changes in the levels of output and employment are largely the result of changes in the level of total spending in the economy.

  d. Not all changes in employment and output which occur in the economy are cyclical; some are due to seasonal and secular influences.

  e. The business cycle affects almost the entire economy, but it does not affect all parts in the same way and to the same degree: The production of capital and durable consumer goods fluctuates more than the production of consumer nondurable goods during the cycle because

  (1) the purchase of capital and durable consumer goods can be postponed.

  (2) the industries producing these goods are largely dominated by a few large firms that hold prices constant and let production and employment decline when demand falls.

2. Full employment does not mean that all workers in the labor force are employed and that there is no unemployment; some unemployment is normal.

  a. There are at least three types of unemployment.

  (1) **Frictional unemployment** is due to workers searching for new jobs or waiting to take new jobs; this type of unemployment is generally desirable.

  (2) **Structural unemployment** is due to the changes in technology and in the types of goods and services consumers wish to buy; these changes affect the total demand for labor in particular industries or regions.

  (3) **Cyclical unemployment** is due to insufficient total spending in the economy; this type of unemployment arises during the recession phase of the businesss cycle.

  b. Because some frictional and structural unemployment is unavoidable, the full-employment unemployment rate (the **natural rate of unemployment**) is the sum of frictional and structural unemployment, is achieved when cyclical unemployment is zero (the real output of the economy is equal to its potential output), and is about 5.5% of the labor force. This natural rate is not automatically achieved and changes over time.

  c. Surveying some 60,000 households each month, the Bureau of Labor Statistics (BLS) finds the unemployment rate by dividing the number of persons in the labor force who are unemployed by the number of persons in the labor force. The figures collected in the survey have been criticized for at least two reasons:

  (1) They include part-time workers.

  (2) They exclude "discouraged" workers who have left the labor force.

  d. Unemployment has an economic cost.

  (1) The economic cost is the unproduced output (or the **GDP gap**). **Okun's law** is that for every 1% the actual unemployment rate exceeds the natural rate of unemployment, there is a GDP gap of about 2%.

  (2) This cost is unequally distributed among different groups of workers in the labor force.

  e. Unemployment also leads to serious social problems.

3. Over its history, the U.S. economy has experienced not only periods of unemployment but periods of inflation.

  a. *Inflation* is an increase in the general level of prices in the economy; a decline in the level of prices is deflation.

  b. The rate of inflation in any year is equal to the percentage change in the price index between that year and the preceding year. The rule of 70 can be used to calculate the number of years it will take for the price level to double at any given rate of inflation.

  c. The United States has experienced both inflation and deflation, but the past half century has been a period of inflation. Inflation is also experienced by other industrial nations.

  d. There are at least two causes of inflation, and these two causes may operate separately or simultaneously to raise the price level.

  (1) **Demand-pull inflation** is the result of excess total spending in the economy. While increases in total spending do not increase the price level, when the unemployment rate is high (in a depression) they do bring about inflation as the economy nears and reaches full employment.

  (2) **Cost-push** or **supply-side inflation** is the result of factors that raise per unit production costs. This average cost is found by dividing the total cost of the resource inputs by the amount produced. Two variants explain this rise in costs: (*a*) excessive wage increases that push up unit costs, and (*b*) supply shock from an increase in the prices of resource inputs. With cost-push inflation, output and employment decline as the price level rises.

  It is difficult to distinguish between demand-pull and cost-push inflation in the real world.

4. Even if the total output of the economy did not change, inflation would arbitrarily redistribute real income and wealth, and it would benefit some groups and hurt other groups in the economy.

  a. Whether someone benefits or is hurt by inflation is measured by what happens to real income. Inflation injures those whose real income falls and benefits those whose real income rises.

  (1) **Real income** is determined by dividing nominal income by the price level expressed in hundredths.

(2) The percentage change in real income can be approximated by subtracting the percentage change in the price level from the percentage change in nominal income.

b. Inflation injures savers because it decreases the real value of any savings.

c. It benefits debtors and hurts creditors because it lowers the real value of debts.

d. When the inflation is anticipated and people can adjust their nominal incomes to reflect the expected rise in the price level, the redistribution of income and wealth is lessened.

e. Since World War II inflation in the United States has redistributed wealth from the household to the public sector of the economy.

f. If short in duration, inflation acts to tax some groups and to subsidize other groups.

5. Inflation may also affect the total output of the economy, but economists disagree over whether it is likely to expand or contract total output.

a. Mild demand-pull inflation seems likely to expand output and employment in the economy.

b. Cost-push inflation is apt to contract output and employment.

c. Hyperinflation may well lead to the breakdown of the economy.

■ HINTS AND TIPS

1. Some students get confused by the seemingly contradictory term "full-employment unemployment rate" and related unemployment concepts. Full employment does not mean that everyone who wants to work has a job; it means that the economy is achieving its potential output and has a *natural rate of unemployment.* Remember that there are three types of unemployment: frictional, structural, and cyclical. There will always be some unemployment arising from frictional reasons (e.g., people searching for jobs) or structural reasons (e.g., changes in industry demand), and these two types of unemployment are "natural" for an economy. Cyclical reasons (e.g., a downturn in the business cycle) for unemployment, however, are not natural for an economy. Thus, full-employment unemployment rate means that there are no cyclical reasons causing unemployment, only frictional or structural reasons.

2. To verify your understanding of how to calculate the unemployment rate, GDP gap, or inflation rate after reading the chapter, do Problems 1, 2, and 3 in this *Study Guide* chapter.

3. Inflation is a rise in the general level of prices, not just a rise in the prices of a few products. An increase in product price is caused by supply or demand factors. You now know why the prices for many products rise in an economy. The macroeconomic reasons given in Chapter 8 for the increase in the general level of prices are different from the microeconomic reasons for a price increase that you learned about in Chapter 3.

■ IMPORTANT TERMS

business cycle	Okun's law
peak	inflation
recession	deflation
trough	rule of 70
recovery	demand-pull inflation
seasonal variation	cost-push inflation
secular trend	supply-side inflation
unemployment	per unit production cost
frictional unemployment	nominal income
structural unemployment	real income
cyclical unemployment	anticipated inflation
full-employment unemployment rate	unanticipated inflation
natural rate of unemployment	cost-of-living adjustment (COLA)
potential output	inflation premium
unemployment rate	nominal interest rate
labor force	real interest rate
discouraged workers	hyperinflation
GDP gap	

SELF-TEST

■ FILL-IN QUESTIONS

1. The history of the U.S. economy is one of (steady, unsteady) _____ economic growth. At times its growth has been accompanied by price (stability, inflation) _____, and at other times its expansion has been interrupted by (increasing, decreasing) _____ levels of output of goods and services and _____ unemployment of workers.

2. The business cycle is a term which encompasses the recurrent ups, or (decreases, increases) _____, and downs, or _____, in the level of business activity in the economy.

3. The order of the four phases of a typical business cycle are peak, (recovery, trough, recession) _____, _____, and _____.

4. The basic determinant of the levels of employment and output in an economy is the level of (monopoly power, total spending) _____.

5. In addition to the changes brought about by the operation of the business cycle, noncyclical fluctuations in output and employment may be due to (secular, seasonal) _____ variations and a _____ trend.

6. Expansion and contraction of the economy affect to a greater extent the production and employment in the consumer (durables, nondurables) _____ and (capital, consumer) _____ goods industries than they do (durable, nondurable) _____ goods industries, and prices vary to a greater extent in the (low-, high-) _____ concentration industries.

7. When workers are searching for a new job or waiting to start a new job, this type of unemployment is called (structural, frictional, cyclical) _____, but when workers are laid off because of changes in the consumer demand and technology in industries or regions, this unemployment is called _____; when workers are unemployed because of insufficient total spending in the economy, this type of unemployment is called _____.

8. The full-employment unemployment rate is called the (Okun, natural) _____ rate of unemployment. It is equal to the total of (frictional and structural, cyclical and frictional) _____ unemployment in the economy. It is realized when the (frictional, cyclical) _____ unemployment in the economy is equal to zero and when the actual output of the economy is (less than, equal to) _____ its potential output. It is assumed in this chapter to be about (2.5, 5.5, 7.5) _____%.

9. When the economy achieves its natural rate of unemployment, the number of job seekers is (greater than, less than, equal to) _____ the number of job vacancies and the price level is (rising, falling, constant) _____.

10. The *unemployment rate* is found by dividing the number of (employed, unemployed) _____ persons by the (population, labor force) _____ and (multiplying, dividing) _____ by 100.

11. The GDP gap is equal to the potential GDP (minus, plus) _____ the actual GDP. For every percentage point the unemployment rate rises above the natural rate, the GDP gap will, according to Okun's law, (increase, decrease) _____ by (1, 2, 5) _____%.

12. The burdens of unemployment are borne more heavily by (black, white) _____, (adult, teenage) _____, and (white-collar, blue-collar) _____ workers, and the percentage of the labor force unemployed for 15 or more weeks is much (greater, less) _____ than the unemployment rate.

13. Inflation means (an increase, a decrease) ____ _____ in the general level of (unemployment, prices) _____ in the economy. To calculate the rate of inflation from year 1 to year 2, subtract the price index for year 1 from year 2, then (multiply, divide) _____ the result by the price index for year 1, and _____ by 100.

14. To find the approximate number of years it takes the price level to double, (multiply, divide) _____ 70 by the percentage annual increase in the rate of inflation. This approximation is called (Okun's law, rule of 70) _____.

15. Since the 1920s, the experience of the United States with inflation has varied. The price level decreased during the early years of the Great Depression, which means (inflation, deflation) _____ was occurring in the economy. In the United States, the post–World War II period (1945–1948) was characterized by (high, low) _____ rates of inflation, the 1961–1965 period was a period of _____ inflation, and the mid-to-late 1970s was a period of (high, low) _____ inflation.

16. The basic cause of

a. demand-pull inflation is (a(n) (increase, decrease) _____ in total spending beyond the full employment output rate in the economy.

b. cost-push inflation is explained in terms of factors that raise per unit (inflation, production) _____ costs. This type of inflation is also called (demand, supply) _____-side inflation and is caused by (decreases, increases) _____ in wages and prices of nonwage inputs.

c. In practice, it is (easy, difficult) _____ to distinguish the two types of inflation.

17. The amount of goods and services one's nominal income can buy is called (variable, real) _____ income.

a. If one's nominal income rises by 10% and the price level rose by 7%, the percentage of increase in (variable, real) _____ income would be (1, 2, 3) _____.

b. If nominal income was $30,000 and the price index, expressed in hundredths, was 1.06, then (variable, real) _____ income would be ($28,302, $29,855) _____.

18. Inflation hurts those whose nominal incomes are relatively (fixed, flexible) _____, penalizes savers when the inflation is (expected, unexpected) _____, hurts (creditors, debtors) _____ and benefits _____, and has, since World War II, shifted wealth from (the public sector, households) _____ to _____.

19. The redistributive effects of inflation are less severe when it is (anticipated, unanticipated) _____.

  a. Clauses in labor contracts that call for automatic adjustments of workers' income from the effects of inflation are called (unemployment benefits, cost-of-living) _____ adjustments.

  b. The percentage increase in purchasing power that the lender receives from the borrower is the (real rate of interest, nominal rate of interest) _____; the percentage increase in money that the lender receives is the _____.

20. Despite considerable disagreement and uncertainty among economists, it seems that demand-pull inflation, unless there is full employment in the economy, will (increase, decrease) _____ total output and employment, cost-push inflation will _____ output and employment in the economy, and an economic collapse or breakdown can result from (cost-push, hyperinflation) _____.

■ **TRUE-FALSE QUESTIONS**

Circle the T if the statement is true, the F if it is false.

  1. The U.S. economy has always experienced steady economic growth, price stability, and full employment. **T F**

  2. The business cycle is best defined as alternating periods of increases and decreases in the rate of inflation in the economy. **T F**

  3. Individual business cycles tend to be of roughly equal duration and intensity. **T F**

  4. Not all changes which occur in output and employment in the economy are due to the business cycle. **T F**

  5. Industries which are highly concentrated show small relative decreases in output and large relative decreases in prices during a downswing of the business cycle. **T F**

  6. Frictional unemployment is not only inevitable but largely desirable. **T F**

  7. The essential difference between frictionally and structurally unemployed workers is that the former *do not have* and the latter *do have* salable skills. **T F**

  8. When the number of people seeking employment is less than the number of job vacancies in the economy, the actual rate of unemployment is less than the natural rate of unemployment, and the price level will tend to rise. **T F**

  9. If unemployment in the economy is at its natural rate, the actual and potential outputs of the economy are equal. **T F**

10. The natural rate of unemployment in the U.S. economy is a constant 7% of the labor force. **T F**

11. An economy cannot produce an actual real GDP that exceeds its potential real GDP. **T F**

12. The unemployment rate is equal to the number of people in the labor force divided by the number of people who are unemployed. **T F**

13. The percentage of the labor force unemployed for 15 or more weeks is always less than the unemployment rate and tends to rise during a recession. **T F**

14. The economy's GDP gap is measured by deducting its actual GDP from its potential GDP. **T F**

15. The economic cost of cyclical unemployment is the goods and services that are not produced. **T F**

16. Inflation is defined as an increase in the total output of an economy. **T F**

17. From one year to the next, the consumer price index rose from 311.1 to 322.2. The rate of inflation was therefore 5.6%. **T F**

18. If the price level increases by 10% each year, the price level will double every 10 years. **T F**

19. With a moderate amount of unemployment in the economy, an increase in aggregate spending will generally increase both the price level and the output of the economy. **T F**

20. The theory of cost-push inflation explains rising prices in terms of factors which increase per unit production cost. **T F**

21. A person's real income is the amount of goods and services which the person's nominal (or money) income will enable him or her to purchase. **T F**

22. Whether inflation is anticipated or unanticipated, the effects of inflation on the distribution of income are much the same. **T F**

23. Suppose a household has $10,000 on deposit in a savings and loan association and earns 7% interest during a year, and the rate of inflation is 9% in that year. By the end of the year the purchasing power of the $10,000 and the interest it has earned will have decreased to about $9,817. **T F**

24. Unemployment and inflation rates vary among major industrialized nations. **T F**

25. Inflation in the United States has transferred wealth from the public sector to the households of the economy. **T F**

■ **MULTIPLE-CHOICE QUESTIONS**

Circle the letter that corresponds to the best answer.

  1. Which is one of the four phases of an idealized business cycle?

  (a) inflation

(b) recession
(c) unemployment
(d) seasonal variation

2. Most economists believe that the immediate determinant of the levels of domestic output and employment is
(a) the price level
(b) the size of the civilian labor force
(c) the nation's stock of capital goods
(d) the level of total spending

3. Total output in December of this year was greater than total output in December of 1928. This is no doubt due to the effect of
(a) seasonal variations
(b) secular trend
(c) the business cycle
(d) business fluctuations

4. If employment in the agricultural sector of the U.S. economy during August and September is typically 112% of what it normally is in the other months of the year, this is probably a consequence of
(a) seasonal variations
(b) secular trend
(c) the business cycle
(d) both seasonal variations and the business cycle

5. Production and employment in which of the following industries would be least affected by a depression?
(a) nondurable consumer goods
(b) durable consumer goods
(c) capital goods
(d) iron and steel

6. A worker who loses a job at a petroleum refinery because consumers and business firms switch from the use of oil to the burning of coal is an example of
(a) frictional unemployment
(b) structural unemployment
(c) cyclical unemployment
(d) disguised unemployment

7. A worker who has quit one job and is taking 2 weeks off before reporting to a new job is an example of
(a) frictional unemployment
(b) structural unemployment
(c) cyclical unemployment
(d) disguised unemployment

8. Insufficient total spending in the economy results in
(a) frictional unemployment
(b) structural unemployment
(c) cyclical unemployment
(d) disguised unemployment

9. The full-employment unemployment rate in the economy has been achieved when
(a) frictional unemployment is zero
(b) structural unemployment is zero
(c) cyclical unemployment is zero
(d) the natural rate of unemployment is zero

10. Which has decreased the natural rate of unemployment in the United States in recent years?
(a) the increased size of unemployment benefits

(b) more workers covered by unemployment programs
(c) fewer young workers in the labor force
(d) less competition in product and labor markets

11. The labor force includes those who are
(a) less than 16 years of age
(b) in mental institutions
(c) not seeking work
(d) employed

12. The unemployment rate in an economy is 8%. The total population of the economy is 250 million, and the size of the civilian labor force is 150 million. The number of employed workers in this economy is
(a) 12 million
(b) 20 million
(c) 138 million
(d) 140 million

13. The price has doubled in about 14 years. The approximate annual percentage rate of increase in the price level over this period has been
(a) 2%
(b) 3%
(c) 4%
(d) 5%

14. The unemployment data collected by the Bureau of Labor Statistics have been criticized because
(a) part-time workers are not counted in the number of workers employed
(b) discouraged workers are not considered a part of the labor force
(c) it covers frictional unemployment, but not cyclical unemployment, which inflates unemployment figures.
(d) the underground economy may understate unemployment

15. Okun's law predicts that when the actual unemployment rate exceeds the natural rate of unemployment by two percentage points, the GDP gap will equal
(a) 2% of the potential GDP
(b) 3% of the potential GDP
(c) 4% of the potential GDP
(d) 5% of the potential GDP

16. If the GDP gap were equal to 6% of the potential GDP, the actual unemployment rate would exceed the natural rate of unemployment by
(a) two percentage points
(b) three percentage points
(c) four percentage points
(d) five percentage points

17. The burden of unemployment is *least* felt by
(a) white-collar workers
(b) teenagers
(c) blacks
(d) males

18. If the consumer price index was 110 in one year and 117 in the next year, then the rate of inflation from one year to the next was
(a) 3.5%
(b) 4.7%

(c) 6.4%
(d) 7.1%

Use the following graph to answer Question 19.

Real domestic output and employment

19. In which range does the price level begin to rise as the economy either approaches or surpasses the full employment level of output?
(a) range 1
(b) range 2
(c) range 3
(d) range 4

20. Only two resources, capital and labor, are used in an economy to produce an output of 300 million units. If the total cost of capital resources is $150 million and the total cost of labor resources is $50 million, then the per unit production costs in this economy are
(a) $0.67 million
(b) $1.50 million
(c) $2.00 million
(d) $3.00 million

21. If the economy can supply no more resources to production, an increase in aggregate spending will cause
(a) output and employment to increase
(b) output and prices to increase
(c) nominal income and prices to increase
(d) employment and nominal income to increase

22. If the economy is experiencing a depression with substantial unemployment, an increase in total spending will cause
(a) a decrease in the *real* income of the economy
(b) little or no increase in the level of prices
(c) an increase in the *real* income and a decrease in the *nominal* income of the economy
(d) proportionate increases in the price level, output, and income in the economy

23. If a person's nominal income increases by 8% while the price level increases by 10%, the person's real income
(a) increases by 2%
(b) increases by 18%
(c) decreases by 18%
(d) decreases by 2%

24. If the average level of nominal income is $21,000 and the price level index is 154, the average real income would be about

(a) $12,546
(b) $13,636
(c) $15,299
(d) $17,823

25. With no inflation, a bank would be willing to lend a business firm $10 million at an annual interest rate of 8%. But, if the rate of inflation was anticipated to be 6%, the bank would charge the firm an annual interest rate of
(a) 2%
(b) 6%
(c) 8%
(d) 14%

26. Who would be hurt by unanticipated inflation?
(a) those living on incomes with cost-of-living adjustments
(b) those who find prices rising less rapidly than their nominal incomes
(c) those who lent money at a fixed interest rate
(d) those who became debtors when prices were lower

27. Some economists argue that mild demand-pull inflation at less than full employment results in
(a) rising real output and employment
(b) falling real output and employment
(c) a rising price level and falling employment
(d) a falling price level and rising employment

28. Which contributes to cost-push inflation?
(a) an increase in employment and output
(b) an increase in per unit production costs
(c) a decrease in resource prices
(d) an increase in unemployment

29. Which is *not* associated with hyperinflation?
(a) war or its aftermath
(b) rising output in the economy
(c) the hoarding of goods and speculation
(d) a halt to the use of money as both a medium of exchange and a standard of value

30. If an economy has experienced an inflation rate of over 3000% per year, this economic condition would best be described as
(a) a wage-price inflationary spiral
(b) a cost-of-living adjustment
(c) cost-push inflation
(d) hyperinflation

■ **PROBLEMS**

1. The following table gives statistics on the labor force and total employment during year 1 and year 5. Make the computations necessary to complete the table. (Numbers of persons are in thousands.)

	Year 1	Year 5
Labor force	84,889	95,453
Employed	80,796	87,524
Unemployed	_____	_____
Unemployment rate	_____	_____

a. How is it possible that *both* employment and unemployment increased? _____

_____

b. In relative terms, if unemployment increases, employment will decrease. Why? _____

_____

_____

c. Would you say that year 5 was a year of full employment? _____

_____

d. Why is the task of maintaining full employment over the years more than just a problem of finding jobs for those who happen to be employed at any given time?

_____

2. Suppose that in year 1 an economy is at full employment, has a potential and actual real GDP of $3000 billion, and has an unemployment rate of 5.5%.

a. Compute the GDP gap in year 1 and enter it in the table below.

Year	Potential GDP	Actual GDP	GDP gap
1	$3000	$3000.0	$_____
2	3800	3724.0	_____
3	4125	3712.5	_____

b. The potential and actual real GDPs in years 2 and 3 are also shown in the table. Compute and enter into the table the GDP gaps in these 2 years.

c. In year 2, the actual real GDP is _____% of the potential real GDP. (*Hint:* divide the actual real GDP by the potential real GDP and multiply by 100.)

(1) The actual real GDP is _____% *less* than the potential real GDP.
(2) Using Okun's law, the unemployment rate will rise from 5.5% in year 1 and be _____% in year 2.

d. In year 3 the actual real GDP is _____% of the potential real GDP.

(1) The actual real GDP is _____% *less* than the potential real GDP.
(2) The unemployment rate, according to Okun's law, will be _____%.

3. The following table shows the price index in the economy at the end of four different years.

Year	Price index	Rate of inflation
1	100.00	
2	112.00	_____%
3	123.20	_____
4	129.36	_____

a. Compute and enter in the table the rates of inflation in years 2, 3, and 4.
b. Employing the rule of 70, how many years would it take for the price level to double at each of these three inflation rates? _____

_____

c. If nominal income increased by 15% from year 1 to year 2, what was the approximate percentage change in real income? _____
d. If nominal income increased by 7% from year 2 to year 3, what was the approximate percentage change in real income? _____
e. If nominal income was $25,000 in year 2, what was real income that year? _____
f. If nominal income was $25,000 in year 3, what was real income that year? _____
g. If the nominal interest rate was 14% to borrow money from year 1 to year 2, what was the approximate real rate of interest over that period? _____
h. If the nominal interest rate was 8% to borrow money from year 3 to year 4, what was the approximate real rate of interest over that period? _____

4. Indicate in the space below each of the following the most likely effect—beneficial (B), detrimental (D), or indeterminate (I)—of unanticipated inflation on these persons:

a. A retired business executive who now lives each month by spending a part of the amount that was saved and deposited in a fixed-rate savings account for a long term. _____

b. A retired private-school teacher who lives on the dividends received from the shares of stock owned.

_____

c. A farmer borrowed $500,000 from a bank at a fixed rate; the loan must be repaid in the next 10 years.

_____

d. A retired couple whose sole source of income is the pension they receive from a former employer.

_____

e. A widow whose income consists entirely of interest received from the corporate bonds she owns.

_____

f. A public school teacher. _____
g. A member of a union who works for a firm that produces computers. _____

5. Indicate for each of the following situations the effects of an increase in total spending on *real GDP, nominal GDP*, the *unemployment rate,* and the *price level,* respectively, using the following symbols: A, little, or no effect; B, increase; C, decrease; and D, sharp increase.

a. Depression and widespread unemployment

_____ _____ _____ _____

b. Prosperity, but moderate unemployment

_____ _____ _____ _____

c. Prosperity and full employment

_____ _____ _____ _____

6. On the following two graphs, the price *level* is measured along the vertical axis and real *domestic* output is measured along the horizontal axis. The demand for and the supply of domestic output are shown by the curves labeled *D* and *S*.

Real domestic output

Real domestic output

a. Applying the principles of demand and supply which you learned in Chapter 3, the equilibrium price level is the price level at which the domestic output demanded

and the domestic output supplied are _____

and the equilibrium domestic output is _____

_____.

b. On the first graph, draw a new demand curve which represents an *increase* in the demand for domestic output.
(1) The effect of this increase in demand is a rise in

the equilibrium price level and a(n) _____
in the equilibrium domestic output.

(2) This rise in the price level is an example of _____

_____ inflation.

c. On the second graph, draw a new supply curve which represents a *decrease* in the supply of domestic output.

(1) The effect of this decrease in supply is a _____

in the equilibrium price level and a _____
in the equilibrium domestic output.

(2) These effects are an example of _____

_____.

■ SHORT ANSWER AND ESSAY QUESTIONS

1. What is the historical record of the U.S. economy with respect to economic growth, full employment, and price-level stability?

2. Define the business cycle. Why do some economists prefer the term "business fluctuations" to "business cycle"?

3. Describe the four phases of an idealized business cycle.

4. In the opinion of most economists, what is the immediate determinant or cause of the levels of output and employment in the economy?

5. The business cycle is only one of three general causes of changes in output and employment in the economy. What are the other influences which affect these variables?

6. Compare the manner in which the business cycle affects output and employment in the industries producing capital and durable goods with industries producing nondurable goods and services. What causes these differences?

7. Distinguish among frictional, structural, and cyclical unemployment.

8. When is there full employment in the U.S. economy? (Answer in terms of the unemployment rate, the actual and potential output of the economy, and the markets for labor.)

9. What is the natural rate of unemployment? Will the economy always operate at the natural rate? Why is the natural rate subject to revision?

10. How is the unemployment rate measured in the United States? What criticisms have been made of the method the Bureau of Labor Statistics uses to determine the unemployment rate?

11. What is the economic cost of unemployment, and how is this cost measured? What is the quantitative relationship (called Okun's law) between the unemployment rate and the cost of unemployment?

12. What groups in the economy tend to bear the burdens of unemployment? How are women affected by unemployment, and how is the percentage of the labor force unemployed 15 or more weeks related to the unemployment rate in the economy?

13. How does the unemployment rate in the United States compare with those for other industrialized nations in recent years?

14. What is inflation, and how is the rate of inflation measured?

15. What has been the experience of the United States with inflation since the 1920s? How does the inflation rate in the United States compare with those for other industrialized nations in recent years?

16. Compare and contrast demand-pull and cost-push inflation.

17. What groups benefit from and what groups are hurt by inflation, and how has the public sector of the economy been affected by it?

18. What is the difference between the effects of unanticipated and the effects of anticipated inflation on the redistribution of real incomes in the economy?

19. Explain what will tend to happen to employment, output, nominal and real income, and the price level if total spending increases and the resources of the economy are (*a*) widely unemployed, (*b*) moderately unemployed, and (*c*) fully employed. If total spending *decreased* would the effects on employment, output, income, and the price level be just the opposite?

20. Write three scenarios that describe the effects of inflation on the domestic output.

ANSWERS

Chapter 8 Macroeconomic Instability: Unemployment and Inflation

FILL-IN QUESTIONS

1. unsteady, inflation, decreasing, increasing
2. increases, decreases
3. recession, trough, recovery
4. total spending
5. seasonal, secular
6. durable, capital, nondurable, low-
7. frictional, structural, cyclical
8. natural, frictional and structural, cyclical, equal to, 5.5
9. equal to, constant
10. unemployed, labor force, multiplying
11. minus, increase, 2
12. black, teenage, blue-collar, less
13. an increase, prices, divide, multiply
14. divide, rule of 70
15. deflation, high, low, high
16. *a.* an increase; *b.* production, supply, increases; *c.* difficult
17. real; *a.* real, 3; *b.* real, $28,302
18. fixed, unexpected, creditors, debtors, households, the public sector

19. anticipated; *a.* cost-of-living; *b.* real rate of interest, nominal rate of interest
20. increase, decrease, hyperinflation

TRUE-FALSE QUESTIONS

1. F, p. 148	**8.** T, pp. 153-154	**15.** T, p. 156	**22.** F, p. 164
2. F, p. 149	**9.** T, p. 153	**16.** F, p. 159	**23.** T, p. 164
3. F, P. 149	**10.** F, p. 154	**17.** F, p. 160	**24.** T, pp. 159, 161
4. T, p. 150	**11.** F, p. 156	**18.** T, p. 160	**25.** F, p. 165
5. F, p. 151	**12.** F, p. 154	**19.** T, p. 162	
6. T, p. 152	**13.** T, p. 158	**20.** T, p. 163	
7. F, p. 153	**14.** T, p. 156	**21.** T, p. 164	

MULTIPLE-CHOICE QUESTIONS

1. b, p. 149	**11.** d, p. 154	**21.** c, p. 162
2. d, p. 150	**12.** c, pp. 154-155	**22.** b, pp. 161-162
3. b, pp. 150-151	**13.** d, p. 160	**23.** d, p. 164
4. a, pp. 150-151	**14.** b, pp. 155-156	**24.** b, p. 164
5. a, p. 151	**15.** c, p. 156	**25.** d, pp. 165-166
6. b, pp. 152-153	**16.** b, p. 156	**26.** c, p. 165
7. a, p. 152	**17.** a, pp. 156-158	**27.** a, p. 167
8. c, p. 153	**18.** c, p. 160	**28.** b, p. 163
9. c, p. 153	**19.** b, pp. 161-162	**29.** b, pp. 167-169
10. c, p. 154	**20.** a, p. 163	**30.** d, pp. 167-169

PROBLEMS

1. year 1: 4,093, 4.8; year 5: 7,929, 8.3; *a.* the labor force increased more than employment increased; *b.* because unemployment and employment in relative terms are percentages of the labor force and *always* add to 100%, and if one increases the other must decrease; *c.* no economist would argue that the full-employment unemployment rate is as high as 8.3% and year 5 was not a year of full employment; *d.* the number of people looking for work expands
2. *a.* 0; *b.* 76, 412.5; *c.* 98, (1) 2, (2) 6.5; *d.* 90, (1) 10, (2) 10.5
3. *a.* 12, 10, 5; *b.* 5.8, 7, 14; *c.* 3; *d.* −3; *e.* $22,321; *f.* $20,292; *g.* 2; *h.* 3
4. *a.* D; *b.* I; *c.* B; *d.* D; *e.* D; *f.* I; *g.* I
5. *a.* B, B, C, A; *b.* B, B, C, B; *c.* A, D, A, D
6. *a.* equal, the domestic output demanded and supplied at the equilibrium price level; *b.* (1) increase, (2) demand-pull; *c.* (1) rise, fall, (2) cost-push inflation

SHORT ANSWER AND ESSAY QUESTIONS

1. p. 149	**8.** pp. 153-154	**15.** p. 161
2. pp. 149-150	**9.** pp. 153-154	**16.** pp. 161-163
3. p. 149	**10.** pp. 154-156	**17.** pp. 164-165
4. p. 150	**11.** p. 156	**18.** pp. 165-166
5. pp. 150-151	**12.** pp. 156-158	**19.** p. 167
6. p. 151	**13.** p. 159	**20.** pp. 167-169
7. pp. 152-153	**14.** pp. 159-160	

CHAPTER 9

Building the Aggregate Expenditures Model

This chapter is the first of two chapters that develops the first macroeconomic model of the economy presented in the textbook—the *aggregate expenditures model.* In the chapter you will find out what determines the demand for real domestic output (real GDP) and how an economy achieves an equilibrium level of output (and employment).

The first section of Chapter 9 offers a brief historical perspective on the aggregate expenditures model. Here you will learn about classical economics and its conclusion that the economy will automatically function to produce the maximum output it is capable of producing and provide employment for all those who are willing and able to work. This conclusion is based on *Say's law,* which holds that production automatically provides the income necessary to purchase all output, or **supply creates its own demand.**

The Great Depression and the work of John Maynard Keynes showed that there is no guarantee of maximum output and full employment. Depression or inflation can prevail with no automatic tendency for it to be corrected by the economy. **Keynesian** analysis of the expenditure components of the economy became the basis for the aggregate expenditures model.

A major section of the chapter describes the largest component of aggregate expenditures—consumption. An examination of consumption, however, also entails a study of saving because saving is simply the part of disposable income that is not consumed. This section develops the consumption and saving schedules and describes their main characteristics. Other key concepts are also presented: *average propensities to consume* (APC), and *save* (APS), *marginal propensities to consume* (MPC), and *save* (MPS), and the nonincome determinants of consumption and saving.

Investment expenditures is the subject of the next section of the chapter. The purchase of capital goods depends on the rate of return which business firms *expect* to earn from an investment and on the real rate of interest they have to pay for the use of money. Because firms are anxious to make profitable investments and to avoid unprofitable ones, they undertake all investments which have an expected rate of return greater than (or equal to) the real rate of interest and do not undertake an investment when the expected rate of return is less than the real interest rate. This relationship between the real interest rate and the level of investment spending is an inverse one: The lower the interest rate, the greater the investment spending. It is illustrated by an *investment demand curve*

which is downsloping. This curve can also be shifted by five factors which can change the expected rate of return on investment.

The investment decisions of individual firms can be aggregated to construct an investment schedule, which shows the amount firms collectively intend to invest at each possible level of GDP. A simplifying assumption is made that investment is independent of GDP. Unlike the consumption schedule, which is relatively stable over time, the investment schedule is unstable for several reasons and often shifts upward or downward.

The next two sections of the chapter explain the equilibrium level of real GDP with tables and graphs, first by using the *expenditures-output approach* and then by employing the *leakages-injections approach.* These two approaches are complementary and are two different ways of analyzing the same process and reaching the same conclusions. For each approach it is important for you to know, given the consumption (or saving) schedule and the level of investment expenditures, what real GDP will tend to be produced and why this will be the real GDP which will be produced.

The final section discusses the distinction between *planned investment* and *actual investment.* Saving and actual investment are always equal because they are defined in exactly the same way: the output of the economy minus its consumption. But saving and planned investment are not equal by definition. Saving and planned investment are equal only when real GDP is at its equilibrium level. When real GDP is *not* at its equilibrium level, saving and planned investment are *not* equal even though saving and actual investment are, as always, equal because the actual investment includes *un*planned investment or disinvestment. Remember: Equilibrium real GDP is achieved when saving and *planned* investment—*not* saving and *actual* investment—are equal.

The tools and ideas explained in Chapter 9 are important because they are used to form a complete picture of how aggregate expenditures determine the level of GDP in the next chapter.

■ **CHECKLIST**

When you have studied this chapter you should be able to

☐ Describe Say's law and the main ideas of classical economics.

☐ Explain the major ideas of Keynesian economics and how it differs from classical economics.

☐ List four simplifying assumptions in this chapter for building the aggregate expenditures model and two implications of those assumptions.

☐ State what determines the amount of goods and services produced and the level of employment in the Keynesian theory.

☐ Explain how consumption and saving are related to disposable income.

☐ Draw a graph to illustrate the relationship among consumption, saving, and disposable income.

☐ Construct a hypothetical consumption schedule.

☐ Construct a hypothetical saving schedule, and identify the level of break-even income.

☐ Compute the four propensities (APC, APS, MPC, and MPS) when given the necessary data.

☐ State the relationship between APC and APS as income increases.

☐ Demonstrate that MPC is the slope of the consumption schedule and MPS is the slope of the saving schedule.

☐ Explain how each of the four nonincome determinants of consumption and saving affect the consumption and saving schedules.

☐ Explain the difference between a change in the amount consumed (or saved) and a change in the consumption (or saving) schedule.

☐ Describe the marginal benefit and marginal cost in an investment decision.

☐ Draw a graph of an investment demand curve for the business sector.

☐ Explain how each of the five noninterest determinants of investment will shift the investment demand curve.

☐ Construct an investment schedule showing the relationship between intended investment and GDP.

☐ Give two reasons why a higher level of business activity may induce additional investment spending.

☐ Give four explanations of why investment spending tends to be unstable.

☐ When given the necessary data, use a table or graph to find equilibrium GDP using the aggregate expenditures—domestic output approach.

☐ When given the necessary data, use a table or graph to find equilibrium GDP using the leakages-injection approach.

☐ Explain why the economy will tend to produce its equilibrium GDP rather than at some small or larger level real GDP.

☐ State the difference between planned and actual investment.

☐ Explain how it is possible for saving and actual investment to be equal when saving and planned investment are not equal.

☐ State the conditions for inventories and investment at equilibrium GDP.

■ **CHAPTER OUTLINE**

1. The context for the development of the aggregate expenditures model developed in this chapter is historical debate between classical and Keynesian economics.

   a. *Classical economics* concluded that the economy would automatically tend to full employment of resources and maximum output and that laissez faire is the best policy for the government to pursue. These employment and output conclusions are based on Say's law, which states that supply creates its own demand. If there were an excess supply of goods or an excess supply of labor, price and wages would fall until the excesses were eliminated and full employment and maximum output were again achieved.

   b. The Great Depression and the ideas of J. M. Keynes, in *The General Theory of Employment, Interest and Money,* laid the foundation for a rejection of classical economics and the development of the aggregate expenditures model. Keynes challenged Say's law and showed that an economy can be inherently unstable and experience a long period of recession. Wages and prices are inflexible downward, and saving and investment decisions may not be coordinated, so there is no guarantee of full employment and maximum output. The economy is not self-regulating, so government policies are necessary to counteract economic instability.

2. To simplify the explanation of the aggregate expenditures model, four *assumptions* are made: The economy is "closed," government neither spends nor collects taxes, all saving is personal saving, and depreciation and net foreign factor income earned in the United States are zero. These assumptions have two important implications: Only consumption and investment are considered in the model, and output or income measures (GDP, NI, PI, DI) are treated as equal to each other.

3. Aggregate output and employment in the aggregate expenditures theory are directly related to the level of total or aggregate expenditures in the economy. To understand what determines the level of total expenditures at any time, it is necessary to explain the factors which determine the levels of consumption and investment expenditures.

4. Consumption is the largest component of aggregate expenditures, and saving is disposable income not spent for consumer goods.

   a. Disposable income is the most important determinant of both consumption and saving; the relationships between income and consumption and between income and saving are both direct (positive) ones.

   b. The consumption schedule shows the amounts that households plan to spend for consumer goods at various levels of income, given a price level.

   c. The saving schedule indicates the amounts households plan to save at different income levels, given a price level.

   d. The average propensity to consume (APC) and the average propensity to save (APS) and the marginal propensity to consume (MPC) and the marginal propensity to save (MPS) can be computed from the consumption and saving schedules.

   (1) The APC and the APS are, respectively, the percentages of income spent for consumption and saved, and their sum is equal to 1.

(2) The MPC and the MPS are, respectively, the percentages of *additional* income spent for consumption and saved; and their sum is equal to 1.

(3) The MPC is the slope of the consumption schedule, and the MPS is the slope of the saving schedule when the two schedules are graphed.

e. In addition to income, there are several other important determinants of consumption and saving, and changes in these nonincome determinants will cause the **consumption** and **saving schedules** to change. The four nonincome determinants include wealth, expectations, household debt, and taxation.

f. Three other considerations need to be noted:

(1) A change in the amount consumed (or saved) is not the same thing as a change in the consumption (or saving) schedule.

(2) Changes in wealth, expectations, and household debt shift consumption and saving schedules in opposite directions; taxation shifts them in the same direction.

(3) Both consumption and saving schedules tend to be stable over time.

5. The two important determinants of the level of **investment spending** in the economy are the expected rate of return (*r*) from the purchase of additional capital goods and the real rate of interest (*i*).

a. The expected rate of return is directly related to the net profits (revenues less operating costs) that are expected to result from an investment. It is the marginal benefit of investment for a business.

b. The rate of interest is the price paid for the use of money. It is the marginal cost of investment for a business. When the expected real rate of return is greater (less) than the real rate of interest, a business will (will not) invest because the investment will be profitable (unprofitable).

c. For this reason, the lower (higher) the real rate of interest, the greater (smaller) will be the level of investment spending in the economy; the investment demand curve (schedule) indicates this inverse relationship between the real rate of interest and the level of spending for capital goods. The amount of investment by the business sector is determined at the point where the marginal benefit of investment (*r*) equals the marginal cost (*i*).

d. There are at least five noninterest determinants of investment demand, and a change in any of these determinants will shift the investment demand curve (schedule). These determinants include acquisition, maintenance, and operating costs; business taxes; technological change; the stock of capital on hand; and expectations.

e. The investment decisions of businesses in an economy can be aggregated to form an investment schedule which shows the amounts business firms collectively plan to invest at each possible level of GDP. A simplifying assumption is made that investment is independent of disposable income or real GDP.

f. Investment is inherently unstable, and the investment schedule will shift up or down. Factors that contribute to this variability are the durability of capital goods, innovations, changes in profits, and altered expectations.

6. Employing the **aggregate expenditures—domestic output approach,** the equilibrium real GDP is the real GDP at which

a. aggregate expenditures (consumption plus planned investment) equal the real GDP, or

b. in graphical terms, the aggregate expenditures curve crosses the 45 degree line and its slope is equal to the marginal propensity to consume.

7. Using the **leakages-injections approach,** the equilibrium real GDP is the real GDP at which

a. saving and planned investment are equal, or

b. in graphical terms, the saving schedule crosses the planned investment schedule.

8. The **investment schedule** indicates what investors plan to do. Actual investment consists of both planned and unplanned investment (unintended changes in inventory investment).

a. At above equilibrium levels of GDP, saving is greater than planned investment, and there will be unintended or unplanned investment through increases in inventories. At below equilibrium levels of GDP, planned investment is greater than saving, and there will be unintended or unplanned disinvestment through a decrease in inventories.

b. Equilibrium is achieved when planned investment equals saving and there is no unplanned investment.

■ **HINTS AND TIPS**

1. The most important graph in the chapter is the consumption schedule (see Key Graph 9-2). Know how to interpret it. There are two lines on the graph. The 45 degree reference line shows all points where disposable income equals consumption (there is no saving). The consumption schedule line shows the total amount of disposal income spent on consumption at each and every income level. Where the two lines *intersect,* all disposable income is spent (consumed). At all income levels to the right of the intersection, the consumption line lies below the 45 degree line, and not all disposable income is spent (there is saving). To the left of the intersection, the consumption line lies above the 45 degree line and consumption exceeds disposable income (there is dissaving).

2. Always remember that *marginal propensities* sum to 1 (MPC + MPS = 1). The same is true for average propensities (APC + APS = 1). Thus, if you know the value of one marginal propensity (e.g., MPC), you can always figure out the value of the other one (e.g., 1 − MPC = MPS).

3. Do not confuse the *investment demand curve* for the business sector with the *investment schedule* for an economy. The former shows the inverse relationship between the expected rate of return and the amount of total investment by the business sector, whereas the latter shows the collective investment intentions of business firms at each possible level of disposable income or real GDP.

4. The distinction between *actual* and *planned* investment is important for determining the equilibrium level of real GDP. *Actual* investment includes both *planned* and *unplanned* investment. At any level of real GDP, *saving* and *actual* investment will always be equal by definition, but *saving* and *planned* investment may not equal real GDP because there may be *unplanned* investment (unplanned changes in inventories). Only at the equilibrium level of real GDP will *saving* and *planned* investment be equal (this is no *unplanned* investment).

■ **IMPORTANT TERMS**

Say's law	investment schedule
Keynesian economics	aggregate expenditures—
consumption schedule	domestic output approach
saving schedule	aggregate expenditures
break-even income	schedule
average propensity to	equilibrium (real) GDP
consume (APC)	45 degree line
average propensity to	expenditures-output
save (APS)	approach
marginal propensity to	leakages-injections
consume (MPC)	approach
marginal propensity to	leakage
save (MPS)	injection
expected rate of return	planned investment
real rate of interest	actual investment
investment demand curve	

SELF-TEST

■ **FILL-IN QUESTIONS**

1. Classical economists believe a market (or capitalistic) economy will tend to produce an output at which its labor force is (fully, less than fully) _____ employed; Keynesian economists argue it will often tend to produce an output at which its labor force is _____ employed.

2. According to the classical way of thinking, if total output exceeded the level of spending, prices, wages, and interest rates would (rise, fall) _____. These changes would (increase, decrease) _____ consumer spending, _____ employment, _____ investment spending. After these adjustments, the supply of goods and workers would be (greater than, less than, equal to) _____ the demand for them.

3. According to Say's law, the production of goods and services creates an equal (supply of, demand for) _____ these goods and services.

4. J. M. Keynes (accepted, rejected) _____ Say's law and showed that an economy can be inherently (stable, unstable) _____ and experience long periods of (recession, economic growth) _____. According to Keynes, wages and prices are (flexible, inflexible) _____ downward, and thus costly unemployment can occur for (short, long) _____ periods.

5. Four simplifying assumptions used throughout most of the chapter are that the economy is a(n) (open, closed) _____ economy, the economy is (private, public) _____, all saving is (personal, business) _____ saving, and depreciation and net foreign factor income earned in the United States is (positive, negative, zero) _____. Two implications of these assumptions are

   a. Aggregate spending = _____ + _____

   b. GDP = _____ = _____ = _____

6. In modern capitalism, domestic output and employment depend on the level of (marginal, aggregate) _____ expenditures in the economy. The most important determinant of consumption and saving is the economy's disposable (production, income) _____. The consumption schedule shows the various amounts that households plan to (save, consume) _____ at various levels of disposable income, while the saving schedule shows the various amounts that households plan to _____.

7. Both consumption and saving are (directly, indirectly) _____ related to the level of disposable income. At lower levels of disposable income, households tend to spend a (smaller, larger) _____ proportion of this income and save a _____ proportion, but at higher levels of disposable income, they tend to spend a (smaller, larger) _____ proportion of this income and save a _____ proportion. At the break-even income, consumption is (greater than, less than, equal to) _____ disposable income.

8. As disposable income falls, the average propensity to consume (APC) will (rise, fall) _____ and the average propensity to save (APS) will _____. The sum of APC and APS is equal to (0, 1) _____.

9. The marginal propensity to consume (MPC) is the change in (consumption, saving, income) _____ divided by the change in _____; it is the numerical value of the slope of the _____ schedule. The marginal propensity to save (MPS) is the change in (consumption, saving, income) _____ divided by the change in _____; it is the numerical value of the slope of the _____ schedule. The sum of MPC and MPS is equal to (0, 1) _____.

10. The most important determinants of consumption spending, other than the level of income, are

    a. _____

    b. _____

    c. _____

    d. _____

11. A change in the consumption (or saving) schedule means that the amount consumers plan to consume (save) will (be the same, change) _____ at every level of income, but a change in the amount consumed (or saved) means that the level of income has (stayed the same, changed) _____ and that consumers will (not change, change) _____ their planned consumption (saving) as a result.

12. Investment is defined as spending for additional (consumer, capital) _____ goods, and the total amount of investment spending in the economy depends on the expected rate of (interest, return) _____ and the real rate of _____. A business firm will increase the amount of investment if the expected rate of (interest, return) _____ on this investment is (greater, less) _____ than the real rate of (interest, return) _____ it must pay for the use of money.

13. The relationship between the rate of interest and the total amount of investment in the economy is (direct, inverse) _____ and is shown in the investment-(supply, demand) _____ curve. This curve shows that if the real rate of interest rises, the quantity of investment will (increase, decrease) _____, but if the real rate of interest falls, the quantity of investment will _____.

14. Five noninterest determinants of investment demand are

    a. _____

    b. _____

    c. _____

    d. _____

    e. _____

15. The consumption schedule and the saving schedule tend to be (stable, unstable) _____, while investment demand tends to be _____.

16. The demand for new capital goods tends to be unstable because of the (durability, nondurability) _____ of capital goods, the (regularity, irregularity) _____ of innovation, and the (stability, variability) _____ of actual and expected profits.

17. Two complementary approaches used to explain the equilibrium level of real domestic output are

    a. _____

    b. _____

18. Assuming a private and closed economy, the equilibrium level of real GDP is determined where aggregate expenditures are (greater than, less than, equal to) _____ real domestic output, consumption plus investment is _____ real domestic output, and the aggregate expenditures schedule or curve intersects the (90 degree, 45 degree) _____ line.

19. A leakage is (an addition to, a withdrawal from) _____ the income expenditure stream, whereas an injection is _____ to the income expenditure stream. In this chapter, the only leakage considered is (investment, saving) _____, and the only injection considered is _____.

20. At every level of GDP, saving is equal to (planned, actual) _____ gross investment.

    a. If aggregate expenditures are greater than the real domestic output, saving is (greater than, less than, equal to) _____ planned investment, there is unplanned (investment, disinvestment) _____ in inventories, and the real GDP will (rise, fall) _____.

    b. If aggregate expenditures are less than the real domestic output, saving is (greater than, less than, equal to) _____ planned investment, there is unplanned (investment, disinvestment) _____ in inventories, and the real GDP will (rise, fall) _____.

c. If aggregate expenditures are equal to the real domestic output, saving is (greater than, less than, equal to) _____ planned investment, unplanned investment in inventories is (negative, positive, zero) _____, and the real GDP will neither rise nor fall.

■ TRUE-FALSE QUESTIONS

Circle the T if the statement is true, the F if it is false.

1. In the aggregate expenditures model of the economy, the price level is constant. **T F**

2. According to the classical economists, full employment is normal in market economies. **T F**

3. The classical economists believed that when the economy deviated from full employment, there would be automatic adjustments in prices, wages, and interest rates within the market to restore the full-employment equilibrium. **T F**

4. Say's law states that demand for goods and services creates an equal supply of goods and services. **T F**

5. Classical economists contend that prices and wages would be sufficiently flexible to ensure full employment. **T F**

6. The level of saving in the economy, according to the Keynesians, depends primarily on the level of its disposable income. **T F**

7. The consumption schedule used as an analytical tool is also a historical record of the relationship of consumption to disposable income. **T F**

8. Empirical data suggest that households tend to spend a similar proportion of a small disposable income than of a larger disposable income. **T F**

9. The average propensity to save is equal to the level of saving divided by the level of consumption. **T F**

10. The marginal propensity to consume is the change in consumption divided by the change in income. **T F**

11. The slope of the saving schedule is equal to the average propensity to save. **T F**

12. An increase in wealth will increase the consumption schedule (shift the consumption curve upward). **T F**

13. An increase in the taxes paid by consumers will decrease both the amount they spend for consumption and the amount they save. **T F**

14. Both the consumption schedule and the saving schedule tend to be relatively stable over time. **T F**

15. The *real* interest rate is the nominal interest rate minus the rate of inflation. **T F**

16. A business firm will purchase additional capital goods if the real rate of interest it must pay exceeds the expected rate of return from the investment. **T F**

17. An increase in the stock of capital goods on hand will decrease the investment-demand curve. **T F**

18. The relationship between the rate of interest and the level of investment spending is called the investment schedule. **T F**

19. The investment schedule tends to be relatively stable over time. **T F**

20. The irregularity of innovations and the variability of business profits contribute to the instability of investment expenditures. **T F**

21. The equilibrium level of GDP is that GDP level corresponding to the intersection of the aggregate expenditures schedule with the 45 degree line. **T F**

22. Saving is an injection into and investment is a leakage from the income expenditures stream. **T F**

23. The investment schedule is a schedule of planned investment rather than a schedule of actual investment. **T F**

24. Saving and actual investment are always equal. **T F**

25. Saving at any level of real GDP equals planned investment plus unplanned investment (or minus unplanned disinvestment). **T F**

■ MULTIPLE-CHOICE QUESTIONS

Circle the letter that corresponds to the best answer.

1. Classical economics suggests that in capitalist economies
  (a) unemployment may persist for extended periods
  (b) the market system will ensure full employment
  (c) a slump in output will increase prices, wages, and interest rates
  (d) demand creates its own supply

2. From the perspective of classical economics, if total output were greater than total spending, competition would tend to force
  (a) prices and wages up
  (b) prices and wages down
  (c) prices down and wages up
  (d) prices up and wages down

3. Which would be considered part of Keynes' criticism of classical economics?
  (a) Investment spending will increase when the interest rate increases.
  (b) Prices and wages are flexible downward in modern capitalist economies.
  (c) The act of producing goods generates an amount of income equal to the value of the goods produced.
  (d) Saving and investment decisions are not always completely synchronized.

4. If the economy is closed, government neither taxes nor spends, all saving done in the economy is personal saving, and depreciation and net foreign factor income earned in the United States are zero, then

(a) gross domestic product equals personal consumption expenditures

(b) gross domestic product equals personal saving

(c) gross domestic product equals disposable income

(d) disposable income equals personal consumption expenditures

5. The level of output and employment in the economy depends

(a) directly on the level of total expenditures

(b) inversely on the quantity of resources available

(c) inversely on the level of disposable income

(d) directly on the rate of interest

6. As disposable income decreases, *ceteris paribus*

(a) both consumption and saving increase

(b) consumption increases and saving decreases

(c) consumption decreases and saving increases

(d) both consumption and saving decrease

7. If consumption spending increases from $358 to $367 billion when disposable income increases from $412 to $427 billion, it can be concluded that the marginal propensity to consume is

(a) 0.4

(b) 0.6

(c) 0.8

(d) 0.9

8. If disposable income is $375 billion when the average propensity to consume is 0.8, it can be concluded that

(a) the marginal propensity to consume is also 0.8

(b) consumption is $325 billion

(c) saving is $75 billion

(d) the marginal propensity to save is 0.2

9. As the disposable income of the economy increases

(a) both the APC and the APS rise

(b) the APC rises and the APS falls

(c) the APC falls and the APS rises

(d) both the APC and the APS fall

10. The slope of the consumption schedule or line for a given economy is the

(a) marginal propensity to consume

(b) average propensity to consume

(c) marginal propensity to save

(d) average propensity to save

Answer Questions 11 and 12 on the basis of the following diagram.

11. This diagram indicates that

(a) consumption decreases after the $60 billion level of GDP

(b) the marginal propensity to consume decreases after the $60 billion level of GDP

(c) consumption decreases as a percentage of GDP as GDP increases

(d) consumption increases as GDP decreases

12. If the relevant saving schedule were constructed, one would find that

(a) the marginal propensity to save is negative up to the $60 billion level of GDP

(b) the marginal propensity to save increases after the $60 billion level of GDP

(c) saving is zero at the $60 billion level of GDP

(d) saving is $20 billion at the $0 level of GDP

*Answer Questions 13, 14, and 15 on the basis of the following disposable income (**DI**) and consumption (**C**) schedules for a private, closed economy. All figures are in billions of dollars.*

DI	C
$ 0	$ 4
40	40
80	76
120	112
160	148
200	184

13. If plotted on a graph, the slope of the consumption schedule would be

(a) 0.6

(b) 0.7

(c) 0.8

(d) 0.9

14. At the $160 billion level of disposable income, the average propensity to save is

(a) 0.015

(b) 0.075

(c) 0.335

(d) 0.925

15. If consumption increases by $5 billion at each level of disposable income, then the marginal propensity to consume will

(a) change, but the average propensity to consume will *not* change

(b) change, and the average propensity to consume will change

(c) *not* change, but the average propensity to consume will change

(d) *not* change, and the average propensity to consume will *not* change

16. If the slope of a linear saving schedule decreases in a private, closed economy, then it can be concluded that the
(a) MPS has decreased
(b) MPC has decreased
(c) income has decreased
(d) income has increased

17. Which of the following relationships is an inverse one?
(a) the relationship between consumption spending and disposable income
(b) the relationship between investment spending and the rate of interest
(c) the relationship between saving and the rate of interest
(d) the relationship between investment spending and gross domestic product

18. A decrease in the level of investment spending would be a consequence of
(a) a decline in the rate of interest
(b) a decline in the level of wages paid
(c) a decline in business taxes
(d) a decline in expected future sales

19. Which would increase investment demand?
(a) an increase in business taxes
(b) an increase in the cost of acquiring capital goods
(c) a decrease in the rate of technological change
(d) a decrease in the stock of capital goods on hand

20. Which one of the following best explains the variability of investment?
(a) the predictable useful life of capital goods
(b) constancy or regularities in business innovations
(c) instabilities in the level of profits
(d) business pessimism about the future

21. On a graph, the equilibrium real GDP is found at the intersection of the 45 degree line and
(a) the consumption curve
(b) the investment demand curve
(c) the saving curve
(d) the aggregate expenditures curve

22. Which of the following is an injection?
(a) investment
(b) saving
(c) taxes
(d) imports

23. When the economy's real GDP exceeds its equilibrium real GDP,
(a) there is unplanned investment in the economy
(b) planned investment exceeds saving
(c) aggregate expenditures exceed the real domestic output
(d) leakages equal injections

24. If real GDP is $275 billion, consumption is $250 billion, and investment is $30 billion, real GDP
(a) will tend to remain constant
(b) will tend to increase
(c) will tend to decrease
(d) equals aggregate expenditures

25. If saving is greater than planned investment
(a) businesses will be motivated to increase their investments
(b) aggregate expenditures will be greater than the real domestic output
(c) real GDP will be greater than planned investment plus consumption
(d) saving will tend to increase

■ **PROBLEMS**

1. The following table is a consumption schedule. Assume taxes and transfer payments are zero and that all saving is personal saving.

GDP	C	S	APC,%	APS,%
$1500	$1540	$_____	1.027	−.027
1600	1620	_____	1.013	−.013
1700	1700	_____	_____	_____
1800	1780	_____	.989	.011
1900	1860	_____	.979	.021
2000	1940	_____	_____	_____
2100	2020	_____	.962	.038
2200	2100	_____	_____	_____

a. Compute saving at each of the eight levels of GDP and the missing average propensities to consume and to save.

b. The break-even level of income (GDP) is $_____.
c. As GDP rises, the marginal propensity to consume remains constant. Between each two GDPs the MPC can be found by dividing $_____ by $_____, and is equal to _____.
d. The marginal propensity to save also remains constant when the GDP rises. Between each two GDPs the MPS is equal to $_____ divided by $_____, or to _____.
e. Plot the consumption schedule, the saving schedule, and the 45 degree line on the graph on the next page.
(1) The numerical value of the slope of the consumption schedule is _____, and the term that is used to describe it is the _____.
(2) If the relevant saving schedule were constructed, the numerical value of the slope of the saving schedule would be _____, and the term that is used to describe it is the _____.

2. Indicate in the space to the right of each of the following events whether the event will tend to increase (+) or decrease (−) the *saving* schedule.
a. Development of consumer expectations that prices will be higher in the future _____

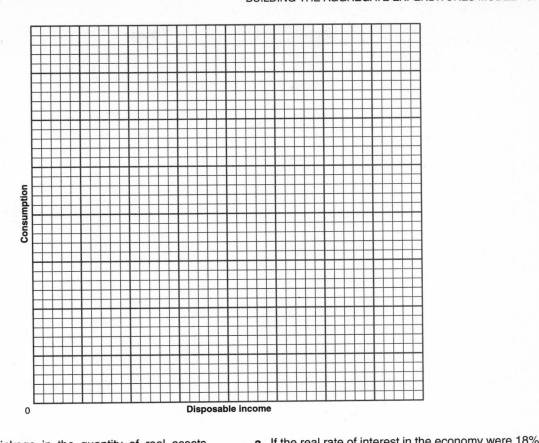

Consumption

0   **Disposable income**

b. Gradual shrinkage in the quantity of real assets owned by consumers _____
c. Increase in the volume of consumer indebtedness

_____

d. Growing belief that disposable income will be lower in the future _____
e. Rumors that a current shortage of consumer goods will soon disappear _____
f. Rise in the actual level of disposable income

_____

g. A build-up in the dollar size of the financial assets owned by consumers _____
h. Development of a belief by consumers that the Federal government can and will prevent recessions in the future _____

3. The following schedule has eight different expected rates of return, and the dollar amounts of the investment projects expected to have each of these return rates.

Expected rate of return profit	Investment projects (billions)
18%	$ 0
16	10
14	20
12	30
10	40
8	50
6	60
4	70

a. If the real rate of interest in the economy were 18%, business firms would plan to spend $_____ billion for investment, but if the real interest rate were 16%, they would plan to spend $_____ for investment.
b. Should the real interest rate be 14%, they would still wish to make the investments they were willing to make at real interest rates of 18% and 16%, they would plan to spend an additional $_____ billion for investment, and their total investment would be $_____ billion.
c. Were the real rate of interest 12% they would make all the investments they had planned to make at higher real interest rates plus an additional $_____ billion, and their total investment spending would be $_____ billion.
d. Complete the following table by computing the amount of planned investment at the four remaining real interest rates.

Real rate of interest	Amount of investment (billions)
18%	$ 0
16	10
14	30
12	60
10	_____
8	_____
6	_____
4	_____

e. Graph the schedule you completed on the following graph. Plot the real rate of interest on the vertical axis and the amount of investment planned at each real rate of interest on the horizontal axis.

0

f. Both the graph and the table show that the relationship between the real rate of interest and the amount of investment spending in the economy is

_____. This means that when the real rate of interest

(1) increases, investment will (increase, decrease)

_____.

(2) decreases, investment will _____.

g. It also means that should we wish to

(1) increase investment, we would need to _____ the real rate of interest.

(2) decrease investment, we would have to _____ the real rate of interest.

h. This graph (or table) is the _____

_____ curve.

4. Indicate in the space to the right of the following events whether the event would tend to increase (+) or decrease (−) investment expenditures.

a. Rising stock market prices _____

b. Development of expectations by business executives that business taxes will be higher in the future

_____

c. Step up in the rates at which new products and new

production processes are being introduced _____

d. Business belief that wage rates may be lower in the future and labor and capital are complementary resources

_____

e. An expectation of a recession _____

f. A belief that business is "too good" and the economy is due for a period of "slow" consumer demand

_____

g. Rising costs in the construction industry _____

h. A rapid increase in the size of the economy's

population _____

i. A period of a high level of investment spending which has resulted in productive capacity in excess of

the current demand for goods and services _____

5. Following are two schedules showing several GDPs and the level of investment spending (*I*) at each GDP. (All figures are in billions of dollars.)

Schedule number 1		Schedule number 2	
GDP	*I*	GDP	*I*
$1850	$90	$1850	$ 75
1900	90	1900	80
1950	90	1950	85
2000	90	2000	90
2050	90	2050	95
2100	90	2100	100
2150	95	2150	105

a. Each schedule is an _____ schedule.

b. When such a schedule is drawn up, it is assumed

that the real rate of interest is _____.

c. In schedule

(1) number 1, GDP and *I* are (unrelated, directly related)

_____.

(2) number 2, GDP and *I* are _____.

d. Should the real rate of interest rise, investment spending at each GDP would (increase, decrease)

_____ and the curve relating GDP and investment spending would shift (upward, downward)

_____.

■ **SHORT ANSWER AND ESSAY QUESTIONS**

1. According to the classical economists, what level of employment would tend to prevail in the economy? Why?

2. In classical analysis, Say's law made it certain that whatever was produced would be sold. How did flexible prices, flexible wages, and competition drive the economy to full employment and maximum output?

3. On what grounds did J. M. Keynes argue that flexible interest rates would not ensure the operation of Say's law?

4. What are the four simplifying assumptions used in this chapter, and what are the two implications of these assumptions?

5. Describe the relationship between consumption and disposable income, called the consumption schedule, and the one between saving the disposable income, known as the saving schedule.

6. Define the two average propensities and the two marginal propensities.

7. Explain briefly how the average propensity to consume and the average propensity to save vary as disposable income varies. Why do APC and APS behave this way? What happens to consumption and saving as disposable income varies?

8. Why do the sum of the APC and the APS and the sum of the MPC and the MPS always equal exactly 1?

9. What is the relationship between MPC and MPS and the consumption and saving schedule?

10. Explain briefly and explicitly *how* changes in the four nonincome determinants will affect the consumption schedule and the saving schedule and *why* such changes will affect consumption and saving in the way you have indicated.

11. Explain the marginal cost and marginal benefit of an investment decision. How is the marginal cost and the marginal benefit of investment measured?

12. Draw an investment demand curve. Use it to explain why investment spending tends to rise when the real rate of interest falls, and vice versa.

13. Identify and explain how five noninterest determinants of investment spending can increase or decrease the amount of investment. Illustrate the changes with a graph.

14. What is the difference between an investment demand curve and an investment schedule?

15. What assumption is made about the relationship between investment and disposable income? Is this assumption a reasonable one?

16. Why does the level of investment spending tend to be highly unstable?

17. Explain why the amount consumers spend and the amount investors spend matter to the performance of the economy.

18. Why is the equilibrium level of real GDP that level of real GDP at which domestic output equals aggregate expenditures? What will cause real GDP to rise if it is below this level, and what will cause it to fall if it is above this level?

19. Explain what is meant by a leakage and by an injection. Which leakage and which injection are considered in this chapter? Why is the equilibrium real GDP the real GDP at which the leakages equal the injections?

20. Why is it important to distinguish between planned and actual investment in explaining how a private, closed economy achieves its equilibrium level of real GDP?

ANSWERS

Chapter 9 Building the Aggregate Expenditures Model

FILL-IN QUESTIONS

1. fully, less than fully
2. fall, increase, increase, increase, equal to
3. demand for
4. rejected, unstable, recession, inflexible, long

5. closed, private, personal, zero; *a.* consumption, investment; *b.* national income, personal income, disposable income
6. aggregate, income, consume, save
7. directly, larger, smaller, smaller, larger, equal to
8. rise, fall, one
9. consumption, income, consumption, saving, income, saving, one
10. *a.* wealth (real and financial assets); *b.* household expectations; *c.* household debt; *d.* taxation of consumer income
11. change, changed, change
12. capital, return, interest, return, greater, interest
13. inverse, demand, decrease, increase
14. *a.* the cost of acquiring, maintaining, and operating the capital goods; *b.* business taxes; *c.* technological change; *d.* the stock of capital goods on hand; *e.* expectations
15. stable, unstable
16. durability, irregularity, variability
17. *a.* aggregate expenditures—domestic output; *b.* leakages-injections
18. equal to, equal to, 45 degree
19. a withdrawal from, an addition to, saving, investment
20. actual; *a.* less than, disinvestment, rise; *b.* greater than, investment, fall; *c.* equal to, zero

TRUE-FALSE QUESTIONS

1. T, p. 172	**10.** T, p. 178	**19.** F, pp. 186-187
2. T, pp. 172-173	**11.** F, p. 179	**20.** T, p. 187
3. T, pp. 172-173	**12.** T, p. 179	**21.** T, p. 190
4. F, p. 173	**13.** T, p. 180	**22.** F, pp. 190-191
5. T, pp. 172-173	**14.** T, p. 181	**23.** T, pp. 185, 188, 193
6. T, p. 175	**15.** T, pp. 181-182	**24.** T, p. 193
7. F, pp. 175-176	**16.** F, p. 182	**25.** T, p. 193
8. F, p. 176	**17.** T, p. 184	
9. F, p. 178	**18.** F, p. 185	

MULTIPLE-CHOICE QUESTIONS

1. b, p. 174	**8.** c, p. 178	**15.** c, p. 178	**22.** a, pp. 190-192
2. b, p. 173	**9.** c, p. 178	**16.** a, p. 179	**23.** a, pp. 193-195
3. d, p. 173	**10.** a, p. 179	**17.** b, pp. 182-184	**24.** b, pp. 189-190
4. c, p. 174	**11.** c, p. 178	**18.** d, pp. 184-185	**25.** c, pp. 192-193
5. a, p. 174	**12.** c, p. 176	**19.** d, pp. 184-185	
6. d, p. 175	**13.** d, p. 178	**20.** c, pp. 186-187	
7. b, p. 178	**14.** b, p. 178	**21.** d, p. 190	

PROBLEMS

1. *a.* S: −40, −20, 0, 20, 40, 60, 80, 100; APC: 1.000, 0.970, 0.955; APS: 0.000, 0.030, 0.045; *b.* 1700; *c.* 80, 100, .8; *d.* 20, 100, .20; *e.* (1) .8, MPC, (2) .2, MPS
2. *a.* −; *b.* +; *c.* −; *d.* +; *e.* +; *f.* none; *g.* −; *h.* −
3. *a.* 0, 10; *b.* 20, 30; *c.* 30, 60; *d.* 100, 150, 210, 280; *f.* inverse, (1) decrease, (2) increase; *g.* (1) lower, (2) raise; *h.* investment-demand
4. *a.* +; *b.* −; *c.* +; *d.* +; *e.* −; *f.* −; *g.* −; *h.* +; *i.* −
5. *a.* investment; *b.* constant (given); *c.* (1) unrelated, (2) directly related; *d.* decrease, downward

SHORT ANSWER AND ESSAY QUESTIONS

1. pp. 172-173	**6.** p. 178	**11.** pp. 181-182	**16.** pp. 186-187
2. pp. 172-173	**7.** p. 178	**12.** pp. 182-184	**17.** pp. 188-190
3. pp. 173-174	**8.** p. 178	**13.** pp. 184-185	**18.** pp. 188-190
4. p. 174	**9.** p. 179	**14.** p. 185	**19.** pp. 190-192
5. pp. 175-176	**10.** pp. 179-180	**15.** pp. 185-186	**20.** pp. 193-195

Aggregate Expenditures: The Multiplier, Net Exports, and Government

Chapter 10 extends the aggregate expenditures model of a private closed economy developed in Chapter 9. You now learn what causes real GDP to rise and fall. Changes in investment spending have an added effect on real GDP because of the multiplier. Including net exports in the aggregate expenditures model transforms the analysis from a closed economy to an open economy, and changes in net exports will change the equilibrium level of real GDP. Government spending and taxation make the economy mixed instead of private, and changes in public spending or taxes also shift the equilibrium real GDP.

The consumption (and the saving) schedule and the investment schedule—especially the latter—are subject to change, and when they change, equilibrium real GDP will also change. The relationship between an initial change in the investment or consumption schedules and a change in equilibrium real GDP is called the **multiplier.** Three things to note here are: how the multiplier is defined, why there is a multiplier effect, and upon what the size of the multiplier depends.

The aggregate expenditures model of the economy can be extended by adding the **net exports** of an economy to the aggregate expenditures schedule. Net exports are nothing more than the economy's exports less its imports of goods and services. Like investment, the exports of a nation are an injection into its circular flow of income and an increase in the flow. But imports are, like saving, a leakage from the circular flow and a decrease in the flow.

The generalization used to find the **equilibrium** real GDP in an open economy (one that exports and imports) is the same one as for a closed economy: The economy will tend to produce a real GDP which is equal to aggregate expenditures. The only difference is that the aggregate expenditures include not only consumption and investment expenditures but the expenditures for net exports. So the equilibrium real GDP will equal $C + I_g + X_n$ (when X_n is the symbol used for net exports). An increase in X_n, like an increase in I_g, will increase the equilibrium real GDP; a decrease in X_n will decrease the equilibrium real GDP. And like a change in I_g, a change in X_n has a multiplier effect on real GDP.

The section titled "Adding the Public Sector" introduces **government** taxing and spending into the analysis of equilibrium real GDP. Government purchases of goods and services add to aggregate expenditures and taxation reduces the disposable income of consumers, thereby reducing both the amount of consumption and the amount of saving that will take place at any level of real GDP. Both

approaches are again employed, and you are warned that you must know what real GDP will tend to be produced and why. Special attention should be directed to the exact effect taxes have on the consumption and saving schedules and to the multiplier effects of changes in government purchases and taxes.

It is important to be aware that the equilibrium real GDP is not necessarily the real GDP at which full employment with inflationary pressures is achieved. Aggregate expenditures may be greater or less than the full-employment noninflationary real GDP; if they are greater there is an **inflationary gap,** and if they are less there exists a **recessionary gap.** Be sure that you know how to measure the size of each gap: the amount by which the aggregate expenditures schedule (or curve) must change to bring the economy to its full-employment real GDP without there being inflation in the economy. Several historical examples—the Great Depression and the Vietnam war inflation—are described to help you see the application of the recessionary and inflationary gaps concepts.

The aggregate expenditures model that you have learned about is a valuable tool for explaining such economic events as recession, inflation, prosperity, and economic growth. The model, however, has limitations. The last section of the chapter describes the major shortcomings and how later chapters address some of these deficiencies.

■ CHECKLIST

When you have studied this chapter you should be able to

☐ Illustrate how equilibrium real GDP changes when the investment schedule shifts upward or downward.
☐ Define the multiplier effect in words, with a ratio, and using an equation.
☐ Make three clarifying points about the multiplier.
☐ Cite two facts on which the multiplier is based.
☐ Discuss the relationship between the multiplier and the marginal propensities.
☐ Find the value of the multiplier when you are given the necessary information.
☐ Explain the difference between the simple and the complex multiplier.
☐ Use the concept of net exports to define aggregate expenditures in an open economy.

☐ Explain what the equilibrium real GDP in an open economy will be when net exports are positive and when net exports are negative.

☐ Find the equilibrium real GDP in an open economy when you are given the appropriate data.

☐ Give examples of how circumstances or policies abroad can affect domestic GDP.

☐ List five simplifying assumptions used to add the public sector to the aggregate expenditures model.

☐ Find the equilibrium real GDP in an economy in which the government purchases goods and services and levies net taxes when you are given the necessary data.

☐ Determine the effect on the equilibrium real GDP of a change in government purchases of goods and services and in net taxes.

☐ Explain why the balanced-budget multiplier is equal to 1.

☐ Distinguish between the equilibrium real GDP and the full-employment noninflationary level of real GDP.

☐ Find the recessionary and the inflationary gaps when you are provided the relevant data.

☐ Apply the concepts of recessionary and inflationary gaps to historical economic events.

☐ Explain four shortcomings of aggregate expenditures theory.

■ **CHAPTER OUTLINE**

1. Changes in investment (or in the consumption and saving schedules) will cause the equilibrium real GDP to change in the same direction by an amount greater than the initial change in investment (or consumption).

   a. This is called the ***multiplier effect;*** the multiplier is equal to the ratio of the change in the real GDP to the initial change in spending.

   (1) The multiplier effect occurs because a change in the dollars spent by one person alters the income of another person in the same direction and because any change in the income of one person will change the person's consumption and saving in the same direction by a fraction of the change in income.

   (2) The value of the simple multiplier is equal to the reciprocal of the marginal propensity to save (1/MPS).

   (3) The significance of the multiplier is that relatively small changes in the spending plans of business firms or households bring about large changes in the equilibrium real GDP.

   (4) The simple multiplier has this value only in an economy in which the only leakage is saving; the complex multiplier takes into account such other leakages as taxes and imports.

2. In an ***open economy*** the exports (***X***) of a nation increase and its imports (***M***) decrease aggregate expenditures in that economy; aggregate expenditures are equal to the sum of consumption spending, investment spending, and net exports (***X_n***) when ***X_n*** is defined as ***X*** minus ***M***.

   a. The equilibrium real GDP in an open economy is the real GDP equal to consumption plus investment plus net exports, and

   b. Any increase (decrease) in its ***X_n*** will increase (decrease) its equilibrium real GDP with a multiplier effect.

   c. In an open economy model, circumstances and policies abroad, such as a change in the level of national incomes of trading partners, changes in tariffs or quotas, or changes in exchange rates can affect domestic GDP.

3. Changes in government spending and tax rates can offset cyclical fluctuations and increase economic growth.

   a. Five assumptions are made in order to simplify the explanation of the effects of government spending and taxes on the equilibrium real GDP.

   b. ***Government purchases*** of goods and services add to the aggregate expenditures schedule and increase equilibrium real GDP; an increase in these purchases has a multiplier effect on equilibrium real GDP.

   c. *Taxes* decrease consumption and the aggregate expenditures schedule by the amount of the tax times the MPC (and decrease saving by the amount of the tax times the MPS); an increase in taxes has a negative multiplier effect on the equilibrium real GDP. When government both taxes and purchases goods and services, the equilibrium GDP is the GDP at which

   (1) aggregate expenditures (consumption + investment + net exports + government purchases of goods and services) = the real domestic output (consumption + saving + taxes), or

   (2) using the leakages-injections approach, at which investment + exports + government purchases of goods and services = saving + imports + taxes.

   d. Equal increases (decreases) in taxes and in government purchases increase (decrease) equilibrium real GDP by the amount of the change in taxes (or in expenditures).

4. The equilibrium level of real GDP may turn out to be an equilibrium at less than full employment, at full employment, or at full employment with inflation.

   a. If the equilibrium real GDP is *less* than the real GDP consistent with full employment, there exists a *recessionary gap;* the size of the recessionary gap equals the amount by which the aggregate expenditures schedule must increase (shift upward) to increase the real GDP to its full-employment noninflationary level.

   b. If equilibrium real GDP is *greater* than the real GDP consistent with stable prices there is an *inflationary gap.* The size of the inflationary gap equals the amount by which the aggregate expenditures schedule must decrease (shift downward) if the economy is to achieve full employment without inflation.

5. The concepts of recessionary and inflationary gaps from the aggregate expenditures model can be applied to two events in U.S. history.

   a. The Great Depression is an example of a severe recessionary (or depressionary) gap as investment spending declined by 82%, thus reducing aggregate expenditures. Four reasons explain this decline in investment spending:

   (1) overcapacity in production and increased business indebtedness during the 1920s

(2) a decline in residential construction in the mid-to-late 1920s

(3) the stock market crash of 1929 and its secondary effects

(4) a sharp decline in the money supply

b. The economic expansion during the Vietnam war produced an inflationary gap in the U.S. economy, as inflation went from 1.6% in 1965 to 5.7% by 1970. This inflationary gap occurred because of various factors that significantly increased aggregate expenditures. These factors included the tax cuts in 1962 and 1964 that increased investment and consumption spending, increased government expenditures from 1965–1968 to pay for the escalating Vietnam war, and a tightened labor market because of the military draft.

6. There are four shortcomings of the aggregate expenditures model: an inability to measure price-level changes or the rate of inflation, no explanation for why demand-pull inflation can occur before the economy reaches its full-employment level of output, no insights into why the economy can expand beyond its full-employment level of real GDP, and no coverage of cost-push inflation. These shortcomings are overcome in the aggregate demand—aggregate supply model of the next chapter.

■ HINTS AND TIPS

1. The multiplier effect is a key concept in this chapter and in the ones that follow, so make sure you understand how it works.

a. The multiplier is simply the ratio of the change in real GDP to the *initial* changes in spending. Multiplying the *initial* change in spending by the multiplier gives you the amount of change in real GDP.

b. The multiplier effect works in both positive and negative directions. An *initial* decrease in spending will result in a larger decrease in real GDP, or an *initial* increase in spending will create a larger increase in real GDP.

c. The multiplier is directly related to the marginal propensities. The multiplier equals 1/MPS. The multiplier also equals 1/ (1 − MPC).

d. The main reason for the multiplier effect is that the *initial* change in income (spending) induces additional rounds of income (spending) that add progressively less each round as some of the income (spending) gets saved because of the marginal propensity to save (see Table 10-1 of the text).

2. There is an important difference between equilibrium and full-employment GDP in the aggregate expenditures model. Equilibrium means no tendency for the economy to change its output (or employment) level. Thus, an economy can experience a low level of output and high unemployment and still be at equilibrium. The recessionary gap shows how much aggregate expenditures need to increase, so that when this increase is multiplied by the multiplier, it will shift the economy to a higher equilibrium and to the full-employment level of real GDP. Remember that you multiply the needed increase in aggregate expenditures (the recessionary gap) by the multiplier to calculate the change in real GDP that moves the economy from below- to full-employment equilibrium.

■ IMPORTANT TERMS

multiplier	**balanced-budget multiplier**
net exports	**recessionary gap**
lump-sum tax	**inflationary gap**

SELF-TEST

■ FILL-IN QUESTIONS

1. An upshift in the aggregate expenditures schedule will (increase, decrease) _____ the equilibrium GDP. The upshift in the aggregate expenditures schedule can result from a(n) (increase, decrease) _____ in the consumption schedule or a(n) _____ in the investment schedule.

2. The multiplier is the change in real GDP (multiplied, divided) _____ by an initial change in spending; when the initial change in spending is _____ by the multiplier, the result equals the change in real GDP.

3. The multiplier has a value equal to 1 divided by the marginal propensity to (consume, save) _____, which is the same thing as 1 divided by the quantity of 1 minus the marginal propensity to _____.

4. The multiplier is based on two facts:

a. an initial increase in spending by business firms or consumers will increase the (debts, income) _____ of households in the economy

b. this increase in (debts, income) _____ will increase and expand the (consumption, investment) _____ spending of households by an amount equal to the incomes times the marginal propensity to (consume, save) _____.

5. When investment spending increases, the equilibrium real GDP (increases, decreases) _____, and when investment spending decreases, the equilibrium real GDP _____.

a. The changes in the equilibrium real GDP are (greater, less) _____ than the changes in investment spending.

b. The size of the multiplier varies (directly, inversely) _____ with the size of the marginal propensity to consume.

6. The (simple, complex) _____ multiplier is 1 divided by the marginal propensity to (consume, save) _____ because it reflects only the leakage of saving. The (simple, complex) _____ multiplier takes into account other leakages such as (exports, imports) _____ or (taxes, government spending) _____ along with saving.

7. In an open economy, a nation's net exports are equal to its exports (plus, minus) _____ its imports. In the open economy, aggregate expenditures are equal to consumption (plus, minus) _____ investment (plus, minus) _____ net exports.

8. What would be the effect—increase (+) or decrease (−)—of each of the following upon an open economy's equilibrium real GDP?

    a. an increase in imports _____

    b. an increase in exports _____

    c. a decrease in imports _____

    d. a decrease in exports _____
    e. an increasing level of national income among trading partners _____

    f. an increase in trade barriers imposed by trading partners _____
    g. a depreciation in the value of the economy's currency _____

9. Increases in public spending will (decrease, increase) _____ the aggregate expenditures schedule and equilibrium real GDP, but decreases in public spending will _____ the aggregate expenditures schedule and equilibrium real GDP.

10. Taxes tend to reduce consumption at each level of real GDP by an amount equal to the taxes multiplied by the marginal propensity to (consume, save) _____; saving will decrease by an amount equal to the taxes multiplied by the marginal propensity to _____.

11. In an economy in which government both taxes and purchases goods and services, the equilibrium level of real GDP is the real GDP at which

    a. aggregate (output, expenditures) _____ equals domestic _____.
    b. real GDP is equal to consumption (plus, minus) _____ investment (plus, minus) _____ net exports (plus, minus) _____ purchases of goods and services by government.

12. When the public sector is added to the model, the equation for the leakages-injection approach shows (consumption, investment) _____ plus (imports, exports) _____, plus purchases of goods and services by government equals (consumption, saving) _____ plus (exports, imports) _____ plus taxes.

13. Equal increases in taxes and government purchases will (increase, decrease) _____ real GDP by an amount equal to the _____ in taxes and government purchases. In this case, the balanced-budget multiplier is (1, 0) _____.

14. A recessionary gap exists when equilibrium real GDP is (greater, less) _____ than the full-employment real GDP. To bring real GDP to the full-employment level, the aggregate expenditures schedule must (increase, decrease) _____ by an amount equal to the difference between the equilibrium and the full-employment real GDP (multiplied, divided) _____ by the multiplier.

15. The amount by which aggregate spending at the full-employment GDP exceeds the full-employment level of real GDP is a(n) (recessionary, inflationary) _____ gap. To eliminate this gap, the aggregate expenditures schedule must (increase, decrease) _____ by the amount by which current GDP exceeds the full-employment noninflationary GDP divided by the multiplier.

16. The Great Depression is a historical example of a(n) (inflationary, recessionary) _____ gap, whereas the period of the escalation of the Vietnam war is a historical example of a(n) _____ gap.

17. List the factors that caused the steep decline in investment spending during the Great Depression.

    a. _____

    b. _____

    c. _____

    d. _____

18. The inflation of the Vietnam war was caused by tax (increases, decreases) _____ during the early-to-mid-1960s, _____ in government spending from 1965−1968, and (increases, decreases) _____ in the demand for labor because of the military draft.

19. One problem with the aggregate expenditures model is that it can explain (cost-push, demand-pull) _____ but not _____ inflation. Another problem is that the model also has no way of measuring the rate of (interest, inflation) _____ because there is no price level.

20. Two other deficiencies of the aggregate expenditures model are its inability to explain premature (demand-pull, cost-push) _____ inflation or how the economy can expand (to, beyond) _____ the full-employment level of output.

■ **TRUE-FALSE QUESTIONS**

Circle the T if the statement is true, the F if it is false.

1. The equilibrium level of GDP will change in response to changes in the investment schedule or the saving-consumption schedules. **T F**

2. If there is a decrease in the investment schedule, there will be an upshift in the aggregate expenditures schedule. **T F**

3. If the expected rate of return from investment increases in an economy, there will most likely be an upshift in the investment schedule for that economy. **T F**

4. A decrease in the real rate of interest will, other things equal, result in a decrease in the equilibrium real GDP. **T F**

5. The multiplier is equal to the change in real GDP multiplied by the initial change in spending. **T F**

6. The initial change in spending for the multiplier refers to an upshift or downshift in the aggregate expenditures schedule due a change in one of its components. **T F**

7. The multiplier effect works only in a positive direction in changing GDP. **T F**

8. The multiplier is based on the idea that any change in income will cause both consumption and saving to vary in the same direction as a change in income and by a fraction of that change in income. **T F**

9. The larger the marginal propensity to consume, the larger the size of the multiplier. **T F**

10. If the slope of a linear consumption schedule is steeper in economy A than economy B, then the MPC is less in economy A than economy B. **T F**

11 The value of the complex multiplier will usually be greater than the value of the simple multiplier because there will be more injections into the economy. **T F**

12. The net exports of an economy equal the sum of its exports and imports of goods and services. **T F**

13. An increase in the volume of a nation's exports, other things being equal, will expand the nation's real GDP. **T F**

14. An increase in the imports of a nation will increase the exports of other nations. **T F**

15. An appreciation of the dollar will increase net exports. **T F**

16. If the MPS were 0.3 and taxes were levied by the government so that consumers paid $20 in taxes at each level of real GDP, consumption expenditures at each level of real GDP would be $14 less. **T F**

17. If taxes are reduced by only $10 at all levels of real GDP and the marginal propensity to save is 0.4, equilibrium real GDP will rise by $25. **T F**

18. Equal increases in government purchases and taxes expand GDP by an amount equal to the increase. **T F**

19. The equilibrium real GDP is the real GDP at which there is full employment in the economy. **T F**

20. The existence of a recessionary gap in the economy is characterized by the full employment of labor. **T F**

21. One major cause of the Great Depression was the decline in the level of government spending. **T F**

22. The main reasons for the inflationary gap that developed in the economy during the 1960s was the increases in investment spending resulting from tax cuts and added government purchases of goods and services for the Vietnam war. **T F**

23. The aggregate expenditures model is valuable because it indicates how much the price level will rise when aggregate expenditures are excessive relative to the economy's capacity. **T F**

24. The aggregate expenditures model bars real GDP beyond the full-employment level of output. **T F**

25. The aggregate expenditures model provides a good explanation for cost-push inflation. **T F**

■ **MULTIPLE-CHOICE QUESTIONS**

Circle the letter that corresponds to the best answer.

Questions 1 and 2 are based on the following consumption schedule.

Real GDP	C
$200	$200
240	228
280	256
320	284
360	312
400	340
440	368
480	396

1. If investment is $60, the equilibrium level of real GDP will be
(a) $320
(b) $360
(c) $400
(d) $440

2. If investment were to increase by $5, the equilibrium real GDP would increase by
  (a) $5.00
  (b) $7.14
  (c) $15.00
  (d) $16.67

3. If the value of the marginal propensity to consume is 0.6 and real GDP falls by $25, this was caused by a decrease in the aggregate expenditures schedule of
  (a) $10.00
  (b) $15.00
  (c) $16.67
  (d) $20.00

4. If the marginal propensity to consume is 0.67 and if both planned gross investment and the saving schedule increase by $25, real GDP will
  (a) increase by $75
  (b) not change
  (c) decrease by $75
  (d) increase by $25

5. If in an economy a $150 billion increase in investment spending creates $150 billion of new income in the first round of the multiplier process and $105 billion in the second round, the multiplier and the marginal propensity to consume will be, respectively
  (a) 5.00 and 0.80
  (b) 4.00 and 0.75
  (c) 3.33 and 0.70
  (d) 2.50 and 0.40

Answer Questions 6, 7, and 8 on the basis of the following table for a private, closed economy. All figures are in billions of dollars.

Expected rate of return	Investment	Consumption	GDP
10%	$ 0	$200	$200
8	50	250	300
6	100	300	400
4	150	350	500
2	200	400	600
0	250	450	700

6. If the real rate of interest is 4%, then the equilibrium level of GDP will be
  (a) $300 billion
  (b) $400 billion
  (c) $500 billion
  (d) $600 billion

7. An increase in the interest rate by 4% will
  (a) increase the equilibrium level of GDP by $200 billion
  (b) decrease the equilibrium level of GDP by $200 billion
  (c) decrease the equilibrium level of GDP by $100 billion
  (d) increase the equilibrium level of GDP by $100 billion

8. The multiplier for this economy is
  (a) 2.00
  (b) 2.50
  (c) 3.00
  (d) 3.33

Use the data in the following table to answer Questions 9, 10, and 11.

Real GDP	$C + I_g$	Net exports
900	$ 913	$3
920	929	3
940	945	3
960	961	3
980	977	3
1,000	993	3
1,020	1,009	3

9. The equilibrium real GDP is
  (a) $960
  (b) $980
  (c) $1,000
  (d) $1,020

10. If net exports are increased by $4 billion at each level of GDP, the equilibrium real GDP would be
  (a) $960
  (b) $980
  (c) $1,000
  (d) $1,020

11. If the marginal propensity to save in this economy is 0.2, a $10 increase in its net exports would increase its equilibrium real GDP by
  (a) $40
  (b) $50
  (c) $100
  (d) $200

12. Other things remaining constant, which of the following would increase an economy's real GDP and employment?
  (a) the imposition of tariffs on goods imported from abroad
  (b) a decrease in the level of national income among the trading partners for this economy
  (c) a depreciation of the dollar relative to foreign currencies
  (d) an increase in the exchange rate for foreign currencies

13. An increase in the real GDP of an economy will, other things remaining constant,
  (a) increase its imports and the real GDPs in other economies
  (b) increase its imports and decrease the real GDPs in other economies
  (c) decrease its imports and increase the real GDPs in other economies
  (d) decrease its imports and the real GDPs in other economies

14. The economy is operating at the full-employment level of output. A depreciation of the dollar will most likely result in
  (a) a decrease in exports
  (b) an increase in imports
  (c) a decrease in real GDP
  (d) an increase in the price level

Questions 15, 16, 17, and 18 are based on the following consumption schedule. Investment figures are for planned investment.

Real GDP	C
$300	$290
310	298
320	306
330	314
340	322
350	330
360	338

15. If taxes were zero, government purchases of goods and services $10, investment $6, and net exports zero, equilibrium real GDP would be
  (a) $310
  (b) $320
  (c) $330
  (d) $340

16. If taxes were $5, government purchases of goods and services $10, investment $6, and net exports zero, equilibrium real GDP would be
  (a) $300
  (b) $310
  (c) $320
  (d) $330

17. Assume investment is $42, taxes are $40, net exports are zero, and government purchases of goods and services zero. If the full-employment level of real GDP is $340, the gap can be eliminated by reducing taxes by
  (a) $8
  (b) $10
  (c) $13
  (d) $40

18. Assume that investment is zero, taxes are zero, net exports are zero, and the government purchases of goods and services are $20. If the full-employment level of real GDP is $330, the gap can be eliminated by decreasing government expenditures by
  (a) $4
  (b) $5
  (c) $10
  (d) $20

19. If the marginal propensity to consume is 0.67 and both taxes and government purchases of goods and services increase by $25, real GDP will
  (a) fall by $25
  (b) rise by $25
  (c) fall by $75
  (d) rise by $75

20. Which of the following policies would do the *most* to reduce inflation?
  (a) increase taxes by $5 billion
  (b) reduce government purchases of goods and services by $5 billion
  (c) increase taxes and government expenditures by $5 billion
  (d) reduce both taxes and government purchases by $5 billion

21. If MPS is 0.10, a simultaneous increase in both taxes and government spending of $30 billion will
  (a) reduce consumption by $27 billion, increase government spending by $27 billion, and increase GDP by $30 billion
  (b) reduce consumption by $27 billion, increase government spending by $30 billion, and increase GDP by $27 billion
  (c) reduce consumption by $24 billion, increase government spending by $30 billion, and increase GDP by $30 billion
  (d) reduce consumption by $24 billion, increase government spending by $24 billion, and increase GDP by $24 billion

Answer Questions 22, 23, and 24 on the basis of the following diagram.

22. The size of the multiplier associated with changes in government spending in this economy is approximately
  (a) 0.29
  (b) 1.50
  (c) 2.50
  (d) 3.50

23. If this were an open economy without a government sector, the level of GDP would be
  (a) $100
  (b) $170
  (c) $240
  (d) $310

24. In this diagram it is assumed that investment, net exports, and government expenditures
  (a) vary inversely with GDP
  (b) vary directly with GDP
  (c) are independent of GDP
  (d) are all negative

25. If the MPC in an economy is 0.75, government could eliminate a recessionary gap of $50 billion by decreasing taxes by

(a) $33.3 billion
(b) $50 billion
(c) $66.7 billion
(d) $80 billion

26. In which of the following situations for an open mixed economy will the level of GDP contract?

(a) when $C_a + S + M$ is less than $I_g + X + T$
(b) when $I_g + M + T$ is less than $C + X + S$
(c) when $S_a + M + T$ is less than $I_g + X + G$
(d) when $I_g + X + G$ is less than $S_a + M + T$

27. If the economy's full-employment real GDP is $1200 and its equilibrium real GDP is $1100, there is a recessionary gap of

(a) $100
(b) $100 divided by the multiplier
(c) $100 multiplied by the multiplier
(d) $100 times the reciprocal of the marginal propensity to consume

28. To eliminate an inflationary gap of $50 in an economy in which the marginal propensity to save is 0.1, it will be necessary to

(a) decrease the aggregate expenditures schedule by $50
(b) decrease the aggregate expenditures schedule by $5
(c) increase the aggregate expenditures schedule by $50
(d) increase the aggregate expenditures schedule by $5

29. Which of the following contributed to the decline in investment spending that led to the Great Depression?

(a) a decrease in the business capacity during the 1920s
(b) an increase in business indebtedness during the 1920s
(c) a decrease in net exports during the 1930s
(d) an increase in the money supply during the 1930s

30. One of the deficiencies of the aggregate expenditures model is that it

(a) fails to account for demand-pull inflation
(b) gives more weight to cost-push then demand-pull inflation
(c) explains recessionary gaps but not inflationary gaps
(d) has no way of measuring the rate of inflation

■ **PROBLEMS**

1. Assume the marginal propensity to consume is 0.8 and the change in investment is $10. Complete the following table modeled after Table 10-1 in the textbook.

	Change in income	Change in consumption	Change in saving
Increase in gross investment of $10	$ + 10	$_____	$_____
Second round	_____	_____	_____
Third round	_____	_____	_____
Fourth round	_____	_____	_____
Fifth round	_____	_____	_____
All other rounds	16.38	13.10	3.28
Totals	_____	_____	_____

2. The following table shows consumption and saving at various levels of real GDP. Assume the price level is constant, the economy is closed to international trade, and there is no government, no business savings, no depreciation, and no net foreign factor income earned in the United States.

Real GDP	C	S	I_g	$C + I_g$	UI
$1,300	$1,290	$10	$22	$1312	−12
1,310	1,298	12	22	1320	−10
1,320	1,306	14	_____	_____	_____
1,330	1,314	16	_____	_____	_____
1,340	1,322	18	_____	_____	_____
1,350	1,330	20	_____	_____	_____
1,360	1,338	22	_____	_____	_____
1,370	1,346	24	_____	_____	_____
1,380	1,354	26	_____	_____	_____
1,390	1,362	28	22	1384	+6
1,400	1,370	30	22	1392	+8

a. The next table is an investment demand schedule which shows the amounts investors plan to invest at different rates of interest. Assume the rate of interest is 6%. In the previous table, complete the gross investment, the consumption-plus-investment, and the unplanned investment (*UI*) columns—showing unplanned investment with a + and unplanned disinvestment with a −.

Interest rate	I_g
10%	$ 0
9	7
8	13
7	18
6	22
5	25

b. The equilibrium real GDP will be $ _____.

c. The value of the marginal propensity to consume in this problem is _____, and the value of the marginal propensity to save is _____.

d. The value of the simple multiplier is _____.

e. If the rate of interest should fall from 6% to 5%, investment would (increase, decrease) _____

0   **Real GDP**

by $_____; and the equilibrium real GDP

would, as a result, (increase, decrease) _____

by $_____.

f. Suppose the rate of interest were to rise from 6%

to 7%. Investment would _____ by

$_____, and the equilibrium real GDP would

_____ by $ _____.

g. Assume the rate of interest is 6%,
(1) on the following graph, plot **S** and **I**$_g$ and indicate
the equilibrium real GDP, and

0   **Real GDP**

(2) on the above graph, plot **C, C + I**$_g$, and the 45 degree line, and indicate the equilibrium real GDP.

3. Following is a saving and investment schedule (**I**$_g$) indicating that planned investment is constant.

Real GDP	S	I$_g$
320	9	15
330	11	15
340	13	15
350	15	15
360	17	15
370	19	15

a. The equilibrium real GDP is $ _____

and saving and investment are both $ _____.

b. The marginal propensity to save is _____,

and the simple multiplier is _____.

c. A $2 rise in the **I**$_g$ schedule will cause real GDP to

rise by $ _____.

d. Use the investment schedule given in the table and
assume a $2 increase in the saving schedule in the
table—that is, saving at every real GDP increases by $2.

(1) Equilibrium real GDP will _____ to

$_____, and at this real GDP, saving will be

$_____.

(2) The amount by which real GDP changes depends
on the size of the change in the saving schedule and

the size of _____.

Possible levels of real GDP (billions)	Aggregate expenditures, closed economy (billions)	Exports (billions)	Imports (billions)	Net exports (billions)	Aggregate expenditures, open economy (billions)
$ 750	$ 776	$90	$86	$_____	$_____
800	816	90	86	_____	_____
850	856	90	86	_____	_____
900	896	90	86	_____	_____
950	936	90	86	_____	_____
1,000	976	90	86	_____	_____
1,050	1,016	90	86	_____	_____

4. Above is a schedule showing what aggregate expenditures (consumption plus investment) would be at various levels of real domestic product in a closed economy.

a. Were this economy to become an open economy, the volume of exports would be a constant $90 billion, and the volume of imports would be a constant $86 billion. At each of the seven levels of real GDP, net exports would be $_____ billion.

b. Compute aggregate expenditures in this open economy at the seven real GDP levels and enter them in the table.

c. The equilibrium real GDP in this open economy, would be _____ billion.

d. The value of the multiplier in this open economy is equal to _____.

e. A $10 billion increase in

(1) exports would (increase, decrease) _____ the equilibrium real GDP by $_____ billion.

(2) imports would (increase, decrease) _____ the equilibrium real GDP by $_____ billion.

5. Following are consumption and saving schedules.

a. Assume government levies a lump sum tax of $100. Also assume that imports are $5.

(1) Because the marginal propensity to consume in this problem is _____, the imposition of this tax will reduce consumption at all levels of real GDP by

$_____. Complete the C_a column to show consumption at each real GDP after this tax has been levied.

(2) Because the marginal propensity to save in this problem is _____, this tax will reduce saving at all levels of real GDP by $_____

_____. Complete the S_a column to show saving at each real GDP after this tax has been levied.

b. Compute the (after-tax) saving-plus-imports-plus-taxes at each real GDP and put them in the $S_a + M + T$ column.

c. Suppose that investment is $150, exports are $5, and government purchases of goods and services equal $200. Complete the investment-plus-exports-plus-government-purchases column ($I_g + X + G$) and the (after-tax) consumption-plus-investment-plus-net-exports-plus-government-purchases column ($C_a + I_g + X_n + G$).

d. The equilibrium real GDP is $_____.

e. On the two graphs on p. 111, plot

(1) C_a, $I_g + X_n + G$, $C_a + I_g + X_n + G$, and the 45 degree line. Show the equilibrium real GDP.

(2) $S_a + M + T$ and $I_g + X + G$. Show the real equilibrium GDP. (To answer the questions that follow, it is *not* necessary to recompute C, S, $S + M + T$, $I_g + X + G$, or $C + I_g + X_n + G$. They can be answered by using the multipliers.)

Real GDP	C	S	C_a	S_a	$S_a + M + T$	$I_g + X + G$	$C_a + I_g + X_n + G$
$1,500	$1,250	$250	$_____	$_____	$_____	$_____	$_____
1,600	1,340	260	_____	_____	_____	_____	_____
1,700	1,430	270	_____	_____	_____	_____	_____
1,800	1,520	280	_____	_____	_____	_____	_____
1,900	1,610	290	_____	_____	_____	_____	_____
2,000	1,700	300	_____	_____	_____	_____	_____
2,100	1,790	310	_____	_____	_____	_____	_____

Real GDP

0

Real GDP

0

f. If taxes remained at $100 and government purchases rose by $10, the equilibrium real GDP would (rise, fall) _____ by $ _____.

g. If government purchases remained at $200 and the lump-sum tax increased by $10, the equilibrium real GDP would _____ by $ _____.

h. The combined effect of a $10 increase in government purchases *and* a $10 increase in taxes is to _____ real GDP by $ _____.

6. Here are consumption and saving schedules for a closed economy. Assume that the level of real GDP at which full employment without inflation is achieved is $590.

Real GDP	C	S
$550	$520	$30
560	526	34
570	532	38
580	538	42
590	544	46
600	550	50
610	556	54
620	562	58
630	568	62

a. The value of the multiplier is _____.

b. If investment is $58, the equilibrium nominal GDP is $ _____ and exceeds the full-employment noninflationary real GDP by $_____. There is a(n) _____ gap of $ _____.

c. If investment is $38, the equilibrium real GDP is $ _____ and is less than full-employment real GDP by $ _____. There is a(n) _____ gap of $ _____.

■ **SHORT ANSWER AND ESSAY QUESTIONS**

1. Why does the equilibrium level of real GDP change?

2. What is the multiplier effect?

3. Give a rationale for the multiplier effect.

4. How is the multiplier effect related to the marginal propensities? Explain in words and equations.

5. Explain the difference between the simple and complex multiplier.

6. How do exports and imports get included in the aggregate expenditures model?

7. What happens to the aggregate expenditures schedule when net exports increase or decrease?

8. Give some examples of international economic linkages affecting the domestic level of GDP.

9. Explain the five simplifying assumptions used to include the public sector in the aggregate expenditures model.

10. Describe how government expenditures affect equilibrium GDP.

11. What effect will taxes have on the consumption schedule? On the saving schedule?

12. Explain why, with government taxing and spending, the equilibrium real GDP is the real GDP at which real GDP equals consumption plus investment plus net exports plus government purchases of goods and services. Also explain why in this case saving plus imports plus taxes equals investment plus exports plus government purchases.

13. How will changes in the different components of aggregate expenditures cause GDP to move to its equilibrium level?

14. If both taxes and government purchases increase by equal amounts, real GDP will increase by that amount. Why does this happen?

15. Explain what is meant by a recessionary gap.

16. Describe the economic conditions that create an inflationary gap.

17. What factors influenced investment spending during the 1920s and early 1930s? How did these conditions contribute to the Great Depression? Explain using an aggregate expenditures graph.

18. What events led to the Vietnam war inflation of the 1960s? How can this event be characterized using the aggregate expenditures model?

19. What are the limitations of the aggregate expenditures model in terms of the measurement of the price level or demand-pull inflation?

20. Is it possible for the economy to expand beyond its full-employment level of real GDP? How does the aggregate expenditures model handle this situation?

ANSWERS

Chapter 10 Aggregate Expenditures: The Multiplier, Net Exports, and Government

FILL-IN QUESTIONS

1. increase, increase, increase
2. divided, multiplied
3. save, consume
4. *a.* income; *b.* income, consumption, consume
5. increases, decreases; *a.* greater; *b.* directly
6. simple, save, complex, imports, taxes
7. minus, plus, plus
8. *a.* −; *b.* +; *c.* +; *d.* −; *e.* +; *f.* −; *g.* +
9. increase, decrease
10. consume, save
11. *a.* expenditures, output; *b.* plus, plus, plus
12. investment, exports, saving, imports
13. increase, increase, one
14. less, increase, divided
15. inflationary, decrease
16. recessionary, inflationary

17. *a.* overcapacity and business indebtedness; *b.* decline in residential construction; *c.* the stock market crash; *d.* shrinking money supply (any order)
18. decreases, increases, increases
19. demand-pull, cost-push, inflation
20. demand-pull, beyond

TRUE-FALSE QUESTIONS

1. T, p. 199	10. F, p. 203	19. F, p. 213
2. F, pp. 200-201	11. F, pp. 203-204	20. F, p. 213
3. T, p. 200	12. F, p. 204	21. F, pp. 214-217
4. F, pp. 200-201	13. T, pp. 205-206	22. T, p. 217
5. F, p. 201	14. T, pp. 206-207	23. F, p. 217
6. T, p. 201	15. F, p. 207	24. T, p. 218
7. F, p. 201	16. T, pp. 209-210	25. F, p. 218
8. T, p. 201	17. F, pp. 209-210	
9. T, p. 203	18. T, p. 212	

MULTIPLE-CHOICE QUESTIONS

1. c, pp. 199-200	11. b, pp. 205-206	21. a, pp. 212-213
2. d, pp. 199-200	12. c, p. 207	22. d, p. 201
3. a, pp. 202-203	13. a, p. 206	23. c, p. 205
4. b, pp. 202-203	14. d, p. 207	24. c, p. 207
5. c, pp. 201-202	15. c, pp. 207-208	25. c, pp. 209-210
6. c, pp. 199-200	16. b, pp. 200-210	26. d, pp. 211-212
7. b, pp. 199-200	17. b, p. 213	27. b, p. 213
8. a, p. 201	18. a, p. 213	28. a, p. 213
9. b, p. 204	19. b, pp. 212-213	29. b, p. 215
10. c, p. 204	20. b, pp. 212-213	30. d, p. 217

PROBLEMS

1. Change in income: 8.00, 6.40, 5.12, 4.10, 50; Change in consumption: 8.00, 6.40, 5.12, 4.10, 3.28, 40.00; Change in saving: 2.00, 1.60, 1.28, 1.02, 0.82, 10.00
2. *a.* I_g: 22, 22, 22, 22, 22, 22, 22; $C + I_g$: 1,328, 1,336, 1,344, 1,352, 1,360, 1,368, 1,376; *UI*: −8, −6, −4, −2, 0, +2, +4; *b.* 1,360; *c.* 0.8, 0.2; *d.* 5; *e.* increase, 3, increase, 15; *f.* decrease, 4, decrease, 20
3. *a.* 350, 15; *b.* 0.20, 5; *c.* 10; *d.* (1) decrease, 340, 15, (2) the multiplier
4. *a.* $4 (and put $4 in each of the seven net exports values in the table); *b.* $780, 820, 860, 900, 940, 980, 1,020; *c.* $900; *d.* 5; *e.* (1) increase, $50, (2) decrease, $50
5. *a.* (1) 0.9, 90; C_a: 1,160, 1,250, 1,340, 1,430, 1,520, 1,610, 1,700, (2) 0.1, 10, S_a: 240, 250, 260, 270, 280, 290, 300; *b.* $S_a + M + T$: 345, 355, 365, 375, 385, 395, 405; *c.* $I_g + X + G$: 355, 355, 355, 355, 355, 355, 355; $C_a + I_g + X_n + G$: 1510, 1600, 1690, 1780, 1870, 1960, 2050; *d.* 1600; *f.* rise, 100; *g.* fall, 90; *h.* raise, 10
6. *a.* 2 1/2; *b.* 620, 30, inflationary, 12; *c.* 570, 20, recessionary, 8

SHORT ANSWER AND ESSAY QUESTIONS

1. pp. 199-201	8. pp. 206-207	15. p. 213
2. p. 201	9. p. 207	16. p. 213
3. pp. 201-202	10. pp. 207-208	17. pp. 214-217
4. pp. 202-203	11. pp. 209-210	18. p. 217
5. pp. 203-204	12. pp. 211-212	19. p. 217
6. pp. 204-205	13. pp. 199-213	20. p. 218
7. pp. 205-206	14. pp. 212-213	

Aggregate Demand and Aggregate Supply

Chapter 11 introduces another macro model of the economy, one based on aggregate demand and aggregate supply. This model overcomes a limitation of the aggregate expenditures model because **the price level is allowed to vary rather than be fixed.** The aggregate demand–aggregate supply model allows you to both determine the size of real domestic output or the level of prices at any time and understand what causes output and the price level to change.

The *aggregate demand (AD) curve* is **downsloping** because of the wealth, interest rate, and foreign-purchases effects on changes in the price level. With a downsloping aggregate demand curve, changes in the price level have an inverse effect on the level of spending by domestic consumers, businesses, government, and foreign buyers, and thus on real domestic output, assuming *other things equal.* This change would be equivalent to a movement along an existing aggregate demand curve: A lower price level increases the quantity of real domestic output, and a higher price level decreases the quantity of real domestic output.

Although the aggregate expenditures model is a fixed-price level model and the aggregate demand–aggregate supply model is a variable-price level model, there is a close relationship between the two models. The important thing to understand is that prices can be fixed or constant at different levels. The AD curve can be derived from the aggregate expenditures model by letting price be **constant at different levels.** In this case, the lower (the higher) the level at which prices are constant in the aggregate expenditures model, the larger (the smaller) will be the equilibrium real GDP in that model of the economy. Various output-price level combinations can be traced to derive an AD curve that slopes downward.

The **aggregate demand curve can increase or decrease.** The curve shifts because of a change in the nonprice level determinants of aggregate demand. The determinants include changes in factors affecting consumer, investment, government, or net export spending. These determinants are similar to the components of the aggregate expenditures model. It is easy to show the relationship between the shifts in the two models. A change in spending will cause a shift (upward or downward) in the aggregate expenditures schedule. The initial change in spending when multiplied times the multiplier would be equal to the size of the horizontal shift in AD, assuming a constant price level.

The *aggregate supply (AS) curve* differs from the shape of the aggregate demand curve because it reflects what happens to per unit production costs as real domestic output increases or decreases. For the purposes of this analysis, it has three ranges: (1) At a low level of real domestic output, the price level is relatively constant, so the aggregate supply curve in this range is horizontal; (2) at a high level of real domestic output, the aggregate supply curve is vertical; and (3) in the intermediate range, the level of real domestic output rises along with the price level, so the curve is upsloping.

You should remember that an assumption has also been made that other things are equal when one moves along an aggregate supply curve. When other things change, then the aggregate supply curve can shift. The determinants of aggregate supply include changes in input prices, changes in productivity, and changes in the legal and institutional environment for production.

The **intersection** of the aggregate demand and aggregate supply curves determines *equilibrium output* and the *price level.* Assuming that the determinants of aggregate demand and aggregate supply do not change, there are competitive pressures that will tend to keep the economy at equilibrium. If, however, a determinant changes, then aggregate demand, aggregate supply, or both, can shift.

When aggregate demand increases, this can lead to changes in real domestic output and the price level, depending on the range on the aggregate supply curve in which the economy is operating. In the intermediate and vertical ranges of AS, a change in AD demand will cause an increase in the price level. Thus, in these ranges the change in AD may not have its full multiplier effect on the real GDP of the economy, and it will result in demand-pull inflation.

There can also be a decrease in aggregate demand, but it is less certain what the effects will be. Some economists think that there is a *ratchet effect* that occurs because prices are inflexible downward. This effect may arise for several reasons, as you will learn from the chapter.

Aggregate supply may also increase or decrease. An increase in aggregate supply gives a double bonus for the economy because the price level falls and output (and employment) increase. Conversely, a decrease in aggregate supply doubly harms the economy because the price level increases and output (and employment) falls, and thus the economy experiences cost-push inflation.

The aggregate demand–aggregate supply model is an important framework for determining the equilibrium level of real domestic output and prices in an economy. The model will be used extensively throughout the next eight chapters to analyze how different parts of the economy function.

■ CHECKLIST

When you have studied this chapter you should be able to

☐ Contrast the aggregate expenditures and the aggregate demand–aggregate supply models by comparing the variability of the price level and real GDP.
☐ Define aggregate demand.
☐ Explain why the aggregate demand curve slopes downward.
☐ Derive the aggregate demand curve from the aggregate expenditures model.
☐ Identify the four major spending determinants of aggregate demand and their underlying components.
☐ Explain how the four major spending determinants of aggregate demand and their underlying components can increase or decrease aggregate demand.
☐ Explain the effect of a change in aggregate expenditures on the aggregate demand curve.
☐ Define aggregate supply.
☐ Describe the shape of the aggregate supply curve and name the three ranges on it.
☐ Identify the three major spending determinants of aggregate supply and their underlying components.
☐ Explain how the three major determinants of aggregate supply and their underlying components can increase or decrease aggregate supply.
☐ Explain what the real domestic output and price level will be in equilibrium and why the economy will tend to produce this output and price level (rather than another combination).
☐ State the effects on the real domestic output and on the price level of an increase in aggregate demand when the economy is in the horizontal, vertical, and intermediate ranges.
☐ Explain what determines how large the multiplier effect on the equilibrium real GDP will be in the aggregate demand–aggregate supply model.
☐ Use a graph to illustrate the operation of the ratchet effect.
☐ Give six reasons for downward price-level inflexibility.
☐ Predict the effects of a change in aggregate supply on the price level and the equilibrium real GDP.

■ CHAPTER OUTLINE

1. This chapter introduces the aggregate demand–aggregate supply model of the economy to explain why real domestic output *and* the price level fluctuate. This model has an advantage over the aggregate expenditures model because it allows the price level to vary (rise and fall) rather than be constant or fixed as in the aggregate expenditures model.

2. Aggregate demand is a curve which shows the total quantity of goods and services that will be purchased (demanded) at different price levels.
  a. The aggregate demand curve slopes downward for three reasons:
  (1) Wealth effect: An increase in the price level also decreases the purchasing power of financial assets with a fixed money value, and because those who own such assets are now poorer, they spend less for goods and services; a decrease in the price level has the opposite effects.
  (2) Interest-rate effect: With the supply of money fixed, an increase in the price level increases the demand for money, increases interest rates, and as a result reduces those expenditures (by consumers and business firms) which are sensitive to increased interest rates; a decrease in the price level has the opposite effects.
  (3) Foreign purchases effect: An increase in the price level (relative to foreign price levels) will reduce U.S. exports, expand U.S. imports, and decrease the quantity of goods and services demanded in the U.S. economy; a decrease in the price level (relative to foreign price levels) will have opposite effects.
  b. The aggregate demand curve is derived from the intersections of the aggregate expenditures curves and the 45 degree curve. As the price level falls, the aggregate expenditures curve shifts upward and the equilibrium real GDP increases, but as the price level rises, the aggregate expenditures curve shifts downward and the equilibrium real GDP decreases. The inverse relationship between the price level and equilibrium real GDP is the aggregate demand curve. Note that for the aggregate expenditures model, changes in
  (1) wealth increase or decrease the consumption schedule;
  (2) the interest rate increase or decrease the investment schedule;
  (3) imports or exports shift the net export schedule.

3. Spending by domestic consumers, businesses, government, and foreign buyers that is independent of changes in the price level shifts aggregate demand, as outlined in Figure 11-3.
  a. For domestic consumers, increases in wealth, improved expectations, reductions in indebtedness, or lower taxes can increase consumer spending and aggregate demand; decreases in consumer wealth, less positive expectations, increases in indebtedness, and higher taxes decrease consumer spending and aggregate demand.
  b. For businesses, lower interest rates, higher expected returns on investment, lower taxes, improved technology, and less excess capacity may increase investment spending and aggregate demand, whereas higher interest rates, lower expected returns on investment, higher taxes, and more excess capacity may retard investment spending and aggregate demand.
  c. More government spending tends to increase aggregate demand and less government spending will

decrease it, assuming that tax collections and interest rates do not change as a result.

d. Net export spending and aggregate demand are increased by increases in the national incomes of other nations and by a dollar depreciation; declines in the incomes of foreign buyers and a dollar appreciation tend to reduce net exports and aggregate demand.

e. If the price level is constant, any change in the nonprice-level determinants of consumption and planned investment that shifts the aggregate expenditures curve upward (downward) will increase (decrease) the equilibrium real GDP and shift the AD curve to the right (left) by an amount equal to the initial increase (decrease) in aggregate expenditures times the multiplier.

4. Aggregate supply is a curve that shows the total quantity of goods and services that will be produced (supplied) at different price levels. The curve has three ranges:

a. In the horizontal range (when the economy is in a severe recession or depression), the aggregate supply curve is horizontal; the price level need not rise to induce producers to supply larger quantities of goods and services.

b. In the vertical range (when the economy is at full employment), the aggregate supply curve is vertical; a rise in the price level cannot result in an increase in the quantity of goods and services supplied.

c. Between these two ranges is the intermediate range in which the supply curve slopes upward; the price level must rise to induce producers to supply larger quantities of goods and services.

5. Factors that shift the aggregate supply curve include changes in the prices of inputs for production, changes in productivity, and changes in the legal and institutional environment in the economy, as outlined in Figure 11-6.

a. Lower prices for productive domestic resources (land, labor, capital, and entrepreneurial ability) and imported resources tend to reduce unit costs of production and increase aggregate supply, whereas higher input prices, which may be brought about by more market power on the part of resource suppliers, will tend to decrease aggregate supply.

b. As productivity improves, per-unit production costs fall and aggregate supply increases; the converse occurs when productivity falls.

c. A decrease in the level of business taxation or reduced regulation of business may improve the business environment and increase aggregate supply; the opposite actions may reduce aggregate supply.

6. The equilibrium real domestic output and the equilibrium price level are at the intersection of the aggregate demand and the aggregate supply curves. Were the actual output greater (less) than the equilibrium output, producers would find that their inventories were increasing (decreasing), and they would contract (expand) their output to the equilibrium output.

7. The aggregate demand and aggregate supply curves shift to change equilibrium.

a. An increase in aggregate demand in

(1) the horizontal range would result in an increase in real output, but the price level would remain unchanged,

(2) the vertical range would result in an increase in the price level, but the real domestic output would remain unchanged,

(3) the intermediate range would result in an increase in both real domestic output and the price level.

b. If the economy is operating along the

(1) horizontal range of the AS curve, an increase in AD will have no effect on the price level and the increase in the equilibrium real GDP will equal the full multiplier effect of the increase in aggregate expenditures,

(2) intermediate range the increase in AD will increase the price level and the increase in the equilibrium real GDP will be less than the full multiplier effect of the increase in aggregate expenditures,

(3) vertical range the increase in AD will increase the price level and have no effect on the equilibrium real GDP.

c. But a decrease in aggregate demand may not have the opposite effect on the price level because prices tend to be inflexible (sticky) downward. This ratchet effect occurs for at least six interrelated reasons: long-term wage contracts, efficiency wages, investments in training, the minimum wage, menu costs, and fear of price wars.

d. A decrease in aggregate supply means there will be a decrease in real domestic output (economic growth) and employment along with a rise in the price level, or cost-push inflation.

e. An increase in aggregate supply, however, has the beneficial effects of improving real domestic output and employment while simultaneously reducing the price level.

■ **HINTS AND TIPS**

1. Demand and supply are the tools used to explain what determines the economy's real output and price level. These tools, however, are different from the demand and supply used in Chapter 3 to explain what determines the output and price of a *particular* product. Instead of thinking about the quantity of a *particular* good or service demanded or supplied, it is necessary to think about the total or *aggregate* quantity of all final goods and services demanded (purchased) and supplied (produced). You will have no difficulty with the way demand and supply are used in this chapter once you switch from thinking about a *particular* good or service and its price to the *aggregate* of all final goods and services and its average price.

2. The aggregate supply curve has a strange shape because there are three ranges—horizontal, upsloping (intermediate), and vertical. Make sure you understand the rationale for each range. Also, the shape of the aggregate supply curve means that graphically an *increase* in aggregate supply will move aggregate supply both *downward* (in the horizontal range) and *outward* (in the upsloping and vertical ranges). The opposite is the case for a decrease in aggregate supply. Check your understanding of this point by referring to Figure 11-6 in the text.

3. Make sure you know the difference between a movement along an aggregate demand or supply curve and a shift in an aggregate demand or supply curve. Figures 11-3 and 11-6 in the text are extremely valuable summaries of the determinants of aggregate demand and aggregate supply that shift each curve.

■ IMPORTANT TERMS

aggregate demand (AD) curve

wealth or real balances effect

interest-rate effect

foreign purchases effect

determinants of aggregate demand

aggregate supply (AS) curve

determinants of aggregate supply

productivity

horizontal range

vertical range

intermediate range

equilibrium price level

equilibrium real domestic output

demand-pull inflation

ratchet effect

efficiency wages

menu costs

cost-push inflation

SELF-TEST

■ FILL-IN QUESTIONS

1. In the aggregate demand–aggregate supply model, the price level is (fixed, variable) _____, but in the aggregate expenditures model, the price level is

_____.

2. Aggregate demand and aggregate supply together determine the equilibrium real domestic (price, output) _____ and the equilibrium _____ level.

3. The aggregate demand curve shows the quantity of goods and services that will be (supplied, demanded) _____ or purchased at various price levels. It slopes (upward, downward) _____ because of the (wealth, consumption) _____ effect, the (profit, interest) _____-rate effect, and the (domestic, foreign) _____ purchases effects.

4. For the aggregate demand curve, an increase in the price level leads to a(n) (increase, decrease) _____ in the quantity of real domestic output, whereas a decrease in the price level leads to a(n) _____ in the quantity of real domestic output, assuming other things equal.

5. In the aggregate expenditures model, a lower price level would (raise, lower) _____ the consumption, investment, and aggregate expenditures curves, and the equilibrium level of real GDP would (rise, fall) _____. A higher price level would (raise, lower) _____ the consumption, investment, and aggregate expenditures curves, and the equilibrium level of real GDP would (rise, fall) _____. This (direct, inverse) _____ relationship between the price level and equilibrium real GDP in the aggregate expenditures model can be used to derive the aggregate (demand, supply) _____ curve (or schedule).

6. In the aggregate demand curve, when the price level changes, there is a (movement along, change in) _____ the curve. When the entire aggregate demand curve shifts, there is a change in (the quantity of real output demanded, aggregate demand) _____.

7. List the determinants of aggregate demand from changes in consumer spending:

a. _____

b. _____

c. _____

d. _____

8. List the determinants of aggregate demand from changes in investment spending:

a. _____

b. _____

c. _____

d. _____

e. _____

9. Aggregate demand can also shift because of changes in government (spending, regulation) _____; it may also shift because of a change in national income abroad or exchange rates that affect net (import, export) _____ spending.

10. If the price level were constant, an increase in the aggregate expenditures curve would shift the aggregate demand curve to the (right, left) _____ by an amount equal to the upward shift in aggregate expenditures times the (interest rate, multiplier) _____. A decrease in the aggregate expenditures curve would shift the aggregate demand curve to the (right, left) _____ by an amount equal to the (upward, downward) _____ shift in aggregate expenditures times the (interest rate, multiplier) _____.

11. The aggregate supply curve shows the quantity of goods and services that will be (demanded, supplied) _____ or produced at various price levels. In the horizontal range of the aggregate supply curve, as domestic output increases, the price level (is constant, increases) _____; in the intermediate range, as domestic output increases, the price level _____; and in the vertical range, domestic output remains constant and the price level _____.

12. The basic cause of a decrease in aggregate supply is a(n) (increase, decrease) _____ in the per-unit costs of producing goods and services, and the basic cause of an increase in aggregate supply is a(n) _____ in the per-unit costs of production, all other things equal.

13. Aggregate supply shift may result from
a. a change in input prices caused by a change in

(1) _____

(2) _____

(3) _____
b. from a change in (consumption, productivity) _____

_____
c. from a change in the legal and institutional environment caused by a change in

(1) _____

(2) _____

14. The equilibrium real domestic output and price level are found at the (zero values, intersection) _____ of the aggregate demand and the aggregate supply curves. At this price level, the aggregate quantity of goods and services purchased (demanded) is (greater than, less than, equal to) _____ the aggregate quantity of goods and services produced (supplied). And at this real domestic output, the prices producers are willing to (pay, accept) _____ are equal to the prices buyers are willing to _____.

15. Were the actual real domestic output greater than the equilibrium domestic output, producers would find that their inventories were (increasing, decreasing) _____ and they would (expand, reduce) _____ their production. At less than the equilibrium domestic output, producers would find that their inventories were (increasing, decreasing) _____ and they would (expand, reduce) _____ their production.

16. When the economy is producing in the horizontal range of aggregate supply, an increase in aggregate demand will (increase, decrease, have no effect on) _____ real domestic output and will _____ the price

level; in the intermediate range, an increase in aggregate demand will _____ real domestic output and will _____ the price level; and in the vertical range, an increase in aggregate demand will _____ real domestic output and will _____ the price level.

17. Were aggregate demand to increase, the flatter the aggregate supply curve, the (greater, smaller) _____ would be the multiplier effect on the real equilibrium GDP and the _____ would be the effect on the equilibrium price level; the steeper the aggregate supply curve, the _____ would be the multiplier effect on the equilibrium real GDP and the _____ would be the effect on the equilibrium price level.

18. The tendency for prices to be inflexible downward when aggregate demand decreases is called the (interest-rate, ratchet) _____ effect. This effect occurs because wage contracts are (short, long) _____-term, workers are paid (efficiency, inefficiency) _____ wages, businesses have (invested in, reduced) _____ training for workers, there is a (maximum, minimum) _____ wage, businesses experience menu (benefits, costs) _____, and there is fear of (price, cold) _____ wars.

19. An increase in aggregate supply will (increase, decrease) _____ real domestic output and _____ the price level. A decrease in aggregate supply will (increase, decrease) _____ real output and _____ the price level.

20. Demand-pull inflation is the result of a(n) (increase, decrease) _____ in aggregate demand and is accompanied by a (rise, fall) _____ in real output, but cost-push inflation is the result of a(n) _____ in aggregate supply and is accompanied by a _____ in real output.

■ **TRUE-FALSE QUESTIONS**

Circle the T if the statement is true, the F if it is false.

1. Aggregation in macroeconomics is the process of combining all the prices of individual products and services into a price level and merging all the equilibrium quantities into real domestic output. **T F**

2. The aggregate demand curve slopes downward. **T F**

3. A fall in the price level increases the real value of financial assets with fixed money values and, as a result, increases spending by the holders of these assets. **T F**

4. A fall in the price level reduces the demand for money in the economy and drives interest rates upward. **T F**

5. A rise in the price level of an economy (relative to foreign price levels) tends to increase that economy's exports and to reduce its imports of goods and services. **T F**

6. The higher the price level, the smaller the wealth of consumers and the lower the consumption schedule (curve). **T F**

7. An increase in the price level will shift the aggregate expenditures schedule upward. **T F**

8. A change in aggregate demand is caused by a change in the price level, *other things equal.* **T F**

9. A fall in excess capacity, or unused existing capital goods, will retard the demand for new capital goods and therefore reduce aggregate demand. **T F**

10. The wealth effect is one of the determinants of aggregate demand. **T F**

11. A high level of household indebtedness will tend to increase consumption spending and aggregate demand. **T F**

12. Appreciation of the dollar relative to foreign currencies will tend to increase net exports and aggregate demand. **T F**

13. The aggregate supply curve has a downsloping range. **T F**

14. When the determinants of aggregate supply change, they alter the per-unit production cost and thereby aggregate supply. **T F**

15. Productivity is a measure of real output per unit of input. **T F**

16. A change in the degree of market power or monopoly power held by sellers of resources can affect input prices and aggregate supply. **T F**

17. Per-unit production cost is determined by dividing total input cost by units of output. **T F**

18. At the equilibrium price level, the real domestic output purchased is equal to the real domestic output produced. **T F**

19. In the intermediate range on the aggregate supply curve, an increase in aggregate demand will increase both the price level and the real domestic output. **T F**

20. In the horizontal range on the aggregate supply curve, an increase in aggregate demand will have no effect on the real equilibrium GDP of the economy and will raise its price level. **T F**

21. The greater the increase in the price level that results from an increase in aggregate demand, the greater will be the increase in the equilibrium real GDP. **T F**

22. Inflation has no effect on the strength of the multiplier. **T F**

23. A decrease in aggregate demand will lower the price level by the same amount as an equal increase in aggregate demand would have raised it because of the ratchet effect. **T F**

24. An increase in aggregate supply increases both the equilibrium real domestic output and the full-employment output of the economy. **T F**

25. A decrease in aggregate supply is "doubly good" because it increases the real domestic output and prevents inflation. **T F**

■ **MULTIPLE-CHOICE QUESTIONS**

Circle the letter that corresponds to the best answer.

1. The aggregate demand curve is the relationship between the
  (a) price level and the real domestic output purchased
  (b) price level and the real domestic output produced
  (c) price level and what producers will supply
  (d) real domestic output purchased and the real domestic output produced

2. When the price level rises,
  (a) holders of financial assets with fixed money values increase their spending
  (b) the demand for money and interest rates rise
  (c) spending which is sensitive to interest-rate changes increases
  (d) holders of financial assets with fixed money values have more purchasing power

3. The slope of the aggregate demand curve is the result of
  (a) the wealth effect
  (b) the interest-rate effect
  (c) the foreign purchases effect
  (d) all of the above effects

4. If the price level in the aggregate expenditures model were lower, the consumption and aggregate expenditures curves would be
  (a) lower, and the equilibrium real GDP would be smaller
  (b) lower, and the equilibrium real GDP would be larger
  (c) higher, and the equilibrium real GDP would be larger
  (d) higher, and the equilibrium real GDP would be smaller

5. A decrease in the price level will shift the
  (a) consumption, investment, and net exports curves downward
  (b) consumption, investment, and net exports curves upward
  (c) consumption and investment curves upward, but the net exports curve downward
  (d) consumption and net export curves upward, but the investment curve downward

6. The aggregate demand curve will tend to be increased by
(a) a decrease in the price level
(b) an increase in the price level
(c) an increase in the excess capacity of factories
(d) a depreciation in the value of the U.S. dollar

7. A sharp decline in the real value of stock prices, which is independent of a change in the price level, would best be an example of
(a) the wealth effect
(b) the real balance effect
(c) a change in real wealth
(d) a change in household indebtedness

8. An increase in aggregate expenditures shifts the aggregate demand curve to the
(a) right by the amount of the increase in aggregate expenditures
(b) right by the amount of the increase in aggregate expenditures times the multiplier
(c) left by the amount of the increase in aggregate expenditures
(d) left by the amount of the increase in aggregate expenditures times the multiplier

9. The aggregate supply curve is the relationship between the
(a) price level and the real domestic output purchased
(b) price level and the real domestic output produced
(c) price level which producers are willing to accept and the price level purchasers are willing to pay
(d) real domestic output purchased and the real domestic output produced

10. In the intermediate range, the aggregate supply curve is
(a) upsloping
(b) downsloping
(c) vertical
(d) horizontal

Suppose that real domestic output in an economy is 50 units, the quantity of inputs is 10, and the price of each input is $2. Answer Questions 11, 12, 13, and 14 on the basis of this information.

11. The level of productivity in this economy is
(a) 5
(b) 4
(c) 3
(d) 2

12. The per unit cost of production is
(a) $0.40
(b) $0.50
(c) $2.50
(d) $3.50

13. If real domestic output in the economy rose to 60 units, then per-unit production costs would
(a) remain unchanged and aggregate supply would remain unchanged
(b) increase and aggregate supply would decrease

(c) decrease and aggregate supply would increase
(d) decrease and aggregate supply would decrease

14. All else equal, if the price of each input increases from $2 to $4, productivity would
(a) decrease from $4 to $2 and aggregate supply would decrease
(b) decrease from $5 to $3 and aggregate supply would decrease
(c) decrease from $4 to $2 and aggregate supply would increase
(d) remain unchanged and aggregate supply would decrease

15. If the prices of imported resources increase, then this event would most likely
(a) decrease aggregate supply
(b) increase aggregate supply
(c) increase aggregate demand
(d) decrease aggregate demand

16. If Congress passed much stricter laws to control the air pollution from business, this action would tend to
(a) increase per-unit production costs and shift the aggregate supply curve to the right
(b) increase per-unit production costs and shift the aggregate supply curve to the left
(c) increase per-unit production costs and shift the aggregate demand curve to the left
(d) decrease per-unit production costs and shift the aggregate supply curve to the left

17. An increase in business taxes will tend to
(a) decrease aggregate demand but not change aggregate supply
(b) decrease aggregate supply but not change aggregate demand
(c) decrease aggregate demand and decrease aggregate supply
(d) decrease aggregate supply and increase aggregate demand

18. If the real domestic output is less than the equilibrium real domestic output, producers find
(a) their inventories decreasing and expand their production
(b) their inventories increasing and expand their production
(c) their inventories decreasing and contract their production
(d) their inventories increasing and contract their production

Answer Questions 19, 20, 21, and 22 on the basis of the following aggregate demand–aggregate supply schedule for a hypothetical economy.

Real domestic output demanded (in billions)	Price level	Real domestic output supplied (in billions)
$1,500	170	$4,000
$2,000	150	$4,000
$2,500	125	$3,500
$3,000	100	$3,000
$3,500	75	$2,500
$4,000	75	$2,000

19. The equilibrium price level and quantity of real domestic output will be
   (a) 100 and $2,500
   (b) 100 and $3,000
   (c) 125 and $3,500
   (d) 150 and $4,000

20. The horizontal range of the aggregate supply curve is associated with the quantity supplied of
   (a) $4,000
   (b) $4,000 and $3,500
   (c) $3,500 and $3,000
   (d) $2,500 and $2,000

21. If the quantity of real domestic output demanded increased by $2,000 at each price level, the new equilibrium price level and quantity of real domestic output would be
   (a) 175 and $4,000
   (b) 150 and $4,000
   (c) 125 and $3,500
   (d) 100 and $3,000

22. Using the original data from the table, if the quantity of real domestic output demanded *increased* by $500 and the quantity of real domestic output supplied *decreased* by $500 at each price level, the new equilibrium price level and quantity of real domestic output would be
   (a) 175 and $4,000
   (b) 150 and $4,000
   (c) 125 and $3,000
   (d) 100 and $3,500

23. When the economy is in the horizontal range, an increase in aggregate demand will
   (a) increase the price level and have no effect on real domestic output
   (b) increase the real domestic output and have no effect on the price level
   (c) increase both real output and the price level
   (d) increase the price level and decrease the real domestic output

24. An increase in aggregate demand will increase the equilibrium real GDP if the economy is operating in the
   (a) horizontal range only
   (b) intermediate range only
   (c) horizontal or intermediate ranges
   (d) vertical range only

25. An increase in aggregate demand will increase both the equilibrium real GDP and the price level if the economy is operating in the
   (a) horizontal range
   (b) intermediate range
   (c) intermediate or vertical ranges
   (d) vertical range

26. In the aggregate demand–aggregate supply model, an increase in the price level will
   (a) increase the marginal propensity to consume
   (b) increase the strength of the multiplier
   (c) decrease the strength of the multiplier
   (d) have no effect on the strength of the multiplier

27. If aggregate demand decreases but the price level does not fall as much as would be expected if price were flexible, then this situation could be the result of
   (a) an increase in aggregate supply
   (b) the foreign purchases effect
   (c) lower interest rates
   (d) a ratchet effect

28. The ratchet effect is the result of
   (a) a price level that is inflexible upward
   (b) a price level that is inflexible downward
   (c) a domestic output that cannot be increased
   (d) a domestic output that cannot be decreased

29. An increase in aggregate supply will
   (a) reduce the price level and real domestic output
   (b) reduce the price level and increase the real domestic output
   (c) increase the price level and real domestic output
   (d) reduce the price level and have no effect on real domestic output

30. If there were cost-push inflation in the economy that decreased aggregate supply,
   (a) both the real domestic output and the price level would decrease
   (b) the real domestic output would increase and rises in the price level would become smaller
   (c) the real domestic output would decrease and the price level would rise
   (d) both the real domestic output and rises in the price level would become greater

■ **PROBLEMS**

1. Following is an aggregate supply schedule.

Price level	Real domestic output supplied
250	2,000
225	2,000
200	1,900
175	1,700
150	1,400
125	1,000
125	500
125	0

   a. The economy is in the
   (1) horizontal range when the real domestic output is
   between _____ and _____.
   (2) vertical range when the real domestic output is
   _____ and the price level is _____
   or more.
   (3) intermediate range when the real domestic output
   is between _____ and _____.
   b. Plot this aggregate supply schedule on the accompanying graph.
   c. The following table has three aggregate demand schedules.

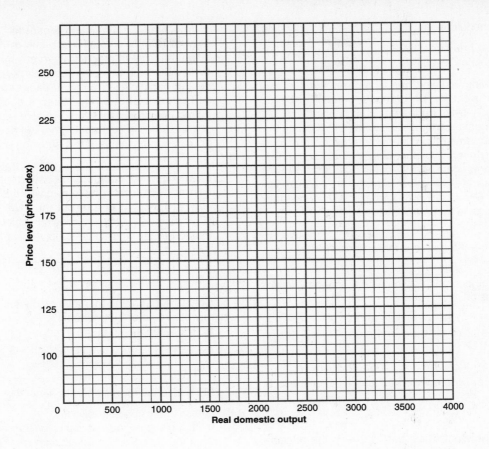

Price level (1)	*Real domestic output demanded*		
	(2)	(3)	(4)
250	1,400	1,900	400
225	1,500	2,000	500
200	1,600	2,100	600
175	1,700	2,200	700
150	1,800	2,300	800
125	1,900	2,400	900
100	2,000	2,500	1,000

(1) On the graph, plot the aggregate demand curve shown in columns 1 and 2; label this curve **AD₁**. At this level of aggregate demand, the equilibrium real domestic output is _____

and the equilibrium price level is _____.
(2) On the same graph, plot the aggregate demand curve shown in columns 1 and 3; label this curve

AD₂. The equilibrium real domestic output is _____

and the equilibrium price level is _____.
(3) On the same graph, plot the aggregate demand curve shown in columns 1 and 4; label it **AD₃**. The equi-

librium real domestic output is _____

and the equilibrium price level is _____.

2. Column 1 of the following table shows the real GDP an economy might produce.

(1) Real GDP	(2) $AE_{1.20}$	(3) $AE_{1.00}$	(4) $AE_{0.80}$
$2,100	$2,110	$2,130	$2,150
2,200	2,200	2,220	2,240
2,300	2,290	2,310	2,330
2,400	2,380	2,400	2,420
2,500	2,470	2,490	2,510
2,600	2,560	2,580	2,600

a. If the price level in this economy were $1.20, the aggregate expenditures (AE) at each real GDP would be those shown in column 2 and the equilibrium real

GDP would be $_____.
b. If the price level were $1.00, the aggregate expenditures at each real GDP would be those shown in column

3 and the equilibrium real GDP would be $_____.
c. If the price level were $0.80, the aggregate expenditures at each real GDP would be those shown in column

4 and the equilibrium real GDP would be $_____.
d. Show in the following schedule the equilibrium real GDP at each of the three price levels.

Price level	Equilibrium real GDP
$1.20	$_____
1.00	_____
0.80	_____

(1) This schedule is the _____ schedule.

(2) The equilibrium real GDP is _____ related to the price level.

3. In the following list, what will most likely happen as a result of each event to (1) aggregate demand (AD); (2) aggregate supply (AS); (3) the equilibrium price level (*P*); and (4) equilibrium real domestic output (*Q*)? Assume that all other things remain constant when the event occurs and that the economy is operating in the intermediate range of the aggregate supply curve. Use the following symbols to indicate the expected effects: *I* = increase, *D* = decrease, *S* = remains the same, and *U* = uncertain.
 a. A decrease in labor productivity.

AD_____   AS_____   *P*_____   *Q*_____
 b. A fall in the interest rate for business loans.

AD_____   AS_____   *P*_____   *Q*_____
 c. Consumer incomes decline as the economy moves into a recession.

AD_____   AS_____   *P*_____   *Q*_____
 d. The price of oil on the world market falls to a low level.

AD_____   AS_____   *P*_____   *Q*_____
 e. There is an appreciation in the value of the U.S. dollar.

AD_____   AS_____   *P*_____   *Q*_____

4. Following are hypothetical data showing the relationships between the real domestic output and the quantity of input resources needed to produce each level of output.

Output	Input	Productivity		Per unit cost		
		(1)	(2)	(3)	(4)	(5)
2500	500	____	____	____	____	____
2000	400	____	____	____	____	____
1500	300	____	____	____	____	____

 a. In column 1, compute the level of productivity at each level of real domestic output.
 b. In column 2, compute the level of productivity if there is a doubling in the quantity of inputs required to produce each level of output.

 c. In column 3, compute the per-unit production cost at each level of output if each unit of input costs $15, given the level of productivity in column 1.
 d. In column 4, compute the new per-unit production cost at each level of output if each unit of input costs $15, given that there has been a doubling in the required quantity of inputs to produce each level of output as shown in column 2. What will happen to the aggregate supply curve if this situation occurs?_____

_____

 e. In column 5, compute the new per-unit production cost at each level of output, given that input price is now $10 instead of $15 but the level of productivity stays as it was originally shown in column 1. What will happen to the aggregate supply curve if this situation occurs?_____

_____

5. Columns 1 and 2 in the table below are the aggregate supply schedule of an economy.
 a. The economy is in the

(1) vertical range when its real GDP is $_____

and the price level is $_____ or higher.

(2) horizontal range when its real GDP is $_____

or less and its price level is $_____.
 b. If the aggregate demand in the economy were columns 1 and 3, the equilibrium real GDP would be

$_____ and the equilibrium price level would be

$_____, and if aggregate demand should increase by $100 to that shown in columns 1 and 4,

the equilibrium real GDP would increase by $_____

and the price level would be _____.
 c. Should aggregate demand be that shown in columns 1 and 5, the equilibrium real GDP would be

$_____ and the equilibrium price would be

$_____, and if aggregate demand should increase by $100 to that shown in columns 1 and 6,

the equilibrium real GDP would increase by $_____

and the price level would rise to $_____.

(1) Price level	(2) Real GDP	(3) AD$_1$	(4) AD$_2$	(5) AD$_3$	(6) AD$_4$	(7) AD$_5$	(8) AD$_6$
$2.60	$2,390	$ 840	$ 940	$1,900	$2,000	$2,190	$2,290
2.40	2,390	940	1,040	2,000	2,100	2,290	2,390
2.20	2,390	1,040	1,140	2,100	2,200	2,390	2,490
2.00	2,390	1,140	1,240	2,200	2,300	2,490	2,590
1.90	2,350	1,190	1,290	2,250	2,350	2,540	2,640
1.80	2,300	1,240	1,340	2,300	2,400	2,590	2,690
1.60	2,200	1,340	1,440	2,400	2,500	2,690	2,790
1.40	2,090	1,440	1,540	2,500	2,600	2,790	2,890
1.20	1,970	1,540	1,640	2,600	2,700	2,890	2,990
1.00	1,840	1,640	1,740	2,700	2,800	2,990	3,090
1.00	1,740	1,640	1,740	2,700	2,800	2,990	3,090
1.00	1,640	1,640	1,740	2,700	2,800	2,990	3,090

d. And if aggregate demand were that shown in columns 1 and 7, the equilibrium real GDP would be

$ _____ and the equilibrium price level would

be $ _____, but if aggregate demand increased by $100 to that shown in columns 1 and 8, the price level would rise to $ _____ and the equilibrium real GDP would _____.

6. The following diagram shows an aggregate supply curve and six aggregate demand curves.

a. The movements of the aggregate demand curves from AD_1 to AD_2, from AD_3 to AD_4, and from AD_5 to AD_6 all portray (increases, decreases) _____ in aggregate demand.

(1) The movement from AD_1 to AD_2 increases the (real domestic output, price level) _____ but does not change the _____.

(2) The movement from AD_3 to AD_4 will (raise, lower) _____ the price level and will (expand, contract) _____ the real domestic output.

(3) The movement from AD_5 to AD_6 will _____

_____.

b. The movements of the aggregate demand curves to the left all portray (increases, decreases) _____ in aggregate demand.

(1) If prices are flexible in a downward direction, what effects will these changes in aggregate demand have upon the real domestic output and the price level?

_____

_____

(2) If prices are *not* flexible in a downward direction, what effects will these changes in aggregate demand have? _____

_____

7. The following diagram shows two aggregate supply curves and three aggregate demand curves.

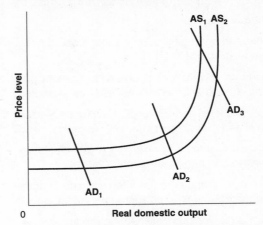

a. The movement of the aggregate supply curve from AS_1 to AS_2 represents a(n) (increase, decrease) _____ in aggregate supply.

(1) If the price level is flexible downward and upward, this change in aggregate supply in each of the three ranges along the aggregate supply curve will (raise, lower) _____ the price level and (expand, contract) _____ the real domestic output.

(2) But if prices are inflexible in a downward direction, this change in aggregate supply will (increase, decrease) _____ real domestic output but (will, will not) _____ affect the price level.

b. The movement of aggregate supply from AS_2 to AS_1 portrays a(n) _____ in aggregate supply and in each of the three ranges will _____ the price level and _____ the real domestic output.

■ **SHORT ANSWER AND ESSAY QUESTIONS**

1. What is the aggregate demand curve? Draw a graph of one and explain its features.

2. Explain
  (a) the interest-rate effect
  (b) the wealth effect
  (c) the foreign purchases effect of a change in the price level on the quantity of goods and services demanded in an economy

3. What roles do the expectations of consumers and businesses play in influencing aggregate demand?

4. Explain the difference between the wealth effect and "a change in the real value of consumer wealth" for the interpretation of aggregate demand.

5. What is the effect of an increase in aggregate expenditures on the aggregate demand curve? Explain in words and with a graph.

6. The aggregate supply curve is divided into three distinct ranges. Describe the slope of this curve in each of the three ranges. What conditions prevail in the economy in each of the ranges?

7. Why does the aggregate supply curve slope upward in the intermediate range?

8. How does an increase or decrease in per-unit production costs change aggregate supply? Give examples.

9. How does the legal and institutional environment affect the price level and real domestic output? Give examples.

10. Explain how a change in business taxes affects aggregate demand and aggregate supply.

11. Describe how changes in the international economy influence aggregate demand or aggregate supply.

12. What is the relationship between the production possibilities curve and aggregate supply?

13. What real domestic output is the equilibrium real domestic output? Why will business firms that produce the domestic output reduce or expand their production when they find themselves producing more or less than the equilibrium output?

14. What are the effects on the real domestic output and the price level when aggregate demand increases in each of the three ranges along the aggregate supply curve?

15. How are the three ranges of the aggregate supply curve, the price level, and the multiplier related? What is the relationship between the effect of an increase in aggregate demand on real GDP and the rise in the price level that accompanies it?

16. If prices were as flexible downward as they are upward, what would be the effects on real domestic output and the price level of a decrease in aggregate demand in each of the three ranges along the aggregate supply curve?

17. Prices in the economy tend to be "sticky" or inflexible in a downward direction. Why? Explain in terms of wages, prices, and costs.

18. What are the effects on the real domestic output and the price level of a decrease in aggregate supply? What are the effects of an increase in aggregate supply on the real domestic output, the price level, and the maximum real output the economy is able to produce?

19. Why is a decrease in aggregate supply "doubly bad" and an increase in aggregate supply "doubly good"?

20. Using the aggregate demand and aggregate supply concepts, explain the difference between demand-pull and cost-push inflation.

ANSWERS

Chapter 11 Aggregate Demand and Aggregate Supply

FILL-IN QUESTIONS

1. variable, fixed
2. output, price
3. demanded, downward, wealth, interest, foreign
4. decrease, increase
5. raise, rise, lower, fall, inverse, demand
6. movement along, aggregate demand
7. *a.* consumer wealth; *b.* consumer expectations; *c.* household indebtedness; *d.* personal taxes (any order)
8. *a.* interest rates; *b.* expected returns on investment; *c.* business taxes; *d.* technology; *e.* degree of excess capacity (any order)
9. spending, export
10. right, multiplier, left, downward, multiplier
11. supplied, is constant, increases, increases
12. increase, decrease
13. *a.* (1) domestic resource availability, (2) prices of imported resources, (3) market power (any order); *b.* productivity; *c.* (1) business taxes and subsidies, (2) government regulation (either order)
14. intersection, equal to, accept, pay
15. increasing, reduce, decreasing, expand
16. increase, have no effect on, increase, increase, have no effect on, increase
17. greater, smaller, smaller, greater
18. ratchet, short, efficiency, invested in, minimum, costs, price
19. increase, decrease, decrease, increase
20. increase, rise, decrease, fall

TRUE-FALSE QUESTIONS

1. T, p. 221	**10.** F, p. 225	**19.** T, p. 234
2. T, pp. 221-222	**11.** F, p. 225	**20.** F, p. 234
3. T, p. 222	**12.** F, p. 227	**21.** F, pp. 234-236
4. F, pp. 222-223	**13.** F, pp. 228-229	**22.** F, pp. 234-236
5. F, p. 223	**14.** T, p. 229-230	**23.** F, p. 236
6. T, p. 223	**15.** T, p. 232	**24.** T, p. 239
7. F, p. 223	**16.** T, pp. 231-232	**25.** F, pp. 237-239
8. F, pp. 223-224	**17.** T, pp. 232	
9. F, p. 226	**18.** T, pp. 233-234	

MULTIPLE-CHOICE QUESTIONS

1. a, pp. 221-222	**11.** a, p. 232	**21.** b, p. 234
2. b, pp. 222-223	**12.** a, p. 232	**22.** c, pp. 234, 237-239
3. d, pp. 222-223	**13.** c, p. 232	**23.** b, p. 234
4. c, p. 223	**14.** d, p. 232	**24.** c, p. 234
5. b, p. 223	**15.** a, p. 231	**25.** b, p. 234
6. d, pp. 226-227	**16.** b, p. 232	**26.** c, pp. 234-236
7. c, pp. 224-225	**17.** c, p. 232	**27.** d, p. 236
8. b, p. 227	**18.** a, p. 234	**28.** b, p. 236
9. b, p. 227	**19.** b, pp. 233-234	**29.** b, pp. 237-239
10. a, p. 229	**20.** d, pp. 228-229	**30.** c, pp. 237-239

PROBLEMS

1. *a.* (1) 0, 1,000, (2) 2,000, 225, (3) 1,000, 2,000; *c.* (1) 1,700, 175, (2) 2,000, 225, (3) 900, 125

2. *a.* 2,200; *b.* 2,400; *c.* 2,600; *d.* 2,200, 2,400, 2,600, (1) aggregate demand, (2) inversely

3. *a.* S, D, I, D; *b.* I, S, I, I; *c.* D, S, D, D; *d.* I, I, U, I; *e.* D, I, D, U

4. *a.* 5, 5, 5; *b.* 2.5, 2.5, 2.5; *c.* $3, $3, $3; *d.* $6, $6, it will decrease; *e.* $2, $2, $2, it will increase

5. *a.* (1) 2,390, 2.00, (2) 1,840, 1.00; *b.* 1,640, 1.00, 100, remain constant; *c.* 2,300, 1.80, 50, 1.90; *d.* 2,390, 2.20, 2.40, remain constant

6. *a.* increases, (1) real domestic output, price level, (2) raise, expand, (3) increase the price level but will not affect domestic output; *b.* decreases, (1) decrease the price level in the vertical and intermediate ranges and decrease domestic output in the intermediate and horizontal ranges, (2) decrease only output in the intermediate, vertical, and horizontal ranges

7. *a.* increase, (1) lower, expand, (2) increase, will not; *b.* decrease, increase, decrease

SHORT ANSWER AND ESSAY QUESTIONS

1. pp. 221-222
2. pp. 222-223
3. pp. 225-226
4. pp. 224-225
5. pp. 227-228
6. pp. 228-229
7. p. 229
8. pp. 230-231
9. p. 232
10. pp. 226, 232
11. pp. 226-227, 231
12. p. 239
13. pp. 233-234
14. p. 234
15. pp. 234-236
16. p. 236
17. pp. 236-237
18. pp. 237-239
19. pp. 237-239
20. pp. 234, 237

CHAPTER 12

Fiscal Policy

Principles of economics are generalizations about how the economy works. These principles are studied to help devise policies to solve real problems. Over the past 100 years or so, the most serious macroeconomic problems have been those resulting from the swings of the business cycle. Learning what determines the equilibrium level of real output and prices in an economy and what causes them to fluctuate makes it possible to find ways to achieve maximum output, full employment, and stable prices. In short, macroeconomic principles suggest policies to lessen both recession and inflation in an economy.

As you will discover in Chapter 12, government can use *fiscal policy* to influence the economy's output, employment, and price level. These policies involve the use of the Federal government's spending and taxing powers to improve economic conditions. The brief first section of this chapter explains how Congress, in the Employment Act of 1946, committed the Federal government to achieving three goals: economic growth, full employment, and stable prices. This act also established the Council of Economic Advisors (CEA) to advise the president and the Joint Economic Committee (JEC) to advise Congress on national economic policies.

The second section of the chapter discusses *discretionary fiscal policy,* which can be either *expansionary* or *contractionary.* Here you will learn how these fiscal policies affect aggregate demand and the Federal budget. Expansionary fiscal policy is used to stimulate the economy and pull it out of a slump or recession. This type of policy can be achieved by increasing government spending, decreasing taxes, or some combination of the two. Contractionary fiscal policy is enacted to counter inflationary pressure in the economy. The policy actions taken to dampen inflation include cutting government spending, raising taxes, or a combination of the two. As you will learn, each policy can have a significant effect on aggregate demand and the Federal budget. If the government has a budget deficit or surplus, the way the government finances it can affect the economy's operation as much as the size of the deficit or surplus.

Discretionary fiscal policy requires that Congress take action to change tax rates, transfer payment programs, or purchases of goods and services. *Non*discretionary fiscal policy does not require Congress to take any action and is a *built-in stabilizer* of the economy. You should be sure that you understand *why* net taxes increase when the GDP rises and decrease when the GDP falls and *how* this tends to stabilize the economy.

Unfortunately, nondiscretionary fiscal policy by itself may not be able to eliminate any recessionary or inflationary gap that might develop, and discretionary fiscal policy may be necessary if the economy is to produce its full-employment GDP and avoid inflation. The built-in stabilizers make it more difficult to use discretionary fiscal policy to achieve this goal because they create the illusion that the Federal government's policy is expansionary or contractionary when in fact its policy is just the opposite.

The illusions created by the built-in stabilizers have led economists to develop a *full-employment budget* and to distinguish between a *cyclical deficit* and a *structural deficit.* This analysis enables economists to determine whether Federal fiscal policy is expansionary or contractionary and to determine what policy should be enacted to improve the economy's economic performance.

Fiscal policy is not without its *problems, criticisms,* or *complications.* There are timing problems in getting it implemented, and there are political problems in getting it accepted. In addition, there are three major criticisms of or complications with fiscal policy. Some economists are concerned that expansionary fiscal policy, which requires the Federal government to borrow money, will raise interest rates and crowd out investment spending, thus reducing the expansionary effect of the fiscal policy. A second complication arises from the connection of the domestic economy to the world economy. Aggregate demand shocks from abroad or a net export effect may increase or decrease the effectiveness of a given fiscal policy. The third concern is whether an expansionary fiscal policy might actually increase the price level and have little effect on real output, especially if the economy is operating near its full-employment level of output.

Most of the discussion of fiscal policy focuses on its effects on aggregate demand. Some economists, however, argue that a reduction in tax rates will not only increase aggregate demand but also expand *aggregate supply.* In this way, fiscal policy can be used to increase real GDP with little or no rise in the price level.

By mastering this chapter on fiscal policy, you will gain an understanding of one of the two major policies used to influence outcomes from the economy. Mastery of this chapter will also prepare you for learning about monetary policy, a topic for Part 3 of the text.

■ **CHECKLIST**

When you have studied this chapter you should be able to

☐ State the responsibility imposed on the Federal government by the Employment Act of 1946 and the roles of the CEA and JEC in fulfilling this responsibility.

☐ Distinguish between discretionary and nondiscretionary fiscal policy.

☐ Explain expansionary fiscal policy and the effect of different policy options on aggregate demand.

☐ Describe contractionary fiscal policy and the effect of different policy options on aggregate demand.

☐ Explain how the expansionary effect of a budget deficit depends on the method used to finance it.

☐ Describe how the deflationary effect of a budget surplus depends on the method used to finance it.

☐ Assess whether it is preferable to use government spending or taxes to eliminate recession and inflation.

☐ Indicate how the built-in stabilizers help to eliminate recession and inflationary pressures.

☐ Describe the relationship among progressive, proportional, and regressive tax systems and the built-in stability of the economy.

☐ Distinguish between the actual budget and the full-employment budget.

☐ Define structural deficit and cyclical deficit and relate them to the full-employment budget.

☐ Make historical comparisons between the full-employment budget and actual budget since 1962.

☐ Evaluate the economic effects of a balanced-budget amendment.

☐ Outline three timing problems that may arise with fiscal policy.

☐ Discuss four political problems with fiscal policy.

☐ Explain and use a graph to illustrate the crowding-out effect of an expansionary fiscal policy.

☐ State the major criticisms of the crowding-out effect.

☐ Show with a graph how the effects of an expansionary fiscal policy differ across different ranges of the aggregate supply curve.

☐ Describe two ways that the effectiveness of fiscal policy changes from interdependency with the world economy.

☐ Explain how supply-side fiscal policy affects real GDP and the price level.

■ **CHAPTER OUTLINE**

1. Fiscal policy is the manipulation by the Federal government of its expenditures and tax receipts in order to expand or contract the economy; and by doing this manipulation, the Federal government either increases its real output (and employment) or decreases its rate of inflation.

2. The Employment Act of 1946 set the goals of fiscal policy in the United States and provided for a Council of Economic Advisers to the president and the Joint Economic Committee.

3. *Discretionary fiscal policy* involves changes in government spending or taxation by Congress which is designed to change the level of real GDP, employment, incomes, or the price level. Specific action needs to be taken by Congress to initiate this policy, in contrast to nondiscretionary fiscal policy that occurs automatically (see item 4 below).

a. *Expansionary fiscal policy* is generally used to counteract the negative economic effects of a recession or cyclical downturn in the economy (a decline in real GDP and rising unemployment). The purpose of the policy is to stimulate the economy by increasing aggregate demand. Three policy options are used: an **increase in government spending;** a **reduction in taxes** (which increases consumer spending); or a **combination** of an increase in government spending and a tax reduction. These policy actions will create a ***budget deficit*** if the budget were in balance before the policy actions were taken. The stimulative effect on the economy from the initial increase in spending from the policy change will be increased by the multiplier effect.

b. *Contractionary fiscal policy* is a restrictive form of fiscal policy generally used to control demand-pull inflation. The purpose of this policy is to reduce aggregate demand pressures that increase the price level. Three policy options are used: a **decrease in government spending;** an **increase in taxes** (which reduces consumer spending); or a **combination** of a reduction in government spending and a tax increase. If the government budget is balanced before the policy actions are taken, it will create a ***budget surplus.*** The contractionary effect on the economy from the initial reduction in spending from the policy actions will be reinforced by the multiplier effect.

c. In addition to the size of the deficit or surplus, the manner in which government finances its deficit or disposes of its surplus affects the level of total spending in the economy.

(1) To finance a deficit, the government can either borrow money from the public or issue new money to creditors, with the latter action being more expansionary.

(2) Budget surpluses may be used for debt reduction, or the funds may be impounded, with the latter action being more contractionary.

d. Whether government purchases or taxes should be altered to reduce recession and inflation depends to a large extent on whether an expansion or a contraction of the public sector is desired.

4. In the U.S. economy, net tax revenues (tax revenues minus government transfer payments) are not a fixed amount or lump sum; they increase as the GDP rises and decrease as the GDP falls.

a. This net tax system serves as a *built-in stabilizer* of the economy because it reduces purchasing power during periods of inflation and expands purchasing during periods of recession.

(1) As GDP increases, the average tax rates will increase in progressive systems, remain constant in proportional systems, and decrease in regressive systems;

there is more built-in stability for the economy in progressive tax systems.

(2) Built-in stabilizers can only reduce and cannot eliminate economic fluctuations.

b. The *full-employment budget* is a better index than the actual budget of the direction of government fiscal policy because it indicates what the Federal budget deficit or surplus would be if the economy were to operate at full employment. In the case of a budget deficit, the full employment budget

(1) removes the cyclical portion that is produced by swings in the business cycle, and

(2) reveals the size of the structural deficit, indicating how expansionary fiscal policy was that year.

(3) Historical comparisons between the actual budget and full-employment budget show which years the discretionary fiscal policy has been expansionary in recent decades.

c. The large annual deficit the United States has experienced since the 1980s has led to calls for a balanced-budget amendment. In its strict form, this amendment would eliminate the use of discretionary fiscal policy to counter recessions and would be contractionary at a time when expansionary fiscal policy is needed.

5. Certain *problems, criticisms,* and *complications* arise in enacting and applying fiscal policy.

a. There will be problems of timing because it requires time to recognize the need for fiscal policy, to take the appropriate steps in the Congress, and for the action taken there to affect output, employment, and the rate of inflation in the economy.

b. There will also be political problems because

(1) the economy has goals other than full employment and stable prices,

(2) the fiscal policies of state and local government run counter to Federal fiscal policy,

(3) there is an expansionary bias (for budget deficits and against surpluses),

(4) there may be a political business cycle (if politicians lower taxes and increase expenditures before and then do the opposite after elections).

c. An expansionary fiscal policy may, by raising the level of interest rates in the economy, reduce (or crowd out) investment spending and weaken the effect of the policy on real GDP; but this crowding-out effect may be small and can be offset by an expansion in the nation's money supply.

d. The effect of an expansionary fiscal policy on the real GDP will also be weakened to the extent that it results in a rise in the price level (inflation). Aggregate demand and aggregate supply curves can be used to show how crowding out and inflation weaken the effects of an expansionary fiscal policy on real GDP.

e. The connection of the domestic economy to a world economy means that fiscal policy may be inappropriate or less effective because of aggregate demand shocks from the world economy or a net export effect that counteracts or reinforces domestic fiscal policy.

f. But an expansionary fiscal policy that includes a reduction in taxes (tax rates) may, by increasing aggregate supply in the economy, expand real GDP (and employment), and reduce inflation. Many economists, however, are skeptical about these supply-side effects.

■ **HINTS AND TIPS**

1. Fiscal policy is a broad concept that covers various taxation and spending policies of the Federal government; it is not limited to one policy. You will need to know the distinctions between the several kinds of fiscal policies. The main difference is between discretionary and nondiscretionary fiscal policy. *Discretionary* fiscal policy is *active* and means that Congress took specific actions to change taxes or government spending to influence the economy. It can also be *expansionary* or *contractionary. Nondiscretionary* fiscal policy is *passive,* or automatic, because changes in taxes or government spending will occur without specific action by Congress.

2. An increase in government spending that is equal to a cut in taxes will not have an equal effect on real GDP. To understand this point, assume that the MPC is .75, the increase in government spending is $8 billion, and the decrease in taxes is $8 billion. The multiplier would be 4 because it equals 1/(1 − .75). The increase in government spending will increase real GDP by $32 billion ($8 billion × 4). Of the $8 billion decrease in taxes, however, one-quarter of it will be saved ($6 billion × .25 = $2 billion) and just three-quarters will be spent ($8 billion × .75 = $6 billion). Thus, the tax cut results in an increase in *initial* spending in the economy of $6 billion, not $8 billion as was the case with the increase in government spending. The tax cut effect on real GDP is $24 billion ($6 × 4), not $32 billion.

3. A large part of the chapter deals with six problems (or criticisms and complications) of fiscal policy. Do not miss the big picture and get lost in the details of each one. The six include (a) timing, (b) politics, (c) crowding out, (d) inflation reducing the multiplier effect, (e) net export effect offsetting fiscal policy, and (f) supply-side effect offsetting or reinforcing demand-side effects.

■ **IMPORTANT TERMS**

fiscal policy	proportional tax
Employment Act of 1946	regressive tax
Council of Economic Advisers	actual budget
discretionary fiscal policy	full-employment budget
expansionary fiscal policy	cyclical deficit
budget deficit	structural deficit
contractionary fiscal policy	political business cycle
budget surplus	crowding-out effect
built-in stabilizers	net export effect
progressive tax	supply-side fiscal policy

SELF-TEST

■ FILL-IN QUESTIONS

1. The use of monetary and fiscal policy to reduce inflation and recession became national economic policy in the (Employment, Unemployment) _____ Act of 1946. To assist and advise the president, the act established the (Joint Economic Committee, Council of Economic Advisers) _____, and to aid Congress in investigating economic matters, the act established the _____.

2. Policy actions taken by Congress designed to change government spending or taxation are (discretionary, nondiscretionary) _____ fiscal policy, but when the policy takes effect automatically or independent of Congress, then it is _____ fiscal policy.

3. Expansionary fiscal policy is generally designed to (increase, decrease) _____ aggregate demand and thus _____ real GDP and employment in the economy. Contractionary fiscal policy is generally used to (increase, decrease) _____ aggregate demand and _____ the level of prices.

4. Expansionary fiscal policy can be achieved with an increase in (government spending, taxes) _____, a decrease in _____, or a combination of the two; contractionary fiscal policy can be achieved by a decrease in (government spending, taxes) _____, an increase in _____, or a combination of the two.

5. An increase of government spending of $5 billion from an expansionary fiscal policy for an economy ultimately produces an increase in real GDP of $20 billion. This magnified effect occurs because of the (multiplier, crowding-out) _____ effect, which has a size of (4, 5) _____ for this economy.

6. If the Federal budget is balanced and Congress passes legislation supporting an expansionary fiscal policy, then this action is likely to produce a budget (deficit, surplus) _____, but if Congress passes legislation supporting a contractionary fiscal policy, then the action will result in a budget _____.

7. If fiscal policy is to have a countercyclical effect, it probably will be necessary for the Federal government to incur a budget (surplus, deficit) _____ during a recession and a budget _____ during inflation.

8. Of the two principal means available to the Federal government for financing budget deficits, the one that is more expansionary is (borrowing money from the public, creating new money) _____.
Of the two principal means available to the Federal government for using funds from a budget surplus, the one that is more contractionary is (impounding funds, debt reduction) _____.

9. Net taxes equal taxes (plus, minus) _____ transfer payments and are called "taxes" in this chapter. In the United States, as GDP increases, tax revenue will (increase, decrease) _____, and as the GDP decreases, tax revenues will _____.

10. Because tax revenues are (directly, indirectly) _____ related to the GDP, the economy has some (artificial, built-in) _____ stability. If the GDP increases, then tax revenue will increase, and the budget surplus will (increase, decrease) _____, thus (stimulating, restraining) _____ the economy when it is needed. When GDP decreases, tax revenues decrease, and the budget deficit (increases, decreases) _____, thus (stimulating, restraining) _____ the economy when it is needed.

11. As GDP increases, the average tax rates will increase with a (progressive, proportional, regressive) _____ tax, remain constant with a _____ tax, and decrease with a _____ tax. With a progressive tax, there is (more, less) _____ built-in stability for the economy.

12. If there is a deficit in the full-employment budget, then fiscal policy is (contractionary, expansionary) _____. A deficit produced by swings in the business cycle is (structural, cyclical) _____, whereas a deficit produced through government taxation and spending decisions is _____. The full-employment budget deficit is also called the (cyclical, structural) _____ deficit.

13. If government has a balanced-budget requirement and the economy moves into recession, then the government must either (increase, decrease) _____ taxes, _____ government spending, or some combination of the two. These actions would (improve, worsen) _____ economic conditions in the economy.

14. There is a problem of timing in the use of discretionary fiscal policy because of the time between the beginning of a recession or inflation and awareness of it, or a(n) (administrative, operational, recognition) _____ lag; the time needed for Congress to adjust fiscal policy, or a _____ lag; and the time needed for fiscal policy to take effect, or an _____ lag.

15. Political problems arise in the application of discretionary fiscal policy to stabilize the economy because government has (one, several) _____ economic goals, state and local fiscal policies may (reinforce, counter) _____ Federal fiscal policy, voters have a bias in favor of budget (surpluses, deficits) _____, and politicians may use fiscal policies in a way that creates a(n) (international, political) _____ business cycle.

16. When the Federal government employs an expansionary fiscal policy to increase real GDP and employment in the economy, it usually has a budget (surplus, deficit) _____ and (lends, borrows) _____ in the money market. These actions will (raise, lower) _____ interest rates in the economy and (contract, expand) _____ investment spending. This change in investment spending is the (net export, crowding-out) _____ effect of the expansionary fiscal policy, and it tends to (weaken, strengthen) _____ the influence of the expansionary fiscal policy on real GDP and employment.

17. An expansionary fiscal policy when the economy is operating in the intermediate range of the aggregate supply curve will increase the real GDP and employment in the economy and (raise, lower) _____ the price level. This change in the price level will (weaken, strengthen) _____ the impact of the expansionary fiscal policy on output and employment in the economy.

18. Fiscal policy is subject to further complications from (independence from, interdependency with) _____ the world economy. For example, the domestic economy can be influenced by aggregate demand (inflation, shocks) _____ from abroad that alter GDP and might reinforce or offset fiscal policy.

19. International trade can also produce a (crowding-out, net export) _____ effect that influences aggregate demand and partially offsets fiscal policy.
   a. When fiscal policy is expansionary, it tends to (increase, decrease) _____ interest rates, which in turn tends to _____ the value of the dollar, (increase, decrease) _____ net exports, and _____ aggregate demand.
   b. When fiscal policy is contractionary, it tends to (increase, decrease) _____ interest rates,

which in turn tends to _____ the value of the dollar, (increase, decrease) _____ net exports, and _____ aggregate demand.

20. If an expansionary fiscal policy is the result of reduction in taxes, the supply-side effects of the policy may be to (increase, decrease) _____ aggregate supply, to _____ productivity capacity of the economy, to (increase, decrease) _____ real GDP and employment, to _____ the rate of inflation, and to (weaken, strengthen) _____ the impact of the fiscal policy on output and employment.

■ **TRUE-FALSE QUESTIONS**

Circle the T if the statement is true, the F if it is false.

1. The Council of Economic Advisers was established to give economic advice to Congress. **T F**

2. Discretionary fiscal policy is independent of Congress and left to the discretion of state and local governments. **T F**

3. Expansionary fiscal policy during a recession or depression will create a budget deficit or add to an existing budget deficit. **T F**

4. A decrease in taxes is one of the options that can be used to pursue a contractionary fiscal policy. **T F**

5. To increase initial consumption by a specific amount, government must reduce taxes by more than that amount because some of the tax cut will be saved by households. **T F**

6. A full-employment budget deficit is contractionary. **T F**

7. A reduction in taxes and an increase in government spending during a recession would tend to contract the public sector of the economy. **T F**

8. Built-in stabilizers are not sufficiently strong to prevent recession or inflation, but they can reduce the severity of a recession or inflation. **T F**

9. The less progressive the tax system, the greater the economy's built-in stability. **T F**

10. The full-employment budget indicates how much government must spend and tax if there is to be full employment in the economy. **T F**

11. A cyclical deficit is the result of countercyclical actions by government to stimulate the economy. **T F**

12. If an economy achieved a full-employment level of output but tax revenues were less than government expenditures, then a structural deficit is created. **T F**

13. The key to assessing discretionary fiscal policy is to disregard the actual budget deficit and instead observe the change in the full-employment budget. **T F**

14. A balanced-budget requirement will use fiscal policy to lessen the effects of recession and stabilize the economy.   **T F**

15. Recognition, administrative, and operational lags in the timing of Federal fiscal policy make fiscal policies more effective in reducing the rate of inflation and decreasing unemployment in the economy.   **T F**

16. State and local governments' fiscal policies have tended to assist and reinforce the efforts of the Federal government to counter recession and inflation.   **T F**

17. The Federal government spending and taxing policies are designed solely to reduce unemployment and limit inflation in the economy.   **T F**

18. It is generally easier to induce U.S. senators and representatives to vote for decreases in tax rates and for increases in government purchases than for increased taxes and decreased purchases.   **T F**

19. Economists who see evidence of a political business cycle argue that members of Congress tend to increase taxes and reduce expenditures before and to reduce taxes and increase expenditures after elections.   **T F**

20. The crowding-out effect occurs when an expansionary fiscal policy decreases the interest rate, increases investment spending, and strengthens fiscal policy.   **T F**

21. Critics contend that the crowding-out effect will be greatest when the economy is in a recession.   **T F**

22. With an upsloping aggregate supply curve, some portion of the potential effect of an expansionary fiscal policy on real GDP may be lost because of an increase in the price level.   **T F**

23. For a domestic economy, there are gains for specialization and trade but also complications from the interdependency with the world economy.   **T F**

24. A net export effect may partially offset an expansionary fiscal policy.   **T F**

25. Supply-side economists maintain that reduction in tax rates decrease aggregate supply and are, therefore, inflationary.   **T F**

■ **MULTIPLE-CHOICE QUESTIONS**

Circle the letter that corresponds to the best answer.

1. Which of the following was instrumental in assigning to the Federal government the basic responsibility for promoting economic stability in the U.S. economy?
  (a) the Employment Act of 1946
  (b) the Tax Reform Act of 1986
  (c) the Ricardian equivalence theorem
  (d) the balanced-budget multiplier

2. If the government wishes to increase the level of real GDP, it might reduce
  (a) taxes
  (b) its purchases of goods and services

  (c) transfer payments
  (d) the size of the budget deficit

3. If Congress passes legislation to make a substantial increase in government spending to counter the effects of severe recession, this would be an example of a
  (a) supply-side fiscal policy
  (b) contractionary fiscal policy
  (c) discretionary fiscal policy
  (d) nondiscretionary fiscal policy

4. Which combination of policies would be the most expansionary?
  (a) an increase in government spending and taxes
  (b) a decrease in government spending and taxes
  (c) an increase in government spending and a decrease in taxes
  (d) a decrease in government spending and an increase in taxes

5. An economy is in a recession and the government decides to increase spending by $4 billion. The MPC is .8. What would be the full increase in real GDP from the change in government spending assuming the increase would be in the horizontal range of the aggregate supply curve?
  (a) $3.2 billion
  (b) $4 billion
  (c) $16 billion
  (d) $20 billion

6. Which combination of fiscal policies would be the most contractionary?
  (a) an increase in government spending and taxes
  (b) a decrease in government spending and taxes
  (c) an increase in government spending and a decrease in taxes
  (d) a decrease in government spending and an increase in taxes

7. Which is a more expansionary way for government to finance a budget deficit?
  (a) borrowing money in the money market
  (b) decreasing government spending
  (c) creating new money
  (d) increasing taxes

8. Which would be the most contractionary use of funds from a budget surplus?
  (a) cutting tax rates
  (b) impounding the funds
  (c) using the funds to retire outstanding government debt
  (d) increasing government spending on social programs

9. When government tax revenues change automatically and in a countercyclical direction over the course of the business cycle, this is an example of
  (a) the political business cycle
  (b) nondiscretionary fiscal policy
  (c) the full-employment budget
  (d) crowding out

10 If the economy is to have built-in stability, when real GDP falls,

(a) tax revenues and government transfer payments both should fall

(b) tax revenues and government transfer payments both should rise

(c) tax revenues should fall and government transfer payments should rise

(d) tax revenues should rise and government transfer payments should fall

Answer Questions 11, 12, and 13 on the basis of the following diagram.

11. If the slope of the line **T** were steeper, there would be

  (a) more built-in stability for the economy

  (b) less built-in stability for the economy

  (c) no change in the built-in stability for the economy

  (d) the need for more emphasis on discretionary fiscal policy

12. If the slope of the line **T** were flatter, there would be

  (a) larger cyclical deficits produced as GDP moved from Y_3 to Y_2

  (b) smaller cyclical deficits produced as GDP moved from Y_3 to Y_2

  (c) larger structural deficits produced as GDP moved from Y_3 to Y_2

  (d) smaller structural deficits produced as GDP moved from Y_3 to Y_2

13. Actions by the Federal government to raise marginal tax rates would tend to

  (a) flatten the slope of line **T** and increase built-in stability

  (b) flatten the slope of line **T** and decrease built-in stability

  (c) steepen the slope of line **T** and increase built-in stability

  (d) steepen the slope of line **T** and decrease built-in stability

14. With a proportional tax system, as the level of income increases in an economy, the average tax rate will

  (a) increase

  (b) decrease

  (c) remain the same

  (d) either increase or decrease

15. In any given year, the full-employment deficit is equal to the

  (a) structural deficit

  (b) cyclical deficit

  (c) actual deficit

  (d) zero-employment budget

16. If the full-employment budget shows a deficit of about $200 billion and the actual budget shows a deficit of about $250 billion over a several-year period, it can be conducted that there is

  (a) a structural deficit but not a cyclical deficit

  (b) a cyclical deficit but not a structural deficit

  (c) neither a cyclical nor structural deficit

  (d) both a cyclical and structural defict

17. When the actual budget deficit is greater than the full-employment deficit, it can be concluded that

  (a) discretionary fiscal policy is contractionary

  (b) the economy is at less than full employment

  (c) the tax system for the economy is regressive

  (d) the structural deficit has increased

18. A balanced-budget amendment that required the Federal government to balance its budget each year would be

  (a) expansionary at a time when fiscal policy should be contractionary

  (b) contractionary at a time when fiscal policy should be expansionary

  (c) expansionary at a time when fiscal policy should be expansionary

  (d) contractionary at a time when fiscal policy should be contractionary

19. The length of time involved for the fiscal action taken by Congress to affect output, employment, or the price level is referred to as the

  (a) administrative lag

  (b) operational lag

  (c) recognition lag

  (d) fiscal lag

20. The crowding-out effect of an expansionary (deficit) fiscal policy is the result of government borrowing in the money market which

  (a) increases interest rates and net investment spending in the economy

  (b) increases interest rates and decreases net investment spending

  (c) decreases interest rates and increases net investment spending

  (d) decreases interest rates and net investment spending

21. The effect of an expansionary fiscal policy on the real GDP of an economy operating in the horizontal range of the aggregate supply curve is partially or fully

  (a) reinforced by the crowding-out effect

  (b) offset by the crowding-out effect

  (c) reinforced by raising rax rates

  (d) offset by lowering tax rates

22. The effect of an expansionary fiscal policy on the real GDP of an economy operating in the upsloping portion of the aggregate supply curve is

  (a) increased by the net export effect

  (b) decreased by the creation of new money

(c) increased by the crowding-out effect

(d) decreased by a rise in the price level

23. Suppose the United States pursued an expansionary fiscal policy to stimulate its economy and eliminate a recession. The net export effect suggests that net exports would

(a) decrease, thus decreasing aggregate demand and partially offsetting the fiscal policy

(b) decrease, thus increasing aggregate demand and partially offsetting the fiscal policy

(c) increase, thus decreasing aggregate demand and partially offsetting fiscal policy

(d) increase, thus increasing aggregate demand and partially reinforcing the fiscal policy

24. Suppose the United States pursued a contractionary fiscal policy to reduce the level of inflation. The net export effect suggests that net exports would

(a) decrease, thus decreasing aggregate demand and partially reinforcing the fiscal policy

(b) decrease, thus increasing aggregate demand and partially offsetting the fiscal policy

(c) increase, thus decreasing aggregate demand and partially reinforcing the fiscal policy

(d) increase, thus increasing aggregate demand and partially offsetting the fiscal policy

25. Supply-side fiscal policy is generally enacted through

(a) a decrease in tax rates

(b) a decrease in investment spending

(c) an increase in government spending

(d) an increase in automatic stabilizers

■ PROBLEMS

1. Columns 1 and 2 in the following table are the aggregate supply schedule, and columns 1 and 3 are the aggregate demand schedule.

(1) Price level	(2) Real GDP$_1$	(3) AD$_1$	(4) AD$_2$	(5) Real GDP$_2$
220	2,390	2,100	2,200	2,490
200	2,390	2,200	2,340	2,490
190	2,350	2,250	2,350	2,450
180	2,300	2,300	2,400	2,400
160	2,200	2,400	2,500	2,300

a. The equilibrium real GDP is $_____

and the price level is _____.

b. Suppose that an expansionary fiscal policy increases aggregate demand from that shown in columns 1 and 3 to that shown in columns 1 and 4.

(1) If the price level remained constant, the equilibrium real GDP would increase to $_____.

(2) But the increase in aggregate demand does raise the price level to _____, and this rise in the price level results in real GDP increasing to only $_____.

c. If the expansionary fiscal policy that increased aggregate demand also has supply-side effects and increased aggregate supply from that shown in columns 1 and 2 to that shown in columns 1 and 5,

(1) the equilibrium real GDP would increase to $_____.

(2) the price level would _____.

2. The following table shows seven real GDPs and the net tax revenues of government at each real GDP.

Real GDP	Net tax revenues	Government purchases	Government deficit/surplus
$ 850	$170	$_____	$_____
900	180	_____	_____
950	190	_____	_____
1,000	200	_____	_____
1,050	210	_____	_____
1,100	220	_____	_____
1,150	230	_____	_____

a. Looking at the two columns on the left side of the table, it can be seen that

(1) when real GDP increases by $50, net tax revenues (increase, decrease) _____ by $_____.

(2) when real GDP decreases by $100, net tax revenues (increase, decrease) _____ by $_____.

(3) the relationship between real GDP and net tax revenues is (direct, inverse) _____.

b. Assume the simple multiplier has a value of 10 and that investment spending in the economy decreases by $10.

(1) If net tax revenues remained constant, the equilibrium real GDP would decrease by $_____.

(2) But when real GDP decreases, net tax revenues also decrease; and this decrease in net tax revenues will tend to (increase, decrease) _____ the equilibrium real GDP.

(3) And, therefore, the decrease in real GDP brought about by the $10 decrease in investment spending will be (more, less) _____ than $100.

(4) The direct relationship between net tax revenues and real GDP has (lessened, expanded) _____ the impact of the $10 decrease in investment spending on real GDP.

c. Suppose the simple multiplier is also 10 and government wishes to increase the equilibrium real GDP by $50.

(1) If net tax revenues remained constant, government would have to increase its purchases of goods and services by $_____.

(2) But when real GDP rises, net tax revenues also rise, and this rise in net tax revenues will tend to (increase, decrease) _____ the equilibrium real GDP.

(3) The effect, therefore, of the $5 increase in government purchases will also be to increase the equilibrium real GDP by (more, less) _____ than $50.

(4) The direct relationship between net tax revenues and real GDP has (lessened, expanded) _____ the effect of the $5 increase in government purchases, and to raise the equilibrium real GDP by $50, the government will have to increase its purchases by (more, less) _____ than $5.

d. Imagine that the full-employment real GDP of the economy is $1150 and that government purchases of goods and services are $200.

(1) Complete the table on the previous page by entering the government purchases and computing the budget deficit or surplus at each of the real GDPs. (Show a government deficit by placing a minus sign in front of the amount by which expenditures exceed net tax revenues.)

(2) The full-employment surplus equals $_____.

(3) Were the economy in a recession and producing a real GDP of $900, the budget would show a (surplus, deficit) _____ of $_____.

(4) This budget deficit or surplus makes it appear that government is pursuing a(n) (expansionary, contractionary) _____ fiscal policy, but this deficit or surplus is not the result of countercyclical fiscal policy but the result of the _____.

(5) If government did not change its net tax *rates,* it could increase the equilibrium real GDP from $900 to the full-employment real GDP of $1150 by increasing its purchases by (approximately) $70. At the full-employment real GDP the budget would show a (surplus, deficit) _____ of $_____.

(6) If government did not change its purchases, it would increase the equilibrium real GDP from $900 to the full-employment real GDP of $1150 by decreasing net tax revenues at all real GDPs by a lump sum of (approximately) $80. The full-employment budget would have a (surplus, deficit) _____ of $_____.

3. a. Complete the table below by computing the average tax rates, given the net tax revenue data in columns 2, 4, and 6. Calculate the average tax rate in percentage to one decimal place (for example, 5.4%).

b. As real GDP increases in column 1, the average tax rate (increases, decreases, remains the same) _____ in column 3, _____ in column 5, and _____ in column 7. The tax system is (progressive, proportional, regressive) _____ in column 2, _____ in column 4, and _____ in column (6).

c. On the graph below, plot the real GDP, net tax revenue, and government spending data given in columns 1, 2, 4, 6, and 8.

(1) Real GDP	(2) Net tax revenue	(3) Average tax rate	(4) Net tax revenue	(5) Average tax rate	(6) Net tax revenue	(7) Average tax rate	(8) Government spending
$1,000	$100	_____%	$100	_____%	$100	_____%	$120
$1,100	$120	_____	$110	_____	$108	_____	$120
$1,200	$145	_____	$120	_____	$115	_____	$120
$1,300	$175	_____	$130	_____	$120	_____	$120
$1,400	$210	_____	$140	_____	$123	_____	$120

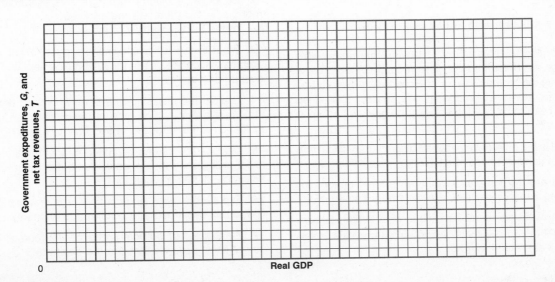

(1) Year	(2) Actual budget surplus (+) or deficit (−)	(3) Full-employment budget surplus (+) or deficit (−)	(4) Direction of fiscal policy
1	−$10 billion	+$10 billion	_____
2	+$10 billion	−$20 billion	_____
3	−$20 billion	+$0 billion	_____
4	−$120 billion	−$120 billion	_____
5	−$150 billion	−$130 billion	_____

Tax revenue system with the steepest slope is found in column _____, and it is (progressive, proportional, regressive) _____ while the one with the flattest slope is found in column _____, and it is _____.

4. a. Complete the table above by stating whether the direction of discretionary fiscal policy was contractionary, expansionary, or had no effect, given the hypothetical budget data for an economy.

b. The best gauge of the direction of fiscal policy is the (actual, full-employment) _____ budget deficit or surplus because it removes the (cyclical, structural) _____ component from the discussion of the budget situation.

c. (1) In what years were there cyclical deficits, and what was the amount of the cyclical deficit in each of those years? _____

_____

(2) In what years were there cyclical deficits, and what was the size of the cyclical deficits in each of those years? _____

_____

■ **SHORT ANSWER AND ESSAY QUESTIONS**

1. In the Employment Act of 1946, (*a*) what responsibility was given to the Federal government, (*b*) what tasks were assigned to the Council of Economic Advisers and the Joint Economic Committee, and (*c*) what specific kinds of policy were to be used to achieve the goals established by the act?

2. What is the difference between discretionary fiscal policy and nondiscretionary fiscal policy?

3. What are the Federal government's three options for conducting expansionary or contractionary fiscal policy?

4. Under what economic conditions would expansionary or contractionary fiscal policy be used? What would be the effect on the Federal budget?

5. Compare and contrast the effect of expansionary and contractionary fiscal policy on aggregate demand. Draw a graph to illustrate the likely effects.

6. What is the effect of the simple multiplier on the initial change in spending from fiscal policy? When the government wants to increase initial consumption by a specific amount, why must the government reduce taxes by more than that amount?

7. In the real world, is the purpose of fiscal policy to restore a previously lower price level? How do "sticky" prices affect events?

8. What are the alternative means of financing deficits and disposing of surpluses available to the Federal government? What is the difference between these methods insofar as their expansionary and contractionary effect is concerned?

9. Explain the fiscal policy that would be advocated during a recession and during a period of inflation by those who (*a*) wish to expand the public sector and (*b*) wish to contract the public sector.

10. What is a built-in stabilizer? How do the built-in stabilizers work to reduce rises and falls in the level of nominal GDP?

11. What is the economic importance of the direct relationship between tax receipts and GDP?

12. Supply a definition of a progressive, proportional, and regressive tax. What are the implications of each type of tax for the built-in stability of the economy?

13. What is the full-employment budget? What was the problem which the use of the full-employment budget was designed to solve?

14. Explain the distinction between a cyclical deficit and structural deficit. Which type of deficit provides the best indication of the direction of fiscal policy? Why?

15. Discuss effects of a balanced-budget requirement on fiscal policy and the economy. Would this requirement be advisable during a recession?

16. Explain the three kinds of time lags that make it difficult to use fiscal policy to stabilize the economy.

17. What are four political problems that complicate the use of fiscal policy to stabilize the economy?

18. How do (*a*) crowding out and (*b*) inflation reduce the effect of an expansionary (deficit) fiscal policy on real GDP and employment?

19. What complications for fiscal policy arise from interdependency with the world economy? Explain how aggregate demand shocks from abroad and the net export effect influence fiscal policy.

20. What might be the supply-side effects of a reduction in tax rates on the capacity output of the economy, the equilibrium levels of real GDP and employment, and the price level?

ANSWERS

Chapter 12 Fiscal Policy

FILL-IN QUESTIONS

1. Employment, Council of Economic Advisers, Joint Economic Committee
2. discretionary, nondiscretionary
3. increase, increase, decrease, decrease
4. government spending, taxes, government spending, taxes
5. multiplier, 4
6. deficit, surplus
7. deficit, surplus
8. creating new money, impounding funds
9. minus, increase, decrease
10. directly, built-in, increase, restraining, increases, stimulating
11. progressive, proportional, regressive, more
12. expansionary, cyclical, structural, structural
13. increase, decrease, worsen
14. recognition, administrative, operational
15. several, counter, deficits, political
16. deficit, borrows, raise, contract, crowding-out, weaken
17. raise, weaken
18. interdependency with, shocks
19. net export *a.* increase, increase, decrease, decrease; *b.* decrease, decrease, increase, increase
20. increase, increase, increase, decrease, strengthen

TRUE-FALSE QUESTIONS

1. F, p. 244	**10.** F, p. 250	**19.** F, p. 254
2. F, p. 244	**11.** F, p. 250	**20.** F, p. 254
3. T, p. 244	**12.** T, p. 250	**21.** F, p. 255
4. F, p. 245	**13.** T, p. 250	**22.** T, pp. 255-256
5. T, p. 245	**14.** F, p. 251-252	**23.** T, p. 256
6. F, pp. 250-251	**15.** F, p. 253	**24.** T, p. 256
7. F, pp. 245-246	**16.** F, p. 253	**25.** F, pp. 257-258
8. T, p. 249	**17.** F, pp. 253	
9. F, p. 249	**18.** T, pp. 253-254	

MULTIPLE-CHOICE QUESTIONS

1. a, pp. 243-244	**10.** c, pp. 248-249	**19.** b, p. 253
2. a, p. 245	**11.** a, p. 249	**20.** b, p. 254
3. c, p. 244	**12.** b, pp. 249-250	**21.** b, pp. 254-255
4. c, pp. 244-246	**13.** c, p. 249	**22.** d, pp. 255-256
5. d, pp. 244-245	**14.** c, p. 249	**23.** a, pp. 256-257
6. d, pp. 246-247	**15.** a, p. 250	**24.** d, pp. 256-257
7. c, p. 247	**16.** d, pp. 249-250	**25.** a, pp. 257-258
8. b, p. 247	**17.** b, pp. 249-250	
9. b, p. 248	**18.** b, p. 252	

PROBLEMS

1. *a.* 2,300, 180; *b.* (1) 2,400, (2) 190, 2,350; *c.* (1) 2,400, (2) remain constant.
2. *a.* (1) increase, $10, (2) decrease, $20, (3) direct; *b.* (1) $100, (2) increase, (3) less, (4) lessened; *c.* (1) $5, (2) decrease, (3) less, (4) lessened, more; *d.* (1) government expenditures are $200 at all GDPs, government surplus or deficit: −30, −20, −10, 0, 10, 20, 30, (2) $30, (3) deficit, $20, (4) expansionary, recession, (5) deficit, $40, (6) deficit, $50
3. *a.* column 3: 10.0, 10.9, 12.1, 13.5, 15.0; column 5: 10.0 at each GDP level; column 7: 10.0, 9.8, 9.6, 9.2, 8.8; *b.* increases, remains the same, decrease; progressive, proportional, regressive; *c.* 2, progressive, 6, regressive
4. *a.* contractionary, expansionary, no effect, expansionary, expansionary; *b.* full-employment, cyclical; *c.* (1) year 1 ($20 billion), year 3 ($20 billion), year 5 ($20 billion), (2) year 2 ($20 billion), year 4 ($120 billion), year 5 ($130 billion)

SHORT ANSWER AND ESSAY QUESTIONS

1. pp. 243-244	**8.** p. 247	**15.** pp. 251-252
2. pp. 244, 248	**9.** pp. 247-248	**16.** p. 253
3. pp. 244-247	**10.** pp. 248-249	**17.** pp. 253-254
4. pp. 244-247	**11.** p. 248	**18.** pp. 254-256
5. pp. 244-247	**12.** p. 249	**19.** p. 256
6. pp. 244-245	**13.** pp. 249-250	**20.** pp. 257-258
7. p. 246	**14.** pp. 249-250	

Money and Banking

Chapter 13 explains how the financial system affects the operation of the economy. The chapter is largely descriptive and factual. Pay particular attention to the following: (1) what money is and the functions it performs, what types of money exist in the U.S. economy and their relative importance, and how the three measures of the money supply ($M1$, $M2$, and $M3$) are defined; (2) what gives value to or backs U.S. money; (3) why people want to have money in their possession and what determines how much money they want to have on hand at any time; (4) how the total demand for money and the money supply together determine the equilibrium rate of interest; and (5) the principal institutions of the U.S. financial system and their functions.

Several points are worth repeating here because so much depends on your full understanding of them. First, money is whatever performs the three functions of money, and in the United States money consists largely of the debts (promises to pay) of the Federal Reserve Banks and depository institutions. In the United States, this money is backed by the goods and services for which its owners can exchange it and not by gold.

Second, the total **demand for money** is made up of a **transactions demand for money** and an **asset demand for money.** Because money is used as a medium of exchange, consumers and business firms wish to have money on hand to use for transaction purposes. The quantity of money they demand for this purpose is directly related to the size of the economy's nominal (or money) gross domestic product. This means that when either the price level or the real gross domestic product increases, they will want to have more money on hand to use for transactions.

Money is also used as a store of value. Consumers and firms who own assets may choose to have some of their assets in the form of money (rather than in stocks, bonds, goods, or property). There is, therefore, also an asset demand for money. Holding money, however, imposes a cost on those who hold it. This cost is the interest they lose when they own money rather than, as an example, bonds. This means that people will demand less money for asset purposes when the rate of interest (the cost of holding money) is high and more when the rate of interest is low: the quantity of money demanded for this purpose is inversely related to the interest rate.

The total demand for money is the sum of the transactions demand and the asset demand, and therefore, it is affected by both nominal GDP and the rate of interest.

It is this total demand and the supply of money that determines interest rates in the money market. The inverse relationship between bond prices and interest rates help this market adjust to shortages or surpluses.

Third, the **central bank** in the United States consists of the 12 Federal Reserve Banks and the Board of Governors of the Federal Reserve System which oversees their operation. These banks, while privately owned by the commercial banks, are operated more or less as an agency of the Federal government. They are not for profit but are primarily to regulate the nation's money supply in the best interests of the economy as a whole and secondarily to perform other services for the banks, the government, and the economy. They are able to perform their primary function because they are bankers' banks in which depository institutions (commercial banks and the thrifts) can deposit and borrow money. They do not deal directly with the public.

Fourth, these depository institutions accept deposits and make loans, but they also are able to create money by lending checkable deposits. Because they are able to do this, they have a strong influence on the size of the money supply and the value of money. The Federal Reserve Banks exist primarily to regulate the money supply and its value by influencing and controlling the amount of money depository institutions create.

The final section of Chapter 13 discusses recent developments in money and banking, of which three are particularly noteworthy. Since the early 1980s, the relative decline of banks and thrifts has significantly altered the financial services industry. Also, financial markets are now global and more highly integrated than in previous decades. In addition, technological advances have changed the character of money. As you will learn, each development has and will continue to shape money and banking in the United States and other nations.

■ **CHECKLIST**

When you have studied this chapter you should be able to

☐ List and explain the three functions of money.
☐ Give an $M1$ definition of money that explains its two major components.
☐ Describe the two major types of institutions offering checkable deposits.

☐ Give an *M*2 definition of money that explains its relationship to *M*1 and four near-money components.

☐ Give an *M*3 definition of money and its major components.

☐ State three reasons why near-monies are important.

☐ Distinguish between credit cards and money.

☐ Explain why money is debt in the U.S. economy and who holds that debt.

☐ State three reasons why currency and checkable deposits are money and have value.

☐ Use an equation to explain the relationship between the value of money and the price level.

☐ Explain what role government plays in maintaining or stabilizing the value of money.

☐ Give a definition of the transactions demand for money that describes how it varies with nominal GDP.

☐ Give a definition of the asset demand for money that describes how it varies with the rate of interest.

☐ Illustrate graphically how the transactions and asset demands for money combine to form the total money demand.

☐ Describe the money market and what determines the equilibrium rate of interest.

☐ Explain how changes in nominal GDP and in the money supply affect the interest rate.

☐ Illustrate with an example how disequilibrium in the money market is corrected through changes in bond prices.

☐ Describe the relationship between the major units of the Federal Reserve System.

☐ Explain why the Federal Reserve Banks are central, quasipublic, and bankers' banks.

☐ List and explain the seven major functions of the Federal Reserve System and indicate which one is most important.

☐ Discuss both sides of the controversy over the independence of the Federal Reserve.

☐ Explain the relative decline of banks and thrifts and the three types of actions that have been taken to respond to it.

☐ Describe the globalization of financial markets.

☐ Explain how technological progress has changed the characteristics of money.

■ **CHAPTER OUTLINE**

1. Money is whatever performs the three basic functions of money: a medium of exchange, a unit of account, and a store of value.

2. In the U.S. economy, *money* is whatever is generally used as a medium of exchange and consists of the debts of the Federal government and of commercial banks and other financial institutions.

    a. The narrowly defined money supply is called *M*1 and has two principal components.

    (1) The smaller component is currency: coins which are token money and paper money largely in the form of Federal Reserve Notes.

    (2) The larger and more important component is checkable deposits in commercial banks and thrift institutions.

    (3) These checkable deposits include demand deposits (checking accounts), negotiable order of withdrawal (NOW) accounts, automatic transfer service (ATS) accounts, and share draft accounts, all of which give the depositor the ability to write checks.

    (4) Currency and checkable deposits owned by the Federal government, commercial banks and savings institutions, and the Federal Reserve Banks are not, however, included in *M*1 or any of the more broadly defined money supplies.

    b. *M*2 and *M*3 are the more broadly defined money supplies and include not only the currency and checkable deposits in *M*1 but such near-monies as noncheckable savings deposits and time deposits in commercial banks and savings institutions.

    (1) *M*2 includes *M*1 plus noncheckable savings deposits plus small time deposits (less than $100,000) plus money market deposit accounts (MMDA) plus money market mutual funds (MMMF).

    (2) *M*3 includes *M*2 plus large time deposits ($100,000 or more).

    (3) There are advantages to each of the different measures of money, but since *M*1 is included in all the definitions and the principles that apply to it are applicable to the other measures, that narrow definition is used for the textbook discussion unless noted otherwise.

    c. Near-monies held by the public are important because they affect spending habits, serve as a stabilizing force in economic activity, and provide different definitions of money for the conduct of monetary policy.

    d. Credit cards are not money but are a device by which the cardholders obtain a loan (credit) from the issuer of the card.

3. In the United States,

    a. Money is the promise of a commercial bank, a savings (thrift) institution, or a Federal Reserve Bank to pay, but these debts cannot be redeemed for anything tangible.

    b. Money has value only because people can exchange it for desirable goods and services.

    c. The value of money is inversely related to the price level.

    d. Money is backed by the confidence which the public has that the value of money will remain stable; the Federal government can use monetary and fiscal policy to keep the value of money relatively stable.

4. Business firms and households wish to hold and, therefore, demand money for two reasons.

    a. Because they use money as a medium of exchange, they have a transactions demand which is directly related to the nominal gross domestic product of the economy.

    b. Because they also use money as a store of value, they have an asset demand which is inversely related to the rate of interest.

    c. Their *total demand for money* is the sum of the transactions and asset demands.

5. In the *money market,* the demand for money and the supply of money determine the interest rate. Graphically, the demand for money is a downsloping line and the supply of money is a vertical line, and their intersection determines the interest rate. Disequilibrium in this market is corrected by changes in bond prices and their inverse relationship with interest rates.

> **a.** If there is a shortage of money, bonds will be sold. The increase in supply of bonds will drive down bond prices, causing interest rates to rise until the shortage is eliminated.
>
> **b.** If there is a surplus of money, bonds will be bought. The increased demand for bonds will drive up bond prices, causing interest rates to fall until the surplus is eliminated.

6. The financial sector of the economy is significantly influenced by the **Federal Reserve System (Fed)** and the nation's banks and thrift institutions.

> **a.** The banking system remains centralized and regulated by government because historical problems led to different kinds of money and the mismanagement of the money supply.
>
> **b.** The Board of Governors of the Fed exercises control over the supply of money and the banking system. The U.S. president appoints the seven members of the Board of Governors.
>
> **c.** Four important bodies help the Board of Governors establish and conduct policy: the *Federal Open Market Committee* (*FOMC*), which establishes policy over the buying and selling of government securities; and three *Advisory Councils* that provide input from commercial banks, thrift institutions, and consumer-related organizations.
>
> **d.** The 12 Federal Reserve Banks of the Fed serve as central banks, quasipublic banks, and bankers' banks.
>
> **e.** The U.S. banking system contains thousands of commercial banks and thrift institutions that are directly affected by the Fed's decisions.
>
> **f.** The Fed performs seven functions: issuing currency, setting reserve requirements and holding reserves, lending money to banks and thrifts, collecting and processing checks, serving as the fiscal agent for the Federal government, supervising banks, and controlling the money supply. The last function is the most important.
>
> **g.** There is a continuing controversy about the independence of the Fed because it limits congressional and presidential control, but most economists think this is necessary to protect the Fed from strong political pressure and from making poor economic decisions.

7. Three *recent developments* have affected money and banking in the United States.

> **a.** There has been a relative decline in the number of banks and thrift institutions since the early 1980s. Three responses to this change have been the expansion of services by banks and thrifts, an increase in the number of bank and thrift mergers, and a push for regulatory reform to deregulate banks and thrifts and permit more competition in the financial services industry.
>
> **b.** Financial markets are now more globalized and integrated because of advances in computer and communications technology.

> **c.** The character of money has changed with the shift to use of electronic money and other forms of payment.

■ **HINTS AND TIPS**

1. Most students think of currency as the major component of the money supply, but it is a very small component relative to checkable deposits. Actually, there are several definitions of the **money supply** that you must know about, from the narrow *M*1 to the broader *M*2 and *M*3.

2. Spend extra time learning how the total demand for money is determined (see Figure 13-2 in the text). The total demand for money is composed of a transactions and an asset demand for money. The transactions demand is influenced by the level of nominal GDP and not affected by the interest rate, so it *is graphed as a vertical line.* The asset demand for money is affected by the interest rate, so it *is graphed as a downsloping curve.* The total demand for money is also graphed as a *downsloping curve* because of the influence of asset demand, but the curve is shifted farther to the right than the asset demand curve because of the influence of transactions demand.

3. One of the most difficult concepts to understand is the inverse relationship between bond prices and interest rates. The simple explanation is that interest yield from a bond is the ratio of the *fixed* annual interest payment to the bond price. The numerator is fixed, but the denominator (bond price) is variable. If the bond price falls, the interest yield on the bond rises because the fixed annual interest payment is being divided by a smaller denominator.

■ **IMPORTANT TERMS**

medium of exchange	time deposits
unit of account	money market mutual funds
store of value	
money supply	legal tender
*M*1, *M*2, and *M*3	fiat money
token money	transactions demand for money
intrinsic value	
Federal Reserve Note	asset demand for money
checkable deposit	total demand for money
thrift (savings) institutions	money market
savings and loan associations	bonds
	Federal Reserve System
mutual savings banks	Board of Governors
credit unions	Federal Open Market Committee (*FOMC*)
near-monies	Advisory Councils
noncheckable savings account	Federal Reserve Banks
money market deposit accounts	commercial banks
	state banks
national banks	smart cards
E-cash (electronic money)	

⊙

SELF-TEST

■ **FILL-IN QUESTIONS**

1. When money is usable for buying and selling goods and services, it functions as (a unit of account, a store of value, a medium of exchange) _____ _____, but when money serves as a measure of relative worth, it functions as _____, and when money serves a liquid asset it functions as a _____.

2. All coins in circulation in the United States are (paper, token) _____ money, which means that their intrinsic value is (less, greater) _____ than the face value of the coin.

3. Paper money and coins are considered (currency, checkable deposits) _____. The major component of *M*1 is (currency, checkable deposits) _____, and the minor component is _____.

4. *M*2 is equal to (*M*1, *M*3) _____ plus (checkable, noncheckable) _____ savings deposits, (small, large) _____ time deposits, and money market (deposit accounts, mutual funds) _____ and _____.

5. *M*3 is equal to *M*2 plus (small, large) _____ time deposits. These deposits have a face value of (less than $100,000; $100,000 or greater) _____.

6. List three reasons why the existence of near-monies is important.

a. _____
_____

b. _____
_____

c. _____
_____

7. Credit cards (are, are not) _____ considered money but rather a form of (paper money, loan) _____ from the institution that issued the card.

8. Paper money is the circulating debt of (banks and thrifts, the Federal Reserve Banks) _____ _____, while checkable deposits are the debts of _____. In the United States, currency and checkable deposits (are, are not) _____

backed by gold and silver.

9. Money has value because it is (unacceptable, acceptable) _____ in exchange for products and resources, because it is (legal, illegal) _____ tender, and because it is relatively (abundant, scarce) _____.

10. The value of money varies (directly, inversely) _____ with the price level. To find the value of $1 (multiply, divide) _____ 1 by the price level.

11. The transactions demand varies (directly, inversely) _____ with (the rate of interest, nominal GDP) _____, and asset demand varies (directly, inversely) _____ with (the rate of interest, nominal GDP) _____.

12. The sum of the transactions and asset demands for money is the total (demand, supply) _____ of money, and the intersection of it with the _____ of money determines the equilibrium (interest rate, price level) _____.

13. When the quantity of money demanded exceeds the quantity of money supplied, bond prices (increase, decrease) _____ and interest rates _____. When the quantity of money demanded is less than the quantity of money supplied, bond prices (increase, decrease) _____ and interest rates _____.

14. The Federal Reserve System is composed of the Board of (Control, Governors) _____ that is assisted by the powerful (U.S. Mint, Federal Open Market Committee) _____ and (3, 12) _____ Advisory Councils. There are also (10, 12) _____ Federal Reserve Banks.

15. The Federal Reserve Banks are (private, quasipublic) _____ banks, serve as (consumers', bankers') _____ banks, and are (local, central) _____ banks whose policies are coordinated by the Board of Governors.

16. The workhorses of the U.S. banking system are the more than 9,000 (thrifts, commercial banks) _____, two-thirds of which are (national, state) _____, banks and one-third of which are _____ banks.

17. The seven major functions of the Fed are

a. _____

_____

b. _____

_____

c. _____

_____

d. _____

_____

e. _____

_____

f. _____

_____

g. _____

_____

Of these, the most important function is _____

_____.

18. The independence of the Fed is a matter of continuing controversy. Opponents say that it is (democratic, undemocratic) _____, while supporters contend that the Fed must be protected from political pressure if it is to control (recession, inflation) _____.

19. Banks and thrifts have responded to their relative decline in recent years by (contracting, expanding) _____ financial services, (starting up, merging with) _____ other banks and thrifts, and pushing for (bankruptcy, regulatory) _____ reform.

20. Two other recent developments in money and banking are the (localization, globalization) _____ of financial markets, and the use of (paper, electronic) _____ money.

■ **TRUE-FALSE QUESTIONS**

Circle the T if the statement is true, the F if it is false.

1. When the price of a product is stated in terms of dollars and cents, then money is functioning as a unit of account.   **T F**

2. The money supply designated $M1$ is the sum of currency and noncheckable deposits.   **T F**

3. The currency component of $M1$ includes both coins and paper money.   **T F**

4. If a coin is token money, its face value is less than its intrinsic value.   **T F**

5. Both commercial banks and thrift institutions accept checkable deposits.   **T F**

6. The checkable deposits of the Federal government at the Federal Reserve Banks are a component of $M1$.   **T F**

7. $M2$ exceeds $M1$ by the amount of noncheckable savings, small time deposits, and money market deposit accounts and money market mutual funds.   **T F**

8. A *small* time deposit is one that is less than $100,000.   **T F**

9. $M2$ is less than $M3$ by the amount of small time deposits in depository institutions.   **T F**

10. Economists and public officials are in general agreement on how to define the money supply in the United States.   **T F**

11. A near-money is a medium of exchange.   **T F**

12. Currency and checkable deposits are money because they are acceptable to sellers in exchange for goods and services.   **T F**

13. If money is to have a fairly stable value, its supply must be limited relative to the demand for it.   **T F**

14. There is a transactions demand for money because households and business firms use money as a store of value.   **T F**

15. An increase in the price level would, *ceteris paribus,* increase the transactions demand for money.   **T F**

16. An increase in the nominal GDP, other things remaining the same, will increase both the total demand for money and the equilibrium rate of interest in the economy.   **T F**

17. Bond prices and interest rates are inversely related.   **T F**

18. Members of the Board of Governors of the Federal Reserve System are appointed by the president of the United States and confirmed by the Senate.   **T F**

19. The Federal Open Market Committee (FOMC) is responsible for keeping the stock market open and regulated.   **T F**

20. The Federal Reserve Banks are owned and operated by the U.S. government.   **T F**

21. Federal Reserve Banks are bankers' banks because they make loans to and accept deposits from depository institutions.   **T F**

22. At times, the Fed lends money to banks and thrifts, charging them an interest rate called the *bank and thrift rate.*   **T F**

23. Defenders of Fed independence contend that the Fed must be protected from political pressure so that it can effectively control the money supply and maintain price stability. **T F**

24. In recent years, banks and thrifts have increased their share of the financial services industry and control of financial assets. **T F**

25. It is expected that electronic cash and smart cards will reduce problems for the Federal Reserve in controlling the money supply. **T F**

■ MULTIPLE-CHOICE QUESTIONS

Circle the letter that corresponds to the best answer.

1. Which one is an economic function of money?
 (a) a medium of communications
 (b) a factor of production
 (c) a store of bonds
 (d) a unit of account

2. The largest element of the currency component of *M*1 is
 (a) coins
 (b) United States Notes
 (c) silver certificates
 (d) Federal Reserve Notes

3. Which of the following constitutes the largest element in the *M*1 money supply?
 (a) currency
 (b) Federal Reserve Notes
 (c) time deposits
 (d) checkable deposits

4. Checkable deposits are money because they are
 (a) legal tender
 (b) fiat money
 (c) token money
 (d) a medium of exchange

5. The supply of money *M*1 consists almost entirely of the debts of
 (a) the Federal government
 (b) the Federal Reserve Banks
 (c) depository institutions
 (d) the Federal Reserve Banks and depository institutions

Use the following table to answer Questions 6, 7, and 8 about the money supply, given the following hypothetical data for the economy.

Item	Billions of dollars
Checkable deposits	1,775
Small time deposits	345
Currency	56
Large time deposits	1,230
Noncheckable savings deposits	945
Money market deposit accounts	256
Money market mutual funds	587

6. The size of the *M*1 money supply is
 (a) $1,775
 (b) $1,831
 (c) $2,176
 (d) $3,019

7. The size of the *M*2 money supply is
 (a) $2,176
 (b) $3,146
 (c) $3,964
 (d) $4,532

8. The size of the *M*3 money supply is
 (a) $4,532
 (b) $5,194
 (c) $5,339
 (d) $6,007

9. Which of the following *best* describes the backing of money in the United States?
 (a) the gold bullion stored in Fort Knox, Kentucky
 (b) the belief of holders of money that it can be exchanged for desirable goods and services
 (c) the willingness of banks and the government to surrender something of value in exchange for money
 (d) the faith and confidence of the public in the ability of government to pay its debts

10. If the price level increases 20%, the value of money decreases
 (a) 14.14%
 (b) 16.67%
 (c) 20%
 (d) 25%

11. To keep the value of money fairly constant, the Federal Reserve
 (a) uses price and wage controls
 (b) employs fiscal policy
 (c) controls the money supply
 (d) buys stock

12. The total quantity of money demanded is
 (a) directly related to nominal GDP and the rate of interest
 (b) directly related to nominal GDP and inversely related to the rate of interest
 (c) inversely related to nominal GDP and directly related to the rate of interest
 (d) inversely related to nominal GDP and the rate of interest

13. There is an asset demand for money because money is
 (a) a medium of exchange
 (b) a measure of value
 (c) a store of value
 (d) a standard of deferred payment

14. If the dollars held for transactions purposes are, on the average, spent five times a year for final goods and services, then the quantity of money people will wish to hold for transactions is equal to
 (a) five times the nominal GDP
 (b) 20% of the nominal GDP

(c) five divided by the nominal GDP

(d) 20% divided by the nominal GDP

15. An increase in the rate of interest would increase

(a) the opportunity cost of holding money

(b) the transactions demand for money

(c) the asset demand for money

(d) the prices of bonds

Use the table below to answer Questions 16 and 17.

Interest rate	Asset demand (billions)
14%	$100
13	150
12	200
11	250

16. Suppose the transactions demand for money is equal to 10% of the nominal GDP, the supply of money is $450 billion, and the asset demand for money is that shown in the table. If the nominal GDP is $3,000 billion, the equilibrium interest rate is

(a) 14%

(b) 13%

(c) 12%

(d) 11%

17. If the nominal GDP remains constant, an increase in the money supply from $450 billion to $500 billion would cause the equilibrium interest rate to

(a) rise to 14%

(b) fall to 11%

(c) fall to 12%

(d) remain unchanged

18. The stock of money is determined by the Federal Reserve System and does not change when the interest rate changes; therefore the

(a) supply of money curve is downward sloping

(b) demand for money curve is downward sloping

(c) supply of money curve is upward sloping

(d) supply of money curve is vertical

19. If the legal ceiling on the interest rate was set below equilibrium, the

(a) quantity of money demanded would be greater than the quantity of money supplied

(b) quantity of money demanded would be less than the quantity of money supplied

(c) supply of money would increase and the demand for money would decrease

(d) demand for money would increase and the supply of money would decrease

20. Which one of the following points would be true?

(a) Bond prices and the interest rate are directly related.

(b) A lower interest rate raises the opportunity cost of holding money.

(c) The supply of money is directly related to the interest rate.

(d) The total demand for money is inversely related to the interest rate.

Answer Questions 21 and 22 on the basis of the following information: Bond price = $10,000; bond fixed annual interest payment = $1,000; bond annual rate of interest = 10%.

21. If the price of this bond decreases by $2,500, the interest rate in effect will

(a) decrease by 1.1 percentage points

(b) decrease by 1.9 percentage points

(c) increase by 2.6 percentage points

(d) increase by 3.3 percentage points

22. If the price of this bond increases by $2,000, the interest rate in effect will

(a) decrease by 1.7 percentage points

(b) decrease by 2.4 percentage points

(c) increase by 1.1 percentage points

(d) increase by 2.9 percentage points

23. The Federal Open Market Committee (FOMC) of the Federal Reserve System is primarily responsible for

(a) supervising the operation of banks to make sure they follow regulation and monitoring banks so they do not engage in fraud

(b) handling the Fed's collection of checks and adjusting legal reserves among banks

(c) setting the Fed's monetary policy and directing the buying and selling of government securities

(d) acting as the fiscal agent for the Federal government and issuing currency

24. The most important function of the Federal Reserve System is

(a) issuing currency

(b) controlling the money supply

(c) supervising commercial banks

(d) lending money to banks and thrifts

25. According to the text, which would be a recent development in the banking industry?

(a) an increase in the number of banks and thrifts

(b) increased integration of world financial markets

(c) increased use of coins and currency as a medium of exchange

(d) a decrease in the financial services and activities of banks and thrifts

■ **PROBLEMS**

1. From the figures in the following table it can be concluded that

Item	Billions of dollars
Small time deposits	630
Large time deposits	645
Money market deposit accounts	575
Money market mutual funds	425
Checkable deposits	448
Noncheckable savings deposits	300
Currency	170

a. *M*1 is equal to the sum of $_____ and $_____, so it totals $_____ billion.

b. M2 is equal to M1 plus $_____ and

$_____ and $_____ and

$_____, so it totals $_____ billion.

c. M3 is equal to M2 plus $_____, so

it totals $_____ billion.

2. Complete the following table showing the relationship between a percentage change in the price level and the percentage change in the value of money. Calculate the percentage change in the value of money to one decimal place.

Change in price level	Change in value of money
a. *rise* by:	
5%	−_____.___%
10%	−_____.___
15%	−_____.___
20%	−_____.___
25%	−_____.___
b. *fall* by:	
5%	+_____.___%
10%	+_____.___
15%	+_____.___

3. The total demand for money is equal to the transaction plus the asset demand for money.

a. Assume each dollar held for transaction purposes is spent (on the average) four times per year to buy final goods and services.

(1) This means that transaction demand for money will be equal to (what fraction or percent)

_____ of the nominal GDP, and,

(2) if the nominal GDP is $2000 billion, the transaction demand will be $_____ billion.

b. The following table shows the number of dollars demanded for asset purposes at each rate of interest.

(1) Given the transactions demand for money in (a), complete the table.

(2) On the graph below, plot the *total* demand for money (Dm) at each rate of interest.

Interest rate	Amount of money demanded (billions)	
	For asset purposes	Total
16%	$ 20	$_____
14	40	_____
12	60	_____
10	80	_____
8	100	_____
6	120	_____
4	140	_____

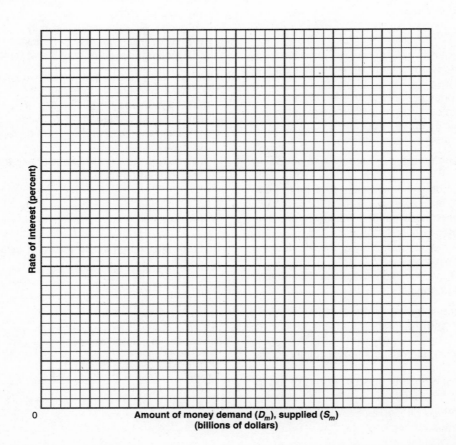

Rate of interest (percent)

0

Amount of money demand (Dm), supplied (Sm)
(billions of dollars)

c. Assume the money supply (S_m) is $580 billion.
(1) Plot this money supply on the graph.
(2) Using either the graph or the table, the equilibrium

rate of interest is _____ %.
d. Should the money supply
(1) increase to $600 billion, the equilibrium interest

rate would (rise, fall) _____ to _____ %.
(2) decrease to $540 billion, the equilibrium interest

rate would _____ to _____ %.
e. If the nominal GDP
(1) increased by $80 billion, the total demand for

money would (increase, decrease) _____

by $_____ billion at each rate of
interest and the equilibrium rate of interest would (rise,

fall) _____ by _____ %.
(2) decreased by $120 billion, the total demand for

money would _____ by $_____
billion at each rate of interest and the equilibrium in-

terest rate would _____ by _____ %.

4. Suppose a bond with no expiration date pays a fixed
$500 annually and sells for its face value of $5,000.
  a. Complete the following table and calculate the interest rate (to one decimal place) that would be obtained from the bond when the bond price is given or
  calculate the bond price when the interest rate is given.

Bond price	Interest rate
$4,000	_____._____%
$_____	11.0
$5,000	_____._____
$5,500	_____._____
$_____	8.0

  b. Based on the results of the table, as the price increases on a bond with a fixed annual payment, the
  interest yield on the bond (decreases, increases)

  _____, but when the price of a bond de-

  creases, the interest yield _____. Given
  this situation in an economy, you can conclude that a

  higher price for bonds _____ interest rates

  and that a lower price for bonds _____ interest rates.

■ **SHORT ANSWER AND ESSAY QUESTIONS**

1. How would you define money based on its three functions?

2. What are the components of the **M**1 supply of money
in the United States? Which of these components is larger?

3. What are checkable deposits, and what are the different types of institutions offering checkable deposits?

4. What is a near-money? What are the more important
near-monies in the U.S. economy?

5. Define **M**2 and **M**3, and explain why the existence of
near-monies is important.

6. For what reasons are checkable deposits included in
the money supply?

7. What backs the money used in the United States?
What determines the value of money?

8. Explain the relationship between the value of money
and the price level.

9. What must government do if it is to stabilize the value
of money?

10. What are the two reasons people wish to hold money?
How are these two reasons related to the functions of
money?

11. Explain the determinant of each of the two demands
for money and how a change in the size of these determinants will affect the amount of money people wish to
hold.

12. The rate of interest is a price. Of what good or service is it the price? Explain how demand and supply determine this price.

13. Describe how changes in bond prices correct disequilibrium in the money market. What is the relationship
between bond prices and interest rates?

14. Outline the structure of the Federal Reserve System
and explain the chief functions of each of the four parts
of the system.

15. As briefly as possible, outline the three characteristics of the Federal Reserve Banks and explain the meaning of these characteristics.

16. What are the chief functions the Federal Reserve
Banks perform? Explain briefly the meaning of each function. Which of the chief functions is the most important?

17. What are the basic arguments for and against the
independence of the Federal Reserve System?

18. Describe three different responses by banks and
thrifts to the relative decline of these institutions in recent
years.

19. Discuss the meaning and effects of increased integration of world financial market.

20. Explain how electronic money changes the way
money is stored and transferred and how these changes
will affect banks, thrifts, and the Federal Reserve.

ANSWERS

Chapter 13 Money and Banking

FILL-IN QUESTIONS

1. a medium of exchange, unit of account, store of value
2. token, less

3. currency, checkable deposits, currency

4. *M*1, noncheckable, small, deposit accounts, mutual funds (either order for the last two)

5. large, $100,000 or greater

6. *a.* they influence consuming-saving habits; *b.* conversion from near-money to money or from money to near-money may affect the stability of the economy; *c.* they are important when monetary policy is to be used

7. are not, loan

8. the Federal Reserve Banks, banks and thrifts, are not

9. acceptable, legal, scarce

10. inversely, divide

11. directly, nominal GDP, inversely, the rate of interest

12. demand, supply, interest rate

13. decrease, increase, increase, decrease

14. Governors, Federal Open Market Committee, 3, 12

15. quasipublic, bankers', central

16. commercial banks, state, national

17. *a.* issuing currency; *b.* setting reserve requirements and holding reserves; *c.* lending money to banks and thrifts; *d.* collecting and processing checks; *e.* serving as fiscal agent for the Federal government; *f.* bank supervision; *g.* controlling the money supply; controlling the money supply

18. undemocratic, inflation

19. expanding, merging with, regulatory

20. globalization, electronic

TRUE-FALSE QUESTIONS

1. T, p. 265	**10.** F, p. 265	**19.** F, p. 277
2. F, p. 265	**11.** F, p. 267	**20.** F, p. 278
3. T, p. 265	**12.** T, pp. 269-270	**21.** T, p. 278
4. F, p. 265	**13.** T, pp. 270-272	**22.** F, p. 279
5. T, pp. 266-267	**14.** F, p. 272	**23.** T, pp. 279-280
6. F, pp. 266-267	**15.** T, p. 272	**24.** F, p. 280
7. T, p. 267	**16.** T, p. 274	**25.** F, p. 284
8. T, p. 267	**17.** T, pp. 274-275	
9. F, p. 267-268	**18.** T, pp. 276-277	

MULTIPLE-CHOICE QUESTIONS

1. d, p. 265	**10.** b, pp. 270-271	**19.** a, pp. 274-275
2. d, p. 266	**11.** c, pp. 271-272	**20.** d, p. 274
3. d, p. 266	**12.** b, pp. 272-274	**21.** d, pp. 274-275
4. d, p. 266	**13.** c, pp. 272-273	**22.** a, pp. 274-275
5. d, p. 269	**14.** b, p. 272	**23.** c, p. 277
6. b, p. 266	**15.** a, p. 274	**24.** b, p. 279
7. c, p. 266	**16.** b, pp. 273-275	**25.** b, p. 282
8. b, p. 266	**17.** c, pp. 273-275	
9. b, pp. 269-270	**18.** d, p. 274	

PROBLEMS

1. *a.* 170, 448 (either order), 618; *b.* 300, 630, 575, 425 (either order), 2,548; *c.* 645, 3,193

2. *a.* 4.8, 9.1, 13, 16.7, 20; *b.* 5.3, 11.1, 17.6

3. *a.* (1) 1/4 (25%), (2) 500; *b.* (1) 520, 540, 560, 580, 600, 620, 640; *c.* (2) 10; *d.* (1) fall, 8, (2) rise, 14; *e.* (1) increase, 20, rise, 2, (2) decrease, 30, fall, 3

4. *a.* 12.5%, $4,545, 10.0%, 9.1%, $6,250; *b.* decreases, increases, decreases, increases

SHORT ANSWER AND ESSAY QUESTIONS

1. pp. 264-265	**8.** pp. 270-271	**15.** pp. 277-278
2. pp. 265-266	**9.** pp. 271-272	**16.** p. 279
3. pp. 266-267	**10.** pp. 272-274	**17.** pp. 279-280
4. p. 267	**11.** pp. 272-274	**18.** pp. 280-282
5. pp. 267-268	**12.** pp. 273-275	**19.** pp. 282-283
6. p. 266	**13.** pp. 274-275	**20.** pp. 282-284
7. pp. 269-270	**14.** pp. 276-278	

CHAPTER 14

How Banks Create Money

Chapter 13 explained the institutional structure of banking in the United States today, the functions which banks and the other depository institutions and money perform, and the composition of the money supply. Chapter 14 explains how banks create money—*demand-deposit* money—and the factors which determine and limit the money-creating ability of commercial banks. The other depository institutions also create checkable deposits, but this chapter focuses on the commercial banks because they have created and will continue to create a very large part of the total amount of money created by all depository institutions in the United States.

The convenient and simple device used to explain commercial banking operations and money creation is the *balance sheet.* All banking transactions affect this balance sheet, and the first step to understanding how money is created is to understand how various simple and typical transactions affect the commercial bank balance sheet.

In reading this chapter you must analyze for yourself the effect of each and every banking transaction discussed on the balance sheet. The important items in the balance sheet are demand deposits and reserves because **demand deposits are money,** and the ability of a bank to create new demand deposits is determined by the amount of reserves the bank has. Expansion of the money supply depends on the possession by commercial banks of excess reserves. Excess reserves do not appear explicitly in the balance sheet but do appear there implicitly because excess reserves are the difference between the actual reserves and the required reserves of commercial banks.

Two cases—the single commercial bank and the banking system—are presented to help you build an understanding of banking and money creation. It is important to understand that the money-creating potential of a single commercial bank differs from the money-creating potential of the entire banking system; it is equally important to understand how the money-creating ability of many single commercial banks is *multiplied* and influences the money-creating ability of the banking system as a whole.

Certain assumptions are used throughout most of this chapter to analyze money creation; in certain instances these assumptions may not be completely realistic and may need to be modified. The chapter concludes with a discussion of how the earlier analysis must be modified—but not changed in its essentials—to take account of slightly unrealistic assumptions.

You will also learn that the money-creating actions of banks have a procyclical effect on the economy which needs to be controlled by the Federal Reserve System—a topic discussed in more detail in the next chapter.

■ **CHECKLIST**

When you have studied this chapter you should be able to

☐ Define the basic items in a bank's balance sheet.
☐ Recount the story of how goldsmiths came to issue paper money and became bankers who created money and held fractional reserves.
☐ Cite two significant characteristics of the fractional reserve banking system today.
☐ Explain the effects of the deposit of currency in a checking account on the composition and size of the money supply.
☐ Compute a bank's required and excess reserves when you are given the needed balance-sheet figures.
☐ Explain why a commercial bank is required to maintain a reserve and why this reserve is not sufficient to protect the depositors from losses.
☐ Indicate how the deposit of a check drawn on one commercial bank and deposited into another will affect the reserves and excess reserves of the two banks.
☐ Show what happens to the money supply when a commercial bank makes a loan (or buys government securities).
☐ Show what happens to the money supply when a loan is repaid (or a bank sells government securities).
☐ Explain what happens to a commercial bank's reserves and demand deposits after it has made a loan, a check has been written on the newly created demand deposit and deposited in another commercial bank and cleared, and explain what happens to the reserves and demand deposits of the commercial bank in which the check was deposited.
☐ Describe what would happen to a commercial bank's reserves if it made loans (or bought government securities) in an amount that exceeded its excess reserves.
☐ State the money-creating potential of a commercial bank (the amount of money a commercial bank can safely create by lending or buying securities).

☐ Explain how the Federal funds market helps reconcile the goals of profits and liquidity for commercial banks.

☐ State the money-creating potential of the banking system.

☐ Explain how it is possible for the banking system to create an amount of money which is a multiple of its excess reserves when no individual commercial bank ever creates money in an amount greater than its excess reserve.

☐ Compute the size of the monetary multiplier and the money-creating potential of the banking system when you are provided with the necessary data.

☐ Illustrate with an example using the monetary multiplier how money can be destroyed in the banking system.

☐ List the two leakages which reduce the money-creating potential of the banking system.

☐ Explain why the size of the money supply needs to be controlled by the Federal Reserve System.

■ **CHAPTER OUTLINE**

1. The *balance sheet* of the commercial bank is a statement of the assets, liabilities, and net worth (capital stock) of the bank at a specific time; and in the balance sheet, the bank's assets equal its liabilities plus its net worth.

2. The history of the early goldsmiths illustrates how paper money came into use in the economy. This history also shows how goldsmiths became bankers when they began making loans and issuing money in excess of their gold holdings. The goldsmiths' fractional reserve system is similar to today's fractional banking system, which has two significant characteristics:

a. Banks can create money in such a system.

b. Banks are subject to "panics" or "runs" in a fractional banking system and thus need government regulation.

3. By examining the ways the balance sheet of the commercial bank is affected by various transactions, it is possible to understand how a *single commercial bank* in a multibank system can create money.

a. Once a commercial bank has been founded,

(1) by selling shares of stock and obtaining cash in return;

(2) and acquiring the property and equipment needed to carry on the banking business;

(3) the deposit of cash in the bank does not affect the total money supply; it only changes its composition by substituting demand deposits for currency in circulation;

(4) three reserve concepts are vital to an understanding of the money-creating potential of a commercial bank.

(a) The **legal reserve deposit** (required reserve), which a bank *must* maintain at its Federal Reserve Bank (or as vault cash—which can be ignored), equals the reserve ratio multiplied by the deposit liabilities of the commercial bank;

(b) the **actual reserves** of a commercial bank are its deposits at the Federal Reserve Bank (plus the vault cash which is ignored);

(c) the **excess reserves** equal to the actual reserves less the required reserve.

(5) The writing of a check on the bank and its deposit in a second bank results in a loss of reserves and deposits for the first and a gain in reserves and deposits for the second bank.

b. When a single commercial bank lends or buys government securities, it increases its own deposit liabilities and therefore the supply of money by the amount of the loan or security purchase. But the bank only lends or buys securities in an amount equal to its excess reserves because it fears the loss of reserves to other commercial banks in the economy.

c. When a single commercial bank receives loan repayments or sells government securities, its deposit liabilities and therefore the supply of money are described by the amount of the loan repayments or securities sale.

d An individual commercial bank balances its desire for profits (which result from the making of loans and the purchase of securities) with its desire for liquidity or safety (which it achieves by having excess reserves or vault cash).

e. The Federal funds market allows banks with excess reserves to lend funds overnight to banks which are short of reserves. The interest rate paid on the overnight loans is the Federal funds rate.

4. The ability of a *banking system* composed of many individual commercial banks to lend and to create money is a multiple (greater than 1) of its excess reserves and is equal to the excess reserves of the banking system multiplied by the demand-deposit (or monetary) multiplier.

a. The banking system as a whole can do this even though no single commercial bank ever lends an amount greater than its excess reserve because the banking system, unlike a single commercial bank, does not lose reserves.

b. The monetary (or demand-deposit) multiplier is equal to the reciprocal of the required reserve ratio for demand deposits, and the maximum expansion of demand deposits is equal to the excess reserves in the banking system times the monetary multiplier.

c. The potential lending ability of the banking system may not be fully achieved if there are leakages because borrowers choose to have additional currency or bankers choose to have excess reserves.

d If bankers lend as much as they are able during periods of prosperity and less than they are able during recessions, they add to the instability of the economy. To reduce this instability, the Federal Reserve Banks must control the size of the money supply.

■ **HINTS AND TIPS**

1. Note that several terms are used interchangeably in this chapter: (1) "Commercial bank" (or "bank") is sometimes called "thrift institution"; (2) "checkable deposit" is sometimes called "demand deposit" or "depository institution."

2. A bank's balance sheet must balance. The bank's assets are either claimed by owners (net worth) or by nonowners (liabilities). Assets = liabilities + net worth.

3. Make a running balance sheet in writing for yourself as you read about each of the eight transactions in the text for the Wahoo Bank. Then determine if you understand the material by telling yourself (or a friend) the story for each transaction without using the text.

4. The maximum amount of **demand-deposit expansion** is determined by multiplying two factors: the excess reserves by the monetary multiplier. Each factor, however, is affected by the required reserve ratio. The monetary multiplier is calculated by dividing one by the required reserve ratio. Excess reserves are determined by multiplying the required reserve ratio by the amount of new deposits. Thus, a change in the required reserve ratio will change the monetary multiplier *and* the amount of excess reserves. For example, a required reserve ratio of 25% gives a monetary multiplier of 4. For $100 in new money deposited, required reserves are $25 and excess reserves are $75. The maximum demand-deposit expansion is $300 (4 × $75). If the reserve ratio drops to 20%, the monetary multiplier is 5 and excess reserves are $80, so the maximum demand-deposit expansion is $400. Both factors have changed.

5. Be aware that the monetary multiplier can result in money destruction as well as money creation in the banking system. You should know how the monetary multiplier reinforces effects in one direction or the other.

■ IMPORTANT TERMS

balance sheet	reserve ratio
assets	actual reserve
liabilities	excess reserve
net worth	Federal funds rate
fractional reserve system of banking	commercial banking system
vault cash (till money)	monetary (demand-deposit) multiplier
required reserves	

SELF-TEST

■ FILL-IN QUESTIONS

1. In this chapter, a commercial bank may also be called a (checkable, thrift) _____ institution and a demand deposit may also be called a _____ deposit.

2. The balance sheet of a commercial bank is a statement of the bank's (gold account, assets) _____, the claims of the owners of the bank, [called (net worth, liabilities) _____], and claims of the nonowners (called _____). This relationship would be written in equation form as:

_____.

3. The banking system used today is a (total, fractional) _____ reserve system, which means that (100%, less than 100%) _____ of the money deposited in a bank is kept on reserve.

4. There are two significant characteristics to the banking system of today.

a. Banks can create (reserves, money) _____ depending on the amount of _____ they hold.

b. Banks are susceptible to (panics, regulation) _____ or "runs," and to prevent this situation from happening, banks are subject to government _____.

5. The coins and paper money which a bank has in its possession are (petty, vault) _____ cash or (till, capital) _____ money.

6. When a person deposits cash in a commercial bank and receives a demand deposit in return, the size of the money supply has (increased, decreased, not changed) _____.

7. The legal reserve of a commercial bank (ignoring vault cash) must be kept on deposit at (a branch of the U.S. Treasury, its district Federal Reserve Bank) _____

_____.

8. The reserve ratio is equal to the commercial bank's (required, gold) _____ reserves divided by its demand deposit (assets, liabilities) _____.

9. The authority to establish and vary the reserve ratio within limits legislated by Congress is given to the (U.S. Treasury, Fed) _____.

10. If commercial banks are allowed to accept (or create) deposits in excess of their reserves, the banking system is operating under a system of (fractional, currency) _____ reserves.

11. The excess reserves of a commercial bank equal its (actual, required) _____ reserves minus its _____ reserves.

12. The basic purpose for having member banks deposit a legal reserve in the Federal Reserve Bank in their district is to provide (liquidity for, control of) _____ the banking system by the Fed.

13. When a commercial bank deposits a legal reserve in its district Federal Reserve Bank, the reserve is (a liability, an asset) _____ to the commercial bank and _____ to the Federal Reserve Bank.

14. When a check is drawn on Bank X, deposited in Bank Y, and cleared, the reserves of Bank X are (increased, decreased, not changed) _____ and the reserves of Bank Y are _____; deposits in Bank X are (increased, decreased, not changed) _____ and deposits in Bank Y are _____.

15. A single commercial bank in a multibank system can safely make loans or buy government securities equal in amount to the (required, excess) _____ reserves of that commercial bank.

16. When a commercial bank makes a new loan of $10,000, the supply of money (increases, decreases) _____ by $_____, but when a loan is repaid, the supply of money (increases, decreases) by $_____.

17. When a commercial bank sells a $10,000 government bond to a securities dealer, the supply of money (increases, decreases) _____ $_____, but when a commercial bank buys a $10,000 government bond from a securities dealer, the supply of money (increases, decreases) _____ by $_____.

18. A bank ordinarily pursues two conflicting goals; one goal is the desire to make money, or (profits, liquidity) _____, and the other goal is the need for safety, or _____.

19. When a bank lends temporary excess reserves held at its Federal Reserve Bank to other commercial banks that are temporarily short of legal reserves, it is participating in the (government securities, Federal funds) _____ market. The interest rate paid on these overnight loans is called the (government securities, Federal funds) _____ rate.

20. The monetary multiplier is equal to 1 divided by the (excess, required) _____ reserve ratio.

21. The greater the reserve ratio, the (larger, smaller) _____ the monetary multiplier.

22. The banking system can make loans (or buy government securities) and create money in an amount equal to its (required, excess) _____ reserves multiplied by the (required reserve ratio, monetary multiplier) _____.

23. Assume that the required reserve ratio is 16.67% and the banking system is $6 million short of required reserves. If the banking system is unable to increase its re-

serves, the banking system must (increase, decrease) _____ the money supply by ($6, $36) _____ million.

24. The money-creating potential of the commercial banking system is lessened by the (addition, withdrawal) _____ of currency from banks and by banks not lending (required, excess) _____ reserves.

25. Commercial banks in the past have kept excess reserves during periods of (prosperity, recession) _____ and have kept few or no excess reserves during periods of _____. By acting this way, they have made the economy (more, less) _____ stable, which has given rise to the need for monetary control by the Federal Reserve System.

■ TRUE-FALSE QUESTIONS

Circle the T if the statement is true, the F if it is false.

1. The balance sheet of a commercial bank shows the transactions in which the bank has engaged during a given period of time. **T F**

2. A commercial bank's assets plus its net worth equal the bank's liabilities. **T F**

3. Goldsmiths increased the money supply when they accepted deposits of gold and issued paper receipts to the depositors. **T F**

4. Modern banking systems use gold as the basis for the fractional reserve system. **T F**

5. Cash held by a bank is sometimes called vault cash. **T F**

6. Mary Lynn, a music star, deposits a $30,000 check in a commercial bank and receives a demand deposit in return; 1 hour later the Manfred Iron and Coal Company borrows $30,000 from the same bank. The money supply has increased $30,000 as a result of the two transactions. **T F**

7. A commercial bank may maintain its legal reserve either as a deposit in its Federal Reserve Bank or as government bonds in its own vault. **T F**

8. The legal reserve which a commercial bank maintains must equal at least its own deposit liabilities multiplied by the required reserve ratio. **T F**

9. Legal reserves permit the Board of Governors of the Federal Reserve System to influence the lending ability of commercial banks. **T F**

10. The actual reserves of a commercial bank equal excess reserves plus required reserves. **T F**

11. The reserve of a commercial bank in the Federal Reserve Bank is an asset of the Federal Reserve Bank. **T F**

12. A check for $1,000 drawn on bank X by a depositor and deposited in bank Y will increase the excess reserves in bank Y by $1,000. **T F**

13. A single commercial bank can safely lend an amount equal to its excess reserves multiplied by the monetary multiplier ratio. **T F**

14. When a borrower repays a loan of $500, either in cash or by check, the supply of money is reduced by $500. **T F**

15. The granting of a $5,000 loan and the purchase of a $5,000 government bond from a securities dealer by a commercial bank have the same effect on the money supply. **T F**

16. The selling of a government bond by a commercial bank will increase the money supply. **T F**

17. A commercial bank seeks both profits and liquidity, but these are conflicting goals. **T F**

18. The Federal funds rate is the interest rate at which the Federal government lends funds to commercial banks. **T F**

19. The reason that the banking system can lend by a multiple of its excess reserves, but each individual bank can only lend "dollar for dollar" with its excess reserves, is that reserves lost by a single bank are not lost to the banking system as a whole. **T F**

20. The monetary multiplier is excess reserves divided by required reserves. **T F**

21. The maximum demand-deposit expansion is equal to excess reserves divided by the monetary multiplier. **T F**

22. If the banking system has $10 million in excess reserves and if the reserve ratio is 25%, it can increase its loans by $40 million. **T F**

23. When borrowers from a commercial bank wish to have cash rather than demand deposits, the money-creating potential of the banking system is increased. **T F**

24. A desire by banks to hold excess reserves may reduce the size of the monetary multiplier. **T F**

25. There is a need for the Federal Reserve System to control the money supply because profit-seeking banks tend to make changes in the money supply that are pro-cyclical. **T F**

■ **MULTIPLE-CHOICE QUESTIONS**

Circle the letter that corresponds to the best answer.

1. The fractional reserve system of banking started when goldsmiths began
 (a) accepting deposits of gold for safe storage
 (b) issuing receipts for the gold stored with them
 (c) using deposited gold to produce products for sale to others
 (d) issuing paper money in excess of the amount of gold stored with them

2. When cash is deposited in a demand-deposit account in a commercial bank, there is

 (a) a decrease in the money supply
 (b) an increase in the money supply
 (c) no change in the composition of the money supply
 (d) a change in the composition of the money supply

3. A commercial bank has actual reserves of $9000 and liabilities of $30,000, and the required reserve ratio is 20%. The excess reserves of the bank are
 (a) $3,000
 (b) $6,000
 (c) $7,500
 (d) $9,000

4. The primary reason commercial banks must keep required reserves on deposit at the Federal Reserve Banks is to
 (a) protect the deposits in the commercial bank against losses
 (b) provide the means by which checks drawn on the commercial bank and deposited in other commercial banks can be collected
 (c) add to the liquidity of the commercial bank and protect it against a "run" on the bank
 (d) provide the Fed with a means of controlling the lending ability of the commercial bank

5. A depositor places $750 in cash in a commercial bank, and the reserve ratio is 33 1/3%; the bank sends the $750 to the Federal Reserve Bank. As a result, the *reserves* and the *excess reserves* of the bank have been increased, respectively, by
 (a) $750 and $250
 (b) $750 and $500
 (c) $750 and $750
 (d) $500 and $500

6. A commercial bank has no excess reserves until a depositor places $600 in cash in the bank. The bank then adds the $600 to its reserves by sending it to the Federal Reserve Bank. The commercial bank then lends $300 to a borrower. As a consequence of these transactions the size of the money supply has
 (a) not been affected
 (b) increased by $300
 (c) increased by $600
 (d) increased by $900

7. A commercial bank has excess reserves of $500 and a required reserve ratio of 20%; it grants a loan of $1,000 to a borrower. If the borrower writes a check for $1,000 which is deposited in another commercial bank, the first bank will be short of reserves, after the check has been cleared, in the amount of
 (a) $200
 (b) $500
 (c) $700
 (d) $1,000

8. A commercial bank sells a $1,000 government security to a securities dealer. The dealer pays for the bond in cash, which the bank adds to its vault cash. The money supply has
 (a) not been affected
 (b) decreased by $1,000

(c) increased by $1,000
(d) increased by $1,000 multiplied by the reciprocal of the required reserve ratio

9. A commercial bank has deposit liabilities of $100,000, reserves of $37,000, and a required reserve ratio of 25%. The amount by which a *single commercial bank* and the amount by which the *banking system* can increase loans are, respectively
  (a) $12,000 and $48,000
  (b) $17,000 and $68,000
  (c) $12,000 and $60,000
  (d) $17,000 and $85,000

10. If the required reserve ratio were 12 1/2%, the value of the monetary multiplier would be
  (a) 5
  (b) 6
  (c) 7
  (d) 8

11. The commercial banking system has excess reserves of $700, makes new loans of $2,100, and is just meeting its reserve requirements. The required reserve ratio is
  (a) 20%
  (b) 25%
  (c) 30%
  (d) 33 1/3%

12. The commercial banking system, because of a recent change in the required reserve ratio from 20% to 30%, finds that it is $60 million short of reserves. If it is unable to obtain any additional reserves it must decrease the money supply by
  (a) $60 million
  (b) $180 million
  (c) $200 million
  (d) $300 million

13. Only one commercial bank in the banking system has an excess reserve, and its excess reserve is $100,000. This bank makes a new loan of $80,000 and keeps an excess reserve of $20,000. If the required reserve ratio for all banks is 20%, the potential expansion of the money supply is
  (a) $80,000
  (b) $100,000
  (c) $400,000
  (d) $500,000

14. The money-creating potential of the banking system is reduced when
  (a) bankers choose to hold excess reserves
  (b) borrowers choose to hold none of the funds they have borrowed in currency
  (c) the Federal Reserve lowers the required reserve ratio
  (d) bankers borrow from the Federal Reserve

15. The excess reserves held by banks tend to
  (a) rise during periods of prosperity
  (b) fall during periods of recession
  (c) rise during periods of recession
  (d) fall when interest rates in the economy fall

16. Unless controlled, the money supply will
  (a) fall during periods of prosperity
  (b) rise during periods of recession
  (c) change in a procyclical fashion
  (d) change in an anticyclical fashion

Use the following balance sheet for the First National Bank to answer Questions 17, 18, 19, 20, and 21. Assume the required reserve ratio is 20%.

Assets		Liabilities and Net Worth	
Reserves	$ 50,000	Demand Deposits	$150,000
Loans	70,000	Capital Stock	100,000
Securities	30,000		
Property	100,000		

17. This commercial bank has excess reserves of
  (a) $10,000
  (b) $20,000
  (c) $30,000
  (d) $40,000

18. This bank can safely expand its loans by a maximum of
  (a) $50,000
  (b) $40,000
  (c) $30,000
  (d) $20,000

19. Using the original bank balance sheet, assume that the bank makes a loan of $10,000 and has a check cleared against it for the amount of the loan; then its reserves and demand deposits will now be
  (a) $40,000 and $140,000
  (b) $40,000 and $150,000
  (c) $30,000 and $150,000
  (d) $60,000 and $140,000

20. Using the original bank balance sheet, assume that the bank makes a loan of $15,000 and has a check cleared against it for the amount of the loan; then it will have excess reserves of
  (a) $5,000
  (b) $10,000
  (c) $15,000
  (d) $20,000

21. If the original bank balance sheet was for the commercial banking *system,* rather than a single bank, loans and deposits could have been expanded by a maximum of
  (a) $50,000
  (b) $100,000
  (c) $150,000
  (d) $200,000

22. The claims of the owners of the bank against the bank assets is the bank's
  (a) net worth
  (b) liabilities
  (c) balance sheet
  (d) fractional reserves

23. The selling of government bonds by commercial banks is most similar to the

(a) making of loans by banks because both actions increase the money supply

(b) making of loans by banks because both actions decrease the money supply

(c) repayment of loans to banks because both actions decrease the money supply

(d) repayment of loans to banks because both actions increase the money supply

Answer Questions 24 and 25 on the basis of the following consolidated balance sheet for the commercial banking system. All figures are in billions. Assume that the required reserve ratio is 12.5%.

Assets		Liabilities and Net Worth	
Reserves	$ 40	Demand Deposits	$200
Loans	80	Capital Stock	120
Securities	100		
Property	200		

24. The maximum amount by which this commercial banking system can expand the supply of money by lending is

(a) $120 billion

(b) $240 billion

(c) $350 billion

(d) $440 billion

25. If there is a deposit of $20 billion of new currency into checking accounts in the banking system, excess reserves will increase by

(a) $16.5 billion

(b) $17.0 billion

(c) $17.5 billion

(d) $18.5 billion

■ **PROBLEMS**

1. The following table shows the simplified balance sheet of a commercial bank. Assume that the figures given show the bank's assets and demand-deposit liabilities *prior to each of the following four transactions.* Draw up the balance sheet as it would appear after each of these transactions is completed and place the balance-sheet figures in the appropriate column. Do *not* use the figures you place in columns a, b, and c when you work the next part of the problem; start all parts of the problem with the printed figures.

		(a)	(b)	(c)	(d)
Assets:					
Cash	$100	$____	$____	$____	$____
Reserves	200	____	____	____	____
Loans	500	____	____	____	____
Securities	200	____	____	____	____
Liabilities and net worth:					
Demand deposits	900	____	____	____	____
Capital stock	100	100	100	100	100

a. A check for $50 is drawn by one of the depositors of the bank, given to a person who deposits it in another bank, and cleared (column a).

b. A depositor withdraws $50 in cash from the bank, and the bank restores its vault cash by obtaining $50 in additional cash from its Federal Reserve Bank (column b).

c. A check for $60 drawn on another bank is deposited in this bank and cleared (column c).

d. The bank sells $100 in government bonds to the Federal Reserve Bank in its district (column d).

2. Following are five balance sheets for a single commercial bank (columns 1a–5a). The required reserve ratio is 20%.

a. Compute the required reserves (A), ignoring vault cash, the excess reserves (B) of the bank (if the bank is short of reserves and must reduce its loans or obtain additional reserves, show this by placing a minus sign in front of the amounts by which it is short of reserves), and the amount of new loans it can extend (C).

	(1a)	(2a)	(3a)	(4a)	(5a)
Assets:					
Cash	$ 10	$ 20	$ 20	$ 20	$ 15
Reserves	40	40	25	40	45
Loans	100	100	100	100	150
Securities	50	60	30	70	60
Liabilities and net worth:					
Demand deposits	175	200	150	180	220
Capital stock	25	20	25	50	50
A. Required reserve	$____	$____	$____	$____	$____
B. Excess reserve	____	____	____	____	____
C. New loans	____	____	____	____	____

b. In the following table, draw up for the individual bank the five balance sheets as they appear after the bank has made the new *loans* that it is capable of making.

	(1b)	(2b)	(3b)	(4b)	(5b)
Assets:					
Cash	$____	$____	$____	$____	$____
Reserves	____	____	____	____	____
Loans	____	____	____	____	____
Securities	____	____	____	____	____
Liabilities and net worth:					
Demand deposits	____	____	____	____	____
Capital stock	____	____	____	____	____

3. The table on the top of the next page shows several reserve ratios. Compute the monetary multiplier for each reserve ratio and enter the figures in column 2. In column 3 show the maximum amount by which a single commercial bank can increase its loans for each dollars worth of excess reserves it possesses. In column 4 indicate the maximum amount by which the banking system can increase its loans for each dollar's worth of excess reserves in the system.

(1)	(2)	(3)	(4)
12 1/2%	$_____	$_____	$_____
16 2/3%	_____	_____	_____
20%	_____	_____	_____
25%	_____	_____	_____
30%	_____	_____	_____
33 1/3%	_____	_____	_____

4. At the bottom of the page is the simplified consolidated balance sheet for *all* commercial banks in the economy. Assume that the figures given show the banks' assets and liabilities *prior to each of the following three transactions* and that the reserve ratio is 20%. Do *not* use the figures you placed in columns 2 and 4 when you begin parts **b** and **c** of the problem; start parts **a, b,** and **c** of the problem with the printed figures.

    a. The public deposits $5 in cash in the banks and the banks send the $5 to the Federal Reserve, where it is added to their reserves. Fill in column 1. If the banking system extends the maximum amount of new loans which it is capable of extending, show in column 2 the balance sheet as it would then appear.

    b. The banking system sells $8 worth of securities to the Federal Reserve. Complete column 3. Assuming the system extends the maximum amount of credit of which it is capable, fill in column 4.

    c. The Federal Reserve lends $10 to the commercial banks; complete column 5. Complete column 6 showing the condition of the banks after the maximum amount of new loans which the banks are capable of making is granted.

■ SHORT ANSWER AND ESSAY QUESTIONS

1. Why does a bank's balance sheet balance?

2. How did the early goldsmiths come to issue paper money and then become bankers?

3. Explain the difference between a 100% and fractional reserve system of banking.

4. What are two significant characteristics of a fractional reserve system of banking?

5. Explain what happens to the money supply when a bank accepts deposits of cash.

6. What are legal reserves? How are they determined? How are legal reserves related to the reserve ratio?

7. Define the meaning of excess reserves. How are they calculated?

8. Explain why bank reserves can be an asset to the depositing commercial bank but a liability to the Federal Reserve Bank receiving them.

9. Commercial banks seek both profits and safety. Explain how the balance sheet of the commercial banks reflects the desires of bankers for profits and for liquidity.

10. What is the Federal funds rate?

11. Discuss how the Federal funds market helps banks reconcile the two goals of profits and liquidity.

12. Do the reserves held by commercial banks satisfactorily protect the bank's depositors? Are the reserves of commercial banks needed? Explain your answers.

13. Explain why the granting of a loan by a commercial bank increases the supply of money. Why does the repayment of a loan decrease the supply of money?

14. How does the buying or selling of government securities by commercial banks influence the money supply?

15. The owner of a sporting goods store writes a check on his account in a Kent, Ohio, bank and sends it to one of his suppliers who deposits it in his bank in Cleveland, Ohio. How does the Cleveland bank obtain payment from the Kent bank? If the two banks were in Kent and New York City, how would one bank pay the other? How are the excess reserves of the two banks affected?

16. Why is a single commercial bank able to lend safely only an amount equal to its excess reserves?

		(1)	(2)	(3)	(4)	(5)	(6)
Assets:							
Cash	$ 50	$_____	$_____	$_____	$_____	$_____	$_____
Reserves	100	_____	_____	_____	_____	_____	_____
Loans	200	_____	_____	_____	_____	_____	_____
Securities	200	_____	_____	_____	_____	_____	_____
Liabilities and net worth:							
Demand deposits	500	_____	_____	_____	_____	_____	_____
Capital stock	50	50	50	50	50	50	50
Loans for Federal Reserve	0	_____	_____	_____	_____	_____	_____
Excess reserves		_____	_____	_____	_____	_____	_____
Maximum possible expansion of the money supply		_____	_____	_____	_____	_____	_____

17. No one commercial bank ever lends an amount greater than its excess reserve, but the banking system as a whole is able to extend loans and expand the money supply by an amount equal to the system's excess reserves multiplied by the reciprocal of the reserve ratio. Explain why this is possible and how the multiple expansion of deposits and money takes place.

18. What is the monetary multiplier? How does it work?

19. On the basis of a given amount of excess reserves and a given reserve ratio, a certain expansion of the money supply may be possible. What are two reasons why the potential expansion of the money supply may not be fully achieved?

20. Why is there a need for monetary control in the U.S. economy?

ANSWERS

Chapter 14 How Banks Create Money

FILL-IN QUESTIONS

1. thrift, checkable
2. assets, net worth, liabilities, assets = liabilities + net worth
3. fractional, less than 100%
4. *a.* money, reserves; *b.* panics, regulation
5. vault, till
6. not changed
7. its district Federal Reserve Bank
8. required, liabilities
9. Fed
10. fractional
11. actual, required
12. control of
13. an asset, a liability
14. decreased, increased, decreased, increased
15. excess
16. increases, 10,000, decreases, 10,000
17. decreases, 10,000, increases, 10,000
18. profits, liquidity
19. Federal funds, Federal funds
20. required
21. smaller
22. excess, monetary multiplier
23. decrease, $36
24. withdrawal, excess
25. recession, prosperity, less

TRUE-FALSE QUESTIONS

1. F, p. 287
2. F, pp. 287-288
3. F, p. 288
4. F, p. 288
5. T, p. 289
6. T, pp. 289, 293-294
7. F, p. 290
8. T, p. 290
9. T, p. 291
10. T, p. 291
11. F, p. 291
12. F, pp. 291-293
13. F, p. 295
14. T, p. 295
15. T, p. 295
16. F, p. 296
17. T, p. 296
18. F, p. 296
19. T, pp. 296-299
20. F, p. 299
21. F, p. 299
22. T, p. 299
23. F, p. 300
24. T, p. 300
25. T, pp. 300-302

MULTIPLE-CHOICE QUESTIONS

1. b, p. 288
2. d, pp. 289
3. a, pp. 290-291
4. d, pp. 291
5. b, pp. 291-293
6. b, p. 293-294
7. b, pp. 293-295
8. b, pp. 295-296
9. a, pp. 296-299
10. d, p. 299
11. d, p. 299
12. c, p. 299
13. c, pp. 299-300
14. a, p. 300
15. c, p. 302
16. c, p. 302
17. b, pp. 290-291
18. d, pp. 293-295
19. b, pp. 293-294
20. a, pp. 293-294
21. b, p. 299
22. a, pp. 287-288
23. c, p. 295
24. a, pp. 291, 299
25. c, p. 291

PROBLEMS

1.

	(a)	(b)	(c)	(d)
Assets:				
Cash	$100	$100	$100	$100
Reserves	150	150	260	300
Loans	500	500	500	500
Securities	200	200	200	100
Liabilities and net worth:				
Demand deposits	850	850	960	900
Capital stock	100	100	100	100

2. a.

	(1a)	(2a)	(3a)	(4a)	(5a)
A. Required reserve	$35	$40	$30	$36	$44
B. Excess reserve	5	0	−5	4	1
C. New loans	5	0	*	4	1

b.

	(1b)	(2b)	(3b)	(4b)	(5b)
Assets:					
Cash	$ 10	$ 20	$ 20	$ 20	$ 15
Reserves	40	40	25	40	45
Loans	105	100	*	104	151
Securities	50	60	30	70	60
Liabilities and net worth:					
Demand deposit	180	200	*	184	221
Capital stock	25	20	25	50	50

*If an individual bank is $5 short of reserves it must either obtain additional reserves of $5 by selling loans, securities, or its own IOUs to the reserve bank or contract its loans by $25.

3.

(1)	(2)	(3)	(4)
12 1/2%	$8	$1	$8
16 2/3%	6	1	6
20%	5	1	5
25%	4	1	4
30%	3 1/3	1	3 1/3
33 1/3%	3	1	3

4. see top of following page

SHORT ANSWER AND ESSAY QUESTIONS

1. pp. 287-288
2. p. 288
3. p. 288
4. p. 288
5. pp. 289-290
6. p. 290
7. p. 291
8. pp. 291-292
9. p. 296
10. p. 296
11. p. 296
12. p. 291
13. pp. 293-295
14. pp. 295-296
15. pp. 292-293
16. pp. 293-295
17. pp. 296-299
18. pp. 299-300
19. p. 300
20. pp. 300-302

	(1)	(2)	(3)	(4)	(5)	(6)
Assets:						
Cash	$ 50	$ 50	$ 50	$ 50	$ 50	$ 50
Reserves	105	105	108	108	110	110
Loans	200	220	200	240	200	250
Securities	200	200	192	192	200	200
Liabilities and net worth:						
Demand deposit	505	525	500	540	500	550
Capital stock	50	50	50	50	50	50
Loans from Federal						
Reserve	0	0	0	0	10	10
Excess reserves	4	0	8	0	10	0
Maximum possible expansion						
of the money supply	20	0	40	0	50	0

CHAPTER 15

Monetary Policy

Chapter 15 is the third chapter dealing with money and banking. It explains how the Board of Governors of the Federal Reserve System and the Federal Reserve Banks affect output, income, employment, and the price level of the economy. Central-bank policy designed to affect these variables is called monetary policy, the goal of which is full employment without inflation.

The first half of the chapter explains how the *Federal Reserve* achieves its basic goal. In this discussion, attention should be paid to the following: (1) the important items on the balance sheet of the Federal Reserve Banks; (2) the three major controls available to the Federal Reserve, and how the employment of these controls can affect the reserves, excess reserves, actual money supply, and money-creating potential of the banking system; (3) the actions the Federal Reserve would take if it were pursuing a **tight money policy** to curb inflation, and the actions it would take if it were pursuing an **easy money policy** to reduce unemployment, and (4) the relative importance of the three major controls which the Federal Reserve uses or has used to influence the economy.

Following the examination of "The Tools of Monetary Policy," Professors McConnell and Brue explain how the demand for and the supply of money determine the interest rate (in the "money market"), and how the interest rate and the investment-demand schedule determine the level of equilibrium GDP. How an easy money policy and a tight money policy work through this cause-effect chain is illustrated with examples and summarized in Table 15-3.

This explanation of monetary policy makes it clear that the effect of a change in the money supply depends on just how steep or flat the money-demand and investment-demand curves are. There may also be feedback effects from an easy money policy because the increased economic activity may cause interest rates to rise and partially offset interest-rate decreases started by the easy money policy. Changes in monetary policy and aggregate demand also have different output and price-level outcomes depending on the range of the aggregate supply curve where the changes in aggregate demand occur.

A major section of the chapter discusses the strengths and shortcomings of or problems with monetary policy as a stabilization tool. Its strengths are related to its speed, flexibility, and its isolation from political pressures. Its weaknesses are its potential ineffectiveness during recessions, while changes in the velocity of money can offset the policy effects.

Monetary policy can be used in different ways in the real world, and it can be subject to complications. In recent years, the Federal Reserve has made changes in monetary policy by adjusting its targets for the Federal fund rates. These rates in turn have an effect on other interest rates in the economy, such as the prime interest rate. The effectiveness of monetary policy is also complicated by linkages with the international economy. Monetary policy can affect exchange rates and net exports, which in turn can strengthen or weaken its intended effects.

The final section of the chapter is short but extremely important. Figure 15-3 in that section gives you an overview of the economic factors and government policies that affect aggregate demand and supply. It summarizes much of the economic theory and policy that have been discussed in this chapter and the eight others that preceded it.

■ CHECKLIST

When you have studied this chapter you should be able to

☐ State the fundamental objective of monetary policy.
☐ List the important assets and liabilities of the Federal Reserve Banks.
☐ Identify the three tools of monetary policy.
☐ Explain how the Federal Reserve expands or contracts the money supply by buying or selling government bonds.
☐ Describe how an increase or decrease in reserve requirement can increase or decrease the money supply.
☐ Illustrate how an increase or decrease in the discount rate increases or decreases the money supply.
☐ Describe three actions the Fed can take to pursue an easy money policy.
☐ Describe three actions the Fed can take to pursue a tight money policy.
☐ Discuss the relative importance of monetary policy tools.
☐ Draw the demand-for-money and the supply-of-money curves and use them to show how a change in the supply of money will affect the interest rate.
☐ Draw an investment-demand curve to explain the effects of changes in the interest rate on investment spending.
☐ Construct an aggregate supply and demand graph to show how aggregate demand and the equilibrium level of

GDP are affected by changes in interest rates and investment spending.

☐ Use a cause-effect chain to explain the links between a change in the money supply and a change in the equilibrium level of GDP when there is an easy money policy and a tight money policy.

☐ State precisely how the steepness of the demand-for-money and of the investment-demand curves affects the impact of a change in the money supply on the equilibrium GDP.

☐ Explain the feedback effects from different monetary policies.

☐ Use the ranges of the aggregate supply curve to explain how a change in aggregate demand is divided between changes in real output and the price level.

☐ List three strengths of monetary policy.

☐ Discuss five shortcomings of or problems with monetary policy.

☐ Describe the relationship among the Federal funds rate, the prime interest rate, and monetary policy in recent years.

☐ Describe how the effectiveness of an easy money policy or a tight money policy is influenced by net exports and how these policies affect international trade deficits.

☐ Use Figure 15-4 to summarize the key factors and policies affecting aggregate supply and demand, and the level of output, employment, income, and prices in an economy.

■ CHAPTER OUTLINE

1. The fundamental *objective* of monetary policy is full employment without inflation. The Federal Reserve can accomplish this objective by exercising control over the amount of excess reserves held by commercial banks and thereby influencing the size of the money supply and the level of aggregate expenditures.

2. By examining the consolidated *balance sheet* and the principal assets and liabilities of the Federal Reserve Banks, an understanding of the ways the Federal Reserve can control and influence the reserves of commercial banks and the money supply can be obtained.

  a. The principal assets of the Federal Reserve Banks (in order of size) are U.S. government securities and loans to commercial banks.

  b. Their principal liabilities are Federal Reserve Notes, the reserve deposits of commercial banks, and U.S. Treasury deposits.

3. The Federal Reserve Banks use *three principal tools* (techniques or instruments) to control the reserves of banks and the size of the money supply.

  a. The Federal Reserve can buy and sell government securities in the open market.

  (1) Buying securities in the open market from either banks or the public increases the reserves of banks.

  (2) Selling securities in the open market to either banks or the public decreases the reserves of banks.

  b. It can raise or lower the reserve ratio.

  (1) Raising the reserve ratio decreases the excess reserves of banks and the size of the monetary (demand-deposit) multiplier.

  (2) Lowering the reserve ratio increases the excess reserves of banks and the size of the monetary multiplier.

  c. It can also lower the discount rate to encourage banks to borrow reserves from the Fed and raise it to discourage them from borrowing reserves from the Fed.

  d. Monetary policy can be easy or tight.

  (1) An easy money policy can be implemented by actions of the Federal Reserve to buy government bonds in the open market, decrease the discount rate, or decrease the reserve ratio.

  (2) A tight money policy can be implemented by actions of the Federal Reserve to sell government bonds in the open market, increase the discount rate, or increase the reserve ratio.

  e. Open-market operations are the most important of the three monetary tools.

4. Monetary policy affects the equilibrium GDP in many ways.

  a. In the money market the demand-for- and the supply-of-money curves determine the real interest rate, the investment-demand curve and this rate of interest determine investment spending, and investment spending affects aggregate demand and the equilibrium levels of real output and prices.

  b. If unemployment and deflation are the problems, the Federal Reserve takes policy actions to increase the money supply, causing the interest rate to fall and investment spending to increase, thereby increasing aggregate demand and increasing real GDP by a multiple of the increase in investment.

  c. But if inflation is the problem, the Federal Reserve uses its tools to decrease the money supply, causing the interest rate to rise and investment spending to decrease, thereby reducing aggregate demand and inflation.

  d. There are refinements and feedback effects to monetary policy that must be considered.

  (1) The steeper the demand-for-money curve and the flatter the investment-demand curve, the greater will be the effect on the equilibrium GDP of a change in the money supply.

  (2) Changes in the equilibrium GDP that result from a change in the money supply will alter the demand for money and dampen the effect of the change in the money supply on the GDP.

  e. The aggregate supply curve will influence how the change in investment spending and aggregate demand is divided between change in real output and changes in the price level.

5. Whether monetary policy is effective in promoting full employment without inflation is a debatable question because monetary policy has both *strengths* and *shortcomings* or problems in fighting recession and inflation.

  a. Its strengths are that it can be more quickly changed than fiscal policy, it is more isolated from political pressure than fiscal policy, and it has been successful when it was used in recent situations.

  b. Its five shortcomings or problems are that it

  (1) may be subject to less control by the Federal Reserve because of recent changes in banking practices,

(2) is more effective in fighting inflation than it is in curbing recession,

(3) can be offset by changes in the velocity of money,

(4) may not have a significant effect on investment spending, and

(5) may produce changes in interest income and expenses that have offsetting effects.

c. The recent focus of the monetary policy of the Federal Reserve has been interest rates.

(1) The Federal Reserve can influence the ***Federal funds rate*** by buying or selling bonds. When the Federal Reserve buys bonds, it becomes cheaper for banks to borrow excess reserves overnight because the Federal funds rate falls; conversely, when the Federal Reserve sells bonds, the Federal funds rates rise and it becomes more expensive for banks to borrow funds.

(2) The ***prime interest rate*** is the rate that banks charge their most creditworthy customers; it tends to rise and fall with the Federal funds rate.

d. There are **international linkages** to monetary policy.

(1) An easy money policy to bring the economy out of recession or slow growth will tend to lower domestic interest rates and cause the dollar to depreciate. In this situation, net exports will increase, thus increasing aggregate demand and reinforcing the effect of the easy money policy.

(2) A tight money policy to reduce inflation will tend to raise domestic interest rates and cause the dollar to appreciate. These events will decrease net exports and reduce aggregate demand, thereby strengthening the tight money policy.

(3) An easy policy is compatible with the goal of correcting a balance of trade deficit, but a tight money policy conflicts with this economic goal.

6. The equilibrium levels of output, employment, income, and prices are determined by the interaction of aggregate supply and demand.

a. There are four expenditure components of aggregate demand: consumption, investment, net export spending, and government spending.

b. There are three major components of aggregate supply: the prices of inputs or resources, factors affecting the productivity with which resources are used, and the legal and institutional environment.

c. Fiscal, monetary, or other government policies may have an effect on the components of aggregate demand or supply, which in turn affect the level of output, employment, income, and prices.

■ **HINTS AND TIPS**

1. To acquire a thorough knowledge of how the Federal Reserve transactions affect reserves, excess reserves, the actual money supply, and the potential money supply, carefully study each of the sets of balance sheets which are used to explain these transactions. The items to watch are the reserves and demand deposits. Be sure that you

know why a change is made in each balance sheet, and be able to make the appropriate balance-sheet entries as you trace through the effects of each transaction. Problem 2 in this chapter provides additional practice.

2. You must understand and remember the cause-effect chain of monetary policy. The best way to learn it is to draw your own chain (diagram or table) that shows the links for an easy money policy and a tight money policy. Then check your work against Table 15-3 in the text. Draw another chain for describing monetary policy and the net export effect. Check your cause-effect chain against Table 15-4 in the text.

3. The single most important figure for the macroeconomics part of the textbook is probably Figure 15-4. It gives an excellent overview and summary of the determinants of aggregate supply and demand and identifies the key policy variables that have been discussed in this chapter and Chapters 7–14.

■ **IMPORTANT TERMS**

monetary policy	**tight money policy**
open-market operations	**velocity of money**
reserve ratio	**Federal funds rate**
discount rate	**prime interest rate**
easy money policy	

SELF-TEST

■ **FILL-IN QUESTIONS**

1. The objective of monetary policy in the United States is a full-employment (inflationary, noninflationary) _____ level of total output. Responsibility for monetary policy rests with the (Secretary of the Treasury, Federal Board of Governors) _____, and they are put into effect by the 12 (largest commercial banks, Federal Reserve Banks) _____.

2. The two important assets of the Federal Reserve Banks are (Treasury deposits, government securities) _____ and (reserves of, loans to) _____ commercial banks. The three major liabilities are (Treasury deposits, government securities) _____; (reserves of, loans to) _____ commercial banks, and (government securities, Federal Reserve Notes) _____.

3. The three tools the monetary authority uses to control the money supply are (open, closed) _____-market operations, changing the (loan, reserve) _____ ratio, and changing the (prime interest, discount) _____ rate.

4. When the Federal Reserve Banks buy government securities in the open market, the reserves of commercial banks will (increase, decrease) _____ and when they sell government securities in the open market, the reserves of commercial banks will _____.

5. If the Federal Reserve Banks were to sell $10 million in government bonds to the *public* and the reserve ratio were 25%, the supply of money would immediately be reduced by $_____, the reserves of commercial banks would be reduced by $_____, and the excess reserves of the banks would be reduced by $_____. But if these bonds were sold to the commercial banks, the supply of money would immediately be reduced by $_____, the reserves of the banks would be reduced by $_____, and the excess reserves of the banks would be reduced by $_____.

6. An increase in the reserve ratio will (increase, decrease) _____ the size of the monetary multiplier and _____ the excess reserves held by commercial banks, thus causing the money supply to (increase, decrease) _____. A decrease in the reserve ratio will (increase, decrease) _____ the size of the monetary multiplier and _____ the excess reserves held by commercial banks, thus causing the money supply to (increase, decrease) _____.

7. If the Federal Reserve Banks were to lower the discount rate, commercial banks would tend to borrow (more, less) _____ from them, and this would (increase, decrease) _____ their excess reserves.

8. To increase the supply of money, the Federal Reserve Banks should (raise, lower) _____ the reserve ratio, (buy, sell) _____ securities in the open market, and/or (increase, decrease) _____ the discount rate.

9. An easy money policy would be characterized by actions of the Federal Reserve to (increase, decrease) _____ the discount rate, _____ reserve ratios, and (buy, sell) _____ government bonds, whereas a tight money policy would include actions taken to (increase, decrease) _____ the discount rate, _____ reserve ratios, and (buy, sell) _____ government bonds.

10. The most effective and most often used tool of monetary policy is a change in (the discount rate, the reserve ratio, open-market operations) _____, and a rarely used tool is a change in _____; an announcement effect is created by a change in _____, but it is relatively weak because banks may not be inclined to borrow even at a lower rate.

11. There is cause-effect chain of monetary policy.
  a. In the money market, the demand for and the supply of money determine the equilibrium rate of (discount, interest) _____.
  b. This rate in turn determines the level of (government, investment) _____ spending based on the _____-demand curve.
  c. This spending in turn affects aggregate (demand, supply) _____, and the intersection of aggregate supply and demand determine the equilibrium level of real (interest, GDP) _____ and the (discount, price) _____ level.
  d. When there is an increase in the supply-of-the money curve, the real interest rate will (increase, decrease) _____, investment spending will _____, aggregate demand will (increase, decrease) _____, and real GDP will _____.

12. To eliminate inflationary pressures in the economy, the traditional view holds that the monetary authority should seek to (increase, decrease) _____ the reserves of commercial banks; this would tend to _____ the money supply and to (increase, decrease) _____ the rate of interest, and this in turn would cause investment spending, aggregate demand, and GDP to _____. This action by monetary authorities would be considered a(n) (easy, tight) _____ money policy.

13. If there were a serious problem with unemployment in the economy, the traditional view would be that the Federal Reserve should pursue a(n) (easy, tight) _____ money policy, in which case the Federal Reserve would (buy, sell) _____ government bonds as a way of (increasing, decreasing) _____ the money supply, and thereby _____ interest rates; these events would have the effect of (increasing, decreasing) _____ investment spending and thus _____ real GDP.

14. The effect of a $1 billion increase or decrease in the money supply upon the equilibrium GDP is greater the (flatter, steeper) _____ the demand-for-money curve and the _____ the investment-demand curve.

15. An increase in the money supply will shift the aggregate (supply, demand) _____ curve to the (right, left) _____.

    a. In the horizontal (or recession) range along the aggregate supply curve, this increase in the money supply will have a (small, large) _____ effect on real domestic output and a _____ effect on the price level.

    b. In the vertical range along the aggregate supply curve, this increase in the money supply will have a (small, large) _____ effect on real domestic output and a _____ effect on the price level.

16. Monetary policy has strengths. Compared to fiscal policy, monetary policy is speedier and (more, less) _____ flexible, _____ isolated from political pressure, and (more, less) _____ successfully used to counter inflation and recession in recent years.

17. Monetary policy has shortcomings or problems, too.

    a. It may be subject to (more, less) _____ control by the Federal Reserve because of recent changes in banking practices that give the Fed _____ control of the money supply.

    b. It may be more effective in counteracting (recession, inflation) _____ than _____.

    c. It may be offset when the velocity of money changes in the (same, opposite) _____ direction as the money supply.

    d. It will not be effective if changes in the interest rate have (little, significant) _____ effect on investment spending.

    e. It will cause changes in interest income that (offset, reinforce) _____ the intended effects on consumer or investment spending.

18. The interest rate that banks charge one another for overnight loans is the (prime interest, Federal funds) ' _____ rate, but the rate banks charge their most creditworthy customers is the _____ rate. The (prime interest, Federal funds) _____ rate has been the recent focus of the monetary policy of the Federal Reserve.

19. An easy money policy (increases, decreases) _____ net exports; a tight money policy _____ net exports. The net export effect from an easy money policy thus (strengthens, weakens) _____ domestic monetary policy, and the net export effect from a tight money policy _____ it.

20. An easy money policy is (compatible, incompatible) _____ with the economic goal of reducing a balance of trade deficit, but a tight money policy is _____ with this economic goal.

■ **TRUE-FALSE QUESTIONS**

Circle the T if the statement is true, the F if it is false.

1. The fundamental goal of monetary policy is to stabilize interest rates. **T F**

2. The securities owned by the Federal Reserve Banks are almost entirely U.S. government bonds. **T F**

3. If the Federal Reserve Banks buy $15 in government securities from the public in the open market, the effect will be to increase the excess reserves of commercial banks by $15. **T F**

4. When the Federal Reserve sells bonds in the open market, the price of these bonds falls. **T F**

5. A change in the reserve ratio will affect the multiple by which the banking system can create money, but it will not affect the actual or excess reserves of member banks. **T F**

6. If the reserve ratio is lowered, some required reserves are turned into excess reserves. **T F**

7. When commercial banks borrow from the Federal Reserve Banks, they increase their excess reserves and their money-creating potential. **T F**

8. If the monetary authority wished to follow a tight money policy, it would sell government bonds in the open market. **T F**

9. An increase in the required reserve ratio tends to reduce the profits of banks. **T F**

10. The least effective and used tool of monetary policy is the open-market operation, in which government securities are bought and sold. **T F**

11. The equilibrium rate of interest is found at the intersection of the demand-for-money and the supply-of-money curves. **T F**

12. An increase in the equilibrium GDP will shift the demand-for-money curve to the left and increase the equilibrium interest rate. **T F**

13. Consumer spending is more sensitive to changes in the rate of interest than is investment demand. **T F**

14. There can be a feedback effect from an easy money policy because an increase in GDP resulting from the policy will also cause an increase in the demand for money, partially offsetting the interest-reducing effect of the policy. **T F**

15. When the economy is at or near full employment, an increase in the money supply tends to be inflationary. **T F**

16. It is generally agreed that fiscal policy is more effective than monetary policy in controlling the business cycle because fiscal policy is more flexible. **T F**

17. Monetary policy is subject to more political pressure than fiscal policy. **T F**

18. A tight money policy suffers from a "You can lead a horse to water, but you can't make him drink" problem. **T F**

19. A combination of a relatively flat money-demand curve and a relatively steep investment-demand curve will mean that a particular change in the money supply will cause a large change in investment and, thus, a large change in equilibrium GDP. **T F**

20. When interest rates increase, the reduction in spending for purchases of capital goods, homes, and autos is partially offset by the increase in spending by those who receive increased interest income. **T F**

21. In recent years, the Federal Reserve has announced its changes in monetary policy by changing its targets for the Federal funds rate. **T F**

22. The prime interest rate is the rate that banks charge other banks for overnight loans of excess reserves at Federal Reserve banks. **T F**

23. An easy money policy decreases net exports. **T F**

24. A tight money policy will tend to cause the dollar to appreciate. **T F**

25. A tight money policy is compatible with the goal of correcting a trade deficit. **T F**

■ **MULTIPLE-CHOICE QUESTIONS**

Circle the letter that corresponds to the best answer.

1. The agency directly responsible for monetary policy in the United States is
   (a) the 12 Federal Reserve Banks
   (b) the Board of Governors of the Federal Reserve System
   (c) the Congress of the United States
   (d) the U.S. Treasury

2. The largest single asset in the Federal Reserve Banks' consolidated balance sheet is
   (a) securities
   (b) the reserves of commercial banks

   (c) Federal Reserve Notes
   (d) loans to commercial banks

3. The largest single liability of the Federal Reserve Banks is
   (a) securities
   (b) the reserves of commercial banks
   (c) Federal Reserve Notes
   (d) loans to commercial banks

4. Assuming that the Federal Reserve Banks sell $20 million in government securities to commercial banks and the reserve ratio is 20%, then the effect will be
   (a) to reduce the actual supply of money by $20 million
   (b) to reduce the actual supply of money by $4 million
   (c) to reduce the potential money supply by $20 million
   (d) to reduce the potential money supply by $100 million

5. Which of the following is the most important control used by the Federal Reserve Banks to regulate the money supply?
   (a) changing the reserve ratio
   (b) open-market operations
   (c) changing the discount rate
   (d) changing the Federal funds rate

6. Assume that there is a 20% reserve ratio and that the Federal Reserve buys $100 million worth of government securities. If the securities are purchased from the public, this action has the potential to increase bank lending by a maximum of
   (a) $500 million, but only by $400 million if the securities are purchased directly from commercial banks
   (b) $400 million, but by $500 million if the securities are purchased directly from commercial banks
   (c) $500 million, and also by $500 million if the securities are purchased directly from commercial banks
   (d) $400 million, and also by $400 million if the securities are purchased directly from commercial banks

7. In the traditional or Keynesian chain of cause and effect between changes in the excess reserves of commercial banks and the resulting changes in output and employment in the economy,
   (a) an increase in excess reserves will decrease the money supply
   (b) a decrease in the money supply will increase the rate of interest
   (c) an increase in the rate of interest will increase aggregate demand
   (d) an increase in aggregate demand will decrease output and employment

8. Which of the following is more likely to be affected by changes in the rate of interest?
   (a) consumer spending
   (b) investment spending

(c) the spending of the Federal government

(d) the exports of the economy

9. The economy is experiencing inflation and the Federal Reserve decides to pursue a tight money policy. Which set of actions by the Fed would be most consistent with this policy?

(a) buying government securities and lowering the discount rate

(b) buying government securities and lowering the reserve ratio

(c) selling government securities and raising the discount rate

(d) selling government securities and lowering the discount rate

10. A newspaper headline reads: "Fed Cuts Discount Rate for Third Time This Year." This headline indicates that the Federal Reserve is most likely trying to

(a) reduce inflationary pressures in the economy

(b) increase the Federal funds rate

(c) reduce the cost of credit and stimulate the economy

(d) increase the value of the dollar

11. A change in the money supply has the *least* effect on the equilibrium GDP when

(a) both the demand-for-money and the investment-demand curves are steep

(b) both the demand-for-money and the investment-demand curves are flat

(c) the demand-for-money curve is flat and the investment-demand curve is steep

(d) the demand-for-money curve is steep and the investment-demand curve is flat

12. Which explanation best describes the feedback effects of an easy money policy? The increase in GDP resulting from the policy will

(a) decrease the demand for money, and partially offset the interest-reducing effect of the policy

(b) increase the demand for money, and partially offset the interest-increasing effect of the policy

(c) increase the demand for money, and partially offset the interest-reducing effect of the policy

(d) decrease the demand for money, and partially offset the interest-increasing effect of the policy

13. An increase in the money supply will have little or no effect on the price level in

(a) the horizontal range of the aggregate supply curve

(b) the intermediate range of the aggregate supply curve

(c) the vertical range of the aggregate supply curve

(d) any of the three ranges of the aggregate supply curve

Use the following graph to answer Questions 14, 15, and 16.

14. A shift from AD_1 to AD_2 would be most consistent with

(a) an increase in the prime interest rate

(b) an increase in the discount rate by the Federal Reserve

(c) the buying of securities by the Federal Reserve

(d) the selling of securities by the Federal Reserve

15. Which shift would be most consistent with the potential effects of tight money policy in an inflationary period in an economy where prices are flexible?

(a) AD_1 to AD_2

(b) AD_3 to AD_4

(c) AD_4 to AD_3

(d) AD_2 to AD_1

16. If the Federal Reserve adopted an easy money policy in a period of high unemployment, the situation can best be characterized by a shift from

(a) AD_1 to AD_2

(b) AD_3 to AD_4

(c) AD_4 to AD_3

(d) AD_2 to AD_1

17. Which one is considered a *strength* of monetary policy compared to fiscal policy?

(a) feedback effects

(b) cyclical asymmetry

(c) isolation from political pressure

(d) effect on changes in the velocity of money

18. An increase in the money supply is *least* effective in stimulating aggregate expenditures when the velocity of money

(a) falls as the money supply increases

(b) remains constant

(c) rises as the money supply increases

(d) is equal to 5

19. A shortcoming of monetary policy is that actions taken to increase the interest rate

(a) decrease investment spending and decrease interest income, thus doubling the effect

(b) increase investment spending and increase interest income, thus doubling the effect

(c) decrease investment spending but increase interest income, thus offsetting the effect

(d) increase investment spending but decrease interest income, thus offsetting the effect

20. The Federal funds rate is the rate that
(a) banks charge for overnight use of excess reserves held at the Federal Reserve banks
(b) banks charge for loans to the most creditworthy customers
(c) the Federal Reserve charges for short-term loans to commercial banks
(d) government bonds are sold at in the open-market operations of the Federal Reserve

21. When the Federal Reserve uses open-market operations to reduce the Federal funds rate it is pursuing a(n)
(a) easier money policy
(b) tighter money policy
(c) prime interest rate policy
(d) discretionary fiscal policy

22. When the Federal Reserve Banks decide to buy government bonds, the demand for government bonds will
(a) decrease, bond prices will decrease, and the interest rate will decrease
(b) increase, bond prices will increase, and the interest rate will decrease
(c) increase, bond prices will increase, and the interest rate will increase
(d) decrease, bond prices will increase, and the interest rate will decrease

23. A tight money policy in the United States is most likely to
(a) increase domestic interest rates and cause the value of the dollar to depreciate
(b) decrease domestic interest rates and cause the value of the dollar to appreciate
(c) increase domestic interest rates and cause the value of the dollar to appreciate
(d) decrease domestic interest rates and cause the value of the dollar to depreciate

24. Which policy combination would tend to reduce net exports?
(a) tight money policy and expansionary fiscal policy
(b) easy money policy and expansionary fiscal policy
(c) tight money policy and contractionary fiscal policy
(d) easy money policy and contractionary fiscal policy

25. A tight money policy that is used to reduce inflation in the domestic economy
(a) is best conducted by reducing the required reserve ratios at commercial banks
(b) increases net exports and the effectiveness of the policy
(c) conflicts with the economic goal of correcting a trade deficit
(d) causes the dollar to depreciate

■ **PROBLEMS**

1. Assume that the following consolidated balance sheet is for all commercial banks. Assume also that the required reserve ratio is 25% and that cash is *not* a part of the commercial banks' legal reserve.

Assets		Liabilities	
Cash	$ 50	Demand deposits	$400
Reserves	100	Loans from Federal	
Loans	150	Reserve	25
Securities	200	Net worth	75
	$500		$500

a. To *increase* the supply of money by $100, the Fed could (buy, sell) _____ securities worth $_____ in the open market.

b. To *decrease* the supply of money by $50, the Fed could (buy, sell) _____ securities worth $_____ in the open market.

2. On the next page are the consolidated balance sheets of the Federal Reserve and of the commercial banks. Assume that the reserve ratio for commercial banks is 25%, that cash is *not* a part of a bank's legal reserve, and that the figures in column 1 show the balance sheets of the Federal Reserve and the commercial banks *prior to each of the following five transactions.* Place the new balance-sheet figures in the appropriate columns and complete A, B, C, D, and E in these columns. Do *not* use the figures you place in columns 2 through 5 when you work the next part of the problem; start all parts of the problem with the printed figures in column 1.

a. The Federal Reserve Banks sell $3 in securities to the public, which pays by check (column 2).

b. The Federal Reserve Banks buy $4 in securities from the commercial banks (column 3).

c. The Federal Reserve Banks lower the required reserve ratio for commercial banks to 20% (column 4).

d. The U.S. Treasury buys $5 worth of goods from U.S. manufacturers and pays the manufacturers by checks drawn on its accounts at the Federal Reserve Banks (column 5).

e. Because the Federal Reserve Banks have raised the discount rate, commercial banks repay $6 which they owe to the Federal Reserve (column 6).

3. On the following graph is the demand-for-money curve which shows the amounts of money consumers and firms

	(1)	(2)	(3)	(4)	(5)	(6)
Federal Reserve Banks						
Assets:						
Gold certificates	$ 25	$___	$___	$___	$___	$___
Securities	30	___	___	___	___	___
Loans to commercial banks	10	___	___	___	___	___
Liabilities:						
Reserves of commercial banks	50	___	___	___	___	___
Treasury deposits	5	___	___	___	___	___
Federal Reserve Notes	10	___	___	___	___	___
Commercial Banks						
Assets:						
Reserves	$ 50	$___	$___	$___	$___	$___
Securities	70	___	___	___	___	___
Loans	90	___	___	___	___	___
Liabilities:						
Demand deposits	200	___	___	___	___	___
Loans from Federal Reserve	10	___	___	___	___	___
A. Required reserves		___	___	___	___	___
B. Excess reserves		___	___	___	___	___
C. How much has the money supply changed?		___	___	___	___	___
D. How much *more* can the money supply change?		___	___	___	___	___
E. What is the total of C and D?		___	___	___	___	___

wish to hold at various rates of interest (when the nominal GDP in the economy is given).

a. Suppose the supply of money is equal to $300 billion. (1) Draw the supply-of-money curve on the graph on page 168. (2) The equilibrium rate of interest in the economy is_____ %.

b. Below is a graph of an investment-demand curve which shows the amounts of planned investment at various rates of interest. Given your answer to (2) above, how much will investors plan to spend for capital goods? $_____ billion.

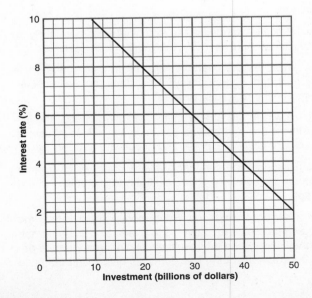

c. The following figure shows the aggregate supply (**AS**) curve in this economy. On the graph, draw an aggregate demand curve (**AD₁**) so that it crosses the **AS** curve in the horizontal range of aggregate supply. Label the price level (**P₁**) and output level (**Q₁**) associated with the intersection of **AD₁** and **AS**.

Real domestic product, GDP (billions of dollars)

d. Now assume that monetary authorities increase the money supply to $400.
(1) On the graph on page 168, plot the new money supply curve. The new equilibrium interest rate is _____ %.
(2) On the investment graph, determine the level of investment spending that is associated with this new interest rate: $_____ billion. By how much

has investment spending increased as a result of the change in the interest rate? $_____ billion.
(3) Assume that the marginal propensity to consume is .75. What is the multiplier? _____ By how much will the new investment spending increase aggregate demand? $_____ billion.
(4) On the previous figure, indicate how the change in investment spending affects aggregate demand. Draw a new aggregate demand curve (**AD₂**) so that it crosses the **AS** curve in the intermediate range of aggregate supply at the output level (**Q_f**). Also label the new price level (**P₂**) associated with the intersection of **AD₂** and **AS**.

4. Columns 1 and 2 of the following table show the aggregate supply schedule. (The price level is a price index, and real domestic output is measured in billions of dollars.)

(1) Price level	(2) Real output	(3) AD₁	(4) AD₂	(5) AD₃	(6) AD₄	(7) AD₅	(8) AD₆
.30	$1500	$1600	$1700	$2070	$2400	$2920	$3020
.30	1600	1600	1700	2070	2400	2920	3020
.30	1700	1600	1700	2070	2400	2920	3020
.40	1790	1500	1600	1970	2300	2820	2920
.50	1870	1400	1500	1870	2200	2720	2820
.60	1940	1300	1400	1770	2100	2620	2720
.70	2000	1200	1300	1670	2000	2520	2620
.80	2050	1100	1200	1570	1900	2420	2520
.90	2090	1000	1100	1470	1800	2320	2420
1.00	2120	900	1000	1370	1700	2220	2320
1.10	2120	800	900	1270	1600	2120	2220
1.20	2120	700	800	1170	1500	2020	2120

a. The horizontal range on this aggregate supply schedule is from a real domestic output of zero to $_____ billion.
b. The vertical range on this aggregate supply curve is at the real domestic output of $_____ billion.
c. If the aggregate demand schedule were that shown in columns 1 and 3, the equilibrium real domestic output would be $_____ billion and the price level would be _____.
d. If the aggregate demand schedule increased from that shown in columns 1 and 3 to the one shown in columns 1 and 4, the equilibrium real domestic output would _____ and the price level would

_____.

e. If the aggregate demand schedule increased from that shown in columns 1 and 5 to the one shown in columns 1 and 6, the equilibrium real domestic output would _____ and the price level would

_____.

f. If the aggregate demand schedule increased from that shown in columns 1 and 7 to the one shown in columns 1 and 8, the equilibrium real domestic output

would _____ and the price level would

_____.

■ **SHORT ANSWER AND ESSAY QUESTIONS**

1. What is the basic goal of monetary policy? What actions are taken to achieve this goal during recession or during a period of high inflation?

2. What are the important assets and liabilities of the Federal Reserve Banks?

3. Explain how the monetary policy tools of the Federal Reserve Banks would be used to contract the supply of money. How would they be used to expand the supply of money?

4. What is the difference between the effects of the Federal Reserve's buying (selling) government securities in the open market from (to) commercial banks and from (to) the public?

5. Which of the monetary policy tools available to the Federal Reserve is most effective? Why is it more important than other tools?

6. Using three graphs, explain what determines (a) the equilibrium interest rate, (b) investment spending, and (c) the equilibrium GDP. Now use these three graphs to show the effects of a decrease in the money supply upon the equilibrium GDP.

7. Using your answers to Question 6, (a) what determines how large the effect of the decrease in the money supply on the equilibrium GDP will be, and (b) how would the change in the equilibrium GDP affect the demand-for-money curve, the interest rate, investment spending, and the GDP itself?

8. Explain how the Board of Governors and the Federal Reserve Banks can influence income, output, employment, and the price level. In your explanation, employ the following concepts: reserves, excess reserves, the supply of money, the availability of bank credit, and the rate of interest.

9. Why are changes in the rate of interest more likely to affect investment spending than consumption and saving?

10. What are the characteristics of an easy money policy or a tight money policy? How does the Federal Reserve implement such policies?

11. How will the shape of the money-demand and investment-demand curves influence the effectiveness of monetary policy? Explain, and show with a graph.

12. Describe the feedback effects that result from a change in monetary policy. Illustrate this problem with a graph.

13. How does a change in the money supply affect the aggregate demand curve? How will a change in the money supply and the resulting shift in the aggregate demand curve affect the real domestic output and the price

level in (*a*) the horizontal range and (*b*) the vertical range, along the aggregate supply curve?

14. What are the major strengths of monetary policy?

15. How might recent changes in banking practices affect control of monetary policy?

16. Why is monetary policy more effective in controlling inflation than in reducing unemployment?

17. Why might a change in velocity reduce the effectiveness of monetary policy?

18. What is the prime interest rate, and how is it related to the Federal funds rate? What happens to the Federal funds rate when the Federal Reserve expands or contracts the money supply through open-market operations?

19. Explain how the net export effect influences the effectiveness of a tight or an easy money policy.

20. What type of monetary policy would you recommend to correct a balance of trade deficit? Why?

ANSWERS

Chapter 15 Monetary Policy

FILL-IN QUESTIONS

1. noninflationary, Federal Board of Governors, Federal Reserve Banks
2. government securities, loans to, Treasury deposits, reserves of, Federal Reserve Notes
3. open, reserve, discount
4. increase, decrease
5. 10 million, 10 million, 7.5 million, 0, 10 million, 10 million
6. decrease, decrease, decrease, increase, increase, increase
7. more, increase
8. lower, buy, decrease
9. decrease, decrease, buy, increase, increase, sell
10. open-market operations, the reserve ratio, the discount rate

11. *a.* interest; *b.* investment, investment; *c.* demand, GDP, price; *d.* decrease, increase, increase, increase
12. decrease, decrease, increase, decrease, tight
13. easy, buy, increasing, decreasing, increasing, increasing
14. steeper, flatter
15. demand, right; *a.* large, small; *b.* small, large
16. more, more, more
17. *a.* less, less; *b.* inflation, recession; *c.* opposite; *d.* little; *e.* offset
18. Federal funds, prime interest, Federal funds
19. increases, decreases, strengthens, strengthens
20. compatible, incompatible

TRUE-FALSE QUESTIONS

1. F, p. 306	**10.** F, p. 313	**19.** F, p. 320
2. T, p. 306-307	**11.** T, pp. 314-316	**20.** T, p. 320
3. F, p. 308-309	**12.** F, pp. 314-316	**21.** T, pp. 320-321
4. T, pp. 310-311	**13.** F, p. 316	**22.** F, p. 321
5. F, pp. 311-312	**14.** T, p. 318	**23.** F, pp. 322-323
6. T, p. 311	**15.** T, p. 318	**24.** T, pp. 322-323
7. T, p. 312	**16.** F, p. 318	**25.** F, pp. 323-324
8. T, p. 313	**17.** F, p. 319	
9. T, p. 313	**18.** F, pp. 319-320	

MULTIPLE-CHOICE QUESTIONS

1. b, p. 305	**10.** c, pp. 316-317	**19.** c, p. 320
2. a, pp. 306-307	**11.** c, p. 318	**20.** a, pp. 320-321
3. c, pp. 306-307	**12.** c, p. 318	**21.** a, pp. 320-321
4. d, pp. 309-310	**13.** a, p. 318	**22.** b, pp. 310-311
5. b, p. 313	**14.** c, pp. 315-317	**23.** c, pp. 322-323
6. b, pp. 307-309	**15.** c, pp. 315, 317	**24.** a, pp. 322-323
7. b, pp. 314-316	**16.** a, pp. 315-317	**25.** c, pp. 323-324
8. b, p. 316	**17.** c, p. 319	
9. c, p. 313	**18.** a, p. 320	

PROBLEMS

1. *a.* buy, 25; *b.* sell, 12 1/2
2. see below

	(2)	(3)	(4)	(5)	(6)
	Federal Reserve Banks				
Assets:					
Gold certificates	$ 25	$ 25	$ 25	$ 25	$ 25
Securities	27	34	30	30	30
Loans to commercial banks	10	10	10	10	4
Liabilities:					
Reserves of commercial banks	47	54	50	55	44
Treasury deposits	5	5	5	0	5
Federal Reserve Notes	10	10	10	10	10
	Commercial Banks				
Assets:					
Reserves	$ 47	$ 54	$ 50	$ 55	$ 44
Securities	70	66	70	70	70
Loans	90	90	90	90	90
Liabilities:					
Demand deposits	197	200	200	205	200
Loans from Federal Reserve	10	10	10	10	4
A. Required reserves	49.25	50	40	51.25	50
B. Excess reserves	−2.25	4	10	3.75	−6
C. How much has the money supply changed?	−3	0	0	+5	0
D. How much *more* can the money supply change?	−9	+16	+50	+15	−24
E. What is the total of C and D?	−12	+16	+50	+20	−24

3. *a.* (2) 8; *b.* 20; *c.* see Figure 15-2 in text; *d.* (1) 6, (2) 30, 10, (3) 4, 40, (4) see Figure 15-2 in text

4. *a.* 1700; *b.* 2120; *c.* 1600, .30; *d.* rise to $1700 billion, remain constant; *e.* rise from $1870 billion to $2000 billion, rise from .50 to .70; *f.* remain constant at $2120 billion, rise from 1.10 to 1.20

SHORT ANSWER AND ESSAY QUESTIONS

1. p. 306	**6.** pp. 314-317	**11.** p. 318	**16.** pp. 319-320
2. pp. 306-307	**7.** pp. 317-318	**12.** p. 318	**17.** p. 320
3. pp. 312-313	**8.** pp. 314-317	**13.** p. 318	**18.** pp. 320-321
4. pp. 307-311	**9.** p. 316	**14.** pp. 318-319	**19.** pp. 322-323
5. p. 313	**10.** pp. 316-317	**15.** p. 319	**20.** pp. 323-324

CHAPTER 16

Extending the Analysis of Aggregate Supply

Chapter 16 extends the basic aggregate demand–aggregate supply (AD–AS) model first introduced in Chapter 11. This addition will give you the analytical tools to improve your understanding of the relationship between unemployment and inflation. The chapter also offers different economic perspectives on the appropriateness of government policy for controlling inflation and reducing unemployment.

The major extension to the AD–AS model is the distinction between the short-run aggregate supply curve and the long-run aggregate supply curve. In the **short run,** nominal wages are fixed, so an increase in the price level increases business profits and real output. In the **long run,** nominal wages are flexible, so business profits and employment return to their original level. Thus, the **long-run aggregate supply curve** is vertical at the full-employment level of output.

The distinction between the short-run and long-run aggregate supply curve requires a reinterpretation of **demand-pull inflation** and **cost-push inflation.** Although demand-pull inflation will increase the price level and real output in the short run, once nominal wages increase, the temporary increase in output is gone, but the price level will be higher at the full-employment level of output. Cost-push inflation will increase the price level and decrease real output in the short run, but again, once nominal wages fall, output and the price level will return to their original positions. If government policymakers try to counter cost-push inflation by increasing aggregate demand, they may make matters worse by increasing the price level and causing the short-run aggregate supply curve to decrease, thereby setting off an inflationary spiral.

The relationship between inflation and unemployment has been studied for many years. One influential observation, supported by data from the 1950s and 1960s, was embodied in the **Phillips Curve,** which suggested that there was a stable and predictable tradeoff between the rate of inflation and the unemployment rate. During the 1960s, it was thought that this tradeoff could be used for formulating sound monetary and fiscal policy to manage the economy.

The **stagflation** of the 1970s, however, called into question the shape and stability of the Phillips Curve because the economy was experiencing both higher rates of inflation and unemployment. One widely accepted explanation of events was that the aggregate supply shocks of this period shifted the Phillips Curve rightward. When these shocks dissipated in the 1980s, the Phillips Curve began to shift back to its original position.

An alternative explanation of the stagflation of the 1970s and early 1980s came from the **natural rate hypothesis.** Two variants of this hypothesis were **adaptive expectations theory** and **rational expectations theory (RET).** Both theories contend that the downsloping Phillips Curve is actually a vertical line in the long run at the natural rate of unemployment. In this view, government attempts to reduce the unemployment rate below the natural rate simply result in inflation. The major difference between adaptive and rational expectations is that the former believes there are time lags in wage and price adjustments in the economy which can bring about a decline in unemployment in the short run, whereas the latter sees no distinction between short-run and long-run adjustments.

Another perspective on aggregate supply comes from **supply-side economics,** which gained visibility during the Reagan administration (1981–1988). Supply-side economists pointed to the role of the Federal government in causing the slump in productivity and economic growth in the 1970s. The solutions, which became the program of Reaganomics, were to come from large cuts in personal and corporate income taxes and reduced government regulation. It was thought that the tax cuts would increase incentive to work, save, and invest, thus increasing productivity and aggregate supply. Despite its successes, this economic program has been criticized for the failure of the tax cuts to increase aggregate supply beyond its historical rate.

Chapter 16 is important because it provides the analytical foundation for understanding disputes over macroeconomic theory and policy. These disputes will be the focus of Chapter 17.

■ CHECKLIST

When you have studied this chapter you should be able to

☐ Give a definition of the short run and long run in macroeconomics.

☐ Distinguish between a change in real wages and a change in nominal wages.

☐ Draw the short-run aggregate supply curve and describe its characteristics.

☐ Explain how the long-run aggregate supply curve is determined.

☐ Draw a graph that illustrates equilibrium in the extended AD-AS model.

☐ Explain demand-pull inflation using the extended AD-AS model and identify its short-run and long-run outcomes.

☐ Describe cost-push inflation using the extended AD-AS model.

☐ Give two generalizations about the policy dilemma for government in dealing with cost-push inflation.

☐ Explain recession and the process of adjustment using the extended AD-AS model.

☐ Describe how to derive a Phillips Curve from an AD-AS model.

☐ Draw a Phillips Curve and identify the basic tradeoffs.

☐ Define stagflation and contrast it with the conclusion from the Phillips Curve.

☐ Explain how aggregate supply shocks contributed to the stagflation of the 1970s and how they might have shifted the Phillips Curve.

☐ List events that contributed to stagflation's demise and their effect on the price level and output.

☐ Contrast the traditional view of the Phillips Curve with the natural rate hypothesis.

☐ Use adaptive expectations theory and its view of the short and long-run Phillips Curve to explain inflation and disinflation.

☐ Describe how rational expectations theory differs from adaptive expectations theory.

☐ Discuss the changing interpretations of the Phillips Curve and the current perspective on the issue.

☐ List the three tax-transfer disincentives identified by supply-side economists.

☐ Use the Laffer Curve to explain the hypothesized relationship between marginal tax rates and tax revenues.

☐ State three criticisms of the Laffer Curve.

☐ Give examples of how overregulation adversely affects the economy.

☐ Describe how supply-side economics was embodied in Reaganomics.

☐ Evaluate the effectiveness of Reaganomics.

■ **CHAPTER OUTLINE**

1. The aggregate supply curve has short- and long-run characteristics. The short-run curve also shifts because of an increase in nominal wages. These factors make the analysis of aggregate supply and demand more complex.

  a. The short run is a period in which nominal wages (and other input prices) remain fixed as the price level changes. The long run is a period in which nominal wages are fully responsive to changes in the price level.

  b. The *short-run aggregate supply curve* is upward sloping: An increase in the price level increases business revenues and profits because nominal wages are fixed; in contrast, when the price level decreases, business revenue and profits decline, and so does real output.

  c. The *long-run aggregate supply curve* is vertical at the potential level of output. Increases in the price level will increase nominal wages and cause a decrease (shift left) in the short-run aggregate supply curve, or declines in the price level reduce nominal wages and

increase (shift right) the short-run aggregate supply curve. In either case, although the price level changes, output returns to its potential level, and the long-run aggregate supply curve is vertical at the full-employment level of output.

  d. Equilibrium in the extended AD-AS model occurs at the price level and output where the aggregate demand crosses the long-run aggregate supply curve and also crosses the short-run aggregate supply curve.

2. The extended AD-AS model can be applied to explain conditions of inflation and recession in an economy.

  a. *Demand-pull inflation* will increase (shift right) the aggregate demand curve, which increases the price level and causes a temporary increase in real output. In the long run, workers will realize that their real wages have fallen and will demand raises in their nominal wages. The short-run aggregate supply curve, which was based on fixed nominal wages, now decreases (shifts left), resulting in an even higher price level and with real output returning to its initial level.

  b. *Cost-push inflation* will decrease (shift left) the short-run aggregate supply curve. This situation will increase the price level and temporarily decrease real output, causing a recession. It creates a policy dilemma for government.

  (1) If government takes actions to counter the cost-push inflation and recession by increasing aggregate demand, the price level will move to an even higher level, and the actions may set off an inflationary spiral.

  (2) If government takes no action, the recession will eventually reduce nominal wages, and eventually the short-run aggregate supply curve will shift back to its original position.

  c. If aggregate demand decreases, it will result in a recession. If prices and wages are flexible downward, the price level will fall and increase real wages. Eventually, nominal wages will fall to restore the original real wages. This change will increase short-run aggregate supply and end the recession, but not without a long period of high unemployment and lost output.

3. The *Phillips Curve* is important for examining the short- and long-run relationship between inflation and unemployment.

  a. If aggregate supply is constant and the economy is operating in the upsloping range of aggregate supply, then the greater the rate of increase in aggregate demand, the higher the rate of inflation (and output) and the lower the rate of unemployment. This inverse relationship between the rate of inflation and unemployment is known as the Phillips Curve.

  b. In the 1960s, economists thought there was a predictable tradeoff between unemployment and inflation. All society had to do was to choose the combination of inflation and unemployment on the Phillips Curve.

  c. Events of the 1970s and 1980s called into question the stability of the Phillips Curve. In that period, the economy experienced both higher rates of inflation and unemployment (*stagflation*). The data suggested that the Phillips Curve had either shifted right or that there was no dependable tradeoff between inflation and unemployment.

d. The stagflation of the 1970s and early 1980s was most likely caused by aggregate supply shocks from an increase in resource prices (oil), shortages in agricultural production, higher wage demands, and declining productivity. These shocks decreased the short-run aggregate supply curve, which increased the price level and decreased output (and unemployment).

e. The demise of stagflation came in the 1982–1989 period because of such factors as a severe recession in 1981–1982 that reduced wage demands, increased foreign competition that restrained price increases, and a decline in OPEC's monopoly power. The short-run aggregate supply curve increased, and the price level and unemployment rate fell. This meant that the Phillips Curve may have shifted back (left). Recent unemployment-inflation data are now similar to the Phillips Curve of the 1960s.

4. The *natural rate hypothesis* questions the existence of a downsloping Phillips Curve and views the economy as stable in the long run at the natural rate of unemployment. There are two variants to this hypothesis.

a. *Adaptive expectations theory* suggests that an increase in aggregate demand sponsored by government may temporarily reduce unemployment as the price level increases and profits expand, but the actions also set into motion other events.

(1) The increase in the price level reduces the real wages of workers who demand and obtain higher nominal wages; these actions return unemployment to its original level.

(2) Back at the original level, there is now a higher actual and expected rate of inflation for the economy, so the short-run Phillips Curve has shifted upward.

(3) The process is repeated when government tries again to reduce unemployment, and the rise in the price level accelerates as the short-run Phillips Curve shifts upward.

(4) In the long run, the Phillips Curve is stable only as a vertical line at the natural rate of unemployment; there is no tradeoff between unemployment and inflation.

b. *Rational expectations theory (RET)* assumes that workers fully anticipate that government policies to reduce unemployment will also be inflationary, and they increase their nominal wage demands to offset the expected inflation; thus there will not even be a temporary decline in unemployment or even a short-run Phillips Curve.

c. The interpretations of the Phillips Curve have changed over the past three decades based on the adaptive and rational expectations analysis. This consensus view of economists is that there is a short-run tradeoff between unemployment and inflation, but not a long-run tradeoff. Most economists also now acknowledge that both aggregate supply shocks and misguided government policies contributed to the stagflation of the 1970s.

5. *Supply-side economics* views aggregate supply as active rather than passive in explaining changes in the price level and unemployment.

a. It argues that higher marginal tax rates and a widespread system for public transfer payments reduce incentives to work and that high taxes also reduce incentives to save and invest. These policies lead to a misallocation of resources, less productivity, and a decrease in aggregate supply. To counter these effects, supply-side economists call for a cut in marginal tax rates.

b. The Laffer Curve suggests that it is possible to lower tax rates and increase tax revenues, thus avoiding a budget deficit because the policies will result in less tax evasion and reduced transfer payments.

c. Critics of *supply-side economics* and the Laffer Curve suggest that the policy of cutting tax rates will not work because

(1) It has only a small and uncertain effect on incentives to work (or on aggregate supply).

(2) It would increase aggregate demand relative to aggregate supply and thus reinforce inflation when there is full employment.

(3) The expected tax revenues from tax rate cuts depend on assumptions about the position on the Laffer Curve. If tax cuts reduce tax revenues, it only contributes to problems with existing budget deficits.

d. Another tenet of supply-side economics is that over-regulation of the economy by government (both industrial and social regulation) has decreased productivity, led to higher costs, and reduced economic growth.

e. The economic program of the Reagan administration (1981–1988), or *Reaganomics,* was based on supply-side ideas. This program reduced government regulation and cut personal and corporate income taxes.

(1) The record shows that by the late 1980s, there was a reduction in inflation and interest rates, an economic expansion, and the achievement of full employment.

(2) The supply-side approach can also be criticized. There is little evidence to show that the tax cuts increased aggregate supply beyond its historic pace, or provided strong incentives to work, or increased saving or investment. The economic expansion may also be attributed to the expansionary effect of the tax cuts on aggregate demand. The tax cuts also increased U.S. budget deficits and were not financed by increasing tax revenues as predicted by the Laffer Curve.

■ **HINTS AND TIPS**

1. Chapter 16 is a more difficult chapter because the AD-AS model is made more complex. Spend extra time mastering this material, but do not try to read everything at once. Break the chapter into its logical sections, and practice drawing each graph.

2. Be sure you understand the distinction between the short-run and long-run aggregate supply curve. Then use these ideas to explain demand-pull inflation, cost-push inflation, and recession. Doing problem 2 will be especially helpful.

3. Be sure you understand the different perspectives on the shape and stability of the controversial Phillips Curve.

4. Use Figure 16-9 in the text to help you understand the distinction between adaptive and rational expectations. Problem 4 will help your understanding of this complicated graph.

■ **IMPORTANT TERMS**

short-run aggregate supply curve

long-run aggregate supply curve

Phillips Curve

stagflation

aggregate supply shocks

natural rate hypothesis

adaptive expectations theory

disinflation

rational expectations theory (RET)

supply-side economics

Laffer Curve

Reaganomics

SELF-TEST

■ **FILL-IN QUESTIONS**

1. In an AD-AS model with a stable aggregate supply curve, when the economy is producing in the upsloping portion of the aggregate supply curve, an increase in aggregate demand will (increase, decrease) _____ real output and employment, but a decrease in aggregate supply will _____ real output and employment.

2. In the short run, nominal wages are (fixed, variable) _____, and in the long run, nominal wages are _____. In the short run, the aggregate supply curve is (upsloping, vertical) _____, and in the long run the curve is _____.

3. Demand-pull inflation will shift the aggregate demand curve (right, left) _____, which will (decrease, increase) _____ the price level and temporarily _____ real output. As a consequence, the (short-run, long-run) _____ aggregate supply curve will shift left because of a rise in (real, nominal) _____ wages, producing a (lower, higher) _____ price level at the original level of real output.

4. Cost-push inflation will shift the short-run aggregate supply curve (right, left) _____; thus the price level will (increase, decrease) _____ and real output will temporarily _____.

5. If government takes no actions to counter the cost-push inflation, the resulting recession will (increase, decrease) _____ nominal wages and shift the short-run aggregate supply curve back to its original position, yet if the government tries to counter the cost-push inflation and recession with a(n) _____ in aggregate demand, the price level will move even higher.

6. A recession will occur when there is a(n) (increase, decrease) _____ in aggregate demand. If the controversial assumption is made that prices and wages are flexible downward, then the price level (rises, falls) _____. Real wages will then (increase, decrease) _____, but eventually nominal wages will _____ and the aggregate supply curve will (increase, decrease) _____ and end the recession.

7. Along the upsloping portion of the short-run aggregate supply curve, the greater the increase in aggregate demand, the (greater, smaller) _____ the increase in the rate of inflation, the _____ the increase in real output, and the (greater, smaller) _____ the unemployment rate.

8. The Phillips Curve indicates that there will be a(n) (direct, inverse) _____ relationship between the rate of inflation and the unemployment rate. This means that high rates of inflation will be associated with a (high, low) _____ unemployment rate, or that low rates of inflation will be associated with a _____ unemployment rate.

9. The policy tradeoff based on a stable Phillips Curve was that for the economy to reduce the unemployment rate, the rate of inflation must (increase, decrease) _____, and to reduce the rate of inflation, the unemployment rate must _____.

10. During the 1970s and early 1980s, the Phillips Curve was (stable, unstable) _____ because of aggregate (demand, supply) _____ shocks. These shocks produced (demand-pull, cost-push) _____ inflation that resulted in a simultaneous increase in the inflation rate and the unemployment rate.

11. Factors that contributed to stagflation's demise during the 1982–1989 period include the 1981–1982 (inflation, recession) _____ largely caused by a(n) (tight, easy) _____ money policy. There was also (increased, decreased) _____ foreign competition and the _____ monopoly power of OPEC. These factors (increased, decreased) _____ the short-run aggregate supply curve; thus the inflation _____ and the unemployment rate (increased, decreased) _____.

12. The standard explanation for the Phillips Curve is that during the stagflation of the 1970s, the Phillips Curve shifted (right, left) _____, and during the demise of stagflation from 1982–1989, the Phillips Curve shifted _____. In this view, there is a trade-off between the unemployment rate and rate of inflation, but changes in (short-run, long-run) _____ aggregate supply can shift the Phillips Curve.

13. Another explanation for stagflation is the (inflation, natural) _____ rate hypothesis. It suggests that the inverse relationship between the rate of inflation and the rate of unemployment (does, does not) _____ exist in the long run, and the economy is stable at its natural rate of (unemployment, inflation) _____.

14. The theory of adaptive expectations suggests that people form their expectations of inflation based on experience and (immediately, gradually) _____ change expectations. With this theory, the (short-run, long-run) _____ Phillips Curve may be downsloping, but the _____ Phillips Curve is vertical at the natural rate of unemployment, and attempts by government to reduce the unemployment rate result in a(n) (increase, decrease) _____ in the rate of inflation.

15. In the view of adaptive expectations, when the actual rate of inflation is higher than the expected rate, profits temporarily (fall, rise) _____ and the unemployment rate temporarily falls, but when the actual rate of inflation is lower than the expected rate, profits temporarily _____ and the unemployment rate temporarily rises. The latter case would occur during a period of (inflation, disinflation) _____.

16. Rational expectations theory suggests that the inflation resulting from a government policy to reduce the unemployment rate will be (unanticipated, anticipated) _____, and this will (reinforce, offset) _____ the intent of the government policy. Workers will try to keep their (real, nominal) _____ wages constant by obtaining an increase in their _____ wages. This action brings about (a rise, a fall, no change) _____ in the price level and _____ in the unemployment rate.

17. It is the view of supply-side economics that high marginal tax rates (increase, decrease) _____ incentives to work, save, invest, and take risks. According to supply-side economists, the remedy for stagflation is a substantial (increase, decrease) _____ in marginal tax rates that would _____ economic growth through a(n) (increase, decrease) _____ in aggregate supply.

18. The Laffer Curve depicts the relationship between tax rates and tax revenues. In theory, as the tax rates increase from 0%, tax revenues will (increase, decrease) _____ to some maximum level, after which tax revenues will _____ as the tax rates increase, or as tax rates are reduced from 100%, tax revenues will (increase, decrease) _____ to some maximum level, after which tax revenues will _____ as tax rates decrease.

19. Criticisms of the Laffer Curve are that the effects of a cut in tax rates on incentives to work, save, and invest are (large, small) _____; the tax cuts generate an increase in aggregate (demand, supply) _____ that outweigh any increase in aggregate _____ and may lead to inflation in a full-employment situation; and tax cuts can produce a (gain, loss) _____ in tax revenues that only adds to a budget deficit.

20. The two principal elements of Reaganomics were calls for (more, less) _____ regulation by government and _____ taxation of personal and corporate incomes. These changes were designed to increase productivity and economic growth by stimulating aggregate (demand, supply) _____. The evidence suggests that supply-side economics ideas (did, did not) _____ work as proposed in Reaganomics. The cut in tax rates primarily (increased, decreased) _____ aggregate demand, and the tax cuts _____ tax revenues that added to budget deficits. The effect of tax cuts on saving, investment, and productivity was (minimal, substantial) _____.

■ TRUE-FALSE QUESTIONS

Circle the T if the statement is true, the F if it is false.

1. The short run in macroeconomics is a period in which nominal wages are fully responsive to changes in the price level.   **T F**

2. The short-run aggregate supply curve has a negative slope.   **T F**

3. The long-run aggregate supply curve is vertical because nominal wages eventually change by the same amount as changes in the price level.   **T F**

4. Demand-pull inflation will increase the price level and real output in the short run, but in the long run, only the price level will increase.   **T F**

5. Cost-push inflation results in a simultaneous increase in the price level and real output.   **T F**

6. When the economy is experiencing cost-push inflation, an inflationary spiral is likely to result when the government enacts policies to maintain full employment.   **T   F**

7. A recession is the result of an increase in the short-run aggregate supply curve.   **T   F**

8. If the economy is in a recession, prices and nominal wages will presumably fall, and the short-run aggregate supply curve will increase, so that real output returns to its full-employment level.   **T   F**

9. The Phillips Curve shows an inverse relationship between the rate of inflation and the unemployment rate.   **T   F**

10. Stagflation refers to a situation in which both the price level and the unemployment rate are rising.   **T   F**

11. The data from the 1970s suggest that the Phillips Curve shifted to the left.   **T   F**

12. One important explanation for the stagflation of the 1970s and early 1980s was a series of aggregate supply shocks.   **T   F**

13. The factors that contributed to the demise of stagflation during the 1980s tended to shift the Phillips Curve to the right.   **T   F**

14. The natural rate hypothesis suggests that there is a natural rate of inflation for the economy.   **T   F**

15. The adaptive expectations theory indicates that there may be a short-run tradeoff between inflation and unemployment, but no long-run tradeoff.   **T   F**

16. From the adaptive expectations perspective, when the actual rate of inflation is higher than the expected rate, the unemployment rate will rise.   **T   F**

17. Adaptive expectations theory can be used to explain disinflation.   **T   F**

18. An implication of rational expectations theory is that labor will anticipate the inflationary effects of government policies to reduce unemployment and increase its wage demands, so the policy will increase inflation.   **T   F**

19. According to rational expectations theory, the Phillips Curve is horizontal at the current rate of inflation.   **T   F**

20. Most economists reject the idea of a short-run tradeoff between the unemployment and inflation rates but accept the long-run tradeoff.   **T   F**

21. Supply-side economists contend that aggregate demand is the active factor in determining the price level and real output in an economy.   **T   F**

22. One proposition of supply-side economics is that the marginal tax rates on earned income should be reduced to increase the incentives to work.   **T   F**

23. The Laffer Curve suggests that lower tax rates will increase the rate of inflation.   **T   F**

24. The economic effects of overregulation on the economy is an increase in costs and prices and a decrease in economic growth.   **T   F**

25. There is considerable evidence that the tax cuts made as part of Reaganomics increased aggregate supply more rapidly than its historical pace.   **T   F**

■ MULTIPLE-CHOICE QUESTIONS

Circle the letter that corresponds to the best answer.

1. For macroeconomics, the short run is a period in which nominal wages
  (a) remain fixed as the price level stays constant
  (b) change as the price level stays constant
  (c) remain fixed as the price level changes
  (d) change as the price level changes

2. Once sufficient time has elapsed for wage contracts to expire and nominal wage adjustments to occur, the economy enters
  (a) the short run
  (b) the long run
  (c) a period of inflation
  (d) a period of unemployment

3. A graph of the short-run aggregate supply curve is
  (a) downsloping, and a graph of the long-run aggregate supply is upsloping
  (b) upsloping, and a graph of the long-run aggregate supply is vertical
  (c) upsloping, and a graph of the long-run aggregate supply is downsloping
  (d) vertical, and a graph of the long-run aggregate supply is upsloping

4. Assume that initally your nominal wage was $10 an hour and the price index was 100. If the price level increases to 110, then your
  (a) real wage has increased to $11.00
  (b) real wage has decreased to $9.09
  (c) nominal wage has increased to $11.00
  (d) nominal wage has decreased to $9.09

5. In the extended AD-AS model, demand-pull inflation occurs because of an increase in aggregate demand that will eventually produce
  (a) an increase in real wages, thus a decrease in the short-run aggregate supply curve
  (b) an increase in nominal wages, thus an increase in the short-run aggregate supply curve
  (c) a decrease in nominal wages, thus a decrease in the short-run aggregate supply curve
  (d) an increase in nominal wages, thus a decrease in the short-run aggregate supply curve

6. In the short run, demand-pull inflation increases real
  (a) output and decreases the price level
  (b) wages and nominal wages
  (c) output and the price level
  (d) wages and decreases nominal wages

7. In the long run, demand-pull inflation
  (a) decreases real wages
  (b) increases the price level
  (c) increases the unemployment rate
  (d) decreases real output

8. A likely result of the government trying to reduce the unemployment associated with cost-push inflation through stimulative fiscal policy or monetary policy is

(a) an inflationary spiral
(b) stagflation
(c) a recession
(d) disinflation

9. What will occur if the government adopts a hands-off approach to cost-push inflation?

(a) an increase in real output
(b) a fall in unemployment
(c) demand-pull inflation
(d) a recession

10. If prices and wages are flexible, a recession will increase real wages as the price level falls. Eventually, nominal wages will

(a) fall to the previous real wages, and the short-run aggregate supply will increase
(b) rise to the previous real wages, and the short-run aggregate supply will increase
(c) fall to the previous real wages, and the short-run aggregate supply will decrease
(d) rise to the previous real wages, and the short-run aggregate supply will decrease

11. The traditional Phillips Curve is based on the idea that with a constant short-run aggregate supply curve, the greater the increase in aggregate demand

(a) the greater the increase in the unemployment rate
(b) the greater the increase in the rate of inflation
(c) the greater the increase in real output
(d) the smaller the increase in nominal wages

12. The traditional Phillips Curve shows the

(a) inverse relationship between the rate of inflation and the unemployment rate
(b) inverse relationship between the nominal and the real wage
(c) direct relationship between unemployment and demand-pull inflation
(d) tradeoff between the short run and the long run

13. Supply shocks which cause a leftward shift in the aggregate supply curve, aggregate demand remaining constant, will

(a) decrease the price level
(b) decrease the unemployment rate
(c) increase real output
(d) increase both the price level and the unemployment rate

14. Which would be a factor contributing to the demise of stagflation during the 1982–1989 period?

(a) a lessening of foreign competition
(b) a strengthening of the monopoly power of OPEC
(c) a recession brought on largely by a tight monetary policy
(d) an increase in regulation of airline and trucking industries

15. The shift in the Phillips Curve during the 1982–1989 period was the consequence of a

(a) rightward shift in aggregate demand
(b) rightward shift in aggregate supply
(c) leftward shift in aggregate demand
(d) leftward shift in aggregate supply

16. The natural rate hypothesis suggests that the economy is stable only in the

(a) short run at the natural rate of unemployment
(b) short run at the natural rate of inflation
(c) long run at the natural rate of unemployment
(d) long run at the natural rate of inflation

17. The adaptive expectations theory suggests that if increases in nominal wage rates lag behind increases in the price level and government attempts to reduce unemployment by using fiscal and monetary policies, then employment

(a) and the price level increase in the long run
(b) remains constant and the price level increases in the short run
(c) increases and the price level remains constant in the short run
(d) remains constant and the price level increases in the long run

18. The rational expectations theorists contend that when government attempts to reduce unemployment by using monetary and fiscal policies, unemployment decreases

(a) temporarily and the price level rises
(b) permanently and the price level rises
(c) both temporarily and permanently and the price level rises
(d) neither temporarily nor permanently and the price level rises

19. In the view of natural rate theorists, the long-run Phillips Curve is

(a) horizontal
(b) vertical
(c) upsloping
(d) downsloping

20. Disinflation, or reductions in the rate of inflation, can be explained based on the natural rate conclusion that when the

(a) actual rate of inflation is lower than the expected rate, the unemployment rate will rise to bring the expected and actual rates into balance
(b) expected rate of inflation is lower than the actual rate, the unemployment rate will rise to bring the expected and actual rates into balance
(c) actual rate of inflation is higher than the expected rate, the unemployment rate will fall to bring the expected and actual rates into balance
(d) expected rate of inflation is higher than the actual rate, the unemployment rate will fall to bring the expected and actual rates into balance

21. The natural rate theory suggests that the aggregate supply curve

(a) is stable in the short run so long as nominal wages do not increase in the short run in response to the increase in the price level
(b) is stable in the long run because real wages are continually changing

(c) will shift to the right when the price of capital increases

(d) will shift to the right when nominal wages increase

22. Supply-side economists contend that the U.S. system of taxation reduces

(a) unemployment but causes inflation

(b) incentives to work, save, and invest

(c) transfer payments to the poor

(d) the effects of cost-push inflation

23. Based on the Laffer Curve, a cut in the tax rate from 100% to a point before the maximum level of tax revenue will

(a) increase the price level

(b) increase tax revenues

(c) decrease real output

(d) decrease the real wages

24. In the case of cuts in tax rates, most economists think that

(a) the demand-side effects exceed the supply-side effects

(b) the supply-side effects exceed the demand-side effects

(c) the demand-side and supply-side effects offset each other

(d) there are only supply-side effects

25. One general criticism of Reaganomics of the 1981–1988 period was that it failed to have a significant effect on

(a) cuts in personal and corporate income tax rates

(b) increases in saving and investment

(c) reductions in government regulation

(d) renewed interest in entrepreneurship

■ **PROBLEMS**

1. In columns 1 and 2 of the following table is a portion of a short-run aggregate supply schedule. Column 3 shows the number of full-time workers (in millions) that would have to be employed to produce each of the seven real domestic outputs (in billions) in the short-run aggregate supply schedule. The labor force is 80 million workers and the full-employment output of the economy is

$_____.

a. If the aggregate demand schedule were that shown in columns 1 and 4,

(1) the price level would be _____ and the

real output would be $_____.

(2) the number of workers employed would be

_____, the number of workers unemployed would be _____ , and the unemployment *rate* would be _____%.

b. If aggregate demand were to increase to that shown in columns 1 and 5 and short-run aggregate supply remained constant,

(1) the price level would rise to _____

and the real output would rise to $_____.

(2) employment would increase by _____ workers and the unemployment rate would fall to

_____%.

(3) the price level would increase by _____ and

the rate of inflation would be _____%.

c. If aggregate demand were to decrease to that shown in columns 1 and 6 and short-run aggregate supply remained constant,

(1) the price level would fall to _____

and the real output would fall to $_____.

(2) employment would decrease by _____ compared with situation a, and workers and the unemployment rate would rise to _____%.

(3) the price level would decrease and the rate of inflation would be (positive, negative) _____.

2. On the top of the next page is an aggregate demand and aggregate supply model. Assume that the economy is initially in equilibrium at **AD₁** and **AS₁**. The price level

will be _____ and the real domestic output will

be _____.

a. If there is demand-pull inflation, then

(1) in the short run, the new equilibrium is at point

_____, with the price level at _____

and real output at _____;

(2) in the long run, nominal wages will rise so the aggregate supply curve will shift from _____ to

_____. The equilibrium will be at point

_____ with the price level at _____

and real output at _____, so the increase in

(1) Price level	(2) Real output supplied	(3) Employment (in millions)	(4) Real output demanded	(5) Real output demanded	(6) Real output demanded
130	$ 800	69	$2300	$2600	$1900
140	1300	70	2200	2500	1800
150	1700	72	2100	2400	1700
160	2000	75	2000	2300	1600
170	2200	78	1900	2200	1500
180	2300	80	1800	2100	1400
190	2300	80	1700	2000	1300

aggregate demand has only moved the economy along

its _____ curve.

b. Now assume that the economy is initially in equilibrium at point **W**, where **AD₁** and **AS₁** intersect. If there is cost-push inflation, then

(1) in the short run, the new equilibrium is at point

_____, with the price level at _____

and real output at _____.

(2) if the government tries to counter the cost-push inflation with expansionary monetary and fiscal policy,

then aggregate demand will shift from _____

to _____, with the price level becoming

_____ and real output _____, but this policy has a trap because the price level has shifted

from _____ to _____ and the new

level of inflation might shift _____ leftward.

(3) if government does not counter the cost-push inflation, the price level will eventually move to _____

and real output to _____ as the recession reduces nominal wages and shifts the aggregate supply

curve from _____ to _____.

c. Now assume that the economy is initially in equilibrium at point **Y**, where **AD₂** and **AS₂** intersect. If there is a recession that reduces investment spending, then

(1) aggregate demand decreases and real output

shifts from _____ to _____,

and, assuming that prices and wages are flexible downward, the price level shifts from _____ to

_____.

(2) these events cause real wages to (rise, fall)

_____, and eventually nominal wages

_____ to restore the previous real wages.

(3) when this happens, the short-run aggregate supply

curve shifts from _____ to _____

to its new equilibrium at point _____. The

equilibrium price level is _____ and the equilibrium level of output is _____ at the long-run aggregate supply curve _____.

3. Following is a traditional Phillips Curve.

a. At full employment (a 4% unemployment rate) the

price level would rise by _____% each year.

b. If the price level were stable (increasing by 0% a

year), the unemployment rate would be _____%.

c. Which of the combinations along the Phillips Curve

would you choose for the economy? _____

Why would you select this combination? _____

_____

4. Following is an adaptive expectations model of the short- and long-run Phillips Curve.

a. Suppose you begin at point **X₁** and an assumption is made that nominal wages are set on the original expectation that a 3% rate of inflation will continue in the economy.

(1) If government invokes expansionary monetary and fiscal policy to reduce the unemployment rate from 6% to 3%, then the actual rate of inflation will move to

_____%. The higher product prices will lift profits of firms and they will hire more workers; thus in the short run the economy will temporarily move to point

_____.

(2) If workers demand and receive higher wages to compensate for the loss of purchasing power from higher than expected inflation, then business profits will fall from previous levels and firms will reduce employment; therefore, employment will move from point

_____ to point _____ on the graph.

The short-run Phillips Curve has shifted from _____

to _____ on the graph.

(3) If government again tries to stimulate aggregate demand with monetary and fiscal policy to reduce the unemployment rate from 6% to 3%, then prices will rise before nominal wages, and output and employment will increase, so that there will be a move from point

_____ to point _____ on the graph.

(4) But when workers get nominal wage increases, profits fall, and employment moves from point

_____ at _____% to point

_____ at _____%. The short-run

Phillips Curve has now shifted from _____

to _____ on the graph.

(5) The long-run Phillips Curve is the line _____.

b. Suppose you begin at point X_3, where the expected and actual rate of inflation is 9% and the unemployment rate is 6%.

(1) If there should be a decline in aggregate demand because of a recession and if the actual rate of inflation should fall to 6%, well below the expected rate of 9%, then business profits will fall and the unemployment rate will decrease to 9% as shown by the movement from point X_3 to point _____.

(2) If firms and workers adjust their expectation to the 6% rate of inflation, the nominal wages will fall, profits will rise, and the economy will move from point

_____ to point _____. The short-run

Phillips Curve has shifted from _____ to

_____.

(3) If this process is repeated, the long-run Phillips

Curve will be traced as line _____.

5. Following is a Laffer Curve.

a. The point of maximum tax revenue is _____. As tax rates decrease from 100% to point **B**, tax revenues will (increase, decrease) _____. As

tax rates increase from 0% to point **B**, tax revenues

will _____.

b. Supply-side economists would contend that it would be beneficial for government to cut tax rates if they are

(below, above) _____ point **B**, whereas critics of supply-side economics contend that it would be harmful for government to cut tax rates if they are

_____ point **B**.

■ **SHORT ANSWER AND ESSAY QUESTIONS**

1. What distinguishes the short run from the long run in macroeconomics?

2. Identify the basic difference between a short-run and a long-run aggregate supply curve. Explain what happens to aggregate supply when an increase in the price level results in an increase in nominal wages.

3. Explain how to find equilibrium in the extended AD-AS model.

4. Describe the process of demand-pull inflation in the short run and in the long run. How does demand-pull inflation influence the aggregate supply curve?

5. What two generalizations emerge from the analysis of cost-push inflation? Describe the two scenarios that provide the basis for the generalizations.

6. What is a Phillips Curve? Explain how a Phillips Curve with a negative slope may be derived by holding aggregate supply constant and mentally increasing aggregate demand.

7. What policy dilemma does the traditional Phillips Curve illustrate? Does the manipulation of aggregate demand through monetary and fiscal policy move the Phillips Curve or cause a movement along the Phillips Curve?

8. Were the rates of inflation and of unemployment consistent with the Phillips Curve in the 1960s? What do these two rates suggest about the curve in the 1970s and early 1980s?

9. What were the aggregate supply shocks to the U.S. economy during the 1970s and early 1980s? How did these shocks affect the Phillips Curve in the United States?

10. Describe the factors that contributed to stagflation's demise during the 1982–1989 period. What do many economists contend happened to the Phillips Curve during this period compared to the 1970s and early 1980s?

11. Explain the natural rate hypothesis, and briefly describe the two variants of the interpretation of the unemployment-inflation rate data of the 1970s and early 1980s.

12. What does "adaptive" refer to in the adaptive expectations theory? Illustrate how this theory is used to explain both inflation and disinflation in the economy.

13. What are the views of the adaptive expectations theory on the
(a) effects of expansionary monetary and fiscal policy on employment in the short run and on the short-run Phillips Curve, and
(b) long-run Phillips Curve? How does it reach these conclusions?

14. How does rational expectations theory explain expansionary monetary and fiscal policy effects on the price level and employment in the short run and the long run? What assumptions are made to reach this conclusion?

15. Compare and contrast the theories of rational expectations and adaptive expectations in terms of views on inflationary expectations, the interpretation of the Phillips Curve, and the effectiveness of monetary policy and fiscal policy.

16. Discuss three ways that supply-side economists contend there are tax and transfer payment disincentives in the economy.

17. Draw a Laffer Curve showing the relationship between tax rates and tax revenues. Outline the three criticisms of the ideas expressed in the Laffer Curve.

18. What are the two types of government regulation? How might this regulation affect economic growth?

19. Identify the major feature of Reaganomics. Make a case for its success.

20. Discuss the evidence on the effects of Reaganomics on saving, investment, productivity, economic growth, and aggregate supply. Did supply-side economics work during the 1980s?

ANSWERS

Chapter 16 Extending the Analysis of Aggregate Supply

FILL-IN QUESTIONS

1. increase, decrease
2. fixed, variable, upsloping, vertical

3. right, increase, increase, short-run, nominal, higher
4. left, increase, decrease
5. decrease, increase
6. decrease, falls, increase, decrease, increase
7. greater, greater, smaller
8. inverse, low, high
9. increase, increase
10. unstable, supply, cost-push
11. recession, tight, increased, decreased, increased, decreased, decreased
12. right, left, short-run
13. natural, does not, unemployment
14. gradually, short-run, long-run, increase
15. rise, fall, disinflation
16. anticipated, offset, real, nominal, a rise, no change
17. decrease, decrease, increase, increase
18. increase, decrease, increase, decrease
19. small, demand, supply, loss
20. less, less, supply, did not, increased, decreased, minimal

TRUE-FALSE QUESTIONS

1. F, p. 331	10. T, pp. 337-338	19. F, p. 342
2. F, pp. 331-332	11. F, p. 338	20. F, p. 342
3. T, p. 332	12. T, pp. 338-339	21. F, p. 343
4. T, p. 333	13. F, p. 339	22. T, p. 343
5. F, pp. 334-335	14. F, pp. 339-340	23. F, pp. 343-344
6. T, p. 335	15. T, pp. 340-341	24. T, p. 345
7. F, pp. 335-336	16. F, p. 341	25. F, p. 345
8. T, pp. 335-336	17. T, pp. 341-342	
9. T, pp. 336-337	18. T, p. 342	

MULTIPLE-CHOICE QUESTIONS

1. c, p. 331	10. a, pp. 335-336	19. b, p. 341
2. b, p. 331	11. b, pp. 336-337	20. a, pp. 341-342
3. b, pp. 332-333	12. a, pp. 336-337	21. a, p. 340
4. b, p. 331	13. d, pp. 338-339	22. b, p. 343
5. d, p. 333	14. c, p. 339	23. b, pp. 343-344
6. c, p. 333	15. b, p. 339	24. a, p. 344
7. b, pp. 333-334	16. c, pp. 339-340	25. b, p. 345
8. a, p. 335	17. d, pp. 340-341	
9. d, p. 335	18. d, p. 342	

PROBLEMS

1. 2300; *a.* (1) 160, 2,000, (2) 75, 5, 6.25; *b.* (1) 170, 2,200, (2) 3, 2.5, (3) 6.25; *c.* (1) 150, 1,700, (2) 3, 10, (3) negative
2. P_1, Q_p; *a.* (1) X, P_2, Q_2, (2) AS_1, AS_2, Y, P_3, Q_p, AS_{LR}; *b.* (1) Z, P_2, Q_1, (2) AD_1, AD_2, P_3, Q_p, P_2, P_3, AS_2, (3) P_1, Q_p, AS_2, AS_1; *c.* (1). Q_p, Q_1, P_3, P_2, (2) rise, fall, (3) AS_2, AS_1, W, P_1, Q_p, AS_{LR}
3. *a.* 20; *b.* 9
4. *a.* (1) 6, Y_1; (2) Y_1, X_2, PC_1, PC_2, (3) X_2, Y_2, (4) Y_2, 3, X_3, 6, PC_2, PC_3, (5) PC_{LR}; *b.* (1) Z_2, (2) Z_2, X_2, PC_3, PC_2, (3) PC_{LR}
5. *a.* B, increase, decrease; *b.* above, below

SHORT ANSWER AND ESSAY QUESTIONS

1. p. 331	8. pp. 337-338	15. pp. 340-342
2. pp. 331-333	9. pp. 338-339	16. p. 343
3. p. 333	10. p. 339	17. pp. 343-344
4. pp. 333-334	11. pp. 340-342	18. p. 345
5. pp. 334-335	12. pp. 340-342	19. p. 345
6. pp. 336-337	13. pp. 340-342	20. p. 345
7. pp. 336-337	14. p. 342	

CHAPTER 17

Disputes in Macro Theory and Policy

Now that you understand the basic theory and models of the macro economy, you are ready to learn about different perspectives on how the economy functions and the major disputes in macro theory and policy.

Economics has always been an arena in which conflicting theories and policies oppose each other. This field of intellectual combat, in major engagements, has seen Adam Smith do battle with the defenders of a regulated economy. It witnessed the opposition of Karl Marx to the orthodox economics of his day. In the 1930s, it saw Keynes oppose the classical economists. Around the major engagements have been countless minor skirmishes between opposing viewpoints. Out of these major and minor confrontations have emerged not winners and losers but the advancement of economic theory and the improvement of economic policy.

Chapter 17 sets the foundation for understanding the modern debates by comparing **classical** and **Keynesian** views of macroeconomic theory. The now familiar aggregate demand–aggregate supply model is used to illustrate the classical view that aggregate supply is vertical and aggregate demand relatively stable. Keynesians, however, saw aggregate supply as being horizontal (to full-employment output), aggregate demand as being highly unstable, and a need for government intervention to stabilize the macro economy.

The chapter then turns to the first of three major questions: *What causes macro instability in the economy?* Four different perspectives on the issues are given. First, from the Keynesian-based *mainstream* view, this instability arises primarily from volatility in investment that shifts aggregate demand or from occasional shocks to aggregate supply. Second, *monetarists* focus on the money supply and assume that the competitive market economy has a high degree of stability, except when there is inappropriate monetary policy. The monetarist analysis is based on the equation of exchange and the assumption that the velocity of money is stable. Changes in the money supply, therefore, directly affect the level of nominal GDP. Third, *real-business-cycle* theorists see instability as coming from the aggregate supply side of the economy and from real factors that affect the long-term growth rather than monetary factors that affect aggregate demand. Fourth, some economists think that macroeconomic instability is the result of *coordination failures* that do not permit people to act jointly to determine the optimal level of output, and the equilibrium in the economy changes as expectations change.

The next question the chapter discusses is: *Does the economy self-correct its macro instability?* The view of new classical economics is that internal mechanisms in the economy allow it to self-correct. The two variants of this new classical perspective are based on **monetarism** and **rational expectations theory (RET)**. Monetarists think the economy will self-correct to its long-run level of output, although there can be short-run changes in the price level and real output. Rational expectations theory suggests that the self-correction process is quick and does not change the price level or real output, except when there are price-level surprises.

By contrast, mainstream economists contend that the downward inflexibility of wages limits the self-correction mechanisms in the economy. Several explanations are offered for this inflexibility. There can be long-term wage contracts that support wages. Firms may also pay an efficiency wage to encourage work effort, reduce turnover, and prevent shirking. Firms may also be concerned about maintaining the support and teamwork of key workers (insiders), so they do not cut wages even when other workers (outsiders) might be willing to accept a lower wage.

The different perspectives on macro instability and self-correction set the stage for discussion of the third and final question: *Should the macro economy be guided by policy rules or discretion?* To restrict monetary policy, monetarists and rational expectations economists call for a monetary rule that would have monetary authorities allow the money supply to grow in proportion to the long-term growth in the productive capacity of the economy. Both monetarists and rational expectations economists also oppose the use of fiscal policy, and a few call for a balanced budget requirement to limit the use of discretionary fiscal policy.

Mainstream economists see value in discretionary monetary and fiscal policy. They suggest that a monetary rule would be ineffective in achieving growth and would destabilize the economy. A balanced-budget requirement would also have a procyclical effect that would reinforce recessionary or inflationary tendencies in the economy. And, since government has taken a more active role in the economy, the historical record shows that discretionary monetary and fiscal actions have reduced macro instability.

As was the case in the past, macroeconomic theory and policy have changed because of the debates among economists. The disputes among mainstream economists, monetarists, rational expectationists, and real business cycle theorists have produced new insights about how the macro economy operates. In particular, it is now recognized that "money matters" and that the money supply has a significant effect on the economy. More attention is also being given to the influence of people's expectations on policy and coordination failures in explaining macroeconomic events. The factors that influence aggregate supply and long-term growth in the economy are also being considered. The disputes in macroeconomics in the past 30 years forced economists to reconsider previous conclusions and led to the incorporation of new ideas into mainstream thinking about macro theory and policy.

■ CHECKLIST

When you have studied this chapter you should be able to

☐ Compare and contrast the classical and Keynesian views of the aggregate demand curve and the aggregate supply curve.
☐ Describe the mainstream view of stability in the macro economy and the two potential sources of instability.
☐ Explain the monetarist view of stability in the macro economy.
☐ Write the equation of exchange and define each of the four terms in the equation.
☐ Explain why monetarists think the velocity of money is stable.
☐ Write a brief scenario which explains what monetarists believe will happen to change the nominal GDP and to *V* (velocity of money) when *M* (money supply) is increased.
☐ Discuss the monetary causes of instability in the macro economy.
☐ Describe the real-business-cycle view of stability in the macro economy.
☐ Give a noneconomic and macroeconomic example of the coordination failures view of stability in the macro economy.
☐ Use a graph to explain the new classical view of self-correction in the macro economy.
☐ Discuss the differences between the monetarist and rational expectations views on the speed of adjustment for self-correction in the macro economy.
☐ State the two basic assumptions of the rational expectations theory (RET).
☐ Use a graph to explain how RET views unanticipated and fully anticipated changes in the price level.
☐ Describe the mainstream view of self-correction in the macro economy.
☐ Give two reasons why there may be downward wage inflexibility.
☐ State three reasons why a higher wage might result in greater efficiency.
☐ Use ideas from insider-outsider theory to explain the downward inflexibility of wages.
☐ State the rationale for why monetarists think there should be a monetary rule, and illustrate it using an aggregate demand and aggregate supply model.
☐ Describe how monetarists and new classical econo-

mists view the effectiveness of fiscal policy.
☐ Offer a mainstream defense of discretionary stabilization policy and a critique of a monetary rule and balanced-budget requirement.
☐ Describe the possible reasons for increased stability in the macro economy since 1946.
☐ Offer a summary of the four alternative views on issues affecting the macro economy.

■ CHAPTER OUTLINE

1. Classical and Keynesian economics can be compared by examining their aggregate demand–aggregate supply models of the economy.
  a. In the *classical model,*
  (1) the aggregate supply curve is vertical at the economy's full-employment output, and a decrease in aggregate demand will lower the equilibrium price level and have no effect on the real output (or employment) in the economy because of Say's law and flexible, responsive prices and wages.
  (2) the aggregate demand curve slopes downward because (with a fixed money supply in the economy) a fall in the price level increases the purchasing power of money and enables consumers and business firms to purchase a larger real output. Aggregate demand will be reasonably stable if the nation's monetary authorities maintain a constant supply of money to accomodate long-term growth.
  b. In the *Keynesian model,*
  (1) the aggregate supply curve is horizontal at the current price level, and a decrease in aggregate demand will lower the real output (and employment) in the economy and have no effect on the equilibrium price level because of the downward inflexibility of prices and wages.
  (2) aggregate demand is viewed as being unstable over time, even if the supply of money is held constant, partly because of fluctuations in investment spending. A decline in aggregate demand decreases real domestic output but has no effect on the price level, thereby causing output to stay permanently below the full-employment level.

2. There are four different views among economists on stability and instability in the macro economy.
  a. The *mainstream view* is Keynesian-based and holds that instability in the economy arises from
  (1) the volatility in investment spending that makes aggregate demand unstable, and
  (2) occasional aggregate supply shocks which cause cost-push inflation and recession.
  b. *Monetarists* focus on the money supply. They think markets are highly competitive and that government intervention destabilizes the economy.
  (1) In monetarism, the equation of exchange is $MV = PQ$, where M is the money supply, V the velocity of money, P the price level, and Q the quantity of goods and services produced.
  (2) Monetarists think that velocity is stable or that the quantity of money demanded is a stable percentage of

GDP (GDP/**M** is constant). If velocity is stable, there is a predictable relationship between **M** and nominal GDP (= **PQ**). An increase in **M** will leave firms and households with more money than they wish to have, so they will increase spending and boost aggregate demand. This causes nominal GDP and the amount of money they wish to hold to rise until the demand for money is equal to **M** and nominal GDP/**M** = **V**.

(3) Monetarists view macroeconomic instability as a result of inappropriate monetary policy. An increase in the money supply will increase aggregate demand, output, and the price level; it will also reduce unemployment. Eventually, nominal wages rise to restore real wages and real output, and the unemployment rate falls back to its natural level at long-run aggregate supply.

c. *Real-business-cycle theorists* see macroeconomic instability as being caused by real factors influencing aggregate supply instead of monetary factors causing shifts in aggregate demand. Changes in technology and resources will affect productivity and thus the long-run growth rate of aggregate supply.

d. A fourth view of instability in the macro economy attributes the reasons to *coordination failures.* These failures occur when people are not able to coordinate their actions to achieve an optimal equilibrium. A self-fulfilling prophecy can lead to recession because if households and firms expect it, they individually cut back on spending and employment. If, however, they were to act jointly, they could take actions to counter the recession expectations to achieve an optimal equilibrium.

3. Economists also debate the issue of *whether the macro economy self-corrects.*

a. The *new classical view* of economics, held by monetarists and rational expectations economists, is that the economy may deviate from the full-employment level of output, but it eventually returns to this output level because there are self-corrective mechanisms in the economy.

(1) Graphically, if aggregate demand increases, it temporarily raises real output and the price level. Nominal wages rise and productivity falls, so short-run aggregate supply decreases, thus bringing the economy back to its long-run output level.

(2) There is disagreement about the speed of adjustment. The monetarists adopt the adaptive expectations view that there will be a slower, temporary change in output but that in the long run it will return to its natural level. Other new classical economists adopt the *rational expectations theory (RET)* view that there will be a rapid adjustment with little or no change in output. RET is based on two assumptions: People understand how the economy works so that they quickly anticipate the effect on the economy of an economic event, and all markets in the economy are so competitive that equilibrium prices and quantities quickly adjust to changes in policy.

(3) In RET, unanticipated price-level changes, called price-level surprises, cause short-run changes in real output because they cause misperceptions about the economy among workers and firms.

(4) In RET, fully anticipated price-level changes do not change real output even in the short run because workers and firms anticipate and counteract the effects of the changes.

b. The *mainstream view of self-correction* suggests that price and wages may be inflexible downward in the economy.

(1) Graphically, a decrease in aggregate demand will decrease real output but not the price level because nominal wages will not decline and cause the short-run aggregate supply curve to shift right.

(2) Downward wage inflexibility primarily arises because of wage contracts and the legal minimum wage, but they may also occur from efficiency wages and insider-outsider relationships, according to new Keynesian economics.

(3) An efficiency wage minimizes the firm's labor cost per unit of output but may be higher than the market wage. This higher wage may result in greater efficiency because it stimulates greater work effort, requires less supervision costs, and reduces job turnover.

(4) Insider-outsider relationships may also produce downward wage inflexibility. During a recession, outsiders (who are less essential to the firm) may try to bid down wages to try to keep their jobs, but the firm may not lower wages because it does not want to alienate insiders (who are more essential to the firm) and disrupt the cooperative environment in the firm needed for production.

4. The debates over macro policy also focus on the need for *policy rules* or *discretion.*

a. Monetarists and new classical economists argue for policy rules to reduce government intervention in the economy. They believe this intervention causes macroeconomic instability.

(1) In regard to monetary policy, monetarists have proposed a monetary rule that the money supply be increased at the same annual rate as the potential annual rate of increase in the real GDP. A monetary rule would shift aggregate demand rightward to match a shift in the long-run aggregate supply curve that occurs because of economic growth, thus keeping the price level stable over time.

(2) Monetarists and new classical economists question the value of fiscal policy, and some would like to see a balanced Federal budget over time. An expansionist fiscal policy will tend to crowd out investment and cause only a temporary increase in output. RET economists also think that fiscal policy is ineffective and that people will anticipate it and their acts will counteract its intended effects.

b. Mainstream economists think that discretionary fiscal and monetary policy can be effective and are opposed to a monetary rule and a balanced-budget requirement.

(1) They see the velocity of money as relatively unstable and a loose link beween changes in the money supply and aggregate demand. This means that a monetary rule might produce too great a shift in aggregate demand (and demand-pull inflation) or too small a shift

(and deflation) to match the shift in aggregate supply. Such a rule would contribute to price instability, not price stability.

(2) They support the use of fiscal policy during a recession or to counter growing inflation. Fiscal policy, however, should be reserved for those situations where monetary policy is relatively ineffective. They also oppose a balanced-budget amendment because its effects would be procyclical rather than countercyclical and would reinforce recessionary or inflationary tendencies.

c. Mainstream ecconomists also note that there has been greater stability in the macro economy since 1946, when discretionary monetary and fiscal policy was more actively used to moderate the effects of the business cycle.

5. The *disputes* in macroeconomics in the past two decades have led to the incorporation of several ideas from monetarism, rational expectations theory, real-business-cycle theory, and supply-side economics into mainstream thinking about macroeconomics. First, monetarists have gotten mainstream economists to recognize that changes in the money supply are important in explaining long-lasting and rapid inflation. Second, mainstream economists now recognize that expectations matter because of rational expectations theory and that there are coordination failures in the economy. Third, real-business-cycle theory and supply-side economics have forced mainstream economists to give more attention to government policies that promote long-run economic growth. Table 17-1 summarizes the four alternative views of macroeconomics.

■ HINTS AND TIPS

1. The chapter may appear complex because many alternative viewpoints are presented. To simplify matters, first focus on the three questions that the chapter addresses: What causes macro instability in the economy? Does the economy self-correct? Should policymakers use rules or discretion? For each question, identify how different types of economists answer each question.

2. Review the discussions of aggregate demand and aggregate supply in Chapters 11 and 16 as preparation for the comparison of alternate views of the macro economy presented in this chapter.

3. Monetarist and mainstream views of the macro economy are two approaches of looking at the same thing. The similarities can best be seen in equations in nominal form. The monetarist equation of exchange is $MV = PQ$. The Keynesian-based mainstream equation is $C_a + I_g + X_n + G = GDP$. The MV term is the monetarist expression for the mainstream equilibrium $C_a + I_g + X_n + G$. The PQ term is the monetarist expression for GDP. Monetarists give more emphasis to the role of money and assume that velocity is relatively stable. Mainstream economists give more emphasis to the instability caused by investment spending and to influences on GDP from consumption, net export, and government spending.

■ IMPORTANT TERMS

classical economics	**price-level surprises**
Keynesianism	**new Keynesian economics**
monetarism	**efficiency wage**
equation of exchange	**insider-outsider theory**
velocity	**monetary rule**
real-business-cycle theory	**rational expectations theory (RET)**
coordination failures	
new classical economics	

SELF-TEST

■ FILL-IN QUESTIONS

1. The aggregate supply curve of the classical economists is (horizontal, vertical) _____, and the aggregate supply curve of the Keynesian economists is _____ up to the full-employment level of output. Therefore, a decrease in aggregate demand will have no effect on price level and will decrease output and employment in the (classical, Keynesian) _____ model, but a decrease in aggregate demand will decrease the price level and have no effect on output and employment in the _____ model.

2. In the classical way of thinking, changes in the money supply shift the aggregate (demand, supply) _____ curve. If the money supply increases, then the curve will (increase, decrease) _____, and if the money supply decreases, then the curve will _____. If the nation's monetary authorities maintain a constant supply of money, this curve will be (stable, unstable) _____.

3. From the Keynesian perspective, aggregate demand is (stable, unstable) _____, even if there are no changes in the supply of money, largely because of the volatility in (investment, government) _____ spending.

4. The mainstream view is that macro instability is caused by changes in investment spending which shift the aggregate (demand, supply) _____ curve. If it increases too rapidly, then (inflation, recession) _____ can occur, but if it decreases, then the economy can experience _____. Occasionally, adverse aggregate (demand, supply) _____ shocks also cause instability.

5. Monetarists argue that capitalism is inherently (stable, unstable) _____ because most of its markets are (competitive, noncompetitive) _____.

They believe that government intervention in the economy has contributed to macroeconomic (stability, instability) _____ and has promoted (flexibility, inflexibility) _____ in wages.

6. The basic equation of the monetarists is _____ = _____. Indicate what each of the four letters in the following equation represents:
  a. M: _____
  b. V: _____
  c. P: _____
  d. Q: _____

7. Monetarists believe that **V** is (stable, unstable) _____ because people have a _____ desire to hold money relative to holding other financial and real assets or for making purchases. The amount of money people will want to hold will depend on the level of (real, nominal) _____ GDP.

8. An increase in **M**, to the monetarist's way of thinking, will leave the public with (more, less) _____ money than it wishes to have, induce the public to (increase, decrease) _____ its spending for consumer and capital goods, which will result in a(n) _____ in aggregate demand and nominal GDP until nominal GDP equals **MV.**

9. Monetarists believe that the most significant cause of macroeconomic instability has been inappropriate (fiscal, monetary) _____ policy. Too rapid increases in **M** cause (recession, inflation) _____; insufficient growth of **M** causes _____.

10. The theory that changes in resource availability and technology (real factors), which alter productivity, are the main causes of instability in the macro economy is held by (real-business-cycle, rational expectations) _____ _____ economists. In this theory, shifts in the economy's long-run aggregate (demand, supply) _____ curve change real output. As a consequence, money demand and money supply change, shifting the aggregate demand curve in the (opposite, same) _____ direction as the initial change in long-run aggregate supply. Real output thus can change (with, without) _____ a change in the price level.

11. A coordination failure is said to occur when people (do, do not) _____ reach a mutually beneficial equilibrium because they lack some way to jointly coordinate their actions. In this view, there is (one, a number of) _____ equilibrium position(s) in the economy. Macroeconomic instability is the result of changing (the money supply, expectations) _____ that result in changing in the equilibrium position(s).

12. Monetarists and rational expectations economists view the economy as (capable, incapable) _____ of self-correction when it deviates from the full-employment level of real output. Monetarists suggest that this adjustment occurs (gradually, rapidly) _____, while rational expectations economists argue that it occurs _____.

13. Rational expectations theory assumes that with sufficient information, peoples' beliefs about future economic outcomes (are, are not) _____ accurate reflections of the likelihood of the outcomes occurring. It also assumes that markets are highly competitive, meaning that prices and wages are (flexible, inflexible) _____.

14. In rational expectations theory, changes in aggregate demand that change the price level and real output are (anticipated, unanticipated) _____, while changes in aggregate demand that only change in the price level and not real output are _____.

15. The view of mainstream economists is that many prices and wages are (flexible, inflexible) _____ downward for (short, long) _____ periods of time. This situation (increases, decreases) _____ the ability of the economy to automatically self-correct for deviations from full-employment output.

16. A higher wage can result in more efficiency because of results in (greater, less) _____ work effort, supervision costs that are (lower, higher) _____, and (more, less) _____ turnover in jobs. Efficiency wages (increase, decrease) _____ the downward inflexibility of wages because it makes firms more reluctant to cut wages when aggregate demand declines.

17. Monetarists and rational expectations economists support a monetary rule because they believe that discretionary monetary policy tends to (stabilize, destabilize) _____ the economy. With this rule the money supply would be increased at a rate (greater than, less than, equal to) _____ the long-run growth of potential GDP; graphically, this can be shown by a shift in aggregate demand that would be _____ the shift in long-run aggregate supply resulting from economic growth.

18. Proponents of the rational expectations theory contend that discretionary monetary policy is (effective, ineffective) _____ and like the monetarists favor (rules, discretion) _____. When considering discretionary fiscal policy, most monetarists and RET economists (do, do not) _____ advocate its use.

19. Mainstream economists (support, oppose) _____ a monetary rule and a balanced-budget requirement. They view discretionary monetary policy as (effective, ineffective) _____, and think discretionary fiscal policy is _____ but should be held in reserve when monetary policy works too slowly. They say the use of discretionary monetary and fiscal policy since 1946 has produced (more, less) _____ stability in the macro economy.

20. Many ideas from alternative views of the macro economy have been absorbed into mainstream thinking about macroeconomics. There is more recognition that excessive growth of the money supply is a major cause of (recession, inflation) _____, that expectations and coordination failures are (important, unimportant) _____, and that government needs to focus more attention on policy that shifts aggregate (demand, supply) _____.

■ **TRUE-FALSE QUESTIONS**

Circle the T if the statement is true, the F if it is false.

1. The classical view is that the aggregate supply curve is vertical. **T F**

2. Classical economists consider the aggregate demand curve to be unstable. **T F**

3. Keynesians think that the aggregate supply curve is horizontal (to full-employment output). **T F**

4. Keynesians suggest that full employment is the norm in the economy. **T F**

5. The mainstream view is that macro instability is caused by the volatility of investment spending, which shifts the aggregate demand curve. **T F**

6. Monetarists argue that the market system would provide for macroeconomic stability were it not for government interference in the economy. **T F**

7. In the equation of exchange, the left side, *MV*, represents the total amount received by sellers of output, while the right side, *PQ*, represents the total amount spent by purchasers of that output. **T F**

8. Monetarists argue that *V* in the equation of exchange is stable and that a change in *M* will bring about a direct and proportional change in *PQ*. **T F**

9. Most monetarists believe that an increase in the money supply has no effect on real output and employment in the short run. **T F**

10. In the monetarist view, a major cause of the Great Depression was the decline in investment spending. **T F**

11. Real-business-cycle theory views changes in resource availability and technology, which alter productivity, as the main cause of macroeconomic instability. **T F**

12. In real-business-cycle theory, real output changes only with a change in the price level. **T F**

13. A coordination failure is said to occur when people do not reach a mutually beneficial equilibrium because they lack some way to jointly coordinate their actions to achieve it. **T F**

14. Peoples' expectations have no effect on coordination failures. **T F**

15. Neoclassical economists see the economy as automatically correcting itself when disturbed from its full-employment level of real output. **T F**

16. Rational expectations theory assumes that both product and resource markets are uncompetitive and that wages and prices are inflexible. **T F**

17. In rational expectations theory, a fully anticipated price-level change results in a change in real output. **T F**

18. Mainstream economists contend that wages are inflexible downward. **T F**

19. An efficiency wage is a below-market wage that spurs greater work effort and gives the firm more profits because of lower wage costs. **T F**

20. Insider-outsider theory offers one explanation for the downward inflexibility of wages in the economy. **T F**

21. Monetarists believe that a monetary rule would reduce instability in the macro economy. **T F**

22. Rational expectations economists argue that monetary policy should be left to the discretion of government. **T F**

23. Monetarists support the use of fiscal policy, especially as a means of controlling inflation. **T F**

24. Mainstream economists believe that discretionary monetary policy is an effective tool for stabilizing the economy. **T F**

25. The mainstream view of the economy since 1946 believes that it has become inherently less stable because of the use of fiscal policy. **T F**

■ **MULTIPLE-CHOICE QUESTIONS**

Circle the letter that corresponds to the best answer.

1. Classical economists suggest that full employment is
   (a) best achieved through government interventions
   (b) not possible in an unstable market economy
   (c) inversely related to the price level
   (d) the norm in a market economy

2. The aggregate supply curve of classical economists
   (a) is vertical
   (b) is horizontal

(c) slopes upward

(d) slopes downward

3. Classical theory concludes that the production behavior of firms will *not* change when the price level decreases because input costs would

(a) rise along with product prices to leave real profits and output unchanged

(b) fall along with product prices to leave real profits and output unchanged

(c) fall, but product prices would rise, offsetting any change in real profits or output

(d) rise, but product prices would rise, offsetting any change in real profits or output

4. In classical economics, a decrease in aggregate demand results in

(a) a decrease in both the price level and domestic output

(b) a decrease in the price level and no change in domestic output

(c) no change in the price level and a decrease in domestic output

(d) no change in either the price level or domestic output

5. The aggregate supply curve in the Keynesian model is

(a) vertical at the full-employment output level

(b) horizontal to the full-employment output level

(c) positively sloped to the full-employment output level

(d) negatively sloped to the full-employment output level

6. In the Keynesian model, a decrease in aggregate demand results in

(a) a decrease in both the price level and domestic output

(b) a decrease in the price level and no change in domestic output

(c) no change in the price level and a decrease in domestic output

(d) no change in either the price level or domestic output

7. The mainstream view of the economy holds that

(a) government intervention in the economy is not desirable

(b) product and labor markets are highly competitive and flexible

(c) changes in investment spending lead to changes in aggregate demand

(d) economic growth is best achieved through implementation of a monetary rule

8. In the monetarist perspective

(a) discretionary monetary policy is the most effective way to moderate swings in the business cycle

(b) government policies have reduced macroeconomic stability

(c) macroeconomic stability results from adverse aggregate supply shocks

(d) markets in a capitalistic economy are largely noncompetitive

9. Which is the equation of exchange?

(a) $PQ/M + V = GDP$

(b) $V = M + PQ$

(c) $MV = PQ$

(d) $V + I_g + M = GDP$

10. In the equation of exchange, if V is stable, an increase in M will necessarily increase

(a) the demand for money

(b) government spending

(c) nominal GDP

(d) velocity

11. When nominal gross domestic product (GDP) is divided by the money supply (M), then you will obtain the

(a) velocity of money

(b) monetary multiplier

(c) equation of exchange

(d) monetary rule

12. Monetarists argue that the amount of money the public will want to hold depends primarily on the level of

(a) nominal GDP

(b) investment

(c) consumption

(d) prices

13. Real-business-cycle theory suggests that

(a) velocity changes gradually and predictably; thus it is able to accommodate the long-run changes in nominal GDP

(b) the volatility of investment is the main cause of the economy's instability

(c) inappropriate monetary policy is the single most important cause of macroeconomic instability

(d) changes in technology and resources affect productivity, and thus the long-run growth of aggregate supply

14. In real-business-cycle theory, if the long-run aggregate supply increased, then aggregate demand would increase by

(a) an equal amount, so real output and the price level would increase

(b) less than an equal amount, so real output would increase and the price level would decrease

(c) greater than an equal amount, so real output and the price level would increase

(d) an equal amount, so real output would increase and the price level would be unchanged

15. If aggregate demand declined and the economy experienced a recession due to a self-fulfilling prophecy, this would be an example of

(a) real-business-cycle theory

(b) insider-outsider theory

(c) a coordination failure

(d) a change in velocity

16. In the new classical view, when the economy diverges from its full-employment output,

(a) internal mechanisms within the economy would automatically return it to its full-employment output
(b) discretionary monetary policy is needed to return it to its full-employment output
(c) discretionary fiscal policy is needed to return it to its full-employment output
(d) the adoption of an efficiency wage in the economy would return it to its full-employment output

17. The views about the speed of adjustment for self-correction in the economy suggest that
(a) monetarists think it would be gradual and rational expectations economists think it would be quick
(b) monetarists think it would be quick and rational expectations economists think it would be gradual
(c) monetarists and mainstream economists think it would be quick
(d) real-business-cycle theorists and rational expectations economists think it would be gradual

18. Proponents of rational expectations theory argue that people
(a) are not as rational as monetarists assume them to be
(b) make forecasts that are based on poor information, causing economic policy to be driven by a self-fulfilling prophecy
(c) form beliefs about future economic outcomes that accurately reflect the likelihood that those outcomes will occur
(d) do not respond quickly to changes in wages and prices, causing a misallocation of economic resources in the economy

19. In the rational expectations theory, a temporary change in real output would occur from a
(a) fully anticipated price-level change
(b) downward wage inflexibility
(c) coordination failure
(d) price-level surprise

20. The conclusion mainstream economists draw about the downward price and wage inflexibility is that
(a) the effects can be reversed relatively quickly
(b) efficiency wages do not contribute to the problem
(c) the economy can be mired in recession for long periods
(d) wage and price controls are needed to counteract the situation

21. According to mainstream economists, which contributes to the downward inflexibility of wages?
(a) price-level surprises
(b) insider-outsider relationships
(c) adverse aggregate supply shocks
(d) inadequate investment spending

22. The rule suggested by the monetarists is that the money supply should be increased at the same rate as the
(a) price level
(b) interest rate
(c) velocity of money
(d) potential growth in real GDP

23. To stabilize the economy, monetarist and rational expectations economists advocate
(a) the use of price-level surprises and adoption of an efficiency wage
(b) a monetary rule and a balanced-budget requirement
(c) the use of discretionary fiscal policy instead of discretionary monetary policy
(d) the use of discretionary monetary policy instead of discretionary fiscal policy

24. Mainstream economists support
(a) increasing the money supply at a constant rate
(b) eliminating insider-outsider relationships in business
(c) the use of discretionary monetary and fiscal policy
(d) a balanced-budget requirement and a monetary rule

25. Which would be an idea from monetarism which has been absorbed into mainstream macroeconomics?
(a) how changes in investment spending change aggregate demand
(b) the importance of money and the money supply in the economy
(c) using discretion rather than rules for guiding economic policy
(d) building the macro foundations for microeconomics

■ **PROBLEMS**

1. Assume that you are a monetarist in this problem and that **V** is stable and equal to 4. In the following table is the aggregate supply schedule: the real output **Q** which producers will offer for sale at seven different price levels **P**.

P	Q	PQ	MV
$1.00	100	$____	$____
2.00	110	____	____
3.00	120	____	____
4.00	130	____	____
5.00	140	____	____
6.00	150	____	____
7.00	160	____	____

a. Compute and enter in the table above the seven values of **PQ**.
b. Assume **M** is $90. Enter the values of **MV** on each of the seven lines in the table. The equilibrium

(1) nominal domestic output (**PQ** or **MV**) is $_____.

(2) price level is $_____.

(3) real domestic output (**Q**) is $_____.
c. When **M** increases to $175, **MV** at each price level

is $_____ and the equilibrium

(1) nominal domestic output is $_____.

(2) price level is $_____.

(3) real domestic output is $_____.

2. Indicate what perspective(s) of economics would be most closely associated with each position. Use the following abbreviations: **MAI** (mainstream economics), **MON** (monetarism), **RET** (rational expectations theory), and **RBC** (real-business-cycle theory).

   a. macro instability from investment spending

                        _____

   b. macro instability from inappropriate monetary policy

                        _____

   c. macro instability from changes in resource availability and technology   _____

   d. equation of exchange   _____

   e. fiscal policy can be effective   _____

   f. unanticipated price-level changes   _____
   g. downward inflexibility of wages and prices

                        _____

   h. monetary rule   _____

   i. neutral fiscal policy   _____

   j. economy automatically self-corrects   _____

   k. monetary policy is effective   _____

3. Following are price-level (PL) and output (Q) combinations to describe aggregate demand and aggregate supply curves: (1) PL and Q_1 is AD_1. (2) PL and Q_2 is AD_2. (3) PL and Q_3 is AS_{LR1}. (4) PL and Q_4 is AS_{LR2}.

PL	Q_1	Q_2	Q_3	Q_4
250	0	200	400	600
200	200	400	400	600
150	400	600	400	600
100	600	800	400	600
50	800	1,000	400	600

   a. Use the following to graph AD_1, AD_2, AS_{LR1}, and AS_{LR2}. Label the vertical axis as the price level and the horizontal axis as real output (Q).

0

   b. If the economy is initially in equilibrium where AD_1 and AS_{LR1} intersect, the price level will be _____ and real output will be _____.

   c. If, over time, the economy grows from AS_{LR1} to AS_{LR2}, the equilibrium price level will be _____ and real output will be _____.

   d. Assume a monetary rule is adopted that increases the money supply proportionate to the increase in aggregate supply. Aggregate demand will increase from AD_1 to AD_2, making the price level _____ and real output _____.

   e. Mainstream economists would argue that velocity is unstable, so a constant increase in the money supply might not shift AD_1 all the way to AD_2. In this case, the price level would fall below the target of _____. It might also be the case that the constant increase in the money supply might shift AD_1 beyond AD_2, so the price level would rise above the target of _____.

■ **SHORT ANSWER AND ESSAY QUESTIONS**

1. What is the difference between the classical and Keynesian aggregate supply curve? Draw a graph showing the difference. What is the justification for each viewpoint?

2. What is the effect of a decrease in aggregate demand on the price level and real domestic output in the classical and Keynesian model? Show the change in a graph.

3. Why did classical economists consider the aggregate demand curve to be stable? What is the response of Keynesians to this position?

4. Why does the classical aggregate demand curve have a negative (downward) slope?

5. Explain the two causes of macroeconomic instability in the view of mainstream economists.

6. What do monetarists see as the cause of economic instability in the economy? Explain, using the equation of exchange, how a change in the money supply will affect nominal GDP.

7. Why do monetarists argue that the velocity of money is stable? If the money supply increases, how will people respond from a monetarist perspective?

8. Compare and contrast the monetarist and mainstream view on the causes of macroeconomic instability. How do monetarists explain the Great Depression?

9. Explain the real-business-cycle view of macroeconomic instability using an aggregate demand and supply graph.

10. Give a macroeconomic example of how coordination failures cause macroeconomic instability.

11. Explain the monetarist view of self-correction in the macro economy. Contrast that perspective with that of rational expectations in terms of the real output, the price level, and the speed of adjustment.

12. Describe the two assumptions on which rational expectations is based. How realistic is to expect that people will be able to accurately forecast economic outcomes?

13. Use a graph to illustrate and explain the mainstream view of self-correction in the macro economy.

14. Why would an efficiency wage lead to downward inflexibility in prices?

15. Give an example of insider-outsider relationships and explain how it affects wage flexibility.

16. What is the monetary rule? Why do monetarists suggest this rule to replace discretionary monetary policy?

17. What is the perspective of rational expectations economists on a monetary rule and the conduct of monetary policy?

18. What is the position of some monetarist and rational expectations economists on a requirement for a balanced budget? Why do they adopt such a position?

19. How do mainstream economists defend the use of discretionary monetary and fiscal policy? What interpretation do mainstream economists make of the historical evidence on the relationship between macroeconomic policy and instability?

20. What influence has monetarism, rational expectations theory, real-business-cycle theory, and supply-side economics had on mainstream macroeconomic theory and policy? Give three examples of ideas that have changed mainstream thinking.

ANSWERS

Chapter 17 Disputes in Macro Theory and Policy

FILL-IN QUESTIONS

1. vertical, horizontal, Keynesian, classical
2. demand, increase, decrease, stable
3. unstable, investment
4. demand, inflation, recession, supply
5. stable, competitive, instability, inflexibility
6. *MV = PQ;* a. the money supply; b. the velocity of money; c. the average price of each unit of physical output; d. the physical volume of goods and services produced
7. stable, stable, nominal
8. more, increase, increase
9. monetary, inflation, recession
10. real-business-cycle, supply, same, without

11. do not, a number of, expectations
12. capable, gradually, rapidly
13. are, flexible
14. unanticipated, anticipated
15. inflexible, long, decreases
16. greater, lower, less, increase
17. destabilize, equal to, equal to
18. ineffective, rules, do not
19. oppose, effective, effective, more
20. inflation, important, supply

TRUE-FALSE QUESTIONS

1. T, p. 351
2. F, p. 350
3. T, P. 352
4. F, p. 352
5. T, p. 353
6. T, p. 353
7. F, p. 353
8. T, p. 354
9. F, p. 354
10. F, p. 355
11. T, p. 355
12. F, p. 355
13. T, p. 356
14. F, p. 356
15. T, pp. 356-357
16. F, p. 358
17. F, p. 358
18. T, p. 359
19. F, p. 359
20. T, p. 360
21. T, pp. 360-361
22. F, p. 361
23. F, pp. 361-362
24. T, p. 363
25. F, p. 363

MULTIPLE-CHOICE QUESTIONS

1. d, p. 351
2. a, p. 351
3. b, p. 351
4. b, pp. 351-352
5. b, p. 352
6. c, pp. 351-352
7. c, p. 353
8. b, p. 353
9. c, p. 353
10. c, p. 354
11. a, p. 354
12. a, p. 354
13. d, p. 355
14. d, p. 355
15. c, p. 356
16. a, p. 356
17. a, pp. 357-358
18. c, pp. 357-358
19. d, p. 358
20. c, p. 359
21. b, pp. 359-360
22. d, p. 360
23. b, pp. 360-361
24. c, p. 363
25. b, p. 364

PROBLEMS

1. *a.* 100, 220, 360, 520, 700, 900, 1120; *b.* 360, 360, 360, 360, 360, 360, 360, (1) 360, (2) 3.00, (3) 120; *c.* 700, (1) 700, (2) 5.00, (3) 140
2. *a.* MAI; *b.* MON, RET; *c.* RBC; *d.* MON; *e.* MAI; *f.* RET; *g.* MAI; *h.* MON, RET; *i.* MON, RET; *j.* MON, RET; *k.* MAI
3. *a.* graph similar to Figure 17-4 in the text; *b.* 150, 400; *c.* 100, 600; *d.* 150, 600; *e.* 150, 150

SHORT ANSWER AND ESSAY QUESTIONS

1. pp. 350-352
2. pp. 351-352
3. p. 352
4. p. 352
5. p. 353
6. pp. 353-354
7. p. 354
8. pp. 353-355
9. p. 355
10. p. 356
11. pp. 356-358
12. pp. 357-358
13. pp. 358-359
14. p. 359
15. p. 360
16. pp. 360-361
17. p. 361
18. pp. 361-363
19. pp. 363-364
20. p. 364

Economic Growth

The United States has experienced an impressive record of economic growth since 1900. In Chapter 18 you will learn about the major factors that have contributed to this long-term economic growth.

The chapter begins by defining economic growth and explaining its significance. The text then analyzes the six factors that make growth possible. The four **supply factors** increase the output potential of the economy. Whether the economy actually produces its full potential—that is, whether the economy has both full employment and full production—depends upon two other factors: the level of aggregate demand (the **demand factor**) and the efficiency with which the economy allocates resources (the **efficiency factor**).

The next section of the chapter places the factors contributing to economic growth in graphical perspective with the use of two familiar models. The **production possibilities model** was originally presented in Chapter 2 and is now used to discuss how the two major supply factors—labor input and labor productivity—shift the production possibilities curve outward. The second model is the **aggregate demand–aggregate supply model** that was first explained in Chapter 11 and was discussed in more detail in Chapter 16. Here you learn how both the short-run and the long-run shifts in aggregate supply combined with shifts in aggregate demand (and the factors underlying those shifts) affect the output and the price level.

The growth record of the United States has been impressive both in terms of increases in real GDP and in real GDP per capita. What accounts for this long-term economic growth of the United States? First, the U.S. population and the size of its labor force have grown. Second and more important, the productivity of the labor force in the United States has increased. The increase in the productivity of labor is the result of technological advances, the expansion of the stock of capital goods in the U.S. economy, the improved education and training of its labor force, economies of scale, the reallocation of resources, the generous quantities of natural resources with which the U.S. economy was endowed, and its social, cultural, and political environment. (Note, however, that the regulations of government tend to slow the rates at which the productivity of labor and the output of the economy grows.) In addition, macroeconomic instability has limited the economy from achieving its full potential output.

The rate of increase in labor productivity was less in the 1970s and 1980s compared with previous decades and also less when compared with some of our major trading partners. This slowdown in labor productivity is significant for several reasons related to our standard of living, inflation, and the competitiveness of the United States in world markets. As you will learn, the decline stems from at least five major problems experienced by the economy in the past two decades.

Although productivity growth has increased modestly in recent years, the resurgence may be transitory and low productivity may continue to limit the long-term potential for economic growth. It is still too early to tell if the recent upsurge in productivity and economic growth heralds a "new economy" or is a short-term change to be followed by macroeconomic instability.

The last section of the chapter describes two major types of growth policies. The demand-side policies include discretionary monetary and fiscal policies that you learned about in previous chapters. The supply-side policies are varied and include efforts to improve education and training, and changes in tax policies to increase incentives to work, save, and invest. These policies may also include deregulation of industries or international trade agreements both of which increase the long-term growth potential of the economy.

■ CHECKLIST

When you have studied this chapter you should be able to

☐ Define economic growth in two different ways.
☐ Explain why economic growth is important to any economy.
☐ Use the rule of 70 to demonstrate how different growth rates affect real domestic output over time.
☐ Identify four supply factors in economic growth.
☐ Explain demand and efficiency factors in economic growth.
☐ Show graphically how economic growth shifts the production possibilities curve.
☐ Explain the equation for total output.
☐ Illustrate graphically how economic growth shifts the short-run and long-run aggregate supply curve and the aggregate demand curve.
☐ Describe the growth record of the U.S. economy since 1940 and its rates of economic growth since 1948.

☐ Compare the relative importance of the two major means of increasing the real GDP in the United States since 1929.

☐ List the sources of growth in the productivity of labor in the United Sates since 1929, and state their relative importance.

☐ Identify the chief detriment to growth and indicate how much it has reduced real output in the United States since 1929.

☐ Describe the other contributing factors which affect an economy's growth rate.

☐ Explain why the actual rate of growth in the United States has been less than its potential rate of growth and why it has been unstable.

☐ Give three reasons why the slowdown in productivity is significant.

☐ Enumerate the five principal causes of the slowdown in the rate of labor productivity in the United States.

☐ Discuss whether there has been a resurgence of productivity growth and the development of a "new economy."

☐ Outline two growth policies and give examples of each.

■ CHAPTER OUTLINE

1. *Growth economics* deals with the long-run changes in production capacity over time.

   a. *Economic growth* means an increase in the per capita real output of an economy and is measured in terms of the annual percentage rate of growth of per capita real output.

   b. Economic growth is important because it lessens the burden of scarcity; it provides the means of satisfying existing wants more fully and fulfilling new wants.

   c. One or two percentage point differences in the rate of growth result in substantial differences in annual increases in the economy's output.

2. Whether economic growth *can* occur depends on supply, demand, and efficiency factors:

   a. *supply factors* include the quantity and quality of resources (natural, human, and capital), and technology;

   b. *demand factors* influence the level of aggregate demand in the economy that is important for sustaining full employment of resources; and

   c. *efficiency factors* affect the efficient use of resources to obtain maximum production of goods and services (productive efficiency) and allocates them to their highest and best use by society (allocative efficiency).

3. Two familiar economic models can be used for the analysis of economic growth.

   a. In the *production possibilities model*, economic growth shifts the production possibilities curve outward because of improvement in supply factors that

   (1) increase real output by increasing the labor inputs and by increasing the productivity of labor (in equation terms: total output = worker-hours × labor productivity);

   (2) however, whether the economy operates on the frontier of the curve depends on demand factors affecting the full employment of resources efficiency factors affecting full production.

   b. In the *aggregate demand–aggregate supply model*, economic growth is also affected by these supply, demand, and efficiency factors.

   (1) Supply factors that contribute to economic growth shift the vertical long-run aggregate supply to the right in the model.

   (2) But since the price level has increased over time, this suggests that the increase in potential output has been accompanied by an even greater shift in aggregate demand (and its underlying demand and allocative factors).

4. Over the past 50 years, the *growth record* of the U.S. economy has been impressive, but economic growth in America has been less impressive than the record of many advanced industrialized nations in recent decades.

   a. Economic well-being may be understated by economic growth figures because the figures do not take into account improvements in product quality or increase in leisure time.

   b. But growth may have adverse effects on the environment or the quality of life that are not reflected in growth figures, thus the figures may overstate the benefits of growth.

5. Many factors account for the economic growth of the United States since 1929.

   a. Two-thirds of this growth was the result of the increased productivity of labor, and one-third of it was the result of the increased quantity of labor employed in the economy.

   b. During this period the U.S. population and its labor force expanded, and despite decreases in the length of the workweek and birthrates, the increased participation of women in the labor force and the growth of its population continue to expand the size of the labor force by two million workers a year.

   c. Technological advance is combining given amounts of resources in new ways that result in a larger output, and since 1929, it accounted for 28% of the increase in real national income.

   d. Saving and investment have expanded the U.S. economy's stock of capital; increased the quantity of tools, equipment, and machinery with which each worker has to work; and accounted for 20% of the increase in real national income since 1929.

   e. Increased investment in human capital (in the training and education of workers) expands the productivity of workers, and accounted for 12% of the increase in real national income.

   f. Economies of scale *and* the improved allocation of resources also expand the productivity of workers; since 1929, each has contributed 8% to the U.S. real national income.

   g. But such detriments (or deterrents) to the growth of productivity as the government regulation of industry, pollution, and worker health and safety divert investment away from productivity-increasing additions to capital. They accounted for a *negative* 9% of the increased real national income since 1929.

h. Other factors that are difficult to quantify, such as a general abundance of natural resources and social-cultural-political environment, have also contributed to economic growth in the United States.

i. While the actual economic growth in the United States averaged 2.9% per year since 1929, it would have been higher by .2 to .3 percentage points if the economy had achieved its potential level of output and not experienced depression or recession.

6. The annual rates of growth in labor productivity in the United States declined substantially during the 1970s and rose only modestly during the 1980s and early 1990s. Productivity rates achieved in the United States are also less than those found in other major industrial nations such as Japan or Germany.

   a. The slowdown in the growth of labor productivity is significant because it affects the standard of living, inflation, and the prices of U.S. goods in world markets.

   b. The suggested causes of the productivity slowdown have included

   (1) *labor quality*—a decline in the quality (education, training, and experience) of the U.S. labor force;

   (2) *less technological progress*—a decline in research and development expenditures as a percentage of GDP;

   (3) *low investment*—reduced investment in capital goods as a percentage of GDP than in previous periods stemming from low saving rates, import competition, regulation, and less spending for infrastructure;

   (4) *high energy prices*—higher prices in 1973–1975 and 1978–1980 increased production costs and had inflationary and adverse macro policy effects on the economy;

   (5) *low growth of service productivity*—the lack of substitute resources, less competitive pressure, and the demand for higher quality services contributed to this condition.

7. Productivity and economic growth showed substantial improvement in the 1990s compared with the 1970s and 1980s. These developments caused some economists to wonder whether a "new economy" has developed based on improvements in computer technology, communications, and global capitalism. The question is whether these increases in the rates of productivity and economic growth represent a long-run trend or a short-run boom to be followed by macroeconomic instability.

8. Two economic policies have been discussed for achieving more economic growth in the United States.

   a. *Demand-side policies* focus on the use of monetary and fiscal policies to influence aggregate demand and maintain full employment and full production of resources.

   b. *Supply-side policies* call for expansion of the economy's output potential and often involve changes in education and training and new tax policies to increase investment, saving, and work effort.

■ HINTS AND TIPS

1. Chapter 18 contains very little economics that should be new to you. You learned about real GDP and how to measure its growth in Chapter 7. Chapter 2 introduced you to the production possibilities model that is now discussed in more detail. In Chapters 11 and 16 you learned about the aggregate demand–aggregate supply models that are now used to discuss economic growth. You might review these concepts and models from previous chapters before reading Chapter 18.

2. Table 18-2 is important if you want to understand the factors that influence economic growth in the United States. The figures in the table indicate the relative importance of each factor. About two-thirds of American economic growth comes from eight factors that affect labor productivity, and one-third comes from the increase in the quantity of labor.

■ IMPORTANT TERMS

economic growth	labor productivity
supply factor	labor force participation rate
demand factor	
efficiency factor	infrastructure

SELF-TEST

■ FILL-IN QUESTIONS

1. Growth economics is concerned with an economy whose productive capacity (increases, decreases) _____ over time.

2. Economic growth is best measured either by an increase in (nominal, real) _____ GDP over a time period or by an increase in _____ GDP per capita over a time period.

3. A rise in real output per capita (increases, decreases) _____ the standard of living and _____ the burden of scarcity in the economy.

4. Assume an economy has a GDP of $3600 billion. If the growth rate is 5%, real GDP will increase by ($360, $180) _____ billion next year; but if the rate of growth is only 3%, the annual increase in GDP will be ($54, $108) _____ billion. A two percentage point difference in the growth rate results in a ($72, $254) _____ billion difference in the annual increase in GDP.

5. The four supply factors in economic growth are

   a. _____

b. _____

c. _____

d. _____

6. To realize its growing production potential, a nation must fully employ its expanding supplies of resources, which is the (efficiency, demand) _____ factor in economic growth, and it must also achieve productive and allocative _____, the other factor contributing to economic growth.

7. In the production possibilities model, economic growth increases primarily because of (demand, supply) _____ factors that shift the production possibilities curve to the (left, right) _____; but if there is less than full employment and production, the economy (may, may not) _____ realize its potential.

8. Real GDP of any economy in any year is equal to the quantity of labor employed (divided, multiplied) _____ by the productivity of labor. The quantity of labor is measured by the number of (workers, hours of labor) _____ employed. Productivity is equal to real GDP per (capita, worker-hour) _____.

9. The quantity of labor employed in the economy in any year depends on the size of the (unemployed, employed) _____ labor force and the length of the average workweek. The size element depends on the size of the working-age population and the labor-force (unemployment, participation) _____ rate.

10. In the aggregate demand–aggregate supply framework, economic growth is illustrated by an (increase, decrease) _____ in the long-run aggregate supply curve; when the price level also increases, it indicates that the aggregate demand curve has increased (more, less) _____ rapidly than the long-run aggregate supply.

11. Since 1940, real GDP has increased (threefold, sixfold) _____ and real GDP per capita has increased _____. These figures do not fully account for (better, worse) _____ products and services, (more, less) _____ leisure, (positive, negative) _____ environmental effects, and the fact that the growth rate in the United States is (less, more) _____ impressive than many other industrial nations.

12. Economist Edward Denison studied economic growth in the United States since 1929 and found that the increase in the quantity of labor accounted for (one-third, two-thirds) _____ of economic growth and increases in

labor productivity accounted for _____ of economic growth.

13. Factors contributing to labor productivity include

a. technological _____

b. increases in the quantity of _____ employed and in the quantity employed per _____

c. the improved _____ and _____ of workers

d. economies of _____

e. the improved _____ of resources.

14. An increase in the stock of capital of a nation is the result of saving and (consumption, investment) _____. In the United States the stock of capital has historically grown (more, less) _____ rapidly than the quantity of labor employed.

15. The principal detriment to growth of real output since 1929 seems to have been government regulations which diverted (consumption, investment) _____ spending away from uses that would have increased the (cost, productivity) _____ of labor.

16. Two other factors that have led to economic growth in the United States are its abundant (labor, natural) _____ resources and its social-cultural-political (parties, environment) _____.

17. Denison's analysis is designed to explain (actual, potential) _____ real national income, but when there is macroeconomic instability such as a recession the _____ rate of economic growth falls short of the (actual, potential) _____ rate.

18. In the 1970s and to a lesser extent the 1980s, the annual rates of increase in the productivity of labor (rose, fell) _____. The significance of this development is that it can cause a (rise, fall) _____ in the standard of living and a _____ in inflationary pressure. It can also result in a loss of international markets for (United States, foreign) _____ producers of goods and services.

19. The slowdown in productivity growth is a result of problems with labor (quantity, quality) _____, (more, less) _____ technological progress, relatively (high, low) _____ levels of investment spending as a percent of GDP, energy prices that are (high, low) _____ in certain years, and (faster, slower) _____ growth in service productivity. Some of these problems have lessened in the past two decades, and productivity has (increased, decreased) _____ as a consequence, but it is not known whether the change is permanent and signals the development of a (new, old) _____ economy.

20. Two basic types of growth policies have been suggested for stimulating economic growth in the United States. Policies that involve the use of discretionary monetary and fiscal policies to sustain and expand full employment in the economy are (supply, demand) _____-side policies, whereas _____-side policies focus primarily on tax changes to stimulate work, saving, investment, education, and training policies.

■ TRUE-FALSE QUESTIONS

Circle the T if the statement is true; the F if it is false.

1. Growth economics examines why an economy's production capacity increases over time. **T F**

2. The better of the two definitions of economic growth for comparing living standards is an increase in the per capita real output of the economy. **T F**

3. Suppose two economies both have GDPs of $500 billion. If the GDPs grow at annual rates of 3% in the first economy and 5% in the second economy, the difference in their amounts of growth in 1 year is $10 billion. **T F**

4. If the rate of growth in real GDP averages 2.5% a year, it will take about 28 years for real GDP to double. **T F**

5. The potential of an enhanced productive capacity in an economy will not be completely realized unless there is full employment of resources and full production in the economy. **T F**

6. An increase in economic growth will increase the long-run aggregate supply curve and the short-run aggregate supply curve, but will decrease the aggregate demand curve. **T F**

7. The demand factor in economic growth refers to the ability of the economy to expand its production as the demand for products grows. **T F**

8. To reach its production potential, a nation must achieve not only full employment but also economic efficiency. **T F**

9. The real GDP of an economy in any year is equal to its input of labor divided by the productivity of labor. **T F**

10. Real GDP has tended to increase more rapidly than real per capita GDP in the United States. **T F**

11. Growth and rates-of-growth estimates generally attempt to take account of changes in the quality of goods produced and in the amount of leisure members of the economy enjoy. **T F**

12. Increased labor productivity has been more important than increased labor inputs in the growth of the U.S. economy since 1929. **T F**

13. Since 1929 improved technology has accounted for about 28% of the increase in real output in the United States. **T F**

14. More often than not technological progress requires the economy to invest in new machinery and equipment. **T F**

15. The single most important source of the growth of labor productivity in the United States since 1929 has been the increase in the size of the U.S. labor force. **T F**

16. The expanded regulation of industry, the environment, and worker health and safety tends to reduce the rate at which labor productivity grows. **T F**

17. The availability of natural resources in the United States has been a significant factor in the growth of the U.S. economy. **T F**

18. Over the past 60 years, the U.S. social, cultural, and political environment has slowed the economic growth of the United States. **T F**

19. Increases in labor productivity can, at least in the U.S. economy, be taken pretty much for granted because the rate of increase has been nearly constant for well over half a century. **T F**

20. Productivity growth is the basic source of improvements in real wage rates and the standard of living. **T F**

21. Productivity increases offset increases in nominal wage rates, partly or fully lessening cost-push inflationary pressures. **T F**

22. There was a significant improvement in the education, employment training, and work experience of workers in the 1970s and 1980s that contributed to increased labor productivity in those decades. **T F**

23. During the 1970s and 1980s the United States invested a larger percentage of its GDP in capital goods. **T F**

24. The slowdown in U.S. productivity growth has been greater in the manufacturing sector than in the service sector. **T F**

25. An example of a supply-side policy for economic growth would be programs for education and training of the labor force. **T F**

■ MULTIPLE-CHOICE QUESTIONS

Circle the letter that corresponds to the best answer.

1. Which of the following is a benefit of real economic growth to a society?

(a) Everyone enjoys a greater nominal income.
(b) The standard of living increases.
(c) The burden of scarcity increases.
(d) The society is less able to satisfy new wants.

2. If the real output of an economy were to increase from $2,000 billion to $2,100 billion in 1 year, the rate of growth of real output during that year would be
(a) 0.5%
(b) 5%
(c) 10%
(d) 50%

3. Suppose an economy has a real GDP of $700 billion and an annual growth rate of 5%. Over a 2-year period real GDP will increase by
(a) $14 billion
(b) $35 billion
(c) $70 billion
(d) $71 3/4 billion

4. If a nation's real GDP is growing by 2% per year, then approximately how many years will it take for real GDP to double?
(a) 25 years
(b) 30 years
(c) 35 years
(d) 40 years

5. Which of the following is *not* a supply factor in economic growth?
(a) an expansion in purchasing power
(b) an increase in the economy's stock of capital goods
(c) more natural resources
(d) technological progress

Use the following graph to answer Questions 6 and 7.

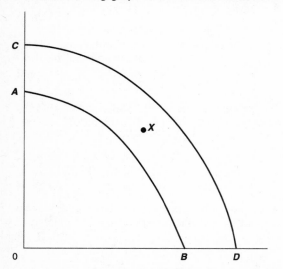

6. If the production possibilities curve of an economy shifts from **AB** to **CD**, it is most likely caused by
(a) supply factors
(b) demand factors
(c) efficiency factors
(d) industrial policy

7. If the production possibilities curve for an economy is at **CD** but the economy is operating at point **X**, the reasons are most likely to be because of
(a) supply and environmental factors
(b) demand and efficiency factors
(c) labor inputs and labor productivity
(d) technological progress

8. Total output or real GDP in any year is equal to
(a) labor inputs divided by resource outputs
(b) labor productivity multiplied by real output
(c) worker-hours multiplied by labor productivity
(d) worker-hours divided by labor productivity

9. Assume that an economy has 1,000 workers, each working 2,000 hours per year. If the average real output per worker-hour is $9, then total output or real GDP will be
(a) $2 million
(b) $9 million
(c) $18 million
(d) $24 million

Use the graph below to answer Questions 10 and 11.

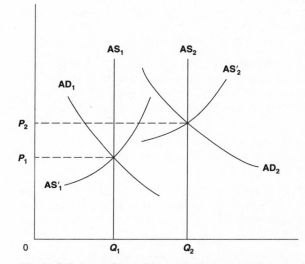

10. A shift from Q_1 to Q_2 is caused by a shift in the
(a) level of prices
(b) aggregate demand curve
(c) short-run aggregate supply curve
(d) long-run aggregate supply curve

11. Which combination would best explain a shift in the price level from P_1 to P_2 and an increase in real domestic output from Q_1 to Q_2?
(a) an increase in the long-run aggregate supply (AS_1 to AS_2) and in short-run aggregate supply (AD_1 to AD_2).
(b) an increase in aggregate demand (AD_1 to AD_2) and a decrease in long-run aggregate supply (AS_2 to AS_1).
(c) an increase in the long-run aggregate supply (AS_1 to AS_2), an increase in aggregate demand (AD_1 to AD_2), and an increase in short-run aggregate supply (AS_1' to AS_2').
(d) a decrease in the long-run aggregate supply (AS_2 to AS_1), a decrease in aggregate demand (AD_2 to

AD_1), and a decrease in short-run aggregate supply (AS'_2 to AS'_1)

12. Since 1940 real GDP in the United States has increased about
(a) onefold
(b) twofold
(c) fourfold
(d) sixfold

13. The real GDP of the U.S. economy since 1948 increased at an average *annual* rate of about
(a) .5%
(b) 2.1%
(c) 3.1%
(d) 5.4%

14. Real GDP per capita in the United States since 1948 increased at an average annual rate of about
(a) 1%
(b) 2%
(c) 3%
(d) 4%

15. Data on real GDP, real GDP per capita, and the respective growth rates of those measured in the United States take into account
(a) improvement in product quality
(b) increases in available leisure time
(c) environmental problems
(d) changes in domestic output

16. About what fraction of the growth in the real national income of the United States since 1929 has been due to increases in the quantity of labor employed?
(a) one-fourth
(b) one-third
(c) one-half
(d) two-thirds

17. The factor accounting for the largest increase in the productivity of labor in the United States since 1929 has been
(a) economies of scale
(b) technological advance
(c) the quantity of capital
(d) the education and training of workers

18. A major factor that has negatively affected economic growth since 1929 has been
(a) the decreased quantity of labor
(b) education and training
(c) diseconomies of scale
(d) government regulation

19. The average annual growth rate in the United States has been
(a) increased by periods of recession
(b) increased by periods of inflation
(c) decreased by periods of recession
(d) not affected by periods of inflation

20. Which labor factor contributed to the slowdown in the growth rate of productivity in the 1970s and 1980s?
(a) a decline in the number of high school dropouts
(b) a decline in the level of work experience
(c) a decline in the size of the labor force
(d) a rise in the number of jobs

21. Which best explains why there was a lower level of capital investment in the United States in the 1970s and 1980s?
(a) less regulation of business practices
(b) less competition from imported goods
(c) greater spending for infrastructure
(d) lower rates of saving

22. A factor that helped slow the growth rate of productivity in the 1970s and 1980s was
(a) a rise in the growth rate of manufacturing productivity
(b) a fall in the growth rate of service productivity
(c) a rise in the quality of labor
(d) a fall in energy prices

23. Which factor has contributed to the resurgence of productivity growth in recent years?
(a) increased inflation
(b) higher energy prices
(c) more experienced workers
(d) greater government regulation

24. If the Federal Reserve acted to cut interest rates to stimulate investment, this would be an example of
(a) a supply-side policy
(b) a demand-side policy
(c) an industrial policy
(d) a fiscal policy

25. A program which provides tuition tax credits that are designed to increase college enrollment would be an example of
(a) monetary policy
(b) regulatory policy
(c) supply-side policy
(d) demand-side policy

■ **PROBLEMS**

1. The table below shows the quantity of labor (measured in hours) and the productivity of labor (measured in real GDP per hour) in a hypothetical economy in three different years.

Year	Quantity of labor	Productivity of labor	Real GDP
1	1000	$100	$ _____
2	1000	105	_____
3	1100	105	_____

a. Compute the economy's real GDP in each of the three years and enter them in the table.
b. Between years 1 and 2, the quantity of labor remained constant, but

(1) the productivity of labor increased by _____%, and

(2) as a consequence, real GDP increased by _____%.

c. Between years 2 and 3, the productivity of labor remained constant, but

(1) the quantity of labor increased by _____%, and
(2) as a consequence, real GDP increased by _____%.

d. Between years 1 and 3

(1) real GDP increased by _____%, and
(2) this rate of increase is approximately equal to the sum of the rates of increase in the _____ and the _____ of labor.

2. Suppose the real GDP and the population of an economy in seven different years were those shown in the next table.

Year	Population, million	Real GDP, billions of dollars	Per capital real GDP
1	30	$ 9	$ 300
2	60	24	_____
3	90	45	_____
4	120	66	_____
5	150	90	_____
6	180	99	_____
7	210	105	_____

a. How large would the real per capita GDP of the economy be in each of the other six years? Put your figures in the table.

b. What would have been the size of the optimum population of this economy? _____

c. What was the *amount* of growth in real GDP between year 1 and year 2? $ _____

d. What was the *rate* of growth in real GDP between year 3 and year 4? _____ %

3. Given the hypothetical data in the table below, calculate the average annual rates of growth in real GDP and real per capita GDP over the period given.

Year	Real GDP	Annual growth in %	Real GDP per capita	Annual growth in %
1	$2,416	_____	$11,785	_____
2	2,695	_____	12,593	_____
3	3,187	_____	13,978	_____
4	3,618	_____	15,139	_____
5	3,995	_____	16,240	_____
6	4,545	_____	17,110	_____

■ SHORT ANSWERS AND ESSAY QUESTIONS

1. What is meant by economic growth? Why should the citizens of the United States be concerned with economic growth?

2. What are the six basic ingredients of economic growth? What is the essential difference between the supply factors and the other two factors? Is there any relationship between the strength of the supply factors and the strength of the demand factor?

3. What is the relationship between the real GDP produced in any year and the quantity of labor employed and labor productivity?

4. In what units are the quantity of labor and the productivity of labor measured?
(a) What are the two principal determinants of the quantity of the labor input?
(b) What determines the size of the labor force?

5. How does economic growth affect production possibilities? What demand and efficiency assumptions are necessary to achieve maximum productive potential?

6. Describe how economic growth can be illustrated in an aggregate demand–aggregate supply framework. What has happened to aggregate demand compared to long-run aggregate supply when the price level and real domestic output both increase?

7. What has been the growth record of the U.S. economy? Compare recent U.S. growth rates with those in other nations.

8. What have been the sources of the growth of the real national income in the United States since 1929? What has tended to slow the increase in labor productivity and in real national income?

9. What changes have occurred in the size of the U.S. population and labor force since 1929? What factor has slowed the rate of growth of the former, and what factor has speeded the growth of the latter?

10. What is the relationship between investment and the stock of capital? What is the connection between increases in the capital stock and the rate of economic growth?

11. What is technological advance, and why are technological advance and capital formation closely related processes?

12. What tends to increase the "quality" of labor? How is this quality usually measured?

13. What are the economic consequences if the economy fails to achieve its potential output year after year? What are the long-term consequences of this macroeconomic instability?

14. By how much did the annual increases in the productivity of labor decline in the United States between the mid-1960s and 1981? What are three significant features of this decline in this productivity growth?

15. What are five causes of the slowdown in the growth of labor productivity since the mid-1960s? Explain how each cause affects productivity.

16. How might changes in labor quality dampen productivity growth? What factors in the United States have contributed to this situation?

17. What is the relationship between the capital investment and productivity growth? What four conditions in the United States have affected the relative level of investment?

18. Explain the three possible reasons for slower productivity growth in services relative to manufacturing since the 1970s.

19. Has there been a resurgence in economic growth? What trends are suggested by the evidence? Do you think this is a long-term or short-term development in the economy?

20. What are the basic differences between demand-side and supply-side policies to stimulate economic growth? Give examples of each type.

ANSWERS

Chapter 18 Economic Growth

FILL-IN QUESTIONS

1. increases
2. real, real
3. increases, decreases
4. $180, $108, $72
5. *a.* quantity and quality of natural resources; *b.* quantity and quality of human resources; *c.* the supply or stock of capital goods; *d.* technology (any order for a–d)
6. demand, efficiency
7. supply, right, may not
8. multiplied, hours of labor, worker-hour
9. employed, participation
10. increase, more
11. sixfold, threefold, better, more, negative, less
12. one-third, two-thirds
13. *a.* progress (advance); *b.* capital, worker; *c.* education, training; *d.* scale; *e.* allocation
14. investment, more
15. investment, productivity
16. natural, environment
17. actual, actual, potential
18. fell, fall, rise, United States
19. quality, less, low, high, slower, increased, new
20. demand, supply

TRUE-FALSE QUESTIONS

1. T, p. 368	**10.** T, p. 372	**19.** F, p. 378
2. T, pp. 368-369	**11.** F, p. 373	**20.** T, p. 378
3. T, pp. 368-369	**12.** T, pp. 373-374	**21.** T, p. 378
4. T, p. 369	**13.** F, p. 374	**22.** F, pp. 378-379
5. T, pp. 369-370	**14.** T, p. 374	**23.** F, p. 380
6. F, pp. 371-372	**15.** F, pp. 373-376	**24.** T, pp. 381-382
7. F, p. 369	**16.** T, p. 376	**25.** T, p. 383
8. T, pp. 369-370	**17.** T, p. 377	
9. F, pp. 370-371	**18.** F, p. 377	

MULTIPLE-CHOICE QUESTIONS

1. b, p. 369	**10.** d, pp. 371-372	**19.** c, p. 377
2. b, p. 369	**11.** c, pp. 371-372	**20.** b, p. 379
3. d, p. 369	**12.** d, p. 372	**21.** d, p. 380
4. c, p. 369	**13.** c, p. 373	**22.** b, pp. 381-382
5. a, p. 369	**14.** b, p. 373	**23.** c, p. 382
6. a, p. 370	**15.** d, p. 373	**24.** b, p. 383
7. b, p. 370	**16.** b, pp. 373-374	**25.** c, p. 383
8. c, pp. 370-371	**17.** b, p. 374	
9. c, pp. 370-371	**18.** d, p. 376	

PROBLEMS

1. *a.* 100,000, 105,000, 115,500; *b.* (1) 5, (2), 5; *c.* (1) 10, (2) 10; *d.* (1) 15.5, (2) quantity, productivity
2. *a.* 400, 500, 550, 600, 550, 500; *b.* 150 million; *c.* $15 billion; *d.* 46.7%
3. *real GDP:* years 1–2 (2.3%); years 2–3 (3.7%); years 3–4 (2.7%); years 4–5 (3.5%); years 5–6 (4.6%); *real GDP per capita:* years 1–2 (1.4%); years 2–3 (2.2%); years 3–4 (1.7%); years 4–5 (2.4%); years 5–6 (1.8%)

SHORT ANSWER AND ESSAY QUESTIONS

1. pp. 368-369	**8.** pp. 373-377	**15.** pp. 378-382
2. pp. 369-370	**9.** p. 374	**16.** p. 379
3. pp. 370-371	**10.** pp. 374-375	**17.** p. 380
4. pp. 370-371	**11.** p. 374	**18.** pp. 381-382
5. p. 370	**12.** p. 375	**19.** pp. 382-383
6. pp. 371-372	**13.** p. 377	**20.** pp. 383
7. pp. 372-373	**14.** p. 378	

CHAPTER 19

Budget Deficits and the Public Debt

Over the past 35 years, the Federal government has had budget deficits in all but one year. In the past decade these budget deficits have grown quite large and have caused problems for the U.S. economy. Chapter 19 looks at the data and issues surrounding **budget deficits** and the related **public debt.**

The Federal government can operate with a budget deficit, a budget surplus, or a balanced budget during a year. Any budget surplus or deficit affects the size of the public (sometimes called national) debt; surpluses decrease it and deficits increase it. After a budget deficit and the public debt have been defined, three budget philosophies are discussed. Be aware that the philosophies the Federal government adopts have a significant impact on output and employment in the economy and on the public debt.

The chapter then discusses how four major *factors— wars, recessions, tax cuts,* and *lack of political will*—have contributed to increases in the public debt since 1929. The increased public debt resulting from these factors is placed into perspective with a quantitative description of the size of the public debt (and interest payments for it) relative to the size of the economy (GDP), how the public debt in the United States compares with that in other industrial nations, who owns the debt, and measurement problems caused by accounting and inflation.

The two middle sections of the chapter examine the economic implications or consequences of the public debt and deficits. These economic problems do not include bankrupting the Federal government because the government has three ways that it can meet its obligations. Nor does the public debt simply shift the economic burden to future generations because the public debt is a public credit for the many people who hold that debt in the form of government bonds. Rather, the public debt and payment of interest on the debt contribute to five important problems: increased inequality in income, reduced incentives for work and production, decreased standard of living when part of the debt is paid to foreigners, curbs on fiscal policy, and less capital investment.

The crowding out of investment in plant and equipment in the United States is probably the most serious of these five problems. You should understand how crowding out works and how it may impose a burden on future generations by reducing the growth of the nation's capital stock. Whether it does impose a burden on a future generation depends on how the increased government spending is financed. Raising taxes to pay for increased spending imposes a burden on the current taxpayers, whereas gov-

ernment borrowing to finance increased spending tends to reduce private investment and future capital stock.

The final sections of the chapter offer an extensive discussion of the macroeconomic problems with the Federal deficits of the past two decades. The recent deficits are of great concern because of their relatively large size, high interest cost, and the problems they pose for domestic macroeconomic and trade policy. Be sure that you study each link in the chain of events that lead to the contractions of output and employment in the U.S. economy as a result of large deficits. There is not any new economic theory in this discussion, just an application of theory you learned in previous chapters. The chapter then concludes with an explanation of three different policy responses to eliminate or reduce Federal budget deficits.

■ CHECKLIST

When you have studied this chapter you should be able to

☐ Define a budget deficit and the public debt, and explain how they are related.

☐ List three budget philosophies.

☐ Describe the characteristics of an annually balanced budget.

☐ State the rationale for a cyclically balanced budget.

☐ Explain how functional finance works as a budget philosophy.

☐ Identify the four principal causes of the public debt and discuss their relative importance.

☐ Describe the absolute and relative sizes of the public debt and interest payments since 1929.

☐ Compare the relative size of the public debt to those of other industrial nations.

☐ State who owns the public debt.

☐ Explain how inflation and accounting issues affect the public debt.

☐ Give three reasons why a large public debt will not bankrupt the government.

☐ Discuss whether the public debt imposes a burden on future generations.

☐ List five substantive issues related to the public debt.

☐ State the effect of the public debt on income distribution.

☐ Explain how the public debt affects incentives.

☐ Compare the effects of an internal debt with the effects of an external debt on the economy.

☐ Explain how large budget deficits curb the use of fiscal policy.

☐ Describe the crowding-out effect from a public debt.

☐ Compare taxation with borrowing as a way to finance a public debt and and qualify this comparison in two ways.

☐ Describe five concerns with the budget deficits and the public debt during the past two decades.

☐ Discuss the cause and effect linkage between the budget deficits and the balance of trade deficits and three related complications.

☐ Explain three major policy responses to large budget deficits and the expanding public debt.

☐ State how the public debt plays a positive role in the economy.

■ CHAPTER OUTLINE

1. The *budget deficit* of the Federal government is the amount by which its expenditures exceed its revenues in any year, and the *public debt* at any time is the sum of the Federal government's previous annual deficits (less any annual surpluses).

2. If the Federal government uses fiscal policy to combat recession and inflation, its budget is not likely to be balanced in any particular year. Three *budget philosophies* may be adopted by the government; the adoption of any of these philosophies will affect employment, real output, and the price level of the economy.

a. Proponents of an ***annually balanced budget*** would have government expenditures and tax revenues equal in every year. Such a budget is pro- rather than countercyclical; but conservative economists favor it to prevent the expansion of the public sector (and the contraction of the private sector) of the economy without the increased payment of taxes by the public.

b. Those who advocate a ***cyclically balanced budget*** propose matching surpluses (in years of prosperity) with deficits (in depression years) to stabilize the economy, but there is no assurance that the surpluses will equal the deficits over the years.

c. Advocates of ***functional finance*** contend that deficits, surpluses, and the size of the debt are of minor importance and that the goal of full employment without inflation should be achieved regardless of the effects of the necessary fiscal policies on the budget and the size of the public debt.

3. Any government deficit increases the size of the public debt. The public debt has grown substantially since 1929.

a. There are four basic *causes of the debt:*

(1) *wars* require increased Federal borrowing to finance the war effort;

(2) *recessions* result in budget deficits because of the built-in stability of the economy (tax revenues fall and domestic spending rises);

(3) *cuts in tax rates* without offsetting reductions in expenditures contribute to budget deficits, as occurred during the early 1980s; and

(4) *a lack of political will* to control expenditures for popular entitlement programs or raise taxes to pay for them adds to budget deficits.

b. The public debt in 1997 was $5.4 trillion.

(1) The size of the debt as a percentage of the economy's GDP did not grow as rapidly as the absolute size of the debt between 1940 and 1997, but relative to the GDP, it has increased significantly since the early 1980s.

(2) Other industrial nations have relative public debts similar to or greater than the United States.

(3) Since the 1970s the interest payments on the debt (because of increases in the size of the debt and higher interest rates in the economy) have also increased significantly, and interest payments as a percentage of the economy's GDP have grown dramatically.

(4) More than one-third (37%) of the public debt is owed to government agencies and the Federal Reserve Banks. Less than two-thirds (63%) is owed to others, including 23% owed to foreign citizens, firms, and governments.

(5) Because the accounting system the Federal government uses records its debts but not its assets, the public debt is not a true picture of its financial position. Adjusting for inflation further decreases the size of budget deficits and the public debt.

4. The contentions that a large debt will eventually *bankrupt* the government and that borrowing to finance expenditures passes the cost on to future generations are false.

a. The debt cannot bankrupt the government because the government

(1) need not retire (reduce) the debt and can refund (or refinance) it,

(2) has the constitutional authority to levy and collect taxes, and

(3) can always print (or create) money to pay both the principal and the interest on it.

b. The debt cannot shift the burden of the debt to future generations because the debt is largely internally held, and repayment of any portion of the principal and the payment of interest on it does not reduce the wealth or purchasing power of U.S. citizens.

5. The public debt does create real and potential problems in the economy.

a. The payment of interest on the debt probably increases the extent of income inequality.

b. The payment of taxes to finance these interest payments may reduce the incentives to bear risks, to innovate, to invest, and to save, and therefore they slow economic growth in the economy.

c. The portion of the debt that is externally held (by foreign citizens and institutions) requires the repayment of principal and the payment of interest to foreign citizens and institutions. This transfers a part of the real output of the U.S. economy to them.

d. It creates political problems for the use of fiscal policy as an antirecessionary measure because increasing government expenditures or cutting taxes during a recession adds to the public debt.

e. An increase in government spending may or may not impose a burden on future generations.

(1) If the increase in government spending is financed by increased personal taxes, the burden of the in-

creased spending is on the present generation whose consumption is reduced, but if it is financed by an increased public debt, the increased borrowing of the Federal government will raise interest rates and crowd out investment spending, and future generations will inherit a smaller stock of capital goods.

(2) The burden imposed on future generations is lessened if the increase in government expenditures is for real or human capital or if the economy were initially operating at less than full employment (and it stimulates an increase in investment demand).

6. Federal budget deficits during the past two decades have been the focus of national interest for many economic reasons.

    a. The absolute size of the annual Federal budget deficit grew enormously during the 1980s and 1990s.

    b. Recent budget deficits may be understated because surpluses from social security are being used to offset current government spending.

    c. Interest costs of the debt have risen.

    d. The deficits have taken place in an economy operating close to full employment, which means there is great potential for the crowding out of real private investment and for demand-pull inflation.

    e. Large budget deficits make it difficult for a nation to achieve a balance in its international trade.

7. These large Federal budget deficits produced a cause-and-effect chain of events with the *balance of trade deficits.*

    a. They increased interest rates, which crowded out real private investment and increased foreign financial investment in the United States. The greater foreign investment increased the international value of the dollar, which in turn reduced U.S. exports and increased U.S. imports, resulting in trade deficits.

    b. There are three loose ends to the complex chain of events as described in **a:**

    (1) The inflow of foreign funds helped keep interest rates lower than would otherwise be the case and diminished the size of the crowding-out effect.

    (2) High interest rates in the United States resulting from large deficits placed an increased burden on developing countries, thereby contributing to the world debt problem and banking problems in the United States.

    (3) The unfavorable trade balance meant that the United States had to borrow heavily from other nations and to sell assets to foreign investors, thereby affecting the course of economic growth in the future.

8. Several *policy responses* have lessened the effect of the large Federal budget deficits and the expanding public debt.

    a. Deficit reduction legislation has been passed in recent years, including the Deficit Reduction Act of 1993 and a 1996 tax and spending package designed to reduce the deficit to zero by 2002.

    b. In 1995 Congress gave the president authority to veto individual spending items.

    c. Congress has considered an amendment to the U.S. Constitution that would require Congress to balance the Federal budget each year.

9. Private and public debt play a positive role in the economy. As an economy grows, saving increases. This saving is borrowed and spent by consumers and businesses, and private debt is created. If, however, consumers and businesses do not borrow sufficient amounts, the public debt will need to be increased to absorb some saving so that the economy can maintain full employment and achieve its growth potential.

■ HINTS AND TIPS

1. Make sure you know the difference between the public debt and the budget deficit. The two are often confused.

2. The best way to gauge public debt and budget deficit is to calculate each one as a percentage of real GDP. The absolute size of the public debt or the deficit is not a good indicator of whether it causes problems for the economy.

3. Try to understand the real rather than the imagined problems caused by the public debt. The debt will not cause the country to go bankrupt, nor will it be the burden on future generations that people often state that it will. Carefully read the section on the false issues and the real issues.

■ IMPORTANT TERMS

public debt	external debt
annually balanced budget	public investments
cyclically balanced budget	balanced budget amendment
functional finance	
entitlement programs	line-item veto

SELF-TEST

■ FILL-IN QUESTIONS

1. The Federal government's budget deficit in any year is equal to its (expenditures, revenues) _____ less its _____ in that year. The public debt is equal to the sum of the Federal government's past budget (deficts, surpluses) _____ minus its budget _____.

2. An annually balanced budget is (pro, counter) _____-cyclical because governments would have (raised, lowered) _____ taxes and _____ their purchases of goods and services during a recession (and have done just the opposite during an inflation).

3. A cyclically balanced budget suggests that to ensure full employment without inflation, the government would incur deficits during periods of (inflation, recession)

_____ and surpluses during periods of _____, with the deficits and surpluses equaling each other over the business cycle.

4. The budget philosophy that has as its main goal the achievement of full employment without inflation is (external debt, functional finance) _____. It regards budget deficits and increases in the public debt as of (primary, secondary) _____ importance to this goal.

5. The principal causes of the public debt are the expense of paying for (wars, inflation) _____, changes in the economy such as (a recession, an expansion) _____, tax rate (cuts, increases) _____ without offsetting reductions in government expenditures, and the lack of (monopoly power, political will) _____ to control entitlement spending or increase taxes to balance the budget.

6. There are several quantitative aspects to the public debt.

   a. The most meaningful way to measure the public debt is relative to (interest rates, GDP) _____, and in 1997 it was _____%.

   b. In 1997 the public debt as a percentage of GDP was (higher, lower) _____ in Japan and Canada and _____ in Britain and Australia.

   c. Federal government agencies and our central banks hold about (one-third, two-thirds) _____ of the debt, and commercial banks, financial institutions, state and local governments, and foreign individuals and institutions hold about_____ of the debt.

   d. Most of the public debt is (internal, external) _____ because foreigners hold only about _____% of the public debt.

   e. The public debt and budget deficits are subject to measurement problems because the accounting procedures the Federal government uses reflect (assets, debts) _____ but do not reflect _____.

   f. If the Federal government used a capital budget which included depreciation costs, the Federal budget deficit would be (increased, decreased) _____; if the Federal budget was adjusted for the effects of inflation, the budget deficit would be _____.

7. The possibility that the Federal government will go bankrupt is a false issue. It does not need to reduce its debt; it can retire maturing securities by (taxing, refinancing) _____ them or by (destroying, creating) _____ money. The government can also pay its debts by increasing (interest, taxes) _____.

8. As long as the government expenditures which lead to the increase in the public debt are not financed by borrowing from foreigners, the public debt of the United States is a(n) (liability, asset) _____ of the U.S. citizens who own government securities; the cost of a government program financed by borrowing from the U.S. public is equal to the public's decreased consumption of goods and services and is a burden on the (present, future) _____ generation.

9. The public debt is a burden on an economy if it is (internally, externally) _____ held. Also, it and the payment of interest on it may (increase, decrease) _____ income inequality in the economy, _____ the incentives to work, take risks, save, and invest in the economy, and (increase, decrease) _____ the crowding out of private investment.

10. A public debt which is internally held imposes a burden on future generations if the borrowing done to finance an increase in government expenditures (increases, decreases) _____ interest rates, _____ investment spending, and (increases, decreases) _____ the stock of capital goods for future generations.

11. If the increased government expenditures are financed by an increase in the taxes on personal income, the present generation will have (more, less) _____ consumer goods, and the burden of the increased government expenditures will be on the (future, present) _____ generation.

12. The size of the burden of increased government expenditures financed by borrowing on future generations is weakened if the government expenditures finance (increases, decreases) _____ in physical or human capital or if the economy had been operating at (full, less than full) _____ employment.

13. The increased concern of the public about the Federal deficit and the expanding public debt in the past two decades is the result of the (small, large) _____ size of these deficits, the use of funds from (external debt, social security) _____ that offset and understate the deficit, the fact that interest costs have (fallen, risen) _____, the use of macroeconomic policies that were (appropriate, inappropriate) _____ for dealing with the economy, and the difficulty of achieving a (surplus, balance) _____ in international trade.

14. Large deficits during times of full employment raise two problems. First, there is great potential for crowding out or (increasing, decreasing) _____ real private investment. Second, the stimulus to the economy from the deficits may create the conditions for (cost-push, demand-pull) _____ inflation.

15. Large budget deficits create an unfavorable balance of trade by (increasing, decreasing) _____ imports and _____ exports. This trade imbalance has contributed to making the United States a (creditor, debtor) _____ nation and (increased, decreased) _____ the selling of domestic assets to foreign investors.

16. The deficits of the Federal government tend to (increase, decrease) _____ interest rates in the money markets.

   a. This change in interest rates (expands, contracts) _____ private investment spending and makes financial investments by foreigners in the United States (more, less) _____ attractive.

   b. This change in the financial investments of foreigners in the United States (increases, decreases) _____ the external debts of the United States and (raises, lowers) _____ the international value of the dollar.

   c. This change in the international value of the dollar (expands, contracts) _____ U.S. exports, _____ U.S. imports, and (expands, contracts) _____ *net* exports.

17. Other complications must be considered in the chain of events from the budget deficits of the 1980s. First, the inflow of funds from abroad (raised, lowered) _____ domestic interest rates and therefore (strengthened, weakened) _____ the crowding-out effect. Second, the high interest rates in the United States placed greater burden on (developed, developing) _____ countries that trade with the United States. Third, the value of imports became greater than exports, so the United States had to (lend, borrow) _____ from foreigners and (buy, sell) _____ more assets.

18. In 1993, the Congress passed the Deficit Reduction Act, which was designed to (decrease, increase) _____ tax revenues by $250 billion over a 5-year period and _____ government spending by a similar amount.

19. In 1995 Congress passed a (balanced-budget amendment, line-item veto) _____ to give the president more budget control. Congress has also considered the merit of a more extreme proposal, a _____, as another policy response to budget deficits.

20. Public and private debts play a positive role if they absorb a sufficient amount of (investment, saving) _____ to enable an economy that is (stationary, growing) _____ to remain at full employment.

■ **TRUE-FALSE QUESTIONS**

Circle the T if the statement is true, the F if it is false.

1. The budget deficit of the Federal government in any year is equal to its revenues less its expenditures. **T F**

2. An annually balanced budget is economically neutral in its effects on the economy. **T F**

3. A cyclically balanced budget is procyclical, not countercyclical. **T F**

4. Proponents of functional finance argue that a balanced budget, whether it is balanced annually or over the business cycle, is of minor importance when compared with the objective of full employment without inflation. **T F**

5. A major reason for the increase in the public debt since 1929 is the government spending associated with recessions. **T F**

6. One reason for the growth in the public debt is the difficulty of getting political support for specific proposals to cut government spending or raise taxes to pay for government programs. **T F**

7. The defense spending for new weapons programs by the U.S. government is an example of an entitlement program. **T F**

8. The public debt as a percentage of GDP is higher in the United States than in most other industrial nations. **T F**

9. Interest payments as a percent of GDP reflect the level of taxation (average tax rate) required to service the public debt. **T F**

10. Most of the public debt is owned by foreign individuals and institutions. **T F**

11. Inflation increases the real value of the public debt. **T F**

12. A large public debt will bankrupt the Federal government. **T F**

13. The public debt is a public credit. **T F**

14. The payment of interest on the public debt probably increases income inequality. **T F**

15. The additional taxes required to pay the interest on the public debt increase incentives to work, save, invest, and bear risks. **T F**

16. Selling government securities to foreigners to finance increased expenditures by the Federal government imposes a burden on future generations. **T F**

17. A large and growing public debt makes it politically difficult to use fiscal policy during a recession.   **T F**

18. The crowding-out effect is caused by a rise in interest rates resulting from an increase in government borrowing in the money market to finance government expenditures.   **T F**

19. The crowding-out effect increases the investment-demand curve and investment in capital goods.   **T F**

20. If government spending is for investment-type projects, then this spending can increase the economy's future production capacity.   **T F**

21. The size of recent annual Federal budget deficits may be understated because they include items such as the social security surplus that offsets some current government spending.   **T F**

22. Large budget deficits can increase interest rates and lead to an appreciation in the value of the dollar that contributes to trade deficits.   **T F**

23. The 1993 Deficit Reduction Act is a constitutional amendment that requires a balanced Federal budget by the year 2010.   **T F**

24. In 1995, Congress gave the president the authority to veto individual spending items in legislation passed by Congress.   **T F**

25. The process by which saving is transferred to spenders in an economy is debt creation, and it plays a positive role in a growing economy.   **T F**

■ **MULTIPLE-CHOICE QUESTIONS**

Circle the letter that corresponds to the correct answer.

1. The public debt is the sum of all previous
(a) expenditures of the Federal government
(b) budget deficits of the Federal government
(c) budget deficits less the budget surpluses of the Federal government
(d) budget surpluses less the current budget deficit of the Federal government

2. Which of the following would involve reducing government expenditures and increasing tax rates during a recession?
(a) an annually balanced budget policy
(b) functional finance
(c) a cyclically balanced budget policy
(d) a policy employing built-in stability

3. A cyclically balanced budget philosophy is
(a) procyclical
(b) countercyclical
(c) functional finance
(d) economically neutral

4. What three factors largely explain why the public debt has increased since 1929?
(a) interest payments on the public debt, spending for social security, and depreciation of the dollar

(b) deficit spending to finance a war, effects of automatic stabilizers on the budget during recessions, and tax cuts not offset by spending cuts
(c) deficit spending caused by depressions, borrowing funds from other nations, and increased government spending to cover economic problems such as the saving and loan bailout
(d) interest payments on the public debt, government spending for welfare programs, and the crowding out of investment spending

5. Since the 1980s, the public debt relative to GDP has
(a) increased and interest payments relative to GDP have increased
(b) decreased and interest payments relative to GDP have decreased
(c) decreased, but interest payments relative to GDP have decreased
(d) increased, but interest payments relative to GDP have decreased

6. To place the public debt in perspective based on the wealth and productive capacity of the economy, it is more meaningful to
(a) examine its absolute size
(b) calculate the interest payments on the debt
(c) measure it relative to the gross domestic product
(d) compare it to import, exports, and the trade deficit

7. The public debt of the United States as a percentage of its GDP is
(a) larger than all other industrial nations
(b) smaller than all other industrial nations
(c) less than all other industrial nations except Japan
(d) greater than some industrial nations but less than others

8. Foreign individuals and institutions hold about what percentage of the public debt?
(a) 5%
(b) 14%
(c) 23%
(d) 34%

9. The accounting procedures the Federal government uses record
(a) only its assets
(b) only its debts
(c) both its assets and debts
(d) its net worth

10. Inflation is a tax on the
(a) holders of the public debt, and it reduces the real size of the public debt
(b) holders of the public debt, and expands the real size of the public debt
(c) Federal government, and reduces the real size of the public debt
(d) Federal government, and expands the real size of the public debt

11. The public debt cannot bankrupt the Federal government because the Federal government
(a) has the power to levy taxes

(b) is able to refinance the debt

(c) can create money to repay the debt and pay the interest on it

(d) all of the above

12. Incurring an internal debt to finance a war does not pass the cost of the war on to future generations because

(a) the opportunity cost of the war is borne by the generation that fights it

(b) the government need not pay interest on internally held debts

(c) there is never a need for government to refinance the debt

(d) wartime inflation reduces the relative size of the debt

13. Which would be a consequence of the retirement of the internally held portion of the public debt?

(a) a reduction in the nation's productive capacity

(b) a reduction in the nation's standard of living

(c) a redistribution of the nation's wealth among its citizens

(d) an increase in aggregate expenditures in the economy

14. Which of the following is an important consequence of the public debt of the United States?

(a) It increases incentives to work and invest.

(b) It transfers a portion of the U.S. output of goods and services to foreign nations.

(c) It reduces income inequality in the United States.

(d) It leads to greater saving at every level of disposable income.

15. A large and growing public debt creates political problems for the Congress and the president to adopt

(a) an easy money policy

(b) a tight money policy

(c) an antirecessionary fiscal policy

(d) a trade policy calling for increased U.S. exports and decreased U.S. imports

16. The crowding-out effect of borrowing in the money market to finance an increase in government expenditures

(a) reduces current private investment expenditures

(b) decreases the rate at which the privately owned stock of real capital increases

(c) imposes a burden on future generations

(d) does all of the above

17. The crowding-out effect from government borrowing is reduced

(a) when the economy is operating at less than full employment

(b) when the expenditures expand human capital in the economy

(c) when the government's deficit financing improves the profit expectations of business firms

(d) when any one or more of the above are true

18. Which is *not* one of the sources of the concern with the deficits of the Federal government and the growth of the public debt during the past two decades?

(a) the large increases in the size of the deficits and in the public debt

(b) the operation of the economy substantially below full employment throughout the decade

(c) the rising interest costs of the debt

(d) problems with the balance of trade

19. Deficits in the early 1990s were primarily increased by

(a) an increase in spending for social security

(b) a recession and a bailout of the savings and loan industry

(c) an increased demand by foreigners for government securities

(d) an easy money policy of the Federal Reserve

20. The increased foreign demand for U.S. securities that results from higher interest rates in the United States

(a) increases the external debts of the United States and the international value of the dollar

(b) increases the external debts of the United States and decreases the international value of the dollar

(c) decreases the external debts of the United States and increases the international value of the dollar

(d) decreases the external debts of the United States and the international value of the dollar

21. When the international value of the dollar rises,

(a) U.S. exports tend to increase

(b) U.S. imports tend to decrease

(c) U.S. net exports tend to decrease

(d) U.S. net exports tend to increase

22. High interest rates in the United States which were related to Federal budget deficits

(a) contributed to the debt burden of developing nations that traded with the United States

(b) reduced the flow of funds from foreign nations to the United States

(c) increased the long-term economic growth and domestic investment of foreign nations that transferred funds to the United States

(d) enabled the United States to become a major creditor nation

23. The Deficit Reduction Act of 1993 was legislation passed by Congress and signed by the president; it was designed to

(a) decrease marginal tax rates on personal income, but increase corporate income taxes and the Federal tax on gasoline

(b) increase taxes on personal income and corporations and hold all discretionary government spending to 1993 nominal levels

(c) use fiscal policy to stimulate the sluggish U.S. economy during 1993

(d) coordinate fiscal policy with the monetary policy of the Federal Reserve to achieve a budget balance by the year 2010

24. A serious proposal to eliminate annual Federal budget deficits that Congress has recently considered is

(a) the changing of accounting procedures

(b) a balanced-budget amendment

(c) a moratorium on debt payments

(d) a reduction in interest rates

25. The process by which saving is transferred to spenders is
(a) public investment
(b) functional finance
(c) debt creation
(d) crowding out

■ **PROBLEMS**

1. The following table gives data on the public debt and the GDP for selected 5-year periods from 1961–1997. Data for the public debt and the GDP are in billions of dollars.

Year	Debt	GDP	Debt/GDP
1961	$ 292.6	$ 531.8	_____ %
1966	328.5	769.8	_____
1971	408.2	1097.2	_____
1976	629.0	1768.4	_____
1981	994.3	3030.6	_____
1986	2120.1	4268.6	_____
1991	3599.0	5671.8	_____
1996	4921.0	7265.4	_____
1997	5369.7	8083.4	_____

a. Calculate the ratio of the public debt to GDP expressed as a percentage of GDP. Enter the numbers into the last column of the table.
b. On the graph below, plot the year on the horizontal axis and plot the public debt as a percentage of GDP on the vertical axis.
c. Explain what happened to the public debt as a percentage of GDP from 1961–1997.

_____

_____

_____

2. The following table gives data on interest rates and investment demand (in billions of dollars) in a hypothetical economy.

Interest rate	I_{d1}	I_{d2}
10%	$250	$300
8	300	350
6	350	400
4	400	450
2	450	500

a. Use the I_{d1} schedule. Assume that the government needs to finance a budget deficit and this public borrowing increases the interest rate from 4% to 6%. How much crowding out of private investment will occur?

_____

b. Now assume that the deficit is used to improve the performance of the economy and that, as a consequence, the investment-demand schedule changes from I_{d1} to I_{d2}. At the same time, the interest rate rises from 4% to 6% as the government borrows money to finance the deficit. How much crowding out of private investment will occur in this case? _____
c. Graph the two investment-demand schedules on the graph on page 213 and show the difference between the two events. Put the interest rate on the vertical axis and the quantity of investment demanded on the horizontal axis.

3. Columns 1 and 2 in the following table are the investment-demand schedules and show planned investment (I) at different rates of interest (i). Assume the marginal propensity to consume in the economy is 0.8.

(1) i	(2) I	(3) I'
.08	$115	$125
.07	140	150
.06	165	175
.05	190	200
.04	215	225

a. If the Federal government were to spend an additional $20 for goods and services, the equilibrium real

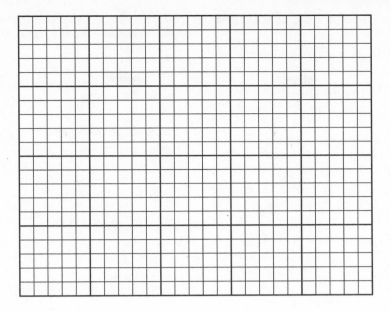

GDP would (increase, decrease) _____

by $_____.

b. If the Federal government had obtained the additional $20 by

(1) increasing taxes by $20, the equilibrium real GDP

would have (increased, decreased) _____

by a total of $ _____;

(2) borrowing $20 in the money market and this borrowing had increased the interest rate from 5% to 6%,

(a) planned investment spending would have (increased, decreased) _____ by $_____,

(b) the equilibrium real GDP would have _____

by $ _____, and

(c) the net effect of the increased government spending of the $20 borrowed in the money market would

have been to _____ the equilibrium real

GDP by $_____.

c. But if the government deficit spending had improved business profit expectations and shifted the investment-demand schedule to the one shown in columns 1 and 3 in the preceding table, the total effect of the increased government spending of the $20 borrowed in the money market would have been to _____

the equilibrium real GDP by $_____.

■ **SHORT ANSWER AND ESSAY QUESTIONS**

1. What is the difference between the (Federal) budget deficit and the public debt?

2. Explain why an annually balanced budget is not neutral and how it can intensify, rather than reduce, the tendencies for GDP to rise and fall.

3. How does a cyclically balanced budget philosophy differ from the philosophy of functional finance? Why do advocates of functional finance argue that budget deficits and a mounting national debt are of secondary importance?

4. What are the four basic causes of the public debt over the past 55 years?

5. How does the lack of political will and entitlement programs affect the public debt and Federal budget deficits?

6. How big is the public debt of the United States absolutely and relative to the GDP? How large are the interest payments on this debt absolutely and relative to the GDP? What has happened to the size of the debt and the interest payments on it absolutely and relatively since 1930 and since 1980? Why have these changes occurred?

7. In what way do the accounting procedures of the Federal government misstate its actual financial position (its net worth)? How does inflation effect the *real* size of the public debt and the real size of the Federal government's budget deficits?

8. Why can't the public debt result in the bankruptcy of the Federal government?

9. Explain the difference between an internally held and an externally held public debt. If the debt is internally held, government borrowing to finance a war does not pass the cost of the war on to future generations. Why?

10. How does the public debt and the payment of interest on this debt affect

(a) the distribution of income and

(b) incentives?

11. Who owns the public debt? What percentage is held by the two major groups? What percentage of the public debt is held by foreigners? What are the economic implications of the portion of the public debt held by foreigners?

12. Why can a large and growing public debt put curbs on the use of fiscal policy?

13. How does the crowding out of investment impose a burden on future generations?

14. Does it matter to future generations whether increases in government spending are financed by taxation or increased public debt?

15. What two qualifications might lessen the crowding-out effect on the size of the economic burden that has shifted to future generations?

16. What are four reasons for the heightened concern about Federal budget deficits during the past two decades?

17. How do budget deficits and the increase in the public debt affect interest rates, domestic investment, foreign financial investment in the United States, the international value of the dollar, and the trade deficit?

18. Explain three complications arising from the relationship between budget and trade deficits.

19. Describe the major policy responses to concerns about large budget deficits and the expanding public debt.

20. How does debt play a positive role in a growing economy?

ANSWERS

Chapter 19 Budget Deficits and the Public Debt

FILL-IN QUESTIONS

1. expenditures, revenues, deficits, surpluses
2. pro, raised, lowered
3. recession, inflation
4. functional finance, secondary
5. wars, a recession, cuts, political will
6. *a.* GDP, 66; *b.* higher, lower; *c.* one-third, two-thirds; *d.* internal, 23; *e.* debts, assets; *f.* decreased, decreased
7. refinancing, creating, taxes
8. asset, present
9. externally, increase, decrease, increase
10. increases, decreases, decreases
11. less, present
12. increases, less than full
13. large, social security, risen, inappropriate, balance
14. decreasing, demand-pull
15. increasing, decreasing, debtor, increased
16. increase; *a.* contracts, more; *b.* increases, raises; *c.* contracts, expands, contracts
17. lowered, weakened, developing, borrow, sell
18. increase, decrease
19. line-item veto, balanced-budget amendment
20. saving, growing

TRUE-FALSE QUESTIONS

1. F, p. 386	**10.** F, pp. 390-391	**19.** F, pp. 394-395
2. F, p. 387	**11.** F, p. 391	**20.** T, p. 394
3. F, p. 387	**12.** F, p. 391	**21.** T, pp. 395-396
4. T, p. 388	**13.** T, p. 392	**22.** T, pp. 396-397
5. T, p. 389	**14.** T, p. 393	**23.** F, pp. 398-399
6. T, p. 389	**15.** F, p. 393	**24.** T, p. 399
7. F, p. 389	**16.** T, p. 393	**25.** T, p. 400
8. F, p. 390	**17.** T, p. 393	
9. T, p. 390	**18.** T, p. 393	

MULTIPLE-CHOICE QUESTIONS

1. c, p. 386	**10.** a, p. 391	**19.** b, p. 395
2. a, p. 387	**11.** d, pp. 391-392	**20.** a, pp. 396-397
3. b, p. 387	**12.** a, p. 392	**21.** c, pp. 396-397
4. b, pp. 389-390	**13.** c, pp. 392-393	**22.** a, p. 397
5. a, pp. 388, 390	**14.** b, p. 393	**23.** b, pp. 398-399
6. c, p. 390	**15.** c, p. 393	**24.** b, p. 400
7. d, p. 390	**16.** d, p. 393	**25.** c, p. 400
8. c, p. 390	**17.** d, pp. 394-395	
9. b, p. 391	**18.** b, pp. 395-396	

PROBLEMS

1. *a.* 55, 43, 37, 36, 33, 50, 63, 69, 68, 66; *c.* The debt as a percentage of GDP fell from 1961 to 1981 and then rose substantially from 1981 to 1995. It has fallen slightly since 1995.
2. *a.* $50 billion; *b.* none
3. *a.* increase, 100; *b.* (1) increased, 20 (2) (a) decreased, 25, (b) decreased, 125 (c) decrease, 25; *c.* increase, 25

SHORT ANSWER AND ESSAY QUESTIONS

1. p. 386	**8.** pp. 391-392	**15.** pp. 394-395
2. p. 387	**9.** pp. 392-393	**16.** pp. 395-396
3. pp. 387-388	**10.** pp. 392-393	**17.** pp. 396-397
4. pp. 389-390	**11.** pp. 390-391, 393	**18.** pp. 397-398
5. pp. 389-390	**12.** p. 393	**19.** pp. 398-400
6. pp. 388, 390	**13.** p. 393	**20.** p. 400
7. p. 391	**14.** pp. 393-394	

CHAPTER 20

International Trade

In Chapter 6 you learned about the role of the United States in the global economy and the basic principles of international trade. Chapter 20 extends that analysis in several ways. It gives you a more advanced understanding of comparative advantage. It uses the tools of supply and demand to explain the equilibrium prices and quantities of imports and exports and the economic effects of tariffs and quotas. It examines the fallacious arguments for trade protectionism and the cost of this protection on U.S. society.

After a brief review of the facts of international trade presented in Chapter 6, the text uses graphical analysis to explain why nations trade: to take advantage of the benefits of specialization. Nations specialize in and export those goods and services in the production of which they have a **comparative advantage.** A comparative advantage means that the opportunity cost of producing a particular good or service is lower in that nation than in another nation. These nations will avoid producing and importing the goods and services that other nations have a comparative advantage in producing. In this way all nations are able to obtain products which are produced as inexpensively as possible. Put another way, when nations specialize in those products in which they have a comparative advantage, the world as a whole can obtain more goods and services from its resources; each nation of the world can enjoy a standard of living higher than it would have if it did not specialize and export and import.

The principle of comparative advantage tells us why nations trade, but what determines the **equilibrium prices** and **quantities** of the imports and exports resulting from trade? To answer this question, the text uses the supply and demand analysis, originally presented in Chapter 3, to explain equilibrium in the world market for a product. A simplified two-nation and one-product model of trade is used to construct export supply curves and import demand curves for each nation. Equilibrium occurs where one nation's export supply curve intersects another nation's import demand curve.

Regardless of the advantages of specialization and trade among nations, people in the United States and throughout the world for well over 200 years have debated whether **free trade** or **protection** was the better policy for their nation. Economists took part in this debate and, with few exceptions, argued for free trade and against protection. Those who favor free trade contend that free trade benefits both the nation and the world as a whole. "Free traders" argue that tariffs, import quotas, and other barriers to international trade prevent or reduce specialization and decrease both a nation's and the world's production and standard of living.

But nations have and continue to erect *barriers to trade* with other nations. The latter part of this chapter focuses attention on (1) what motivates nations to impose tariffs and to limit the quantities of goods imported from abroad; (2) the economic effects of protection on a nation's own prosperity and on the prosperity of the world economy; (3) the kinds of arguments those who favor protection use to support their position (on what grounds do they base their contention that their nation will benefit from the erection of barriers which reduce imports from foreign nations); and (4) the costs of protectionism for the United States.

The chapter's final section is a brief review of the *international trade policy* of the United States. Three general approaches to trade policy are identified in the discussion. First, the United States has participated in a generalized liberalization of trade as a result of **General Agreements on Tariffs and Trade (GATT)** negotiations and regional accords such as the **North American Free Trade Agreement (NAFTA).** Second, the United States has pursued an aggressive policy of promoting exports. The U.S. government has subsidized exports, supported export-oriented industries, and lobbied other nations to purchase U.S. exports, all in an effort to increase U.S. exports. Third, bilateral negotiations have been conducted between the United States and other nations. In recent years, the United States has held bilateral negotiations with China and Japan to resolve major trade disputes.

Whether the direction of the international trade policy in the United States will be toward freer trade or more protectionism is a question that gets debated as each new trade issue is presented to the U.S. public. The decision on each issue may well depend on your understanding of the advantages of free trade and the costs of trade protection for the nation and the world economy.

■ CHECKLIST

When you have studied this chapter you should be able to

☐ Cite some key facts about international trade.
☐ State the two economic circumstances which make it desirable for nations to specialize and trade.
☐ Compute the costs of producing two commodities when you are given the necessary data in a two-nation example.

☐ Determine which nation has the comparative advantage in the production of each commodity using the cost data you computed for the two-nation example.

☐ Calculate the range in which the terms of trade will occur in the two-nation example.

☐ Explain how nations benefit from trade and specialization based on the two-nation example.

☐ Discuss how increasing costs affect specialization in the two-nation example.

☐ Restate the case for free trade.

☐ Construct domestic supply and demand curves for two nations that trade a product.

☐ Construct export supply and import demand curves for two nations that trade a product.

☐ Use supply and demand analysis to explain how the equilibrium prices and quantities of exports and imports are determined for two nations that trade a product.

☐ Identify the four principal types of artificial barriers to international trade and the motive for erecting these barriers.

☐ Explain the economic effects of a protective tariff on resource allocation, the price of the commodity, the total production of the commodity, and the outputs of foreign and domestic producers of the commodity.

☐ Analyze the economic effects of an import quota and compare them with the economic effects of a tariff.

☐ Enumerate six arguments used to support the case for protection and find the weakness in each argument.

☐ Offer a summation of the arguments for and against trade protection.

☐ Discuss the costs of trade protectionism for society.

☐ Explain how trade protectionism affects income distribution.

☐ Describe actions taken to promote trade liberalization.

☐ Cite examples of export promotion undertaken by the United States.

☐ Discuss the issues involved in the bilateral trade negotiations of the United States.

■ **CHAPTER OUTLINE**

1. Some facts about international trade presented in Chapter 6 are worth reviewing.

   a. About 12% of the total output of the United States is accounted for by exports of goods and services, a percentage which has more than doubled since 1965. The percentage of exports is much higher in other industrially advanced nations (e.g., 56% in the Netherlands, 38% in Canada), but the size of the U.S. economy means that it has the largest volume of imports and exports in the world.

   b. The United States has a trade deficit in goods, a trade surplus in services, and a trade deficit in goods and services.

   c. The principal exports of the United States are chemicals, computers, consumer durables, and aircraft, while its major imports are petroleum, automobiles, and clothing. Most of the trade occurs with other industrially advanced nations. Canada is the largest trading partner for the United States.

   d. Factors that have facilitated trade since World War II include improvements in transportation and communications technology along with a general decline in tariffs and worldwide conflict.

   e. The major participants in international trade are the United States, Japan, and the nations of western Europe. Newer participants include the "Asian tigers" (Hong Kong, Singapore, South Korea, and Taiwan) and China. The collapse of the former Soviet Union has changed trade patterns for Russia and the nations of eastern Europe.

   f. International trade policy has been a subject of recent concern as evidenced by the North American Free Trade Agreement (NAFTA), the conclusion of negotiations on the General Agreements on Tariffs and Trade (GATT), and bilateral negotiations between the United States and Japan.

2. Specialization and trade among nations is advantageous because the world's resources are not evenly distributed and the efficient production of different commodities necessitates different methods and combinations of resources.

3. The principle of *comparative advantage,* first presented in Chapter 6 to explain the gains from trade, can now be reexamined with the aid of graphical analysis.

   a. Suppose the world is composed of only two nations, each of which is capable of producing two different commodities and in which the production possibilities curves are different straight lines (whose opportunity cost ratios are constant but different).

   (1) With different opportunity cost ratios, each nation will have a comparative (cost) advantage in the production of one of the two commodities, and if the world is to use its resources economically, each nation must specialize in the commodity in the production of which it has a comparative advantage.

   (2) The ratio at which one product is traded for another—the terms of trade—lies between the opportunity cost ratios of the two nations.

   b. Each nation gains from this trade because specialization permits a greater total output from the same resources and a better allocation of the world's resources.

   c. If opportunity cost ratios in the two nations are not constant (if there is increasing cost), specialization may not be complete.

   d. The basic argument for free trade among nations is that it leads to a better allocation of resources and a higher standard of living in the world, but it also increases competition and deters monopoly in these nations.

4. *Supply and demand analysis* can be used to explain how the equilibrium price and quantity of exports and imports for a product (e.g., aluminum) are determined when there is trade between two nations (e.g., the United States and Canada).

   a. For the United States, there will be domestic supply and demand as well as export supply and import demand for aluminum.

   (1) The price and quantity of aluminum are determined by the intersection of the *domestic* demand and supply curves in a world without trade.

(2) In a world with trade, the **export supply curve** for the United States shows the amount of aluminum that U.S. producers will export at each world price above the domestic equilibrium price. U.S. exports will increase when the world price rises relative to the domestic price.

(3) The **import demand curve** for the United States shows the amount of aluminum that U.S. citizens will import at each world price below the domestic equilibrium price. U.S. imports will increase when world prices fall relative to the domestic price.

b. For Canada, there will be domestic supply and demand as well as export supply and import demand for aluminum. The description of these supply and demand curves is similar for those of the United States described in point **a.**

c. The *equilibrium* world price and equilibrium world levels of exports and imports can be determined with further supply and demand analysis. The export supply curves of the two nations can be plotted on one graph. The import demand curves of both nations can be plotted on the same graph. In this two-nation model, equilibrium will be achieved when one nation's import demand curve intersects another nation's export supply curve.

5. Nations, however, limit international trade by erecting *artificial barriers.* Tariffs, import quotas, a variety of non-tariff barriers, and voluntary export restrictions are the principal barriers to trade.

a. Special-interest groups benefit from protection and persuade their nations to erect trade barriers, but the costs to consumers of this protection exceed the benefits to the economy.

b. The imposition of a **tariff** on a good imported from abroad has both direct and indirect effects on an economy.

(1) The tariff increases the domestic price of the good, reduces its domestic consumption, expands its domestic production, decreases foreign production, and transfers income from domestic consumers to government.

(2) It also reduces the income of foreign producers and the ability of foreign nations to purchase goods and services in the nation imposing the tariff, causes the contraction of relatively efficient industries in that nation, decreases world trade, and lowers the real output of goods and services.

c. The imposition of a *quota* on an imported product has the same direct and indirect effects as that of a tariff on that product, with the exception that a tariff generates revenue for government use whereas an import quota transfers that revenue to foreign producers.

6. The arguments for *protectionism* are many, but often they are of questionable validity.

a. The military self-sufficiency argument can be challenged because it is difficult to determine which industry is "vital" to national defense and must be protected; it would be more efficient economically to provide a direct subsidy to military producers rather than impose a tariff.

b. Trade barriers do not necessarily increase domestic employment because

(1) imports may eliminate some jobs, but create others, so imports may change only the composition of employment, not the overall level of employment;

(2) the exports of one nation become the imports of another, so tariff barriers can be viewed as "beggar thy neighbor" policies;

(3) other nations are likely to retaliate against the imposition of trade barriers that will reduce domestic output and employment; and

(4) they create a less efficient allocation of resources by shielding protected domestic industries from the rigors of competition.

c. Using tariff barriers to permit diversification for stability in the economy is not necessary for advanced economies such as the United States, and there may be economic costs to diversification in developing nations.

d. It is alleged that infant industries need protection until they are sufficiently large to compete, but the argument may not apply to developed economies: It is difficult to select which industries will prosper; protectionism tends to persist long after it is needed; and direct subsidies may be more economically efficient. For advanced nations, a variant of this argument is strategic trade policy. It justifies barriers that protect the investment in high risk, growth industries for a nation, but these policies often lead to retaliation and similar policies from other trading nations.

e. Sometimes protection is sought against the "dumping" of excess foreign goods on U.S. markets. Dumping is a legitimate concern and is restricted under U.S. trade law, but to use dumping as an excuse for widespread tariff protection is unjustified and the number of documented cases is few. If foreign companies are more efficient (low cost) producers, what may appear to be dumping may actually be comparative advantage at work.

f. Protection is sometimes sought because of the cheap foreign labor argument; it should be realized that nations gain from trade based on comparative advantage, and without trade, living standards will be lower.

g. In summary, most protectionist arguments are fallacious or based on half-truths. The only points that have some validity, under certain conditions, are the infant industry and military-sufficiency arguments, but both are subject to abuse. The historical evidence suggests that free trade promotes and protectionism deters prosperity and economic growth in the world.

7. There are *costs to trade protectionism* for the United States.

a. There is a significant cost to society:

(1) It raises product prices by raising the imported price of the product, causes some consumers to switch to higher-priced domestic products, and increases the price of domestic products.

(2) The benefits for businesses and workers from trade protection are outweighed by the costs to U.S. society. The net cost to U.S. citizens was more than $15 billion annually in the mid-1990s.

b. There is an effect on income distribution because import restrictions are more costly for low-income families than for high-income families.

8. The *trade policies* of the United States in recent years can be categorized in three ways.

a. The United States has participated in regional and global agreements to liberalize trade. Two examples are the North American Free Trade Agreement (NAFTA) and the completion of the Uruguay round of the General Agreements on Tariffs and Trade (GATT).

b. Export promotion policies have included governmental lobbying for contracts, relaxation of export controls, advantageous loans through the U.S. Export-Import Bank, increased support for an industrial policy, and retaliatory tariffs.

c. Bilateral trade negotiations have been used to resolve trade differences with trading partners. These negotiations were used with China over most-favored-nation status and with Japan over persistent trade deficits.

■ **HINTS AND TIPS**

1. In the discussion of comparative advantage, the assumption of a constant-cost ratio means the production possibilities "curves" for each nation can be drawn as straight lines. The slope of the line in each nation is the opportunity cost of one product (wheat) in terms of the other product (coffee). The reciprocal of the slope of each line is the opportunity cost of the other product (coffee) in terms of the first product (wheat).

2. The export supply and import demand curves in Figures 20-3 and 20-4 in the text look different from the typical supply and demand curves that you have seen so far, so you should understand how they are constructed. The export supply and import demand curves for a nation do not intersect. Each curve meets at the price point on the *Y* axis showing the equilibrium price for domestic supply and demand. At this point there are no exports or imports.

a. The *export supply curve* is upsloping from that point because as world prices rise above the domestic equilibrium price, there will be increasing domestic surpluses produced by a nation that can be exported. The export supply curve reflects the positive relationship between rising world prices (above the domestic equilibrium price) and the increasing quantity of exports.

b. The *import demand curve* is downsloping from the domestic equilibrium price because as world prices fall below the domestic equilibrium price, there will be increasing domestic shortages that need to be covered by increasing imports. The import demand curve reflects the inverse relationship between falling world prices (below the domestic price) and the increasing quantity of imports.

3. One of the most interesting sections of the chapter discusses the arguments for and against trade protection. You have probably heard people give one or more of the arguments for trade protection, but now you have a chance to use your economic reasoning to expose the weaknesses in these arguments. Most are half-truths and special pleadings.

■ **IMPORTANT TERMS**

labor-intensive goods	**revenue tariff**
land-intensive goods	**protective tariff**
capital-intensive goods	**import quota**
cost ratio	**nontariff barrier**
principle of comparative advantage	**voluntary export restriction**
terms of trade	**strategic trade policy**
trading possibilities line	**dumping**
gains from trade	**World Trade Organization**
world price	**export controls**
domestic price	**export subsidy**
export supply curve	**most-favored-nation (MFN) status**
import demand curve	
tariff	

SELF-TEST

■ **FILL-IN QUESTIONS**

1. Exports of goods and services account for about (12, 24) _____% of total output in the United States and have more than (doubled, quadrupled) _____ since 1965.

2. Other industrially advanced nations such as the Netherlands and Canada have a (larger, smaller) _____ percentage of imports and exports than the United States, but the United States' volume makes it the world's (largest, smallest) _____ importing and exporting nation.

3. Nations tend to trade among themselves because the distribution of economic resources among them is (even, uneven) _____ and the efficient production of various goods and services necessitates (the same, different) _____ technologies or combinations of resources.

4. Comparative advantage means total world output will be greatest when each good is produced by that nation having the (highest, lowest) _____ opportunity cost. The nations of the world tend to specialize in the production of those goods in which they (have, do not have) _____ a comparative advantage and then export them, and they import those goods in which they _____ a comparative advantage in production.

5. If the cost ratio in country X is 4 Panama hats equal 1 pound of bananas, while in country Y 3 Panama hats equal 1 pound of bananas, then

    a. country X hats are relatively (expensive, inexpensive) _____ and bananas relatively

_____,

    b. country Y hats are relatively (expensive, inexpensive) _____ and bananas relatively

_____,

    c. X has a comparative advantage and should specialize in the production of (bananas, hats)

_____, and Y has a comparative advantage and should specialize in the production of

_____.

    d. when X and Y specialize and trade, the terms of trade will be somewhere between (1, 2, 3, 4)

_____ and _____ hats for each pound of bananas and will depend on world demand and supply for hats and bananas.

    e. When the actual terms of trade turn out to be 3 1/2 hats for 1 pound of bananas, the cost of obtaining (1) 1 Panama hat has been decreased from (2/7, 1/3)

_____ to _____ pounds of bananas in Y. (2) 1 pound of bananas has been decreased from

(3 1/2, 4) _____ to _____ Panama hats in X.

    f. International specialization will not be complete if the opportunity cost of producing either good (rises, falls) _____ as a nation produces more of it.

6. The basic argument for free trade based on the principle of (bilateral negotiations, comparative advantage)

_____ is that it results in a (more, less) _____ efficient allocation of resources and a (lower, higher) _____ standard of living.

7. The world equilibrium price is determined by the interaction of (domestic, world) _____ supply and demand, while the domestic equilibrium price is determined by _____ supply and demand.

8. When world prices fall relative to domestic prices in a nation, the nation will (increase, decrease) _____ its imports, and when world prices rise relative to domestic prices, the nation will _____ its exports.

9. In a two-nation model for a product, the equilibrium price and quantity of imports and exports occurs where one nation's import demand intersects another nation's export (supply, demand) _____ curve. In a highly competitive world market, there can be (multiple, only one) _____ price(s) for a standardized product.

10. Excise taxes on imported products are (quotas, tariffs) _____, whereas limits on the maximum amount of a product that can be imported are import _____. Tariffs applied to a product not produced domestically are (protective, revenue) _____ tariffs, but tariffs designed to shield domestic producers from foreign competition are _____ tariffs.

11. There are other types of trade barriers. Imports that are restricted through the use of a licensing requirement or bureaucratic red tape are (tariff, nontariff) _____ barriers. When foreign firms voluntarily limit their exports to another country, this would represent a voluntary (import, export) _____ restraint.

12. Nations erect barriers to international trade to benefit the economic positions of (consumers, domestic producers) _____ even though these barriers (increase, decrease) _____ economic efficiency and trade among nations and the benefits to that nation are (greater, less) _____ than the costs to it.

13. When the United States imposes a tariff on a good which is imported from abroad, the price of that good in the United States will (increase, decrease) _____, the total purchases of the good in the United States will _____, the output of U.S. producers of the good will (increase, decrease) _____, and the output of foreign producers will _____. The ability of foreigners to buy goods and services in the United States will (increase, decrease) _____ and, as a result, output and employment in U.S. industries that sell goods and services abroad will _____.

14. When comparing the effects of a tariff with the effects of a quota to restrict the U.S. imports of a product, the basic difference is that with a (tariff, quota) _____ the U.S. government will receive revenue, but with a _____ foreign producers will receive the revenue.

15. List the six arguments which protectionists use to justify trade barriers.

    a. _____

    b. _____

    c. _____

    d. _____

    e. _____

    f. _____

16. Most arguments for protectionism are (strong, weak) _____ and are designed to benefit (consumers, domestic producers) _____. If these arguments were followed, it would create (losses, gains) _____ for protected industries and their workers at the expense of _____ for the economy.

17. Protectionism will raise the price of a product by (increasing, decreasing) _____ the imported price of the product, _____ consumer purchases of the domestically produced product, and thus _____ the demand and the price of the domestically produced product.

18. Studies indicate that the cost to consumers of protected products are substantially (less, greater) _____ than the benefits to producers and government. Import restrictions also hurt low-income consumers (more, less) _____ than high-income consumers.

19. Participation of the United States in the General Agreements on Tariffs and Trade (GATT) is an example of (export promotion, trade liberalization) _____, whereas increased government funding for the U.S. Import-Export Bank is an example of _____; both activities are part of the U.S. international trade policies.

20. Another U.S. trade policy is to hold discussions on trade issues directly with particular nations using (regional agreements, bilateral negotiations) _____. Examples of this policy would be the annual review of most-favored-nation status for (Japan, China) _____ and the discussion about the large trade deficit with _____.

■ **TRUE-FALSE QUESTIONS**

Circle the T if the statement is true, the F if it is false.

1. The bulk of U.S. export and import trade is with other industrially advanced nations. **T F**

2. Two factors serve as the economic basis for world trade: the even distribution of resources and the fact that efficient production of various goods requires similar techniques or combinations of resources. **T F**

3. Mutually advantageous specialization and trade are possible between any two nations if they have the same domestic opportunity-cost ratios for any two products. **T F**

4. The principle of comparative advantage is that total output will be greatest when each good is produced by that nation which has the higher domestic opportunity cost. **T F**

5. By specializing based on comparative advantage, nations can obtain larger real incomes with fixed amounts of resources. **T F**

6. The terms of trade determine how the increase in world output resulting from comparative advantage is shared by trading nations. **T F**

7. Increasing production costs tend to prevent specialization among trading nations from being complete. **T F**

8. Trade among nations tends to bring about a more efficient use of the world's resources and a higher level of material well-being. **T F**

9. Free trade among nations tends to increase monopoly and lessen competition in these nations. **T F**

10. A nation will export a particular product if the world price is less than the domestic price. **T F**

11. In a two-country model, equilibrium in world prices and quantities of exports and imports will occur where one nation's export supply curve intersects the other nation's import demand curve. **T F**

12. A tariff on coffee in the United States is an example of a protective tariff. **T F**

13. The imposition of a tariff on a good imported from abroad will raise the price of the good and lower the quantity of how much of that good is bought and sold. **T F**

14. The major difference between a tariff and a quota on an imported product is that a quota produces revenue for the government. **T F**

15. To advocate tariffs which would protect domestic producers of goods and materials essential to national defense is to substitute a political-military objective for the economic objectives of efficiently allocating resources. **T F**

16. Tariffs and import quotas meant to achieve domestic full employment achieve short-run domestic goals by making trading partners poorer. **T F**

17. One-crop economies may be able to make themselves more stable and diversified by imposing tariffs on goods imported from abroad, but these tariffs are also apt to lower the standard of living in these economies. **T F**

18. Protection against the "dumping" of foreign goods at low prices on the U.S. market is one good reason for widespread, permanent tariffs. **T F**

19. The only argument for tariffs that has, in the appropriate circumstances, any economic justification is the increase-domestic-employment argument. **T F**

20. The cost of protecting U.S. firms and employees from foreign competition is the rise in the prices of products produced in the United States, and this cost almost always exceeds its benefits. **T F**

21. Trade protectionism has no effect on income distribution. **T F**

22. An example of trade liberalization is General Agreements on Tariffs and Trade (GATT). **T F**

23. The World Trade Organization was established by the United Nations to encourage purchases of products from developing nations.   **T F**

24. It is a myth that the global marketplace is a battleground for supremacy where one nation wins and the other loses. Every nation is both a seller and buyer in the world market. Gains from trade come from the increased consumable output shared by the trading countries.   **T F**

25. The United States uses bilateral trade negotiations to resolve trade disputes with the U.S. Export-Import Bank.
                                                          T F

■ **MULTIPLE-CHOICE QUESTIONS**

Circle the letter that corresponds to the best answer.

1. Which nation leads the world in the volume of exports and imports?
  (a) Japan
  (b) Germany
  (c) United States
  (d) United Kingdom

2. Which group of nations dominates world trade?
  (a) Saudi Arabia and other OPEC nations
  (b) Hong Kong, Singapore, South Korea, and Taiwan
  (c) United States, Japan, and the nations of western Europe
  (d) China, Russia, and the nations of eastern Europe

3. Nations need to engage in trade because
  (a) world resources are evenly distributed among nations
  (b) world resources are unevenly distributed among nations
  (c) all products are produced from the same technology
  (d) all products are produced from the same combinations of resources

Use the following tables to answer Questions 4, 5, 6, and 7.

NEPAL PRODUCTION POSSIBILITIES TABLE

Product	Production alternatives					
	A	B	C	D	E	F
Yak fat	0	4	8	12	16	20
Camel hides	40	32	24	16	8	0

KASHMIR PRODUCTION POSSIBILITIES TABLE

Product	Production alternatives					
	A	B	C	D	E	F
Yak fat	0	3	6	9	12	15
Camel hides	60	48	36	24	12	0

4. The data in the table show that production in
  (a) both Nepal and Kashmir are subject to increasing opportunity costs
  (b) both Nepal and Kashmir are subject to constant opportunity costs

  (c) Nepal is subject to increasing opportunity costs and Kashmir to constant opportunity costs
  (d) Kashmir is subject to increasing opportunity costs and Nepal to constant opportunity costs

5. If Nepal and Kashmir engage in trade, the terms of trade will be
  (a) between 2 and 4 camel hides for 1 unit of yak fat
  (b) between 1/3 and 1/2 units of yak fat for 1 camel hide
  (c) between 3 and 4 units of yak fat for 1 camel hide
  (d) between 2 and 4 units of yak fat for 1 camel hide

6. Assume that prior to specialization and trade Nepal and Kashmir both choose production possibility C. Now if each specializes according to its comparative advantage, the resulting gains from specialization and trade will be
  (a) 6 units of yak fat
  (b) 8 units of yak fat
  (c) 6 units of yak fat and 8 camel hides
  (d) 8 units of yak fat and 6 camel hides

7. Each nation produced only one product in accordance with its comparative advantage, and the terms of trade were set at 3 camel hides for 1 unit of yak fat. In this case, Nepal could obtain a maximum combination of 8 units of yak fat and
  (a) 12 camel hides
  (b) 24 camel hides
  (c) 36 camel hides
  (d) 48 camel hides

8. What happens to a nation's imports or exports of a product when world prices rise relative to domestic prices?
  (a) Imports of the product increase.
  (b) Imports of the product stay the same.
  (c) Exports of the product increase.
  (d) Exports of the product decrease.

9. What happens to a nation's imports or exports of a product when world prices fall relative to domestic prices?
  (a) Imports of the product increase.
  (b) Imports of the product decrease.
  (c) Exports of the product increase.
  (d) Exports of the product stay the same.

10. Which one of the following is characteristic of tariffs?
  (a) They prevent the importation of goods from abroad.
  (b) They specify the maximum amounts of specific commodities which may be imported during a given period of time.
  (c) They often protect domestic producers from foreign competition.
  (d) They enable nations to reduce their exports and increase their imports during periods of depression.

11. The motive for barriers to the importation of goods and services from abroad is to
  (a) improve economic efficiency in that nation
  (b) protect and benefit domestic producers of those goods and services
  (c) reduce the prices of the goods and services produced in that nation
  (d) expand the export of goods and services to foreign nations

12. When a tariff is imposed on a good imported from abroad,
(a) the demand for the good increases
(b) the demand for the good decreases
(c) the supply of the good increases
(d) the supply of the good decreases

Answer Questions 13, 14, 15, 16, and 17 on the basis of the following diagram, where S_d and D_d are the domestic supply and demand for a product and P_w is the world price of that product.

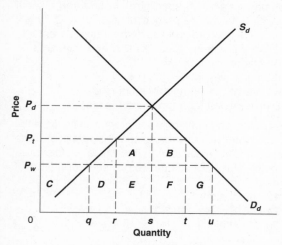

13. In a closed economy (without international trade), the equilibrium price would be
(a) P_d, but in an open economy, the equilibrium price will be P_t
(b) P_d, but in an open economy, the equilibrium price will be P_w
(c) P_w, but in an open economy, the equilibrium price will be P_d
(d) P_w, but in an open economy, the equilibrium price will be P_t

14. If there is free trade in this economy and no tariffs, the total revenue going to the foreign producers is represented by
(a) area C
(b) areas A and B combined
(c) areas A, B, E, and F combined
(d) areas D, E, F, and G combined

15. If a per unit tariff was imposed in the amount of P_wP_t then domestic producers would supply
(a) q units and foreign producers would supply qu units
(b) s units and foreign producers would supply su units
(c) r units and foreign producers would supply rt units
(d) t units and foreign producers would supply tu units

16. Given a per unit tariff in the amount of P_wP_t, the amount of the tariff revenue paid by consumers of this product is represented by
(a) area A
(b) area B
(c) areas A and B combined
(d) areas D, E, F, and G combined

17. Assume an import quota of rt units is imposed on the foreign nation producing this product. The amount of *total* revenue going to foreign producers is represented by areas
(a) $A + B$
(b) $E + F$
(c) $A + B + E + F$
(d) $D + E + F + G$

18. Tariffs lead to
(a) the contraction of relatively efficient industries
(b) an overallocation of resources to relatively efficient industries
(c) an increase in the foreign demand for domestically produced goods
(d) an underallocation of resources to relatively inefficient industries

19. "The nation needs to protect itself from foreign countries that sell their products in our domestic markets at less than the cost of production." This quotation would be most closely associated with which protectionist argument?
(a) diversification for stability
(b) increase domestic employment
(c) protection against dumping
(d) cheap foreign labor

20. Which argument for protection is the least fallacious and most pertinent in the United States today?
(a) the military self-sufficiency argument
(b) the increase-domestic-employment argument
(c) the cheap foreign labor argument
(d) the infant industry argument

21. Which of the following is the likely result of the United States using tariffs to protect its high wages and standard of living from cheap foreign labor?
(a) an increase in U.S. exports
(b) a rise in the U.S. real GDP
(c) a decrease in the average productivity of U.S. workers
(d) a decrease in the quantity of labor employed by industries producing the goods on which tariffs have been levied

22. Which is a likely result of imposing tariffs to increase domestic employment?
(a) a short-run increase in domestic employment in import industries
(b) a decrease in the tariff rates of foreign nations
(c) a long-run reallocation of workers from export industries to protected domestic industries
(d) a decrease in consumer prices

23. The infant industry argument for tariffs
(a) is especially pertinent for the European Economic Community
(b) generally results in tariffs that are removed after the infant industry has matured
(c) makes it rather easy to determine which infant industries will become mature industries with comparative advantages in producing their goods
(d) might better be replaced by an argument for outright subsidies for infant industries

24. Trade protectionism is costly to consumers because
(a) the price of the imported good rises
(b) the supply of the imported good increases
(c) import competition increases for domestically produced goods
(d) consumers shift purchases away from domestically produced goods

25. What international trade policy has the United States pursued in recent years?
(a) increasing the level of tariffs
(b) increasing import quotas
(c) export promotion
(d) import subsidies

■ **PROBLEMS**

1. Shown below are the production possibilities curves for two nations: the United States and Chile. Suppose these two nations do not currently engage in international trade

or specialization, and suppose that points **A** and **a** show the combinations of wheat and copper they now produce and consume.

a. The straightness of the two curves indicates that the cost ratios in the two nations are (changing, constant) _____.

b. Examination of the two curves reveals that the cost ratio in

(1) the United States is _____ million tons of wheat for _____ thousand pounds of copper.

(2) Chile is _____ million tons of wheat for _____ thousand pounds of copper.

c. If these two nations were to specialize and trade wheat for copper,

(1) The United States would specialize in the production of wheat because _____

_____.

(2) Chile would specialize in the production of copper because _____.

d. The terms of trade, if specialization and trade occur, will be greater than 2 and less than 4 million tons of wheat for 1,000 pounds of copper because _____

_____.

e. Assume the terms of trade turn out to be 3 million tons of wheat for 1,000 pounds of copper. Draw in the trading possibilities curve for the United States and Chile.

f. With these trading possibilities curves, suppose the United States decides to consume 5 million tons of wheat and 1,000 pounds of copper while Chile decides to consume 3 million tons of wheat and 1,000 pounds of copper. The gains from trade to

(1) the United States are _____ million tons of wheat and _____ thousand pounds of copper.

(2) Chile are _____ million tons of wheat and

_____ thousand pounds of copper.

2. Following are tables showing the domestic supply and demand schedule and the export supply and import demand schedule for two nations (**A** and **B**).

NATION A

Price	Q_{dd}	Q_{sd}	Q_{di}	Q_{se}
$3.00	100	300	0	200
2.50	150	250	0	100
2.00	200	200	0	0
1.50	250	150	100	0
1.00	300	100	200	0

a. For nation **A,** the first column of the table is the price of a product. The second column is the quantity demanded domestically (Q_{dd}). The third column is the quantity supplied domestically (Q_{sd}). The fourth column is the quantity demanded for imports (Q_{di}). The fifth column is the quantity of exports supplied (Q_{se}).

(1) At a price of $2.00, there (will, will not) _____

be a surplus or shortage and there _____ be exports or imports.

(2) At a price of $3.00, there will be a domestic (shortage, surplus) _____ of _____

units. This domestic _____ will be eliminated

by (exports, imports) _____ of _____ units.

(3) At a price of $1.00, there will be a domestic (shortage, surplus) _____ of _____

units. This domestic _____ will be eliminated

by (exports, imports) _____ of _____ units.

b. For nation **B**, the first column is the price of a product. The second column is the quantity demanded domestically (Q_{dd}). The third column is the quantity supplied domestically (Q_{sd}). The fourth column is the quantity demanded for imports (Q_{di}). The fifth column is the quantity of exports supplied (Q_{se}).

NATION B

Price	Q_{dd}	Q_{sd}	Q_{di}	Q_{se}
$2.50	100	300	0	200
2.00	150	250	0	100
1.50	200	200	0	0
1.00	250	150	100	0

(1) At a price of $1.50, there (will, will not) _____

be a surplus or shortage and there _____ be exports or imports.

(2) At a price of $2.50, there will be a domestic (shortage, surplus) _____ of _____

units. This domestic _____ will be eliminated

by (exports, imports) _____ of _____ units.

(3) At a price of $1.00, there will be a domestic (shortage, surplus) _____ of _____

units. This domestic _____ will be eliminated

by (exports, imports) _____ of _____ units.

c. The following table shows a schedule of the import demand in Nation **A** and the export supply in Nation **B** at various prices. The first column is the price of the product. The second column is the quantity demanded for imports (Q_{diA}) in Nation **A**. The third column is the quantity of exports supplied (Q_{seB}) in Nation **B**.

Price	Q_{diA}	Q_{seB}
$2.00	0	100
1.75	50	50
1.50	100	0

(1) If the world price is $2.00, then Nation (**A, B**)

_____ will want to import _____ units

and Nation _____ will want to export _____ units of the product.

(2) If the world price is $1.75, then Nation (**A, B**)

_____ will want to import _____ units

and Nation _____ will want to export _____ units of the product.

(3) If the world price is $1.50, then Nation (**A, B**)

_____ will want to import _____ units

and Nation _____ will want to export _____ units of the product.

3. The following table shows the quantities of woolen gloves demanded (**D**) in the United States at several different prices (**P**). Also shown in the table are the quantities of woolen gloves that would be supplied by U.S. producers (S_a) and the quantities that would be supplied by foreign producers (S_f) at the nine different prices.

P	D	S_a	S_f	S_t	S'_f	S'_t
$2.60	450	275	475	___	___	___
2.40	500	250	450	___	___	___
2.20	550	225	425	___	___	___
2.00	600	200	400	___	___	___
1.80	650	175	375	___	___	___
1.60	700	150	350	___	___	___
1.40	750	125	325	___	___	___
1.20	800	0	300	___	___	___
1.00	850	0	0	___	___	___

a. Compute and enter in the table the total quantities that would be supplied (S_t) by U.S. and foreign producers at each of the prices.

b. If the market for woolen gloves in the United States is a competitive one the equilibrium price for woolen

gloves is $_____ and the equilibrium quan-

tity is _____.

c. Suppose now that the United States government imposes an 80 cent ($.80) tariff per pair of gloves on all gloves imported into the United States from abroad. Compute and enter into the table the quantities that would be supplied (S'_t) by foreign producers at the nine different prices. (*Hint:* If foreign producers were willing to supply 300 pairs at a price of $1.20 when there was no tariff and they are now willing to supply 300 pairs at $2.00 (the $.80 per pair tariff plus the $1.20 they will receive for themselves). The quantities supplied at each of the other prices may be found in a similar fashion.)

d. Compute and enter into the table the total quantities that would be supplied (S'_t) by U.S. and foreign producers at each of the nine prices.

e. As a result of the imposition of the tariff the equi-

librium price has risen to $_____ and the

equilibrium quantity has fallen to _____.

f. The number of pairs sold by

(1) U.S. producers has (increased, decreased)

_____ by _____.

(2) foreign producers has (increased, decreased)

_____ by _____.

g. The total revenues (after the payment of the tariff) of

(1) U.S. producers—who *do not* pay the tariff—have

(increased, decreased) _____ by $_____.

(2) foreign producers—who *do* pay the tariff—have

(increased, decreased) _____ by $_____.

h. The total amount spent by U.S. buyers of woolen

gloves has _____ by $_____.

i. The total number of dollars earned by foreigners

has _____ by $_____, and, as a

result, the total foreign demand for goods and services

produced in the United States will _____ by

$_____.

j. The tariff revenue of the United States government

has _____ by $_____.

k. If an import quota were imposed that had the same effect as the tariff on price and output, the amount of

the tariff revenue, $_____, would now be

received as revenue by _____ producers.

■ **SHORT ANSWER AND ESSAY QUESTIONS**

1. Describe the quantity of imports and exports for the United States in absolute and relative terms. How has the quantity of imports and exports changed over time?

2. What are the major imports and exports of the United States? With which nations does the United States trade?

3. What role does the United States play in international trade? Who are the other major players in international trade?

4. What two facts—one dealing with the distribution of the world's resources and the other related to the technology of producing different products—are the basis for the trade among nations?

5. Explain
(a) the theory or principle of comparative advantage;
(b) what is meant by and what determines the terms of trade; and
(c) the gains from trade.

6. What is the case for free trade?

7. Explain how the equilibrium prices and quantities of exports and imports are determined.

8. Why will exports in a nation increase when world prices rise relative to domestic prices?

9. What motivates nations to erect barriers to the importation of goods from abroad, and what types of barriers do they erect?

10. Suppose the United States increases the tariff on automobiles imported from Germany (and other foreign countries). What is the effect of this tariff-rate increase on
(a) the price of automobiles in the United States;
(b) the total number of cars sold in the United States during a year;
(c) the number of cars produced by and employment in the German automobile industry;
(d) production by and employment in the U.S. automobile industry;
(e) German income obtained by selling cars in the United States;
(f) the German demand for goods produced in the U.S.;
(g) the production of and employment in those U.S. industries which now export goods to Germany;
(h) the standards of living in the U.S. and in Germany;
(i) the allocation of resources in the U.S. economy; and
(j) the allocation of the world's resources?

11. Compare and contrast the economic effects of a tariff with the economic effects of an import quota on a product.

12. Critically evaluate the military self-sufficiency and infant industry arguments (including strategic trade policy) as a basis for protectionism.

13. Can a strong case for protectionism be made on the basis of one of the following reasons: increasing domestic employment, diversifying for stability, defending against the "dumping" of products, or shielding domestic workers from competition from "cheap" foreign labor? Summarize the case for and the case against protectionism.

14. How costly have trade barriers been for the United States? What are the costs to society? What are the benefits from trade barriers?

15. What is the effect of trade protectionism on income distribution in society? Explain, and give an example.

16. Describe the three types of international trade policies the United States conducts.

17. What are the major provisions of the General Agreements on Tariffs and Trade (GATT)?

18. Describe at least three examples of how the United States has pursued a trade policy of aggressive export promotion in recent years.

19. What are the issues involved in the renewal of most-favored-nation status for China?

20. Why did the United States participate in bilateral negotiations with Japan in recent years? What were the arguments and the results?

ANSWERS

Chapter 20 International Trade

FILL-IN QUESTIONS

1. 12, doubled
2. larger, largest

3. uneven, different
4. lowest, have, do not have
5. *a.* inexpensive, expensive; *b.* expensive, inexpensive; *c.* hats, bananas; *d.* 3, 4; *e.* (1) 1/3, 2/7, (2) 4, 3 1/2; *f.* rises
6. comparative advantage, more, higher
7. world, domestic
8. increase, increase
9. supply, only one
10. tariffs, quotas, revenue, protective
11. nontariff, export
12. domestic producers, decrease, less
13. increase, decrease, increase, decrease, decrease, decrease
14. tariff, quota
15. *a.* military self-sufficiency; *b.* infant industry; *c.* increase domestic employment; *d.* diversification for stability; *e.* protection against dumping; *f.* cheap foreign labor (any order for a–f)
16. weak, domestic producers, gains, losses
17. increasing, increasing, increasing
18. greater, more
19. trade liberalization, export promotion
20. bilateral negotiations, China, Japan

TRUE-FALSE QUESTIONS

1. T, p. 405	**10.** F, pp. 411-414	**19.** F, p. 419
2. F, pp. 405-406	**11.** T, pp. 414-415	**20.** T, p. 420
3. F, pp. 406-408	**12.** F, p. 415	**21.** F, p. 420
4. F, p. 407	**13.** T, pp. 415-416	**22.** T, pp. 417-418
5. T, p. 411	**14.** F, p. 417	**23.** F, pp. 418-419
6. T, p. 408	**15.** T, p. 417	**24.** T, p. 421
7. T, pp. 410-411	**16.** T, p. 416	**25.** F, pp. 423-425
8. T, p. 411	**17.** T, p. 417	
9. F, p. 411	**18.** F, pp. 416-417	

MULTIPLE-CHOICE QUESTIONS

1. c, p. 404	**10.** c, p. 415	**19.** c, p. 419
2. c, p. 405	**11.** b, pp. 415-417	**20.** a, p. 420
3. b, p. 405	**12.** d, pp. 415-416	**21.** c, p. 420
4. b, p. 407	**13.** b, pp. 415-416	**22.** c, pp. 417-418
5. a, pp. 407-408	**14.** d, p. 416	**23.** d, pp. 418-419
6. a, pp. 408-410	**15.** c, p. 416	**24.** a, p. 421
7. c, pp. 408-410	**16.** c, p. 416	**25.** c, pp. 423-425
8. c, pp. 411-414	**17.** c, p. 417	
9. a, pp. 411-414	**18.** a, pp. 416-417	

PROBLEMS

1. *a.* constant; *b.* (1) 8, 2, (2) 4, 2; *c.* (1) it has a comparative advantage in producing wheat (its cost of producing wheat is less than Chile's), (2) it has a comparative advantage in producing copper (its cost of producing copper is less than the United States'); *d.* one of the two nations would be unwilling to trade if the terms of trade are outside this range; *f.* (1) 1, 0, (2) 1, 0
2. *a.* (1) will not, will not, (2) surplus, 200, surplus, exports, 200, (3) shortage, 200, shortage, imports, 200; *b.* (1) will not, will not, (2) surplus, 200, surplus, exports, 200, (3) shortage, 100, shortage, imports, 100; *c.* (1) A, 0, B, 100, (2) A, 50, B, 50, (3) A, 100, B, 0
3. *a.* 750, 700, 650, 600, 550, 500, 450, 300, 0; *b.* $2.00, 600; *c.* 375, 350, 325, 300, 0, 0, 0, 0, 0; *d.* 650, 600, 550, 500, 175, 150, 125, 0, 0; *e.* $2.20, 550; *f.* (1) increased, 25, (2) decreased, 75; *g.* (1) increased, $95, (2) decreased, $345; *h.* increased, $10; *i.* decreased, $345, decreased, $345; *j.* increased, $260; *k.* $260, foreign

SHORT ANSWER AND ESSAY QUESTIONS

1. pp. 404-405	**8.** pp. 412-413	**15.** p. 422
2. p. 405	**9.** pp. 415-417	**16.** pp. 422-423
3. pp. 405-406	**10.** pp. 415-417	**17.** pp. 422-423
4. pp. 405-406	**11.** p. 417	**18.** p. 423
5. pp. 407-410	**12.** pp. 417-419	**19.** pp. 423-425
6. p. 411	**13.** pp. 417-420	**20.** p. 425
7. pp. 414-415	**14.** pp. 421-422	

CHAPTER 21

Exchange Rates, the Balance of Payments, and Trade Deficits

In the last chapter you learned *why* nations engage in international trade and *why* they erect barriers to trade with other nations. In Chapter 21 you will learn *how* nations using different currencies are able to trade with each other.

The means nations use to overcome the difficulties that result from the use of different currencies is fairly simple. When the residents of a nation (its consumers, business firms, or governments) wish to buy goods or services or real or financial assets from, make loans or gifts to, or pay interest and dividends to the residents of other nations, they *buy* some of the currency used in that nation. They pay for the foreign money with some of their own currency. In other words, they *exchange* their own currency for foreign currency.

When the residents of a nation sell goods or services or real or financial assets to, receive loans or gifts from, or are paid dividends or interest by the residents of foreign nations and obtain foreign currencies, they **sell** this foreign currency—often called foreign exchange—in return for some of their own currency. That is, they **exchange** foreign currency for their own currency.

The markets in which one currency is sold and is paid for with another currency are called **foreign exchange markets.** The price that is paid (in one currency) for a unit of another currency is called the **foreign exchange rate** (or the **rate of exchange**). And like most prices, the foreign exchange rate for any foreign currency is determined by the demand for and the supply of that foreign currency.

As you know from Chapter 20, nations buy and sell large quantities of goods and services across national boundaries. But the residents of these nations also buy and sell such financial assets as stocks and bonds and such real assets as land and capital goods in other nations, and the governments and individuals in one nation make gifts (remittances) in other nations. At the end of a year, nations summarize their foreign transactions with the rest of the world. This summary is called the nation's *international balance of payments:* a record of how it obtained foreign currency during the year and what it did with this foreign currency.

Of course, all foreign currency obtained was used for some purpose—it did not evaporate—consequently the balance of payments *always* balances. The international balance of payments is an extremely important and useful device for understanding the amounts and kinds of international transactions in which the residents of a nation engage. But it also enables us to understand the meaning of a balance of payments imbalance (a deficit or a surplus), the causes of these imbalances, and how to deal with them.

Probably the most difficult section of this chapter is concerned with **balance of payments deficits** and **surpluses.** A balance of payments deficit (surplus) is found when the receipts of foreign currency are less (greater) than the payments of foreign currency and the nation must reduce (expand) its official reserves to make the balance of payments balance. Pay particular attention to the way in which a system of *flexible* exchange rates and a system of *fixed* exchange rates will correct balance of payments deficits and surpluses and the advantages and disadvantages of these two alternative methods of eliminating imbalances.

As examples of these two types of exchange-rate systems, the third section of the chapter examines the gold standard, the Bretton Woods system, and the managed floating exchange-rate system. In the first two systems exchange rates are fixed, and in the third system exchange rates are fixed in the short run (to obtain the advantages of fixed exchange rates) and flexible in the long run (to enable nations to correct balance of payments deficits and surpluses).

The final section of the chapter examines the **trade deficits** of the United States during the 1990s. As you will learn, these deficits were the result of several factors—differences in national growth rates, large Federal budget deficits, and a declining saving rate—that contributed to imports rising faster than exports. They also have several implications, such as increased current consumption at the possible expense of future consumption and increased U.S. indebtedness to foreigners.

■ CHECKLIST

When you have studied this chapter you should be able to

☐ Explain how U.S. exports create a foreign demand for dollars that in turn generates a supply of foreign currencies.
☐ Describe how U.S. imports create a domestic demand for foreign currencies that in turn generates a supply of dollars.
☐ Give a definition of a nation's international balance of payments.
☐ Use the items in the current account to calculate the balance of trade, balance on goods and services, and balance on the current account when given the necessary data.

☐ Describe how balance is achieved in the capital account.

☐ Explain the relationship between the current account, capital account, and official reserves account.

☐ Indicate how the official reserve account is used to determine whether there is a balance of payment deficit or surplus.

☐ Use a supply and demand graph to illustrate how a flexible exchange-rate system works to establish the price and quantity of a currency.

☐ Describe the depreciation and appreciation of a nation's currency under a flexible exchange-rate system.

☐ Identify the five principal determinants of the demand for and supply of a particular foreign currency and explain how they alter exchange rates.

☐ List three disadvantages of flexible exchange rates.

☐ Use a supply and demand graph to illustrate how a fixed exchange-rate system functions.

☐ Discuss the objectives and limitations of using official reserves, trade policies, exchange controls, and domestic stabilization policies to maintain a fixed exchange rate.

☐ Identify three different exchange-rate systems used by the world's nations in recent years.

☐ List three conditions a nation had to fulfill if it were to be on the gold standard.

☐ Explain how the gold standard worked to maintain fixed exchange rates.

☐ Give reasons for the demise of the gold standard.

☐ Explain how the Bretton Woods system attempted to stabilize exchange rates and establish orderly changes in exchange rates for correcting balance of payment deficits.

☐ State reasons for the demise of the Bretton Woods system.

☐ Describe the current system of managed floating exchange rates.

☐ Discuss the pros and cons of the system of managed floating exchange rates.

☐ Describe the causes of recent trade deficits in the United States.

☐ Explain the economic implications of recent trade deficits in the United States.

■ CHAPTER OUTLINE

1. Trade between two nations differs from domestic trade because the nations use different currencies. This problem is resolved by the existence of *foreign exchange markets,* in which the currency used by one nation can be purchased and paid for with the currency of the other nation.

  a. United States exports create a foreign demand for dollars, and the satisfaction of this demand increases the supply of foreign currencies in the foreign exchange market.

  b. United States imports create a domestic demand for foreign currencies, and meeting this demand decreases the supplies of foreign currencies in the foreign exchange market.

2. The ***international balance of payments*** for a nation is an annual record of all its transactions with the other nations in the world; it records all the payments received from and made to the rest of the world.

  a. The ***current account*** section of a nation's international balance of payments records its trade in currently produced goods and services. Within this section
(1) the trade balance of the nation is equal to its exports of goods (merchandise) less its imports of goods (merchandise);
(2) the balance on goods and services is equal to its exports of goods and services less its imports of goods and services; and
(3) the balance on the current account is equal to its balance on goods and services plus its net investment income (dividends and interest) from other nations and its net private and public transfers to other nations, and minus this balance may be either a surplus or a deficit.

  b. The ***capital account*** section of a nation's international balance of payments records its sales of real and financial assets (which earn it foreign currencies) and its purchases of real and financial assets (which use up foreign currencies). The nation has a ***capital account surplus (deficit)*** if its sales are greater (less) than its purchases of real and financial assets.

  c. The ***official reserves*** account consists of the foreign currencies owned by the central bank. These reserves decrease when they are used to finance a net deficit on the combined current and capital accounts. The reserves increase when a nation has a net surplus on its current and capital account. The three components of the balance of payments—the current account, the capital account, and the official reserves account—must equal zero.

  d. A nation has a balance of payments *deficit* when imbalances in the combined current and capital accounts lead to a decrease in official reserves. A balance of payments *surplus* arises when imbalances in the combined current and capital accounts result in an increase in official reserves.

3. There are flexible (floating) and fixed *exchange-rate systems* that nations use to correct imbalances in the balance of payments. If the foreign exchange rate *floats freely,* the demand for and the supply of foreign exchange determine foreign exchange rates. The exchange rate for any foreign currency is the rate at which the quantity of that currency demanded is equal to the quantity of it supplied.

  a. A change in the demand for or the supply of a foreign currency will cause a change in the exchange rate for that currency. When there is an increase in the price paid in dollars for a foreign currency, the dollar has depreciated and the foreign currency has appreciated in value. Conversely, when there is an decrease in the price paid in dollars for a foreign currency, the dollar has appreciated and the foreign currency has depreciated in value.

  b. Changes in the demand for or supply of a foreign currency are largely the result of changes in tastes, relative incomes, relative price levels, relative interest rates, and speculation.

  c. Flexible exchange rates can be used to eliminate a balance of payments deficit or surplus.
(1) When a nation has a payment deficit, foreign exchange rates will increase, thus making foreign goods and services more expensive and decreasing imports.

These events will make a nation's goods and services less expensive for foreigners to buy, thus increasing exports.

(2) With a payment surplus, the exchange rates will increase, thus making foreign goods and services less expensive and increasing imports. This situation makes a nation's goods and services more expensive for foreigners to buy, thus decreasing exports.

d. But a flexible exchange-rate system increases the uncertainties exporters, importers, and investors face, thus reducing international trade. This system also changes the terms of trade and creates instability in domestic economies.

4. When nations *fix* (or peg) foreign exchange rates, the governments of these nations must intervene in the foreign exchange markets to prevent shortages and surpluses caused by shifts in demand and supply.

a. One way a nation can stabilize foreign exchange is for its government to sell its reserves of a foreign currency in exchange for its own currency (or gold) when there is a shortage of the foreign currency. Conversely, a government would buy a foreign currency in exchange for its own currency (or gold) when there is a surplus of the foreign currency; however, currency reserves may be limited and inadequate for handling large and persistent deficits or surpluses, so it may use other means to maintain fixed exchange rates.

(1) A nation might adopt trade policies that discourage imports and encourage exports.

(2) A nation might impose exchange rate controls and rationing, but these policies tend to distort trade, lead to government favoritism, restrict consumer choice, and create black markets.

b. Another way a nation can stabilize foreign exchange rates is to use monetary and fiscal policy to reduce its national income and price level and raise interest rates relative to those in other nations. These events would lead to a decrease in demand for and increase in the supply of different foreign currencies.

5. In their recent history, the nations of the world have used three different exchange-rate systems.

a. Under the **gold standard,** each nation must define its currency in terms of a quantity of gold, maintain a fixed relationship between its gold and its money supply, and allow gold to be imported or exported without restrictions.

(1) The potential gold flows between nations would ensure that exchange rates remained fixed.

(2) Payment deficits and surpluses would be eliminated through macroeconomic adjustments. For example, if a nation has a balance of payments deficit and gold flowing out of the country, its money supply would decrease. This event would increase interest rates and decrease total spending, output, employment, and the price level. The opposite would happen in the other country because it has a payments surplus. The changes in both nations would eliminate any payments deficit or surplus.

(3) During the worldwide depression of the 1930s nations felt that remaining on the gold standard threatened their recoveries, and the policy of devaluating

their currencies to boost exports led to the breakdown and abandonment of the gold standard.

b. From the end of World War II until 1971 the **Bretton Woods system,** committed to the adjustable-peg system of exchange rates and managed by the **International Monetary Fund (IMF),** kept foreign exchange rates relatively stable.

(1) The adjustable-peg system required the United States to sell gold to other member nations at a fixed price and the other members of the IMF to define their monetary units in terms of either gold or dollars (which established fixed exchange rates among the currencies of all member nations) and required the other member nations to keep the exchange rates for their currencies from rising by selling foreign currencies, selling gold, or borrowing on a short-term basis from the IMF.

(2) The system also provided for orderly changes in exchange rates to correct a fundamental imbalance (persistent and sizable balance of payments deficits) by allowing a nation to devalue its currency (increase its defined gold or dollar equivalent).

(3) The other nations of the world used gold and dollars as their international monetary reserves in the Bretton Woods system. For these reserves to grow, the United States had to continue to have balance of payments deficits, but to continue the convertibility of dollars into gold it had to reduce the deficits, and, faced with this dilemma, in 1971 the United States suspended the convertibility of the dollar, brought an end to the Bretton Woods system of fixed exchange rates, and allowed the exchange rates for the dollar and the other currencies to float.

c. Exchange rates today are managed by individual nations to avoid short-term fluctuations and allowed to float in the long term to correct balance of payments deficits and surpluses. This new system of **managed floating exchange rates** is favored by some and criticized by others.

(1) Its proponents contend that this system has not led to any decrease in world trade and has enabled the world to adjust to severe economic shocks.

(2) Its critics argue that it has resulted in volatile exchange rates, has not reduced balance of payments deficits and surpluses, and is a "nonsystem" that a nation may use to achieve its own domestic economic goals.

6. During the 1990s, the United States has had large and persistent trade deficits.

a. These trade deficits were the result of several factors:

(1) more rapid growth in the domestic economy than in the economies of several major trading partners, which caused imports to rise more than exports;

(2) recent large deficits in the Federal budget which drove up real interest rates, increased the international value of the dollar, and increased imports and decreased exports; and

(3) a decline in the rate of saving and a capital account surplus, which allowed U.S. citizens to consume more imported goods.

b. The trade deficits of the United States have had two principal effects: They increased current domestic consumption and allowed the nation to operate outside its production possibilities frontier, and they increased the indebtedness of U.S. citizens to foreigners. A possible implication of these persistent trade deficits is that they will lead to permanent debt and foreign ownership of domestic assets, or large sacrifices of future domestic consumption.

■ HINTS AND TIPS

1. The chapter is filled with many new terms, some of which are just special words used in international economics to mean things with which you are already familiar. Other terms are new to you, so you must spend time learning them if you are to understand the chapter.

2. The terms *depreciation* and *appreciation* can be confusing when applied to foreign exchange markets.
    a. First, know the related terms. "Depreciate" means decrease or fall, whereas "appreciate" means increase or rise.
    b. Second, think of depreciation or appreciation in terms of quantities:
    (1) what *decreases* when the currency of Country A *depreciates* is the *quantity* of Country B's currency that can be purchased for *1 unit* of Country A's currency;
    (2) what increases when the currency of Country A *appreciates* is the *quantity* of Country B's currency that can be purchased for *1 unit* of Country A's currency.
    c. Third, consider the effect of changes in exchange rates:
    (1) when the exchange rate for Country B's currency *rises,* this means that Country A's currency has *depreciated* in value because 1 unit of Country A's currency will now purchase a smaller quantity of Country B's currency;
    (2) when the exchange rate for Country B's currency *falls,* this means that Country A's currency has *appreciated* in value because 1 unit of Country A's currency will now purchase a larger quantity of Country B's currency.

3. The meaning of the balance of payments can be confusing also because of the number of accounts in the balance sheet. Remember that the balance of payments must always balance and sum to zero because one account in the balance of payments can be in surplus, but it will be offset by a deficit in another account. However, when people talk about a *balance of payments surplus* or *deficit,* they are referring to the sum of the current and capital account balances. If the total is positive, there is a balance of payments surplus, but if it is negative, there is a balance of payments deficit.

■ IMPORTANT TERMS

international balance of payments

current account

trade balance

balance on goods and services

balance on current account

capital account

balance on the capital account

official reserves

balance of payments deficit

balance of payments surplus

flexible (floating) exchange-rate system

fixed exchange-rate system

purchasing power parity theory

gold standard

devaluation

Bretton Woods system

International Monetary Fund (IMF)

managed floating exchange rate

SELF-TEST

■ FILL-IN QUESTIONS

1. The rate of exchange for the French franc is the amount in (francs, dollars) _____ which a U.S. citizen must pay to obtain 1 (franc, dollar) _____. If the rate of exchange for the French franc is (5 francs, $.20) _____, the rate of exchange for the U.S. dollar is _____.

2. U.S. exports create a foreign (demand for, supply of) _____ dollars and generate a _____ foreign currencies owned by U.S. banks and available to domestic buyers; U.S. imports create a domestic (demand for, supply of) _____ foreign currencies and reduces the _____ foreign currencies held by U.S. banks and available for domestic consumers.

3. The balance of payments of a nation records all payments (domestic, foreign) _____ residents make to and receive from _____ residents. Any transaction that *earns* foreign exchange for that nation is a (debit, credit) _____, and any transaction that *uses up* foreign exchange is a _____. A debit is shown with a (+, −) _____ sign, and a credit is shown with a _____ sign.

4. If a nation has a deficit in its balance of trade, its exports are (greater, less) _____ than its imports of goods, and if it has a deficit in its balance on goods and services, its exports of these items are _____ than its imports of them. The current account is equal to the balance on goods and services (plus, minus) _____ net investment income and _____ net transfers.

5. The capital account records the capital inflows and capital outflows of a nation. The capital inflows are the expenditures made (in that nation, abroad) _____ by residents of (that nation, other nations) _____

_____, and the capital outflows are the expenditures made (in that nation, abroad) _____ by residents of (that nation, other nations) _____

_____ for real and financial assets. A nation has a capital account surplus when its capital account inflows are (greater, less) _____ than its outflows.

6. A nation may finance a current account deficit by (buying, selling) _____ assets or by (borrowing, lending) _____ abroad and may use a current account surplus to (buy, sell) _____ assets or to (borrow, lend) _____ abroad.

7. The official reserves of a nation are the quantities of (foreign currencies, its own money) _____ owned by its central bank. If that nation has a deficit on the current and capital accounts, its official reserves (increase, decrease) _____, but with a surplus on the current and capital accounts, its official reserves _____. The sum of the current, capital, and official reserve accounts must equal (0, 1) _____.

8. A country has a balance of payments deficit if the sum of its current and capital accounts balance is (positive, negative) _____ and its official reserves (increase, decrease) _____. A country has a payments surplus when the sum of its current and capital accounts balance is (positive, negative) _____ and its official reserves (increase, decrease) _____.

9. If foreign exchange rates float freely and a nation has a balance of payments *deficit*, that nation's currency in the foreign exchange markets will (appreciate, depreciate) _____ and foreign currencies will _____. As a result of these changes in foreign exchange rates, the nation's imports will (increase, decrease) _____, its exports will _____, and the size of its deficit will (increase, decrease) _____.

10. What effect would each of the following have on the appreciation (**A**) or depreciation (**D**) of the French franc in the foreign exchange market (*ceteris paribus*)?
  a. The increased preference in the United States for domestic wines over wines produced in France: _____

  b. A rise in the U.S. national income: _____

  c. An increase in the price level in France: _____
  d. A rise in real interest rates in the United States: _____

  _____

e. The belief of speculators in France that the dollar will appreciate in the foreign exchange market: _____

11. There are three disadvantages of freely floating foreign exchange rates: the risks and uncertainties associated with flexible rates tend to (expand, diminish) _____ trade between nations; when a nation's currency depreciates, its terms of trade with other nations are (worsened, improved) _____; and fluctuating exports and imports can (stabilize, destabilize) _____ an economy.

12. To fix or peg the rate of exchange for the German mark when the exchange rate for the mark is rising, the United States would (buy, sell) _____ marks in exchange for dollars, and when the exchange rate for the mark is falling, the United States would _____ marks in exchange for dollars.

13. Under a fixed exchange-rate system, a nation with a balance of payments deficit might attempt to eliminate the deficit by (taxing, subsidizing) _____ imports or by _____ exports. The nation might use exchange controls and ration foreign exchange among those who wish to (export, import) _____ goods and services and require all those who _____ goods and services to sell the foreign exchange they earn to the (businesses, government) _____.

14. If the United States has a payments deficit with Japan and the exchange rate for the Japanese yen is rising, under a fixed exchange-rate system the United States might adopt (expansionary, contractionary) _____ fiscal and monetary policies to reduce the demand for the yen, but this would bring about (inflation, recession) _____ in the United States.

15. When the nations of the world were on the gold standard exchange, rates were relatively (stable, unstable) _____. When a nation had a payments deficit, gold flowed (into, out of) _____ the nation, its money supply (increased, decreased) _____, its interest rates _____, and output, employment, income, and perhaps prices (increased, decreased) _____; thus its payments deficit _____.

16. The Bretton Woods system was established to bring about (flexible, fixed) _____ exchange rates. Under the Bretton Woods system, a member nation defined its monetary unit in terms of (oil, gold) _____ or dollars. Each member nation stabilized the exchange rate for its currency and prevented it from rising by (buying, selling) _____ foreign currency which it obtained from its official reserves, by (buying, selling) _____ gold or by (borrowing from, lending to) _____ the International Monetary Fund. A nation with a deeply rooted payments deficit could (devalue, revalue) _____ its currency. The system was designed so that in the short run exchange rates would be (stable, flexible) _____ enough to promote international trade and in the long run they would be _____ enough to correct balance of payments imbalances.

17. The role of the dollar as a component of international monetary reserves under Bretton Woods produced a dilemma. For the dollar to remain an acceptable international monetary reserve, the U.S. payments deficits had to be (eliminated, continued) _____, but for international monetary reserves to grow to accommodate world trade, the U.S payments deficits had to be _____. These deficits caused an acceptability problem because they resulted in a(n) (decrease, increase) _____ in the foreign holding of U.S. dollars and a(n) _____ in the U.S. reserves of gold, which contributed to a(n) (decrease, increase) _____ in the ability of the United States to convert dollars into gold and the willingness of foreigners to hold dollars as if they were as good as gold. In 1971, the United States essentially ended this system when it (adopted, suspended) _____ the convertibility of dollars into gold and allowed the value of the dollar to be determined by markets.

18. Since then the international monetary system has moved to a system of managed (fixed, floating) _____ exchange rates. This means that exchange rates of nations are (restricted from, free to) _____ find their equilibrium market levels, but nations may occasionally (leave, intervene in) _____ the foreign exchange markets to stabilize or alter market exchange rates.

19. The advantages of the current system are that the growth of trade (was, was not) _____ accommodated as well as under the Bretton Woods system and that it has survived much economic (stability, turbulence) _____. Its disadvantages are its (equilibrium, volatility) _____ and the lack of guidelines for nations that make it a (bureaucracy, nonsystem) _____.

20. The major problem with foreign trade in the United States concerns U.S. merchandise and current account (surpluses, deficits) _____ which were brought about by the sharp increases in its (exports, imports) _____ and the small increases in its _____. One cause has been (stronger, weaker) _____ economic growth in the United States relative to _____ economic growth in Europe and Japan which would (increase, decrease) _____ U.S. imports more than exports. Other contributing factors are (small, large) _____ deficits in the annual Federal budget and a (rising, falling) _____ saving rate. One effect of the trade deficits of the United States has been (decreased, increased) _____ current domestic consumption that allows the nation to operate outside its production possibility frontier, and another effect was a (rise, fall) _____ in the indebtedness of U.S. citizens to foreigners.

■ TRUE-FALSE QUESTIONS

Circle the T if the statement is true, the F if it is false.

1. The importation of goods and services by U.S. citizens from abroad creates a supply of dollars in the foreign exchange market.　　　　　**T F**

2. The international balance of payments of the United States records all the payments its residents receive from and make to the residents of foreign nations.　**T F**

3. Exports are a debit item and are shown with a plus sign (+), and imports are a credit item and are shown with a minus sign (−) in the international balance of payments of a nation.　　　　　**T F**

4. The United States would have a balance of payments surplus if the balances on its current and capital accounts were positive.　　　　　**T F**

5. Any nation with a balance of payments deficit must reduce its official reserves.　　　　　**T F**

6. The sum of a nation's current account balance, its capital account balance, and the change in its official reserves in any year is always equal to zero.　**T F**

7. The purchasing power parity theory basically explains why there is an inverse relationship between the price of dollars and the quantity demanded.　　　**T F**

8. The expectations of speculators in the United States that the exchange rate for the Japanese yen will fall in the future will increase the supply of yen in the foreign exchange market and decrease the exchange rate for the yen.　　　　　**T F**

9. If a nation has a balance of payments deficit and exchange rates are flexible, the price of that nation's currency in the foreign exchange markets will fall; this will reduce its imports and increase its exports.　　**T F**

10. Were the United States' terms of trade with Nigeria to worsen, Nigeria would obtain a greater quantity of U.S.

goods and services for every barrel of oil it exported to the United States. **T F**

11. If a nation wishes to fix (or peg) the foreign exchange rate for the Swiss franc, it must buy Swiss francs with its own currency when the rate of exchange for the Swiss franc rises. **T F**

12. If exchange rates are stable or fixed and a nation has a payments surplus, prices and currency incomes in that nation will tend to rise. **T F**

13. A nation using exchange controls to eliminate a balance of payments surplus might depreciate its currency. **T F**

14. If country A defined its currency as worth 100 grains of gold and country B defined its currency as worth 20 grains of gold, then, ignoring packing, insuring, and shipping charges, 5 units of country A's currency would be worth 1 unit of country B's currency. **T F**

15. Under the gold standard, the potential free flow of gold between nations would result in exchange rates which are fixed. **T F**

16. In the Bretton Woods system, a nation could not devalue its currency by more than 10% without the permission of the International Monetary Fund. **T F**

17. In the Bretton Woods system, a nation with persistent balance of payments surpluses had an undervalued currency and should have increased the pegged value of its currency. **T F**

18. To accommodate expanding world trade in the Bretton Woods system, the U.S. dollar served as a reserve medium of exchange and the United States ran persistent balance of payments deficits. **T F**

19. A basic shortcoming of the Bretton Woods system was its inability to bring about the changes in exchange rates needed to correct persistent payments deficits and surpluses. **T F**

20. Using the managed floating system of exchange rates, a nation with a persistent balance of payments surplus should allow the value of its currency in foreign exchange markets to decrease. **T F**

21. Two criticisms of the current managed floating exchange-rate system are its potential for volatility and its lack of clear policy rules or guidelines for nations to manage exchange rates. **T F**

22. The foreign trade deficits experienced by the U.S. economy in the 1990s were caused by sharp increases in U.S. exports and slight increases in U.S. imports. **T F**

23. Improved economic growth in the major economies of the major trading partners of the United States would tend to worsen the trade deficit. **T F**

24. High real interest rates in the United States would tend to increase the attractiveness of financial investment in the United States to foreigners and the foreign demand for U.S. dollars. **T F**

25. The negative net exports of the United States have increased the indebtedness of U.S. citizens to foreigners. **T F**

■ **MULTIPLE-CHOICE QUESTIONS**

Circle the letter that corresponds to the best answer.

1. If a U.S. citizen could buy £25,000 for $100,000, the rate of exchange for the pound would be
(a) $40
(b) $25
(c) $4
(d) $.25

2. U.S. residents demand foreign currencies to
(a) produce goods and services exported to foreign countries
(b) pay for goods and services imported from foreign countries
(c) receive interest payments on investments in the United States
(d) have foreigners make real and financial investments in the United States

3. A nation's balance of trade is equal to its exports less its imports of
(a) goods
(b) goods and services
(c) financial assets
(d) official reserves

4. A nation's balance on the current account is equal to its exports less its imports of
(a) goods and services
(b) goods and services, plus U.S. purchases of assets abroad
(c) goods and services, plus net investment income and net transfers
(d) goods and services, minus foreign purchases of assets in the United States

5. The net investment income of the United States in its international balance of payment is the
(a) interest income it receives from foreign residents
(b) dividends it receives from foreign residents
(c) excess of interest and dividends it receives from foreign residents over what it paid to them
(d) excess of public and private transfer payments it receives from foreign residents over what it paid to them

6. A nation may be able to correct or eliminate a persistent (long-term) balance of payments deficit by
(a) lowering the barriers on imported goods
(b) reducing the international value of its currency
(c) expanding its national income
(d) reducing its official reserves

7. If exchange rates float freely, the exchange rate for any currency is determined by the
(a) demand for it
(b) supply of it
(c) demand for and the supply of it
(d) official reserves that back it

8. If a nation had a balance of payments surplus and exchange rates floated freely, the foreign exchange rate for its currency would

   (a) rise, its exports would increase, and its imports would decrease

   (b) rise, its exports would decrease, and its imports would increase

   (c) fall, its exports would increase, and its imports would decrease

   (d) fall, its exports would decrease, and its imports would increase

9. Assuming exchange rates are flexible, which of the following should increase the dollar price of the Swedish krona?

   (a) a rate of inflation greater in Sweden than in the United States

   (b) real interest rate increases greater in Sweden than in the United States

   (c) national income increases greater in Sweden than in the United States

   (d) the increased preference of Swedish citizens for U.S. automobiles over Swedish automobiles

10. Which of the following would be one of the results associated with the use of freely floating foreign exchange rates to correct a nation's balance of payments surplus?

   (a) The nation's terms of trade with other nations would be worsened.

   (b) Importers in the nation who had made contracts for the future delivery of goods would find that they had to pay a higher price than expected for the goods.

   (c) If the nation were at full employment, the decrease in exports and the increase in imports would be inflationary.

   (d) Exporters in the nation would find their sales abroad had decreased.

11. When exchange rates are fixed and a nation at full employment has a balance of payments surplus, the result in that nation will be

   (a) a declining price level

   (b) falling currency income

   (c) inflation

   (d) rising real income

12. The use of exchange controls to eliminate a nation's balance of payments deficit results in decreasing the nation's

   (a) imports

   (b) exports

   (c) price level

   (d) income

13. Which condition did a nation have to fulfill if it were to be under the gold standard?

   (a) use only gold as a medium of exchange

   (b) maintain a flexible relationship between its gold stock and its currency supply

   (c) allow gold to be freely exported from and imported into the nation

   (d) define its monetary unit in terms of a fixed quantity of dollars

14. If the nations of the world were on the gold standard and one nation has a balance of payments surplus,

   (a) foreign exchange rates in that nation would rise

   (b) gold would tend to be imported into that country

   (c) the level of prices in that country would fall

   (d) employment and output in that country would fall

15. Which was the principal disadvantage of the gold standard?

   (a) unstable foreign exchange rates

   (b) persistent payments imbalances

   (c) the uncertainties and decreased trade that resulted from the depreciation of gold

   (d) the domestic macroeconomic adjustments experienced by a nation with a payments deficit or surplus

16. The objective of the adjustable-peg system was exchange rates which were

   (a) adjustable in the short run and fixed in the long run

   (b) adjustable in both the short and long run

   (c) fixed in both the short and long run

   (d) fixed in the short run and adjustable in the long run

17. Which is the best definition of international monetary reserves in the Bretton Woods system?

   (a) gold

   (b) dollars

   (c) gold and dollars

   (d) gold, dollars, and British pounds

18. The major dilemma created by the persistent U.S. payments deficits under the Bretton Woods system was that to maintain the status of the dollar as an acceptable international monetary reserve, the deficits had to

   (a) decrease, but to expand reserves to accommodate world trade, the deficits had to continue

   (b) continue, but to expand reserves to accommodate world trade, the deficits had to be eliminated

   (c) increase, but to expand reserves to accommodate world trade, the deficits had to be reduced

   (d) decrease, but to expand reserves to accommodate world trade, the deficits had to be eliminated

19. "Floating" the dollar means

   (a) the value of the dollar is determined by the demand for and the supply of the dollar

   (b) the dollar price of gold has been increased

   (c) the price of the dollar has been allowed to crawl upward at the rate of one-fourth of 1% a month

   (d) the IMF decreased the value of the dollar by 10%

20. A system of managed floating exchange rates

   (a) allows nations to stabilize exchange rates in the short term

   (b) requires nations to stabilize exchange rates in the long term

   (c) entails stable exchange rates in both the short and long term

   (d) fixes exchange rates at market levels

21. Floating exchange rates

   (a) tend to correct balance of payments imbalances

   (b) reduce the uncertainties and risks associated with international trade

(c) increase the world's need for international monetary reserves

(d) tend to expand the volume of world trade

22. The foreign trade problem facing the United States is
(a) its balance of trade and current account surpluses
(b) its balance of trade deficit and current account surpluses
(c) its balance of trade and current account deficits
(d) its balance of trade surplus and current account deficit

23. Which is one of the causes of the growth of U.S. trade deficits during the 1990s?
(a) protective tariffs imposed by the United States
(b) slower economic growth in the United States
(c) direct foreign investment in the United States
(d) a declining saving rate in the United States

24. What would be the effect on U.S. imports and exports when the United States experiences strong economic growth but its major trading partners experience sluggish economic growth?
(a) U.S. imports will increase more than U.S. exports
(b) U.S. exports will increase more than U.S. imports
(c) U.S. imports will decrease but U.S. exports will increase
(d) there will be no effect on U.S. imports and exports

25. Two major outcomes from the trade deficits of the 1990s were
(a) decreased domestic consumption and U.S. indebtedness
(b) increased domestic consumption and U.S. indebtedness
(c) increased domestic consumption but decreased U.S. indebtedness
(d) decreased domestic consumption but increased U.S. indebtedness

■ **PROBLEMS**

1. Assume a U.S. exporter sells $3 million worth of wheat to an importer in Colombia. If the rate of exchange for the Colombian peso is $.02 (2 cents), the wheat has a total value of 150 million pesos.
a. There are two ways the importer in Colombia may pay for the wheat. It might write a check for 150 million pesos drawn on its bank in Botogá and send it to the U.S. exporter.
(1) The American exporter would then sell the check to its bank in New Orleans and its demand deposit there would increase by $_____ million.
(2) This New Orleans bank now sells the check for 150 million pesos to a correspondent bank (a U.S. commercial bank that keeps an account in the Botogá bank).
   (a) The New Orleans bank's account in the correspondent bank increases by _____ million (dollars, pesos) _____; and

(b) the correspondent bank's account in the Botogá bank increases by _____ million (pesos, dollars) _____.

b. The second way for the importer to pay for the wheat is to buy from its bank in Botogá a draft on a U.S. bank for $3 million, pay for this draft by writing a check for 150 million pesos drawn on the Botogá bank, and send the draft to the U.S. exporter.
(1) The U.S. exporter would then deposit the draft in its account in the New Orleans bank and its demand deposit account there would increase by $_____ million.
(2) The New Orleans bank collects the amount of the draft from the U.S. bank on which it is drawn through the Federal Reserve Banks.

   (a) Its account at the Fed increases by $_____ million; and
   (b) the account of the bank on which the draft was drawn decreases by $_____ million.

c. Regardless of the way used by the Colombian importer to pay for the wheat,
(1) the export of the wheat created a (demand for, supply of) _____ dollars and a _____ pesos.
(2) The number of dollars owned by the U.S. exporter has (increased, decreased) _____ and the number of pesos owned by the Colombian importer has _____.

2. The following table contains hypothetical international balance of payments data for the United States. All figures are in billions.

Current account	
(1) U.S. merchandise exports	$+150
(2) U.S. merchandise imports	−200
(3) Balance of trade	_____
(4) U.S. exports of services	+75
(5) U.S. imports of services	−60
(6) Balance on goods and services	_____
(7) Net investment income	+12
(8) Net transfers	−7
(9) Balance on current account	_____
Capital account	
(10) Capital inflows to the U.S.	+80
(11) Capital outflows from the U.S.	−55
(12) Balance on capital account	_____
(13) Current and capital account balance	_____
(14) Official reserves	_____
	$ 0

a. Compute with the appropriate sign (+ or −) and enter in the table the six missing items.
b. The United States had a payments (deficit, surplus) _____ of $_____.

3. The following table shows the supply and demand schedules for the British pound.

Quantity of pounds supplied	Price	Quantity of pounds demanded
400	$5.00	100
360	4.50	200
300	4.00	300
286	3.50	400
267	3.00	500
240	2.50	620
200	2.00	788

a. If the exchange rates are flexible
(1) what will be the rate of exchange for the pound?

$_____

(2) what will be the rate of exchange for the dollar?

£_____

(3) how many pounds will be purchased in the market?

_____

(4) how many dollars will be purchased in the market?

_____

b. If the U.S. government wished to fix or peg the price of the pound at $5.00, it would have to (buy, sell)

_____ (how many) _____ pounds

for $_____.

c. And if the British government wishes to fix the price of the dollar at £ 2/5, it would have to (buy, sell)

_____ (how many) _____ pounds

for $_____.

■ **SHORT ANSWER AND ESSAY QUESTIONS**

1. What is foreign exchange and the foreign exchange rate? Who are the demanders and suppliers of a particular foreign exchange, say, the French franc? Why is a buyer (demander) in the foreign exchange markets always a seller (supplier) also?

2. What is meant when it is said that "A nation's exports pay for its imports"? Do nations pay for all their imports with exports?

3. What is an international balance of payments? What are the principal sections in a nation's international balance of payments, and what are the principal "balances" to be found in it?

4. How can a nation finance a current account deficit, and what can it do with a current account surplus?

5. How does a nation finance a balance of payments deficit, and what does it do with a balance of payments surplus?

6. What types of events cause the exchange rate for a foreign currency to appreciate or to depreciate? How will each event affect the exchange rate for a foreign currency and for a nation's own currency?

7. How can freely floating foreign exchange rates eliminate balance of payments deficits and surpluses? What are the problems associated with this method of correcting payments imbalances?

8. How may a nation use its international monetary reserves to fix or peg foreign exchange rates? Be precise. How does a nation obtain or acquire these monetary reserves?

9. What kinds of trade controls may nations with payments deficits use to eliminate their deficits?

10. How can foreign exchange controls be used to restore international equilibrium? Why do such exchange controls necessarily involve the rationing of foreign exchange? What effect do these controls have on prices, output, and employment in nations that use them?

11. If foreign exchange rates are fixed, what kind of domestic macroeconomic adjustments are required to eliminate a payments deficit? To eliminate a payments surplus?

12. When were the major nations on the gold standard? How did the international gold standard correct payments imbalances?

13. What were the disadvantages of the gold standard for eliminating payments deficits and surpluses?

14. What did nations use as international monetary reserves under the Bretton Woods system? Why was the dollar used by nations as an international money, and how could they acquire additional dollars?

15. Explain the dilemma created by the need for expanding international monetary reserves and for maintaining the status of the dollar.

16. Why and how did the United States shatter the Bretton Woods system in 1971?

17. Explain what is meant by a managed floating system of foreign exchange rates. When are exchange rates managed and when are they allowed to float?

18. Explain the arguments of the proponents and the critics of the managed floating system.

19. What were the causes of the trade deficits of the United States during the 1990s?

20. What were the effects of the trade deficits of the 1990s on the U.S. economy?

ANSWERS

Chapter 21 Exchange Rates, the Balance of Payments, and Trade Deficits

FILL-IN QUESTIONS

1. dollars, franc, $.20, 5 francs
2. demand for, supply of, demand for, supply of
3. domestic, foreign, credit, debit, −, +
4. less, less, plus, minus
5. in that nation, other nations, abroad, that nation, greater

6. selling, borrowing, buy, lend
7. foreign currencies, decrease, increase, zero
8. negative, decrease, positive, increase
9. depreciate, appreciate, decrease, increase, decrease
10. *a.* D; *b.* A; *c.* D; *d.* D; *e.* D
11. diminish, worsened, destabilize
12. sell, buy
13. taxing, subsidizing, import, export, government
14. contractionary, recession
15. stable, out of, decreased, increased, decreased, decreased
16. fixed, gold, buying, selling, borrowing from, devalue, stable, flexible
17. eliminated, continued, increase, decrease, decrease, suspended
18. floating, free to, intervene in
19. was, turbulence, volatility, nonsystem
20. deficits, imports, exports, stronger, weaker, increase, large, falling, increased, rise

TRUE-FALSE QUESTIONS

1. T, pp. 429-431	10. T, p. 439	19. T, p. 443
2. T, p. 431	11. F, pp. 439-440	20. F, pp. 444-445
3. F, pp. 431-432	12. T, p. 440	21. T, p. 445
4. T, pp. 432-434	13. F, p. 440	22. F, pp. 446-447
5. T, p. 434	14. F, p. 441	23. F, p. 446
6. T, p. 434	15. T, p. 441	24. T, p. 446
7. F, p. 434	16. T, p. 443	25. T, p. 447
8. T, pp. 434-435	17. T, p. 443	
9. T, pp. 435-438	18. T, p. 443	

MULTIPLE-CHOICE QUESTIONS

1. c, pp. 429-430	10. d, pp. 438-439	19. a, p. 444
2. b, pp. 430-431	11. c, pp. 439-441	20. a, pp. 444-445
3. a, p. 432	12. a, p. 440	21. a, pp. 444-445
4. c, pp. 432-433	13. c, p. 441	22. c, pp. 446-447
5. c, p. 439	14. b, pp. 441-442	23. d, pp. 446-447
6. b, pp. 437-438	15. d, pp. 441-442	24. a, pp. 446-447
7. c, p. 434	16. d, pp. 442-443	25. b, p. 447
8. b, pp. 437-438	17. c, p. 443	
9. b, pp. 436-437	18. a, p. 443	

PROBLEMS

1. *a.* (1) 3, (2) (a) 3, dollars, (b) 150, pesos; *b.* (1) 3, (2) (a) 3, (b) 3; *c.* (1) demand for, supply of, (2) increased, decreased
2. *a.* −50, −35, −30, +25, −5, +5; *b.* deficit, 5
3. *a.* (1) 4.00, (2) 1/4, (3) 300, (4) 1,200; *b.* buy, 300, 1,500; *c.* sell, 380, 950

SHORT ANSWER AND ESSAY QUESTIONS

1. pp. 429-431	8. pp. 439-440	15. p. 443
2. p. 431	9. p. 440	16. pp. 443-445
3. pp. 431-434	10. p. 440	17. pp. 444-445
4. p. 434	11. p. 440	18. p. 445
5. p. 434	12. pp. 441-442	19. pp. 446-447
6. pp. 435-437	13. p. 442	20. p. 447
7. pp. 435-439	14. pp. 442-443	

CHAPTER 22

The Economics of the Developing Countries

This chapter looks at the critical problem of raising the *standard of living* in **developing countries** (DVCs) of the world. About three-fourths of the world's population live in these 107 nations. The development problems in these nations are extensive: low literacy rates, low levels of industrialization, high dependence on agriculture, rapid rates of population growth, and widespread poverty. In addition, the income gap between these developing nations and the 26 industrially advanced nations of the world is growing.

Economic growth in both developing and **industrially advanced countries** (IACs) requires that the economic resources base be expanded and these resources be used efficiently. As you will discover in one of the major sections of the chapter, developing nations trying to apply these principles face *obstacles* quite different from those that limit growth in the United States and other industrially advanced nations. Developing nations have many problems with natural, human, and capital resources and with technology, all of which combine to hinder economic growth. In addition, certain social, cultural, and institutional factors create a poor environment for economic development.

These obstacles do not mean that it is impossible to increase the living standards of these DVCs. What they do indicate is that to encourage growth, the DVCs must do things that do not need to be done in the United States or other industrially advanced nations. Population pressures need to be managed, and labor resources have to be better used. Steps must be taken to encourage capital investment. Governments must take an active role in promoting economic growth and limiting the public sector problems for economic development. Dramatic changes in social practices and institutions are required. If these and other actions are not taken, it may not be possible to reduce the major obstacles to growth and break the vicious circle of poverty in the DVCs.

No matter how successful the DVCs are in overcoming these obstacles, they still will not be able to grow very rapidly without the help of industrially advanced countries. These countries can lower trade barriers that limit sales of products from developing countries, and they can provide foreign aid in the form of government grants and loans. This foreign aid is subject to criticism, and it is declining, as you will learn from the chapter. The banks, corporations, and other businesses in industrially advanced nations can provide private capital in the form of loans or direct foreign investment. These private capital flows are also subject to problems, as the debt crisis of the 1980s

illustrates. This crisis is now over, and changes have been made, but the conditions for another crisis also exist.

The final section of the chapter is a fitting ending to the discussion of economic problems in developing nations. It focuses on specific policies to promote economic growth in the DVCs and examines the issue from two sides. One side offers a set of policies from the perspective of developing countries, and the other side lists things industrially advanced countries can do to foster economic growth in developing nations.

■ CHECKLIST

When you have studied this chapter you should be able to

☐ Describe income disparity among nations.

☐ Compare industrially advanced countries (IACs) and developing countries (DVCs) in terms of economic growth and population.

☐ Discuss the human implications of poverty in DVCs.

☐ Identify two basic avenues for economic growth in IACs and DVCs.

☐ Describe natural resource problems in DVCs.

☐ Identify the three specific problems related to human resources that plague the DVCs.

☐ Explain the difficulties for economic growth that are created by population growth in DVCs.

☐ Compare the traditional and demographic transition view of population and economic growth in DVCs.

☐ Describe the conditions of unemployment and underemployment in DVCs.

☐ State reasons for low labor productivity in DVCs.

☐ Present three reasons for the emphasis on capital formation in the DVCs.

☐ Identify obstacles to domestic capital formation through saving.

☐ List obstacles to domestic capital formation through investment.

☐ Explain why transferring the technologies used in the industrially advanced countries to the DVCs may not be a realistic method of improving the technology of the latter nations.

☐ Identify three potential sociocultural factors that can inhibit economic growth.

☐ Describe the institutional obstacles to growth.

☐ Explain why poverty in the poor nations is a vicious circle.

☐ List five reasons why governments in the DVCs will have to play a crucial role if the vicious circle of poverty is to be broken.

☐ Describe the problems with the public sector in fostering economic development.

☐ Identify the three ways the industrially advanced countries may help the DVCs grow economically.

☐ Explain the importance of a reduction in international trade barriers to economic growth in DVCs.

☐ Describe the two sources of foreign aid for DVCs.

☐ Give three criticisms of foreign aid to DVCs.

☐ Explain why foreign aid to DVCs has declined.

☐ Describe what groups in IACs provide private capital to DVCs.

☐ Give four reasons for the debt crisis of the 1980s.

☐ Explain how the debt crisis was resolved in the 1990s.

☐ Evaluate the prospects for future debt problems in DVCs.

☐ Discuss nine DVC policies for promoting economic growth.

☐ Explain five actions that IACs can take to encourage growth in DVCs.

■ **CHAPTER OUTLINE**

1. There is considerable income inequality among countries. The richest 20% of the world's population receive about 83% of the world's income.

Countries can also be classified into two main groups. *Industrially advanced countries* (IACs) are characterized by well-developed market economies based on large stocks of capital goods, advanced technology for production, and well-educated workers. Among these 26 high-income nations are the United States, Canada, Japan, Australia, New Zealand, and most of the nations of western Europe. These countries averaged $24,930 per capita income in 1995.

Developing countries (DVCs) are poor, not highly industrialized, heavily dependent on agriculture, have high population growth, and have low rates of literacy. These countries comprise about three-fourths of the world's population. Of the 107 DVCs, 68 are middle-income countries with an average income per capita of $2,390; 49 low-income countries have an average income per capita of $430. This latter group is dominated by India, China, and most of the sub-Saharan nations of Africa.

a. There are disparities in the growth rates of nations, resulting in sizable income gaps. Some DVC nations have been able to improve their economic conditions over time and become IACs. Other DVCs are now showing high rates of economic growth, but still other DVCs have experienced a decline in economic growth and standard of living. If growth rates were the same for high- and low-income nations, the gap in per capita income would widen because the income base is higher in high-income nations.

b. The human implications of extreme poverty are important. Compared with IACs, DVCs have not only lower per capita incomes but also lower life expectancies, higher infant mortality, lower literacy rates, more

of the labor force in agriculture, and fewer nonhuman sources of energy.

2. Economic growth requires that DVCs use their existing resources more efficiently and that they expand their available supplies of resources. The physical, human, and socioeconomic conditions in these nations are the reasons why DVCs experience different rates of economic growth.

a. Many DVCs possess inadequate *natural resources*. This limited resource base is an obstacle to growth. Also, the agricultural products which DVCs typically export are subject to significant price variation on the world market, creating variations in national income.

b. The circumstances for *human resources* in DVCs is difficult for three reasons.

(1) DVCs tend to be overpopulated and have high rates of population growth. These growing populations reduce the DVCs' capacity to save, invest, and increase productivity. They also overuse land and natural resources, and the migration of rural workers to cities creates urban problems.

(2) DVCs often experience both unemployment and underemployment, which wastes labor resources.

(3) DVCs have low levels of labor productivity because of insufficient physical capital and lack of investment in human capital.

c. DVCs have an inadequate amount of **capital goods,** and so find it difficult to accumulate capital. Domestic capital formation occurs through saving and investing. The potential for saving is low in many DVCs because the nations are too poor to save. There is also capital flight of saving from DVCs to more stable IACs. The investment obstacles include a lack of investors and entrepreneurs and a lack of incentives to invest in DVC economies. The infrastructure is poor in many DVCs.

d. *Technological advance* is slow in DVCs. Although these nations might adopt the technologies of industrial nations, these technologies are not always appropriate for the resource endowments of the DVCs, so they must learn to develop and use their own technologies.

e. It is difficult for DVCs to alter the *social, cultural,* and *institutional* factors to create a good environment for achieving economic growth.

3. In summary, DVCs save little and therefore invest little in real and human capital because they are poor, and because they do not invest, their outputs per capita remain low and they remain poor. Even if the vicious circle were to be broken, a rapid increase in population would leave the standard of living unchanged.

4. There are differing views about the role that government plays in fostering economic growth in DVCs.

a. The positive view holds that in the initial stages of economic development, government action is needed to help overcome such obstacles as the lack of law and order, entrepreneurship, and infrastructure. Government policies may also assist capital formation and help resolve social and institutional problems.

b. Problems and disadvantages with government involvement in promoting growth include bureaucratic impediments, corruption, maladministration, and the importance of political objectives over economic goals. Central planning does not work because it restricts competition and individual incentives, which are important ingredients in the growth process.

5. Industrially advanced nations of the world can help the DVCs develop in a number of ways.

a. They can lower the trade barriers which prevent the DVCs from selling their products in the developed countries.

b. Loans and grants from governments and international organizations such as the World Bank also enable the DVCs to accumulate capital. This foreign aid has been criticized because it increases dependency, bureaucracy, and corruption. For these reasons, and because of the end of the cold war, foreign aid to DVCs is declining.

c. DVCs can also receive flows of private capital from IACs. These flows come from banks, corporations, and financial investment companies.

(1) In the 1980s, DVCs experienced a debt crisis in which they found they could not repay their loans. The factors contributing to this crisis were high prices for imported oil, a tight monetary policy in the United States, an appreciating dollar, and unproductive investments by DVCs. The flow of private lending and investments in DVCs virtually ceased during this period.

(2) In the 1990s, the flow of private lending and investing increased as DVC debts were restructured and some DVC economies were reformed to control budget deficits and inflation. More of the flows are now in the form of direct foreign investment in DVCs rather than loans to their governments; however, the flow of most private capital goes to selective nations, and it is still not certain that the debt crisis is over in some DVCs.

6. There are several policies that DVCs and IACs might undertake to foster economic development in DVCs. Two perspectives are offered.

a. DVC policies for promoting growth include establishing the rule of law, opening economies to international trade, controlling population growth, encouraging direct foreign investment, building human capital, making peace with neighbors, establishing independent central banks, making realistic exchange-rate policies, and privatizing state industries.

b. IAC policies for encouraging economic growth in DVCs are directing foreign aid to the poorest of the DVCs, reducing tariffs and import quotas, providing debt relief to DVCs, allowing more low-skilled immigration and discouraging brain drains, and limiting arm sales to DVCs.

■ **HINTS AND TIPS**

1. This chapter offers a comprehensive look at the various factors affecting growth and economic development. No one factor explains why some nations prosper and others remain poor. The chapter should give you insights into how natural, human, and capital resources together with government policies may influence a nation's economic development.

2. Several economic and demographic statistics for comparing rich and poor nations appear in the chapter's tables. You need not memorize the numbers, but you should try to get a sense of the magnitude of the differences between IACs and DVCs on several key indicators. To do this, ask yourself questions calling for relative comparisons. For example, how many times larger is per capita income in IACs than in low-income DVCs? Answer: 58 times greater ($24,930/$430 = 58).

3. The chapter ends with policy suggestions for increasing economic growth in DVCs. Be sure to look at these policies from the perspective of both DVCs and IACs. Identify those that you think are most important, and explain your reasoning.

■ **IMPORTANT TERMS**

industrially advanced countries (IACs)	**capital-saving technology**
	capital-using technology
developing countries (DVCs)	**the will to develop**
demographic transition view	**capricious universe view**
	land reform
underemployment	**vicious circle of poverty**
brain drain	**World Bank**
capital flight	**direct foreign investment**
infrastructure	

SELF-TEST

■ **FILL-IN QUESTIONS**

1. There is considerable income inequality among nations. The richest 20% of the world's population receive about (43, 83) _____% of world income, while the poorest 20% of the world's population receive about (1, 10) _____% of world income.

2. High-income nations can be classified as (industrially advanced, developing) _____ countries, or (IACs, DVCs) _____, and the middle- or low-income nations as _____ countries, or (DVCs, IACs) _____. In 1995, the average income per capita in high-income nations was ($24,930, $55,460) _____, in middle-income nations it was ($2,390, $9,650) _____, and in low-income nations it was ($430, $5,170) _____.

3. IACs have a (higher, lower) _____ starting base for per capita income than DVCs, so the same percentage growth rate for both IACs and DVCs means a(n) (increase, decrease) _____ in the absolute income gap.

4. Low per capita income in DVCs means that there is (lower, higher) _____ life expectancies, _____ adult literacy, (lower, higher) _____ daily calorie supply, _____ energy consumption, and (lower, higher) _____ infant mortality.

5. The process for economic growth is the same for IACs and DVCs. It involves (less, more) _____ efficient use of existing resources and obtaining _____ productive resources.

6. The distribution of natural resources among DVCs is (even, uneven) _____; many DVCs lack vital natural resources. Although oil resources have been used for economic growth in (OPEC, DVCs) _____, IACS own or control much of the natural resources in _____. Also, exports of products from DVCs are subject to (small, large) _____ price fluctuations in the world market, and that tends to make DVC incomes (more, less) _____ stable.

7. In terms of human resources,

a. many DVCs are (under, over) _____ populated and have (higher, lower) _____ population growth rates than IACs. Rapid population growth can cause per capita income to (increase, decrease) _____.

b. In DVCs, many people are unable to find jobs, so there is (underemployment, unemployment) _____, and many people are employed for fewer hours than they desire or work at odd jobs, so there is _____.

c. In DVCs, labor productivity is very (high, low) _____, partly because these countries have not been able to invest in (stocks and bonds, human capital) _____; when the best-trained workers leave DVCs to work in IACs, there is a (demographic transition, brain drain) _____ that contributes to the decline in skill level and productivity.

8. Capital accumulation is critical to the development of DVCs. If there were more capital goods, this would improve (natural resources, labor productivity) _____ and help boost per capita output. An increase in capital goods is necessary because the (demand for, supply of) _____ arable land is limited. The process

of capital formation is cumulative, investment increases the (output, natural resources) _____ of the economy, and this in turn makes it possible for the economy to save more and invest more in capital goods.

9. The formation of domestic capital requires that a nation save and invest.

a. Saving is difficult in DVCs because of a (high, low) _____ potential for saving, and investment is difficult because of (many, few) _____ investors or entrepreneurs, and (strong, weak) _____ incentives to invest. The is also the problem of private savings being transferred to IACs; this transfer is called (brain drain, capital flight) _____.

b. Many DVCs do not have the infrastructure or (private, public) _____ capital goods that are necessary for productive _____ investment by businesses.

c. Nonfinancial (or in-kind) investment involves the transfer of surplus labor from (agriculture, industry) _____ to the improvement of agricultural facilities or the infrastructure.

10. The technologies used in the advanced industrial countries might be borrowed by and used in the DVCs, but

a. the technologies used in the advanced countries are based on a labor force that is (skilled, unskilled) _____, labor that is relatively (abundant, scarce) _____, and capital that is relatively _____, and their technologies tend to be (labor, capital) _____-using, while

b. the technologies required in developing countries must be based on a labor force that is (skilled, unskilled) _____, labor that is relatively (abundant, scarce) _____, and capital that is relatively _____, and their technologies tend to be (labor, capital) _____-using.

c. If technological advances make it possible to replace a worn-out plow, costing $10 when new, with a new $5 plow, the technological advance is capital (saving, using) _____.

11. Other obstacles to economic growth in DVCs include those dealing with problems of national unity, religion, and customs, or (institutional, sociocultural) _____ problems, and those dealing with such issues as political corruption, poor school systems, and land reform, or _____ problems.

12. In most DVCs, there is a vicious circle of poverty. Saving is low because the income per capita is (high, low) _____, and because saving is low, investment in real and human capital is _____. For this reason the productivity of labor and output (income) per capita remain (high, low) _____.

13. List five ways that government can serve a positive role in fostering economic growth in DVCs, especially during the early phases of growth:

a. _____

b. _____

c. _____

d. _____

e. _____

14. Government involvement in the economy of DVCs creates public sector problems because government bureaucracy can (foster, impede) _____ social and economic change, government planners can give too much emphasis to (political, economic) _____ objectives, and there can be (good, poor) _____ administration and corruption.

15. Three major ways that IACs can assist in the economic development in DVCs is by (increasing, decreasing) _____ international trade barriers, _____ foreign aid, and _____ the flow of private capital investment.

16. Direct foreign aid for DVCs generally comes from individual nations in the form of (private, public) _____ loans, grants, and programs. It can also come from the (Bank of America, World Bank), _____ which is supported by (12, 180) _____ member nations. This organization is a (first, last) _____ resort lending agency for DVCs and provides (military, technical) _____ assistance for DVCs.

17. Foreign aid has been criticized in recent years because it may (increase, decrease) _____ dependency in a nation instead of creating self-sustained growth, may _____ government bureaucracy and control over a nation's economy, and may _____ the misuse of funds or corruption. These criticisms and the end of the cold war have led to a(n) _____ in the amount of foreign aid to DVCs.

18. The causes of the DVC debt problem were due to world events during the 1970s and early 1980s. Oil prices (rose, fell) _____ during the 1970s, and thus the borrowing needs of DVCs _____ to pay for imported oil. In the early 1980s, the United States had a(n) (tight, easy) _____ monetary policy that

increased interest rates and the cost to DVCs of servicing debts. The international value of the dollar (appreciated, depreciated) _____, which meant that DVCs had to pay (more, less) _____ for imports and receive _____ in return for exports. Some DVCs borrowed funds and used them for (consumption, investment) _____ that was not productive.

19. Actions taken to resolve the debt crisis have (raised, lowered) _____ foreign private investment in DVCs in the 1990s. The reason for this change is that many DVCs have reformed their economies and adopted policies that (limit, encourage) _____ economic growth and _____ direct foreign investment. Nevertheless, the flow of private capital to DVCs is (selective, widespread) _____, and it is (correct, premature) _____ to say that the crisis is resolved.

20. DVCs can adopt policies to encourage economic growth. They can (open, close) _____ economies to international trade, (encourage, discourage) _____ direct foreign investment and the development of human capital, and (expand, control) _____ population growth. IACs can also adopt policies to help DVCs. They can (raise, lower) _____ trade barriers, (encourage, discourage) _____ immigration of the brightest and best-educated, and direct foreign aid to the (middle-income, low-income) _____ DVCs.

■ **TRUE-FALSE QUESTIONS**

Circle the T if the statement is true, the F if it is false.

1. The richest 20% of the world's population receive about 50% of the world's income while the poorest 20% receive only about 20% of the world's income.   **T   F**

2. Developing countries generally have high unemployment, low literacy rates, rapid population growth, and a labor force committed to agricultural production.   **T   F**

3. The United States has about 5% of the world's population and produces about one-fourth of the world's output.   **T   F**

4. The absolute income gap between DVCs and industrially advanced countries has decreased over the past 30 years.   **T   F**

5. Economic growth in both IACs and DVCs requires using economic resources more efficiently and increasing the supplies of some of these resources.   **T   F**

6. It is impossible to achieve a high standard of living with a small supply of natural resources. **T F**

7. DVCs have low population densities and low population growth relative to IACs. **T F**

8. The demographic transition view of population growth is that rising incomes must first be achieved and only then will slower population growth follow. **T F**

9. A major factor contributing to the high unemployment rates in urban areas of DVCs is the fact that the migration from rural areas to cities has greatly exceeded the growth of urban job opportunities. **T F**

10. Saving in DVCs is a smaller percentage of domestic output than in IACs, and this is the chief reason total saving in DVCs is small. **T F**

11. Before private investment can be increased in DVCs, it is necessary to reduce the amount of investment in infrastructure. **T F**

12. Technological advances in DVCs will be made rapidly because the advances do not require pushing forward the frontiers of technological knowledge, and the technologies used in IACs can be easily transferred to all DVCs.
T F

13. When technological advances are capital saving, it is possible for an economy to increase its productivity without any *net* investment in capital goods. **T F**

14. A critical, but intangible, ingredient in economic development is the "will to develop." **T F**

15. The capricious universe view is that there is a strong correlation between individual effort and results. **T F**

16. Land reform is one of the institutional obstacles to economic growth in many developing countries. **T F**

17. The situation in which poor nations stay poor because they are poor is a description of the vicious circle of poverty. **T F**

18. The creation of an adequate infrastructure in a nation is primarily the responsibility of the private sector. **T F**

19. Governments always play a positive role in fostering the economic growth of DVCs. **T F**

20. One effective way that IACs can help DVCs is to raise trade barriers so that DVCs become more self-sufficient.
T F

21. The World Bank is the organization to which DVCs turn for the majority of foreign aid, loans, and grants. **T F**

22. Two reasons why foreign aid is viewed as harmful are that it tends to promote dependency and reduce market activity. **T F**

23. One reason for the debt crisis of the 1980s is that loans to DVCs frequently went to projects that were not productive investments. **T F**

24. In recent years, a smaller proportion of private capital flows to DVCs has been direct foreign investment rather than loans to DVC governments. **T F**

25. One policy suggested for promoting economic growth in DVCs is the establishment of independent central banks (where they do not already exist) to keep inflation in check and control the money supply. **T F**

■ **MULTIPLE-CHOICE QUESTIONS**

Circle the letter that corresponds to the best answer.

1. Data on per capita income from the nations of the world indicate that there is considerable
 (a) income equality
 (b) income inequality
 (c) stability in the income growth
 (d) deterioration in incomes for most developing nations

2. Which nation would be considered a developing nation?
 (a) India
 (b) Italy
 (c) Singapore
 (d) New Zealand

3. If the per capita income is $600 a year in a DVC and $12,000 in an IAC, then a 2% growth rate in each nation will increase the absolute income gap by
 (a) $120
 (b) $228
 (c) $240
 (d) $252

4. A DVC would probably exhibit a high level of
 (a) literacy
 (b) life expectancy
 (c) infant mortality
 (d) per capita energy consumption

5. The essential paths for economic growth in any nation are expanding the
 (a) size of the population and improving agriculture
 (b) role of government and providing jobs for the unemployed
 (c) supplies of resources and using existing resources more efficiently
 (d) amount of tax subsidies to business and tax credits for business investment

6. Based on the rule of 70, if the United States has an annual rate of population increase of 1% and a DVC has one of 2%, how many years will it take for the population to double in each nation?
 (a) 140 years for the United States and 70 years for the DVC
 (b) 35 years for the United States and 70 years for the DVC
 (c) 70 years for the United States and 35 years for the DVC
 (d) 70 years for the United States and 140 years for the DVC

7. Assume the total real output of a developing country increases from $100 billion to $115.5 billion while its population expands from 200 to 210 million people. Real per capital income has increased by
 (a) $50

(b) $100
(c) $150
(d) $200

8. An increase in the total output of consumer goods in a DVC may not increase the average standard of living because it may increase
(a) capital flight
(b) population growth
(c) disguised unemployment
(d) the quality of the labor force

9. Which best describes unemployment found in DVCs?
(a) the cyclical fluctuations in the nation's economy
(b) the migration of agricultural workers from rural areas to seek jobs in urban areas
(c) workers being laid off by large domestic or multinational corporations during periods of economic instability
(d) the education and training of workers in the wrong types of jobs and for which there is little demand

10. Which is an obstacle to economic growth in DVCs?
(a) the low demand for natural resources
(b) the low supply of capital goods
(c) the decline in demographic transition
(d) a fall in population growth

11. Which is a reason for placing special emphasis on capital accumulation in DVCs?
(a) the flexible supply of arable land in DVCs
(b) the high productivity of workers in DVCs
(c) the high marginal benefits of capital goods
(d) the greater opportunities for capital flight

12. Which is a factor limiting saving in DVCs?
(a) The output of the economy is too low to permit a large volume of saving.
(b) Those who do save make their savings available only to their families.
(c) Governments control the banking system and set low interest rates.
(d) There is an equal distribution of income in most nations.

13. When citizens of developing countries transfer savings to or invest savings in industrially advanced countries, this is referred to as
(a) brain drain
(b) capital flight
(c) savings potential
(d) in-kind investment

14. Which is a major obstacle to capital formation in DVCs?
(a) lack of oil resources
(b) lack of entrepreneurs
(c) lack of government price supports for products
(d) an excess of opportunities for financial investments

15. If it is cheaper to use a new fertilizer that is better adapted to a nation's topography, this is an example of
(a) a capital-using technology
(b) a capital-saving technology
(c) capital consumption
(d) private capital flows

16. Which is an example of infrastructure?
(a) a farm
(b) a steel plant
(c) an electric power plant
(d) a deposit in a financial institution

17. Which seems to be the most acute *institutional* problem that needs to be resolved by many DVCs?
(a) development of strong labor unions
(b) an increase in natural resources
(c) the adoption of birth control
(d) land reform

18. Which is a major positive role for government in the early stage of economic development?
(a) providing an adequate infrastructure
(b) conducting central economic planning
(c) improving the efficiency of tax collection
(d) creating marketing boards for export products

19. In recent years, many DVCs have come to realize that
(a) there are few disadvantages from government involvement in economic development
(b) competition and economic incentives for individuals are necessary for economic growth
(c) the World Bank is an institutional barrier to economic growth
(d) private capital is not essential for economic growth

20. Industrially advanced countries can best help DVCs by
(a) letting them raise tariffs and quotas to protect domestic markets
(b) reducing foreign grant aid but increasing loan aid
(c) increasing the flows of private capital
(d) increasing control over their capital markets

21. The major objective of the World Bank is to
(a) maximize its profits for its worldwide shareholders
(b) assist developing countries in achieving economic growth
(c) provide financial backing for the operation of the United Nations
(d) maintain stable exchange rates in the currencies of developing countries

22. A major criticism of foreign aid to developing nations is that it
(a) provides incentives for capital flight
(b) is capital using rather than capital saving
(c) encourages growth in government bureaucracy
(d) gives too much power and control to the World Bank

23. An event that occurred in the early 1980s that contributed to the debt crisis in DVCs was a
(a) sharp decline in the price of oil charged by OPEC
(b) depreciation in the international value of the dollar
(c) tight monetary policy in the United States
(d) fall in interest rates in Japan

24. A suggested policy for DVCs to implement that promotes economic growth is
(a) reducing the control of monetary policy by central banks

(b) obtaining more low-interest loans from the World Bank
(c) encouraging more direct foreign investment
(d) expanding state industries

25. Which is a suggested policy for industrially advanced countries to adopt to foster economic growth in DVCs?
(a) increased appreciation of currencies in DVCs
(b) increased debt relief in DVCs
(c) elimination of the International Monetary Fund
(d) elimination of the OPEC oil cartel

■ **PROBLEMS**

1. Suppose that the real per capita income in the average industrially advanced country is $8,000 per year and in the average DVC $500 per year.
a. The gap between their standards of living is

$_____ per year.

b. If GDP per capita were to grow at a rate of 5% during a year in both the industrially advanced and the DVC,
(1) the standard of living in the IACs would rise to

$_____ in a year;
(2) the standard of living in the DVCs would rise to

$_____ in a year; and
(3) the gap between their standards of living would

(narrow, widen) _____ to $_____
in a year.

2. While economic conditions are not identical in all DVCs, certain conditions are common to or typical of most of them. In the space after each of the following characteristics, indicate briefly the nature of this characteristic in most DVCs.

a. Standard of living (per capita income): _____

b. Average life expectancy: _____

c. Extent of unemployment: _____

d. Literacy: _____

e. Technology: _____
f. Percentage of the population engaged in agriculture: _____

g. Size of the population relative to the land and capital available: _____

h. The birthrates and death rates: _____

i. Quality of the labor force: _____
j. Amount of capital equipment relative to the labor force: _____

k. Level of saving: _____

l. Incentive to invest: _____

m. Amount of infrastructure: _____

n. Extent of industrialization: _____

o. Size and quality of the entrepreneurial class and the supervisory class: _____
p. Per capita public expenditures for education and per capita energy consumption: _____

q. Per capita consumption of food: _____

r. Disease and malnutrition: _____

3. Suppose it takes a minimum of 5 units of food to keep a person alive for a year, the population can double itself every 10 years, and the food supply can increase every 10 years by an amount equal to what it was in the beginning (year 0).
a. Assume that both the population and the food supply grow at these rates. Complete the following table by computing the size of the population and the food supply in years 10 through 60.

Year	Food supply	Population
0	200	20
10	_____	_____
20	_____	_____
30	_____	_____
40	_____	_____
50	_____	_____
60	_____	_____

b. What happens to the relationship between the food supply and the population in the 30th year?_____
_____
_____

c. What would actually prevent the population from growing at this rate following the 30th year?_____
_____
_____

d. Assuming that the actual population growth in the years following the 30th does not outrun the food supply, what would be the size of the population in

(1) Year 40:_____
(2) Year 50:_____
(3) Year 60:_____
e. Explain why the standard of living failed to increase in the years following the 30th even though the food supply increased by 75% between years 30 and 60.

_____

■ **SHORT ANSWER AND ESSAY QUESTIONS**

1. What is the degree of income inequality among nations of the world?

2. How do the overall level of economic growth per capita and the rates of economic growth compare among rich nations and poor countries? Why does the income gap widen?

3. What are the human implications of poverty found in DVCs? (Use the socioeconomic indicators in Table 39-3 of the text to contrast the quality of life in IACs and DVCs).

4. Describe the basic paths of economic growth. Do these avenues differ for IACs and DVCs?

5. How would you describe the natural resource situation for DVCs? In what ways do price fluctuations affect DVC exports? Is a weak natural resource base an obstacle to economic growth?

6. Describe the implications of the high rate of growth in population and its effects on the standard of living. Can the standard of living be raised merely by increasing the output of consumer goods in DVCs? What is the meaning of the cliché "the rich get richer and the poor get children," and how does it apply to DVCs?

7. Compare and contrast the traditional view of population and economic growth with the demographic transition view.

8. What is the distinction between unemployment and underemployment? How do these concepts apply to DVCs?

9. What are the reasons for the low level of labor productivity in DVCs?

10. How does the brain drain affect DVCs?

11. What are the reasons for placing special emphasis on capital accumulation as a means of promoting economic growth in DVCs?

12. Why is domestic capital accumulation difficult in DVCs? Answer in terms of both the saving side and the investment side of capital accumulation. Is there capital flight from DVCs?

13. In addition to the obstacles which limit domestic investment, what other obstacles tend to limit the flow of foreign capital into DVCs? What role does infrastructure play in capital formation?

14. How might the DVCs improve their technology without engaging in slow and expensive research? Why might this be an inappropriate method of improving the technology used in the DVCs?

15. What is meant by the "will to develop"? How is it related to social and institutional change in DVCs?

16. Explain the vicious circle of poverty in the DVCs. How does population growth make an escape from this vicious circle difficult?

17. Why is the role of government expected to be a positive one in the early phases of development in DVCs? What have been the problems with the involvement of government in economic development?

18. What are three ways that IACs help DVCs?

19. How is it possible for the United States to assist DVCs without spending a penny on foreign aid? Is this type of aid sufficient to ensure rapid and substantial development in DVCs?

20. Discuss the World Bank in terms of its purposes, characteristics, sources of funds, promotion of private capital flows, and success. What are its affiliates and their purposes?

21. Discuss three criticisms of foreign aid to DVCs.

22. Describe the dimension and basic causes of the DVC debt crisis.

23. In the 1990s, what were the results and reforms from the debt crisis for DVCs?

24. Describe the variety of suggested policies that DVCs can adopt to promote economic growth.

25. Explain what IACs can do to assist DVCs in fostering economic growth.

ANSWERS

Chapter 22 The Economics of Developing Countries

FILL-IN QUESTIONS

1. 83, 1
2. industrially advanced, IACs, developing, DVCs, $24,930; $2,390; $430
3. higher, increase
4. lower, lower, lower, lower, higher
5. more, more
6. uneven, OPEC, DVCs, large, less
7. *a.* over, higher, decrease; *b.* unemployment, underemployment; *c.* low, human capital, brain drain
8. *a.* labor productivity, supply of, output
9. *a.* low, few, weak, capital flight; *b.* public, private; *c.* agriculture
10. *a.* skilled, scarce, abundant, capital; *b.* unskilled, abundant, scarce, labor; *c.* saving
11. sociocultural, institutional
12. low, low, low
13. *a.* establishing effective law and order; *b.* encouraging entrepreneurship; *c.* improving the infrastructure; *d.* promoting saving and investment; *e.* dealing with the social-institutional obstacles (any order for *a–e*)
14. impede, political, poor
15. decreasing, increasing, increasing
16. public, World Bank, 180, last, technical
17. increase, increase, increase, decrease
18. rose, rose, tight, appreciated, more less, investment
19. raised, encourage, encourage, selective, premature
20. open, encourage, control, lower, discourage, low-income

TRUE-FALSE QUESTIONS

1. F, pp. 452-453	**10.** F, pp. 459-460	**19.** F, p. 464
2. T, pp. 452-453	**11.** F, p. 460	**20.** F, p. 465
3. T, p. 453	**12.** F, p. 461	**21.** F, pp. 465-466
4. F, p. 453	**13.** T, p. 461	**22.** T, p. 466
5. T, p. 455	**14.** T, p. 461	**23.** T, p. 467
6. F, pp. 455-456	**15.** F, p. 462	**24.** F, p. 468
7. F, p. 458	**16.** T, p. 462	**25.** T, pp. 468-469
8. T, p. 458	**17.** T, pp. 462-463	
9. T, p. 458	**18.** F, p. 464	

MULTIPLE-CHOICE QUESTIONS

1. b, pp. 452-453	**10.** b, p. 459	**19.** b, p. 465
2. a, pp. 452-454	**11.** c, p. 459	**20.** c, p. 465
3. b, p. 453	**12.** a, pp. 459-460	**21.** b, p. 466
4. c, pp. 454-455	**13.** b, p. 460	**22.** c, p. 466
5. c, p. 455	**14.** b, p. 460	**23.** c, p. 467
6. c, pp. 456-458	**15.** b, p. 461	**24.** c, p. 469
7. a, p. 456	**16.** c, p. 460	**25.** b, pp. 469-470
8. b, p. 456	**17.** d, p. 462	
9. b, p. 458	**18.** a, pp. 460, 464	

PROBLEMS

1. *a.* 7,500; *b.* (1) 8,400, (2) 525, (3) widen, 7,875

2. *a.* low; *b.* short; *c.* widespread; *d.* low; *e.* primitive; *f.* large; *g.* large; *h.* high; *i.* poor; *j.* small; *k.* low; *l.* absent; *m.* small; *n.* small, *o.* small and poor; *p.* small; *q.* low; *r.* common

3. *a.* Food supply: 400, 600, 800, 1,000, 1,200, 1,400; Population: 40, 80, 160, 320, 640, 1,280; *b.* the food supply is just able to support the population; *c.* the inability of the food supply to support a population growing at this rate; *d.* (1) 200, (2) 240, (3) 280; *e.* the population increased as rapidly as the food supply

SHORT ANSWER AND ESSAY QUESTIONS

1. pp. 452-453	**10.** p. 459	**19.** p. 465
2. p. 453	**11.** p. 459	**20.** p. 466
3. pp. 453-455	**12.** pp. 459-460	**21.** pp. 466-467
4. p. 455	**13.** pp. 460-461	**22.** p. 467
5. pp. 455-456	**14.** p. 461	**23.** pp. 467-468
6. pp. 456-457	**15.** p. 461	**24.** pp. 468-469
7. p. 458	**16.** pp. 462-463	**25.** pp. 469-470
8. p. 458	**17.** pp. 463-465	
9. pp. 458-459	**18.** p. 465	

Transition Economies: Russia and China

In the years following the Russian Revolution of 1917, many people in the United States were convinced that the economic system of the Soviet Union was unworkable and that it would break down sooner or later—proof that Marx and Lenin were unrealistic dreamers—and that the reconversion of the Soviet economy to a market system would follow. Now, over 80 years after the revolution, the Russian economy is being transformed into a market economy and a democracy.

China is also undergoing a rapid transition from a centrally planned economy to a market-based economy, but its experience differs from that of Russia. The transition in China has been longer and more gradual. The economic outcomes have also been very positive, with strong economic growth, rising productivity, and a significantly increased standard of living; however, problems remain because the Communist party retains dictatorial political control and economic development is uneven throughout the country.

Chapter 23 provides insights into the profound turn of events in both Russia and China. The first two sections of the chapter explain the basic ideas behind *Marxian ideology,* which gave rise to these command economies. They also discuss two basic institutional features of the former Soviet Union and pre-reform China: These economies operated under a system of state ownership of property resources; central planning was used to set prices, restrict consumption, and direct investment to heavy industry and the military.

Although central planning served as a powerful form of economic decision making in the former Soviet Union and pre-reform China, it had two serious problems, as you will discover in the third section. The first problem was one of *coordination,* which resulted in production bottlenecks and managers and bureaucrats missing production targets. Central planning also created an *incentive problem* because it sent out incorrect and inadequate signals for directing the efficient allocation of an economy's resources and gave workers little reason to work hard. The lack of incentives killed entrepreneurship and stifled innovation and technological advance.

The slowing of economic growth in the Soviet economy in the 1970s and 1980s set the stage for the failure of communism and the *collapse* of its command economy. Certainly other factors contributed to the economy's deterioration, as you will discover in the fourth section of the chapter. Production was of poor quality, and there were inadequate or limited consumer goods to meet consumer demand. The economy was overly burdened by govern-

ment leaders' desire to support a large military. Agricultural inefficiencies were a drain on resources and restricted investment for other sectors of the economy.

The fifth section of the chapter explains the five elements of market reform in the Russian economy and its problems and prospects. The transition has led to the privatization of property resources, the promotion of competition, the decontrol of prices, and better connections to the international economy. The hyperinflation problem was solved by the establishment of a Russian central bank and the adoption of an anti-inflation monetary policy. Other problems continue to plague the economy. Real output, as well as living standards, fell significantly during the transition. Income inequality has grown, and government instability and social unrest give organized crime the opportunity to flourish. In spite of these problems, Russia is likely to succeed in becoming an advanced market economy, but much work remains to be done.

The market reform in China is the focus of the sixth section of the chapter. As already noted, China's reform efforts differed significantly from those of Russia because they started earlier and have been more gradual and experimental. Partial decontrol of land and prices in agriculture unleashed the rural economy and made it more market oriented. State-owned enterprises are being consolidated and forced to become more competitive and operate like corporations. The formation of private businesses has been encouraged. New foreign investment is encouraged to help capital formation and to gain access to advanced technology.

The results from Chinese economic reforms have been impressive, as described in the final section of the chapter. The economy has grown at a 9% annual rate since 1978. The standard of living has risen fourfold and at a much faster rate than population growth. Nevertheless, China's transition to a market economy continues to face significant problems. Property rights are ill-defined. The economy has experienced periods of high inflation and is not well-integrated into the world economy. Economic development across the nation is uneven, and the average income remains low by DVC standards.

The transformations of Russian and Chinese economies into market economies are among the most important economic events of recent decades. The sweeping changes in these economies from centrally planned economies to market economies should deepen your understanding of the principles of economics and how the market system works. These dramatic developments are a fitting topic to conclude your study of economics.

■ CHECKLIST

When you have studied this chapter you should be able to

☐ Outline the key elements of Marxian ideology.

☐ Identify two institutional characteristics of the former Soviet Union (prior to collapse) and China (prior to market reforms).

☐ Make seven generalizations about the central planning goals and techniques in the former Soviet Union and China.

☐ Compare how a market economy coordinates economic activity with how it works in a centrally planned economy.

☐ Explain how a market economy provides incentives and the problems with incentives in a centrally planned economy.

☐ Identify five factors that contributed to the collapse of the Soviet economy.

☐ List five factors that are important for the transition of Russia's economy to a market economy.

☐ Explain the effects of privatization in Russia.

☐ Use a supply and demand graph to discuss the difficulties that price reforms pose in the Russian transition.

☐ Describe the promotion of competition in Russia.

☐ Explain the importance of Russia joining the world economy.

☐ Describe the need for price-level stabilization in Russia.

☐ Explain two major problems the Russian economy has experienced during the transition.

☐ Evaluate the future prospects for Russia's transition to a market economy.

☐ Contrast China's path to market reforms with that of Russia.

☐ Describe agricultural and price reform in China.

☐ Discuss the reform of urban industries and the use of special economic zones in China.

☐ Describe how the Chinese government has developed supporting institutions and transformed state-owned enterprises.

☐ State the positive outcomes from the reform of the Chinese economy.

☐ Identify four significant problems in the Chinese transition to a market economy.

■ CHAPTER OUTLINE

1. The centrally planned economies of the former Soviet Union and pre-reform China were based on Marxian ideology. The government was viewed as a dictatorship of the proletariat (or working class) and the peasantry. Especially important was the Marxian concept of a *labor theory of value,* which held that only labor creates value in production and that profits are a surplus value expropriated from workers by capitalists who, because of the institution of private property, were able to control the means of production (capital goods). The purpose of communism was to overthrow capitalism and end this exploitation of workers (and peasants) by eliminating private property and creating a classless society.

2. The two major institutional features of the pre-collapse Soviet and pre-reform Chinese economies were *state-owned enterprises* of all property resources and *central economic planning.* The command economy based most economic decisions on bureaucrats' choices rather than relying on market forces to direct economic activity.

    a. The central planning functioned differently in the former Soviet Union and pre-reform China.

    (1) The former Soviet Union attached great importance to rapid industrialization and military strength, whereas China emphasized rural development.

    (2) Each economy overcommitted its available resources, and they often missed planning targets.

    (3) Each economy mobilized resources by increasing the quantity of resources rather than using given resources more productively.

    (4) Directives were used rather than markets and prices to allocate inputs for production in each economy.

    (5) Government fixed and controlled prices.

    (6) Each economy emphasized self-sufficiency of the nation, viewed capitalist nations as hostile, and restricted trade.

    (7) Each economy passively used monetary and fiscal policies; unemployment was limited or disguised; the price level was controlled through government price fixing.

3. There are two basic problems with a centrally planned economy.

    a. The *coordination problem* involves the difficulty of coordinating the economy's many interdependent segments and avoiding the chain reaction that would result from a bottleneck in any one of the segments. This coordination problem became even more difficult as the economy grew larger and more complex, and more economic decisions had to be made in the production process. There were also inadequate measures of economic performance to determine the degree of success or failure of enterprises or to give clear signals to the economy.

    b. The second problem was *economic incentives.* In a command economy, incentives are ineffective for encouraging economic initiative and work and for directing the most efficient use of productive resources. In a market economy, profits and losses signal what firms should produce, how they should produce, and how productive resources should be allocated to best meet the wants of a nation. Central planning in the two economies also lacked entrepreneurship and stifled innovation, both of which are important forces for achieving long-term economic growth. Individual workers lacked much motivation to work hard because pay was limited and there were either few consumer goods to buy or they were of low quality.

4. The *collapse of the Soviet economy* stemmed largely from the failure of central economic planning.

    a. Economic growth declined in the 1970s and 1980s. Real output also fell sharply in the few years before the country's breakup.

    b. Technology in manufacturing lagged by western standards, and consumer goods were of poor quality.

c. Consumers received few material benefits from years of sacrifice for rapid industrialization and the military, and consumer goods were in short supply.

d. The large financial burden for military expenditures diverted valuable resources from the production of consumer and capital goods to military production.

e. Agriculture acted as a drag on economic growth and hurt productivity in other sectors of the economy.

5. The *transition* of the former Soviet Union, particularly Russia, from a centrally planned to a market economy is occurring in several ways.

a. A market economy relies on private property rights and limited government control of business. Private property rights have been established to encourage entrepreneurship, and much government property has been transferred to private ownership. This privatization was initially achieved through government distribution of vouchers that could be used to purchase businesses; it is now done through the direct sale of state enterprises. This change has stimulated foreign investment and the flow of foreign capital to Russia; however, market reforms in agriculture have been limited.

b. Soviet government controls on prices led to a serious misallocation of resources and poor economic incentives. Most price controls were eliminated (about 90%) in 1992, so prices for goods and services were free to change and reflect relative scarcities. The value of the ruble is now established by supply and demand on foreign exchange markets.

c. For a market economy to work properly, competition must be promoted by splitting up or restructuring large state-owned enterprises to reduce the potential for monopoly power from having one privatized business in an industry. Progress in this area has been slow, but joint ventures and foreign investment may stimulate more business competition in the Russian economy.

d. The Soviet economy was restricted from actively participating in international trade. Action has been taken to open the economy to international trade and finance by making the ruble a convertible currency.

e. The transition to a market economy brought hyperinflation. Contributing factors included price decontrols, the ruble overhang (excess currency saved when there were few consumer goods to purchase), large government budget deficits, and the printing of money to finance the deficits. A Russian central bank has been created, and an anti-inflation money policy was adopted to eliminate hyperinflation and keep prices relatively stable.

f. Several major problems continue to affect the transition.

(1) Real output and living standards fell during the reforms, although the decline bottomed out in 1992. Inflation, reduced international trade, bankruptcy and the closing of state enterprises, and the massive reallocation of resources and reductions in government and military spending precipitated the decline in output.

(2) Economic inequality and social costs increased during the transition. Market reforms enriched some groups and hurt others. Economic insecurity and instability resulting from the transition raised tensions among workers and other groups, reduced the quality of life and life expectancy, and stimulated the rise of organized crime and "crony" capitalism.

g. The *prospects* for Russia's transition to a market economy are still a matter of concern. The pessimistic view is that the government remains weak in enforcing laws, public debt is mounting, and there is an inability to provide basic public services. Excessive government spending and borrowing combined with a banking crisis might lead to a collapse of the economy. The more optimistic view is that the fall in real output has ended and that the rate of inflation is now under control. Market reforms are now taking hold, and the economy will eventually prosper. Although the transitional problems are present, prospects are good for Russia to become an advanced market economy.

6. The path of *economic reform in China* differed significantly from that in Russia. China's market reforms began earlier and were more gradual and experimental. The Communist Party in China retained dictatorial control, while in Russia the party was replaced with democratic leadership. Russia has privatized much of the economy and sold off state enterprises, whereas China has protected its state enterprises while encouraging competing private enterprises. Russia experienced a significant decline in real output; China's output has continued to grow at high rates.

a. Agricultural reform in China began in 1978 with the leasing of land to individual farmers and permission to sell the output at competitive rather than government-controlled prices. This decollectivization and price reform provided a market basis for Chinese agriculture and the economy and released labor resources to private rural manufacturing firms (township and village enterprises).

b. Market reforms were also established in urban industries to give state-owned enterprises (SOEs) more control over production and employment. Enterprises could retain profits and sell more of their output at market prices rather than government-set prices. Urban collectives were formed that operated as private firms jointly owned by managers and workers. The collectives competed strongly with state enterprises and stimulated productivity in the economy.

c. Special enterprise zones were established that were open to foreign investment, private ownership, and international trade. They attracted foreign capital and increased Chinese exports. These areas undercut the support for central planning.

d. Supporting institutions have been developed to facilitate the transition to a market economy. The Chinese central bank was established to regulate the banking system and control the money supply. The enterprise tax system replaced the profit transfer from state enterprises. Foreign exchange can be swapped as needed between enterprises. A stock market has been established.

e. State-owned enterprises have been transformed; they operate more like corporations and respond to market needs rather than to social directives. The major SOEs have been consolidated into 1,000 enterprises. Government plans call for stock to be issued and for the SOEs to become shareholder owned and operate like corporations, with the government retaining control. Other SOEs will be sold or permitted to go bankrupt.

7. There are positive outcomes from China's market-based reforms, but the transition to a market economy is still incomplete.

   a. China has an impressive record of growth. It has averaged 9% annually since 1978, among the highest on record for such a period. Real output and incomes have quadrupled in less than two decades. Capital formation has increased productivity, and labor resources have been shifted from lower areas of productivity (agriculture) to higher areas of productivity (manufacturing). International trade has expanded exports and the imports of critical consumer and capital goods. Foreign investment has resulted in access to new technology that can be used to further increase productivity.
   b. There are economic problems in China's development.
   (1) Property rights are incomplete because the privatization of farmland is opposed by the Communist Party, and such a policy leads to less investment in agriculture.
   (2) China has experienced periods of high inflation because the financial and monetary control system is weak. The banking system is owed substantial sums by state-owned enterprises.
   (3) China is not fully integrated into the world economy. It is not a member of the World Trade Organization, and it has high tariffs on many products. There is weak enforcement of intellectual property rights.
   (4) Economic growth is geographically uneven throughout China. Hong Kong is now part of China and has high per capita income. Although people living in enterprise zones and the coastal areas near Hong Kong have experienced substantial growth in incomes and living standards, people in poorer regions still receive low incomes. Overall, China is still considered a low-income developing country.

■ **HINTS AND TIPS**

1. This chapter applies your knowledge of economics to explain the transformation of Russia and China from centrally planned to market-oriented economies. Throughout this chapter you will be comparing a market economy with a command economy. Review Chapter 4 before you read this chapter to make sure you have a good understanding of how capitalism works and its major characteristics.

2. View the chapter as a culminating exercise in your study of economics that gives you a chance to *review, apply,* and *integrate* many of the economic concepts and ideas you learned from the text. Only a few terms and concepts will be new to you in this chapter (they apply to Marxian ideology or the reforms in China or Russia).

3. Supply and demand analysis is used to explain price controls in Figure 23-1 in the text. The figure differs from those you saw in a previous chapter (Chapter 3) because there are two supply curves. One is vertical (perfectly inelastic) because it assumes fixed government control of production and no effect on quantity supplied as price controls are lifted. The upsloping supply curve shows an increase in quantity supplied as price controls are lifted.

■ **IMPORTANT TERMS**

labor theory of value

surplus value

state ownership

central economic planning

coordination problem

incentive problem

township and village enterprises

state-owned enterprises

urban collectives

special economic zones

SELF-TEST

■ **FILL-IN QUESTIONS**

1. The ideology behind the central planning in the former Soviet Union and pre-reform China was that the value of any commodity is determined by the amount of (capital, labor) _____ required to produce it. In capitalist economies, capital was (privately, publicly) _____ owned, and capitalists exploited workers by paying them a wage that was (greater than, less than) _____ the value of their production and obtained (shortage, surplus) _____ value at the expense of workers.

2. In a communist economy, capital and other property resources would be (publicly, privately) _____ owned and society would be (segregated, classless) _____. The Communist Party would serve as the representative of the (capitalists, proletariat) _____ and peasantry and would redistribute the surplus value of workers in the form of (tax cuts, subsidies) _____ for public and quasipublic goods. In reality, the Communist Party was (democratic, a dictatorship) _____.

3. One major institution of the former Soviet Union and pre-reform China was the ownership of property resources by (the state, property owners) _____. Another institutional feature was (central, decentralized) _____ economic planning.

4. Economic planning in the former Soviet Union and pre-reform China functioned in several ways. In the former

Soviet Union, plans sought to achieve rapid (population growth, industrialization) _____ and provision of (civilian, military) _____ goods. In China, emphasis was on (urban, rural) _____ development. In both nations, the planning policies created an (over, under)_____commitment of the economy's resources and resulted in an _____ production of goods for consumers.

5. Economic growth was achieved by (importing, mobilizing) _____ resources and by reallocating surplus labor from (industry, agriculture) _____ to _____. The government allocated inputs among industries by (prices, directives) _____, and the government set fixed _____ for goods and services and inputs.

6. Each nation also viewed itself as a (capitalist, socialist) _____ nation surrounded by hostile _____ nations, and central plans were designed to achieve economic (freedom, self-sufficiency) _____. Macroeconomic policies were (active, passive) _____.

7. Coordination and decision making in a market economy are (centralized, decentralized) _____, but in the Soviet and pre-reform Chinese economies it was _____. The market system tends to produce a reasonably (efficient, inefficient) _____ allocation of resources, but in centrally planned economies it was _____ and resulted in production bottlenecks and failures to meet many production targets. Central planning became (more, less) _____ complex and difficult as each economy grew and changed over time. Indicators of economic performance were (adequate, inadequate) _____ for determining the success or failure of economic activities.

8. Another problem with central planning was that economic incentives were (effective, ineffective) _____ for encouraging work or for giving signals to planners for efficient allocation of resources in the economy. The centrally planned system also lacked the (production targets, entrepreneurship) _____ which is so important to technological advance. Innovation (fostered, lagged) _____ because there was no competition.

9. A number of factors contributed to the collapse of the Soviet economy. The economy experienced (rise, decline) _____ in economic growth in the

1970s and 1980s. Consumer goods were of (good, poor) _____ quality, and there were widespread (shortages, surpluses) _____. There was a large (consumer, military) _____ burden on the economy that diverted resources from the production of (consumer, investment) _____ goods. Agriculture was (efficient, inefficient) _____ and (helped, hurt) _____ economic growth and productivity in other sectors of the economy.

10. The Russian transition to a market economy has resulted in major reforms. Property rights have been (revoked, established) _____, and government property has been transferred to (foreign, private) _____ ownership. In Soviet Russia, the prices of goods and services were kept at low levels through price (competition, controls) _____, so the marginal cost of a product (was, was not) _____ equal to its marginal benefit. This pricing policy led to (efficient, inefficient) _____ use of resources to make products and to (surpluses, shortages) _____ of many consumer goods. Today, most prices in Russia are (still fixed, free to vary) _____ _____.

11. Russia is also promoting competition by (forming, dismantling) _____ state-owned enterprises to reduce the potential for (rivalry, monopoly) _____. Russia has (opened, closed) _____ the economy to international trade and finance. One example of this policy is making the ruble a (fixed, convertible) _____ currency on international markets.

12. The Russian transition to a market economy was accompanied by (inflation, deflation) _____. It was high because of price (controls, decontrols) _____, a ruble (under, over) _____hang, and government budget (surpluses, deficits) _____. In response to this problem, the nation created an independent central (account, bank) _____ to provide control over (fiscal, monetary) _____ policy.

13. Major problems remain for Russia's transition. There has been a (falling, rising) _____ level of real output and a _____ standard of living. Economic inequality has (increased, decreased) _____ and led to _____ economic security and (increased, decreased) _____ and _____ crime.

14. Compared with Russia, China's market reforms began (later, earlier) _____ and were more (rapid, gradual) _____. China asserts that communist dictatorship and markets are (incompatible, compatible) _____, while Russia views them as _____. China instituted its market reforms and experienced (growth, depression) _____, while Russia experienced _____ in its transition to a market economy. Russia (sold, protected) _____ state enterprises, while China _____ them but encouraged competing private enterprises.

15. Agricultural reform in China began in 1978 with the (selling, leasing) _____ of land to individual farmers and permission for _____ the agriculture products at (market, government) _____ prices. The reform released (capital, labor) _____ resources to private rural manufacturing firms called township and village enterprises.

16. Market reforms were also established in Chinese urban industries to give state-owned enterprises (less, more) _____ decision making about production and employment. Urban (cartels, collectives) _____ were formed that operated as private firms jointly owned by managers and workers. The competition of state and nonstate enterprises (increased, decreased) _____ productivity and innovation in the economy.

17. China created special economic zones that were (open, closed) _____ to foreign investment, private ownership, and international trade. A Chinese central bank was established to regulate the (trading, banking) _____ system and control the (import, money) _____ supply. Profit transfers from state enterprises to the central government were replaced with an enterprise (spending, tax) _____ system. Foreign exchange can be (hoarded, swapped) _____ as needed between enterprises.

18. There has been a transformation of Chinese state-owned enterprises (SOEs). They operate more like (bureaucracies, corporations) _____ and respond to (social directive, the market) _____. Plans call for the major 100 SOEs to issue (money, stock) _____ and operate more like corporations under government control. Other smaller SOEs will be (bought, sold) _____ by the government or permitted to go bankrupt.

19. The transition to a market economy in China shows positive outcomes. Economic growth in China averaged (2, 9) _____% annually since 1978. Real output and income have (doubled, quadrupled) _____ in less than two decades. China's real GDP and real income have grown much (more, less) _____ rapidly than its population.

20. Problems remain with China's transition. Privatization of farmland is (supported, opposed) _____ by the Communist Party, and this policy leads to (more, less) _____ investment in agriculture. Limited financial and monetary control has resulted in periods of severe (inflation, deflation) _____. Substantial sums are (paid, owed) _____ by state-owned enterprises to the banking system. China (is, is not) _____ fully integrated into the world economy, _____ a member of the World Trade Organization, and has (low, high) _____ tariffs on many products. Economic growth is (even, uneven) _____, and China is still considered a (low, middle) _____-income developing country.

■ TRUE-FALSE QUESTIONS

Circle the T if the statement is true, the F if it is false.

1. The labor theory of value is the Marxian idea that the value of any good is determined solely by the amount of labor required for its production.　　**T　F**

2. Surplus value in Marxian ideology is the value or price of a commodity at equilibrium in a competitive market.　　**T　F**

3. The economies of the former Soviet Union and pre-reform China were characterized by state ownership of resources and authoritarian central planning.　　**T　F**

4. The former Soviet Union was dedicated to the task of rapid industrialization and building economic self-sufficiency.　　**T　F**

5. Pre-reform China emphasized rural economic development.　　**T　F**

6. Economic resources tended to be undercommitted in both the former Soviet Union and pre-reform China.　　**T　F**

7. Both the former Soviet Union and pre-reform China actively used monetary and fiscal policies to manipulate levels of employment, output, and prices.　　**T　F**

8. A centrally planned economy is significantly affected by missed production targets and bottlenecks.   **T   F**

9. The problems of central planning become easier and less complex as an economy grows over time.   **T   F**

10. Profit is the key indicator of success and failure in a centrally planned economy.   **T   F**

11. Central planning provided weak or inaccurate incentives for allocating resources to achieve economic efficiency and encourage hard work.   **T   F**

12. Centrally planned economies encourage entrepreneurship and technological advance under the directive of the Communist Party.   **T   F**

13. In the former Soviet Union, greater productivity and technological progress in the civilian sector were often sacrificed or limited by the demands to support a large military.   **T   F**

14. As part of the transition to a market economy, Russia has taken major steps to privatize its economy and establish property rights.   **T   F**

15. Price decontrol was a minor problem in the conversion of the Russian economy to capitalism because the prices the Soviet government established over the years were very similar to the economic value established in a competitive market.   **T   F**

16. The transition to a market economy in Russia has required the breakup of large industries and coordinated actions to promote competition.   **T   F**

17. A major accomplishment during the Russian transition to a market economy was limited inflation because of balanced budgets and a tight control of the money supply.   **T   F**

18. Two major problems Russia experienced during its transition to capitalism were a decline in the standard of living and increased economic inequality.   **T   F**

19. The Chinese economy used a "shock" approach to economic reform to make its transition to a market economy.   **T   F**

20. Collectivization and price controls were instrumental in strengthening production incentives and moving the Chinese economy toward a market-based agriculture.   **T   F**

21. The Chinese government has encouraged the formation of nonstate enterprises, called urban collectives, which are jointly owned by workers and managers.   **T   F**

22. China has created special economic zones that are open to foreign investment, private ownership, and international trade.   **T   F**

23. A major limitation of Chinese economic reform is the failure to create a stock market for the exchange of shares of newly created corporations.   **T   F**

24. China's economic growth has declined over the past two decades because of the instability caused by its economic reforms.   **T   F**

25. One continuing economic problem in China is the uneven regional economic development.   **T   F**

■ MULTIPLE-CHOICE QUESTIONS

Circle the letter that corresponds to the best answer.

1. Which was an element in Marxian ideology?
  (a) the creation of surplus value by government
  (b) dictatorship over the business class
  (c) the private ownership of property
  (d) the labor theory of value

2. Marxian ideology was highly critical of capitalist societies because in those societies capitalists
  (a) reduced the productivity of workers by not investing their profits in new capital goods
  (b) paid workers a wage that was less than the value of their production
  (c) shared surplus value with the government
  (d) were not taxed as much as the workers

3. The institution that was most characteristic of the former Soviet Union and pre-reform China was
  (a) private ownership of property
  (b) authoritarian central planning
  (c) a system of markets and prices
  (d) consumer sovereignty

4. Industrialization, rapid economic growth, and military strength in the former Soviet Union and pre-reform China were primarily achieved by
  (a) mobilizing larger quantities of resources
  (b) joining the international economy
  (c) making currencies convertible
  (d) using an easy-money policy

5. Both the former Soviet Union and pre-reform China viewed themselves as socialist nations surrounded by hostile capitalist nations, and as a consequence central planning stressed the need for
  (a) hoarding gold
  (b) flexible prices
  (c) consumer sovereignty
  (d) economic self-sufficiency

6. In the former Soviet Union and pre-reform China, monetary policy
  (a) was active and fiscal policy was passive
  (b) was passive and fiscal policy was active
  (c) and fiscal policy were both passive
  (d) and fiscal policy were both active

7. In the system of central planning, the outputs of some industries became the inputs for other industries, but a failure of one industry to meet its production target would cause
  (a) widespread unemployment
  (b) inflation in wholesale and retail prices
  (c) profit declines and potential bankruptcy of firms
  (d) a chain reaction of production problems and bottlenecks

8. What was the major success indicator for Soviet and Chinese state enterprises?
(a) profits
(b) the level of prices
(c) production targets
(d) the enterprise tax

9. The centrally planned system in the former Soviet Union and pre-reform China lacked
(a) price controls
(b) entrepreneurship
(c) economic growth
(d) allocation by directives

10. In the last year or two before the Soviet economic system collapsed, real output
(a) increased slightly
(b) decreased significantly
(c) remained relatively constant
(d) increased faster than the rate of population growth

11. Which was evidence of the Soviet economy's economic failure?
(a) a tight monetary policy
(b) an oversupply of most products
(c) the poor quality of consumer goods
(d) higher productivity in agriculture than industry

12. What was the size of expenditures for the military as a percentage of domestic output in the former Soviet Union (**SU**) and the United States (**U.S.**)?

	SU %	U.S., %
(a)	26–30	18
(b)	21–25	12
(c)	15–20	6
(d)	10–14	3

13. Which was a cause of low productivity in agriculture in the former Soviet Union?
(a) inability to make productive use of the abundance of good farmland in the country
(b) failure to construct an effective incentive system for agriculture
(c) increase in the length of the growing season
(d) overuse of certain chemical fertilizers on crops

14. Which helped Russia make a transition to a market economy?
(a) ruble overhang
(b) price controls
(c) privatization
(d) hyperinflation

15. The effect of price controls on most consumer goods in the former Soviet Union was that
(a) surpluses developed because the quantity consumers demanded was greater than the quantity supplied at the price set by government
(b) prices fell because the quantity consumers demanded was greater than the quantity supplied
(c) prices rose because the quantity consumers demanded was less than the quantity supplied

(d) shortages developed because the quantity consumers demanded was greater than the quantity supplied at the price set by government

16. Which set of factors most likely contributed to hyperinflation as Russia made its transition to a market economy?
(a) the breakup of state monopolies, land reform, and the poor quality of consumer goods
(b) increased military spending, investment in new technology, and the convertibility of the ruble
(c) central planning, production targets, and production bottlenecks
(d) government deficits, the ruble overhang, and price decontrols

17. Which two significant problems did Russia encounter in its transition to a market system?
(a) rising taxes and increasing life expectancies
(b) a loose monetary policy and a strict fiscal policy
(c) falling real output and declining living standards
(d) greater military spending and more environmental pollution

18. Compared with Russia, market reforms in China
(a) occurred over a longer time and were more gradual
(b) focused primarily on industry rather than agriculture
(c) relied more on monetary policy than fiscal policy
(d) were less successful and more disruptive

19. The key elements of the 1978–1984 rural economic reforms in China
(a) were passive macroeconomic policies
(b) was formation of special economic zones
(c) were foreign investment and loans to state-owned enterprises
(d) were decollectivization and creation of a two-track price system

20. Privately owned rural manufacturing firms in China are called
(a) town and village enterprises
(b) special economic zones
(c) incentive collectives
(d) farm cooperatives

21. Chinese enterprises in urban areas that are jointly owned by their managers and workers are
(a) industrial unions
(b) urban collectives
(c) business operating units
(d) manufacturing cooperatives

22. Which would be a supporting institution for market reform in China?
(a) a price control authority
(b) a profit transfer system
(c) a farm collective
(d) a central bank

23. Since market reforms began, real output and real income in China have
(a) doubled
(b) tripled
(c) quadrupled
(d) quintupled

24. The shift of employment from agriculture toward rural and urban manufacturing in China has increased
  (a) inflation
  (b) productivity
  (c) bankruptcies
  (d) unemployment

25. One significant problem China faces in its transition to a market economy is
  (a) establishing a stock market
  (b) establishing a central bank
  (c) incomplete privatization of land
  (d) creation of special economic zones

■ **PROBLEMS**

1. In the following table are several major institutions and characteristics of a capitalistic economy, such as that in the United States, and a centrally planned economy, such as that in the former Soviet Union or pre-reform China. In the appropriate space, name the corresponding institution or characteristic of the other economy.

Capitalist institution or characteristic	Socialist institution or characteristic
a. _____	labor theory of value
b. _____	surplus value
c. private ownership of economic resources	_____
d. a market economy	_____
e. _____	state-owned enterprises
f. privately owned farms	_____
g. _____	government price controls
h. _____	passive macroeconomic policies
i. representative democracy	_____

2. Answer the following set of questions based on the table below. The columns show the price, quantity demanded (Q_d) by consumers, and a fixed quantity supplied by government (Q_{s1}) for a product in the former Soviet Union. The column for Q_{s2} shows the supply curve for the product *after* privatization in the industry producing the product.

Price (in rubles)	Q_d	Q_{s1}	Q_{s2}
90	25	25	55
80	30	25	50
70	35	25	45
60	40	25	40
50	45	25	35
40	50	25	30
30	55	25	25

  a. When only the government supplies the product as shown in the Q_{s1} schedule, the equilibrium price will be _____ rubles and the equilibrium quantity will be _____ units.

  b. If the government tries to make the product more accessible to lower-income consumers by setting the price at 30 rubles, then the quantity demanded will be _____ units and the quantity supplied will be _____ units, producing a shortage of _____ units.

  c. If the government decontrolled prices but did not privatize industry, then prices would rise to _____ rubles and the government would still produce _____ units.

  d. With privatization, there will be a new quantity supplied schedule (Q_{s2}). The equilibrium price will be _____ rubles and the equilibrium quantity will be _____ units. The equilibrium price has risen by _____ rubles and the equilibrium quantity by _____ units.

3. Match the terms from China's economic reform with the phrase using the appropriate number.

  1. special economic zone   5. enterprise tax system
  2. urban collective   6. state-owned enterprise
  3. two-track price system
  4. town and village enterprises

  a. Privately owned rural manufacturing firms
  _____

  b. Replaced the system of profit transfers from state enterprises to the central government   _____
  c. Areas in coastal regions that are open to foreign investment, private ownership, and international trade
  _____

  d. Nonstate enterprises jointly owned by managers and their work forces in urban areas   _____
  e. Gives farmers ability to sell output at market-determined prices   _____
  f. Enterprises that are controlled by the government
  _____

■ **SHORT ANSWER AND ESSAY QUESTIONS**

  1. What are the essential features of Marxian ideology on which the Soviet Union's command economy was based?

  2. What were the two principal economic institutions of the pre-reform and pre-collapse economies of China and Russia? How do these institutions compare with those in the United States?

  3. Describe how central planning functioned in the former Soviet Union and pre-reform China. What generalizations can you make about resource use, directives, prices, self-sufficiency, and macroeconomic policies?

4. Why does central planning result in a coordination problem? Compare the operation of central planning with the use of markets and prices for economic decision making.

5. How does central economic planning produce a significant incentive problem? What types of economic incentives for business, workers, and consumers exist in a market economy? How are those incentives different in a centrally planned economy?

6. Discuss the five factors that help explain or contributed to the collapse of the Soviet economy.

7. What action has Russia taken to privatize the economy?

8. Why was there a need for price reform in Russia in its transition to a market economy? What has been the *general* effect of this change? Use a supply and demand graph to explain the effect of the price decontrol on a specific product.

9. Discuss what is being done in Russia to promote competition. To what extent are public monopolies a problem?

10. What major problem is confronting Russia as it seeks to join the world economy?

11. How have high rates of inflation affected Russia's transition to a market economy? What has been the shift in macroeconomic policy?

12. What major problems has Russia encountered in its transition to a market economy?

13. Evaluate the prospects for the transformation of Russia into a market economy.

14. How did China's approach to market reforms differ from that in Russia?

15. Describe how China has tried to transform agriculture and rural production.

16. What market-based changes has the Chinese government made in urban industries?

17. What actions has the Chinese government taken to encourage foreign investment and establish institutions that support a market-based economy?

18. Describe the economic transformation of state-owned enterprises in China.

19. What are the positive outcomes of China's economic reform?

20. Discuss four significant economic problems that China continues to face in its transition to a market economy.

ANSWERS

Chapter 23 Transition Economies: Russia and China

FILL-IN QUESTIONS

1. labor, privately, less than, surplus
2. publicly, classless, proletariat, subsidies, a dictatorship
3. the state, central
4. industrialization, military, rural, over, under
5. mobilizing, agriculture, industry, directives, prices
6. socialist, capitalist, self-sufficiency, passive
7. decentralized, centralized, efficient, inefficient, more, inadequate
8. ineffective, entrepreneurship, lagged
9. decline, poor, shortages, military, consumer, inefficient, hurt
10. established, private, controls, was not, inefficient, shortages, free to vary
11. dismantling, monopoly, opened, convertible
12. inflation, decontrols, over, deficits, bank, monetary
13. falling, falling, increased, decreased, increased
14. earlier, gradual, compatible, incompatible, growth, depression, sold, protected
15. leasing, selling, market, labor
16. more, collectives, increased
17. open, banking, money, tax, swapped
18. corporations, the market, stock, sold
19. 9, quadrupled, more
20. opposed, less, inflation, owed, is not, is not, high, uneven, low

TRUE-FALSE QUESTIONS

1. T, p. 475	**10.** F, pp. 477-478	**19.** F, p. 483
2. F, p. 475	**11.** T, pp. 477-478	**20.** F, pp. 483-484
3. T, pp. 475-476	**12.** F, pp. 477-478	**21.** T, p. 484
4. T, p. 476	**13.** T, p. 478	**22.** T, p. 484
5. T, p. 476	**14.** T, pp. 479-480	**23.** F, p. 484
6. F, p. 476	**15.** F, pp. 480-481	**24.** F, p. 485
7. F, pp. 476-477	**16.** T, p. 481	**25.** T, pp. 486-487
8. T, p. 477	**17.** F, p. 481	
9. F, p. 477	**18.** T, pp. 481-482	

MULTIPLE-CHOICE QUESTIONS

1. d, p. 475	**10.** b, p. 479	**19.** d, pp. 483-484
2. b, p. 475	**11.** c, p. 479	**20.** a, p. 484
3. b, pp. 475-476	**12.** c, p. 479	**21.** b, p. 484
4. a, p. 476	**13.** b, p. 479	**22.** a, p. 484
5. d, p. 476	**14.** c, pp. 479-480	**23.** c, p. 485
6. c, pp. 476-477	**15.** d, p. 480	**24.** b, p. 485
7. d, p. 477	**16.** d, p. 481	**25.** c, p. 485
8. c, pp. 477-478	**17.** c, pp. 481-482	
9. b, p. 478	**18.** a, p. 483	

PROBLEMS

1. *a.* supply and demand; *b.* profit; *c.* state ownership of resources; *d.* command or centrally planned economy; *e.* corporations; *f.* collective farms or agricultural cooperatives; *g.* competitive markets and flexible prices; *h.* active or discretionary macroeconomic policies; *i.* dictatorship by the Communist Party
2. a. 90, 25; *b.* 55, 25, 30; *c.* 90, 25; *d.* 60, 40, 30, 15
3. a. 4; *b.* 5; *c.* 1; *d.* 2; *e.* 3; *f.* 6

SHORT ANSWER AND ESSAY QUESTIONS

1. pp. 474-475	**8.** pp. 480-481	**15.** pp. 483-484
2. pp. 475-476	**9.** p. 481	**16.** p. 484
3. pp. 476-477	**10.** p. 481	**17.** p. 484
4. p. 477	**11.** p. 481	**18.** p. 484
5. pp. 477-478	**12.** pp. 481-482	**19.** p. 485
6. pp. 478-479	**13.** pp. 482-483	**20.** pp. 485-487
7. pp. 479-480	**14.** p. 483	

Glossary

Note: Terms in *italic* type are defined separately in this glossary.

A

Ability-to-pay principle The idea that those who have greater income (or wealth) should pay a greater proportion of it as taxes than those who have less income (or wealth).

Abstraction Elimination of irrelevant and noneconomic facts to obtain an *economic principle.*

Actual budget A listing of amounts spent by the *Federal government* (to purchase goods and services and for *transfer payments*) and the amounts of tax revenue collected by it in any (fiscal) year.

Actual deficit The size of the Federal government's *budget deficit* actually recorded in any particular year.

Actual investment The amount which *firms* do invest; equal to *planned investment* plus *unplanned investment.*

Actual reserves The funds which a bank has on deposit at the *Federal Reserve Bank* of its district (plus its *vault cash*).

Adaptive expectations theory The idea that people determine their expectations about future events (for example, inflation) on the basis of past and present events (rates of inflation) and only change their expectations as events unfold.

Adjustable pegs The device used in the *Bretton Woods system* to alter *exchange rates* in an orderly way to eliminate persistent payments deficits and surpluses. Each nation defined its monetary unit in terms of (pegged it to) gold or the dollar, kept the *rate of exchange* for its money stable in the short run, and adjusted its rate in the long run when faced with international payments disequilibrium.

Aggregate demand A schedule or curve which shows the total quantity of goods and services demanded (purchased) at different *price levels.*

Aggregate demand—aggregate supply model The macroeconomic model which uses *aggregate demand* and *aggregate supply* to determine and explain the *price level* and the real *domestic output.*

Aggregate expenditures The total amount spent for final goods and services in the economy.

Aggregate expenditures—domestic output approach Determination of the *equilibrium gross domestic product* by finding the real GDP at which aggregate expenditures equal *domestic output.*

Aggregate expenditures schedule A schedule or curve showing the total amount spent for final goods and services at different levels of GDP.

Aggregate supply A schedule or curve showing the total quantity of goods and services supplied (produced) at different *price levels.*

Aggregation Combining individual units or data into one unit or number. For example, all prices of individual goods and services are combined into a *price level,* or all units of output are aggregated into *real gross domestic product.*

Allocative efficiency The apportionment of resources among firms and industries to obtain the production of the products most wanted by society (consumers); the output of each product at which its *marginal cost* and *price* or *marginal benefit* are equal.

Annually balanced budget A budget in which government expenditures and tax collections are equal each year.

Anticipated inflation Increases in the price level (*inflation*) which occur at the expected rate.

Applied economics (See *Policy economics.*)

Appreciation (of the dollar) An increase in the value of the dollar relative to the currency of another nation so that a dollar buys a larger amount of the foreign currency and thus of foreign goods.

"Asian tigers" The newly industrialized and rapidly growing economies of Hong Kong, Singapore, South Korea, and Taiwan.

Asset Anything of monetary value owned by a firm or individual.

Asset demand for money The amount of *money* people want to hold as a *store of value;* this amount varies inversely with the *rate of interest.*

Authoritarian capitalism An economic system in which property resources are privately owned and government extensively directs and controls the economy.

Average product The total output produced per unit of a *resource* employed (*total product* divided by the quantity of that employed resource).

Average propensity to consume Fraction (or percentage) of *disposable income* which households plan to spend for consumer goods and services; *consumption* divided by *disposable income.*

Average propensity to save Fraction (or percentage) of *disposable income* which households save; *saving* divided by *disposable income.*

Average tax rate Total tax paid divided by total (taxable) income, as a percentage.

B

Balanced-budget amendment Proposed constitutional amendment that would require Congress to balance the Federal budget annually.

Balanced-budget multiplier The extent to which an equal change in government spending and taxes changes *equilibrium gross domestic product;* always has a value of 1 since it is equal to the amount of the equal changes in *G* and *T*.

Balance of payments (See *International balance of payments.*)

Balance of payments deficit The amount by which the sum of the *balance on current account* and the *balance on the capital account* is negative in a year.

Balance of payments surplus The amount by which the sum of the *balance on current account* and the *balance on the capital account* is positive in a year.

Balance on current account The exports of goods and services of a nation less its imports of goods and services plus its *net investment income* and *net transfers* in a year.

Balance on goods and services The exports of goods and services of a nation less its imports of goods and services in a year.

Balance on the capital account The *capital inflows* of a nation less its *capital outflows.*

Balance sheet A statement of the *assets, liabilities,* and *net worth* of a firm or individual at some given time.

Bank deposits The deposits which individuals or firms have at banks (or thrifts) or which banks have at the *Federal Reserve Banks.*

Bankers' bank A bank which accepts the deposits of and makes loans to *depository institutions;* in the United States, a *Federal Reserve Bank.*

Bank reserves The deposits of commercial banks and thrifts at *Federal Reserve Banks* plus bank and thrift *vault cash.*

Barter The exchange of one good or service for another good or service.

Base year The year with which other years are compared when an index is constructed, for example, the base year for a *price index.*

Benefit-cost analysis Comparing the *marginal benefits* of a government project or program with the *marginal costs* to decide whether or not to employ resources in that project or program and to what extent.

Board of Governors The 7-member group which supervises and controls the money and banking system of the United States; the Board of Governors of the Federal Reserve System; the Federal Reserve Board.

Bond A financial device through which a borrower (a firm or government) is obligated to pay the principle and interest on a loan at a specific date in the future.

Brain drain The emigration of highly educated, highly skilled workers from a country.

Break-even income The level of *disposable income* at which *households* plan to consume (spend) all their income and to save none of it; also denotes that level of earned income at which subsidy payments become zero in an income transfer program.

Bretton Woods system The international monetary system developed after World War II in which *adjustable* pegs were employed, the *International Monetary Fund* helped to stabilize foreign exchange rates, and gold and the dollar were used as *international monetary reserves.*

Budget deficit The amount by which the expenditures of the Federal government exceed its revenues in any year.

Budget surplus The amount by which the revenues of the Federal government exceed its expenditures in any year.

Built-in stabilizer A mechanism which increases government's budget deficit (or reduces its surplus) during a recession and increases government's budget surplus (or reduces its deficit) during inflation without any action by policymakers; the tax system is one such mechanism.

Business cycle Recurring increases and decreases in the level of economic activity over periods of years. Consists of peak, *recession,* trough, and recovery phases.

Business firm (See *Firm.*)

C

Capital Human-made resources (buildings, machinery, and equipment) used to produce goods and services; goods which do not directly satisfy human wants; also called capital goods.

Capital account The section of a nation's *international balance of payments* statement in which the foreign purchases of assets in the United States (producing money *capital inflows*) and U.S. purchases of assets abroad (producing money *capital outflows* of that nation) are recorded.

Capital account deficit A negative *balance on the capital account.*

Capital account surplus A positive *balance on the capital account.*

Capital flight The transfer of savings from developing countries to industrially advanced countries to avoid government expropriation, taxation, and high rates of inflation or to realize better investment opportunities.

Capital gain The gain realized when securities or properties are sold for a price greater than the price paid for them.

Capital goods (See *Capital.*)

Capital inflow The expenditures made by the residents of foreign nations to purchase real and financial capital from the residents of a nation.

Capital-intensive commodity A product which requires a relatively large amount of *capital* to produce.

Capitalism (See *Pure capitalism.*)

Capital outflow The expenditures made by the residents of a nation to purchase real and financial capital from the residents of foreign nations.

Capital-saving technological advance An improvement in *technology* which permits a greater quantity of a product to be produced with a specific amount of *capital* (or permits the same amount of the product to be produced with a smaller amount of capital).

Capital stock The total available *capital* in a nation.

Capital-using technological advance An improvement in *technology* which requires the use of a greater amount of *capital* to produce a specific quantity of a product.

Causation A relationship in which the occurrence of one or more events brings about another event.

CEA   (See *Council of Economic Advisers.*)

Central bank   A bank whose chief function is the control of the nation's *money supply;* in the United States, the *Federal Reserve System.*

Central economic planning   Government determination of the objectives of the economy and how resources will be directed to attain those objectives.

Ceteris paribus assumption   (See *"Other things equal"* *assumption.*)

Change in demand   A change in the *quantity demanded* of a good or service at every price; a shift of the *demand curve* to the left or right.

Change in supply   A change in the *quantity supplied* of a good or service at every price; a shift of the *supply curve* to the left or right.

Checkable deposit   Any deposit in a *commercial bank* or *thrift institution* against which a check may be written; includes *demand deposits.*

Checking account   A *checkable deposit* in a *commercial bank* or *thrift institution.*

Check clearing   The process by which funds are transferred from the checking accounts of the writers of checks to the checking accounts of the recipients of the checks.

Circular flow model   The flow of resources from *households* to *firms* and of products from firms to households. These flows are accompanied by reverse flows of money from firms to households and from households to firms.

Classical economics   The macroeconomic generalizations accepted by most economists before the 1930s which led to the conclusion that a capitalistic economy was self-regulating and therefore would usually employ its resources fully.

Closed economy   An economy which neither exports nor imports goods and services.

Coincidence of wants   A situation in which the good or service which one trader desires to obtain is the same as that which another trader desires to give up, and an item which the second trader wishes to acquire is the same as that which the first trader desires to surrender.

COLA   (See *Cost-of-living adjustment.*)

Command economy   An economic system (method of organization) in which property resources are publicly owned and government uses *central economic planning* to direct and coordinate economic activities.

Commercial bank   A firm which engages in the business of banking (accepts deposits, offers checking accounts, and makes loans).

Commercial banking system   All *commercial banks* and *thrift institutions* as a group.

Communism   (See *Command economy.*)

Comparative advantage   A lower relative or comparative cost than another producer.

Competing goods   (See *Substitute goods.*)

Competition   The presence in a market of a large number of independent buyers and sellers competing with one another and the freedom of buyers and sellers to enter and leave the market.

Complementary goods   Products and services which are used together; when the price of one falls the demand for the other increases (and conversely).

Complex multiplier   The *multiplier* which exists when changes in the *gross domestic product* change *net taxes* and *imports,* as well as *saving.*

Conglomerate combination   A group of *plants* owned by a single *firm* and engaged at one or more stages in the production of different products (of products that do not compete with each other).

Consumer price index (CPI)   An index which measures the prices of a fixed "market basket" of some 300 goods and services bought by a "typical" consumer.

Consumer sovereignty   Determination by consumers of the types and quantities of goods and services which will be produced with the scarce resources of the economy; consumer direction of production through dollar votes.

Consumption of fixed capital   Estimate of the amount of *capital* worn out or used up (consumed) in producing the *gross domestic product;* also called *depreciation.*

Consumption schedule   A schedule showing the amounts *households* plan to spend for *consumer goods* at different levels of *disposable income.*

Contractionary fiscal policy   A decrease in *government expenditures* for goods and services, an increase in *net taxes,* or some combination of the two, for the purpose of decreasing *aggregate demand* and thus controlling inflation.

Coordination failure   A situation in which people do not reach a mutually beneficial outcome because they lack some way to jointly coordinate their actions; a possible cause of macroeconomic instability.

Corporate income tax   A tax levied on the net income (profit) of corporations.

Corporation   A legal entity ("person") chartered by a state or the Federal government which is distinct and separate from the individuals who own it.

Correlation   A systematic and dependable association between two sets of data (two kinds of events); does not itself indicate causation.

Cost-of-living adjustment (COLA)   An automatic increase in the incomes (wages) of workers when inflation occurs; guaranteed by a collective bargaining contract between firms and workers.

Cost-push inflation   Increases in the price level (inflation) resulting from an increase in resource costs (for example, higher wage rates and raw material prices) and hence in *per-unit production costs;* inflation caused by reductions in *aggregate supply.*

Cost ratio   An equality showing the number of units of two products which can be produced with the same resources; the cost ratio 1 corn $\equiv$ 3 olives shows that the resources required to produce 3 units of olives must be shifted to corn production to produce 1 unit of corn.

Council of Economic Advisers   A group of three persons that advises and assists the President of the United States on economic matters (including the preparation of the annual *Economic Report of the President*).

Credit   An accounting item which increases the value of an asset (such as the foreign money owned by the residents of a nation).

Credit union   An association of persons who have a common tie (such as being employees of the same firm or members of the same labor union) which sells shares to (accepts deposits from) its members and makes loans to them.

Crowding model of occupational discrimination A model of labor markets suggesting that *occupational discrimination* has kept many women and minorities out of high-paying occupations and forced them into a limited number of low-paying occupations.

Crowding-out effect A rise in interest rates and a resulting decrease in *planned investment* caused by the Federal government's increased borrowing in the money market.

Currency Coins and paper money.

Currency appreciation (See *Exchange rate appreciation.*)

Currency depreciation (See *Exchange rate depreciation.*)

Current account The section in a nation's *international balance of payments* which records its exports and imports of goods and services, its *net investment income,* and its *net transfers.*

Customary economy (See *Traditional economy.*)

Cyclical deficit A Federal *budget deficit* which is caused by a recession and the consequent decline in tax revenues.

Cyclical unemployment A type of *unemployment* caused by insufficient total spending (or by insufficient *aggregate demand*).

Cyclically balanced budget The equality of *government expenditures* and *net tax collections* over the course of a *business cycle;* deficits incurred during periods of recession are offset by surpluses obtained during periods of prosperity (inflation).

D

Debit An accounting item which decreases the value of an asset (such as the foreign money owned by the residents of a nation).

Deduction Reasoning from assumptions to conclusions; a method of reasoning which first develops a hypothesis (an assumption) and then tests the hypothesis with economic facts.

Deflating Finding the *real gross domestic product* by decreasing the dollar value of the GDP for a year in which prices were higher than in the *base year.*

Deflation A decline in the economy's *price level.*

Demand A schedule showing the amounts of a good or service buyers (or a buyer) wish to purchase at various prices during some time period.

Demand curve A curve illustrating *demand.*

Demand deposit A deposit in a *commercial bank* or *thrift* against which checks may be written; a *checkable deposit.*

Demand-deposit multiplier (See *Monetary multiplier.*)

Demand factor (in growth) The increase in the level of *aggregate demand* which brings about the *economic growth* made possible by an increase in the production potential of the economy.

Demand management The use of *fiscal policy* and *monetary policy* to increase or decrease *aggregate demand.*

Demand-pull inflation Increases in the price level (inflation) resulting from an excess of demand over output at the existing price level, caused by an increase in *aggregate demand.*

Dependent variable A variable which changes as a consequence of a change in some other (independent) variable; the "effect" or outcome.

Depository institutions Firms which accept the deposits of *money* of the public (businesses and persons); *commercial banks, savings and loan associations, mutual savings banks,* and *credit unions.*

Depreciation (See *Consumption of fixed capital.*)

Depreciation (of the dollar) A decrease in the value of the dollar relative to another currency so that a dollar buys a smaller amount of the foreign currency and therefore of foreign goods.

Derived demand The demand for a resource which depends on the demand for the products it can be used to produce.

Determinants of aggregate demand Factors such as consumption spending, *investment,* government spending, and *net exports* which, if they change, shift the *aggregate demand curve.*

Determinants of aggregate supply Factors such as input prices, *productivity,* and the legal-institutional environment which, if they change, shift the *aggregate supply curve.*

Determinants of demand Factors other than its price which determine the quantities demanded of a good or service.

Determinants of supply Factors other than its price which determine the quantities supplied of a good or service.

Devaluation A decrease in the governmentally defined value of a currency.

Developing countries Many countries of Africa, Asia, and Latin America which are characterized by a lack of capital goods, use of nonadvanced technologies, low literacy rates, high unemployment, rapid population growth, and labor forces heavily committed to agriculture.

Direct foreign investment The building of new factories (or the purchase of existing capital) in a particular nation by corporations of other nations.

Direct relationship The relationship between two variables which change in the same direction, for example, product price and quantity supplied.

Discount rate The interest rate which the *Federal Reserve Banks* charge on the loans they make to *commercial banks* and *thrift institutions.*

Discouraged workers Employees who have left the *labor force* because they have been unable to find employment.

Discrimination According individuals or groups inferior treatment in hiring, occupational access, education and training, promotion, wage rates, or working conditions, even though they have the same abilities, education and skills, and work experience as other workers.

Discretionary fiscal policy Deliberate changes in taxes (tax rates) and government spending by Congress to promote full-employment, price stability, and economic growth.

Diseconomies of scale Increase in the *average total cost* of producing a product as the *firm* expands the size of its *plant* (its output) in the *long run*.

Disinflation A reduction in the rate of *inflation*.

Disposable income *Personal income* less personal taxes; income available for *personal consumption expenditures* and *personal saving*.

Dissaving Spending for consumer goods and services in excess of *disposable income;* the amount by which *personal consumption expenditures* exceed disposable income.

Dividends Payments by a corporation of all or part of its profit to its stockholders (the corporate owners).

Division of labor Dividing the work required to produce a product into a number of different tasks which are performed by different workers; *specialization* of workers.

Dollar votes The "votes" which consumers and entrepreneurs cast for the production of consumer and capital goods, respectively, when they purchase them in product and resource markets.

Domestic capital formation Addition to a nation's stock of *capital* by saving and investing part of its own domestic output.

Domestic output *Gross* (or net) *domestic product;* the total output of *final goods and services* produced in the economy.

Domestic price The price of a good or service within a country, determined by domestic demand and supply.

Double taxation The taxation of both corporate net income (profits) and the *dividends* paid from this net income when they become the personal income of households.

Dumping The sale of products below cost in a foreign country or below the prices charged at home.

Durable good A consumer good with an expected life (use) of 3 or more years.

Dynamic efficiency The development over time of less costly production techniques, improved products, and new products; technological progress.

E

E-cash Electronic money; an entry (usable as money) stored in a computer or a stored-value card ("smart card").

Earnings The money income received by a worker; equal to the *wage* (rate) multiplied by the amount of time worked.

Easy money policy Federal Reserve System actions to increase the *money supply* to lower interest rates and expand *real GDP*.

Economic analysis Deriving *economic principles* from relevant economic facts.

Economic cost A payment which must be made to obtain and retain the services of a *resource;* the income a firm must provide to a resource supplier to attract the resource away from an alternative use; equal to the quantity of other products which cannot be produced when resources are instead used to make a particular product.

Economic efficiency Obtaining the socially optimal amounts of goods and services using minimum necessary resources; entails both *productive efficiency* and *allocative efficiency*.

Economic growth (1) An outward shift in the *production possibilities curve* which results from an increase in resource quantity or quality or an improvement in *technology;* (2) an increase either in real output (*gross domestic product*) or in real output per capita.

Economic integration Cooperation among and the complete or partial unification of the economies of different nations; the elimination of barriers to trade among these nations; the bringing together of the markets in each of the separate economies to form one large (a common) market.

Economic law (See *Economic principle*.)

Economic model A simplified picture of economic reality; an abstract generalization.

Economic perspective A viewpoint which envisions individuals and institutions making rational decisions by comparing the marginal benefits and marginal costs associated with their actions.

Economic policy A course of action intended to correct or avoid a problem.

Economic principle A widely accepted generalization about the economic behavior of individuals and institutions.

Economic profit The *total revenue* of a firm less all its *economic costs;* also called "pure profit" and "above normal profit."

Economic regulation (See *Industrial regulation*.)

Economic rent The price paid for the use of land and other natural resources, the supply of which is fixed (*perfectly inelastic*).

Economic resources The *land, labor, capital,* and *entrepreneurial ability* which are used in the production of goods and services; productive agents; factors of production.

Economics The social science dealing with the use of scarce resources to obtain the maximum satisfaction of society's virtually unlimited material wants.

Economic theory Deriving *economic principles* from relevant economic facts; an *economic principle*.

Economic system A particular set of institutional arrangements and a coordinating mechanism for solving the economizing problem; a method of organizing an economy; of which the *market economy, command economy,* and *traditional economy* are three general types.

Economies of scale Reductions in the *average total cost* of producing a product as the firm expands the size of plant (its output) in the *long run;* the economies of mass production.

Economizing problem The choices necessitated because society's material wants for goods and services are unlimited but the *resources* available to satisfy these wants are limited (scarce).

Efficiency factors (in growth) The capacity of an economy to combine resources effectively to achieve growth of real output which the *supply factors* (of growth) make possible.

Efficient allocation of resources That allocation of the resources of an economy among the production of different products which leads to the maximum satisfaction of the wants of consumers; producing the socially optimal mix of output with society's scarce resources.

Employment Act of 1946 Federal legislation that committed the Federal government to the maintenance of economic stability (a high level of employment, a stable price level, and economic growth); established the *Council of Economic Advisers* and the *Joint Economic Committee;* and required an annual economic report of the President to Congress.

Employment rate The percentage of the *labor force* employed at any time.

Entrepreneurial ability The human resources which combine the other resources to produce a product, make nonroutine decisions, innovate, and bear risks.

Equation of exchange $MV = PQ$, in which M is the supply of money, V is the *velocity of money*, P is the *price level,* and Q is the physical volume of *final goods and services* produced.

Equilibrium real domestic output The *gross domestic product* at which the total quantity of final goods and services purchased (*aggregate expenditures*) is equal to the total quantity of final goods and services produced (the real domestic output); the real domestic output at which the *aggregate demand curve* intersects the *aggregate supply curve.*

Equilibrium price The *price* in a competitive market at which the *quantity demanded* and the *quantity supplied* are equal; where there is neither a *shortage* nor a *surplus;* and where there is no tendency for price to rise or fall.

Equilibrium price level The price level at which the *aggregate demand curve* intersects the *aggregate supply curve.*

Equilibrium quantity (1) The quantity demanded and supplied at the equilibrium price in a competitive market; (2) the profit-maximizing output of a firm.

European Union (EU) An association of European nations initiated in 1958 which has eliminated tariffs and import quotas that existed among them, established common tariffs for goods imported from outside the member nations, allowed the free movement of labor and capital among them, and created other common economic policies.

Excess reserves The amount by which a bank or thrift's *actual reserves* exceed its *required reserves;* actual reserves minus required reserves.

Exchange control (See *Foreign exchange control.*)

Exchange rate The *rate of exchange* of one nation's currency for another nation's currency.

Exchange-rate appreciation An increase in the value of a nation's currency in foreign exchange markets; an increase in the *rate of exchange* for foreign currencies.

Exchange-rate depreciation A decrease in the value of a nation's currency in foreign exchange markets; a decrease in the *rate of exchange* for foreign currencies.

Exchange-rate determinant Any factor other than the *rate of exchange* which determines a currency's demand and supply in the *foreign exchange market.*

Excise tax A tax levied on the production of a specific product or on the quantity of the product purchased.

Exclusion principle The ability to exclude those who do not pay for a product from receiving its benefits.

Exhaustive expenditure An expenditure by government resulting directly in the employment of *economic resources* and in the absorption by government of the goods and services those resources produce; a *government purchase.*

Expanding industry An industry whose firms earn *economic profits* and which experience an increase in output as new firms enter the industry.

Expansionary fiscal policy An increase in *government expenditures* for goods and services, a decrease in *net taxes,* or some combination of the two for the purpose of increasing *aggregate demand* and expanding real output.

Expectations The anticipations of consumers, firms, and others about future economic conditions.

Expected rate of return The increase in profit a firm anticipates it will obtain by purchasing capital (or engaging in research and development), expressed as a percentage of the total cost of the investment (or R&D) activity.

Expenditures approach The method which adds all expenditures made for *final goods and services* to measure the *gross domestic product.*

Expenditures-output approach (See *Aggregate expenditures-domestic output approach.*)

Export controls The limitation or prohibition of the export of certain products on the basis of foreign policy or national security objectives.

Export-Import Bank A Federal institution which provides interest-rate subsidies to foreign borrowers who buy U.S. exports on credit.

Exports Goods and services produced in a nation and sold to customers in other nations.

Export subsidies Government payments to domestic producers to enable them to reduce the *price* of a good or service to foreign buyers.

Export supply curve An upsloping curve showing the amount of a product domestic firms will export at each *world price* above the *domestic price.*

Export transactions A sale of a good or service which increases the amount of foreign currency flowing to the citizens, firms, and governments of a nation.

External benefit (See *Spillover benefit.*)

External cost (See *Spillover cost.*)

External debt Private or public debt owed to foreign citizens, firms, and institutions.

Externality (See *Spillover.*)

F

Face value The dollar or cents value stamped on a U.S. coin.

Factors of production *Economic resources: land, capital, labor,* and *entrepreneurial ability.*

Fallacy of composition Incorrectly reasoning that what is true for the individual (or part) is necessarily true for the group (or whole).

Fallacy of limited decisions The false notion that there are a limited number of economic decisions to be made so that, if government makes more decisions, there will be fewer private decisions to render.

FDIC (See *Federal Deposit Insurance Corporation.*)

Federal Advisory Committee The group of 12 commercial bankers that advises the Board of Governors on banking policy.

Federal Deposit Insurance Corporation (FDIC) The Federally chartered corporation which insures the deposit liabilities of *commercial banks* and *thrift institutions.*

Federal funds rate The interest rate banks and other depository institutions charge one another on overnight loans made out of their *excess reserves.*

Federal government The government of the United States, as distinct from the state and local governments.

Federal Open Market Committee (FOMC) The 12-member group that determines the purchase-and-sale policies of the *Federal Reserve Banks* in the market for U.S. government securities.

Federal Reserve Banks The 12 banks chartered by the U.S. government to control the *money supply* and perform other functions. (See *Central bank, Quasipublic bank,* and *Banker's bank.*)

Federal Reserve Notes Paper money issued by the *Federal Reserve Banks.*

Feedback effects (of monetary policy) The effects that a change in the money supply will have (because it affects the interest rate, planned investment, and the equilibrium GDP) on the demand for money, which is itself directly related to the GDP.

Fiat money Anything which is *money* because government has decreed it to be money.

Final goods and services Goods and services which have been purchased for final use and not for resale or further processing or manufacturing.

Financial capital (See *Money capital.*)

Firm An organization which employs resources to produce a good or service for profit and owns and operates one or more *plants.*

Fiscal federalism The system of transfers (grants) by which the Federal government shares its revenues with state and local governments.

Fiscal policy Changes in government spending and tax collections designed to achieve a full-employment and noninflationary domestic output; also called *discretionary fiscal policy.*

Five fundamental economic questions The 5 questions which every economy must answer: how much to produce, what to produce, how to produce it, how to divide the total output, and how to ensure economic flexibility.

Fixed exchange rate A *rate of exchange* which is set in some way and hence prevented from rising or falling with changes in currency supply and demand.

Flexible exchange rate A *rate of exchange* determined by the international demand for and supply of a nation's money; a rate free to rise or fall (to float).

Floating exchange rate (See *Flexible exchange rate.*)

Foreign competition (See *Import competition.*)

Foreign exchange control The control a government may exercise over the quantity of foreign currency demanded by its citizens and firms and over the *rates of exchange* in order to limit its *outpayments* to its *inpayments* (to eliminate a *payments deficit*).

Foreign exchange market A market in which the money (currency) of one nation can be used to purchase (can be exchanged for) the money of another nation.

Foreign exchange rate (See *Rate of exchange.*)

Foreign purchase effect The inverse relationship between the *net exports* of an economy and its price level relative to foreign price levels.

45-degree line A line along which the value of *GDP* (measured horizontally) is equal to the value of *aggregate expenditures* (measured vertically).

Fractional reserve A *reserve ratio* that is less than 100 percent of the deposit liabilities of a *commercial bank* or *thrift institution.*

Freedom of choice The freedom of owners of property resources to employ or dispose of them as they see fit, of workers to enter any line of work for which they are qualified, and of consumers to spend their incomes in a manner which they think is appropriate.

Freedom of enterprise The freedom of *firms* to obtain economic resources, to use these resources to produce products of the firm's own choosing, and to sell their products in markets of their choice.

Free-rider problem The inability of potential providers of an economically desirable but indivisible good or service to obtain payment from those who benefit because the *exclusion principle* is not applicable.

Free trade The absence of artificial (government-imposed) barriers to trade among individuals and firms in different nations.

Frictional unemployment A type of unemployment caused by workers voluntarily changing jobs and by temporary layoffs; unemployed workers between jobs.

Full employment (1) Use of all available resources to produce want-satisfying goods and services. (2) The situation when the *unemployment rate* is equal to the *full-employment unemployment rate* and there is *frictional* and *structural* but no *cyclical unemployment* (and the *real output* of the economy equals its *potential real output*).

Full-employment budget A comparison of the government expenditures and tax collections which would occur if the economy operated at *full employment* throughout the year.

Full-employment unemployment rate The *unemployment rate* at which there is no *cyclical unemployment* of the *labor force;* equal to about 5.5 percent in the United States because some *frictional* and *structural unemployment* are unavoidable.

Full production Employment of available resources so that the maximum amount of (or total value of) goods and services is produced; occurs when both *productive efficiency* and *allocative efficiency* are realized.

Functional distribution of income The manner in which *national income* is divided among the functions performed to earn it (or the kinds of resources provided to earn it); the division of national income into wages and salaries, proprietors' income, corporate profits, interest, and rent.

Functional finance The use of *fiscal policy* to achieve a noninflationary full employment *gross domestic product* without regard to the effect on the *public debt.*

G

G-7 Nations A group of seven major industrial nations (the United States, Japan, Germany, United Kingdom, France, Italy, and Canada) whose leaders meet regularly to discuss common economic problems and try to coordinate economic policies. (Recently has also included Russia, making it unofficially the G-8.)

Gains from trade The extra output which trading partners obtain through specialization of production and exchange of goods and services.

GDP (See *Gross domestic product.*)

GDP deflator The *price index* found by dividing *nominal GDP* by *real GDP;* a price index used to adjust money (or nominal) GDP to real GDP.

GDP gap The amount by which actual *gross domestic product* falls below *potential gross domestic product.*

General Agreement on Tariffs and Trade (GATT) The international agreement reached in 1947 in which 23 nations agreed to give equal and nondiscriminatory treatment to the other nations, to reduce tariff rates by multinational negotiations, and to eliminate *import quotas.* Now includes most nations and has become the *World Trade Organization.*

Generalization Statement of the nature of the relation between two or more sets of facts.

Gold standard A historical system of fixed exchange rates in which nations defined their currency in terms of gold, maintained a fixed relationship between their stock of gold and their money supplies, and allowed gold to be freely exported and imported.

Government purchases Disbursements of money by government for which government receives a currently produced good or service in return; the expenditures of all governments in the economy for *final goods and services.*

Government transfer payment The disbursement of money (or goods and services) by government for which government receives no currently produced good or service in return.

Gross domestic product (GDP) The total market value of all *final goods and services* produced annually within the boundaries of the United States, whether by U.S. or foreign-supplied resources.

Gross private domestic investment Expenditures for newly produced *capital goods* (such as machinery, equipment, tools, and buildings) and for additions to inventories.

Guiding function of prices The ability of price changes to bring about changes in the quantities of products and resources demanded and supplied.

H

Horizontal axis The "left-right" or "west-east" axis on a graph or grid.

Horizontal combination A group of *plants* in the same stage of production which are owned by a single *firm.*

Horizontal range The horizontal segment of the *aggregate-supply curve* along which the price level is constant as real domestic output changes.

Household An economic unit (of one or more persons) which provides the economy with resources and uses the income received to purchase goods and services that satisfy material wants.

Human capital The accumulation of prior investments in education, training, health, and other factors which increase productivity.

Hyperinflation A very rapid rise in the price level.

Hypothesis A tentative, untested economic principle.

I

IMF (See *International Monetary Fund.*)

Import competition The competition which domestic firms encounter from the products and services of foreign producers.

Import demand curve A downsloping curve showing the amount of a product which an economy will import at each *world price* below the *domestic price.*

Import quota A limit imposed by a nation on the quantity (or total value) of a good which may be imported during some period of time.

Imports Spending by individuals, *firms,* and governments for goods and services produced in foreign nations.

Import transaction The purchase of a good or service which decreases the amount of foreign money held by citizens, firms, and governments of a nation.

Income approach The method that adds all the income generated by the production of *final goods and services* to measure the *gross domestic product.*

Income effect A change in the price of a product changes a consumer's *real income* (*purchasing power*) and thus the quantity of the product purchased.

Income inequality The unequal distribution of an economy's total income among persons or families.

Income-maintenance system Government programs designed to eliminate poverty and reduce inequality in the distribution of income.

Increase in demand An increase in the *quantity demanded* of a good or service at every price; a shift of the *demand curve* to the right.

Increase in supply An increase in the *quantity supplied* of a good or service at every price; a shift of the *supply curve* to the right.

Independent goods Products or services for which there is no relationship between the price of one and the demand for the other; when the price of one rises or falls, the demand for the other remains constant.

Independent variable The variable causing a change in some other (dependent) variable.

Indirect business taxes Such taxes as *sales, excise,* and business *property taxes,* license fees, and *tariffs* which firms treat as costs of producing a product and pass on (in whole or in part) to buyers by charging higher prices.

Individual demand   The demand schedule or *demand curve* of a single buyer.

Individual supply   The supply schedule or *supply curve* of a single seller.

Induction   A method of reasoning which proceeds from facts to *generalization.*

Industrially advanced countries   High-income countries such as the United States, Canada, Japan, and the nations of western Europe which have highly developed *market economies* based on large stocks of technologically advanced capital goods and skilled labor forces.

Industrial policy   Any policy by which government takes a direct and active role in promoting specific firms or industries for purposes of expanding their output and achieving economic growth; called "technology policy" when its goal is to promote *technological advance.*

Industry   A group of (one or more) *firms* which produces identical or similar products.

Inferior good   A good or service whose consumption declines as income rises (and conversely), price remaining constant.

Inflating   Determining *real gross domestic product* by increasing the dollar value of the *nominal gross domestic product* produced in a year in which prices are lower than in a *base year.*

Inflation   A rise in the general level of prices in an economy.

Inflation premium   The component of the *nominal interest rate* which reflects anticipated inflation.

Inflationary expectations   The belief of workers, firms, and consumers that substantial inflation will occur in the future.

Inflationary gap   The amount by which the *aggregate expenditures schedule* must shift downward to decrease the *nominal GDP* to its full-employment noninflationary level.

Infrastructure   The capital goods usually provided by the *public sector* for the use of its citizens and firms (for example, highways, bridges, transit systems, wastewater treatment facilities, municipal water systems, and airports).

Injection   An addition of spending to the income-expenditure stream: *investment, government purchases,* and *net exports.*

In-kind investment   (See *Nonfinancial investment.*)

Innovation   The first commercially successful introduction of a new product, the use of a new method of production, or the creation of a new form of business organization.

Inpayments   The receipts of its own or foreign money which individuals, firms, and governments of one nation obtain from the sale of goods and services abroad, or as investment income, *remittances,* and *capitals inflows* from abroad.

Insider-outsider theory   The hypothesis that nominal wages are inflexible downward because firms are aware that workers ("insiders") who retain employment during recession may refuse to work cooperatively with previously unemployed workers ("outsiders") who offer to work for less than the current wage.

Interest   The payment made for the use of money (of borrowed funds).

Interest income   Payments of income to those who supply the economy with *capital.*

Interest rate   The annual rate at which interest is paid; a percentage of the borrowed amount.

Interest-rate effect   The tendency for increases in the *price level* to increase the demand for money, raise interest rates, and, as a result, reduce total spending in the economy (and the reverse for price level decreases).

Intermediate goods   Products which are purchased for resale or further processing or manufacturing.

Intermediate range   The upsloping segment of the *aggregate supply curve* lying between the *horizontal range* and the *vertical range.*

Internally held public debt   *Public debt* owed to citizens, firms, and institutions of the same nation issuing the debt.

International balance of payments   A summary of all the transactions which took place between the individuals, firms, and government unit of one nation and those in all other nations during a year.

International balance of payments deficit   (See *Balance of payments deficit.*)

International balance of payments surplus   (See *Balance of payments surplus.*)

International Bank for Reconstruction and Development   (See *World Bank.*)

International gold standard   (See *Gold standard.*)

International Monetary Fund (IMF)   The international association of nations which was formed after World War II to make loans of foreign monies to nations with temporary *payments deficits* and, until the early 1970s, to administer the *adjustable pegs;* it now mainly makes loans to nations facing possible defaults on private and government loans.

International monetary reserves   The foreign currencies and such assets as gold a nation may use to settle a *payments deficit.*

International value of the dollar   The price which must be paid in foreign currency (money) to obtain one U.S. dollar.

Intrinsic value   The market value of the metal within a coin.

Inventories   Goods which have been produced but are still unsold.

Inverse relationship   The relationship between two variables which change in opposite directions, for example, product price and quantity demanded.

Investment   Spending for the production and accumulation of *capital* and additions to inventories.

Investment goods   Same as *capital.*

Investment schedule   A curve or schedule which shows the amounts firms plan to invest at various possible values of *real gross domestic product.*

Investment-demand curve   A curve which shows the amount of *investment* demanded by an economy at a series of *real interest rates.*

Investment in human capital   (See *Human-capital investment.*)

Invisible hand The tendency of firms and resource suppliers seeking to further their own self-interests in competitive markets to also promote the interest of society as a whole.

J

Joint Economic Committee (JEC) Committee of Senators and Representatives which investigates economic problems of national interest.

K

Keynesian economics The macroeconomic generalizations which lead to the conclusion that a capitalistic economy is characterized by macroeconomic instability and that *fiscal policy* and *monetary policy* can be used to promote *full employment, price-level stability,* and *economic growth.*

Keynesianism The philosophical, ideological, and analytical views pertaining to *Keynesian economics.*

L

Labor The physical and mental talents and efforts of people which are used to produce goods and services.

Labor force Persons 16 years of age and older who are not in institutions and who are employed or are unemployed (and seeking work).

Labor force participation rate The percentage of the working-age population which is actually in the *labor force.*

Labor-intensive commodity A product requiring a relatively large amount of *labor* to produce.

Labor productivity Total output divided by the quantity of labor employed to produce it; the *average product* of labor or output per worker per hour.

Labor union A group of workers organized to advance the interests of the group (to increase wages, shorten the hours worked, improve working conditions, and so on).

Labor theory of value The Marxian idea that the economic value of any commodity is determined solely by the amount of labor required to produce it.

Laffer curve A curve showing the relationship between tax rates and the tax revenues of government and on which there is a tax rate (between 0 and 100 percent) where tax revenues are a maximum.

Laissez faire capitalism (See *Pure capitalism.*)

Land Natural resources ("free gifts of nature") used to produce goods and services.

Land-intensive commodity A product requiring a relatively large amount of land to produce.

Law of demand The principle that, other things equal, an increase in a product's price will reduce the quantity of it demanded; and conversely for a decrease in price.

Law of increasing opportunity costs As the production of a good increases, the *opportunity cost* of producing an additional unit rises.

Law of supply The principle that, other things equal, an increase in the price of a product will increase the quantity of it supplied; and conversely for a price decrease.

Leakage (1) A withdrawal of potential spending from the income-expenditures stream via *saving,* tax payments, or imports. (2) A withdrawal which reduces the lending potential of the banking system.

Leakages-injections approach Determination of the equilibrium *gross domestic product* by finding the real GDP at which *leakages* are equal to *injections.*

Least-cost combination of resources The quantity of each resource a firm must employ in order to produce a particular output at the lowest total cost; the combination at which the ratio of the *marginal product* of a resource to its *marginal resource cost* (to its *price* if the resource is employed in a competitive market) is the same for the last dollar spent on each resource employed.

Legal reserves The minimum amount a *depository institution* must keep on deposit with the *Federal Reserve Bank* in its district, or in *vault cash.*

Legal tender Anything which government says must be accepted in payment of a debt.

Lending potential of an individual commercial bank The amount by which a single bank can safely increase the *money supply* by making new loans to (or buying securities from) the public; equal to the bank's excess reserves.

Lending potential of the banking system The amount by which the banking system can increase the money supply by making new loans to (or buying securities from) the public; equal to the *excess reserves* of the banking system multiplied by the *monetary multiplier.*

Liability A debt with a monetary value; an amount owed by a firm or an individual.

Limited liability Restriction of the maximum loss to a predetermined amount for the owners (stockholders) of a *corporation;* the maximum loss is the amount they paid for their shares of stock.

Limited-liability company An unincorporated business whose owners are protected by *limited liability.*

Line-item veto The presidential power to delete specific expenditure items from spending legislation passed by Congress.

Liquidity *Money* or things which can be quickly and easily converted into money with little or no loss of purchasing power.

Long run (1) In *microeconomics,* a period of time long enough to enable producers of a product to change the quantities of all the resources they employ; period in which all resources and costs are variable and no resources or costs are fixed. (2) In *macroeconomics,* a period sufficiently long for *nominal wages* and other input prices to change in response to a change in the nation's *price level.*

Long-run aggregate supply curve The *aggregate supply curve* associated with a time period in which input prices (especially *nominal wages*) are fully responsive to changes in the *price level.*

Lump-sum tax A tax which is a constant amount (the tax revenue of government is the same) at all levels of GDP.

M

M1 The most narrowly defined *money supply;* the *currency* and *checkable deposits* not owned by the *Federal government, Federal Reserve Banks,* or *depository institutions.*

M2 A more broadly defined money supply; equal to M1 plus *noncheckable savings deposits, money market deposit accounts,* small *time deposits* (deposits of less than $100,000), and individual *money market mutual fund balances.*

M3 Very broadly defined *money supply;* equal to *M*2 plus large *time deposits* (deposits of $100,000 or more).

Macroeconomics The part of economics concerned with the economy as a whole; with such major aggregates as the household, business, and governmental sectors; and with measures of the total economy.

Managed floating exchange rate An *exchange rate* which is allowed to change (float) as a result of changes in currency supply and demand but at times is altered (managed) by governments via their buying and selling of particular currencies.

Marginal analysis The comparison of marginal ("extra" or "additional") benefits and marginal costs, usually for decision making.

Marginal benefit The extra (additional) benefit of consuming one more unit of some good or service; the change in total benefit when one more unit is consumed.

Marginal cost The extra (additional) cost of producing one more unit of output; equal to the change in *total cost* divided by the change in output (and in the short run to the change in total *variable cost* divided by the change in output).

Marginal propensity to consume The fraction of any change in *disposable income* spent for *consumer goods;* equal to the change in consumption divided by the change in disposable income.

Marginal propensity to save The fraction of any change in *disposable income* which households save; equal to the change in *saving* divided by the change in disposable income.

Marginal tax rate The tax rate paid on each additional dollar of income.

Marginal utility The extra *utility* a consumer obtains from the consumption of one additional unit of a good or service; equal to the change in total utility divided by the change in the quantity consumed.

Market Any institution or mechanism which brings together buyers (demanders) and sellers (suppliers) of a particular good or service.

Market demand (See *Total demand.*)

Market economy An economy in which only the private decisions of consumers, resource suppliers, and firms determine how resources are allocated; the market system.

Market failure The failure of a market to bring about the allocation of resources which best satisfies the wants of society. In particular, the over- or underallocation of resources to the production of a particular good or service because of *spillovers* or informational problems and because markets fail to provide desired *public goods.*

Market socialism An *economic system* (method of organization) in which property resources are publicly owned *and* markets and prices are used to direct and coordinate economic activities.

Market system All the product and resource markets of a *market economy* and the relationships among them; a method which allows the prices determined in these markets to allocate the economy's scarce resources and to communicate and coordinate the decisions made by consumers, firms, and resource suppliers.

Medium of exchange Items sellers generally accept and buyers generally use to pay for a good or service; *money;* a convenient means of exchanging goods and services without engaging in *barter.*

Microeconomics The part of economics concerned with such individual units as *industries, firms,* and *households;* and with individual markets, particular prices, and specific goods and services.

Minimum wage The lowest *wage* employers may legally pay for an hour of work.

Mixed capitalism An economy in which both government and private decisions determine how resources are allocated.

Monetarism The macroeconomic view that the main cause of changes in aggregate output and the price level are fluctuations in the *money supply;* advocates of a *monetary rule.*

Monetary multiplier The multiple of its *excess reserves* by which the banking system can expand *demand deposits* and thus the *money supply* by making new loans (or buying securities); and equal to 1 divided by the *required reserve ratio.*

Monetary policy A central bank's changing of the *money supply* to influence interest rates and assist the economy in achieving a full-employment, noninflationary level of total output.

Monetary rule The rule suggested by *monetarism;* the *money supply* should be expanded each year at the same annual rate as the potential rate of growth of the *real gross domestic product;* the supply of money should be increased steadily from 3 to 5 percent per year.

Money Any item which generally is acceptable to sellers in exchange for goods and services.

Money capital Money available to purchase *capital.*

Money income (See *Nominal income.*)

Money interest rate The *nominal interest rate;* the interest rate which includes an *inflationary premium* (if any).

Money market The market in which the demand for and the supply of money determine the *interest rate* (or the level of interest rates) in the economy.

Money market deposit account (MMDA) Interest-earning accounts at *banks* and *thrift institutions,* which pool the funds of depositors to buy various short-term securities.

Money market mutual funds (MMMF) Interest-bearing accounts offered by investment companies, which pool depositors' funds for the purchase of short-term securities; depositors may write checks in minimum amounts or more against their accounts.

Money supply Narrowly defined *M*1; more broadly defined, *M*2 and *M*3.

Money wage (See *Nominal wage.*)

Money wage rate (See *Nominal wage.*)

Monopoly A market structure in which the number of sellers is so small that each seller is able to influence the total supply and the price of the good or service. (Also see *Pure monopoly.*)

Most-favored-nation (MFN) status An agreement by the United States to allow some other nation's *exports* into the United States at the lowest tariff level levied by the United States, then or at any later time.

Multinational corporation A firm which owns production facilities in other countries and produces and sells its product abroad.

Multiple counting Wrongly including the value of *intermediate goods* in the *gross domestic product;* counting the same good or service more than once.

Multiplier The ratio of a change in the *equilibrium GDP* to the change in *investment* or in any other component of *aggregate expenditures* or *aggregate demand;* the number by which a change in any component of aggregate expenditures or aggregate demand must be multiplied to find the resulting change in the equilibrium GDP.

Multiplier effect The effect on equilibrium GDP of a change in *aggregate expenditures* or *aggregate demand* (caused by a change in the *consumption schedule, investment, government expenditures,* or *net exports*).

Mutual savings bank A firm without stockholders which accepts deposits primarily from small individual savers and lends primarily to individuals to finance the purchases of autos and residences.

Mutually exclusive goals Two or more goals which conflict and cannot be achieved simultaneously.

N

National bank A *commercial bank* authorized to operate by the U.S. government.

National income Total income earned by resource suppliers for their contributions to *gross national product;* equal to the gross domestic product minus *nonincome charges,* minus *net foreign factor income.*

National income accounting The techniques used to measure the overall production of the economy and other related variables for the nation as a whole.

Natural monopoly An industry in which *economies of scale* are so great the product can be produced by one firm at a lower average total cost than if the product were produced by more than one firm.

Natural rate hypothesis The idea that the economy is stable in the long run at the *natural rate of unemployment;* views the long-run *Phillips Curve* as vertical at the *natural rate of unemployment.*

Natural rate of unemployment The *full-employment unemployment rate;* the unemployment rate occurring when there is no *cyclical unemployment* and the economy is achieving its *potential output;* the unemployment rate at which actual inflation equals expected inflation.

Near-money Financial assets, the most important of which are *noncheckable savings accounts, time deposits,* and U.S. short-term securities and savings bonds, which are not a medium of exchange but can be readily converted into money.

Negative relationship (See *Inverse relationship.*)

Net domestic product *Gross domestic product* less the part of the year's output which is needed to replace the *capital goods* worn out in producing the output; the nation's total output available for consumption or additions to the *capital stock.*

Net export effect The idea that the impact of a change in *monetary policy* or *fiscal policy* will be strengthened or weakened by the consequent change in *net exports;* the change in net exports occurs because of changes in real interest rates, which affect exchange rates.

Net exports *Exports* minus *imports.*

Net foreign factor income Payments by a nation of resource income to the rest of the world minus receipts of resource income from the rest of the world.

Net investment income The interest and dividend income received by the residents of a nation from residents of other nations less the interest and dividend payments made by the residents of that nation to the residents of other nations.

Net private domestic investment *Gross private domestic investment* less *consumption of fixed capital;* the addition to the nation's stock of *capital* during a year.

Net taxes The taxes collected by government less *government transfer payments.*

Net transfers The personal and government transfer payments made by one nation to residents of foreign nations, less the personal and government transfer payments received from residents of foreign nations.

Net worth The total *assets* less the total *liabilities* of a firm or an individual; the claims of the owners of a firm against its total assets.

New classical economics The theory that, although unanticipated price level changes may create macroeconomic instability in the short run, the economy is stable at the full-employment level of domestic output in the long run because prices and wages adjust automatically to correct movements away from the full employment, noninflationary output.

Nominal gross domestic product (GDP) The *GDP* measured in terms of the price level at the time of measurement (unadjusted for *inflation*).

Nominal income The number of dollars received by an individual or group for its resources during some period of time.

Nominal interest rate The interest rate expressed in terms of annual amounts currently charged for interest and not adjusted for inflation.

Nominal wage The amount of money received by a worker per unit of time (hour, day, etc.); money wage.

Noncheckable savings account A *savings account* against which a check can *not* be written.

Nondiscretionary fiscal policy (See *Built-in stabilizer*).

Nondurable good A *consumer good* with an expected life (use) of less than 3 years.

Nonexhaustive expenditure An expenditure by government which does not result directly in the employment of economic resources or the production of goods and services; see *Government transfer payment.*

Nonfinancial investment An investment which does not require *households* to save a part of their money incomes; but which uses surplus (unproductive) labor to build *capital goods.*

Nonincome charges *Consumption of fixed capital* and *indirect business taxes;* amounts subtracted from *GDP* (along with *net foreign factor income*) in determining *national income.*

Nonincome determinants of consumption and saving All influences on *consumption* and *saving* other than the level of *GDP*.

Noninterest determinants of investment All influences on the level of investment spending other than the *interest rate.*

Noninvestment transaction An expenditure for stocks, bonds, or second-hand *capital goods.*

Nonmarket transactions The production of goods and services excluded in the measurement of the *gross domestic product* because they are not bought and sold.

Nonproduction transaction The purchase and sale of any item which is not a currently produced good or service.

Nontariff barriers All barriers other than *protective tariffs* which nations erect to impede international trade: include *import quotas,* licensing requirements, unreasonable product-quality standards, and unnecessary red tape in customs procedures.

Normal good A good or service whose consumption increases when income increases and falls when income decreases, price remaining constant.

Normative economics That part of economics involving value judgments about what the economy should be like; concerned with identifying economic goals and promoting them via public policies.

North American Free Trade Agreement (NAFTA) A 1993 agreement establishing, over a 15-year period, a free trade zone composed of Canada, Mexico, and the United States.

O

Official reserves Foreign currencies owned by the central bank of a nation.

Okun's Law The generalization that any one percentage point rise in the *unemployment rate* above the *full-employment unemployment rate* will increase the GDP gap by 2 percent of the *potential output* (GDP) of the economy.

OPEC An acronym for the *Organization of Petroleum Exporting Countries.*

Open economy An economy which exports and imports goods and services.

Open-market operations The buying and selling of U.S. government securities by the *Federal Reserve Banks* for purposes of carrying out *monetary policy.*

Opportunity cost The amount of other products which must be forgone or sacrificed to produce a unit of a product.

Organization of Petroleum Exporting Nations (OPEC) The cartel formed in 1970 by 13 oil-producing countries to control the price and quantity of crude oil exported by its members, and which accounts for a large proportion of the world's export of oil.

Other things equal assumption The assumption that factors other than those being considered are held constant.

Outpayments The expenditures of its own or foreign currency which the individuals, firms, and governments of one nation make to purchase goods and services, for *remittances,* as investment income, and *capital outflows* abroad.

P

Paper money Pieces of paper used as a *medium of exchange;* in the United States, *Federal Reserve Notes.*

Partnership An unincorporated firm owned and operated by two or more persons.

Patent An exclusive right to inventors to produce and sell a new product or machine for a set period of time.

Payments deficit (See *Balance of payments deficit.*)

Payments surplus (See *Balance of payments surplus.*)

Payroll tax A tax levied on employers of labor equal to a percentage of all or part of the wages and salaries paid by them; and on employees equal to a percentage of all or part of the wages and salaries received by them.

Per capita GDP *Gross domestic product* (GDP) per person; the average GDP of a population.

Per capita income A nation's total income per person; the average income of a population.

Personal consumption expenditures The expenditures of *households* for *durable* and *nondurable consumer goods* and services.

Personal distribution of income The manner in which the economy's *personal* or *disposable income* is divided among different income classes or different households.

Personal income The earned and unearned income available to resource suppliers and others before the payment of *personal taxes.*

Personal income tax A tax levied on the *taxable income* of individuals, households, and unincorporated firms.

Personal saving The *personal income* of households less *personal taxes* and *personal consumption expenditures; disposable income* not spent for *consumer goods.*

Per-unit production cost The average production cost of a particular level of output; total input cost divided by units of output.

Phillips Curve A curve showing the relationship between the *unemployment rate* (on the horizontal axis) and the annual rate of increase in the *price level* (on the vertical axis).

Planned economy An economy in which government determines how resources are allocated.

Planned investment The amount which *firms* plan or intend to invest.

Plant A physical establishment which performs one or more functions in the production, fabrication, and distribution of goods and services.

Policy economics The formulation of courses of action to bring about desired economic outcomes or to prevent undesired occurrences.

Political business cycle The alleged tendency of Congress to destabilize the economy by reducing taxes and increasing government expenditures before elections and to raise taxes and lower expenditures after elections.

Positive economics The analysis of facts or data to establish scientific generalizations about economic behavior.

Positive relationship Direct relationship between two variables.

***Post hoc, ergo propter hoc* fallacy** Incorrectly reasoning that when one event precedes another the first event must have caused the second event.

Potential output The real output (*GDP*) an economy can produce when it fully employs its available resources.

Premature inflation A type of inflation which sometimes occurs before the economy has reached *full employment*.

Price The amount of money needed to buy a particular good, service, or resource.

Price index An index number which shows how the weighted average price of a "market basket" of goods changes through time.

Price leadership An informal method which firms in an *oligopoly* may employ to set the price of their product: one firm (the leader) is the first to announce a change in price, and the other firms (the followers) soon announce identical or similar changes.

Price level The weighted average of the prices of all the final goods and services produced in an economy.

Price-level surprises Unanticipated changes in the price level.

Price-level stability A steadiness of the price level from one period to the next; zero or low annual inflation; also called "price stability."

Price-wage flexibility Changes in the *prices* of products and in the *wages* paid to workers; the ability of prices and wages to rise or fall.

Price war Successive and continued decreases in the prices charged by the firms in an oligopolistic industry; each firm lowers its price below rivals' prices, hoping to increase its sales and revenues at its rivals expense.

Prime interest rate The *interest rate* banks charge their most creditworthy borrowers, for example, large corporations with excellent financing credentials.

Principal-agent problem A conflict of interest which occurs when agents (workers or managers) pursue their own objectives to the detriment of the principals' (stockholders) goals.

Private good A good or service which is subject to the *exclusion principle* and which is provided by privately owned firms to consumers who are willing to pay for it.

Private property The right of private persons and firms to obtain, own, control, employ, dispose of, and bequeath *land, capital,* and other property.

Private sector The *households* and business *firms* of the economy.

Production possibilities curve A curve showing the different combinations of two goods or services that can be produced in a *full-employment, full-production* economy in which the available supplies of resources and technology are fixed.

Productive efficiency The production of a good in the least costly way; occurs when production takes place at the output at which *average total cost* is a minimum and at which *marginal product* per dollar's worth of input is the same for all inputs.

Productivity A measure of average output or real output per unit of input. For example, the productivity of labor may be found by dividing real output by hours of work.

Productivity slowdown The decline in the rate at which *labor productivity* in the United States has increased in recent decades.

Product market A market in which products are sold by *firms* and bought by *households.*

Profit The return to the resource *entrepreneurial ability* (see *Normal profit*); *total revenue* minus *total cost* (see *Economic profit*).

Profit sharing plan A compensation device through which workers receive part of their pay in the form of a share of their employer's profit (if any).

Progressive tax A tax whose *average tax rate* increases as the taxpayer's income increases and decreases as the taxpayer's income decreases.

Property tax A tax on the value of property (*capital, land,* stocks and bonds, and other *assets*) owned by *firms* and *households.*

Proportional tax A tax whose *average tax rate* remains constant as the taxpayer's income increases or decreases.

Proprietor's income The net income of the owners of unincorporated firms (proprietorships and partnerships).

Protective tariff A *tariff* designed to shield domestic producers of a good or service from the competition of foreign producers.

Public debt The total amount owed by the Federal government to the owners of government securities; equal to the sum of past government *budget deficits* less government *budget surpluses.*

Public finance The branch of economics which analyzes government revenues and expenditures.

Public good A good or service which is indivisible and to which the *exclusion principle* does not apply; a good or service with these characteristics provided by government.

Public sector The part of the economy which contains all government entities; government.

Purchasing power The amount of goods and services which a monetary unit of income can buy.

Purchasing power parity The idea that exchange rates between nations equate the purchasing power of various currencies; exchange rates between any two nations adjust to reflect the price-level differences between the countries.

Pure capitalism An economic system in which property resources are privately owned and markets and prices are used to direct and coordinate economic activities.

Pure rate of interest An essentially risk-free, long-term interest rate which is free of the influence of market imperfections.

Q

Quantity demanded The amount of a good or service buyers (or a buyer) desire to purchase at a particular price during some period.

Quantity supplied The amount of a good or service producers (or a producer) offer to sell at a particular price during some period.

Quasipublic bank A bank which is privately owned but governmentally (publicly) controlled; each of the U.S. *Federal Reserve Banks.*

Quasipublic good A good or service to which the *exclusion principle* could apply but which has such a large *spillover benefit* that government sponsors its production to prevent an underallocation of resources.

R

R&D Research and development activities undertaken to bring about *technological progress.*

Ratchet effect The tendency for the *price level* to rise when *aggregate demand* increases but not fall when aggregate demand declines.

Rate of exchange The price paid in one's own money to acquire one unit of a foreign currency; the rate at which the money of one nation is exchanged for the money of another nation.

Rate of return The gain in net revenue divided by the cost of an investment or a *R&D* expenditure; expressed as a percentage.

Rational expectations theory The hypothesis that firms and households expect monetary and fiscal policies to have certain effects on the economy and (in pursuit of their own self-interests) take actions which make those policies ineffective.

Rationing function of prices The ability of market forces in a competitive market to equalize *quantity demanded* and *quantity supplied* and to eliminate shortages and surpluses via changes in prices.

Real-balances effect The tendency for increases in the price level to lower the real value (or purchasing power) of financial assets with fixed money value and, as a result, to reduce total spending; and conversely for decreases in the price level; also called the *wealth effect.*

Real business cycle theory A theory that *business cycles* result from changes in technology and resource availability, which affect *productivity* and thus increase or decrease *long-run aggregate supply.*

Real capital (See *Capital.*)

Real gross domestic product (GDP) *Gross domestic product* adjusted for inflation; gross domestic product in a year divided by the *GDP deflator* for that year, expressed as a decimal.

Real GDP (See *Real gross domestic product.*)

Real income The amount of goods and services which can be purchased with *nominal income* during some period of time; nominal income adjusted for inflation.

Real interest rate The interest rate expressed in dollars of constant value (adjusted for *inflation*); and equal to the *nominal interest rate* less the expected rate of inflation.

Real wage The amount of goods and services a worker can purchase with his or her *nominal wage;* the purchasing power of the nominal wage.

Recession A period of declining real GDP, accompanied by lower real income and higher unemployment.

Recessionary gap The amount by which the *aggregate expenditures schedule* must shift upward to increase the *real GDP* to its full-employment, noninflationary level.

Reciprocal Trade Agreements Act A 1934 Federal law which gave the President the authority to negotiate up to 50 percent lower tariffs with foreign nations that agreed to reduce their tariffs on U.S. goods (and which incorporated the *most-favored-nation clause*).

Refinancing the public debt Paying owners of maturing government securities with money obtained by selling new securities or with new securities.

Regressive tax A tax whose *average tax rate* decreases as the taxpayer's income increases, and increases as the taxpayer's income decreases.

Required reserves The funds which banks and thrifts must deposit with the *Federal Reserve Bank* (or hold as *vault cash*) to meet the legal *reserve requirement;* a fixed percentage of the bank or thrift's checkable deposits.

Reserve requirement The specified minimum percentage of its checkable deposits which a bank or thrift must keep on deposit at the Federal Reserve Bank in its district, or in *vault cash.*

Resource market A market in which *households* sell and *firms* buy resources or the services of resources.

Retiring the public debt Reducing the size of the *public debt* by paying money to owners of maturing U.S. government securities.

Revaluation An increase in the governmentally defined value of its currency relative to other nations' currencies.

Revenue tariff A *tariff* designed to produce income for the Federal government.

Roundabout production The construction and use of *capital* to aid in the production of *consumer goods.*

Rule of 70 A method for determining the number of years it will take for some measure to double, given its annual percentage increase. Example: To determine the number of years it will take for the *price level* to double; divide 70 by the annual rate of *inflation.*

S

Sales tax A tax levied on the cost (at retail) of a broad group of products.

Saving Disposable income not spent for consumer goods; equal to *disposable income* minus *personal consumption expenditures.*

Savings deposit An interest-bearing deposit which normally can be withdrawn by the depositor at any time.

Savings and Loan association (S&L) A firm which accepts deposits primarily from small individual savers and lends primarily to individuals to finance purchases such as autos and homes; now nearly indistinguishable from a *commercial bank.*

Saving schedule A schedule which shows the amounts *households* plan to save (plan not to spend for *consumer goods*), at different levels of *disposable income.*

Savings institution A *thrift institution.*

Say's law The largely discredited macroeconomic generalization that the production of goods and service (supply) creates an equal *demand* for these goods and service.

Scarce resources The limited quantities of *land, capital, labor,* and *entrepreneurial ability* which are never sufficient to satisfy the virtually unlimited material wants of humans.

Seasonal variations Increases and decreases in the level of economic activity within a single year, caused by a change in the season.

Secular trend Long-term tendency; change in some variable over a very long period of years.

Self-interest That which each firm, property owner, worker, and consumer believes is best for itself and seeks to obtain.

Seniority The length of time a worker has been employed absolutely or relative to other workers; may be used to determine which workers will be laid off when there is insufficient work for them all, and who will be rehired when more work becomes available.

Separation of ownership and control The fact that different groups of people own a *corporation* (the stockholders) and manage it (the directors and officers).

Service An (intangible) act or use for which a consumer, firm, or government is willing to pay.

Shirking Actions by workers to increase their *utility* or well-being by neglecting or evading work.

Shortage The amount by which the *quantity demanded* of a product exceeds the *quantity supplied* at a particular (below-equilibrium) price.

Short run (1) In *microeconomics,* a period of time in which producers are able to change the quantity of some but not all of the resources they employ; a period in which some resources (usually plant) are fixed and some are variable. (2) In *macroeconomics,* a period in which nominal wages and other input prices do not change in response to a change in the price level.

Short-run aggregate supply curve An aggregate supply curve relevant to a time period in which input prices (particularly *nominal wages*) do not change in response to changes in the *price level.*

Simple multiplier The *multiplier* in an economy in which government collects no *net taxes,* there are no *imports,* and *investment* is independent of the level of income; equal to 1 divided by the *marginal propensity to save.*

Slope of a line The ratio of the vertical change (the rise or fall) to the horizontal change (the run) between any two points on a line. The slope of an upward sloping line is positive, reflecting a direct relationship between two variables; the slope of a downward sloping line is negative, reflecting an inverse relationship between two variables.

Smoot-Hawley Tariff Act Legislation passed in 1930 which established very high tariffs. Its objective was to reduce imports and stimulate the domestic economy, but it only resulted in retaliatory tariffs by other nations.

Social accounting (*See National income accounting.*)

Sole proprietorship An unincorporated *firm* owned and operated by one person.

Special economic zones Regions of China open to foreign investment, private ownership, and relatively free international trade.

Specialization The use of the resources of an individual, a firm, a region, or a nation to produce one or a few goods and services.

Speculation The activity of buying or selling with the motive of later reselling or rebuying for profit.

Spillover A benefit or cost from production or consumption, accruing without compensation to nonbuyers and nonsellers of the product (see *Spillover benefit; Spillover costs*).

Spillover benefit A benefit obtained without compensation by third parties from the production or consumption of sellers or buyers. Example: A beekeeper benefits when a neighboring farmer plants clover.

Spillover cost A cost imposed without compensation on third parties by the production or consumption of sellers or buyers. Example: A manufacturer dumps toxic chemicals into a river, killing the fish sport fishers seek.

Stagflation Inflation accompanied by stagnation in the rate of growth of output and an increase in unemployment in the economy; simultaneous increases in the *price level* and the *unemployment rate.*

State bank A *commercial bank* authorized by a state government to engage in the business of banking.

State-owned enterprises Businesses which are owned by government; the major types of enterprises in Russia and China before their transitions to the market system.

Stock (corporate) An ownership share in a corporation.

Store of value An *asset* set aside for future use; one of the three functions of *money.*

Strategic trade policy The use of trade barriers to reduce the risk inherent in product development by domestic firms, particularly that involving advanced technology.

Structural deficit The extent to which the Federal government's expenditures exceed its tax revenues when the economy is at full employment (or the extent to which its current expenditures exceed the projected tax revenues which would accrue if the economy were at full employment); also known as a full-employment budget deficit.

Structural unemployment Unemployment of workers whose skills are not demanded by employers, they lack sufficient skill to obtain employment, or they cannot easily move to locations where jobs are available.

Subsidy A payment of funds (or goods and services) by a government, firm, or household for which it receives no good or service in return; when made by a government, it is a *government transfer payment.*

Substitute goods Products or services which can be used in place of each other. When the price of one falls the demand for the other falls, and conversely with an increase of price.

Substitution effect (1) A change in the price of a *consumer good* changes the relative expensiveness of that good and hence changes the consumer's willingness to buy it rather than other goods. (2) The effect of a change in the price of a *resource* on the quantity of the resource employed by a firm, assuming no change in its output.

Superior good (*See Normal good.*)

Supply A schedule showing the amounts of a good or service sellers (or a seller) will offer at various prices during some period.

Supply curve A curve illustrating *supply.*

Supply factor (in growth) An increase in the availability of a resource, an improvement in its quality, or an expansion of technological knowledge which makes it possible for an economy to produce a greater output of goods and services.

Supply shock An event which increases production costs, decreases *aggregate supply,* reduces *real GDP,* and increases *unemployment.*

Supply-side economics A view of macroeconomics which emphasizes the role of costs and *aggregate supply* in explaining *inflation, unemployment,* and *economic growth.*

Surplus The amount by which the *quantity supplied* of a product exceeds the *quantity demanded* at a specific (above-equilibrium) price.

Surplus value A Marxian term; the amount by which the value of a worker's daily output exceeds the worker's daily wage; workers' output appropriated by capitalists as profit.

T

Tariff A tax imposed by a nation on an imported good.

Tax An involuntary payment of money (or goods and services) to a government by a *household* or *firm* for which the household or firm receives no good or service directly in return.

Technology The body of knowledge and techniques which can be used to produce goods and services from *economic resources.*

Technological advance New and better goods and services and new and better ways of producing or distributing them.

Terms of trade The rate at which units of one product can be exchanged for units of another product; the price of a good or service; the amount of one good or service which must be given up to obtain one unit of another good or service.

Thrift institution A *savings and loan association, mutual savings bank,* or *credit union.*

Tight money policy *Federal Reserve System* actions which contract, or restrict, the growth of the nation's *money supply* for the purpose of reducing or eliminating inflation.

Till money (See *Vault cash.*)

Time deposit An interest-earning deposit in a *commercial bank* or *thrift institution* which the depositor can withdraw without penalty after the end of a specified period.

Token money Coins having a *face value* greater than their *intrinsic value.*

Total demand The demand schedule or the *demand curve* of all buyers of a good or service; also called market demand.

Total demand for money The sum of the *transactions demand for money* and the *asset demand for money.*

Total product The total output of a particular good or service produced by a firm (or a group of firms or the entire economy).

Total revenue The total number of dollars received by a firm (or firms) from the sale of a product; equal to the total expenditures for the product produced by the firm (or firms); equal to the quantity sold (demanded) multiplied by the price at which it is sold.

Total-revenue test A test to determine elasticity of *demand* between any two prices: Demand is elastic if *total revenue* moves in the opposite direction as price; it is inelastic when it moves in the same direction as price; and it is of unitary elasticity when it does not change when price changes.

Total spending The total amount buyers of goods and services spend or plan to spend; also called *aggregate expenditures.*

Total supply The supply schedule or the supply curve of all sellers of a good or service; also called market supply.

Township and village enterprises Privately owned rural manufacturing firms in China.

Trade balance The export of goods (or goods and services) of a nation less its imports of goods (or goods and services).

Trade bloc A group of nations which lowers or abolishes trade barriers among members. Examples include the *European Union* and the nations of the *North American Free Trade Agreement.*

Trade controls *Tariffs, export subsidies, import quotas,* and other means a nation may use to reduce *imports* and expand *exports.*

Trade deficit The amount by which a nation's *imports* of goods (or goods and services) exceed its *exports* of goods (or goods and services).

Tradeoffs The sacrifice of some or all of one economic goal, good, or service to achieve some other goal, good, or service.

Trade surplus The amount by which a nation's exports of goods (or goods and services) exceed its imports of goods (or goods and services).

Trading possibilities line A line which shows the different combinations of two products an economy is able to obtain (consume) when it specializes in the production of one product and trades (exports) it to obtain the other product.

Traditional economy An economic system in which traditions and customs determine how the economy will use its scarce resources.

Transactions demand for money The amount of money people want to hold for use as a *medium of exchange* (to make payments), and which varies directly with the *nominal GDP.*

Transfer payment A payment of *money* (or goods and services) by a government to a *household* or *firm* for which the payer receives no good or service directly in return.

U

Unanticipated inflation Increases in the price level (*inflation*) at a rate greater than expected.

Underemployment (1) Failure to produce the maximum amount of goods and services which can be produced from the resources employed; failure to achieve *full production.* (2) A situation in which workers are employed in positions requiring less than the amount of education and skill than they have.

Undistributed corporate profits After-tax corporate profits not distributed as dividends to stockholders; corporate or business saving; also called retained earnings.

Unemployment Failure to use all available *economic resources* to produce goods and services; failure of the economy to fully employ its *labor force.*

Unemployment compensation (See *Unemployment insurance.*)

Unemployment insurance The social insurance program which in the United States is financed by state *payroll taxes* on employers and makes income available to workers who become unemployed and are unable to find jobs.

Unemployment rate The percentage of the *labor force* unemployed at any time.

Unit labor cost Labor costs per unit of output; total labor cost divided by total output; also equal to the *nominal wage rate* divided by the *average product* of labor.

Unit of account A standard unit in which prices can be stated and the value of goods and services can be compared; one of the three functions of *money*.

Unlimited liability Absence of any limits on the maximum amount which an individual (usually a business owner) may become legally required to pay.

Unlimited wants The insatiable desire of consumers for goods and services which will give them satisfaction or *utility*.

Unplanned investment Actual investment less *planned investment;* increases or decreases in the *inventories* of firms resulting from production greater than sales.

Urban collectives Chinese enterprises jointly owned by their managers and their workforces, located in urban areas.

Uruguay Round The eighth and most recent round of trade negotiations under *GATT* (now the *World Trade Organization*).

Utility The want-satisfying power of a good or service; the satisfaction or pleasure a consumer obtains from the consumption of a good or service (or from the consumption of a collection of goods and services).

V

Value added The value of the product sold by a *firm* less the value of the products (materials) purchased and used by the firm to produce the product.

Value judgment Opinion of what is desirable or undesirable; belief regarding what ought or ought not to be (regarding what is right or just and wrong or unjust).

Value of money The quantity of goods and services for which a unit of money (a dollar) can be exchanged; the purchasing power of a unit of money; the reciprocal of the *price level.*

Vault cash The *currency* a bank has in its vault and cash drawers.

Velocity The number of times per year the average dollar in the *money supply* is spent for *final goods and services;* nominal GDP divided by the money supply.

Vertical axis The "up-down" or "north-south" axis on a graph or grid.

Vertical combination A group of *plants* engaged in different stages of the production of a final product and owned by a single *firm.*

Vertical intercept The point at which a line meets the vertical axis of a graph.

Vertical range The vertical segment of the aggregate supply curve along which the economy is at full capacity.

Vicious circle of poverty A problem common in some developing countries in which their low per capita incomes are an obstacle to realizing the levels of saving and investment requisite to acceptable rates of economicgrowth.

Voluntary export restrictions Voluntary limitations by countries or firms of their exports to a particular foreign nation to avoid enactment of formal trade barriers by that nation.

W

Wage The price paid for the use or services of *labor* per unit of time (per hour, per day, and so on).

Wage rate (See *Wage.*)

Wealth effect (See *Real balances effect.*)

"Will to develop" Wanting economic growth strongly enough to change from old to new ways of doing things.

World Bank A bank which lends (and guarantees loans) to developing nations to help them increase their *capital stock* and thus achieve *economic growth;* formally, the International Bank for Reconstruction and Development.

World price The international market price of a good or service, determined by world demand and supply.

World Trade Organization An organization established in 1994 to replace *GATT* to oversee the provisions of the *Uruguay round* and resolve any disputes stemming therefrom.

Answers to Key Questions*

Chapter 1

1-1 This behavior can be explained in terms of marginal costs and marginal benefits. At a standard restaurant, items are priced individually—they have a positive marginal cost. If you order more, it will cost you more. You order until the marginal benefit from the extra food no longer exceeds the marginal cost. At a buffet you pay a flat fee no matter how much you eat. Once the fee is paid, additional food items have a zero marginal cost. You therefore continue to eat until your marginal benefit becomes zero.

1-5 Economic theory consists of factually supported generalizations about economic behavior. Economists use two methods to obtain sound theory: induction and deduction. In *deduction* the economist starts with a hypothesis and tests it for accuracy by gathering and examining facts. In *induction,* the economist starts by gathering facts and then examines their relationships, so as to extract a cause and effect pattern: a theory. Regardless of how derived, economic theory enables policymakers to formulate economic policy relevant to real-world goals and problems.

As for the quotation, the opposite is true; any theory not supported by facts is not a good theory. Good economic theory is empirically grounded; it is based on facts and so is highly practical.

1-7 (a), (d), and (f) are macro; (b), (c), and (e) are micro.

1-8 (a) and (c) are positive; (b) and (d) are normative.

1-9 (a) The fallacy of composition is the mistake of believing that something true for an individual part is necessarily true for the whole. Example: A single auto producer can increase its profits by lowering its price and taking business away from its competitors. But matched price cuts by all auto manufacturers will not necessarily yield higher industry profits. (b) The "after this, therefore because of this" fallacy is incorrectly reasoning that when one event precedes another, the first event *necessarily* caused the second. Example: Interest rates rise, followed by an increase in the rate of inflation, leading to the erroneous conclusion that the rise in interest rates caused the inflation. Actually, higher interest rates slow inflation.

Cause-and-effect relationships are difficult to isolate because "other things" are continually changing.

Appendix 1-2 (a) More tickets are bought at each price; the line shifts to the right. (b) and (c) Fewer tickets are bought at each price; the line shifts to the left.

Appendix 1-3 Income column: $0; $5,000; $10,000, $15,000; $20,000. Saving column: −$500; 0; $500; $1,000; $1,500. Slope = 0.1 (= $1,000 − $500)/($15,000 − $10,000). Vertical intercept = −500. The slope shows the amount saving will increase for every $1 increase in income; the intercept shows the amount of saving (dissaving) occurring when income is zero. Equation: $S =$ −$500 + 0.1Y$ (where S is saving and Y is income). Saving will be $750 at the $12,500 income level.

Appendix 1-6 Slopes: at $A = +4$; at $B = 0$; at $C = −40$.

Chapter 2

2-5 Economics deals with the "limited resources–unlimited wants" problem. Unemployment represents valuable resources which could have been used to produce more goods and services—to meet more wants and ease the economizing problem.

Allocative efficiency means that resources are being used to produce the goods and services most wanted by society. The economy is then located at the optimal point on its production possibilities curve where marginal benefit equals marginal cost for each good. *Productive efficiency* means the least costly production techniques are being used to produce wanted goods and services. Example: manual typewriters produced using the least-cost techniques but for which there is no demand.

2-6 (a) See curve *EDCBA* below. The assumptions are full employment and productive efficiency, fixed supplies of resources, and fixed technology.

Question 2-6

(b) 4.5 rockets; .33 automobiles, as determined from the table. Increasing opportunity costs are reflected in the concave-from-the-origin shape of the curve. This means the economy must give up larger and larger amounts of rockets to get constant added amounts of automobiles—and vice versa.

(c) It must obtain full employment and productive efficiency.

2-9 The marginal benefit curve is downsloping; MB falls as more of a product is consumed because additional units of a good yield less satisfaction than previous units. The marginal cost curve is upsloping; MC increases as more of a product is produced because additional units require the use of increasingly unsuitable resources. The optimal amount of a particular product occurs where MB equals MC. If MC exceeds MB, fewer resources should be allocated to this use. The resources are more valuable in some alternative use (as reflected in the higher MC) than in this use (as reflected in the lower MB).

2-10 See the answer for Question 2-6. *G* indicates unemployment, productive inefficiency, or both. *H* is at present unattainable. Economic growth—through more inputs, better inputs, improved technology—must be achieved to attain *H*.

2-11 See the answer for Question 2-6. PPC$_1$ shows improved rocket technology. PPC$_2$ shows improved auto technology. PPC$_3$ shows improved technology in producing both products.

Chapter 3

3-2 Demand increases in (a), (c), (e), and (f); decreases in (b) and (d).

3-5 Supply increases in (a), (d), (e), and (g); decreases in (b), (c), and (f).

3-7 Data, from top to bottom: -13; -7; 0; $+7$; $+14$; and $+21$.
(a) $P_e = \$4.00$; $Q_e = 75,000$. Equilibrium occurs where there is neither a shortage nor surplus of wheat. At the immediately lower price of $3.70, there is a shortage of 7,000 bushels. At the immediately higher price of $4.30, there is a surplus of 7,000 bushels.

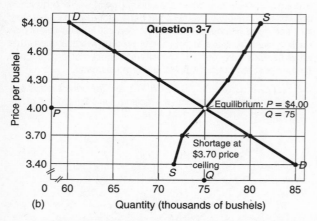

(c) Because at $3.40 there will be a 13,000 bushel shortage which will drive the price up. Because at $4.90 there will be a 21,000 bushel surplus which will drive the price down. Quotation is incorrect; just the opposite is true.
(d) A $3.70 ceiling causes a persistent shortage. Government might want to suppress inflation.

3-8 (a) Price up; quantity down; (b) Price down; quantity down; (c) Price down; quantity up; (d) Price indeterminate; quantity up; (e) Price up; quantity up; (f) Price down; quantity indeterminate; (g) Price up; quantity indeterminate; (h) Price indeterminate and quantity down.

Chapter 4

4-2 "Roundabout" production means using capital goods in the production process, enabling producers to obtain more output than through direct production. The direct way to produce a corn crop is to scatter seed about in an unplowed field. The roundabout way is to plow, fertilize, harrow, and till the field using machinery and then use a seed drill to sow the seeds in rows at the correct depth. The higher yield per acre will more than compensate the farmer for the cost of using the capital goods.

To increase the capital stock at full employment, the current production of consumer goods must decrease. Moving along the production possibilities curve toward more capital goods comes at the expense of current consumption.

No, it can use its previously unemployed resources to produce more capital goods, without sacrificing consumption goods. It can move from a point inside the curve to a point on it, thus obtaining more capital goods.

4-8 (a) Technique 2. Because it produces the output with least cost ($34 compared to $35 each for the other two). Economic profit will be $6 = ($40 $-$34), which will cause the industry to expand. Expansion will continue until prices decline to where total revenue is $34 (equal to total cost).
(b) Adopt technique 4 because its cost is now lowest at $32.
(c) Technique 1 because its cost is now lowest at $27.50.
(d) The statement is logical. Increasing scarcity causes prices to rise. Firms ignoring higher resource prices will become high-cost producers and be competed out of business by firms switching to the less expensive inputs. The market system forces producers to conserve on the use of highly scarce resources. Question 8c confirms this: Technique 1 was adopted because labor had become less expensive.

4-10 The quest for profit led firms to produce these goods. Producers looked for and found the least-cost combination of resources in producing their output. Resource suppliers, seeking income, made these resources available. Consumers, through their dollar votes, ultimately decide on what will continue to be produced.

Chapter 5

5-2 The distribution of income is quite unequal. The highest 20 percent of the residents receive 10 times more income than the lowest 20 percent.

5-4 Sole proprietorship, partnership, and corporation.
Proprietorship advantages: easy to start and provides maximum freedom for the proprietor to do what she or he thinks best. Proprietorship disadvantages: limited financial resources; the owner must be a Jack-or-Jill-of-all-trades; and unlimited liability.
Partnership advantages: easy to organize; greater specialization of management; and greater financial resources. Disadvantages: financial resources are still limited; unlimited liability; possibility of disagreement among the partners; and precarious continuity.

Corporation advantages: can raise large amounts of money by issuing stocks and bonds; limited liability; continuity.

Corporation disadvantages: red tape and expense in incorporating; potential for abuse of stockholder and bondholder funds; double taxation of profits; separation of ownership and control.

The dominant role of corporations stems from the advantages cited, particularly unlimited liability and ability to raise money.

5-9 Public goods are indivisible (they are produced in such large units that they cannot be sold to individuals) and the exclusion principle does not apply to them (once the goods are produced nobody—including free riders—can be excluded from the goods' benefits). The free-rider problem explains the significance of the exclusion principle. The exclusion principle separates goods and services which private firms will supply (because those who do not pay for them can be excluded from their benefits) and goods and services which government must supply (because people can obtain the benefits without paying). Government must levy taxes to get revenues to pay for public goods.

5-10 On the curve, the only way to obtain more public goods is to reduce the production of private goods (from C to B).

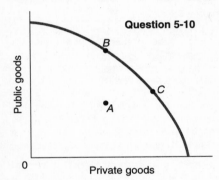

Question 5-10

An economy operating inside the curve can expand the production of public goods without sacrificing private goods (say, from A to B) by making use of unemployed resources.

5-15 Total tax = $13,000; marginal tax rate = 40%; average tax rate = 26%. This is a progressive tax; the average tax rate rises as income goes up.

Chapter 6

6-3 Greater exporting increases domestic output and thus increases revenues to domestic exporting firms. Because these firms would employ more resources, household income would rise. Households would then use part of their greater income to buy more imported goods (imports would rise).

United States exports in 1993 were $457 billion (flow 13) and imports were $590 billion (flow 16).

Flow 14 must equal flow 13. Flow 15 must equal flow 16.

6-4 (a) Yes, because the opportunity cost of radios is less (1R ≡ 1C) in South Korea than in the United States (1R ≡ 2C). South Korea should produce radios and the United States should produce chemicals.

(b) If they specialize, the United States can produce 20 tons of chemicals and South Korea can produce 30,000 radios. Before specialization South Korea produced alternative B and the United States alternative U for a total of 28,000 radios (24,000 + 4,000) and 18 tons of chemicals (6 tons + 12 tons). The gain is 2,000 radios and 2 tons of chemicals.

(c) The limits of the terms of trade are determined by the comparative cost conditions in each country before trade: 1R ≡ 1C in South Korea and 1R ≡ 2C in the United States.

The terms of trade must be somewhere between these two ratios for trade to occur.

If the terms of trade are 1R ≡ 1$\frac{1}{2}$ C, South Korea would end up with 26,000 radios (= 30,000 − 4,000) and 6 tons of chemicals. The United States would have 4,000 radios and 14 tons of chemicals (= 20 − 6). South Korea has gained 2,000 radios. The United States has gained 2 tons of chemicals.

(d) Yes, the world is obtaining more output from its fixed resources.

6-6 The first part of this statement is incorrect. U.S. exports create a domestic *supply* of foreign currencies, not a domestic demand for them. The second part of the statement is accurate. The foreign demand for dollars (from U.S. exports) generates a supply of foreign currencies to the United States.

A decline in U.S. incomes or a weakening of U.S. preferences for foreign goods would reduce U.S. imports, reducing U.S. demand for foreign currencies. These currencies would depreciate (the dollar would appreciate). Dollar appreciation means U.S. exports would decline and U.S. imports would increase.

6-10 GATT is the General Agreement on Tariffs and Trade. It affects nearly everyone around the globe because its trade liberalization applies to 120 nations. Major outcomes: reduced tariffs and quotas, liberalized trade in services, lower agricultural subsidies, enhanced protection of intellectual property rights, creation of the World Trade Organization. The EU and NAFTA are free-trade blocs. GATT reduces tariffs and liberalizes trade for nearly *all* nations. The ascendancy of the EU and the passage of NAFTA undoubtedly encourage nations to reach the latest GATT agreement. The tariff reductions within the EU and NAFTA apply only to sellers from other nations in the blocs. The GATT provisions reduce trade barriers facing *all* exporting nations, including those outside the trade blocs.

Chapter 7

7-3 They are excluded because the dollar value of final goods includes the dollar value of intermediate goods. If intermediate goods were counted, then multiple counting would occur. The value of steel (intermediate good) used in autos is included in the price of the auto (the final product).

This value is not included in GDP because such sales and purchases simply transfer the ownership of existing assets; such sales and purchases are not themselves (economic) investment and thus should not be counted as production of final goods and services.

Used furniture was produced in some previous year; it was counted as GDP then. Its resale does not measure new production.

NDP is GDP less depreciation—the physical capital used up in producing this year's output.

7-6 When gross investment exceeds depreciation, net investment is positive and production capacity expands; the economy ends the year with more physical capital than it started with. When gross investment equals depreciation, net investment is zero and production capacity is said to be static; the economy ends the year with the same amount of physical capital. When depreciation exceeds gross investment, net investment is negative and production capacity declines; the economy ends the year with less physical capital.

The first statement is wrong. Just because *net* investment was a minus $6 billion in 1933 does not mean the economy produced no new capital goods in that year. It simply means depreciation exceeded gross investment by $6 billion. So the economy ended the year with $6 billion less capital.

The second statement is correct. If only one $20 spade is bought by a construction firm in the entire economy in a year and no other physical capital is bought, then gross investment is $20—a positive amount. This is true even if *net* investment is highly negative, because depreciation is well above $20. If not even this $20 spade had been bought, then gross investment would have been zero. But gross investment can never be *less* than zero.

7-8 (a) GDP = $388; NDP = $361; (b) NI = $339; (c) PI = $291; (d) DI = $265.

7-11 Price index for 1984 = 62.5; 60 percent; real GDP for 1984 = $112,000 and real GDP for 1992 = $352,000.

7-12 Values for real GDP, top to bottom of the column: $2,206.5 (inflating); $2,695.1 (inflating); $3,133.8 (inflating); $3,905.6 (inflating); $5,864.8 (inflating); $6,739.7 (deflating).

Chapter 8

8-1 The four phases of a typical business cycle, starting at the bottom, are trough, recovery, peak, and recession. As seen in Figure 8-1, the length of a complete cycle varies from about 2 to 3 years to as long as 15 years.

Normally there is a pre-Christmas spurt in production and sales and a January slackening. This normal seasonal variation does not signal boom or recession. From decade to decade, the long-term trend (the secular trend) of the U.S. economy has been upward. A period of no GDP growth thus does not mean that all is normal but that the economy is operating below its trend growth of output.

Because durable goods last, consumers can postpone buying replacements. This happens when people are worried about a recession and whether there will be a paycheck next month. And firms will soon stop producing what people are not buying. Durable goods industries therefore suffer large output declines during recessions. In contrast, consumers cannot long postpone the buying of nondurables such as food; therefore recessions only slightly reduce nondurable output.

8-3 Labor force = 230 [= 500 − (120 + 150)]; official unemployment rate = 10% [= (23/230) × 100].

8-5 GDP gap = 8% [= (9 − 5) × 2]; forgone output = $40 billion (= 8% of $500 billion).

8-7 This year's rate of inflation is 10% or [(121 −110)/110] × 100.

Dividing 70 by the annual percentage rate of increase of any variable (for instance, the rate of inflation or population growth) will give the approximate number of years for doubling of the variable.

(a) 35 years (= 70/2); (b) 14 years (= 70/5); (c) 7 years (= 70/10).

Chapter 9

9-6 Data for completing the table (top to bottom). Consumption: $244; $260; $276; $292; $308; $324; $340; $356; $372. APC: 1.02; 1.00; .99; .97; .96; .95; .94; .94; .93. APS: −.02; .00; .01; .03; .04; .05; .06; .06; .07. MPC: .80 throughout. MPS: .20 throughout.

(a) See the graphs at the top of the next column.

(b) Break-even income = $260. Households dissave by borrowing or using past savings.

(c) Technically, the APC diminishes and the APS increases because the consumption and saving schedules have positive and negative vertical intercepts respectively (Appendix to Chapter 1). MPC and MPS measure *changes* in consumption and saving as income changes; they are the

slopes of the consumption and saving schedules. For straight-line consumption and saving schedules, these slopes do not change as the level of income changes; the slopes and thus the MPC and MPS remain constant.

9-8 See the graph. Aggregate investment: (a) $20 billion; (b) $30 billion; (c) $40 billion. This is the investment-demand curve because we have applied the rule of undertaking all investment up to the point where the expected rate of return, *r*, equals the interest rate, *i*.

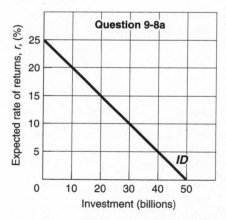

9-10 Saving data for completing the table (top to bottom): $−4; $0; $4; $8; $12; $16; $20; $24; $28.

Equilibrium GDP = $340 billion, determined where (1) aggregate expenditures equal GDP (*C* of $324 billion + *I* of $16 billion = GDP of $340 billion); or (2) where planned *I* = S (*I* of $16 billion = *S* of $16 billion). Equilibrium level of employment = 65 million; MPC = .8; MPS = .2.

9-11 At the $380 billion level of GDP, planned saving = $24 billion; planned investment = $16 billion (from the question). This deficiency of $8 billion of planned investment causes an unplanned $8 billion *increase* in inventories. Actual investment is

$24 billion (= $16 billion of planned investment *plus* $8 billion of unplanned inventory investment), matching the $24 billion of actual saving.

At the $300 billion level of GDP, saving = $8 billion; planned investment = $16 billion (from the question). This excess of $8 billion of planned investment causes an unplanned $8 billion *decline* in inventories. Actual investment is $8 billion (= $16 billion of planned investment *minus* $8 billion of unplanned inventory disinvestment) matching the actual saving of $8 billion.

When unplanned investments in inventories occur, as at the $380 billion level of GDP, businesses revise their production plans downward and GDP falls. When unintended disinvestments in inventories occur, as at the $300 billion level of GDP, businesses revise their production plans upward and GDP rises. Equilibrium GDP—in this case, $340 billion—occurs where planned investment equals saving.

Chapter 10

10-2 The multiplier effect is the magnified increase in equilibrium GDP that occurs when any component of aggregate expenditures changes. The greater the MPC (the smaller the MPS), the greater the multiplier.

MPS = 0,   multiplier = infinity;   MPS = .4,   multiplier = 2.5; MPS = .6, multiplier = 1.67; MPS = 1; multiplier = 1.

MPC = 1;   multiplier = infinity;   MPC = .9,   multiplier = 10; MPC = .67; multiplier = 3; MPC = .5, multiplier = 2; MPC = 0, multiplier = 1.

MPC = .8: Change in GDP = $40 billion (= $8 billion × multiplier of 5); MPC = .67: change in GDP = $24 billion ($8 billion × multiplier of 3). The simple multiplier takes account of only the leakage of saving. The complex multiplier also takes account of leakages of taxes and imports, making the complex multiplier less than the simple multiplier.

10-5 (a) Equilibrium GDP for closed economy = $400 billion.
(b) Net export data for column 5 (top to bottom): $−10 billion in each space. Aggregate expenditure data for column 6 (top to bottom): $230; $270; $310; $350; $390; $430; $470; $510. Equilibrium GDP for the open economy is $350 billion, $50 billion below the $400 billion equilibrium GDP for the closed economy. The $−10 billion of net exports is a leakage which reduces equilibrium GDP by $50 billion. Imports = $40 billion: Aggregate expenditures in the private open economy would fall by $10 billion at each GDP level and the new equilibrium GDP would be $300 billion. Imports = $20 billion: Aggregate expenditures would increase by $10 billion; new equilibrium GDP would be $400 billion. Exports constant, increases in imports reduce GDP; decreases in imports increase GDP.
(d) Since every rise of $50 billion in GDP increases aggregate expenditures by $40 billion, the MPC is .8 and so the multiplier is 5.

10-8 The addition of $20 billion of government expenditures and $20 billion of personal taxes increases equilibrium GDP from $350 to $370 billion. The $20 billion increase in *G raises* equilibrium GDP by $100 billion (= $20 billion × the multiplier of 5); the $20 billion increase in *T reduces* consumption by $16 billion (= $20 billion × the MPC of .8). This $16 billion decline in turn reduces equilibrium GDP by $80 billion (= $16 billion × multiplier of 5). The net change from adding government is $20 billion (= $100 billion −$80 billion.).

10-10 (a) A recessionary gap. Equilibrium GDP is $600 billion, while full employment GDP is $700 billion. Employment will be 20 million less than at full employment. Aggregate expenditures would have to increase by $20 billion (= $700 billion − $680 billion) at each level of GDP to eliminate the recessionary gap.
(b) An inflationary gap. Aggregate expenditures will be excessive, causing demand-pull inflation. Aggregate expenditures would have to *fall* by $20 billion (= $520 billion − $500 billion) at each level of GDP to eliminate the inflationary gap.
(c) MPC = .8 (= $40 billion/$50 billion); MPS = .2 (= 1 −.8); multiplier = 5 (= 1/.2).

Chapter 11

11-4 (a) See the graph. Equilibrium price level = 200. Equilibrium real output = $300 billion. No, the full-capacity level of GDP is $400 billion, where the AS curve becomes vertical.

Question 11-4

Real domestic output ($ billions)

(b) At a price level of 150, real GDP supplied is a maximum of $200 billion, less than the real GDP demanded of $400 billion. The shortage of real output will drive the price level up. At a price level of 250, real GDP supplied is $400 billion, which is more than the real GDP demanded of $200 billion. The surplus of real output will drive down the price level. Equilibrium occurs at the price level at which AS and AD intersect.
(c) See the graph. Increases in consumer, investment, government, or net export spending might shift the AD curve rightward. New equilibrium price level = 250. New equilibrium GDP = $400 billion. The intermediate range.

11-5 (a) Productivity = 2.67 (= 300/112.5). (b) Per-unit cost of production = $.75 (= $2 × 112.5/300). (c) New per-unit production cost = $1.13. The AS curve would shift leftward. The price level would rise and real output would decrease; (d) New per-unit cost of production = $0.375 ($2 × 112.5/600). AS curve shifts to the right; price level declines and real output increases.

11-7 (a) AD curve left; (b) AD curve right; (c) AS curve left; (d) AD curve right; (e) AD curve left; (f) AD curve right; (g) AS curve right; (h) AD curve right; (i) AS curve right; (j) AS curve left; (k) AD curve right; AS curve left; (l) AD curve left; (m) AS curve right.

11-9 (a) Price level rises and no change in real output; (b) price level drops and real output increases; (c) price level does not change, but real output rises; (d) price level does not change, but real output declines; (e) price level increases, but the change in real output is indeterminate; (f) price level does not change, but real output declines.

Chapter 12

12-2 Increase in government spending = $5 billion. Initial spending of $5 billion is still required, but only .8 (= MPC) of a tax cut will be spent. So tax cut = $5/.8 = $6.25 billion. Because part of the tax reduction ($1.25 billion) is saved, not spent. Combination: a $1 billion increase in government spending and a $5 billion tax cut.

12-3 Reduce government spending, increase taxes, or some combination of both. See Figure 12-2. If the price level is flexible downward, it will fall. In the real world, the goal is to reduce *inflation*—to keep prices from rising so rapidly—not to reduce the *price level*. A "conservative" economist might favor cuts in government spending since this would reduce the size of government. A "liberal" economist might favor a tax hike; it would preserve government spending programs.

12-7 The *full-employment budget* is a budget which indicates the amount the Federal deficit or surplus would be *if* the economy operated at full employment throughout the year (whether or not it did). This budget is a useful measure of fiscal policy. An increase in a full-employment deficit (or a decrease in a full-employment surplus) indicates that fiscal policy is expansionary. A decrease in full-employment deficit (or an increase in a full-employment surplus) means that fiscal policy is contractionary. The actual budget simply compares G and T for the year. A *structural deficit* is another name for a full-employment deficit. A cyclical deficit is the difference between G and T caused by tax revenues being below those which are collected when the economy is at full employment.

At GDP_f, the structural deficit is *ab* and the cyclical deficit is zero. Government should raise T or reduce G to eliminate this deficit, but it may want to take this action over several years to avoid pushing the economy into recession.

12-9 It takes time to ascertain the direction in which the economy is moving (recognition lag), to get a fiscal policy enacted into law (administrative lag), and for the policy to have its full effect on the economy (operational lag). Meanwhile, other factors may change, rendering inappropriate a particular fiscal policy. Nevertheless, discretionary fiscal policy is a valuable tool in preventing severe recession or severe demand-pull inflation.

A political business cycle is the concept that politicians are more interested in reelection than in stabilizing the economy. Before the election, they enact tax cuts and spending increases to please voters even though this may fuel inflation. After the election, they apply the brakes to restrain inflation; the economy will slow and unemployment will rise. In this view the political process creates economic instability.

The crowding-out effect is the reduction in investment spending caused by the increase in interest rates arising from an increase in government spending, financed by borrowing. The increase in G was designed to increase AD but the resulting increase in interest rates may decrease I. Thus the impact of the expansionary fiscal policy may be reduced.

The net export effect also arises from the higher interest rates accompanying expansionary fiscal policy. The higher interest rates make U.S. bonds more attractive to foreign buyers. The inflow of foreign currency to buy dollars to purchase the bonds drives up the international value of the dollar, making imports less expensive for the United States, and U.S. exports more expensive for people abroad. Net exports in the United States decline, and like the crowding-out effect, diminish the expansionary fiscal policy.

Chapter 13

13-4 $M1$ = currency (in circulation) + checkable deposits. The largest component of $M1$ is checkable deposits. If the face value of a coin were not greater than its intrinsic (metallic) value, people would remove coins from circulation and sell them for their metallic content. $M2 = M1$ + noncheckable savings deposits +

money market deposit accounts + small time deposits + money market mutual fund balances. $M3 = M2$ + large time deposits (those of $100,000 or more). Near-monies include the components of $M2$ and $M3$ not included in $M1$ and, secondly, other less liquid assets such as Savings bonds and Treasury bills.

Near-monies represent wealth; the more wealth people have, the more they are likely to spend out of current income. Also, the fact that near-monies are liquid adds to potential economic instability. People may cash in their near-monies and spend the proceeds while the monetary authorities are trying to stem inflation by reducing the money supply. Finally, near-monies can complicate monetary policy because $M1$, $M2$, and $M3$ do not always change in the same direction.

The argument for including noncheckable savings deposits in a definition of money is that saving deposits can quickly be transferred to a checking account or withdrawn as cash and spent.

13-6 In the first case, the value of the dollar in year 2, relative to year 1 is $.80 (= 1/1.25); in the second case the value is $2 (= 1/.50). Generalization: The price level and the value of the dollar are inversely related.

13-7 (a) The level of nominal GDP. The higher this level, the greater the amount of money demanded for transactions. (b) The interest rate. The higher the interest rate, the smaller the amount of money demanded as an asset.

On a graph measuring the interest rate vertically and the amount of money demanded horizontally, the two demand for money curves can be summed horizontally to get the total demand for money. This total demand shows the total amount of money demanded at each interest rate. The equilibrium interest rate is determined at the intersection of the total demand for money curve and the supply of money curve.

(a) Expanded use of credit cards: transaction demand for money declines; total demand for money declines; interest rate falls. (b) Shortening of worker pay periods: transaction demand for money declines; total demand for money declines; interest rate falls. (c) Increase in nominal GDP: transaction demand for money increases; total demand for money increases; interest rate rises.

Chapter 14

14-2 Reserves provide the Fed a means of controlling the money supply. It is through increasing and decreasing excess reserves that the Fed is able to achieve a money supply of the size it thinks best for the economy.

Reserves are assets of commercial banks because these funds are cash belonging to them; they are a claim the commercial banks have against the Federal Reserve Bank. Reserves deposited at the Fed are a liability to the Fed because they are funds it owes; they are claims which commercial banks have against it.

Excess reserves are the amount by which actual reserves exceed required reserves: Excess reserves = actual reserves − required reserves. Commercial banks can safely lend excess reserves, thereby increasing the money supply.

14-4 Banks add to checking account balances when they make loans; these checkable deposits are part of the money supply. People pay off loans by writing checks: checkable deposits fall, meaning the money supply drops. Money is "destroyed."

14-8 (a) $2,000. Column 1 of Assets (top to bottom): $22,000; $38,000; $42,000. Column 1 of Liabilities: $102,000.
(b) $2,000. The bank has lent out its excess reserves, creating $2,000 of new demand-deposit money.
(c) Column 2) of assets (top to bottom): $20,000; $38,000; $42,000. Column 2 of Liabilities: $100,000.
(d) $7,000.

14-13 (a) Required reserves = $50 billion (= 25% of $200 billion); so excess reserves = $2 billion (= $52 billion − $50 billion). Maximum amount banking system can lend = $8 billion (= 1/.25 × 2 billion). Column (1) of Assets data (top to bottom): $52 billion; $48 billion; $108 billion. Column (1) of Liabilities data: $208 billion. Monetary multiplier = 4 (= 1/.25).

(b) Required reserves = $40 billion (= 20% of $200 billion); so excess reserves = $12 billion (= $52 billion − $40 billion). Maximum amount banking system can lend = $60 billion (= 1/.20 × $12 billion). Column (1) data for Assets after loans (top to bottom): $52 billion; $48 billion; $160 billion. Column (1) data for Liabilities after loans: $260 billion. Monetary multiplier = 5 (= 1/.20). The decrease in the reserve ratio increases the banking system's excess reserves from $2 billion to $12 billion and increases the size of the monetary multiplier from 4 to 5. Lending capacity become 5 × $12 = $60 billion.

Chapter 15

15-2 (a) Column (1) data, top to bottom: (Commercial banks) $34; $60; $60; $150; $4; (Fed banks) $60; $4; $34; $3; $27.

(b) Column (2) data: (Commercial banks) $30; $60; $60; $147; $3; (Fed banks) $57; $3; $30; $3; $27.

(c) Column (3) data (top to bottom): $35; $58; $60; $150; $3; (Fed banks) $62; $3; $35; $3; $27.

(d1) Money supply (demand deposits) directly changes only in (b), where it decreases by $3 billion; (d2) See balance sheets; (d3) Money-creating potential of the banking system increases by $5 billion in (a); decreases by $12 billion in (b) (not by $15 billion—the writing of $3 billion of checks by the public to buy bonds reduces demand deposits by $3 billion, thus freeing $0.6 billion of reserves. Three billion dollars minus $0.6 billion equals $2.4 billion of reduced reserves, and this multiplied by the monetary multiplier of 5 equals $12 billion); and increases by $10 billion in (c).

15-3 (a) Increase the reserve ratio. This would increase the size of required reserves. If the commercial banks were fully loaned up, they would have to call in loans. The money supply would decrease, interest rates would rise, and aggregate demand would decline.

(b) Increase the discount rate. This would decrease commercial bank borrowing from the Fed. Actual reserves of the commercial banks would fall, as would excess reserves and lending. The money supply would drop, interest rates would rise, and aggregate demand would decline.

(c) Sell government securities in the open market. Buyers of the bonds would write checks to the Fed on their demand deposits. When these checks cleared, reserves would flow from the banking system to the Fed. The decline in reserves would reduce the money supply, which would increase interest rates and reduce aggregate demand.

15-4 The basic objective of monetary policy is to assist the economy in achieving a full-employment, noninflationary level of total output. Changes in the money supply affect interest rates, which affect investment spending and therefore aggregate demand.

(a) A steep demand curve for money makes monetary policy more effective since the steepness of the curve means that only a relatively small change in the money supply is needed to produce large changes in interest rates. A relatively flat investment demand curve aids monetary policy since it means that only a small change in the interest rate is sufficient to change investment sharply. (b) A high MPC (low MPS) yields a large income

multiplier, meaning that a relatively small initial change in spending will multiply into a larger change in GDP.

An easy money policy increases the money supply. The increase in GDP resulting from an easy money policy will also increase the transactions demand for money, partially offsetting the reduction in the interest rate associated with the initial increase in the money supply. Overall, investment spending, aggregate demand, and GDP will not rise by as much. The reverse is true for a tight money policy.

15-5 The Federal funds interest rate is the interest rate banks charge one another on overnight loans needed to meet the reserve requirement. The prime interest rate is the interest rate banks charge on loans to their most creditworthy customers. The tighter the monetary policy, the less the supply of excess reserves in the banking system and the higher the Federal funds rate.

The Fed wanted to reduce excess reserves, slowing the growth of the money supply. This would slow the expansion of aggregate demand and keep inflation from occurring. The prime interest rate went up.

15-6 The intent of a tight money policy would be shown as a leftward shift of the aggregate demand curve and a decline in the price level (or, in the real world, a reduction in the rate of inflation). In an open economy, the interest rate hike resulting from the tight money policy would entice people abroad to buy U.S. securities. Because they would need U.S. dollars to buy these securities, the international demand for dollars would rise, causing the dollar to appreciate. Net exports would fall, pushing the aggregate demand curve farther leftward than in the closed economy.

Chapter 16

16-3 (a) $280; $220. When the price level rises from 100 to 125 [in aggregate supply schedule AS(P_{100})], producers experience higher prices for their products. Because nominal wages are constant, profits rise and producers increase output to Q = $280. When the price level decreases from 100 to 75, profits decline and producers adjust their output to Q = $75. These are short-run responses to changes in the price level.

(b) $250; $250. In the long run, a rise in the price level to 125 leads to nominal wage increases. The AS(P_{100}) changes to AS(P_{125}) and Q returns to $250, now at a price level of 125. In the long run, a decrease in the price level to 75 leads to lower nominal wages, yielding aggregate supply schedule AS(P_{75}). Equilibrium Q returns to $250, now at a price level of 75.

(c) Graphically, the explanation is identical to Figure 16-1b. Short run AS: P_1 = 100; P_2 = 125; P_3 = 75; and Q_1 = $250; Q_2 = 280; Q_3 = $220. Long-run aggregate supply = Q_1 = $250 at each of the three price levels.

16-4 (a) See Figure 16-4 in the chapter. Short run: The aggregate supply curve shifts to the left, the price level rises, and real output declines. Long run: The aggregate supply curve shifts back rightward (due to declining nominal wages), the price level falls, and real output increases.

(b) See Figure 16-3. Short run: The aggregate demand curve shifts to the right, and both the price level and real output increase. Long run: The aggregate supply curve shifts to the left (due to higher nominal wages), the price level rises, and real output declines.

(c) See Figure 16-5. Short run: The aggregate demand curve shifts to the left, both the price level and real output decline. Long run: The aggregate supply curve shifts to the right, the price level falls further, and real output increases.

16-6 Adaptive expectations: People form their expectations of future inflation on the basis of previous and present rates of inflation and only gradually change their expectations as experience unfolds. Rational expectations: People form their expectations by predicting what inflation will be in the future.

With adaptive expectations, an increase in inflation reduces the unemployment rate since prices rise but nominal wages for a time stay constant; thus higher inflation is associated with lower unemployment rates. This is not possible with rational expectations since workers anticipate the higher inflation and immediately take action to increase their nominal wages to avoid suffering a decline in real wages.

Both types of expectations result in a vertical long-run Phillips Curve because workers either *eventually* (adaptive expectations) or *immediately* (rational expectations) adjust their expectations of inflation to the actual rate of inflation. Therefore, no tradeoff between inflation and the unemployment rate exist in the long run.

16-8 Taxes and transfers reduce incentives to work; the economy is overregulated. The Laffer Curve relates tax revenues to tax rates and suggests that tax revenues first rise as tax rates increase, reach a maximum at some particular tax rate, and then decline as tax rates further increase. This curve reflects the supply-side tenet that high taxes create disincentives to work and thus to earn income; reduced income reduces income tax revenue.

Chapter 17

17-1 (a) Classical economists envisioned the AS curve as being perfectly vertical. When prices fall, real profits do not decrease because wage rates fall in the same proportion. With constant real profits, firms have no reason to change the quantities of output they supply. Keynesians viewed the AS curve as being horizontal at outputs less than the full-employment output. Declines in aggregate demand in this range do not change the price level because wages and prices are assumed to be inflexible downward.

(b) Classical economists viewed AD as stable so long as the monetary authorities hold the money supply constant. Therefore inflation and deflation are unlikely. Keynesians viewed the AD curve as unstable—even if the money supply is constant—since investment spending is volatile. Decreases in AD can cause a recession; rapid increases in AD can cause demand-pull inflation. The Keynesian view seems more consistent with the facts of the Great Depression; in that period, real output declined by nearly 40 percent in the United States and remained low for a decade.

17-4 Velocity = 3.5. They will cut back on their spending to try to restore their desired ratio of money to other items of wealth. Nominal GDP will have to fall to $266 billion (= $76 billion of money supply × 3.5) to restore equilibrium.

17-7 See the graph and the decline in aggregate demand from AD_1 to AD_2. RET view: The economy anticipates the decline in the price level and immediately moves from a to d. Mainstream view: The economy first moves from a to b and then to c. In view of historical evidence, the mainstream view seems more plausible to us than the RET view; only when aggregate demand shifts from AD_2 to AD_1 will full-employment output Q_1 be restored.

17-13 (a) RET; (b) MAIN; (c) MON; (d) MAIN; (e) MON.

Chapter 18

18-2 There are four supply factors, a demand factor, and an efficiency factor in explaining economic growth. (1) Supply factors:

Question 17-7

the quantity and quality of natural resources, the quantity and quality of human resources, the stock of capital goods, and technology. (2) Demand factor: maintaining full employment. (3) Efficiency factor: productive and allocative efficiency.

In the long run, a nation must expand its production capacity in order to grow (supply side). But aggregate demand must also expand (demand side) or the extra capacity will stand idle. Economic growth depends on an enhanced ability to produce *and* a greater willingness to buy.

The supply side of economic growth is illustrated by the outward expansion of the production possibilities curve, as from *AB* to *CD* in Figure 18-1. The demand side of economic growth is shown by the movement from a point on *AB* to an optimal point on *CD,* as from *a* to, say, *b* in the figure.

18-3 Growth rate of real GDP = 4 percent (= $31,200 − $30,000)/$30,000). GDP per capita in year 1 = $300 (= $30,000/100). GDP per capita in year 2 = $305.88 (= $31,200/102). Growth rate of GDP per capita is 1.96 percent = ($305.88 − $300)/300).

Question 18-3

"One Possible Graphical Solution"

In the graph, AD_1 and AS_1 intersect for 1959 at a price level of 100 and GDP of 100. The 1997 AD_2 and AS_2 intersect at a price level of 385 (an increase of 285 percent) and at a real GDP of $312 (an increase of 212 percent).

18-5 Increase in labor inputs: 33 percent; increase in labor productivity: 67 percent.

Refer to Table 18-2. Productivity increasing factors in descending order: (1) Technological advance—the discovery of new knowledge which results in the combining of resources in more productive ways. (2) The quantity of capital. (3) Education and training. Since 1940 the proportion of those in the labor force with a high school education has doubled from 40 to 80 percent. And those with a college education have more than doubled from under 10 percent to 20 percent. (4) Economies of scale and (5) improved resource allocation. Workers have been moving out of lower productivity jobs to higher productivity jobs. Part of this is associated with the increased efficiency often derived from production in larger plants in which specialization of labor and productivity-increasing methods are possible.

18-8 Declines in labor quality; a slowing of technological process; declining investment spending as a percentage of GDP; high energy prices during the 1970s and 1980s; and lagging growth of service productivity. The main consequence of the slowdown is a slower rise in the U.S. standard of living (slower increases in real GDP per capita). Other outcomes are greater inflation and loss of competitiveness in world markets.

We are generally optimistic about a resurgence of productivity growth. The most recent productivity growth rates are higher than the averages of the slowdown years. Energy prices are stable and inflation is under control; the baby-boomers are becoming more experienced workers; a surge of innovation is occurring in computers and telecommunications; real interest rates remain low, prompting purchases of capital goods; and international trade barriers are declining. All these factors may result in faster productivity growth than in the slowdown years.

Chapter 19

19-1 (a) There is practically no potential for using fiscal policy as a stabilization tool under an annually balanced budget. In an economic downturn, tax revenues fall. To keep the budget in balance, fiscal policy would require the government to reduce its spending or increase its tax rates, adding to the deficiency in spending and accelerating the downturn. If the economy were booming and tax revenues were mounting, to keep the budget balanced fiscal policy would have to increase government spending or reduce taxes, thus adding to the already excessive demand and accelerating the inflationary pressures. An annually balanced budget would intensify cyclical ups and downs.

(b) A cyclically balanced budget would be countercyclical, as it should be, since it would bolster demand by lowering taxes and increasing government spending during a recession and restrain demand by raising taxes and reducing government spending during an inflationary boom. However, because boom and bust are not always of equal intensity and duration, budget surpluses during the upswing need not automatically match budget deficits during the downswing. Requiring the budget to be balanced over the cycle may necessitate inappropriate changes in tax rates or levels of government expenditures.

(c) Functional finance pays no attention to the balance of deficits and surpluses annually or over the cycle. What counts is the maintenance of a noninflationary full-employment level of spending. Balancing the economy is what counts, not the budget.

19-3 Two ways of measuring the public debt: (1) measure its absolute size; (2) measure its size as a percentage of GDP.

An internally held debt is one in which the bondholders live in the nation having the debt; an externally held debt is one in which the bondholders are citizens of other nations. Paying off an internally held debt would involve boosting taxes or reducing other government spending and using the proceeds to buy the government bonds. This would present a problem of income distribution because holders of the government bonds generally have higher incomes than the average taxpayer. But paying off an internally held debt would not burden the economy as a whole—the money used to pay off the debt would stay within the domestic economy.

In paying off an externally held debt people abroad would use the proceeds of the bonds sales to buy goods from the country paying off its external debt. That nation would have to send some of its output abroad to be consumed by others (with no imported goods in exchange).

Refinancing the public debt simply means rolling over outstanding debt—selling "new" bonds to retire maturing bonds.

19-7 Economists do not, in general, view the large public debt as a burden for future generations. Future generations not only inherit the public debt, they inherit the bonds which constitute the public debt. They also inherit public capital goods, some of which were financed by the debt.

There is one way the debt can be a burden to future generations. Unlike tax financing, debt financing may drive up interest rates since government must compete with private firms for funds in the bond market. Higher interest rates will crowd out some private investment, resulting in a smaller stock of future capital goods and thus a less productive economy for future generations to inherit.

19-8 Cause and effect chain: Government borrowing to finance the debt competes with private borrowing and drives up the interest rate; the higher interest rate induces an inflow of foreign money to buy the now higher-return U.S. bonds; to buy the bonds, the foreign financiers must first buy dollars; the demand for dollars rises and the dollar appreciates; U.S. exports fall and U.S. imports rise; a U.S. trade deficit results.

The U.S. public often blames the large trade deficits on the trade policies of other countries—particularly Japan. But, as noted in the scenario just described, a substantial portion of the large U.S. *trade* deficits may have resulted from the U.S. policy of running large *budget* deficits for the past decade or more.

Chapter 20

20-4 (a) New Zealand's cost ratio is 1 plum $\equiv$ 4 apples (or 1 apple $\equiv \frac{1}{4}$ plum). Spain's cost ratio is 1 plum $\equiv$ 1 apple (or 1 apple $\equiv$ 1 plum).

(b) New Zealand should specialize in apples, Spain in plums.

(c) See the graphs.

(d) Total production before specialization and trade: 40 apples (20 + 20) and 50 plums (10 + 40). After specialization and trade: 60 apples and 60 plums. Gain = 20 apples and 10 plums.

20-6 At $1: import 15,000. At $2: import 7,000. At $3: no imports or exports. At $4: export 6,000. At $5: export 10,000.

The United States will export corn; France will import it.

20-7 See the graph. The United States does not have a comparative advantage in this product because the world price P_w is below the U.S. domestic price P_d. Imports will reduce the price to P_w, increasing consumption from Q_c to Q_e and decreasing domestic production from Q_c to Q_a. See the graph. A tariff of P_wP_t (a) harms domestic consumers by increasing price from P_w to P_t and decreasing consumption from Q_e to Q_d; (b) aids domestic producers through the increase in price from P_w to P_t and the expansion of domestic production from Q_a to Q_b; (c) harms foreign exporters by decreasing exports from Q_aQ_e to Q_bQ_d.

An import quota of Q_bQ_d would have the same effects as the tariff, but there would be no tariff revenues to government from these imports; this revenue would in effect be transferred to foreign producers.

20-11 The major cost of trade protection is reduced efficiency borne by price increases by consumers. Prices of imported goods rise, decreasing levels of competition for domestic firms producing similar goods and allowing them to increase their prices. Prices of products using these goods as inputs also rise. Prices of all other goods increase as consumer spending patterns change. Also, resources are reallocated from more-efficient to less-efficient domestic industries.

The main benefit of protectionist policies is greater profits for the protected firms. Government also benefits from tariff revenues. But empirical studies find that the costs of protectionism greatly exceed the benefits, resulting in a large net cost—or efficiency loss—to society.

Chapter 21

21-2 A demand for francs is created in (a), (c), and (f). A supply of francs is created in (b), (d), (e), and (g).

21-3 Balance of trade = $10 billion surplus (= exports of goods of $40 billion minus imports of goods of $30 billion). Balance on goods and services = $15 billion surplus (= $55 billion of exports of goods and services minus $40 billion of imports of goods and services). Balance on current account = $20 billion surplus (= credits of $65 billion minus debits of $45 billion). Balance on capital account = $30 billion deficit (= Foreign purchases of assets in the United States of $10 billion minus U.S. purchases of assets abroad of $40 billion). Balance of payments = $10 billion deficit.

21-6 The U.S. demand for pesos is downsloping: When the peso depreciates in value (relative to the dollar), the United States find that Mexican goods and services are less expensive in dollar terms and purchase more of them, demanding a greater quantity of pesos in the process. The supply of pesos to the United States is upsloping: As the peso appreciates in value (relative to the dollar), U.S. goods and services become cheaper to Mexicans in peso terms. Mexicans buy more dollars to obtain more U.S. goods, supplying a larger quantity of pesos.

The peso appreciates in (a), (f), (g), and (h) and depreciates in (b), (c), (d), and (e).

21-10 See the graph illustrating the market for Zees.

(a) The decrease in demand for Zees from D_1 to D_2 will create a surplus (bc) of Zees at the $5 price. To maintain the $5 to Z1 exchange rate, the United States must undertake policies to shift the demand-for-Zee curve rightward or shift the supply-of-Zee curve leftward. To increase the demand for Zees, the United States could use dollars or gold to buy Zees in the foreign exchange market, employ trade policies to increase imports from Zeeonia, or enact expansionary fiscal and monetary policies to increased U.S. domestic output and income, thus increasing imports from Zeeonia. Expansionary monetary policy would also reduce the *supply* of Zees: Zeeons would respond to the resulting lower U.S. interest rates by reducing their financial investing in the United States. Therefore, they would not supply as many Zees to the foreign exchange market.

(b) Under a system of flexible exchange rates, the bc surplus of Zees (the U.S. balance of payments surplus) will cause the Zee to appreciate and the dollar to appreciate until the surplus is eliminated (at the $4 = Z1 exchange rate shown in the figure).

Question 21-10

(Graph: Vertical axis "Dollar price of one Zee" with values $5 and $4 marked; horizontal axis "Quantity of Zee" with Q₂ and Q₁ marked. Supply curve S, demand curves D₁ and D₂, points a and b.)

Chapter 22

22-3 Rise in per capita output gap = $135 (= 3% × $5,000 − 3% × $500).

22-6 Demographic transition view: Expanded output and income in developing countries will result in lower birthrates and slower growth of population. As incomes of primary family members expand, they begin to see the marginal cost of a larger family exceeding the marginal benefit. The policy emphasis should therefore be on economic growth; population growth will stabilize. Traditional view: Developing nations should reduce population growth as a first priority. Slow population growth enables the growth of per capita income.

22-7 Capital earns a higher return where it is scarce, *other things equal.* But, when comparing investment opportunities between IACs and DVCs, other things are not equal. Advanced factories filled with specialized equipment require a productive work force. IACs have an abundance of educated, experienced workers; these workers are scarce in DVCs. Also, IACs have extensive public infrastructures which increase the returns on private capital. Example: a network of highways makes it more profitable to produce goods which need to be widely transported. Finally, investment returns must be adjusted for risk. IACs have stable governments and "law and order," reducing the risk of capital being "nationalized" or pilfered by organized crime.

22-13 To describe countries such as Japan and South Korea, we would need to change labels on three boxes, leading to a change in the "results" boxes. "Rapid" population growth would change to "low" rate of population growth; "low" level of saving would change to "high" level of saving; "low" levels of investment in physical and human capital would change to "high" levels of investment in physical and human capital. These three changes would result in higher productivity and higher per capita income, which would produce a rising level of demand. Other factors: stable national government; homogeneous population; extensive investment in infrastructure; "will to develop"; strong private incentives.

Chapter 23

23-5 See Figure 23-1. Because Russia and China set prices and did not allow them to change as supply or demand shifted, prices were below the equilibrium price for most goods and services. When the fixed price, P_f, is below the equilibrium price, P_e, there will be a shortage since the quantity demanded will exceed the quantity supplied.

Black markets are common where prices are fixed below equilibrium levels. People can buy goods at the fixed government prices (or pay off clerks to save such goods to sell to them), and because of the shortages at the low fixed price, resell these goods at a much higher price to those unable to find the goods in government stores at the controlled prices. This reselling is said to occur on the black market.

23-6 Privatization of state-owned businesses; market-determined prices; promotion of competition; integration with the world economy; and price-level stabilization. These reforms are referred to as shock therapy because they were dramatic and quick rather than phased in over many years or decades. Russia's reform has been successful in privatizing the economy, establishing market-determined prices, and setting the stage for future prosperity. But the transition has resulted in declining living standards for many and increasing income inequality.

23-8 (a) leasing of land resulted in individually operated rather than collectivized farms; this greatly increased production incentives and boosted farm output. (b) Price reform established market-based prices. These higher-than-government prices provided incentives for enterprises to expand output; they also enabled market-determined allocation of resources to replace inefficient central planning. (c) Private rural and urban enterprises absorbed workers released by greater productivity in China's agricultural sector and established competition for China's state-owned enterprises. (d) The special economic zones—with their private corporations, free trade, and foreign investment—established the workability and benefits of "near-capitalism." (e) Corporatization focused the goals of state-owned enterprises on providing high-quality, minimum per-unit cost goods desired by consumers.